Lappenberg, Johann

A History of England under the Norman Kings

Lappenberg, Johann Martin

A History of England under the Norman Kings

Inktank publishing, 2018

www.inktank-publishing.com

ISBN/EAN: 9783747703779

A

HISTORY OF ENGLAND

UNDER THE

NORMAN KINGS,

OR,

FROM THE BATTLE OF HASTINGS

TO THE ACCESSION OF

THE HOUSE OF PLANTAGENET:

TO WHICH IS PREFIXED

AN EPITOME OF

THE EARLY HISTORY OF NORMANDY.

TRANSLATED FROM THE GERMAN

OF

DR. J. M. LAPPENBERG, For. F. S. A.

KEEPER OF THE ARCHIVES OF THE CITY OF HAMBURG.

BY

BENJAMIN THORPE,

WITH CONSIDERABLE ADDITIONS AND CORRECTIONS BY
THE TRANSLATOR.

OXFORD:
PRINTED BY JAMES WRIGHT, PRINTER TO THE UNIVERSITY.
SOLD BY JOHN RUSSELL SMITH,
36, SOHO SQUARE, LONDON.
M. DCCC. LVII.

PREFACE.

IN sending forth this volume I do no more than fulfil the intention I expressed in the Preface to Lappenberg's HISTORY OF ENGLAND UNDER THE ANGLO-SAXON KING'S[1], namely, that, in the event of that work finding a favourable reception, it should be followed by a translation of the same author's HISTORY OF ENGLAND UNDER THE NORMAN KINGS, OR, TO THE ACCESSION OF THE HOUSE OF PLANTAGENET. That work having now been long in the hands of many, and repeatedly spoken of in terms of commendation by those capable to appreciate it, I feel no hesitation in offering its continuation to the judgment of the public. That I have not limited my labour to that of a mere translator, will be evident to every one who shall undertake the somewhat tedious task of comparing it with the German original; on the contrary, as in the preceding volumes, I have, as far as my means admitted, tested Lappenberg's work by the old chroniclers, and where I found his text abridged, in consequence of the necessity to be concise, under which he was placed[2], I have restored it to its integrity; where the meaning of the chronicler

---

[1] At the end of the volume are given a few pages of additions to and corrections of the text and notes of that work.

[2] See England under the Anglo-Saxon King, Pref. p. xiii.

appeared to me incorrectly represented, I have corrected the passage; besides which, my additions, both
to the text and notes, are neither few nor far between[1].
What I have here stated applies generally to all the
four reigns contained in the volume, though more
especially to that of Stephen, which, although full of
incident and, on account of the mournful picture it
presents of the state of England during that period of
calamity, and of the romantic events with which it
abounds, is well worthy of the historian's labour, has,
nevertheless, been hitherto more briefly and super-
ficially treated than any other reign during the middle
age. In the present volume much of it has been re-
written.

Hence I venture to entertain the hope, that the
work in its English dress will by every intelligent and
unprejudiced reader be classed if not as the best, at
least not among the worst records of England's sad
story, during a period of tyranny, the natural result of
foreign conquest, exercised by alien sovereigns and an
alien aristocracy over the oppressed and impoverished
Anglo-Saxon population—a tyranny of which happily
but few traces are discernible at the present day.

The outline of early Norman history under the house
of Rolf cannot, I think, be otherwise than welcome to
many readers; to some the subject will, no doubt, be
new, while to none who feel an interest in the History
of England can it be matter of indifference, whence

---

[1] My notes are here, as in the H. of E. under the A. S. Kings, distinguished by the letter T. My additions to and corrections of the text are
too intimately blended with the original matter to admit of distinction.

those princes sprang, how they established themselves in the Frankish province, and what were their exploits and characters, who, directly or indirectly, have given a long line of sovereigns to this country. As a supplement to this "Outline," in which much curious matter will be found, I have added from Depping[1], a chapter on the conditions, manners, etc. of the Scandinavians and of their offspring in France, better known to us under the more familiar denomination of NORMANS, while under their own counts or dukes; also a short paper, from the same author, on local names in Normandy, showing, in numerous instances, their exact identity with those similarly applied in the Scandinavian North. I have, in fact, to a certain extent, though unconsciously to myself, acted in conformity with Southey's advice to his brother, when the latter was meditating a work on the Crusades: he writes, "Omit none of those little circumstances which give life to narration, and bring old manners, old feelings, and old times before your eyes."

In my version and my additions, both to the text and notes, I have anxiously endeavoured to be correct; that in this respect I have frequently failed, is highly probable; but the gentle reader will, I hope, kindly take the will for the deed, and regard with lenity those errors and defects which he may detect in the course of the work.

With this volume, ending at the death of Stephen, Lappenberg's labours terminate; his original intention of continuing them to the Reformation having unfor-

---

[1] See p. 5, note 2.

tunately been frustrated by defective vision, under
which he has for some years been a sufferer; but the
long suspended work is, I rejoice to say, in the hands
of my friend DR. REINOLD PAULI, the able author of
the Life of King Ælfred[1], whose labours already reach
to the reign of Henry VIII. Dr. Pauli's volumes merit
great praise, and are justly held in high estimation both
in England and Germany, as exhibiting deep research
not only among the old chroniclers of this and other
countries, but also among our hitherto too much neglected national records, of which he has availed himself
with an earnestness of purpose that could not fail of
finding its reward in the rectification of many points in
our history, that had previously been set in a false
light. It is to be hoped that Dr. Pauli's work will soon
appear in English from the pen of a competent translator.

To MR. WRIGHT, the Printer to the University, I
have to offer my best thanks for his care and expedition, while the volume was passing through the
Press.

B. T.

---

[1] Koenig Aelfred und seine Stelle in der Geschichte Englands, von Dr.
Reinold Pauli. Berlin, 1851. 8vo. There are two translations of it into
English, one published by Mr. Bentley, the other included in Mr. Bohn's
"Antiquarian Library." The latter, which is said to be by a lady, forms
a volume with king Ælfred's Anglo-Saxon version of Orosius by the
present editor.

CONTENTS.

EARLY HISTORY OF NORMANDY.

CONTENTS.

RICHARD I.

RICHARD II.

RICHARD III.

ROBERT II.

WILLIAM II.

ON THE CONDITION, MANNERS, &c. OF THE SCANDINAVIANS AND NORMANS IN GENERAL*.

* Addition by the translator.

WILLIAM THE FIRST. 1066–1087.

* Addition by the translator.

WILLIAM THE SECOND, 1087–1100.

* Addition by the translator.

HENRY THE FIRST, 1100-1135.

STEPHEN, 1135—1154.

b

LITERARY INTRODUCTION.

THE early history of the Frankish province which, at a subsequent period, bore the name of Normandy, is derived chiefly from the same sources as those which constitute the history of France itself, and which, even after the establishment of the Norman principality, are still necessary to illustrate and correct the exclusive sources of the provincial history. As essential sources of Frankish history, having reference to Normandy and its settlers, we will here name only the Annals of St. Bertin, with the Continuations of Prudentius bishop of Troyes (835—861), and of Hincmar archbishop of Rheims (861—882), and the Annals of St. Vedast; from which four works the Chronicon de Rebus gestis Normannorum is compiled; the Annals of Xanten (640—874); and the Annals of Regino of Prüm, to the year 906[1]. Particularly important are the works of Frodoard (ob. 966). More abounding in matter for our purpose than his Historia Ecclesiæ Remensis is his Chronicon; but in which we have to regret a large chasm, from the year 877 to 917[2]. From the period when Frodoard closes, the Frankish annals are no longer to be regarded as the basis of Norman history, but. like Northern, English, and Flemish chronicles, as well as the historic records of Brittany, Le Maine, and other states bordering on

[1] All in Pertz, Monumenta Historiæ Germ. i. and ii.
[2] Both in the Recueil des Historiens de la France, viii.

b 2

19

Normandy, to be looked on in the light of auxiliaries, to which
we must occasionally have recourse.

The particular sources of the history of Normandy require
a more detailed specification, partly because some of them
have been but little known and incorrectly estimated; partly
because they are, for the most part, very instructive also for
the history of England; although, for that object, they have
hitherto been treated with unjustifiable slight. I hope therefore for indulgence, if the following notices should to some
appear superfluous.

Dudo, canon and dean of St. Quentin, must have stood
early in connection with the court of Rouen. In the year 986,
Adalbert count of Vermandois, sent him, at that time a
canon, with important diplomatic commissions to Richard I.,
count of Normandy, which he successfully executed. He remained in familiar intercourse with count Richard, as well as
with his younger step-brother Ralf, count of Ivry. Two
years before his death, count Richard invited Dudo to com-
pose a work on the history of Normandy and his grandfather,
Rolf. After Richard's death, his son, Richard II, renewed
the request, and count Ralf, by his oral communications,
supplied him with matter[1]. The work is dedicated to Adal-
bero, archbishop of Laon (977—1030), and has besides metrical dedications to the count Richard II., his brother,
Robert archbishop of Rouen, and count Ralf. This history,
which is interrupted by many graphic embellishments, and
swelling with dialectic and other kinds of erudition in vogue

---

[1] Dudonis versus ad Comitem Rodulfum, hujus operis relatorem:
  Cujus quæ constant libro hoc conscripta relatu,
  Digessi....
Wil. Gemmet. lib. i. Epistola ad Willelmum regem:—"e Dudonis pe-
riti viri historia collegi, qui quod posteris propagandum chartæ com-
mendavit a Rudolfo comite, primi Richardi fratre, diligenter exquisivit."
On the death of Richard I. Dudo says: "Hucusque digesta prout a Ro-
dulfo comite, hujus ducis fratre, magno et honesto viro, narrata sunt
collegi."

at the time, is divided into three books, the first of which treats of the Normans before the landing of Rolf, particularly of the expedition of Hasting to Luna, and his return to France.   The events of which Dudo here speaks, without any dates, may, for the most part, be confirmed by trustworthy annals.   With all its faults, Dudo's work does not deserve the contempt heaped on it by the learned Benedictines, but may be said to follow traditions credible in the main, though sometimes incorrectly transmitted, and adorned with much false eloquence.   His second book is exclusively devoted to a life of Rolf.   I have already had occasion to show, that a true interpretation is all that is required for Dudo's justification [1].   In the outline of Rolf's history, in the beginning of this volume, I have endeavoured to give a right interpretation of some points.   The third book comprises the Lives of the counts William I. and Richard I.   Dudo's work is printed complete only in the collection of Du Chesne.

An epitome of Dudo's work was made by William, surnamed Calculus, a monk of Jumièges, in four books, to which he adds, in three books, a history of the successors of Richard I. down to the battle of Senlac.   His work is dedicated to William the Conqueror.   The first edition by Camden (Anglica, Normannica, etc.) contains an eighth book, continuing the Anglo-Norman history to 1137.   The work of William of Jumièges has been much used.   The Roman de Rou consists principally of a free translation of it into French verse. Ordericus Vitalis has also largely availed himself of it.   Radulfus de Diceto, in his "Abbreviationes Chronicorum," John Wallingford, Matthew of Westminster, and the Chroniques de St. Denys, have likewise taken much from William of Jumièges.   See Bouquet, x. p. 306, xi. p. 398.

The monk of the abbey of Bec, who composed the eighth

---

[1] A case in point is the probable substitution of the West Saxon king Æthelstán, for Guthrúm Æthelstán, the Danish ruler of East Anglia. See England under the A. S. Kings, ii. pp. 105 sq.

book above-mentioned, which is strictly a biography of king
Henry I., is, without doubt, Robert of Thorigny, in 1128 a
monk of Bec, afterwards, till 1154, prior there, and lastly
abbot of Mont St. Michel, whence his designation of Robert
de Monte. He died in 1186. To the chronicle of Sigebert
of Gemblours he added similar interpolations and appendices,
to the year 1182, in which he mentions his history of Henry I.
appended to the Chronicle of the Dukes of Normandy[1]: His
additions to Sigebert are, for the most part, excerped from
the chronicle of Henry of Huntingdon; while, on the other
hand, his most valuable matter has been extracted by Matthew Paris.

The Chronica Normanniæ ap. du Chesne. Scriptt. Norm. is
only a bad and somewhat abridged transcript of Robert's appendix to Sigebert, from 1139 to 1168.

The Encomium Emmæ, daughter of count Richard I., and
wife of the Anglo-Saxon king Æthelred II., and of Cnut the
Great, the work of an anonymous but contemporary author,
needs only a short notice. That the writer lived in the time
of Cnut, and was probably an inmate of the abbey of St. Bertin at St. Omer's, he informs us himself[2]. The first edition
of the Encomium is that in Du Chesne's collection. It afterwards appeared, with excellent annotations, in the 2nd volume of Langebek's Scriptores Rerum Danicarum, 1773; and
a third time, with annotations by Baron Maseres, at London,
in 1783, 4to[3].

[1] Historia, quam de ipso rege noviter defuncto edidi, et gestis ducum
Normanniæ adjeci. Prolog. Appendicis ad Sigebertum, coll. ibid. a. 1135.
Cf. also Recueil des Historiens de la France, viii. Præf. No. xvi.

[2] Page 173; edit. Maseres, p. 24.

[3] In the same volume, edited with elaborate and valuable notes by the
venerable and learned Cursitor Baron, are contained portions of William
of Poitiers, Ordericus Vitalis, and other interesting original matter relative
to the Norman conquest. The title is 'Historiæ Anglicanæ circa tempus
conquestus Angliæ a Gulielmo Notho, Normannorum Duce, Selecta Monumenta, excerpta ex magno volumine, cui titulus est 'Historiæ Normannorum Scriptores antiqui,' etc. cum notis plurimis, Anglico sermone, ad

The work of William of Poitiers, archdeacon of Lisieux, chaplain to William the Conqueror, is instructive both for the history of the Normans, and for the subversion of the Anglo-Saxon dynasty. If in Dudo's bombastic prose intermingled with verse we recognise traces of old German and Scandinavian composition, as in the Saxon Chronicle, and later in Saxo Grammaticus and Snorri, so, on the other hand, we find in William of Poitiers' attachment to the Roman classics, particularly Sallust, a new source of the degeneracy of historic narrative, in which, "after the practice of eminent Romans," numerous imaginary speeches are interspersed by the author, and half the truth is sacrificed to sparkling antitheses and other pompous rhetorical corruptions. Robert de Monte was acquainted with the work of William of Poitiers[1], and Orderic has so largely drawn from it, that the chasm between the years 1067 and 1070, at the end of the manuscript of this writer, may, with tolerable certainty, be supplied from the third book of Orderic. William of Malmesbury also follows this work in the third book of his Gesta Regum, and some passages from him have been turned into French verse by Benoît de Ste More. William of Jumièges appears also to have made use of him[2].

A narrative poem on the battle of Hastings (De Bello Hastingensi), in 835 hexameters and pentameters, greatly to the praise of the Conqueror, was composed by Wido, or Guido, bishop of Amiens (ob. 1075)[3], and dedicated to archbishop Lanfranc. This long-lost poem was some years ago recovered by Dr. Pertz at Brussels. From the first two lines,

> "Quem probitas celebrat, sapientia munit et ornat,
> Erigit et decerat, L.... W.... salutat,"

illustrandum textum conscriptis, a *Francisco Maseres*, Anglo, Curiæ Scaccarii Regis Magnæ Britanniæ in Anglia Barone quinto. London, 1807." small 4to.—T.

[1] Ord. Vitalis, pp. 503, 521. Wil. Gemmet. lib. vii. c. 44.

[2] Compare Wil. Gemmet. lib. vii. c. 8, with Guil. Pictav. pp. 178, 212.

[3] Chron. Centulense S. Richarii ap. D'Achery, Spicileg. ii. Bouquet, xi. p. 135, xii. p. 272.

it had been concluded that Lanfranc was the author, and that
the work was dedicated to king William ; but the words both
of Robert de Monte and Orderic, with reference to the poem
of Guido of Amiens[1], have led me to the foregoing conclusion.

Orderic, surnamed Vitalis, son of Odelerius[2], born in 1075
at Attingesham on the Severn, or its tributary stream now
called the Tern, lived a monk in the monastery of St. Evroult
en Ouche (Uticum) in Normandy. Under the title of Historia Ecclesiastica, he has composed, in thirteen books, an
historical work treating chiefly of the acts of the Normans
subsequent to their settlement in France, not only in France
and England, but also in Italy and Palestine. Orderic was
prompted to this comprehensive theme—which proves his
deep-felt interest in those countries—by the circumstance
that Normandy, where he had dwelt from his tenth year, was
become his second native country[3]; while his whole life bound
him to the Church and its affairs, from his fifth year, in which
he was consecrated at Shrewsbury, in the church of St. Peter
and St. Paul, to the service of God. For his Anglo-Saxon
countrymen, with whose language, till his transfer to Normandy, he was alone acquainted, he ever entertained a true-
heartedness, which frequently manifests itself. He continued
his work to 1141, when he was in his sixty-seventh year,
which for the history of his time, both from the extent of his
ken, and his exertions to obtain accurate, particularly genealogical, information, is a highly important source of historic
knowledge for posterity. Also for the ancient history of
Normandy, and of individual monasteries in that duchy, his
work abounds in information, and deserves a stricter examina-

---

[1] W. Gemmet. lib. vii. c. 44. Ord. Vital. p. 504. Comp. also p. 122 of
this volume.

[2] His father was from Orléans, and a vassal of Robert earl of Shrewsbury: "vir ingenio et facundia et litterarum eruditione præpollens; amator
æquitatis fervidus, utilisque comitis (Rogerii Scrobeshuriensis) erat auri-
cularius." After 1094 he became a monk, and died seven years later. See
Orderic. pp. 579—581.

[3] See Introd. to book V. and the end of his work.

tion than it has hitherto undergone, which in proportion to the difficulties arising from Orderic's careless arrangement of his matter, appears the more necessary.

Orderic divides his work into three parts, the first of which contains books I. and II.; the second, books III. and VI.; the third, the remaining seven books. He named it Historia Ecclesiastica, because, according to his own words in the Prologus, he wished to confine it chiefly to ecclesiastical history; but of which object he not unfrequently loses sight. It was written during no fewer than four lives. When it was begun, Roger was living, who had been abbot of St. Evroult since 1091, by whose encouragement Orderic was induced to undertake his praiseworthy task. Roger resigned, on account of ill health, in 1125, and died three years after. To Guarin, his successor, Orderic dedicates his History. When finishing the last book, Guarin had already been succeeded, in 1137, by Richard of Leicester, who in 1140 was followed by abbot Ranulf[1].

Orderic's work appears to have been but little known in the middle age. It has been excerped by an anonymous author, in a tract published by Camden, in his Anglica Normannica, etc. (pp. 29—35), from an ancient manuscript belonging to the abbey of St. Stephen at Caen, under the title De Willielmo Conquestore Fragmentum, which is nothing more than the fragment of Orderic (lib. vii. pp. 646, 647, and 656—663) on the death and burial of William the Conqueror, used by Wace and Benoît de Ste More; also by the author of a Vita S. Waltheofi, Comitis Northamptoniensis et Huntingdoniensis, who transcribes whole passages *verbatim* from Orderic (lib. iv. pp. 534 *sq.*), as well as from Florence of Worcester and William of Malmesbury.

The Roman de Rou of Master Wace, or Gasse, a native of Jersey, and canon of Bayeux (ob. 1184), is in the first half a free metrical version of William of Jumièges: it abounds,

[1] Ord. Vital. pp. 873 *sq.*, 910, 921.

c

25

however, in traditions and narratives of its own. At vv. 2108 *sqq.*, Master Wace cites the historic ballads of the "jugleors," which he had heard in his childhood.

A paraphrase of the Roman de Rou in French prose is contained in the Chroniques de Normandie of the 13th century, extracts from which are given in the Recueil des Historiens de la France (xi. pp. 320 *sq.*, xii. p. 220 *sq.*).

Of the English chroniclers, Bromton has made considerable use of Wace.

The history of the dukes of Normandy, in about 48,000 French riming verses, composed by Master Benoît de Ste More, reaching to the earlier years of the reign of Henry II., has been printed from the only known manuscript, in the British Museum, by M. Francisque Michel, under the auspices of the then Minister of Public Instruction, M. Guizot.

Florence of Worcester. To the foregoing notice of this chronicler[1], it may here be added that, from his death in 1118, his work is continued to 1141 by an anonymous author, most probably John, a monk of Worcester[2].

Eadmer, abbot of St. Alban's, a Benedictine of Canterbury, the disciple and friend of archbishop Anselm, whom he accompanied to Rome, Lyons, etc., wrote a history (chiefly ecclesiastical) from the Conquest to the year 1122, in which he treats largely of the dissensions between his patron, Anselm, and the kings, William Rufus and Henry I.[3] Eadmer was also elected to the see of St. Andrew's, but resigned it on

[1] See England under the Anglo-Saxon Kings, i. Literary Introduction. p. xlvii.

[2] This name we obtain from Ordericus Vitalis p. 504. (edit. Maseres. p. 190), who was apparently ignorant of the author continued by John. believing him to be Marianus Scotus. [The edition of Florence published by the English Historical Society has a further continuation to the year 1295, by John de Taxter and another monk of Bury St. Edmund's.—T.]

[3] "In quo," as John Bale elegantly informs us. "plenis buccis bestiæ Romanæ tuetur partes."—T.

refusing consecration except by the archbishop of Canterbury. Eadmer's history has been edited by John Selden[1].

To the notice of William, a monk and librarian of Malmesbury abbey, already given[2], may be here added, that his Gesta Regum Anglorum, bringing the history down to 1120, is succeeded by his Historia Novella, which concludes with the year 1142, and, like his Gesta, is dedicated to his patron, Robert earl of Gloucester, the illegitimate son of Henry I.

The Magnus Rotulus Scaccarii sive Pipæ is also a source of history not to be passed over without notice. The date of this important roll, which had formerly been assigned to the reign of Stephen, is justly fixed by its editor, the Rev. Joseph Hunter, under the year 1131, or thirty-first of Henry I.

For the history of Stephen, the most abundant source of information is the Gesta Stephani, the work of an ecclesiastic, apparently a foreigner, warmly, though not blindly, attached to that prince. This interesting and valuable biographical monograph has reached us only in one known and imperfect manuscript. It is printed in Du Chesne's collection, and reprinted in a separate volume by the English Historical Society[3].

The first five years of Stephen's reign (1135—1139) are treated of in the short tract of Richard, prior of the Augustines at Hexham. It is printed in Twysden's collection[4].

John, prior of Hexham, continued the chronicle of Simeon

[1] Eadmeri Monachi Cantuariensis Historia Novorum, sive sui Sæculi, libri vi. Londini 1622, folio. To this edition a valuable body of notes is subjoined by the learned editor, under the title: Johannis Seldeni ad Eadmerum et Notæ et Spicilegium.—T.

[2] See England under the A. S. Kings i. Lit. Introd. p. liii.

[3] Gesta Stephani, Regis Anglorum et Ducis Normannorum, incerto Auctore, sed Contemporaneo, olim, ex vetere codice M.S. Episcopatûs Laudunensis ab Andrea Duchesne edita, denuo recensuit, notisque illustravit, Ricardus Clarke Sewel, D.C.L. Collegii Beatæ Magdalenæ apud Oxoniam Socius. Londini: Sumptibus Societatis.

[4] Historia Piæ Memoriæ Ricardi Prioris Hagustaldensis Ecclesiæ, de gestis Regis Stephani, et de Bello Standardii.

of Durham from the year 1130 to 1156. In this continuation the dates after 1140 are erroneously increased by 1. This is, however, to be ascribed solely to the error of a copyist, who has interpolated, after 1140 and under 1141, an account of the council of Rheims, held in 1119, and then, instead of 1141, has continued with 1142, and so on. This is in Twysden's collection.

Gervase, a Benedictine of Canterbury, compiled, in the beginning of the 13th century, a chronicle from the year 1122 to 1199, the portion of which that here concerns us is made up from the chronicles of John of Hexham and Henry of Huntingdon, and also from some special acts of the Church of Canterbury. It is in Twysden's collection.

The chronicle of Henry of Huntingdon concludes, as we have before mentioned, with the death of Stephen in 1154. It is dedicated to one of the prelates so misused by Stephen, Alexander bishop of Lincoln.

EPITOME.

EPITOME

OF THE

EARLY HISTORY OF NORMANDY.

THE battle of Senlac, or of Hastings, as the Normans prefer naming it, after the brightest scene in their historic reminiscences, had introduced new men and new masters into England. Normandy was now an English province, but a province of incalculable importance, and, in consequence of its relations with the ecclesiastical and secular states of the Continent, of vast influence. The Normans did not totally extinguish the nationality of the Saxons, but grafted on it a scion, which modified it as much as was possible without annihilating it ; and thus brought to England's future their adventurous, domineering sons, their wars, their military constitutions, their court poets, their legal language, their dissoluteness, their fashions, in short, all which at all times and in all parts of the earth distinguishes a ruling caste.

In the "History of England under the Anglo-Saxon Kings," it was necessary to cast an occasional glance at Normandy and its inhabitants, in illustration of the earlier history of England ; but it is now indispensable to present to the reader an historic view of that country, as a chief, and even yet not wholly extinct, element of English history during the middle age.

The great public importance of the line of coast where the Continent lies most contiguous to the British Isles, has cast into comparative obscurity the less favourably situated coast lands, so that accounts of that part of Celtic Gaul, the " Provincia Lugdunensis Secunda," where, between the Somme and St. Michael's Bay, the British Channel is broken amid innumerable rocks, have, with the exception of what concerns the ports and points of transit, at all times, been but few, and those seldom of any great general interest. To the oldest known inhabitants of these parts, and their several localities, in the times of Cæsar and those immediately following, the Lexovii, the Rothomagi, the Eburovici, the Abrincati, the Baiocenses, the Viducassi, the Sesuvii, the towns of Lisieux (Noviomagus Lexoviorum), Rouen, Evreux, Avranches, Bayeux, Vieux[1] (not far from Caen), and Séez, bear witness. Theatres, baths, and other edifices of the Romans are also still to be traced in Lillebonne (Julia Bona) and Coutances (Constantia Castra). Their druidism and common Celtic origin maintained between these people and the British a connection, which only the introduction of the Roman language and theology slowly tended to weaken. A settlement, however, of Roman allies, of that race of North Saxons that had given name (Littus Saxonicum[2]) to the coast about Bayeux, contributed to accelerate their separation. It cannot be accurately determined when this defensive establishment, which as early as the end of the third century was found necessary for the protection of those coasts against the plundering Saxons and Franks, and originating in an experiment (fortunate at first) of the Romans, to combat an enemy through himself, by founding the military colony of the Læti, grew finally into a Germanic land. To what extent the wanderings and expeditions of the Saxons and kindred

---

[1] For inscriptions found there see the Abbé Lebeuf in Histoire de l'Académie Royale des Inscriptions et Belles Lettres, t. xvi. pp. 489 sq.

[2] See England under the Anglo-Saxon Kings. i. p. 11.

nations to Britain increased the number of settlers on the Gallic coast by new accessions of their countrymen[1], whether they carried with them many of the earlier settlers, how these strangers maintained and conducted themselves, are questions that must remain unanswered, owing to the dark oblivion in which those events are enveloped. But that they *did* maintain themselves and held themselves apart, with respect both to their language and nationality, is proved by the accounts of the sixth century, of how the Bretons burned to quench their Celtic hatred in Saxon blood (a. 578); how bishop Felix of Nantes made the conversion of their stony hearts his daily occupation, in which he succeeded only at the close of his life. Even in the ninth century we find a small district in those parts named the *Lingua Saxonica*, as other districts were distinguished as the *Langue d'oc* and the *Langue d'ouil*[2]. The Normandy of after times united itself but slowly with the Frankish realm, though it acknowledged, but on a very independent footing, Childebert I. of Paris (511–558), and later, after the death of Charibert (567), Chilperic I. of Soissons and his successors, the kings of Neustria. Avranches, like the Saxon Bayeux, appears, with its territory, to have long enjoyed a distinguished independence. The slight connection of these countries with the royal court is apparent from the scantiness of the accounts of them that have been preserved by historians, and which are limited to notices relative to the archbishops of Rouen, the bishops of Bayeux, Evreux, Lisieux, Coutances, Avranches and Séez, also of some

[1] That frequently not a few Anglian and Frisian families peaceably passed over to the Franks, we learn from Procopius, lib. iv. c. 20. Comp. England under the A. S. Kings, i. p. 115.

[2] Capit. Caroli Calvi in Monum. Hist. Germ. i. p. 426. Others read *Otlingua*. Is this the same word, or may it denote the country of the Saxon Etheling? Comp., with reference to this district, Lebeuf ut sup. p. 507 f. In the year 843, Otlingua Saxonica is called only a *pagellus*. See document ap. Bouquet. viii. p. 446.

B 2

monasteries, as Jumièges, St. Wandrille (648), Fécamp, St.
Peter's at Ouche (Uticum) ; and later, St. Evreuil, Le Bec,
St. Vedast and others.

The districts (pagi), into which this territory was divided,
are easily to be recognised in the departments which Charles
the Bald assigned to his *missi*, according to the capitulary of
the year 853[1], in the seventh of which is found united the
greater part of the later Normandy. In this were comprised :
the Aprincatum (Avranches), Constantinum (the Cotentin
round about Coutances), Bagisinum (Bayeux), Corilisum,
Otlingua Saxonica, Harduini, Oxinicum (L'Hiesmois) Lisui-
num (Lieuvin, the neighbourhood of Lisieux. In the sixth department we find together with Vimeu, Ponthieu, and Amiens,
appertaining hereto, Rotinense (Rouen), which also comprised
the smaller Calcensis pagus (Caux[2]), and Tellau (Talleu, Tal-
vois, on the river Yeres in Normandy). To the missi of the
eighth department, comprising Le Mans, Anjou, and Tours,
Sagisus (Séez) and Corbonisus (Le Corbonnois, between Tours
and Séez) were assigned. From the south-eastern, or ninth
department, between the Seine and the Loire, the pagus
Ebroicensis (Evreux) fell to the share of Normandy. Over
most of these departments special counts were appointed ;
and, in the ninth century, over Rouen[3], Bayeux, Coutances,
Avranches, and Hiesmes.

Rouen on the Seine had, through its commerce, been always
a place of considerable importance, and, consequently, at an
early period became an object for the plundering expeditions
of the Northmen, which, although, for many years past,
oftenest directed to the British Isles, were, nevertheless, more
frequently turned towards Gaul than we find mentioned by

[1] Older mention of many of these *pagi* occurs in the Gesta Abbatum
Fontanellensium, in Monum. Hist. Germ. t. ii.

[2] Dudo, p. 110.

[3] Radulphus, comes Rothomagensis under Dagobert I. (ob. 638). Gesta
Abb. Fontanell. c. 1.

the chroniclers [1]. When the bloody struggles of the sons of Lewis the Pious had irresistibly drawn the flower of France and her bravest nobles to the battle field of Fontenay, the Northman Osker (Asker), with his band of barbarians, appeared before Rouen (May 12th 841), which they plundered and burnt; slew the bishop, and took possession of the abbey of St. Ouen, whose relics were conveyed to Condé, a small village in the neighbourhood of Paris; other relics were carried into Lorraine. On the 16th May they evacuated Rouen, but on their return to the coast, destroyed or laid under contribution the towns and monasteries along the Seine. On the 24th they burnt the abbey of Jumièges, founded by St. Philibert, in the seventh century, on a peninsula in the Seine, and inhabited by a numerous body of monks and laymen. Having secretly buried a portion of their treasures, the monks fled with the rest, together with their relics. For thirty years this once flourishing abbey lay in ruins [2]. The Northmen had destined the same fate for the abbey of Fontenelle; but it redeemed itself for six pounds, but whether of gold or silver is uncertain. The monks of the abbey of St. Denis paid twenty-six pounds for the redemption of sixty-eight captives. On the last day of May the pirates again betook themselves to the sea [3]. Four years later the companions of Osker under Ragnar ventured to advance on Paris; and in the year 851, he himself appeared, probably in the plundering expedition of Godefrid the Dane on the Seine, again at Rouen [4]. From that time the towns and monasteries

---

[1] E. g. the Danes under Cochilaicus (the king Hygelac of Beowulf) about the year 515. See Gregor. Turon. lib. iii. c. 3.

[2] Wil. Gemmet. I. c. 6. ann. 851. Chron. Fontanell. cited by Depping. I use Prof. Petersen's Danish translation of Depping (Histoire des Expéditions Maritimes des Normands, etc.), which has many corrections of, and some additions to, the original, by the translator, an eminent and well-known Northern scholar.—T.

[3] Annales Bertiniani cited by Depping.

[4] Hoscheri and Hoseri. Fragm. Chron. Font. aa. 841 and 851. Annal.

on the Seine and in the neighbouring country were exposed,
more than all the rest of France, to the incessantly repeated
attacks of the Northmen. Whether that Hasting, whom
Dudo, dean of St. Quentin, the chief source of the Norman
chronicles, places at their head, was ever in Normandy, is
by no means certain ; according to the most trustworthy
chronicles we find him on the banks of the Loire[1], afterwards
on the Somme at Argove[2], below Amiens, a few miles from
St. Quentin. To the terror of the monks at this dreaded
proximity the impressions may derive their origin, which
have accumulated on Hasting the deeds of many of his comrades, and from traditions and songs have caused to be
sought out all that could add to his renown[3].

But the most formidable ally of the Northmen was to be
found in the weakness of the Christian kings themselves, who
were not only ever ready to buy the absence of those pirates,
but even submitted to grant them permanent settlements in
their kingdoms. Lewis the Pious had set the pernicious
example, when he ceded to the Danes, Klak-Harald[4] and
Rörik, Dorstadt[5] on the Rhine and the Kennemerland. His

Xantens. a. 845.   Prudent. Trecens. aa. 841, 845, 851.   Rudolf. Fuldens.
a. 850.

[1] Annal. Vedast. a. 882.   Hincmar Remens. a. 882.

[2] Annal. Vedast. aa. 890, 891.   Comp. also England under the A. S.
Kings, ii. pp. 74–80, 35.

[3] That historic ballads on the Northmen existed in his time is confirmed
by Wace, Roman de Rou, ll. 2108 sqq.

> [A jugléors oï en m'eflance chanter
> Ke Willame jadis fist Osmont essorber,
> Et al Conte Riouf li dous oilz crever ;
>
> *   *   *
>
> Ne sai noient de ço, n'en poiz noient trover :
>
> *   *   *

On which M. Pluquet remarks : " Ce passage curieux nous apprend que,
du temps de Wace, les jongleurs chantaient des épisodes de notre histoire
de Normandie, et qu'ils y mêlaient souvent des fables."—T.]

[4] He was a petty king of South Jutland, or Sleswig.—T.

[5] The present Wyk te Duerstede.—T.

son, Lothair, attempted to remove Rörik from this fief, who
found an asylum with Lewis the German, who permitted him
to dwell in Holstein until, with the aid of a body of his countrymen, he regained possession of Dorstadt[1]. His nephew
or cousin, Godefrid, also succeeded, in the year 850, in extorting a portion of land from Charles the Bald[2], the locality
of which is unknown. Either he, or a successor of the same
name at Dorstadt, in the year 882, received, together with
that fief, the hand of Gisele, a natural daughter of Lothair
the Second[3]. Many Northmen, whose names are unknown
to us, received fiefs, only by assuming the outward semblance
of being Christians. As early as the year 853, Charles the
Bald speaks of such grants to the Northmen[4], but of which
the conditions of feudal fidelity and defence of the country
against the Danish pirates had not been fulfilled. Without
doubt the formidable Weland also received a fief, when, in the
year 862, he submitted to be baptized, in like manner with
Hasting, who, we are informed, received the county of
Chartres[5].

ROLF, or ROBERT I.

The 17th November in the year 876[6] is named as the day
on which Rolf (Hrôlfr), or (as he is usually called after the
Latin chroniclers) Rollo[7], first landed in the territory subse-

---

[1] Rudolf. Fuld. a. 850.   Prudent. Trecens. eod. a.

[2] Rudolf. Fuld. eod. a.

[3] Annal. Vedast. a. 882.   Annal. Fuld. a. 885.

[4] Capitul. a. 853. April. ap. Pertz, p. 418.

[5] Houard, Traité sur les Cout. Anglo-Norm. part i. Pref.

[6] This date is given both by Florence and Ordericus Vitalis, (p. 368).
That the Normans arrived at the Seine in this year, is confirmed by the
Annales Vedastini.

[7] [According to Snorri (Heimskringla, c. 24.) Rolf was a son of Rögn-
vald, jarl of Möri in Norway.   He is described as being of so large a
stature that no horse could bear him, and he was compelled to go on foot,
hence his appellation of Hrôlfr gavngr, or Hrolf the ganger or walker.
For his plunderings (strandhug) on the coast of Norway, he was expelled
from that kingdom by king Harald Hárfagri.—T.]   William of Malmes-

quently known as Normandy. He was the chief of a band of
pirates, and had previously passed some time in England,
had there formed an alliance with Guthorm- or Guthrûm-
Æthelstàn, and subsequently attacked the isle of Walcheren
and invaded Hainaut. Dudo's account of Rolf's deeds is
founded on historic facts interwoven with fictions, but which
it is possible to elucidate by the abstraction of some mistakes
in the chronology. The archbishop of Rouen, Franco, is
said by Dudo to have received from Rolf the promise not to
lay waste the neighbouring country. This improbable story
contradicts itself, as that archbishop was not raised to the
dignity till afterwards; so that we must either regard Dudo's
narrative here as very doubtful, or, to save his credit, suppose
the Rolf of the year 876 a different person from him who
appears on the scene more prominently twenty years later[1].
Rolf, it is said, soon returned to England[2], and was probably
in the succeeding years among the Northmen that committed
such dreadful ravages between the Scheldt and the Somme.
It is also probable that he was in the fleet of Northmen who
crossed the Channel (878, 879), wintered at Fulham, and in
the latter of these years proceeded to Walcheren, and up the
Scheldt to Ghent[3]; in the following year entered the Frankish territory[4], wintered in Courtray and plundered Cambrai;
in 881 were defeated by Lewis III. at Vimeu, and in 883

bury (and from him Alberic) says of him, " de nobili, sed per vetustatem
obsoleta prosapia Noricorum editus." Dudo (p. 70) calls him the son of
a downright free man, who for no feudal obligation would place his hands
between those of another. And (p. 82) " Rollo superbo regum ducumque
sanguine natus."

[1] A bishop Franco of Liege (852–901), may have given occasion to the
confusion of the names, Annal. Lobiens. et Vedast.

[2] See Engl. under the A. S. Kings, ii. p. 51.

[3] Asser, Vita Ælfredi. Saxon Chron. aa. 879, 880. Annal. Vedast. a.
879. This last differs from the preceding by a year. Hincmar Remens.
agrees with the former. Comp. Engl. under the A. S. Kings, ii. p. 56.
Annal. Gandenses.

[4] Asser. Sax. Chron. a. 881. Annal. Vedast. a. 880.

passed the winter at the abbey of Condé on the Scheldt, on the southern frontier of Hainaut[1]. Proceeding northwards from Walcheren, Rolf had Radbod to overcome at Aelmere[2], then, turning southwards by Condé, to encounter and defeat Ragnar, surnamed Longneck, count of Hasbach and Hainaut.

Lewis III. had, in the last year of his life, prevailed on Hasting to abstain from rapine and enjoy a peaceful investiture[3], consisting, we are informed, in the county of Chartres. King Carloman also, proceeding in the course already adopted by the Anglo-Saxons, entered, through the mediation of the Dane Sigfred, into a negotiation with the enemy at Amiens, where, in the year 883, they had passed the winter, and who, in consideration of a tribute of twelve thousand pounds of silver, engaged to remain tranquil till October[4]; nevertheless, on the 25th July in the year following, an army of Northmen appeared at Rouen[5], who there embarked for the purpose of proceeding up the Seine to Pont de l'Arche. These met with the French posted on the Eure, who were defeated by them with the loss of Regnald, duke of Maine.

The celebrated siege of Paris was now undertaken by the Northmen, at which no Frankish chronicler, but Dudo alone,

[1] The mention of Walcheren is from Dudo (p. 74); Condé is also named by Dudo (p. 74). Annal. Vedast, Asser, Sax. Chron. I depart from the usual chronology, and even from Dudo, who places the expedition to Walcheren and Condé before 876; though the accordance of so many accounts must justify my statement.

[2] Fluvius Aelmere, in Dudo (p. 74); stagnum Aelmere; Vita S. Bonifacii, cc. 11. 12. fretum Aelmere, ib. The fishery and ship tax (cogschuld) in Aelmere, a part of the present Zuyder zee, were among the revenues of the see of Utrecht. See Heda, pp. 64, 84.

[3] Annal. Vedast. a. 882.

[4] Ibid. a. 883. Sax. Chron. a. 884.

[5] Ibid. a. 885. Dudo, after speaking of Rolf's expeditions to Walcheren, Friesland and Hainaut, says that he afterwards, in the year 876, embarked for the Seine, which is perhaps an error for 886, or a confounding with the above account of 876. To this time also the dreaded attack on Jumièges seems to belong, of which Balderic, in Chron. Cameract. lib. ii. c. 29. makes mention.

names Rolf as the commander. From the inaction of a protracted siege Rolf freed himself by incursions into Normandy. He took Bayeux, although it defended itself with Old-Saxon valour, and made Popa, the daughter of the count Berengar[1], his wife, according to the pagan Danish forms. Evreux also he caused to be attacked, by which exploits he gained considerable sums in the shape of tribute, and, inspired great dread of his name[2]. The Northmen before Paris, having entered into a truce, proceeded, some along the Marne as far as Chézy, others into Burgundy[3], sailing up the Yonne, on the last day of November 886, to the archiepiscopal city of Sens, plundering the neighbouring country and towns, to Clermont (department of the Oise), and Provins (Seine and Marne), southward to the Benedictine abbey of Fleury, which they spared, thence to Etampes and Villeme on the Eure. From this place, (in May 887) Rolf hastened back to the siege of Paris, which not till the autumn of 889, through the mediation of king Eudes, bought off the enemy[4]. who returned to Normandy. where, after a long siege, they took St. Lo, near Coutances, and levelled it with the ground[5]. The valiant Bretons, however, set a bound to their further advance; whereupon the Northmen, some by sea, others by land, proceeded eastward to Liège, Nymwegen, Louvain and Utrecht[6]. Of the ulterior acts of a part of this army, which

[1] In the Chron. Rothomag. a. 911, in Labbæi Biblioth., also in R. de Diceto, Abbrev. Chron. col. 453. she is called a daughter of count Wido of Senlis.

[2] Dudo. Chron. S. Benigni Divion. ap. Bouquet, viii. 241. Comp. Engl. under the A. S. Kings. ii. p. 75.

[3] Sax. Chron. and Asser, a. 887. Annal. Vedast. aa. 886, 887. Regino, a. 888. Annal. S. Columbæ Senonensis, a. 886. in Mon. Hist. Germ. i. p. 104. To this time also belongs the account of the besieging of Le Mans and the attempt on Tours by Rolf. Alberic. a. 882 from Helinand "ex dictis Odonis abbatis Cluniacensis."

[4] Annal. Vedast. a. 889. Regino, a. 890. Sax. Chron. a. 890.

[5] Annal Vedast. aa. 889, 890. Sax. Chron. and Regino, a. 890.

[6] Annal. Vedast. a. 890. Sax. Chron. and Regino. a. 891.

passed over to England, and there remained till the year 896, we have already spoken[1]. Under a leader, Hund (Hunedée), who is called by the chroniclers Hunedeus, they then directed their course along the Seine, while others embarked on the Oise and the Meuse. For two years they plundered Neustria. Hund, who had proceeded up the Seine with some ships, made peace with king Charles, and submitted to baptism (897), a circumstance the more worthy of notice, as on that account he has at an early period been confounded with Rolf[2].

In the years immediately following, we find neither accounts of Rolf nor of Northmen at Rouen or in the later Normandy, nor any particular notices of those bands, with whom, according to the earlier accounts, Rolf appears to have been connected. From the silence of the other chronicles it is highly improbable that Rolf occupied the foremost place in all those expeditions, which Dudo, the poetic author of the Norman Chronicle, assigns to him; even the early establishment at Rouen, at which this chronicler hints, is either contrary to fact, or it was afterwards abandoned. Not till the year 911 do we hear of a defeat which, on the 12th July, Rolf sustained at Chartres, by dukes Richard of Burgundy and Robert of France[3], who fought under the special protection of the Virgin Mary[4]. In an intrenchment at Loches, formed of the carcases and bloody hides of animals[5], the barbarous sons

[1] See Engl. under the A. S. Kings, ii. p. 75.

[2] Annal. Vedast. aa. 896, 897. Chron. Norman. ap. Pertz, i. 536.

[3] He was a brother of king Odo (or Eudes), and is sometimes styled count of Paris.—T.

[4] Annal. Colomb. Senon. a. 911. Comp. Dudo. Annal. Besuenses h. a. in Mon. H. Germ. ["The good bishop, as soon as he had sung mass, went forth, clad in his episcopal ornaments, the cross borne before him, and he himself bearing on the point of a lance the Virgin Mary's chemise, which had been brought from Constantinople by Charles the Bald, and was preserved in the cathedral of Chartres. All the clergy followed, singing psalms in honour of the heavenly Virgin." Depping, p. 352. See Dudo, p. 80, W. Gemmet. p. 230, Rom. de Rou, vv. 1621 sqq.—T.]

[5] Roman de Rou, vv. 1777 sqq.

of the North had long maintained themselves.   It is probable
that Rolf, after the death or return of the other leaders, now
arrived at the supremacy among his countrymen, had for a
considerable time been fortified in Rouen or some place commanding the Seine, as well as in other towns of Normandy,
where king Charles the Simple, convinced of the impossibility
of prolonging the defence of his country, purchased from the
enemy, by the cession of a considerable province of Neustria,
which from that time has borne the name of Normandy, the
safety of his kingdom in that quarter; only a century since
Charles the Great had fixed the Eyder as their boundary.
Flanders, that had in the first instance been offered to him,
the haughty conqueror rejected with scorn, as being too
marshy.   The accounts of the treaty relating to this cession,
which was concluded at St. Clair-sur-Epte, in the year 912,
vary from each other.   At first the Franks would grant to
Rolf Neustria from the Andelle to the sea; but, in a further
negotiation, the rivers Bresle and Epte were fixed as the
eastern boundary.   But that the little river Coisnon, that
runs between Normandy and Brittany, could at that time
have been established as the western limit[1], is refuted by the
history of the Norman acquisitions in the following years,
from which it appears much more probable that the boundary
agreed on at St. Clair was drawn northwards from Evreux,
and in the west by or on this side of Caen.   Of such an inconsiderable beginning was this cession, which was shortly to
become so important for France and England, and of the
former kingdom to raise up the mightiest vassal that the
world had ever known!   The Northmen, however, maintained,
that Brittany also[2], or rather certain rights of suzerainty over

---

[1] Malaterræ Chronica. Guido (ap. Albericum. a. 912.) names the Epte
(Itta) as the boundary; also Frodoard. a. 923. "Itta fluvio transito, ingressus est terram, quæ dudum Nordnannis ad fidem Christi venientibus,
ut hanc fidem colerent et pacem haberent, fuerat data." Eu (Auga) on
the Bresle belonged to the Normans. Frodoard. a. 925.

[2] Dudo (p. 83). W. Gemmet. lib. ii. cc. 17, 19. Comp. on this much

that state, and the revenues arising therefrom, or that the fiefs of Rennes and Dol were ceded to Rolf.   One of Rolf's followers, named Gerlo, received from the king the fief of Mont-de-Blois[1]; another, Heribert, the county of Senlis.   It is probable that the Cotentin was also granted to one of these, who, or whose son, named Riulf, afterwards made war on the son of Rolf.   Like Guthrûm-Æthelstân, Rolf immediately became a convert to Christianity, and received baptism at the hands of Franco, archbishop of Rouen.   His sponsor was Robert, duke of France, who gave him his own name, and the king gave his natural daughter, Gisele, in marriage to his new vassal[2].

The Northmen of the Seine, for so were Rolf and his followers still designated[3], soon strove to extend their dominion.   It is probable that they took part in the attacks on western Brittany, which proceeded from their countrymen encamped on the Loire (a. 919), and in the course of two years led to the cession of the desolated land, and of the district of Nantes[4].

Two years later (a. 923) the Northmen of Rouen again allied themselves with Ragenald, the leader of their brethren on the Loire, for the purpose of plundering the neighbouring districts of Beauvais and Arras.   King Rudolf with an army crossed the Epte, with the design of penetrating into their country, whereupon the Northmen advanced into the unprotected lands beyond the Oise, which they ravaged, in ex-

---

disputed point Daru, Geschichte der Bretagne translated by Schubert. t. i. pp. 80–88.   Licquet, H. de Normandie.

[1] Chron. Sithiense, a. 912. ap. Bouquet, ix. p. 76. Johann. Paris. ib. x. p. 255, n^d.   [2] W. Gemmet. Rom. de Rou, 1914 *sqq.*

[3] Charter of Charles the Simple, a. 918, ap. Bouquet, ix. p. 536. "partem quam adnuimus Nortmannis Sequanensibus, videlicet Rolloni suis comitibus, pro tutela regni."

[4] Frodoardi Chron. aa. 919, 921.   That Rolf's companions received or kept this land, appears from Frodoard, a. 921.   "Ragenoldus cum suis Nordmannis, quia nondum possessionem intra Gallias acceperat."

pectation of extorting the cession of larger territories on the other side of the Seine. Seulf, archbishop of Rheims, and Heribert, count of Vermandois, mediated a truce till May in the following year; whereupon, after the pernicious example already set both in France and England, a danegelt was paid to the Northmen (924), whose territory was, moreover, enlarged by the cession of Le Mans and the Bessin, or Bayeux [1]. The latter was intrusted to Botho, the friend of Rolf [2]. Nevertheless, in the second year (925) Rolf availed himself of a new expedition of Ragenald into Burgundy (in which the latter was killed in the Passe Chailles [3]), to violate the truce: he marched eastwards. Among the casualties of this formidable expedition Amiens and Arras fell a prey to the flames; the suburb of Noyon was fired by the Northmen, who were, however, repulsed by the townsmen. When in this conjuncture intelligence was brought that the men of Beauvais [4] had crossed the Seine, the Parisians with count Hugo's warriors had entered Rouen, and count Helgaud of Ponthieu, or Montreuil, with his coast-Franks, was ravaging the Norman districts, Rolf did not venture to cross the Oise, but returned to his own territory. A thousand of his people, whom he had sent to the frontier to support his fort at Eu [5], were, by Heribert and the vassals of the church of Rheims and count Arnulf of Flanders, massacred without mercy, which they themselves had never known. Duke Hugo concluded a separate peace for himself with the Northmen, who in the following year (926) slew count Helgaud at Arras, and would have captured the wounded king Rudolf, but for the timely aid of count Heribert. Eleven hundred Northmen

---

[1] Frodoard. aa. 923, 924.

[2] "Boton de Baex, Quens des Bessineiz." Rom. de Rou, v. 2162.

[3] Mons. Calaus. From the Itinerary of Albert of Stade (edit. Reineccii, p. 183.), who calls it Mons Catus, it appears that this district lies between La Chapelle and Chambery.

[4] So we are, no doubt, to read instead of Frodoard's Bayeux.

[5] Frodoard. a. 925.

fell in one battle, and the survivers contented themselves with a new danegelt from France and Burgundy, for which they swore to refrain from hostilities under mutual oaths[1].

In the following year (927) new wars led to the cession of Nantes to the Northmen of the Loire. Rolf, on the other hand, began now to connect himself more closely with the other magnates and with the destinies of France. Count Heribert, who for some years had held king Charles the Simple in durance, having quarrelled with the rival king Robert, respecting the investiture of the county of Laon, and suffered his captive to re-appear with kingly dignity, Rolf found it advantageous to let his son, William, receive investiture from king Charles at Eu[2], and to conclude a peace with Heribert. Shortly after, this amicable alliance was extended to duke Hugo, though Odo (Eudes), who was Rolf's hostage, was not restored to his father, until the latter had sworn his oath of allegiance to king Charles[3].

Some years after these events Rolf died (931)[4] well stricken

[1] Frodoard a. 926.

[2] Ibid. a. 927, "Filius Rollonis Karolo se committit."

[3] Ibid. aa. 927, 928.

[4] [He was buried in the church founded by him at Rouen; but his remains were afterwards deposited in a chapel of the present cathedral, where his tomb is yet to be seen with the following epitaph, in the place of an older one:—*Hic positus est Rollo, Normanniæ attritæ, vastatæ, restitutæ primus dux, conditor, pater, a Francone, archiep. Rotom. baptizatus anno 913, obiit anno 917; ossa ipsius in veteri sanctuario nunc capite navis primum condita, translato altari, collocata sunt a B. Maurilio, archiepisc. Rotom.*, an. 1063.—T.] Although Dudo (p. 86) relates that the death of Rolf took place five years after the adoption of his son as co-regent, this space of five years has, however, been reckoned from 912, the year of his baptism; and this error has been repeated not only by Florence of Worcester, but, as may be seen above, in his epitaph at Rouen, and also by Ordericus Vitalis, p. 459. The Saxon Chronicle says "he ruled over Normandy fifty years after his landing," therefore till 926. The Chron. Turon. has 931 for the year of his death, the Chron. Alberici, 928. A later MS. of the Saxon Chronicle says, that a. 928, William began to reign, but without mentioning that Rolf died at that time.

in years; the founder of a splendid race, which in the following century was to be adorned with the ducal mantle and a
royal crown; the leader of the boldest bands, in which the
valour of the North and the culture of the South soon combined to form the model of the knightly virtues of the middle
age.   One consequence of the death of Rolf seems to have
been a rising of the West Bretons against the Northmen,
who, on St. Michael's day 931, under their leader Felecan,
massacred all their oppressors.   Berengar, and Alan, who
had returned from England, were, however, soon driven back [1],
when Incon, the leader of the Northmen on the Loire, combined with his countrymen at Rouen again to reduce Brittany
to subjection [2].

Rolf left his son, instead of the rude intrenchments, in
which he had passed the greater part of a life of plunder and
warfare, a formally acquired marquisate, charged with no
obligation, save that of defending his own territory against
an enemy, and already enlarged by successful enterprise; for
such was the intent and character of his possession, but
which appears seldom so expressed.   At first the ceded territory was transferred to the Northmen in joint possession, as
is confirmed by the language of a charter of king Charles the
Simple [3].   The king of France could not in fact recognise
any one of them as prince, as they themselves regarded all on
an equality [4].   Rolf, although certain of the result, left the
choice of his successor to the Northmen of the highest consideration [5], and contented himself with recommending to
them his son, who had been under the tuition of Botho, the

---

[1] See England under the A. S. Kings, ii. p. 113.

[2] Frodoard. a. 931. Hugo Floriac. ap. Bouquet, viii. p. 319.   Comp.
Dudo, p. 93.

[3] Of the year 918. See p. 13, notes 2 and 3.

[4] "Quo nomine vester (Danorum) senior fungitur?" Responderunt,
"Nullo, quia æqualis potestatis sumus." Dudo, p. 76.

[5] "Vestro consilio vestroque judicio constituatur dux vobis." Dudo,
p. 91.

leader of his army (princeps militiæ). The title of this hereditary prince seems at that time not to have been fixed, nor
even at a later period. Dudo calls him *Dux*[1], *Protector,
Patricius, Comes;* we afterwards find *Rector*[2], *Princeps*[3],
Marchio[4]. In charters the title of *Comes* is the most usual,
and this was given by the king of France[5]; we also meet
with it in the charters of the Norman princes themselves, and
although the proœm of the document, according to the arbitrary practice of the time, may be filled with pompous titles,
or rather attributes, we, nevertheless, find almost always in
the subscriptions, and always on the seals, the legally valid
title of *Count*[6]. The county was at first sometimes denominated from its most considerable city, Rouen[7], and sometimes

[1] Lib. i. 86-91. Rotomagensium dux.   Radulf. Glaber, Lib. iii. a. 942.
Also in the later Balderic. Chron. Camerac. lib. i. cc. 33, 71, 114.

[2] " Normannorum, divina ordinante providentia, dux et rector," Charter
of Robert, a. 1028—1036, in Monast. Angl. vi. 1100.

[3] Charter of 1024. Monast. Angl. vi. 1108. " Dei nutu Normannorum
princeps."

[4] " Willelmus (I.) marchio." Dudo, Præf. lib. iii. p. 105. " Richardus,
comes; marchio, dux, patricius." Ib. pp. 106, 107, 108. Richardus marchisus." Charter of K. Lothair, a. 966. Bouquet ix. p. 629.   In a charter
of 968 he calls himself " Richardus Normannorum marchio." Ib. p. 731.
So likewise his successor in 1014. Charter in d'Achery, Spic. xiii. p. 274 :
and as "dux," in a charter of 1003, cited in Chron. S. Benigni Divion. Ib.
i. p. 457.

[5] Charters of K. Robert of 1005 and 1006, ap. Bouquet, x. pp. 586, 587;
without date ap. Mabillon, Vet. Annal. iii. 441.   William the Conqueror
calls his ancestor : " Ricardus Normannorum comes." Monast. Angl. vi.
p. 1082. The Conqueror himself is in the Saxon Chronicle, a. 1051, called
" Willelm eorl ;" and by Ingulf," comes Normannorum."

[6] In a charter e. g. of William II. of 1042. Mon. Angl. vi. p. 1073 ; in
a charter of Robert, s. a. "comes et dux ;" afterwards : "Robertus comes."
Ib. p. 1108.—"Willelmus comes et Normannorum dux." Ib. p. 1101.
Comp. charters of Robert and others ib. pp. 1073, 1074. These numerous
references will not, it is hoped, be considered superfluous, when it is
recollected that both Thierry and Michelet (Histoire de France, i. p. 419)
speak of the *ducal* title conferred on Rolf in 912.

[7] " Robertus Rotomagensis" says Dudo (p. 86.) speaking of Rolf;
" comes Rodomi" of Richard II. Ademar Caban. a. 1008 Bouquet. x. p

from the race by which it was chiefly occupied; but the name
of a county derived from that race first appears in the eleventh
century[1].

Less clear to us than the history of the princely dignity are
the fortunes of the mass of the settlers, as well as those of
the earlier inhabitants. On the principal Northmen towns
and castles were bestowed, on others, villages, as is easily to
be seen in the names of the Norman aristocracy. According
to ancient accounts, the entire long-desolated country was by
Rolf measured out and distributed[2] among his followers, and
by these and many foreigners invited for the purpose, again
brought into cultivation. Yet the land cannot have been
given to the rugged warriors of the North for them to culti-
vate, but its occupiers must have accompanied the donation,
who paid to them a certain portion of the produce of their
labour for certain privileges of serfdom still continued to
them. We have no accounts to show that any free Franks
remained in the early heritage of the Northmen. Worthy of
notice is the appellation of *hospites*[3], occurring also in the
records of the states occupied by the German conquerors,
which in earlier documents is frequently applied to the Norman husbandmen, thus affording reason for inferring the
existence of similar, though, perhaps, less free and definite,
relations between the lords and the cultivators of the soil.
The same appellation occurs in the Frankish realm, and in
the same sense, in the ninth century, though apparently

151. He is also called "comes Rotomagensium" in a charter of 1024,
cited in Balderici Chron. Camerac. lib. 11. c. 29.

[1] I have first found it in a charter of 1024 (Monast. Angl. vi. p. 1108.)
Of the insertion of the name of the country, instead of that of the name of
the people, in the title of the dukes, I know no older example than the
charter of Henry II. a. 1152. ap. Rymer, i. p. 18. Wittekind, B. 2. a. 937
calls Rouen "Rothomum Danorum;" and Dudo still writes Northmanni.

[2] Dudo, p. 85. "Illam terram suis fidelibus funiculo divisit," etc.

[3] Charter of K. Robert, a. 1006: hospites, quos colonos vocant." Bouquet, x. p. 586. Charter of duke Richard, a. 1024, et alibi.

limited to the north of France and Flanders[1], where mutual necessities created a peasant class, which enjoyed a small possession with greater liberty than other serfs, and in respect of military service were only immediately subject to the lord of the soil[2].

The uncertainty with regard to the first distribution of landed property under the Northmen is the cause that great obscurity hangs over the origin of their nobility and its several degrees. We can, however, clearly perceive that a commonwealth, as in Iceland, and perhaps also in Jomsburg, never existed in Normandy, and that the leaders of the old warrior bands and the court officials of the counts of Rouen soon began to form a privileged, hereditary class of nobles. In the times of the first Norman princes the *majores* were frequently summoned to council, to whose decision the most important matters were committed[3], and the once asserted equality became limited to a small and, perhaps, arbitrarily determined class. It is remarkable, that for a long period the bishops and other prelates do not appear in the accounts of important deliberations unconnected with spiritual concerns.

The most influential official appears to have been the *Princeps militiæ* or *Princeps domus*[4]. Of other court dignities no mention occurs in documents anterior to the conquest of England; though it is not to be assumed that seneschals, constables, sewers, cupbearers, chamberlains, and other court officers were wanting at Rouen in those early times[5]. If

---

[1] Comp. Hincmar Rhem. Ann. a. 866. Du Cange *voce* Hospes. Rapsaet, Recherches, ii. 358. Warnkönig, Flandrische Staats– u. Rechts-Geschichte, i. 246.

[2] Charter of 1165 in Miræi Opp. Diplom. i. 708. Coutumes de Senlis, ap. Du Cange. Dudo, lib. i.

[3] " Leges voluntate principum sancitas et decretas." Dudo, p. 85. " Convocatis Dacorum Britonumque principibus." Ib. p. 86 b. " Convocat majores Dacorum." Ib. p. 82 b. (Willelmus I.) " consultis Dacorum principibus." Ib. p. 93 c. "Optimates regni consulturus." Ib. p. 111 c.

[4] Dudo, pp. 91, 92, 98. W. Gemmet. lib. VII. c. 4.

[5] Dudo, p. 105. mentions a camerarius.

c 2

Dudo's expressions may be trusted, there was even a privy council under the ancient dukes[1].

The denomination of *comites* in the time of Rolf is not to be considered as equivalent to *counts*. If to the prince or leader no higher title than that of count was conceded, his lieges, unless they belonged to his family, must of course bear a subordinate one. Nor do the earlier documents make mention of any other counts, but only of barons[2], and *proceres*[3]. The former counties of Neustria are, in the more precise language of the law, but seldom named, and usually appear as divided into vicecounties[4].

Of the particular legal institutions introduced by Rolf there is very little to relate; although, as founder of the Norman state and first Norman prince, the glory of an ordainer of the legal constitution of his country may less justly be denied him than similar glory to many a celebrated ruler of other lands. We can, however, sufficiently perceive, what is to us of more importance, that the institutions of the Frankish state served as a model to the Northman, in like manner as its language and religion were soon adopted by his countrymen.

WILLIAM I.

SURNAMED LONGSWORD.

The young count William appears in the earlier years of his reign to have been on terms of hostility with his neighbour, king Rudolf. But in the year 933 he swore his oath of homage between that king's hands, from whom he received,

---

[1] " Willelmus assumtis tribus fidis secretariis suis," of whom Botho, the princeps militiæ, was one.

[2] Charter of 1032. Monast. Angl. vi. p. 1073.

[3] Charter s. a. Ib. 1073, 1074.

[4] Charter of 1042. " Vicecomitatus Constantini et Constanciarum :" i. e. the Cotentin and its city, Coutances : " Vicecomitatus Waureti." Ib. p. 1073. "Ranulphus vicecomes." s. a. Ib. p. 1074. " Ricardus, vicecomes Abrincarum." Ib. p. 1064.

in addition to the possessions of his father, a maritime territory of the Bretons[1]. Under this denomination the Cotentin
seems to be understood, whereby Normandy first obtained
her western frontier. This grant was the cause, if, and with
greater probability, it may not be regarded as the consequence, of a rebellion raised by Riulf, a Norman, count of the
Cotentin[2], whose relation to Rolf had been one of brotherhood
rather than of vassalage, and who now demanded the cession
of the greater portion of Norman Neustria, consisting of the
country west of the river Risle, of which he, moreover, took
possession. William's character exhibited a contrast, by no
means rare in life, to that of his father. The clergy, whose
duty it was to impart to the youthful count all that, exclusive
of skill in arms, was called education, had abused their influence over his mind to make of the successor of the energetic Rolf another Lewis the Pious. Shut up by the enemy
in his city of Rouen, he was on the eve of surrender, and only
the threats of the brave old warriors to forsake him and return to their native North induced him to venture a battle,
which three hundred of his faithful vassals won for his salvation, and to the complete overthrow of Riulf. Riulf himself
fled, but was delivered to the conqueror by his own son,
Anschetil, who suffered himself to be deceived by William's
assurances, and was punished with the loss of his eyes[3]. The
birth of his first son and successor, Richard, at Fécamp,
whither the mother, a Breton named Sprote, whom he had
espoused in the Danish manner, had fled, from the apprehension that Riulf might get possession of her child and send
it to England, gave additional gladness to the day which
restored the Norman state[4]. The boy was subsequently sent

[1] "Terram Britonum in ora maritima sitam." Frodoard, a. 933.

[2] "Quens fu de Costentin entre Vire è la mer." So he is styled by
Wace (v. 2123), who had heard the ballads of "Jughéors" about him in
his infancy. (v. 2108.). Dudo, pp. 94 sqq. W. Gemmet. p. 234.

[3] Will. Malm. p. 230. edit. Engl. Hist. Soc.

[4] "Natus de concubina Britanna." Frod. a 942. Dudo, pp. 97, 110.

for education to Bayeux, because Danish was still spoken in
that city, while in Rouen French had already quite superseded
the mother-tongue of the conquerors[1]; a striking fact, which
shows partly the small number of Northmen in Rouen, and
partly indicates an inverse proportion at Bayeux, the earlier
conquest of Rolf, and also sheds some light on the discord
which, after the death of Rolf, ensued between the Danish
inhabitants of that city and those of Rouen.

Brilliant festivals and hunting parties, in the following
years, shed lustre on the court of the young count, who, by
the marriage of his sister Gerloc, also named Adele, with
William, surnamed Tête d'Etoupe, count of Poitou, and by
the hand bestowed on himself of Leutgardis, daughter of
Heribert, the powerful count of Vermandois, as well as
through the friendship of the count of Paris, Hugh the
Great, had closely identified himself with Frankish interests.
Consequently, on the return of the king, Lewis d'Outremer,
he played a conspicuous part. The simultaneous return of
Alan of Brittany (936) proves that the count of Normandy
did not consider himself as superior lord of that territory,
although it was engaged to him for the performance of services, which afforded ground for frequent wars[2].

In the war (939), which had for some years raged between
king Lewis and his vassals, William with his neighbours, the
counts Heribert of Vermandois and Herluin of Ponthieu
(Montreuil), took part with Hugh, who was, moreover, supported by his brother-in-law, the German king, Otto I. We
here find him, through these relations, in hostility with king
Æthelstân of England and Arnulf count of Flanders; and
the ravaging of the territory of the latter called down the
excommunication of those French bishops, who adhered to
their sovereign, upon the son of Rolf. But such was not the
kind of warfare to terrify the Norman warriors, who, but

---

[1] Dudo, p. 112. Benoit de Ste More.

[2] See Engl. under the A. S. Kings, ii. p. 113.

chiefly those of the Cotentin, under the banner of count Herluin, recovered the castle of Montreuil[1], which a short time previously had been taken by the Flemings. Tetger, William's majordomo, was sent on a negotiation to king Otto, who in return deputed to William Conrad the Wise, count of Worms, who about that period was nominated duke of the Franks[2]. William himself assisted at a meeting between Hugh, Heribert, and Arnulf with king Otto, which appears to have taken place at Vouziers on the Aisne, between Laon and Verdun[3]. In the spring of the following year (940) William did homage to king Lewis at Amiens; but no sooner had the king confirmed to the bigoted, but ferocious and faithless chieftain of Rouen[4] the land granted him by his father, Charles, than he again leagued himself with the foes of Lewis, and, with Hugh and his ecclesiastical and secular allies, besieged the archbishop of Rheims, Artald, the friend of the king, in his city, which he captured. From this place William with Hugh appeared before Laon, but which, on receiving intelligence of the king's approach, they abandoned. Hugh and Heribert at this time are said to have done homage to the German king at Attigny; the Norman, it is true, did not follow their example in this instance, though he continued in an alliance repeatedly renewed with the party of Hugh and the king of Germany. Through the mediation of the pope, Stephen IX, William was induced to receive count Rotgar as an envoy from the king. Rotgar died suddenly at the court of William almost immediately after his arrival, though not before he had prevailed on the count to receive the king in Rouen, whereupon a truce was negotiated with the other belligerents, and the king and

---

[1] Frodoard, a. 939. Dudo, p. 103.

[2] I am disposed to identify him with Dudo's "Cono, dux Saxonum."

[3] Frodoard, a. 939.

[4] "Willelmus, Rotomagensium dux ferocissimus." Balderici Chron. Camerac. lib. i. c. 71.

William, as also Hugh, sent hostages to Otto. After the
establishment of a general peace, several private feuds were
also to be accommodated, for which purpose William accepted
an invitation from the count of Flanders to meet him on an
island in the Somme near Péquigny (17th Dec. 942). The
contested points were settled with apparent mutual forbear-
ance, and the kiss of peace sealed the new alliance. When
already on his return home, William was called back by
Arnulf's followers, and not bearing in mind that the promised safe-conduct was no longer valid, he returned without
suspicion, and was treacherously slain by the Flemings[1]. The
assassins were named Balzo the short, Eric, Robert, and
Ridulf, whom an old tradition represents as the avengers of
Anschetil, whom William had caused to be ensnared and
basely murdered[2].

The clergy bitterly deplored the death of William, who
had won their affection by the restoration of the abbey of
St. Philibert at Jumièges, which had been destroyed by the
Northern pirates[3]. But by this unexpected event, the existence of the Normans in France was brought into the utmost
peril, to drive whom from their ill-gotten dominion would
have been an easy task to the magnates of France, had any
degree of unity prevailed among them; as the Anglo-Saxon
king Eadmund, at that time, and probably availing himself
of the weakness of the Danes in Normandy, had expelled
their kinsmen from the north of his realm[4]. Lewis also
was not wanting in attempts to obtain by craft what he

[1] Frodoard, aa. 942, 943. Flor. Wigorn. a. 942. Dudo, lib. iii.

[2] W. Malm. p. 230, and Rom. de Rou, vv. 2108 sqq., where by "Baute
d'Espaigne" Balzo seems to be intended. "Blaso curtus, camerarius."
Chron. Sithiens. ap. Bouquet, ix. p. 78.

[3] Dudo, p. 105. Charter of confirmation by K. Henry II. in Mon. Angl. vi.
p. 1087.

[4] See Engl. under the A. S. Kings, ii. p. 121. That connections always
existed between the Normans and the Danes in England can hardly be
doubted.

was unable to gain by the sword. William had taken care to engage his countrymen to acknowledge his son Richard as his successor[1], and even Lewis, with loud expressions of indignation at the base treachery of Arnulf, confirmed to the boy of hardly ten years the land that had been ceded to the Northmen; yet of the neighbouring barons, who had sworn fidelity to the preceding counts, several now transferred their allegiance to the king, others to count Hugh. The country itself, too, fell into a state of anarchy, when fresh swarms of heathen Northmen landed, to whom many of the old settlers, casting off the inconvenient yoke of Christianity, attached themselves. Even Rouen and Evreux fell into their hands. The pagan king Sihtric, and the renegade Turmod endeavoured also to force the youthful count Richard to apostasy, and to slay king Lewis. The latter, however, succeeded in driving the pagans out of Rouen, the government of which he intrusted to count Herluin, and, under the pretext of educating him, took the young Richard with him as a hostage. Evreux also, of which count Hugh, with the aid of such of its Norman inhabitants as had remained true to the Christian faith, had obtained possession, was by him delivered to the king. Herluin gained a victory over his own and the Normans' foe, count Arnulf, slew Balzo the short, the assassin of count William, and sent the severed hand of the murderer to the vengeance-breathing inhabitants of Rouen. But their minds were soon alienated from the king, in consequence of his reconciliation with count Arnulf[2]. Osmund, to whom the education of the young prince had been committed at the court of Laon, contrived means for the liberation of his pupil. He spread a report that the youth was sick, which was followed by intelligence of his death, whereby those appointed

---

[1] By a second and lawful marriage William had no children. His wife was Leutgardis, a daughter, according to William of Jumièges (p. 235) of Heribert, count of Vermandois.

[2] Frodoard. a. 943. Dudo, pp. 115, 116. W. Gemmet. lib. iv. c. 2.

to keep watch over him were thrown off their guard. Then
having disguised himself, he threw the prince, concealed in a
truss of hay, across a horse, and with the aid of Ivo of Creully,
a royal archer [1], passed out from the walls of Laon and conveyed him to the castle of Coucy [2], the lord of which, Bernard
of Senlis, the young prince's maternal uncle, easily prevailed
on count Hugh to afford protection to the fugitive.

An alliance between Hugh and the Normans [3] was the immediate consequence of this determination, and the result of
the alliance was an attack by the Normans on Brittany, where
many battles were fought with bitter animosity, in which the
recently arrived Danes particularly distinguished themselves.
These had for some time past taken up their quarters in the
Cotentin and Bayeux, and soon received a leader named
Harald, said to be the renowned Danish king, surnamed Blâ-
tand (Black-tooth). Lewis with count Arnulf had made a
second inroad into Normandy and, after a feeble resistance,
rendered himself master of Rouen. Many Normans fled
across the sea, in search of other settlements or to procure
aid from their ancient home [1]. Hugh had in the mean time
marched against Bayeux, which the king had granted to him,
provided he would aid him in subduing the Normans. To
avert the peril to which his country was thus exposed, Bernard of Senlis devised the following stratagem. While his
emissaries were seeking aid in Denmark, he appeared before
the king, to bring him the homage of the Normans. Lewis
received him graciously, proceeded to Rouen, and even took
up his quarters in Bernard's house. His troops had orders
to preserve the strictest discipline. In the mean while the

[1] " Ivo de Credolio, regis balistarius." Ord. Vit. p. 619.

[2] Dudo, pp. 117 sq. W. Gemmet. lib. iv. c. 5. compared with Ord. Vitalis,
pp. 619 sq. Pluquet (Rom. de Rou, p. 161.) remarks that Coucy was a
castle belonging to the archbishop of Rheims; though, as Rheims itself
often was at that time, it might have been in the hands of the king's
enemies.

[3] Frodoard, a. 944.   [1] Frodoard, l. c. Dudo, p. 121.

crafty Bernard persuaded Lewis to believe that the Normans would rather be united under the crown of France than see their country divided ; that all would rather obey the king than that a part of them should be under his vassal, Hugh. Hereupon Lewis, in his eagerness to become master of all Normandy, instantly commanded Hugh to withdraw his forces from the country, and distributed several fiefs among his Frankish courtiers. The count of Paris obeyed, but seeing himself deprived of the fruits of his undertaking by a prince who would reap them alone, he resolved on vengeance. He had an interview with the count of Senlis and engaged to labour for the young count's re-establishment. While all this was passing, the desired succours from Denmark arrived, or had newly equipped themselves at Cherbourg, under Harald, who, as we have seen, was no other than the Danish monarch of that name[1]. Harald, we are informed, landed at the mouth of the Dive, and was received as a deliverer. Warriors from all sides hastened to unite themselves with the chosen band brought by the Dane to the aid of their prince. Harald's progress was soon such as to compel the king to march against him with his vanguard. The royal camp is described as being most costly and splendid ; but a body of good troops would have rendered better service than tents radiant with gold[2]. Not daring to hazard a battle, Lewis had recourse to negotiation. Harald's men had already crossed the Dive, when the two kings met in a tent raised on the river's bank. But the French knew not the foe they were trusting. Some Normans, who observed, among the followers of the king, the count of Ponthieu, Herluin, whose side had been espoused by count William, and who had been the innocent cause of his murder, upbraided him bitterly for taking part with their enemy. From offensive words they proceeded to violence. Herluin and his brother Lantbert

[1] Will. Gemmet. lib. iv. c. 6.   [2] Benoit de Ste More.

were slain, and the conflict between the followers of the two
kings became general.   They slaughtered each other instead
of negotiating ; and the French, being taken by surprise, for
the most part perished.   Lewis fell into the hands of the
Danes, but contrived to escape, and fled to an island in the
Seine ; but no sooner was his hiding-place discovered than
he was recaptured, and would have remained long in durance,
had not count Hugh come to his aid, and had they not feared
the vengeance of the emperor Otto.   He did not, however,
regain his liberty until, in a solemn assembly, he had sworn
to make no further claims to the government of Normandy,
and to require from the count only the simple homage[1].
Lewis then returned home, leaving as hostages his sons,
Lothair and Carloman, the latter of whom died shortly after,
besides the bishops of Soissons and Beauvais and many French
lords.   Some time after, Lewis acknowledged the independence of Normandy in a yet more solemn assembly, in which
both nations were represented by those who constituted the
council of the two princes.   Their last meetings had been
disgraced by base treachery ; the Normans experienced perfidy on the Somme, they requited it on the Dive ; but this
time, at St. Clair-sur-Epte, Richard remained on the Norman
bank and Lewis on the French side, and thus concluded an
agreement with the river between them.   On the spot where
Normandy had been ceded to Rolf, the king of France renewed the cession to his grandson, in return for a simple
feudal homage[2].   Dukes, bishops, counts, and abbots of
France swore to the maintenance of this compact.   On the
opposite bank, the lords of Normandy and Brittany swore
fealty to Richard.   In his relation of this act, Dudo makes

[1] Dudo, p. 123.   W. Gemmet, p. 242.   Wace, i. p. 188.   Frodoard,
Benoît de Ste More.

[2] Dudo (p. 128), makes Hugh to say : " Richardus nec regi nec duci
militat, nec ulli, nisi Deo, obsequi præstat.   Tenet, sicuti rex, monarchiam
Northmannicæ regionis."

mention of the higher clergy among the king of France's followers, while among the Normans he speaks only of laymen[1]. This confirms the remark previously made with reference to the members of the Norman council under the first princes. One historian alleges, that, in virtue of this treaty, the frontier of Normandy was extended from the Andelle to the Epte[2]; but when they concluded the treaty on the Epte, as in the time of Rolf, it is sufficiently evident that that river was always the boundary of Normandy. Also when William Longsword would leave the Normans to proceed to France, Bernard the Dane declared that he would not follow him beyond the Epte, which plainly shews that the French territory commenced at that river. The Normans now placed themselves under the count of Paris, who appointed as his representative Radulf Torta, son of Gautier, bishop of Paris, but who, in consequence of his excessive severity towards, and ill treatment of Richard, was driven from Rouen[3].

Soon after his liberation from the hands of the Normans, the miserable Lewis fell into the power of count Hugh, by whom he was imprisoned at Laon. On his release, through the intervention of the king of England, Eadmund, he and his queen, Gerberge, entered into a combination with her brother, the German king Otto, the object of which was to proceed against Paris, Senlis, and Rouen[4]. In this they were joined by the count of Flanders. At the head of a chosen army Otto appeared before Rouen, of which, being strongly defended by its position, he was unable to gain possession before the severity of winter commenced, and compelled him

[1] " Ipse (rex) et omnes episcopi, comites et abbates reverendi, principesque Franciæ regni......" : and " proceres Britonum et optimates Northmanni." Dudo, p. 126.

[2] Additam. ad W. Gemmet, p. 316.

[3] Dudo, p. 127. W. Gemmet, lib. iv. c. 6. From these it appears that he was neither a royal official, nor a Norman.

[4] Dudo, p. 130. Frodoard, a. 946. Wittekind, lib. iii. Contin. Regin. a. 946. Balderic, lib. i.

to return to Saxony. In this expedition Otto sustained a painful loss in the death of his nephew[1], who fell under the swords of the Normans. Yet this triumph did not immediately lead to the independence of Normandy, as Hugh still appears as its suzerain, perhaps also as Richard's guardian[2].

RICHARD I.
SURNAMED SANS PEUR.

Soon afterwards, an investiture took place, whereby, on the bank of the Epte, Lewis confirmed to count Richard the territories formerly granted to his ancestor Rolf[3]. After the death of king Lewis IV. (954) and of Hugh the Great (956), Richard received the hand of Emma, the daughter of the latter[4], and sister of the future king, Hugh Capet. But even this connection did not establish a good understanding between the French princes and the Norman. Count Theobald ('Thibaut) of Chartres, Tours, and Blois, who had espoused the lawful, but childless wife of William Longsword, raised against him great dissensions with king Lothair, the son and successor of Lewis d'Outremer, with the queen mother Gerberge, and her brother, the archbishop of Cologne. It is said that even a plot was laid against the life of Richard[5]. An assembly of the states at Soissons having been proclaimed by Lothair, Richard attempted by violence to prevent their meeting, but his people were dispersed and put to flight by the faithful followers of the king. In the following year he was more fortunate in totally defeating count Theobald, who fled to Gerberge and her son for protection against Richard

[1] His name does not occur.

[2] In a charter of 968, Richard says: "cum assensu senioris mei Hugonis, Francorum principis." Bouquet, ix. p. 731. "Hugo, collecta suorum, Nordmannorumque manu, Suessionicam aggreditur urbem." Frod. aa. 948, 949. "Hugo, magnus princeps Francorum, Burgundionum, Britonum atque Northmannorum." Annal. Floriac. a. 956.

[3] Dudo, p. 126.

[4] Frodoard, a. 960. Dudo, p. 136.   [5] Dudo, p. 137.

and his powerful brother-in-law, the count of Paris[1]. Lothair succeeded in taking the city of Evreux, which he granted to the count of Chartres, and Theobald advanced as far as Rouen, but was again defeated by Richard, who had in the mean while had recourse to the Danes for aid. An armament of these soon appeared in the Seine, and their presence accelerated the restoration of a long-desired peace. Evreux was delivered back to Richard, and the newly arrived Danes proceeded to Spain, whence, after committing great devastation, they are said to have crossed to Africa.

Richard appears now on friendly terms with Lothair, and composed the difference between him and the younger Arnulf of Flanders, when the king had already taken possession of Arras and Douay, the abbey of St. Amand and all the country as far as the Lys[2].

Shortly after died Richard's consort, Emma, by whom he had no children; but the death of the countess caused no interruption to his friendly relations with Hugh Capet, even after the latter had assumed the kingly crown. Count Adelbert of Vermandois, who had refused to acknowledge the new dynasty (986), but yet feared an attack from the king, was induced by Richard, through the negotiations of his future biographer, Dudo, dean of St. Quentin, to submit to the royal authority.

The latter days of the long reign of Richard were dedicated to the strengthening of the newly acquired lands. Even a war with England (991) shows, through the mediation of the pope[3], that the thought of expelling the Normans from those parts, whence they were soon to conquer the south of Italy and threaten the Castle of St. Angelo itself, could be no longer entertained. The intermixture of the northern set-

---

[1] Frodoard, aa. 961, 962, Dudo, p. 141.

[2] Dudo, p. 155. Comp. with Frodoard, a. 965. Chron. Tornacense S. Martini, a. 966. ap. Bouquet, viii. p. 284.

[3] On this war see Engl. under the A. S. Kings, ii. p. 153 sq.

tlers with Roman-Christian Europe may be inferred from
Richard's great ecclesiastical foundations and donations. He
restored and enlarged the abbey of Fécamp, which a hundred
and fifty years before had been destroyed by the Northmen,
and to which he invited St. William, for the purpose of introducing the rule of Cluny[1]. William continued there thirty
years (ob. 1031), and became, after the superintendence of
other monastic institutions of the country had been intrusted
to him, the founder of the Benedictine rule in those parts.
At an earlier period, Richard, with the confirmation of king
Lothair and of pope John XIII., restored the abbey of Mont
St. Michel[2], and placed in it monks, instead of secular clergy.
He also reconstructed the church of St. Ouen at Rouen. To
the abbey of St. Denis he confirmed the village of Berneval
in the district of Talou, or Tellau (Arques), which his grandfather, Robert, had bestowed on that foundation[3]. Even the
abbey of St. Benignus at Dijon received from him a village
with the church of St. Adelbert at Hiesmes[4].

Of the year of Richard's death the notices are very varying,
a circumstance perhaps to be accounted for by the like name
of his successor. His death probably took place on the 20th
Nov. 996[5]; unless in that year he resigned the government
in favour of his son, and did not die until 1002. The preach-
ing of his monks had reduced the grandson of Rolf to a state

[1] This took place only under Richard II. See Monast. Angl. vi. p.
1082; also Chron. S. Benigni Divion. ap. d'Achéry, Spiceleg. i. pp. 444
sq., 450 sq.

[2] See charter of king Lothair of 966 ap. Bouquet, ix. p. 629.

[3] See charter in Bouquet, ix. p. 731, in which besides his wife, Emma,
his "fideles Osmundus et Radulfus" are named.

[4] Chron. S. Benigni, lib. i. p. 445.

[5] Necrolog. Fiscannense. A later MS. of the Sax. Chron. says 994.
996, Florent. Ademar Caban, ap. Bouquet, x. p. 146. Access. Rob. de
Monte, ib. 269. Chron. S. Michaelis in periculo maris, ib. 247, W.
Gemmet, lib. iv. c. 20. Ord. Vitalis, p. 459. Dudo alone has 1002.
Malmesbury (p. 269) places Richard's death in the eighteenth year of the
reign of king Ethelred, i.e. 1006.

of such deep contrition, that he considered himself unworthy of a grave within the church, but desired to be buried without the walls, under the eaves.

After the death of Emma, Richard espoused Gunnor, a lady of a distinguished Danish race[1]. By her he had five sons and three daughters, of whom may be mentioned: his successor of the like name; Robert, count of Evreux, raised while very young to the archiepiscopal see of Rouen; Emma, to whom the distinction was allotted of becoming the wife of an Anglo-Saxon king, Æthelred II., and afterwards, as that prince's widow, the still greater one of sharing the throne of Cnut, the mighty ruler of the North; lastly Hedvige, the consort of Geoffrey, count of Brittany.

RICHARD II.
SURNAMED THE GOOD.

THE youth of Richard II. was to his country no less a source of peril than that of his father had been, though arising from a totally different cause. The exactions of the Norman barons weighed heavily on the peasant, who still remembered the time when, bound to his lord only for services and dues, he suffered little by imposts, tolls, privileges of the chase, and other restrictions on traffic, as well as on the rights of common. When the arbitrary will of the noble, which did not find full scope for itself in the country, acquired greater liberty after the death of the old count, the peasantry also attempted, by a combination of their powers, to relieve themselves from their iniquitous burthens. They held meetings in various parts of the country, from each of which they sent two deputies to a place of assembly in a central spot. The combination was discovered before it came to an outbreak. Count Raoul, Richard's uncle, surrounded and seized the

---

[1] William of Jumièges (Lib. viii. c. 36) relates that he did not marry her till after the birth of several children, with whom Wace (Rom. de Rou, vv. 5102 5766) agrees. Dudo is silent on the subject of Gunnor.

D

deputies during their deliberations, caused their hands and
feet to be cut off, and sent them to their several villages as
living warnings to all similarly disposed [1].

With equal success an insurrection meditated by William,
count of Hiesmes, an elder son of Richard I. by a concubine,
was suppressed [2]. In this instance, too, count Raoul's energetic conduct prevented a yet greater evil than the one already
mentioned, by causing the rebel to be seized and cast into
the tower of Rouen ; from which, five years after, he made
his escape, and availed himself of his liberty to seek his brother and prince at the chase, throw himself at his feet and
pray for pardon. Richard, whose proved goodness of heart
had earned for him the surname of *the Good*, received him
kindly, bestowed on him the county of Eu, together with the
hand of the beautiful Leceline, daughter of the noble Turketil ;
from which union descended an illustrious race.

The young count, from the beginning of his reign, followed
in the footsteps of his father, by closely attaching himself to
the king and the clergy, a policy which proved so successful,
that, through his influence over king Robert, he became
almost the ruler of France. When after the death of Henry,
duke of Burgundy, that duchy was claimed by king Robert,
it was Richard, who, with thirty thousand men, supplied him
the means of seizing it (1003 [3]). Shortly after (1006) he
entered into an alliance with the king and the emperor,
Henry II., against Baldwin IV. of Flanders, and took part
in the siege of Valenciennes [4].

While Richard appears as the chief stay of the new Capetian

[1] W. Gemmet. lib. v. c. 2. The Roman de Rou is here highly interesting (see vv. 5975 *sqq.*).

[2] In 998, according to the Histoire des Grands Officiers de la Couronne ;
or 997, according to M. Le Prevost, Roman de Rou, p. 313.

[3] Rad. Glaberi. lib. ii. c. 8. Hist. Episcop. Autisid. ap. Scriptt. Rer.
Franc. x. p. 171. W. Gemmet. lib. v. c. 15. Chron. Hugon. Floriac. lib. i.
p. 221. Chron. S. Petri Vivi Senon. ib. p. 222.

[4] Sigebert. n. 1006. Balderici Chron. Cameriac. lib. i. cc. 33, 114.

dynasty and of the kingdom of France, he did not neglect to
strengthen his relations with the Northern kingdoms. The
hand of his sister Emma he had bestowed on king Æthelred,
and the massacre of the Danes on St. Brice's night[1] did not
excite him to take an active part in their retributive expeditions against England. To this he might feel the less disposed, as the Danish pirates had not always spared his
shores[2]. Nevertheless, the visit of the Danish king, Svend
Tveskiæg, and his suite to Rouen, was received by the count
with the splendour befitting the brilliancy of his court.
Richard would not engage in a war against the consort of his
sister, and saw a better prospect of reward for his exertions
in the pursuit of his interests in France. However, on the
strength of the Danish king's promise on oath, that his warriors should not annoy the French coasts, he granted permission to the Danes to dispose of their plunder in his
dominions, as well as the reception and entertainment by his
subjects of wounded Danes[3]. —

In a war, which ensued on the death of Matilda, a sister
of Richard, who had been married to Eudes (Odo) count of
Chartres, on account of the restoration of the town of Dreux,
which had been assigned her as a dowry, Richard resolved on
calling to his aid two Northern chieftains, who had accompanied king Svend on his last expedition to England : one of
these was named Lagman, and called king of Sweden, the other
Olaf, called king of Norway[1]. A hundred years had passed

---

[1] See England under the A. S. Kings, ii. p. 165.

[2] Sax. Chron. Flor. Wigorn. a. 1000.

[3] W. Gemmet. lib. v. c. 7.

[4] Comp. England under the A. S. Kings, ii. p. 178. [Lagman is the
name of an office, Angl. *lawman*. The king of Sweden at this time was
Olaf Skotkonung. Depping and Prevost (Rom. de Rou. i. p. 316) erroneously take the Olaf here mentioned for Olaf Tryggvason, not recol-
lecting that he was slain in the year 1000. (This error is corrected in the
Danish translation.) These events must have taken place about 1013, and
Olaf, the future saint, did not attain the crown till 1015. He was, more-

since duke Rolf received holy baptism, when count Richard
and his brother Robert, archbishop of Rouen, prevailed on
king Olaf, son of Harald Grænski, and descendant of Harald
Härfagri, to enter, as his predecessor, Olaf Tryggvason, had
done in England, into the bosom of the church, in which he
afterwards acquired the glorious titles of saint and martyr.
How Richard gave a hospitable reception to his sister, queen
Ælfgifu-Emma, and her sons, when a fugitive from England,
as well as to her consort, king Æthelred, and how, through
the hand of Emma, he became the brother-in-law of the great
Anglo-Danish sovereign, has been already related [1]. Richard's
friendly relation to the Danes proved also of service to the
French, a proof of which appears in the restoration, through
his influence, to her husband, count Wido of Limoges, of the
countess Emma, after a confinement of three years, who had
been captured by the Danes when on a pilgrimage to Mont
St. Michel [2].

Not long after the settlement of the quarrel between Richard and Eudes respecting Dreux, through the mediation of
king Robert, conformably to which the town was ceded to the
latter, but the surrounding land, together with Tillières (still
a frontier place of Normandy), was adjudged to the former,
a new war burst out between these if not kindred, yet closely
connected princely families. A vassal of count Eudes, a
knight named Walter, had contrived to gain possession of the
castle of Melun, belonging to count Burchard of Corbeil and
Melun, and had delivered it over to his feudal lord. The
king commissioned count Richard to settle the dispute, but
Eudes refused to appear at his summons, because he could
be judged only by an assembly of his peers. Hereupon

over, already a Christian, having been baptized in his infancy by his relative, king Olaf Tryggvason. The chieftains here in question were probably two petty Scandinavian potentates from Ireland.—T.]

[1] See England under the A. S. Kings, ii. pp. 180, 199.
[2] Ademar. Caban. ap. Bouquet, x. p. 151.

Richard with his Normans laid siege to Melun, which held out for some time, but was at length compelled to yield to the well-directed missiles of the besiegers, which played on them both by day and night.

Even in his latter years Richard appears as the maintainer of the tranquillity of France, and the avenger of injured friends. His daughter, Adeliz, was married to count Reinold of Upper Burgundy, son of the powerful Otto William, the great 'archcount' on both sides of the Jura. By treachery Hugh, count of Chartres and bishop of Auxerre, got possession of Reinold's person (1024), cast him into strict confinement, and dismissed with insult the envoys of Richard, who demanded the release of the captive. Richard hereupon assembled a considerable army, the command of which he intrusted to his son of like name. A free passage to Burgundy was effected by amicable negotiation, by which the count of the Vexin acquired many considerable villages in Normandy. But a brighter glory awaited the sacrifices and subsequent exertions of the campaign. The capture of the castle of Mirmande in the Alps was afterwards numbered among the most brilliant feats of arms of the Normans; and bishop Hugh, seeing further resistance vain, cast himself with the profoundest humility and a horse's saddle on his back, at the feet of the youthful victor, and made vows and gave hostages for the liberation of Reinold[1].

Successfully as Richard thus strove to increase the strength and consideration of his dominion, we must nevertheless acknowledge that much of its most preeminent glory consisted in its numerous and valiant chivalry, which, even without the guidance of their prince, in the manner of their forefathers, could gain brilliant military fame and rewards, even crowns more precious than that of the count of Rouen. Among

---

[1] W. Gemmet. lib. v. c. 16, says, " Milmandum seu Milbrandum." Hen. Huntend. lib. vi. p. 762, and Rom. de Rou. v. 7340, " Mirmande."

these Roger of Toesny, son of Ralf, of the race of Malahulk [1], a paternal brother of Rolf, is the first to be named, who in Spain, with unsurpassed valour, but unheard of cruelty, fought against the Arabs, and obtained the hand of Stephania, daughter of the count Raymond Borrel and the widowed countess of Barcelona, Ermensede. Of this Roger contemporary writers relate, that he caused his Moorish prisoners to eat their fellow Moslems, after they had been slaughtered like swine, cut into pieces and boiled. But fortune was not always favourable to him ; even in Barcelona he found enviers and enemies ; and count Richard felt that he had cause to call him to account for the number of his faithful vassals that he had sacrificed to his ambition. But Roger, nevertheless, became reconciled with the count, before whose death he returned to Normandy [2].

Attended with greater results, although humbler in its beginning, was the establishment of Radulf or Raoul [3], another Norman, in the south of Italy, whom a pilgrimage to Jerusalem led through that country and to the church on mount Gargano, dedicated to St. Michael the archangel, the highly venerated patron of Normandy. Here, with others invited from Normandy, he was engaged in military service by two native knights, Melo di Bari and Dattus, and, encouraged by pope Benedict VIII., proceeded against Apulia, where, near Capua, they gained a victory over the Greeks, but were afterwards defeated by Basilius, and many of them sent prisoners to Constantinople. This event afforded occasion to the migration of many other Normans to Naples, whose duke ceded the town of Aversa to the Norman Rainolf. This cession was followed by greater acquisitions, the beginning and extension of which, as far as they concern the Franco-Normans, will be

[1] See Genealogy No. 1. at the end of the volume.

[2] Ademar. Caban. ap. Bouquet, x. p. 151. Chron. St. Petri Vivi Senon. Ib. p. 223.

[3] Ademar. a. 1016. Rad. Glaber. lib. iii. c. 1. Chron. S. Petri Senon. lib. i.

glanced at hereafter. Here, however, mention must be made of Tancred of Hauteville, a knight attached to the court of duke Richard, who, through the valour and might with which he slew a wild boar, acquired both that prince's favour and many valiant followers[1], but his greatest fame through those sons, whom he had formed after his own model, and to whom, as meeds of valour, no less prizes were awarded than Apulia, Calabria and Sicily. Robert Guiscard, William Iron-arm, and Roger, were the sons of this fortunate man. Thus, as Scandinavia had, a century before, been an inexhaustible receptacle of plunderers, threatening the well-being of the several European states, until Normandy afforded a home to those fierce and restless spirits, so was now Normandy itself in a similar condition, which threatened not only its own prince, and all the more flourishing states, but most of all France, with the greatest perils. Apulia was now the salvation of Normandy, Benevento afterwards saved Apulia, and, finally, England rescued France from the power of the Normans.

Richard died (1026) while still in the flower of life, after a reign of thirty years[2] the vigour and wisdom of which needed not the panegyrics of the monks, but which the benevolent and pious disposition of the prince equally merited and received. The abbey of St. Wandrille, or Fontenelle, that had been destroyed by the Northmen, he caused to be rebuilt. and richly endowed it ; he founded the abbey of St. Maurice at Evreux, and his wife, Judith[3], that at Bernay. Foreign churches also received from him valuable donations. Monks from mount Sinai came annually to Rouen to fetch, from him as well as from his predecessors, costly presents. To

---

[1] Gaufred. Malaterra, lib. i. c. 40.

[2] Flor. Wigorn. a. 1026. Tigernach, a. 1027, where he is designated " rex Francorum."

[3] Monast. Angl. vi. pp. 1063, 1107. Bouquet, x. p. 235. See also d'Achery, Spicileg. i. p. 460.

the monks at the grave of the Saviour in Jerusalem he gave
a hundred pounds in gold, and aided and protected all pious
pilgrims on their journey thither[1]. Seeing the end of his
days drawing nigh, he called to him his brother Robert, archbishop of Rouen, and the Norman barons, at Fécamp. With
their counsel[2], he conferred Normandy on his eldest son,
Richard, and the county of Hiesmes on Robert, his second
son. Both these were his children by Judith, a daughter of
Conan, count of Brittany, and sister of his brother-in-law,
Geoffrey, by whose pilgrimage to Jerusalem and premature
death (1008), the guardianship of his sons, Alan and Eudes,
devolved on Richard, who, consequently, ruled over that province as his own[3]. In two other sons of Richard, the old
predilection of the Norman counts for the clergy manifested
itself in their choice of a vocation; of these, William died a
monk at Fécamp, Mauger, the other, succeeded his uncle in
the archbishopric of Rouen ; but of which he proved so little
worthy, that his deposition became a matter of necessity. Of
Richard's daughters, one, the countess of Burgundy, has been
already mentioned ; another was married to Baldwin, count
of Flanders. Mauger, and also a second William, count of
Archies, were sons by a second wife named Papia, whom
Richard espoused after the death of Judith in 1017[4].

RICHARD III.

THE reign of the youthful Richard III. was of short duration. His Burgundian campaign had afforded ground for the
most favourable hopes, and he appears to have flattered him-

---

[1] Rad. Glaber, lib. i. c. 5.

[2] " Consulta sapientum." W. Gemmet. lib. v. c.17.

[3] The marriage contract of Richard and Judith is preserved in Martene,
Anecdot. i. p. 122, and in extract in Scr. Fr. x. p. 188. She founded a
cloister at Bernay near Lisieux, concerning which there is a charter of
Richard II. cited in Scr. Fr. x. p. 235. According to the Gesta Cons.
Andegav. Ibid. p. 255, Judith had been already married and was a widow.

[4] Access. Rob. de Monte, ap. Scr. Fr. x. p. 270. Ord. Vitalis, lib. v. 45.

self with the idea that the king of France, Robert, would give him to wife his daughter, Adele, who had previously been promised to Baldwin count of Flanders [1]. The refractory spirit of his brother Robert compelled the count to besiege him in his town of Falaise; but a peace was concluded between them, and shortly after Richard died of poison [2]. The general suspicion fell upon Robert, as the perpetrator or instigator of the misdeed, on whom, after his brother's death (Aug. 6, 1028), the government of the state devolved [3]. Richard left a very young son, named Nicholas, whom we must regard as illegitimate, it being hardly credible that the chroniclers of the time would have omitted all mention of Richard's lawful marriage. After his father's death he was placed in a monastery, and died as abbot of St. Ouen at Rouen in 1092. Illegitimacy would have been no bar to his pretensions to the succession of his father; but the cause of his exclusion is, perhaps, rather to be sought for in the principle which, setting minors aside, called the next relation of mature age to the government of the state.

ROBERT II.

SURNAMED THE DEVIL.

ROBERT appears to have been sufficiently designated by the surname of "The Devil," which was bestowed on him in an age when that name was not wont to be a subject for jesting. At the outset of his government he met with considerable opposition through and on the part of his uncle, the archbishop of Rouen, who maintained himself

[1] A marriage contract of January 1027 is printed in d'Achery, Spicileg. iii. p. 390. Bouquet, x. p. 270. Richard here styles himself dux; but in a charter of 1024, in Monast. Angl. vi. p. 1108 : Ricardus filius comes.

[2] W. Gemmet. lib. vi. c. 2. Ademar Caban. p. 161. The year of Richard's death cannot be 1027, as his successor, Robert, in November 1032, was in the fifth year of his reign. Monast. Angl. vi. 1073.

[3] W. Malm. p. 294.

against him with arms in Evreux, and, after the capture of
that place, fled to the king of France. Against William of
Belesme, who had fortified himself in Alençon, Robert was
more successful, that noble having made his submission in
the most humiliating manner, bearing a saddle on his back,
and barefooted; whereupon he was re-invested with his town [1].
Hugh, bishop of Bayeux, a son of Raoul, count of Ivry, a step-
brother of count Richard I., also ceased from the resistance
he had offered to his authority, and laid down his arms.   In
the meanwhile the king of France had given his daughter,
Adele, in marriage to the younger Baldwin of Flanders, who,
feeling elated at his fortune, drove the count his father, the
uncle of Robert, from his country.   The old count took
refuge in Rouen, where he was kindly received by his nephew,
who performed the part of his avenger both willingly and
vigorously.   Robert's cousin also, Alan of Brittany, rose
against him, over whom Robert is said to have gained a
victory in Brittany, but which is liable to great doubt, as
Alan had invaded Avranches, but from which county he was
expelled by Néel of St. Sauveur and Auvrai-le-Géant [2].

In his relations with the king of France, Robert followed
in the footsteps of his forefathers.   When, on the death of
king Robert (1031), his widow, Constance, strove to place
her son Robert on the throne, instead of Henry, her first-
born, the latter fled to the count of the Normans at Fécamp.
Robert received his liege lord hospitably and honourably,
assembled his forces under his uncle Mauger, established the
king in his realm, and compelled his brother to be satisfied
with the dukedom of Burgundy.   Count Robert received,
with the concurrence of count Drogo of Mantes, in recompense for his services, the Vexin with Pontoise and Chaumont.
Corbeil was granted to the valiant Mauger [1].

[1] W. Gemmet. lib. vi. c. 4, and Rom. de Rou. vv. 7591 sq.
[2] Ibid. lib. vi. c. 8. Rom. de Rou. vv. 7755 sq.
[1] Ibid. lib. vi. c. 7. Ord. Vital. p. 655. Rom. de Rou. vv. 7685—7752.

Less fortunate was Robert in his relations with England, as has been already related [1]. But nothing in his whole career appears more striking, and, at the same time, more completely characterizes the violent religious excitement of the time, than his resolve, in the company of a few knights, among whom was the brother-in-law of the English king Æthelred, Drogo of Mantes [2], to make a pilgrimage to Jerusalem, leaving his duchy to his illegitimate son, William, of tender age, and his counsellors, and to the protection of the king of France [3]. By the clergy, who were the cause of it, Robert's determination was loudly extolled. He died, on his return from Jerusalem, at Nice in Bithynia (July 22, 1035), poisoned, according to tradition, by Raoul, surnamed Mouin [4]; whereby Normandy was plunged into a state of most perilous confusion.

Robert's violent passions, the suspicion, that hung over him, of fratricide, his penitence, his romantic pilgrimage, but, more than all, his renowned son, whom a concubine at Falaise had borne him, have made him a subject for many stories, the appreciation of which we leave to the historians of the country. In those characteristics, of which we are informed, his courage, his liberality, his love of jest and merriment, his sensuality, condescension, and readiness to serve his friends; above all his somewhat ostentatious contempt of money and possessions—in all this the model of a Norman hero is presented to us. But we may no longer linger over his portraiture, and will merely add, that the best panegyric on his reign is, that the country, which at first suffered under his many wars and follies, in his latter years again stood forth in its pristine might [5]. His government was much under the guidance of ecclesiastics, among whom Richard, abbot of

---

[1] See Engl. under the A. S. Kings, ii. p. 217.

[2] Ib. p. 231.   [3] Rom. de Rou, v. 8127.

[4] W. Malm. p. 295. Chron. Fontan. App. ii. ap. d'Achery, Spicileg. iii. p. 264, edit. 4to.

[5] Ibid. c. 7.

Verdun, is particularly distinguished[1]. The founding of a new abbey, that of. St. Vigor at Cerisy near Bayeux, by Robert the Devil, ought therefore to excite no surprise[2]. To the restoration of peace among his vassals the emigrations to Apulia must have greatly contributed, which relieved the land of a number of turbulent, ambitious spirits, and, by placing them in a career of glory, exalted the fame of the Normans, and rendered the alliances of their prince of greater importance : even the expeditions of individual Normans into Spain contributed not a little to the acquisition of glory and rich rewards by valiant men, who were dissatisfied with their narrow home. Among the most distinguished men that remained in the country was Serlo, one of the sons of Tancred of Hauteville. He had been banished by duke Robert, and was a fugitive in Brittany, when that prince laid siege to Tillières. Deeply vexed at the prohibition of the duke to his Normans to accept the challenge of a French knight, he appeared, unknown to his countrymen, with closed visor, before the champion. He overcame his formidable adversary, and the duke was soon reconciled with so valiant and noble an adherent[3].

WILLIAM II.

SURNAMED THE CONQUEROR.

As long as Robert's return was expected, the Normans had shown themselves obedient to the count Gilbert of Eu, son of Godfrey, and a cousin of Robert, by an illegitimate connection of Richard I.[4], whom Robert had appointed governor of the state and guardian of his young son, William. But no sooner was the intelligence of Robert's death spread abroad, than the before-mentioned Ralf Mouin attempted to

[1] Hugonis Flavign. Chron. Verdunense in Ser. Rer. Fr. xi. p. 142
[2] Charter of 1032 in Monast. Angl. vi. p. 1073.
[3] Gaufrid. Malaterra, lib. i. c. 38 sq.
[4] Guil. Pictav. vii. 2. Ord. Vitalis, p. 656.

seize on the government.   If in the beginning his attempt
proved unsuccessful, he—unless it was another, Ralf of Gassy
(de Waceio), son of archbishop Robert, who died in 1036—
appears shortly after to have attained his object.   At Ralf's
instigation, count Gilbert, together with other barons related
to him, also Turold, the prince's instructor, fell by the hand
of the murderer; whereupon Ralf, supported by no inconsiderable part of the Norman nobility, was appointed to the
guardianship of William[1].   Still was the opposition of many
barons to the pretensions of these illegitimate branches of
the race of Rolf far from ended, and still less the anarchy
engendered by the never-ceasing feuds of the nobles with
each other.   Roger of Toesny, sprung, as before related, from
the noblest Norman race, and who had gained the most renowned name on this side of the Pyrenees, would not serve
the bastard.   William was too feeble to extort obedience,
but Roger of Beaumont, son of Humphrey (de Vetulis) and
ancestor of the earls of Warwick[2], whose father had suffered
great provocation from Roger, slew both him and his two
sons in a very bloody conflict.   Alan V. also, duke of Brittany, whom duke Robert had appointed one of the guardians
of his son, was poisoned during these dissensions; and this
murder, which affected the Normans indiscriminately, was
unjustly attributed to his youthful ward[3].

William's early days were passed amid manifold perils and
privations, which have at all times proved themselves the best
school of princes.   Walter, his maternal uncle, sometimes
saved him, while a boy, from the machinations of his enemies,
by conveying him secretly by night from the princely chamber, and concealing him in the huts of the poor.   Osbern,
son of Herfast and the countess Gunnor, the prince's house

---

[1] W. Gemmet. lib. i. cc. 2, 4, 6.   [2] Ibid. cc. 3, 4.
[3] Ord. Vitalis, p. 567.   Comp. W. Gemmet. lib. vii. c. 33.   It is said
that Alan was poisoned in Brittany, but died in Normandy and was buried
at Fécamp.

steward, was murdered in the apartment of the latter[1]. The
country was in a condition not less deplorable than that into
which it had been thrown by the murder of William I., only
that it now appeared stronger against external foes. Offensive
warfare was not to be thought of, and it ought not to appear
extraordinary that, while their countrymen were making
brilliant conquests in the South, they did not more efficiently
support the æthelings, Eadward and Ælfred, the sons of
Emma[2]; an enterprise which, even under other circumstances, might have been more politic than grateful to the
Normans, as a friendly relation between Danes and Normans
had outlived even the Teutonic tongue of the latter.

A striking proof of internal weakness was not long wanting. King Henry I. of France availed himself of the opportunity of humiliating a vassal, whose very friendship and protection seemed dangerous to him, by demanding from the
Norman prince the demolition of the castle of Tillières.
Gilbert Crespin, who had been invested with the castle by
duke Robert, resisted this demand, with which, nevertheless,
the government at Rouen resolved to comply, and to join
their forces with the king's, for the purpose of delivering into
his hand the key of their country. Gilbert Crespin was forced
to submit, and the king ordered the castle to be demolished,
after having given assurances on oath that it should not be
reconstructed within four years. But he very soon found
occasion for a war, invaded the country of Hiesmes, and
caused Tillières to be fortified anew[3]. Falaise also seemed
on the eve of being lost, when Turstin, surnamed Goz, the
son of Ansfrid the Dane, with the aid of the royal forces,
raised the standard of rebellion; but Ralf of Gassy, hastening to its relief with a body of valiant men, put him to

---

[1] W. Gemmet. lib. vii. c. 2. "Osbernus, procurator principalis domus."
Ord. Vital. p. 655. "Normanniæ dapifer."

[2] See Engl. under the A. S. Kings, ii. p. 225.

[3] W. Gemmet. lib. vii. c. 5.

flight, and preserved the rock-built town to its youthful master[1].

The history of the endless feuds of the Norman barons among themselves, during the minority of William the Bastard, belongs to the provincial history of the country. Although it may present to us the illustrious names of Montfort, Montgomery, and other noble races, to contemplate whose splendour in its first forth-bursting beams, must ever afford delight to their latest posterity; yet is it instructive to us only by showing how the Norman nobility, kept remote from all effeminacy, and passing their youth in the use of arms, never lost the character of a warlike class. Of greater importance was the war which Guy, the second son of Adelaïs, or Alix, whom her brother, Richard III., had married to Rainaud, count of Burgundy, raised against William. The partisans of the latter had hoped to satisfy count Guy by the grant of Brionne[2] and Vernon; but notwithstanding the customary exclusion of the female line, the pretensions of the nearest legitimate descendant found powerful support. Nigel, viscount of Coutances; Ranulf, viscount of Bayeux; Hamon-aux-Dents, lord of Thorigny; Grimoult of Le Plessis, and other powerful barons, particularly from the independent territories of the Cotentin and Bessin, declared in favour of Guy. But king Henry, either from some remaining gratitude towards the Norman princes, or from a desire to maintain the acknowledged right of succession, or, influenced by the wise policy of not suffering the Burgundian house to become too powerful, united his warriors with those of William. At Val-des-Dunes, not far from Caen, the armies met (1047) and fought with all the fury of civil strife[3]. The king himself

---

[1] W. Gemmet. lib. vii. c. 6.

[2] Not St. Brieuc (Dép. Cotes du Nord), as W. Gemmet. (p. 276) has it.

[3] Guil. Pictav. p. 179. H. Hunt. a. 1047. W. Gemmet. lib. vii. c. 17. W. Malm. p. 393. The Roman de Rou, v. 8743 sqq. is very circumstantial on this battle.

was unhorsed by a knight of the Cotentin, but escaped un-
hurt, and won a decisive victory. Of thirty thousand partisans of Guy a third part is said to have fallen, among whom
was Hamon. Nigel and Ranulf submitted to the young
count, who immediately besieged Guy in his strong castle of
Brionne, which was protected by the river Risle. After a
protracted siege, it is said of three years' duration, Guy was
compelled to surrender, and was mildly treated by the conqueror[1]; but finding himself an object of hatred and contempt in Normandy, he voluntarily withdrew to Burgundy,
whence, having involved himself in contests with his elder
brother, the reigning count, he was soon expelled, and came
to an uncertain end[2].

William soon had an opportunity of requiting the king for
the service rendered him, and of acquiring as much honour
and influence as had ever been enjoyed by any of his forefathers. He aided the French monarch against the powerful
Geoffrey II., surnamed Martel, count of Anjou, with a numerous army, and displayed in this campaign, as often afterwards,
an almost fool-hardy bravery that excited the admiration of
his contemporaries, which manifested itself in presents of
horses and knightly equipments from the king of Spain, the
dukes of Gascony, the counts of Auvergne and other distant
princes. No long time, however, had elapsed before Geoffrey
sought to take vengeance on the Normans. He marched
through Le Maine, which he governed under the young count
Hugh, and after his death, as administrator during the minority of his son, Heribert II., and made himself master of
the Norman frontier fortress of Alençon. But William soon
recovered the place, and took cruel vengeance on the garrison,
who had ventured, by beating a skin hung out for show, to

---

[1] So Guil. Pictav. p. 179. According to Ord. Vital. p. 657. Guy lost
his castles and was banished as an enemy to the country.

[2] Guil. Pictav. (p. 180) and from him W. Malm. p. 394. Ord. Vital.
p. 687.

deride him for being the son of a skinner's daughter, thereby proving that the stain of his birth, although overlooked by the nobility, was always regarded as such by the lower class. William did not content himself with merely recovering the town, but entered Le Maine, where he took the strong town of Domfront, which afterwards remained to Normandy[1].

Previously to this war, for the commencement of which his absence from Normandy (1051) had probably presented an opportunity, William had visited king Eadward in England. The moment chosen for this visit, immediately after Eadward's rupture with the family of Godwine and the repudiation of the queen, was selected by William, with the crafty policy, for which his countrymen are so distinguished, in the hope of inducing his imbecile relative to make promises with regard to the succession[2]. Shortly after, William concluded a marriage (1053) with Matilda, a daughter of Baldwin V., count of Flanders[3], and of the daughter of king Robert, who had probably been affianced to count Richard III., an alliance which secured him against hostilities in the north of his dominions, as well as against the prejudicial influence of the house of Godwine over the court of Bruges. The canonical obstacles which existed against this marriage, and which

[1] W. Gemmet. lib. vii. c. 18. G. Pictav. p. 187.

[2] See Engl. under the A. S. Kings, ii. p. 251.

[3] Chron. Turon. a. 1053, [where a wonderful story is told of William's method of wooing and winning his bride: "Then William, duke of Normandy," the said chronicle informs us, "took the daughter of Baldwin, count of Flanders, to wife, in this manner: after she had been often asked by her father about receiving a husband, and William of Normandy had above all others been lauded to her by her father, who had for a long time had the care of him, she answered, that she would never receive a bastard for a husband. Having heard which, duke William, with a few companions, secretly hastens to Bruges, where the maiden abode, and, as she was returning from church, beats and chastises her with fists, heels, and spurs; and so, having mounted his horse, returns with his companions to his country. This having been done, the maiden grieving lies down on her bed, when her father coming, interrogate, and demands of her about

I

called forth a papal interdict, were removed, in the usual way,
by tedious negotiations; they are, nevertheless, rendered
memorable by the circumstance, that the monk who declared
them inviolable was afterwards employed by William as his
negotiator and mediator at the papal court[1], and became so
attached to that prince's interests that, at length, as the
celebrated Lanfranc, he was not alone the only, but also the
all-sufficient, ally, which William, in his later and more active
days, constantly possessed.   On the ducal pair was imposed as
an atonement the founding of two abbeys and four hospitals ;
the former, dedicated to St. Stephen and to the holy Trinity,
were erected in the city of Caen ; the latter at Rouen, Caen.
Cherbourg and Bayeux.

The capture of Domfront soon gave birth to new quarrels.
The king of France must naturally disapprove of such violence, which might also afford a pretext to the discontented
vassals of the Norman chief to rise up against him.   William,
his paternal uncle, a son of Richard II. and Papia, and brother of the evil-disposed archbishop Mauger, had been by

receiving a husband, who in answer says, that she will never have a husband save William, duke of Normandy, which was done."
    Philip Mouskes, in his chronicle, tells the same story.   According to
him, Matilda answered to her father's proposal :

> " La demoiselle vint avant
>   Si leur respondi maintenant,
> ' J'aim mious estre nonne velée
>   Que jou soie à bastart donnée.' "

    The tale, with a variation, has also found its way into the Saga of
St. Eadward, where, in answer to the duke's proposal, Matilda says :
" Ærc ertu vallare, er þú hyggr at ek, komin af konúnga ætt, munu vilja
giptaz einum bastharðe."   *Thou art mad, clown, to think that I, sprung
from kings, will marry a bastard.*   Whereupon William, seizing her by
the hair, felled her to the ground and trampled her under foot, etc.   Saga
Játvarðar Konúngs hins Helga, p. 12. ed. Copenh. 1852.—T.]

    [1] Lanfranc went to Rome on the business of the dispensation during
the papacy of Leo IX., whose death shortly after (April 1054) probably
withdrew attention from the object, which was only accomplished under
his successor, Nicholas II. (1059 1061.)

him invested with the county of Talou, or Tellau, in which, on the summit of a steep mountain, he fortified the castle of Arques[1]. This turbulent and ambitious man had deserted his nephew before Domfront, and having allied himself with other powerful barons, and even with the king of France, declared war against his nephew, while he was in the Cotentin. It cannot now be ascertained how far this war was in connection with the rebellions of other Norman barons; yet in these events we may perceive both the uncertain sway as well as the sagacity and valour of duke William. The count of Arques was compelled by famine to capitulate, and ended his days as a fugitive at the court of Eustace, count of Boulogne, whither he was accompanied by his wife, whose brother Enguerrand, count of Ponthieu, had fallen at the siege of Arques; while Hugh Bardolf and other powerful barons, to the great humiliation of the king, were taken prisoners, and, bowed under the weight of a saddle on their backs, submitted to the victor[2].

But there still remained another opponent to be removed. The archbishop of Rouen had supported his brother, and William availed himself of this war, to his great benefit, by deposing the prelate and banishing him to Mont St. Michel, with the approval of pope Leo IX., who, shortly before his death, after the unfortunate battle of Civitella (1053), was obliged to show compliance with all the wishes of the Normans. A choice, alike favourable to the church and to the interests of William, was made of Maurile as the successor to Manger, who, sprung from a noble family near Rheims, had at Liege acquired a proficiency in the liberal arts, and was afterwards teacher of rhetoric in the rich abbey of Hal-

---

[1] Guil. Pictav. p. 184.   Chron. Fontan. lib. i.   W. Gemmet. lib. vii. c. 7.   Ord. Vit. p. 606.

[2] Guil. Pictav. p. 186.   W. Malm. p. 395.   W. Gemmet. lib. vii. c. 7. Comp. Prevost, Rom. de Rou, v. 8653 note[1].   In Malmesbury the name of Ingelram or Enguerrand is changed to Isembard.

E 2

berstadt ; subsequently, at Fécamp and Florence, professed the strictest Benedictine rule, and thereby opened the path to ecclesiastical dominion[1].

This success was the more extraordinary as, during the siege of Arques, William was deserted by many of his most powerful vassals One of these, Gnimond[2], delivered his town of Moulins to the king, to whom the acquisition appeared of such importance as to induce him to commit it to the hands of Guy, count of Poitiers, who, through his sister Agnes, was brother-in-law to the emperor Henry III. The moment appeared favourable to the French magnates for the suppression of the Norman rule; and that restless foe of the Norman name, Geoffrey Martel, count of Anjou, assembled round the king an army so numerous, from Guienne, Gascony, Burgundy, and other provinces, that the like had seldom been seen united under the royal standard. The king's brothers, Eudes and Rainaud of Clermont, with the body of troops that had been raised between the Rhine and the Seine, invaded the county of Caux, but at Mortemer on the Eaulne (1054) were attacked and almost totally annihilated by the Normans under Robert, count of Eu, Hugh of Gournay, Hugh of Montfort, Walter Giffard, William Crespin, who on that day laid the foundation of that military renown, which was destined shortly after to shine with greater brilliancy beyond the sea. Guy count of Ponthieu was taken prisoner, but the greater number were slaughtered ; the remnant with Eudes saved themselves by flight. William was bitterly irritated at the escape of the leader of the royal forces, Ralf of Mont Desiré, by the connivance of Roger of Mortemer, who was bound to him by personal obligations, but paid for his misdeed with the loss of the town from which he was designated, which was given to his and William's relative, William

---

[1] Acta Archiep. Rothom. ap. Mabillon, Vet. Analecta. W. Gemmet. lib. vii. c. 24. Ord. Vital. p. 566 *sq.*

[2] Guil. Pictav. p. 186. Malmesbury (p. 398) calls him Walter.

of Warenne[1]. With the consideration, which the politic vassal always manifested towards his suzerain, and with the view, by a sort of theatrical surprise, of increasing the terror at such mournful tidings, and turning it to his own advantage, William sent Ralf of Toesny, who, in the darkness of the night, from the top of a tree in a spectral voice, announced his defeat to the king, and commanded him to send carts to Mortemer, to fetch away the corpses of his army. Henry retired to the frontier of Normandy, across which he was followed by the Normans, who two years after, by a treaty of peace with the king, including a liberation of prisoners, acquired the land taken from Geoffrey of Anjou, whereby was probably meant only the small territory of Passais, the capital of which, Domfront, had been taken at an earlier period. William thereupon resolved to extend the frontiers of his territory to Ambrières, not far from Mayenne, and there to erect a strong fortress. In the spirit of chivalry, or bravado, he announced his design to the count of Anjou forty days before its commencement. The fortress was completed, and the combined forces of the count, of count William of Poitiers, and duke Eudes of Brittany, were unable to capture it. They therefore withdrew when duke William with his banner appeared before them, and Geoffrey of Mayenne found himself under the necessity of placing his hands between those of the conqueror and swearing fealty to him[2].

But this victory of William's had only new wars for its consequences. As soon as fresh forces could be collected, for which purpose some years seem hardly to have sufficed, king Henry joined Geoffrey Martel in an invasion secretly planned of Normandy, in which they ravaged with fire and sword the county of Hiesmes, without meeting with any resistance.

---

[1] Ord. Vital. pp. 639, 658. Huntingdon relates (a. 1054) that "Radulphus camerarius, princeps exercitus Francorum," fell at Mortemer.

[2] Guil. Pictav. p. 187 (Maseres, pp. 61, 62). W. Gemmet. lib. vii. cc. 18. 24. Rom. de Rou, vv. 9909 sqq.

They were already boasting that they would march through
Normandy undisturbed as far as the coast and then abandon
it, when they reached the Dive, which a part of the royal
army crossed at a ford. Here William, availing himself of
the moment when the flood from the sea prevented the remainder of the army from crossing, attacked those that had
passed over, and massacred them before the eyes of the king.
The astounded monarch fled together with the count of Anjou. Neither of them saw Normandy again, both dying shortly
after (1060), when that country enjoyed some respite from
the horrors of war. A consequence of this disaster was the
restoration of Tillières to William, which had been taken by
the king many years before, and the destruction of which had
been attempted by the latter through the foundation of the
castle of Breteuil, which he intrusted to the brave William,
son of the deceased seneschal Osbern, whose valour had
already been proved at the taking of Domfront. Tillières
was again granted to the brave and trusty Gilbert Crespin,
in whose family it long continued[1].

William now made an important acquisition in the county
of Le Maine, whose prince, Heribert, wearied with the superiority of the counts of Anjou, which had long weighed heavily
on him and his predecessors, sought an alliance with William,
to which the latter readily assented, and confirmed by the
betrothment of his young daughter. Heribert died prema-
turely (1062) and before the intended marriage, but recommended his subjects voluntarily to swear allegiance to duke
William, whom he appointed his heir, in order not to be
compelled by force to obey a sterner command. One party,
however, which had attached itself to Walter, surnamed the
Old, son of Drogo, count of Mantes, Pontoise, and Chaumont,
and nephew of king Eadward the Confessor, who had married
Biota, the paternal aunt of Heribert, opposed the last wish of

---

[1] De Nobili Genere Crispinorum, p. 53.

that prince. William was sufficiently penetrating to feel reluctant to obtain a province, the possession of which he earnestly coveted, by means of a destructive campaign; by inroads, therefore, on a small scale, he possessed himself of the strong castles, one by one, and at length reduced Walter —who never received the aid promised him by the nephews and successors of Geoffrey Martel—to surrender his strong city of Le Mans. He and his wife were conducted to Falaise, where they shortly after died of poison[1], by which in those times so many individuals perished. Thus did William gain —as he afterwards gained England—partly by inheritance, partly by conquest, the territory of Le Maine, after having repossessed himself of Le Mans, which had formerly been possessed by Rolf. Margaret, the sister of Heribert, he betrothed to his son Robert, and sent her for further education to Fécamp, where she shortly after died. The capture of Le Mans was followed by that of Mayenne. This city, strong by its position on steep rocks, and by a rapid river, and on the opposite side fortified by strong walls, was, after all the enginery of war had been applied in vain, at length reduced by fire cast into it. In the confusion which ensued, the besiegers burst the gates, and streamed into the place, where they found a rich booty in horses, arms, and other valuable effects.

Thus was a vital wish of the house of Rolf attained—the humiliation of the house of Anjou, and a possession which, through its favourable position with regard to Brittany, promised, at no distant period, to place in the hands of the valiant Normans the command over northern and western France. But the fact that Le Maine now, (as little as Brittany in other times,) could not be maintained by the conquerors of the Anglo-Saxons, proves to us that national feelings, both of aversion and predilection, remained powerful enough in

---

[1] Guil. Pictav. p. 189. Ord. Vital. pp. 487, 531.

France, long after the establishment of the several immi-
grants, not to be permanently quelled either by the intrigues
of the clergy[1], which here also had been in full activity for
the Normans, nor even by the power of the sword.

The last considerable campaign undertaken by William
before his expedition to England was against Brittany, the
duke of which, Conan II., a son of that Alan who fell a sacrifice to Norman poison, in alliance with the count of Anjou,
had raised pretensions to Normandy, or perhaps, what seems
more probable, was only desirous of protecting himself against
William's claims on Brittany. This prince, who had ventured,
at a most unpropitious moment, to molest William with his
legal claims, died suddenly. On him were found poisoned
gloves, near him a poisoned drinking horn; and even the
Norman writers do not attempt to clear William of the suspicion of being privy to this misdeed[2].

At this period occurred Harold's visit to Rouen, whence
he accompanied William in his campaign against the Bretons.
With reference both to his relations with the Anglo-Saxons,
as well as to his acts in France, we are now no strangers to
the character of William. We have seen him powerful and,
in the highest degree, crafty, shrinking from no crime that
could serve his ambition, hated alike by his allies and vassals,
whose opposition only served to steel anew his demoniacal
powers. The accounts of him, which have reached our
times, we get only through Normans, or members of cloisters
favoured by him; yet, nevertheless, scarcely does any other
character leave behind it so strongly the impression of an evil
spirit, appointed by the all-wise Governor of the world for the
attainment of grand objects, as this son of Robert the Devil,
whose wonderful energy and extraordinary sagacity—for both

---

[1] For the flight of the bishop of Le Mans, Gervasius, afterwards archbishop of Rheims, to duke William, see Actus Pontificum Cenomann. ap.
Mabillon, Vet. Analect. iii. p. 306.

[2] W. Gemmet. lib. vii. c. 33.

of these are the conditions of that which in great events leads to success—brought him to that point, that subject and king, lay and clerical, virtue and vice, obeyed him, so as to render him the mightiest ruler of his age[1].

We will now cast a transient glance on the changes which took place in the condition and manners of the Scandinavians, while the Northmen, in another part of Europe, became blended with the nation that had received them in its bosom.

In Denmark Gorm, and in Norway Harald Hârfagri had raised themselves to sole and absolute dominion. We have already seen that Harald, the son of Gorm, came to the assistance of duke Richard: he was afterwards deprived of his throne by his son, Svend, surnamed Tveskiæg, and slain by the viking-chieftain, Palnatoki. During Harald's absolute sway in Norway, the malcontents and vanquished emigrated in multitudes, some to the present Swedish provinces on the frontiers of Norway, others to the new and thriving commonwealth in Iceland, while others prosecuted a life of piracy on the northern seas, or the coasts of Scotland, Ireland, England, and France. But they now encountered obstacles which diminished both their hopes and their resources. The king of Norway maintained a considerable fleet, and when he had subjugated the Orkneys, the vikings had but a contracted field of action. In France and England they found colonies of their countrymen, but who, having adopted Christianity, had neither the inclination to resume a roving life, nor to receive adventurers who had no native home. Hakon Jarl and Eric were the last vikings of any note; but when old

---

[1] What follows is not from Lappenberg, but is added from "Normannernes Sötoge og deres Nedsættelse i Frankrig, etc. af G. B. Depping. Med. adskillige Forandringer oversat af N. M. Petersen. Köbenhavn." It is hoped that it will be deemed sufficiently interesting to deserve a place in the volume.—T.

habits and antiquated customs are on the eve of being exploded for ever, we sometimes see them suddenly and for a
moment receive, as it were, a new life; and thus in the North,
in the tenth century, a republic of vikings arose, which called
into remembrance the most daring and formidable expeditions
of the Northmen.   A man, whose lively imagination had
formed to itself the beau ideal of a viking, Palnatoki, was the
founder of such a commonwealth in Jomsburg as might serve
for a model to all future vikings.   No one was admitted to be
a member of this community who had not distinguished himself by exploits on the sea; neither riches, friendship, nor
kinship gave any claim; no woman might abide in the town;
every Jomsburger pledged himself by oath to revenge the
death of a comrade as a brother's.   The booty was in common, was exposed to public sale, and the money it produced
divided into equal parts[1].   This fraternity continued for some
time, but could not maintain the old Northern manners and
usages, which time itself had changed.

The kings of the North had begun to hold brilliant courts;
their connection with England gave encouragement to commerce, industry, and arts; the peasants, no longer oppressed
by the independent jarls, again breathed freely, and cultivated
their lands to more advantage; the great body of the people
assumed gentler manners; the Christian missionaries, who
waited only for a favourable moment for the conversion of
those heathens, who had inflicted so much injury on the
clergy, were no longer driven away as previously; people
listened to them, although at first with reluctance; conver-
sions proceeded slowly, but went on increasing, and the time
was not far distant, when those overbearing men, who had
battled with the elements, and despised their own divinities,
bowed their necks under the ponderous yoke of the priesthood.

Iceland was peopled, it may be said, in a hurry. Freedom,

[1] Jómsvikingasaga, c. 21, ap. Fornmanna Sögur, xi. Kjob. 1828.

which had been driven from Norway, there found an asylum ; but the equality, which had sprung from common misfortune, soon vanished. Those who carried with them to the island wealth or talents, or by daring and good fortune had distinguished themselves as vikings, soon obtained an ascendency over the other emigrants, and became their lords. Many of these bore renowned names that inspired the others with respect, who had been accustomed to consider them as leaders. Such families, who in the midst of the new commonwealth could not forget the pride of birth, composed the aristocracy of the island, introduced an oligarchic constitution, and injured the republic by seeking marks of favour from the court of Norway. They rejoiced in the remembrance of the noble exploits of their forefathers, and encouraged the skalds to preserve the memory of them. It was, moreover, grateful to every Icelander both to hear and to sing the songs that had delighted him in his childhood and honoured his countrymen. While in Europe scholars were striving to regenerate the classic poetry in a dead language, and in the monasteries were heaping up insipid monkish legends, the simple, natural understanding and lively imagination of the Icelanders gave an impulse to narrative composition and poesy, in their own mother-tongue, such as had not till then been in the North : there arose an Icelandic literature, to which we are chiefly indebted for our information respecting the Northern vikings. Neither the extreme severity of the climate, nor the barrenness of the soil, nor the poverty of the islanders themselves could quell this general enthusiasm; a phenomenon that will never appear again.

A century after the colonization of Iceland, the Icelanders' thirst after adventures led them to a continent of whose existence they had not the slightest presentiment : they discovered and peopled Greenland, whither new migrations proceeded from Norway[1]. At the present day scarcely the

[1] See Wormskjold om Grönlands, Vinlands og nogle flere af Forfædrene

poorest European would exchange with a Greenlander; but
the Scandinavians were inured to the most rigorous climate,
and proof against hardships and want; they could live everywhere where they could see the ocean; they related or listened
to sagas, and composed verses, in Iceland, and with the same
hilarity they passed over to the icy shores of Greenland.

Christianity at length struck root over all the North. Cnut
in Denmark and Olaf in Norway gained by their zeal in its
propagation the surname bestowed on them by the clergy of
saint. In Iceland Christianity was solemnly adopted in the
general assembly or *Alting*, only with the reservation, that
they might continue to eat horseflesh and expose their children[1]. Everywhere churches and monasteries were erected;
the bishops gained great influence, and the priests preached
against piracy, and created a more pious feeling. But the
spread of Christianity was accompanied by the thraldom of
the great mass of the people. The nobility and clergy rendered themselves the lords of the peasantry, which previously,
as a free and respected class, had constituted the strength of
the North. The agricultural population fell into contempt,
when the military began to form an hereditary order, and the
court followers appropriated to themselves all fiefs and dignities. To escape from oppression, many peasants saw no
other course than to place themselves and their children
under the protection of a potent noble, or of the church[2]. At
a remoter period the kings themselves could not rule an aristocracy that was grown too powerful, without, as the kings
of France, raising the burgher class as a counterpoise.

Ruggedness of manners gradually disappeared, culture more

kjendte Landes formeentlige Beliggende, in part x. of Skand. Lit. S. Skr.;
Schröder om Skandinavernes fordna upptäcktresor till Nord-Amerika, in
part i. of Svea.

[1] Finni Johannæi Hist. Eccles. Islandiæ. (Heimskringla, in St. Olaf's
Saga, c. 56.)

[2] See on this subject Vedel Simonsens Danske Adels og Ridderstands
Hist. p. 181 *sqq.*

and more gained ground, but, at the same time, the nation's strength was impaired. Torn by internal dissensions, Iceland was subjugated by the Norwegian kings. The old popular poetry was silenced, and, instead of Icelandic sagas, Latin legends came into vogue. The Faroes and Greenland shared the same fate. Instead of enriching themselves by piracy, men rather bestowed their possessions on churches and convents; and the Northmen, who once had been so formidable to other nations, became now, as it were, a stranger to them[1]. With the zeal which usually animates those who adopt a new religion, all old customs were exploded. In Roeskilde, under king Cnut, there arose a sort of fraternity, whose object was to make war on all pirates. Its members seized on ships belonging to others, giving to the owners as an indemnity an eighth of the booty; before they went on board they took the sacrament; they lived soberly, exposed themselves to great hardships, and had no superfluous followers; when in want of money, they had recourse to a loan, either voluntary or forced, from the citizens, whom, on their return, they requited with half the booty. To the Christians found on board the captured vessels they gave liberty, clothed them and sent them home. All Sceland shared in this undertaking, through which, according to Saxo Grammaticus[2], eight hundred viking ships were destroyed. A greater contrast cannot be imagined than that exhibited in the North, as described in the sagas during the time of heathenism, and as Adam of Bremen found it. "After the adoption of Christianity," says that church historian, "these people have learnt to love peace

---

[1] On the progress of civilization in the North, see Nyerups Hist. Stat. Skildring af Danm. og Norge, 1ste D. also Lindhs Undersökning om Folkmängden i Sverige före Digerdöden, i Vitt. Hist. och Ant. Akad. Handl. 11te D. Stokh. 1822.

[2] Lib. xiv. He adds: "Hic piraticæ cultus, Roskildiæ cœptus, ab urbis gremio etiam ad agrestes manavit, ab omni fere Sialandræ parte subsidia mutuatus.... Primum tenuis, magna breviter incrementa contraxit; sed neque ante redditam terris pacem ulla ex parte remissior fuit."

and gentler manners, and to be content with their humble condition; they now dissipate what they before collected, and collect what they before despised. Instead of addicting themselves to scandalous magical arts, they now, like the apostles, acknowledge only the crucified Jesus. They now observe the greatest temperance, and love in a higher degree than others abstemiousness and modesty. They hold priests and churches in such respect, that those who every day, after having heard mass, do not go to the offering, are not considered good Christians. Those who before were barbarians now pay tithes," etc. "These exemplary manners," adds the good canon, "are obscured only, according to what I have heard, by the avarice of the clergy."

Arnold of Lübeck speaks also of the change that had taken place in the manners of the Danes. "Now," says he in his continuation of Helmold's chronicle[1], "now the Danes resemble other people in dress and weapons. Formerly they were clad as sailors, because of their humour to dwell on the sea; now we see them in furs, purple, and fine linen. The annual fishery off Scania supplies them with a considerable revenue; merchants from all the neighbouring countries bring them gold and silver in exchange for herrings, which are caught in great number. On their rich pastures they keep excellent horses, and are distinguished for fighting on horseback and by sea. They have also made progress in the liberal arts; the nobles send their sons to Paris for education, not only for ecclesiastical offices, but also for secular employments."

This chronicler makes no mention of the common people; but we have sufficient testimony to show that they were reduced to serfdom in the north as well as in the south of Europe, and that the feudal yoke pressed on the agricultural class, and bereaved it of all freedom and public spirit.

But as the inhabitants of the North still retained their

[1] Lib. iii. c. 5.

thirst for adventures, a number of them found the way to Constantinople, where they served in the body guard of the Greek emperors, after their forefathers had for so long a period ravaged the Western empire[1].

If the inhabitants of Normandy cared little about their northern native country, the inhabitants of the North, on their part, almost forgot their fugitive kinsmen, who had gained for themselves another home. But of some of these heroes the names outlived this oblivion : on the shores of the Baltic it was remembered with pride, that Hasting, Björn Ironside, and Rolf were Northmen, and the deeds of the first Norman duke were sometimes to be found, with those of the most renowned Northern heroes, represented on the hangings in the chieftain's hall[2].

To the attacks of the Northern vikings England was exposed much longer than France, in consequence of the numerous islands which there afforded them an almost unassailable retreat. In the tenth century king Eadgar began to clear his kingdom of the vikings, by sailing with his fleet twice a year round the island, for the purpose of destroying the piratical ships that plundered along the coasts. He subjugated the Norwegian jarl in the Isle of Man, where the Northmen had settled at an early period, as may be seen by the runic inscriptions found in that island[3]. For the purpose of acting with the greater vigour against the Norwegians in the Orkneys, Eadgar called the Danes to his aid ; but they,

[1] Under the name of Væringer or Varæger, according to Cedreni Chron.—Erichsen, de vet. septentrionalium imprimis Islandorum peregrinationibus. (See Suhm, Hist. af Danm. 2dn D. pp. 91 sqq. Anm. a.)

[2] For this the author adduces as an authority ' Nikulás Leikara-saga', but he could hardly have cited anything worse than this altogether fabulous saga.—Petersen.

[3] Speaking of the runic inscriptions in Man, Mr. Worsaae (from Prof. Munch) observes, that the rune ᚪ, which in most inscriptions signifies o, must in these always be read as b. Danes and Norwegians in England, Scotland and Ireland.—T.

who were as piratical as the Norwegians, plundered his kingdom, after their expeditions against the other vikings. His
successor, Æthelred, endeavoured, as soon as possible, by
money, to get rid of these inconvenient allies.

Towards the end of the tenth century we find Norwegian
vikings plundering the Isle of Anglesey.

On the Scottish and Irish islands colonies of the vikings
continued for some time to maintain their independence.
On the coast of Ireland they possessed Dublin, Waterford,
Limerick and Cork.   At Dublin resided the principal king of
the Northmen ; Waterford had also its kings.   These colonies, that sometimes made war on each other, and at others
combined together against the Irish or the English, preserved
their warlike spirit, by which, although possessing only a few
ports and a small portion of the interior, they were able to
maintain themselves for some centuries.   Christianity had
encompassed them on every side, and in the eleventh century
they adopted it themselves.   Towards the end of the twelfth
century, the English kings, themselves of Norman extraction,
were powerful enough to attack the old viking states in
Ireland, and to subjugate Dublin, Waterford, and the other
ports, which the Northmen had either conquered or created.
The Norman race did not mingle here so speedily as elsewhere
with the other nations : English, Irish, and Northmen formed
three distinct races ; and we have a document of the beginning of the thirteenth century, in which twelve men are
nominated from each nation, to ascertain what lands and
possessions belonged to the church in Limerick[1] ; but at a
later period, mention occurs of two nations only, Irish and
English ; the Ostmen or Northmen having disappeared.   The
Scandinavian state in the Orkneys and in the north of Scotland ceased at the same time.   The last king, Harald, died
in 1206.   About two hundred years previously, the Norwegian

[1] Waraeus de Hibernia et Antiquitatibus ejus. Lond. 1658. c. 24.

king Olaf, landed at the Orkneys with soldiers and missionaries, to compel the king to allow himself to be baptized.
The astonished Sigurd vainly assured him that he was quite
content with the faith of his forefathers. Olaf threatened to
take his isles, if he did not adopt Christianity and allow the
missionaries to preach the Gospel. Sigurd yielded to necessity and suffered himself to be baptized, and chapels immediately rose on the barren rocks that were washed by the
foamy billows; habits became somewhat softened, although
they still retained much of the Scandinavian ruggedness.
But by degrees the sea-rovers of the Orkneys ceased to be
formidable, and to constitute a distinct people. On the
Hebrides there were some petty jarls, who preserved their
independence for two or three centuries later; but when the
great Anglo-Norman vassals acquired those islands, the posterity of the ancient chieftains sank into humble sub-tenants,
and disappeared among the mass of the people.

The Norse tongue was preserved in some of the isles long
after the dominion of the vikings had ceased. In the Orkneys
Norse was spoken in the sixteenth century, and at the end of
the seventeenth, it was still a living tongue in four parishes;
but in the eighteenth, it became extinct, and only remains of
it are to be found in the language of the Orkney and Shetland
isles[1]. The islanders are said to have tales which are easily
understood by the Icelanders. Names of towns and villages
in these islands are for the most part old Norse, which has
left traces of itself on the shores of the Atlantic, from the
mouth of the Loire to the neighbourhood of the Frozen
Ocean.

Rolf and his companions were like those meteors which
traverse the air with incredible swiftness, and in vanishing

---

[1] Barry's History of the Orkney Islands. Lond. 1806. Hibbert's description of the Shetland Islands. Edinb. 1821.

leave behind them long streams of fire which the eye gazes on with amazement. The Northmen who settled in Neustria gradually became lost among the French, a mixture of Gauls and Romans, Franks and Burgundians, West Goths and Saracens, friends and foes, barbarians and civilized nations. Ten sorts of language, and with them, perhaps, as many forms of government were lost amid this mass of peoples. French and foreigners have visited Normandy in search of some traces of the old Scandinavian colonies, or at least of some testimonial of their long sojourn there, and one or other memorial characteristic of this daring people. All have admired the prosperity of the province, to which the fertility of the soil and its manufactures and commerce have contributed; but vainly have they sought for the original Northmen in the present inhabitants: with the exception of some faint resemblances[1], they have met with nothing Norsk. On the contrary, every thing appeared to them either French or of a later time. We will now take a view of Normandy, and consider its monuments, customs, language, poetry, chronicles, and charters; even if we do not discover many traces of the Northmen, we shall, nevertheless, become acquainted with the civilization, whose beneficent hand has obliterated all traces of barbarism.

In the Orkney and Shetland islands, the Hebrides and the north of Scotland, are yet to be found vestiges of ancient fortifications, for the greater number so situated as to protect the landing places, and which are there called *Danish forts, duns* or *burghs*, just as the Icelanders call the old enclosures formed of stones, which they now use for sheep-cots[2], *borgir*.

---

[1] See Estrups Bemærkninger paa en Reise i Normandiet. Kjöbenh. 1821. This writer adduces as resemblances the general use of beer, which in Normandy continued to the sixteenth century; the attention paid to the breeding of horses; the head-gear in the Pays de Caux, which resembles that of the Icelandic women, and, finally, sundry words of Northern origin.

[2] The author's "tours coniques, qui servent maintenant de granges" must be a mistake.—Petersen.

In the Orkneys they call them *wart-* or *wardhills.* There are whole rows of such towers, some of which are surrounded by a ditch. The old fort of Snaburgh on the isle of Unst was surrounded by two ditches, one of which was hewn out of the rock. Round some of these forts similar small buildings were erected, in which the islanders probably took refuge, when the watchmen gave a signal that a viking fleet was approaching[1]. The number of villages and single dwellings on these islands, which are still called *burghs*, render it probable that formerly there were many more of such forts. Some of these ancient structures are built in a singular manner; they are circular, and have also a circular court, round which there is a wall, which with the outer wall forms an enclosed circular space; this is again divided into small spaces or galleries, one of which is sometimes placed above another. These spaces are exceedingly narrow, and the galleries very low; the outer wall sometimes inclines inwards. A low and narrow entrance, which may easily be closed with a heavy stone, was the only ingress to these extraordinary fastnesses, to which the people probably fled, with their cattle and provisions, on the approach of an enemy[2].

[1] Edmonstone's Descript. of the Shetland Islands. Edinb. 1808.—Encyclopædia Britannica, vii. *voce* Duns.

[2] Pennant's Tour in Scotland and voyage to the Hebrides. [On such towers Mr. Worsaae observes: "The numerous round towers or castles of loose flag stones laid together, which are often built on islands in lakes, and which are called by many 'Danish Burghs,' are of Pictish or Celtic origin. They have no resemblance whatever to the old fortresses in the Scandinavian North....The most that can be said is that the Norwegians availed themselves of these buildings after their conquests and settlements in these districts." (*Ut supra* p. 233.) "An ancient Celtic tower, which tradition decidedly states to have been occupied by Norwegians, lies on the little island of Mousa (the ancient Mösey.) The tower is fortunately the best preserved one of the kind in the British islands. It rises to the height of between forty and fifty feet, like an immense and perfectly round stone pillar, but bulging out towards the middle. Its appearance from without is quite plain, and no other opening can be perceived in the wall than the entrance door, which even originally was so low that it was

F 2

No remains of any such monuments are to be found in Normandy, not even in Denmark or Norway, from whence the Normans came; nor is it by any means proved that these fortresses are the works of Northern vikings. This opinion is founded merely on a popular tradition in Scotland; but supposing them to be the works of vikings, it need excite no surprise that similar works are not to be met with in Normandy; for piracy ceased in France nearly two centuries earlier than in Scotland, where, moreover, the ancient monuments built on the rocks must remain much longer than on the banks of the Seine, which were liable to constant changes and improvements.

Remains of ancient encampments are, however, found along the Norman coasts and rivers, but it is difficult to distinguish those ascribed to the Northmen from others. The vikings, too, may occasionally have availed themselves of the old Roman encampments. The only military work that can with certainty be ascribed to the Northmen is the intrenchment called Haguedike on the north-western end of the peninsula of Cotentin. The extensive circumference of this camp contains grave-mounds and remains of towers, in the vicinity of the sea.

We must not look for the fine arts among the Northern vikings. A people whose life was spent in destroying could have but little sense of the beautiful. They had not even money of their own; nor do we meet with any coins of the

necessary to creep through it. . . .The entire tower is about fifty feet in diameter, and consists of two concentric stone walls, the innermost of which encloses an open space of about twenty feet wide. The two concentric walls are each five feet thick, and stand at a distance of five feet from each other. The small space between them formed the habitable part of the tower. From the open yard we ascend a stone staircase, and before we reach the top, seven divisions or stories are passed, separated by large flag stones, which form a ceiling for one story and a floor for the next. In the different compartments, which quite encircle the tower, are small square openings or air-holes, one above the other, and looking out into the inner yard." Ib. pp. 234, 235.—T.]

first Norman dukes. Clumsy dwellings and strong and massive forts are all the buildings they knew how to raise. As heathens, they probably, like the Gauls, held their worship in the open air or under the shade of aged oaks, before vast blocks of stone, either upright or set one on another. Many of this description are still found in the North[1]. It is not known whether some of these stone masses in Normandy are to be ascribed to the Northmen.

After their conversion to Christianity, the Normans found great difficulty to get rid of the bad reputation they were in as destroyers, although they caused an incredible number of churches and chapels[2] to be erected. The abbot of Saint Benignus at Dijon, who, in the year 1001, was invited by the duke of Normandy to reform the degenerate abbey of Fécamp, refused to come, because he had heard say that the Normans were rugged and savage, and more accustomed to demolish churches than to build them, and rather laid waste than gathered and preserved[3]. They became, however, so greatly changed, that there were none in France who so zealously built churches and cloisters as they. By indulgences their clergy encouraged all faithful souls to contribute to the cost; they even established conveyance fraternities for the erection of churches; people took the sacrament, reconciled themselves with their enemies, and united for this object, choosing a chief or king, under whose direction they drew carts loaded with all kinds of building materials. Probably there were also fraternities of masons[4].

There is scarcely any church dating from the tenth century

---

[1] Thorlacius, Bemærkninger over de i Danmark endnu tilværende Hedenolds-Höje og Stensætninger. Skand. Lit. S. Skr. 1809.

[2] " Unusquisque optimatum certabat in prædio suo ecclesias ædificare, et monachos, qui pro se Deum orarent, rebus suis locupletare." W. Gemmet. lib. vi. c. 22.

[3] "Templa subvertere, non ædificare solitos esse." Gallia Christiana, ii.

[4] See letter of archbishop Hugo of 1145. ap. Bessin, Concilia Rothom. Prov. p. 29.

that does not widely deviate from the Roman style of building, which was universal throughout France.   Even in the eleventh century, both buildings and sculpture were in a very barbarous style ; as proofs of which may be cited, the little church at St. Julian, and the so called Clerk's chamber and tower in the garden of the Hôtel de Ville at Rouen[1].   But about this time ideas began to dilate, sculpture became more perfect, and a beginning was now made with those bold structures in the so-called Gothic style, which, adorned and improved, still excite our admiration.   "If we are poor in monuments of the tenth century," says the Norman author of an interesting work on the architecture of the middle age[2], "our country is, on the other hand, perhaps the richest in the world in structures of the eleventh.   In the arrondissements of Caen, Bayeux, and Valognes, no one can travel half a mile without meeting with such.   The stone found in the neighbourhood of these three towns is easy to work on, and can without difficulty be used in sculpture, which favourable circumstance sufficiently shows why these places are richer in monuments than other parts."   I refer the reader to the work of De Caumont for descriptions of churches of that period, as well as for the successive development of the Gothic style in Normandy.   This style in the meantime became prevalent in the religious architecture of the greater part of Europe, without its being yet known for certain whence it came.   The Normans neither invented it nor introduced it into France; but they adopted it at an early period.

The fortresses erected by them in England were distinguished by a tower of several stories (the donjon or keep) : this was placed either at the end of the works or on an eminence in the middle of them[3].   We know not whether the

---

[1] La Quérière, Descript. Historique des maisons de Rouen les plus remarquables. Paris 1821. 8vo.

[2] De Caumont, Essai sur l'Architecture religieuse du moyen âge, particulièrement en Normandie. Caen 1825, with plates.

[3] Rees, Cyclop. art. ' Norman Architecture.'

first castles built by the Normans in France had also this characteristic. Of that inhabited by the first dukes in the neighbourhood of Fécamp there is not a trace remaining; even the spot on which it stood is hardly known. These dukes dwelt also in the ancient Juliobona, now Lillebonne, where they probably converted the remains of the old Roman structures into a place of residence. The oldest part of the ruins still remaining are not older than the Conqueror's time, consisting of the great quadrangular building which we see in the south-west, and which is now roofless.

Not far from Lillebonne lies the old castle of Tancarville, which belonged to the family of Harcourt, who trace their origin from one of the Danish chieftains that accompanied Rolf; but this castle is not from the earliest Norman times. In general, there is little hope of finding any thing Scandinavian among the old monuments of Normandy.

Notwithstanding the conversion of Rolf, the clergy had not at first so much influence in Normandy as in the other provinces of France. The Scandinavians were in fact of too warlike a spirit. In the first century after their settlement, no synod was held in Normandy, nor did the Norman bishops attend those that were held elsewhere[1]. A distinction was made between the clergy of Norman origin and the French. Ordericus Vitalis, who was a monk of St. Evroult, complains, in his Ecclesiastical History, that the highest dignities of the church were bestowed on Norman priests.

The clergy were subject to the law of the land, and we have already seen that they had no seat in the council of the first dukes; but if their acquisition of power proceeded slowly, it was by so much the surer and more lasting. They eventually became masters over the rugged, warlike spirit of the converted nation. In a synod held at Rouen it was resolved,

[1] "Tum quod his necdum assueti essent duces nostri, tum ne forsitan episcopi, quorum summa erat apud principem auctoritas, nonnihil adversus politici regiminis rationem hac occasione molirentur." D. Bessin. Concil. Rothom. Prov. p. 35.

that priests, instead of doing homage to the secular lords of
whom they held fiefs, should only swear an oath of fidelity ;
but which decision was afterwards annulled by the resolute
William the Conqueror, when he commanded the bishops to
do him homage[1].

By appealing to the holy see the clergy gradually contrived
to withdraw themselves from the civil judicature, and the
ecclesiastical writers celebrate as a victory the edict whereby,
in the year 1190, they were withdrawn from secular jurisdiction[2], except for the most flagrant crimes[3].   In many synods
and councils the prelates renewed the prohibition for the
priests to obey the citations of secular magistrates[4] ; bishops,
abbots, and chapters, were the only judges over priests and
ministers of the church[5].   Excommunications launched forth
warned the secular law not to interfere with that which concerned the priestly caste.   The law or custom known as the
cri de Haro bound every inhabitant of the country to watch
over the maintenance of good order ; the clergy withdrew
themselves from this custom[6]; but, on the other hand, represented tithes as a law prescribed by the Gospel[7].   A multi-

[1] Houard, Anc. Lois des Français conservées dans les Coutumes An-
glaises. Rouen 1766, i. p. 117.

[2] "Monachi respondere, se non posse, quia meminissent soli apostolicæ
sedi subditos fore, et post suo abbati." Notic. Excommunic. latæ in Guil-
lelm. Rothom. Episc. a. 1089, in t. xi. Gallia Christ.

[3] "Eodem fere anno liberata est ecclesia Normanniæ a longo servitutis
jugo, quo premebatur, edictumque fuit, ne in posterum a secularibus
apprehendi possent clerici, nisi," etc. Gallia Christ. ii. p.52.   Neustria
Pia, p. 99.

[4] See Ecclesiasticæ libertatis in Normannia leges in 'Neustria Pia,'
p. 29.

[5] "Concessimus archiepiscopo omnia placita et omnem justitiam placi-
torum." Charter confirmed by king John in 1200. Neustria Pia.—"Omnia placita de omnibus querelis hominum suorum, de incendio scilicet, de
murtro et de rapto......in abbatis curia teneantur." Charter of Hen. I.
of 1108. Gallia Christiana, xi.

[6] See Conc. ap. S. Mariam de Prato. Ib. p. 171.

[7] Introd. to a charter of donation to the church of Seez, a. 1060. Gall.
Christ. ii. p. 151.

tude of serfs were compelled to sacrifice their whole life in labouring for monasteries and churches; from all sides these pious foundations were enriched at the cost of the well-being of families and of the public.

Many councils and synods renewed the prohibition for priests to have concubines, and to place their sons in their own churches[1]. At the same time, when a provincial assembly at Rouen (in the middle of the eleventh century) was urging on the clergy the duty of chastity, the mistresses of the priests were exhibiting the most shameless luxury, and the priests had many children, who relieved their fathers in their functions, or, more correctly, appropriated them to themselves, to the great scandal of all believers[2]. The prelates even accepted money to shut their eyes to this abuse[3]. At the synod of Rouen in 1119, archbishop Geoffrey severely upbraided the priests in the assembly for their dissolute course of life; but their murmuring soon gave him to understand that they were more exasperated than touched by his representations: one of the priests even stood up and answered the prelate with bitterness. The bishop caused him to be seized and committed to prison, whereupon the meeting became so stormy that one of the presiding prelates ordered his servants to enter, who dispersed it with their staves. The priests' concubines now raised a riot among the townsfolk; ecclesiastics and laymen ran in a body to storm the church, but were driven back; and with this scene of outrage the synod terminated[4]. Many times it was found necessary to reform chapters and monasteries, in consequence of the

---

[1] See Bessin, Concil. Rothom. Prov. Rouen 1717. folio.

[2] Bessin, Observ. in Conc. Rothom.

[3] " Jam illud obsecro, quale est quod in plerisque diœcesibus rectores parochiorum ex certo et conducto cum suis prælatis pretio passim et publice concubinas tenent." Nic. de Clemengis, De corrupto Ecclesiæ Statu, cited by Bessin, p. 73.

[4] " Et sancta synodus in debacchationem et ludibrium conversa est." Ord. Vitalis, pp. 866, 867.

dissolute manners that had found entrance among them. The prelates themselves set a scandalous example, and few provinces have had so many profligate bishops as Normandy ; the archbishops of Rouen, Robert and Manger, and bishop Odo of Bayeux, may be cited as examples of priests of loose morals. The pope refused to confirm the nomination of bishop Foulon of Avranches, because he had children in all directions[1].

The monasteries were sometimes a scene of frightful disorders. A letter from the bishop of Lisieux to pope Alexander III. gives a detailed description of one of these profligate fraternities[2]. The abbey of Grestain was in bad repute throughout the country : the monks asserted that they could perform miracles, and publicly announced that the ice-cold water of their abbey could restore all the diseased who plunged into it seven times. A poor woman, who was simple enough to believe them, died of cold under their hands. Dissipation, hatred, and sanguinary vengeance polluted the abbey ; many of the monks bore scars of the wounds which they inflicted on each other with knives ; the cook was murdered by one of the brotherhood, whom he had upbraided with paying secret visits to his wife. The purveyor of the abbey, in a drunken fit, attacked and stabbed with his knife two of the monks and was killed by them. The bishop prayed for a speedy reform of this profligate cloister. When the archbishop, according to ancient usage, in 1073, would celebrate mass in the abbey church of St. Ouen at Rouen, the monks dragged him from the altar, rang the alarm-bell, armed the populace, and pursued the prelate, whom they would probably have sacrificed in their frenzy, if the vicomte had not protected him with an armed force[3].

[1] " Et cum filios habeat undecumque. Epist. Innoc." ap. Bessin, Conc. Rothom. Prov. p. 368.

[2] Epist. xxxii. Arnulphi Lexov. Episc. in Biblioth. Patrum, xii., and in Neustria Pia, art. ' Grestanum.'

[3] Chron. Cadomense ap. Bessini Conc. Rothom. Prov. p. 63.

Excommunications, a weapon at that time the more dangerous as being in the hands of an ignorant and fanatical clergy, were grossly abused. Chapters were seen excommunicating their bishops, and prelates barons, in quarrels altogether secular. There is a very frank declaration of a count of Auges, in which he says, that he is tired of hearing himself every Sunday excommunicated from the pulpit; and hopes that the monks will behave themselves better; if not, that he will do them all the injury in his power[1].

Disorder and infamy pervaded all classes. It was found necessary to prohibit dancing in churches and churchyards[2]. The pope authorized the chapter of Rouen to consecrate the cathedral anew, after it had been desecrated by sanguinary quarrels, or still more scandalous excesses[3]. As early as the reign of duke Robert II. there was an overseer of the prostitutes (gardien des courtisans) in the "bordel" at Rouen: Baudry, the duke's chief forester and marshal, had the appointment[4]. Violences and oppressions depopulated the country; the ecclesiastical laws could alone keep them in check. The *peace of God* was established, which forbade all

---

[1] " Nolo amplius ferre sententiam excommunicationis, quæ proinde super me singulis dominicis diebus datur," etc. Gallia Christ. xi. p. 294.

[2] " Prohibeant sacerdotes, sub pœna excommunicationis, choreas induci in cœmeterio vel in ecclesiis." Præcepta Antiqua ap. Bessin, p. 50. At the synod of Bayeux, a. 1370, it was also forbidden: " Ne de cætero fierent ludi vocati *Calmali* seu *Carmari* Gallice, quod nonnulli iniquitatis filii et perditionis alumni bonum matrimonii per vias indirectas impedire satagentes soliti sunt exercere." Ib. p. 243.

[3] " Alexander Papæ, prædecessori nostro, expositum fuerat, quod plerumque contingeret ecclesiam prædictam, quæ in loco civitatis Rothomag. magis populoso consistat, et in qua nonaginta missæ celebrari consueverunt, sanguinis vel seminis effusione ex concursu pollui gentium diversarum." Ib. p. 91.

[4] " Prædictus Baldricus...... custos meretricum in lupanari de Rothomago, et marescallus meus." Letter of duke Robert II., cited under art. 'Custos Meretricum,' in t. ii. of the Glossarium Manuale of Adelung. Halle 1773. The Chartrier des Archevêques de Rouen makes mention of exactions raised by the barons on the public houses. Houard, i p. 19.

attacks on tho inhabitants, with the object of slaying or
plundering them, from Wednesday evening till Monday morning, also in Advent, Lent, and on the fast-days before Ascen-
sion-day, under pain of excommunication, fifty years' penance,
and banishment. Solemn maledictions were pronounced on
those who broke this peace, and blessings on those who kept
it inviolate. Three or four times councils in Normandy proclaimed this peace of God[1]. On the last occasion, in the
year 1096, the festivals of the Holy Virgin and the apostles
were added to the other days named for the observance of
this peace. This council, at the same time, enjoined all
males, as soon as they had attained their twelfth year, to
declare on oath that they would observe this law.

In the first centuries after the establishment of the duchy,
we find in Normandy but few traces of popular superstitions,
at least of such local superstitions as the French provinces at
that time abounded in, and which dated chiefly from the days
of paganism ; for the Normans knew nothing of the old
state of the country, and had forgotten their own native
land.

Although the clergy but too often set bad examples to the
people, it was, nevertheless, they who provided for their instruction and refined their manners, by inspiring them with a
taste for the arts and sciences. Among the numerous abbeys
founded or erected under the dukes, several were distinguished for their erudition. Jumièges, Saint Evroult, Bec,
Saint Wandrille, Fécamp, were nurseries for ecclesiastics and
learned men. Under the first dukes, says Ordericus Vitalis,
no Norman applied himself to study, nowhere was any instruction given ; down to the time of William the Conqueror,
the Normans applied themselves more to war than to reading
and writing[2].

[1] See in Bessin the councils of Caen, 1042, the decrees of which were
renewed in 1061 ; of Lillebonne 1080, of Rouen 1096.

[2] Hist. Eccles. lib. iii., iv., v.

The court of the first dukes, though not exactly wanting in splendour, was, nevertheless, by no means a school for what, at that time, was regarded as refinement of manners. One of the pretexts used by Louis d'Outremer for taking the young duke Richard to his court was, that he might there receive a better education[1]. Dudo relates so diffusely what beautiful speech was taught to the young duke at the court of Laon, that it would seem that the like was not to be found in Normandy. Women appear to have had no influence at the court of Rouen. The dukes were in great measure ruled by the clergy; instead of wives they had concubines.

In these times of barbarism and anarchy a considerable step was made towards social order by application to the sciences. With grateful acknowledgment, therefore, the names of those Normans ought to be recorded who first cultivated them, however imperfect may have been their endeavours[2].

After Lanfranc's entrance into the abbey of Bec, a thirst arose there for scientific instruction; men from all parts flocked thither to hear theological lectures under so able a professor. This learned monk, who afterwards became abbot of St. Stephen's at Caen, then recently founded by William the Conqueror, and who had refused a bishopric, delivered lectures also on jurisprudence. In the same century Richard of Annebaut, a Norman, rendered the Institutes of Justinian into verse. Evil tongues might say that the Normans' taste for law manifested itself at an early period.

Anselm, who succeeded the learned Lanfranc, provided the

---

[1] Seniorem sinite mecum morari, ut facundæ ubertatis colloquio edoctus, discat definire et determinare verba scrupulosæ rei. Plurimarum rerum notitiam melius discat in palatio meo quam commorans in sua domo..... Notitiis regalibus palatinisque facundiis instrueretur...... Multimodis illum sermonibus libenter insignibant, et mellifluo palatinæ sermonicationis dulcamine erudierant. Dudo, lib. iii. p. 114.

[2] Estrups Bidrag til Normandiets Kulturhistorie fra 10 de til 13 de Aarh. in Bd. xvii. af Skand. Lit. S. Skr.

abbey of Bec with medical writings; and an abbot of Fécamp, named John, an Italian by birth, is cited, under the year 1028, for his knowledge in the healing art[1].

The abbey of St. Evroult likewise contributed to the spread of taste for study. This cloister was from its foundation a school for civilization. St. Evroult, of a noble family at the court of king Lothair, had chosen for his dwelling-place a forest that was full of robbers and wild beasts; the robbers, whom he had converted by his piety, were the first monks and labourers in the wilderness; his philanthropic care of the poor and sick could not but touch eventually the hearts even of those men that were hardened by deeds of violence, so that they found it pleasant to live by the labour of their hands, under the rules of one of the benefactors of mankind. After the destruction of the abbey by the Northmen, the spot was again transformed into a wild forest, and every trace of civilization obliterated, the name of the holy man being preserved only in that of a fountain in the neighbourhood. In the reign of William the Conqueror, a few pious men erected the abbey anew. Theodoric, its first abbot, had fortunately a considerable taste for the sciences, and wrote a beautiful hand, in those days an invaluable attainment. He collected a few illiterate priests from the country, a gardener, and some other well-meaning persons, caused them to transcribe books, and so founded a small library and writing school. Young persons were now instructed by these able copyists, and thus books were dispersed among the other monasteries. Theodoric related to his pupils, that a monk who had deeply sinned, but with great assiduity had transcribed a large volume of God's law, was after his death condemned by our Lord; but that against each of his sins angels had set one of the beautiful letters from his book. Fortunately the number of letters exceeded by one that of his sins, and this circumstance freed

[1] W. Gemmet. lib. VII. c. 23. Ord. Vital. pp. 460. 461.

him from eternal damnation. Theodoric was ever repeating to his monks and disciples : " Avoid idleness as a pest; pray, read, sing, and write!" His successors, almost without exception, had the same taste and zeal. One of them transcribed and illuminated manuscripts with great elegance. In the time of Ordericus Vitalis[1] the books written by this abbot were still used in his abbey. Osbern, the third abbot, was not only a transcriber, but also a musician and sculptor, and formed his pupils both by words and blows[2]. He was a declared enemy of all the ignorant and idle, and carried on a perpetual war against them. The fourth abbot, Mainer, was a good grammarian, rhetorician, and logician ; he had ninety monks under his authority, and caused the church to be rebuilt. The fifth abbot, Serlo, had a hundred and fifteen monks, or, more strictly, that number of pupils. The abbey had a species of hospital for six lepers, one of the oldest of such establishments known. A monk of this abbey, named Rudolf, who had resided at Salerno, understood not only grammar, dialectics, astronomy, and music, but was also a good physician. It seems, in general, that the school of Salerno, through the Normans in Naples, had an influence on medical studies in Normandy. Several Norman physicians are mentioned about this time, and William the Conqueror founded four hospitals in the principal cities of the duchy.

Odo, bishop of Bayeux, who had a son at the court of king Henry of England, maintained, nevertheless, good order among his clergy, and sent young clerks to Liege to study philosophy[3]. The bishopric of Coutances, in the tenth century, had neither divine worship nor priests : the chroniclers inform us that heathenism still prevailed there, whence it would seem that not all the Normans who settled in Nor-

---

[1] Hist. Eccles. lib. vi. Neustria Pia, art. Uticum.
[2] " Juvenes valde coercebat, eosque bene legere et psallere atque scribere verbis et verberibus cogebat." lib. iii. p. 485.
[3] Ord. Vital. lib. viii. p. 665.

mandy had with Rolf adopted Christianity. The bishop removed his see to the church of St. Lo in Rouen; but towards the middle of the eleventh century, bishop Geoffrey rebuilt the cathedral, provided it with ornaments and books, and founded a school, to which he invited the most celebrated grammarians and dialecticians, also skilful musicians, and rewarded them liberally.

History was cultivated in the monasteries at an early period. Dudo of St. Quentin, William of Jumièges, Ordericus Vitalis, William of Poitiers (born in Normandy, but educated in Poitou) applied themselves to the history of the country. They strove to imitate the great historic writers of antiquity, but were incapable of raising themselves above the barbarism of the times; instead of being simple and noble, their style is inflated and bombastic. But barbarous as was their style, they could flatter their masters as well as we can in a more civilized age. There was not a duke of Normandy, who, under their pen, did not appear as a model of greatness and virtue; those being especial objects of exaltation, in the estimation of the monks, who most favoured their institutions.

The inmates of the cloister sometimes also displayed a glimmering of imagination, and strove to cull the flowers of poesy; but they applied the language of Virgil and Horace to sing the praise of angels and saints. Aimar, abbot of St. Pierre-sur-Dive, who not only made verses but set them to music, wrote hymns in honour of St. Kilian and St. Catherine. Thibaud of Vernon celebrated in song Robert, abbot of St. Wandrille, and other anchorites.

These attempts in ecclesiastical poetry must, however, soon give place to popular poetry, which availed itself of the French tongue, to express national thoughts and feelings, to disseminate knowledge among the commonalty, to engage and amuse them.

We have seen that the native tongue of the Normans was partially lost under the second duke of Normandy, and spoken only in the Bessin and Cotentin, where paganism for a long time maintained itself. In the country it must also have long continued, as may be inferred from the names of places, of such in particular as were at that time only villages or very small towns, the names of which may in many cases be explained by the old Norse or Icelandic tongue [1].

In the larger towns and the districts bordering on France, intercourse with that kingdom, marriages with French women, together with the influence which the clergy, the greater portion of whom were French, had over the people, contributed greatly to the diffusion of that language, which at length became predominant in the country. It is, however, related, that a Norman count named Henry, who came to the court of William I., king of Sicily, who was also of Norman origin, excused himself for being unable to speak French; but this count was from the Bessin or Cotentin [2]. In Rouen they unquestionably spoke French at that time. We know from history that Edward the Confessor, who took many Normans with him from Normandy to England, introduced French manners and the French language among his countrymen; this tongue may, therefore, have been in general use in the first half of the eleventh century. We know, too, that William the Conqueror afterwards made French the predominant tongue in England, until that of the vanquished, the Anglo-Saxon, gained the ascendency, and from the blending of the two the English language arose.

The first, no doubt, feeble attempts of Norman literature are no longer known; not until the conquest of England did the ideas of the Normans begin to expand themselves; their intercourse with other nations made them acquainted with new branches of knowledge, and contributed to commerce and industry. It was not till this time that the first really national

---

[1] On this subject see more hereafter.

[2] Fulcandus, cited by Bonamy, Dissert. sur les causes de la cessation de la langue Tudesque en France, in Mem. de l'acad. des Inscript. xxiv.

poets arose. William, it is true, had poets at his court; but that which his minstrel or trouvère, Taillefer, sang at the battle of Hastings was not a Norman song, but a Rolandic ballad of French composition; and it may in general be assumed, that from the first the French poets served as models to the Normans. But the natural talent of the latter soon displayed itself, and produced works of every class. Poetry was long in vogue among the people, as several of the poets themselves confirm.

Usages est en Normandie,	A custom 'tis in Normandy,
Que qui hébergiez est, qu'il die	That he who harbour'd is recite
Fable ou chanson à son oste,	A song or fable to his host,

says the trouvère Jehan Chapelain[1], who lived in the thirteenth century; Robert Wace also relates that poems were read or recited at banquets and other joyful assemblies.

But this golden age for poets could not have been of long duration, for even Robert Wace pours forth a lament that stories and poems (romanz è serventoiz) were no longer profitable, and that barons and noble dames had ceased from making beautiful presents to

Cil ki li gestes escriveient,	Those who wrote gests,
E ki li estoires faseient.	And those who composed histories.

Saints, love, history, natural history, and romantic tales were the subjects of Anglo-Norman poetry. Robert Wace and Benoît de Ste More turned the Norman chronicles composed in Latin into French verse; Geoffrey Gaimar produced in the same tongue and in rime the history of the Anglo-Saxons; Dourbault even turned the Coutumier (Law-book)

---

[1] Fabliau du Segretain (Sacristain) de Clugni.

That there were also tales in rime, that were recounted to friends, appears from the conclusion of the fabliau 'Du Prêtre qui ot Mere à force':—

> A cest most fenist cis Fabliaux,
> Que nous avons en rime mis,
> Pour conter devant vos amis.

See Fabliaux, etc. des Poetes Franç. Paris. 1756. T. i.

of Normandy into verse. Robert Wace, whom we have so often cited, chose for a subject of his poetic elaboration, the Life of St. Nicholas and the Institution of the Feast of the immaculate Conception, works which during many centuries excited much emulation among poets. Chardry, who seems to have been a wandering trouvère, composed a poem of five thousand verses on the Life of St. Josaphat, and also another on the Lives of the seven holy sleepers. Landri of Valognes, who resided at the little court of count Baldwin of Guisnes, turned the Song of Solomon into Romance or French verse[1].

Erotic and serious poems (sirventes), narratives and tales (fabliaux) found more favour than even hymns and Lives of Saints. Dionys Pirame, who in his younger days had enjoyed the pleasures of this world, but in his advanced age had piously celebrated in song the sainted king Edward, Richard de Semilly, Rogerin d'Andelys, Gilles-le-Viniers, were the forerunners of Olivier Basselin. Other poets would both benefit and amuse. Thus William of Normandy wrote a poem on animals (bestiaire), William Osmont one on birds (volucraire), and on stones (lapidaire). Ladies gave encouragement to poems of whatever kind they might be. Philip de Thaun dedicated to Adelaide, the queen of Henry I. his Bestiaire; and while Wace was engaged on a metrical chronicle for Henry II., at the same time he also translated from the Latin the romance of Brutus, a fabulous Trojan prince, and patriarch of the Gallic princes, which he dedicated to the queen of the same king, Eleanor.

Ladies also applied themselves to poetry. The ' Lays d'amour' and Fabliaux of Marie of France belong to the most interesting productions of Anglo-Norman poesy[2]. To escape

[1] See De la Rue, ' Diss. sur. quelques Trouvères Anglo-Normands;' and Pluquet, 'Mem. sur les Trouvères Normands,' in Mém. de la Soc. des Antiquaires de Normandie. Part. i. vol. ii.
[2] See the edition of her poems by Roquefort. Paris 1820, 2 vols. 8vo.

from the rule of the French king, Philip Augustus, Marie sought an asylum in England ; while, on the other hand, the poet Alexander, born in Bernay, betook himself to the court of that king, and, although a Norman, nevertheless flattered the French monarch in an allegorical poem on Alexander the Great.

But soon a wider field was opened for the Anglo-Norman poets. The poems of Britain and Brittany, the heroic exploits of the Paladins of Charles the Great, the Eastern fictions, brought to Europe by the Arabians and crusaders, gave to the Anglo-Norman poetry a new impulse; it soared into an imaginary world of wonders, and led people to forget the cares of the real one. Hebert composed a romance named *Dolopathos*, of Indian origin ; Luce du Gast wrote an imitation of the Latin romance of Tristan; Hélis and Robert de Borron translated into French other tales of the Round Table. The large poems, composed by the Anglo-Normans, are the first, at least of that class, that French literature gave to the world [1].

In vain we seek herein imitations of the old Norse poesy, or allusions to the history or customs of Scandinavia. There may, perhaps, exist some resemblance between the heroic sagas of the North and the romances of chivalry of the south of Europe, both having for subjects wonderful adventures, and the praise of heroism and beauty ; but from this resemblance it cannot be concluded that the Anglo-Norman poets have borrowed their fictions from the Northern skalds. We have not a single proof that they were acquainted with any saga or any skaldic composition. All remembrance of their national poetry was as completely obliterated among the posterity of the Northmen in France as if, in traversing the ocean, they had drunk of the water of Lethe. This total oblivion of

---

[1] In this view the Normans have exercised an influence on the literature of France. See Heeren ' über den Einfluss der Normannen auf die Französische Sprache und Literatur,' in his Histor. Schriften. 2den Th.

their original home they have in common with the West
Goths, who in Castilian poesy have not left the faintest trace
of their original manners and opinions. The same remark
has been applied to the Vareger, who founded a royal dynasty
in Russia, and to whom that country, as a Russian author
remarks, is not indebted for a single new idea. The causes
are here the same with those that effected a complete oblivion
of their mother-tongue, namely their inferior civilization, their
intermixture with the natives, their marriages with the women
of the country, who knew no other traditions than those of
their native land. In Normandy, too, the Christian clergy
must have suppressed every memorial of the ancient mythology; though it would seem that the god Thor was not
totally forgotten, if it is true what Wace relates: that a
Norman chieftain, Raoul Tesson, at the battle of Val-des-
Dunes[1], chose for his war-cry *Tur aïe!* (that is, Thor aid!)
while, on the opposite side, William's cry was *Dex aïe!*
(God aid!)[2]

In the Shetland isles the Northern rovers propagated the
belief in Trolls and Dwarfs which is still to be found there.
This belief seems also to have been brought to France by
the Northmen, though it did not last long in that country.
Wace relates that the archbishop of Rouen, Mauger, who
excommunicated William the Conqueror, whom William deposed, and the chroniclers charge with bad morals and sor-
cery, had a familiar called Toret, who obeyed his commands,
but was invisible to all[3]. This was probably the name of

[1] See p. 47.   [2] Rom. de Rou, ii. pp. 32, 34.

[3] Plusors distrent por vérité
Ke un deable aveit privé,
Ne sai s'esteit lutin u non,
Ne sai nient de sa façon;
Toret se feseit apeler
E Toret se feseit nomer.
E quant Maugier parler voleit,
Toret apelout, si veneit;

Plusors

some Northern sprite (Thor?) preserved in Normandy. The
belief in elves or fairies the Northmen had no occasion to
propagate in France, it existed there already. The poetess
Marie of France places the sojourn of the fairies in Brittany,
and Wace tells us very good-humouredly that he made a
journey into that province, for the purpose of ascertaining
whether it were true what was everywhere related about
fairies in the forest of Brecheliant, but that he was a fool
for his pains[1]. It was Brittany, too, that the romance
writers of the middle age made the scene of their fairy-
narratives. De la Rue[2] has endeavoured to prove that the
belief in fairies has prevailed in Brittany from the first
century of our era, and that it was introduced neither by
Arabians nor Normans, and that the trouvères, in the
twelfth, thirteenth, and fourteenth centuries, always borrowed
their poetic beings from the ancient Armorica, and never
from the North. They even sometimes declare that they
have the subjects of their romantic epics from the works of
the Bretons.

The Northmen, who established themselves in France,
must, with the language, naturally lose their old writing. In

> Plusors les poeient oïr,
> Maiz nus d'els nes poet véir.
>> Rom. de Rou, v. 9713 *sqq.*

[Toret is, no doubt, meant as the diminutive of Thor. This is the opinion
also of M. Pluquet; "but another MS. reads 'Turie,' and M. Le Provost
considers the latter to be the true reading, and that the cry was really
Thury, and most probably referred to the chief seat of Raol Tesson." See
"Master Wace," by Edgar Taylor. p. 20, *note.*—T.

> [1] Là alai jo merveilles querre,
> Vis la forest è vis la terre;
> Merveilles quis, maiz nes' trovai;
> Fol m'en revins, fol i alai,
> Fol i alai, fol m'en revins,
> Folie quis, por fol me tins.
>> Rom. de Rou, v. 11534 *sqq.*—T.

[2] Recherches sur les Ouvrages des Bardes de la Bretagne Armoricaine.
Caen 1815.

Normandy no runic stones are to be found, as in the Northern kingdoms; no Northman on the shore of his new country has caused to be cut in stone the name of his father or of the heroes of the land of his birth. When they had acquired possessions in France they forgot both native land and kindred; and when they had also forgotten their mother-tongue, what could they do with runes, which the priests would, no doubt, regard as magical characters, or a device of the devil?

Whatever partiality the Normans may have entertained for history, they, nevertheless, betrayed an almost perfect indifference for their original country. The historians of Normandy describe the heathen North as a den of robbers. After an interval of two centuries, they knew nothing of the events that had caused the founder of their ruling family to forsake the North; they did not even know where Denmark and Norway lay. Benoît de Ste More begins his chronicle with a geographic sketch, in which he takes Denmark for Dacia and places it at the mouth of the Danube, between the extensive countries of the Alani and Getæ, which are always covered with ice, and surrounded by a chain of mountains[1].

Having thus taken a brief survey of the intellectual condition of the Frankish Normans, we will now proceed to a review of their manner of living.

Husbandry, domestic and rural economy could not flourish under a rule of violence. Almost all our knowledge of the subject is derived from charters, whereby the greater portion

[1] Entre Alane, qui mult est lee,
Et Jece, qui n'est senz gelée,
Est Danemarche la plenère,
Lissi assise en telle manière,
Que altre si est cume corone,
Fières montagnes le avironne.

Chron. de Norm. liv. I.

Comp. Dudo, de Mor. et Act. Norm. and W. Gemmet. lib. I. c. 2

of the produce of the soil is transferred to churches and convents. The several sorts of grain were cultivated, also flax, hemp, pulses and fruit[1]. The extensive oak and beech forests yielded a superabundance of food for swine, of which frequent mention occurs in the charters. A lord, at one time, allows a monastery to send from sixty to a hundred swine into his forest[2]; at another, he grants to the monks a tithe of the swine on his farms. An abbot of Cluny, whom duke Richard had sent for to reform the abbey of Fécamp, refused to come unless the duke would allow the abbey free grazing in his forests for swine and cattle[3]. Mention of oxen and cows is not very frequent; in the earliest times swine's flesh must have been the most general food. The culture of the vine must at that time have been more universal in Normandy than it is in our days; it appears from the charters that most abbeys had vineyards[4]. Without doubt, this branch of husbandry was in use there before the settlement of the Northmen, and might have afforded the vikings an additional motive for choosing that province. But as almost everything was given to the churches, it is probable that the wine also fell to the share of the monks, and that the people retained only beer and cider. Wace relates that the French gave the Normans the nicknames of *bigots* and *beer-drinkers*[5].

Although the apple was cultivated in gardens, it seems that the cider was made from the wild fruit. At least we find by a charter of the year 1185, that the count of Meulan allows the monks of Jumièges to gather apples in his forest,

---

[1] Decimam annonæ et vinearum, lini, cannabi, et leguminum. Chart. of Henry to St. Evroult, 1128. Neustria Pia.

[2] Habeant monachi in eodem parco centum porcos, etc. Chart. of donat. of K. Henry to the abbey of Essay. Neust. Pia, p. 618.

[3] Mabillon, Annal. Bened. P. iv. Gallia Christ. P. xi.

[4] Vineam de Tri—decimam vinearum in monte de Calvincourt—quadraginta agros ad vineam faciendam—vineam nostram in terra Jay. etc. Charters in Neust. Pia.

[5] Et claiment bigoz è draschiers. Rom. de Rou, v. 9902.

for the purpose of preparing beverages from them for their own use[1]. Honey was also collected in the forests[2], no doubt from wild bees.

The chase was so productive that a tithe was laid on the game. Rabbit-warrens and deer-parks are mentioned as belonging to the great manors. There were also salt-works or, rather, salt-pits, along the shore and the rivers, as far as the sea-water reached at flood-tides[3]. At the present day it is hardly possible to obtain salt in places along the coast, where it was collected in abundance in the eleventh and twelfth centuries, as the sea-water no longer reaches so far.

There was fishing in the rivers and along the coasts; but the best fish were reserved for the monks: they had a tithe of eels[4]. There is a charter of the count of Eu of 1036, in favour of the abbey of Tréport, by which the porpoises are reserved for St. Michael, that is the cloister of that name; the donor, moreover, adds, that whenever a 'crassus piscis'[5] was taken, one fin and half the tail should belong to the monks[6]. Herrings were caught both in rivers and the sea,

[1] "Præterea dedi et in perpetuum concessi præfatis monachis poma colligenda ad proprium potum eorum et servientium ipsorum per totam forestam meam." Chart. of Robert in Neust. Pia, p. 322.

[2] "Decimam mellis ipsius forestæ, venationis," etc. Bull of P. Eugenius III. a. 1152. Gallia Christ. xi. p. 134.

[3] "Quatuor salinas apud Huneflotam—salinam apud Butellas—salinam apud Girafrevillam—totum meum sal de Veduno." Charters in Neust. Pia.

[4] Habeant monachi unam piscariam in mari et decimam anguillarum" (Chart. in Neustr. Pia).—"Decimas linguarum cenarum quæ capiuntur inter Tar et Tarel fluvios." Bull of Eugene III.

[5] In the document entitled 'De Institutis Lundonie' (Laws of K. Ethelred, ap. Ancient LL. and Inst. p. 127, fol. edit.) mention is made of the toll to be paid at Billingsgate by the men of Rouen, who came with wine or craspice, viz. the twentieth piece (frustum) of the said craspice. The fish here in question, called in other documents craspiscis, is supposed by Spelman to be the grampus, the French name of which, grampoise, he takes to be a contraction of grand poisson, or magnus (crassus) piscis.—T.

[6] Quod si homines abbatis piscem qui vocatur Turium capiant, totus erit Sancti Michaelis; crassus piscis si captus fuerit, ala una et medietas

and there were abbeys and other pious foundations that were
annually supplied with them by thousands, particularly during
Lent[1]. Whether they salted them is not known. The
herring fishery is connected with the history of navigation.
It would be interesting to ascertain whether the Normans
introduced this branch of fishery and the method of salting
into France or not. Some literati have declared for the first
opinion[2], because the catching and salting of herrings must
have been of much earlier date in the North than in France.
The history of the North, too, as early as the year 888, speaks
of the herring-fishery, and of sending a lading of herrings to
England[3]. But all the other accounts of the catching and
salting of herrings are of later date[4]. The oldest document
connected with this branch of industry, having reference to
the Baltic, is not earlier than the fourteenth century. As
the herrings went up the Seine, it would not be extraordinary
that the fishery was carried on before the arrival of the
Northmen in France; but with regard to the sea-fishery, it
is reasonable to suppose it commenced when that seafaring
people established themselves at the mouth of the Seine.
Love of fishing and a marine life was inherited by their posterity; and at a subsequent period there issued from Normandy a multitude of seafarers, who extended the commerce,
civilization, and power of France. Dieppe was not founded

caudæ erit monachis." Chart. of donation, in Neust. Pia, and Gallia
Christ. xi.

[1] " Debent etiam habere vinum, milliare bonorum halectorum et trede-
cim paria sotularium." Chart. to the Hôtel Dieu at Lisieux, a. 1218.—
" Ex dono Walteri comitis Giffardi, allecum sex millia apud Pontem Au-
demari." Chart. of a. 1169 in Neust. Pia et Gall. Christ. xi.

[2] Noël de la Morinière, Statistique du Dép. de la Seine Infér. c. 9.
Hist. des Pêches, i.

[3] Schönings Norges Hist. ii. pp. 139, 455.

[4] Westenberg, Diss. de Piscaturis in oceano boreali; Humble, Diss.
de Pisc. Harengorum in Róslagia. Upsal. 1745, and Enanders Afhandl.
om Svenska Sillfisket, etc. in t. vii. of Vitterh. Hist. och Ant. Akad.
Handl. Stockh. 1802.

before the tenth century; but previously Harfleur, Cherbourg, Barfleur, and some other ports had been frequented by foreign vessels, and even carried on a commerce by sea; still later, other sea-ports enjoyed the same advantages. In the first turbulent centuries, history rarely makes mention of commerce; there was, indeed, some intercourse with Flanders and England, but certainly very little with the North. In the interior of the country there were some markets for the necessaries of life and other articles of trade.

Conquerors usually strive to force their laws on the vanquished; it might, therefore, be expected to find in the first legislation of the Norman dukes vestiges of Scandinavian customs. But of that legislation we have very little knowledge, and probably it was not of any great importance. We have seen that those Northmen who emigrated to Iceland established there a commonwealth; but in Normandy the task was not so easy and simple; there was a new aristocracy, consisting of the companions of Rolf, who had received investments of land; perhaps too there was an older one of the Frankish lords, who held already landed property in Neustria, and of which they probably retained a part. There were also a burgher class, a working class, and a sacerdotal class; ancient laws and customs already existed there, which in great part derived their origin from the Franks, and had, no doubt, great resemblance to those of the North. It would therefore be difficult to distinguish the legal provisions introduced by the first Northmen from those that were already in force when they established themselves in France. The ancient *Coutumier de Normandie*[1], the oldest law-book known

---

[1] Houard supposes this collection to contain the oldest laws of Normandy. "Basnage is of opinion that the ancient *Coutumier* would be the old Norman law, if only it could be shown that its compiler wrote before the time of Philip Augustus. But the accordance of this old coutumier with Littleton's collection of English laws is a far better proof that it contains the old Norman law than the certainty of its compilation before the time of Philip Augustus. This accordance compels us to ascribe to

of that province, but the origin of which is not sufficiently clear, says, that when Rolf had become master of Neustria, he collected the ancient customs, and, when he encountered difficulties, made inquiry of the wisest men, who knew what was law according to old custom and usage[1]. Rolf, who had all his life been a rover on the ocean, could hardly have been much skilled in Northern legislation, and must naturally have found it far easier to continue the ancient customs that the inhabitants had previously followed than to introduce others, particularly if they were not in opposition to those of the Northmen. From the eleventh century, therefore, we find Normandy governed in nearly the same manner as the kingdom of France. Counts and barons administered the law in the towns and districts, at first in the name of the duke, afterwards in their own. The rights of the lord, the duties of the vassal, the feudal spirit, the pernicious consequences of serfdom, were all nearly the same in the duchy as in the kingdom. The police law, known by the name of *clameur de Haro*, was, as I have already remarked, in use also among the French, and yet more among the Anglo-Saxons. It was a law required by necessity in those times of feudal anarchy.

The commonalty, more particularly the rural population, were not more fortunate in Normandy than in other countries. After the disastrous result of the combination against the barons in the time of duke Richard II.[2], they no more ventured on an attempt to cast off the galling yoke. They were bound to the spot of earth on which they were born, and human beings were given to churches and monasteries like other property[3]. They were compelled to follow the

the customs collected in these two works a higher antiquity than the time when the English became acquainted with them and adopted them." Houard, Anc. Lois des Français, i. Introd.

[1] Anc. Coutumier de Normandie, cc. 10, 53, 121.   [2] See page 33.

[3] In charters of donation in Neustria Pia we read: " Unum hortulanum cum terra sua."—" duos homines et mensuras duas.—duos villanos," etc.

banner of their lord, and shed their blood in wars and dissensions that in no way concerned them, and the issue of which made no change in their lot. They paid tithes to their lords or to the church, and consumed in anxiety the bread they were allowed to retain; being never sure of reaping the fruits of their toil.

But notwithstanding all this, usage and habit had already introduced forms sufficient for the protection of property and personal security: according to Houard, written decisions even were in general use in Normandy from the beginning of the twelfth century, that is almost two hundred years earlier than in the rest of France[1]. The burning-iron was deposited in the church, blessed and consecrated by the priests, for the purpose of burning, in the name of God, the hand of such as were guilty of false accusation, or of denying their crimes[2]. It was a great privilege for the churches to possess this iron (ferrum judicii) and the jurisdiction connected with it; they obtained this privilege from the duke, and disputes arose for the possession of the formidable iron[3]. But the legal duel was far more in accordance with the martial spirit of the Normans than the ordeal-iron; nor was there any other province of France where so many single combats took place, both in closed lists (en champ clos) and the open field as in Normandy; it was almost the single combat (holmgang) of the Scandinavians transferred to the French soil. But in Norway and Denmark they fought for booty and honour; in Normandy they fought within lists, according to legal custom,

[1] Anc. Lois des Français, i. Houard cites for his authority, 'Lettres Historiques sur les Parlemens, ii. pp. 32, 39.

[2] " Querelam habuit Gilbertus (abbot of St. Wandrille) cum Guillermo, archiep. Rothomag. de ferro judicii et jurisdictione in quatuor parochias, quæ abbati a Wilhelmo R. adjudicata sunt anno 1082 apud Oxellun."— "Gilbertus perditam probationis ferri machinam anno eodem instauravit, et a Guillelmo, Rothom. antistite, benedictione sacrandam curavit; qua de re actum fuerat in concilio ejusdem anni." Gall. Christ. xi.

[3] Ord. Vitalis and other Norman chroniclers.—Capefigue, Essai sur les Invasions maritimes des Normands dans les Gaules, pp. 340 sq.

and in the open field, consistently with the turbulent spirit or
love of danger, which the nation still retained, on which
account it with difficulty reconciled itself to the usages of
France[1]. The ill will borne by the Normans towards the
French appears evidently in the works of the earliest chroniclers. According to Wace, the Normans inveighed against
the French in their songs and histories, and he says himself
very candidly what he has at heart against them. This prejudice on the part of the Normans probably lasted as long
as their Northern physiognomy, their fair hair[2] and other
characteristics, whereby they were distinguished from the
French. William the Conqueror, who knew his people
thoroughly, is made to say, that they were proud, difficult to
govern, and fond of lawsuits[3]. Malaterra, who had studied
their character in Sicily, found them crafty, vindictive, domineering, eager to leave their country for the sake of greater
gain abroad, dissembling, neither prodigal nor avaricious,
devoted to the study of eloquence, lovers of the chase, hawking, horses, arms, and beautiful attire; in short a people that
must be held in check by the laws[4].

The celebrated tapestry in the cathedral of Bayeux, wrought
by a princess Matilda, whether the wife of the Conqueror or
the daughter of Henry I. is uncertain, and intended to represent the conquest of England[5], is the oldest authentic monument which makes us acquainted with the arms and military
costume of the Normans[6]. The arms and habits are identical with those of the Danes, as they appear in the miniature

---

[1] Wace, Chron. ascend. des Ducs de Normandie.

[2] Wace informs us that some of the first dukes were fair-haired.

[3] Rom. de Rou, v. 14253 *sqq.*   [4] Carusii Bibl. hist. Siciliæ, i.

[5] See Archæologia, xvii. [also xviii. and xix. Montfaucon, Monum.
Fr. i.—Mem. de l'Acad. des Insc. vi. and vii.—Stukeley, Palæogr. Brit.
N°. xi. 1746, 4to.—Turner's Tour in Normandy, ii. pp. 234-242.—Estrups
Reise i Norm. pp. 90 *sq.*—Dibdin's Biogr. Tour, i. pp. 375-386.—P.] See
also the engravings from Stothard's drawings in Monum. Vetusta.

[6] Sam. Rush Meyrick, Critical Inquiry into Ancient Armour, i.
1824, 4to.

paintings of a manuscript of the time of king Cnut, preserved in the British Museum[1], namely shirts of mail, consisting of simple iron rings sewed on the habit; helmets of various forms, lances, swords, bows, iron maces, etc. With few exceptions, similar weapons are found among all the nations of Europe in those early times. Muratori is of opinion, that the Italians learned the art of war of the Normans: he would, perhaps, have been nearer the truth, if he had said, the art of fighting well; for that they understood in perfection, as we have already seen, whereby they acquired duchies and kingdoms.

To the Normans has been ascribed the introduction of chivalry into France; and from the foregoing it will, no doubt, appear that the manners and habits of the Scandinavians, rugged and barbarous as they were, had in them something of the knightly character: in their enthusiastic love of valour and glory, their foster-brotherhood, their carrying off of women, their love of heroic poetry, and their indomitable passions, they were in fact knights, though the Moors possessed the same violent passions, which produce extraordinary deeds of heroism. Hence it is difficult to determine, whether the spirit of chivalry spread itself over the middle of Europe from the north or the south; it probably evolved itself there from the same causes that gave it birth among the Moors and Scandinavians. But Christianity and civilization so greatly changed this spirit, that, at least in France, it became perfectly different from the rough valour of the barbarian nations. We have already remarked that the heroic poetry of France had nothing of a Scandinavian character.

The feudal system was unable to quell the haughty spirit of the Normans; even during its existence they enjoyed more freedom than any other province of France. "In the other provinces," says Houard[2], "the protection of a lord was

---

[1] MS. Cott. Cal. A. vii.? [2] Anc. Lois des Français. i. p. 196.

necessary to secure the commonalty against the loss of liberty; while in Normandy every man and every landed possession were by law free; the duke alone having immediate jurisdiction over all his subjects; and it stood in the power of no lord to alter the condition of the freeman or his possessions." There was formed, though it is not known at what time, a supreme court, under the appellation of the *Exchequer*, consisting of the duke, the seneschal, other judges chosen by the duke, and the most eminent of the ministers of justice in the courts of the nobles. These not only managed the domains of the superior lord, but pronounced judgment in all cases of bad administration by the officials, and other abuses, also received appeals in private cases. The mass of the people grew rich by commerce, arts, and seafaring, and thus became conscious of their own importance. The communities demanded rights, or maintained them under the denomination of privileges. The rights of the freemen were at first but imperfectly made known, and the oldest charters no longer exist. The oldest one known is of the year 1315[1]. In this it is provided that those Normans, who were independent of a lord, were only bound to render to the sovereign certain fixed services and imposts, besides which he could demand nothing; that they were not liable to the torture, except when suspected of capital crimes; that forty years' prescription gave right of possession; that Normans should be judged by their own native judges, etc. In such provisions, nearly the same with those which the English prescribed to their early kings, consisted the Normans' charters of liberties; these were at various times confirmed, together with their other customs, especially when the authorities had intrenched upon them, and after the most serious complaints on the part of the people. But when the French kings, by a series of civil and religious wars, had increased their power, and governed

[1] It is printed in several works, as in Brussels, Traité des Fiefs; Dupuy's Collection; Goubé's Hist. du Duché de Normandie, ii., and elsewhere.

more by their own will than with the states of the realm,
they issued their ordinances "without regard to the *clameur
de Haro* and the Norman charters of liberties," thus setting
at naught the express condition on which Normandy submitted to king Philip. Nevertheless, the province, according
to the last constitutional charter of the kingdom, gained
more than it had lost, if we except its ancient municipal
privileges.

OF LOCAL NAMES IN NORMANDY.

A number of local names in Normandy unquestionably
derive their origin from the Northmen: of these there are
several kinds :

In the first place, local names ending in *ville* (Lat. villa)
consist for the most part of that termination with a foreign
word prefixed, which seems almost in every case to be the
name or surname of the Northman who either dwelt at the
ville or was owner of the village. I will take the first that
present themselves from the department of the Lower Seine,
where such names, formed with the Latin termination and a
Northern name, are very general, no doubt because Rolf
there particularly distributed possessions among his followers:
as Froberville, Beuzeville, Gauzeville, Grainbouville, Henne-
querville, Manniquerville, Rouville, Rolleville, Triguerville,
Bierville, Gueutteville, Houppeville, Tancarville, Varengeville,
Heugleville, Normanville, Norville, Gremonville, Toufreville,
Valliquerville, Alliquerville, Heugueville, Guicorville. In the
name Varengeville, as in Varangerfjord in Norway, we meet
with the word Varanger, Βαραγγος, or the name of those
Northmen who served in the Greek emperor's body guard,
and which is the same word with Væringer or Vareger, an
appellation that may be understood to signify all Northern
vikings in general. It is well known that the Northern people
that visited Russia were so called.

In the North itself there are likewise many local names

H

composed of a personal proper name and the words *sted*, *vig*, *lev* and the like, as Sigersted, Gjedsted, Heinsvig, Jelling, Ormslev[1].

Names of towns in *tot*, derived from the Anglo-Saxon or Icelandic, are almost as frequent, as Yvetot, Raffetot, Garnetot, Criquetot, Houdetot, Louvetot. In the neighbourhood of Godarville, in the department of the Lower Seine, most of the villages, as Noel remarks[2], have this termination, as Ansetot, Turretot, Sassetot, Eculetot, Tiboutot, Prétot, Valletot, etc. The name Sassetot seems to signify a Saxon settlement.

The termination *bec* is, without doubt, the O. Nor. bekr, Dan. bæc, Engl. beck (a brook). It is found in Bolbec, Bec, Caudebec[3], Foulbec, Carbec, etc. A little river that flows through Rouen is named Robec. In Denmark there is also Holbek (Engl. Holbeach?), Vedbek, etc.

Names in *eu* and *eur*, which are found so frequently along the coast, as Eu, Cantaleu, are to be explained only by the O. Nor. ey. Dan. ö (isle), and aur, eyri, Dan. ör, öre (strand, shore), which so frequently occur in the North[4]. Those in *fleur*, as Harfleur, Barfleur, Figuefleur, Vittefleur, in their older form, bore a still closer resemblance to their Scandinavian parents. Instead of Harfleur, for instance, it was called Herifloium and Herosfluet; Witeflue, instead of Vitefleur; Harflue instead of Harfleur. Wace writes Barbeflue for Barbeflot[5], and Benoît de Sᵗᵉ More Barreflo for

[1] See Olufsens Bidrag til oplysning om Danmarks indvortes Forfatning i de ældre Tider, in the Vid. S. phil. og hist. Afh. i. p. 377. [The termination *lev* is the A. S. hlæw, Engl. low, Scot. law; vig is Engl. wick (wich); sted in Engl. stead.—T.]

[2] Essai sur le Départ. de la Seine Infér. [There seems no need of recourse to the Anglo-Saxon for the interpretation of *tot*: it is no doubt a corruption of the O. Nor. and Dan. toft.—T.]

[3] Answering no doubt to the Engl. Coldbrook.—T.

[4] Answering to the A. S. ig, Engl. ey (ea), as in Ceortes-ig, *Chertsey*, Battersea.—T.

[5] See Rom. de Rou, v. 6241.

Barfleur. In Odericus Vitalis we find: "in portu qui Barbeflot dicitur;" and in the Chron. Norm.: "Cum esset apud
Barbefluvium;" in R. Hoveden: "apud Barbeflet[1]." All this
plainly points to the O. Nor. fljôt, *a river*, A.S. flôd, Engl. fleet,
as in Northfleet, Bamfleet, etc. But both the pronunciation
and orthography vary in various localities, so that the Northern ey, ö in places on the coast of Normandy became *eu, eur;*
in the names of the isles west of Normandy, *ey*, as Jersey,
Guernsey, Alderney, Chausey; in the names of the Hebrides,
it is *a*, as Jura, Ila; of the Orkneys *ay*, as Ronaldsay,
Strathsay; in Holland, perhaps, *o*, as Borculo, Hengelo,
Almelo, etc.[2]

The termination *beuf*, as in Painbeuf, Marbeuf, Criquebeuf,
Quittebeuf, Quillebeuf, corresponds unquestionably to the Dan.
by or *bo* Engl. *by* (O. Nor. bær, bû). In former times Penteboe
was said instead of Painbeuf, also Dalboe, Balboe, Kilboe (for
Quillebeuf), which was likewise written Cuilebœf; Criquebot
and Criqueboe were also said for Criquebeuf.

The O. Nor. skôgr, Dan. Skov, Engl. Scot. *shaw*, is found
in the name of the old forest of Eskoves, in the department
of the Lower Seine.

Some names have the Northern termination *dal*, (O. Nor.
dalr, *dale*). Besides the two *dals* to the right and left of
Sassetot (Dep. Lower Seine), which are especially called *Dalles*
(*grandes Dalles* and *petites Dalles*), we meet also with Oudales
near Beaucamp, Crodale, Danestal, Darnetal (Dep. Calva-
dos), Dieppedal, Croixdal, Bruquedalle (Dep. L. Seine).

The O. Nor. garðr (Engl. *garth, yard*), which originally sig-
nified every kind of inclosure; and afterwards, a yard, court,
mansion, in town or country, is found also in Norman local
names, as Auppegard and Epegard (Dep. Eure).

---

[1] Noel, Essai sur le Départ. de la Seine Infér. ii. c. 4.

[2] This is a mistake. The *lo* belongs to the second component: Borcu-lo,
Alme-lo, Ven-lo Wester-lo, etc. " Loo, lo. *inquit Becanus*. Locus altus
adjacens stagnis, torrentibus aut paludibus." Kilian, *s. v.* T.

H 2

The point of land the *Hoe* at the mouth of the Lizard, also the promontory of La Hogue, derive their name from the Dan. huk, *an angle, hook*. The Scandinavians have also the word *næs*, of the same signification, whence probably are derived the names of French and English promontories ending in *nez* or *ness*, (*naze*), as Blanenez, Grisnez, Nez de Carteret, Nez de Tancarville, Holderness, Sheerness, etc.

Houlme near Rouen is evidently the O. Nor. hôlmi, Dan. holm, *an islet*, as Bornholm, Stockholm.

Many other names of places are to be found in Normandy, which derive their origin from the Old Norse: e. g. Terhoulde (also Torholt in Flanders, anciently Turhold) Thor's holt? Estrand (O. Nor. strönd, *strand*); Ebe (Ebbe), etc. [1]

---

[1] For further information on this subject see Auguste Le Prevost, Dictionnaire des anciens noms de lieu du département de l'Eure.—T.

A
HISTORY OF ENGLAND

UNDER THE

NORMAN KINGS.

WILLIAM THE FIRST,

SURNAMED THE CONQUEROR.

CONTEMPORARY SOVEREIGNS.

GERMANY.	FRANCE.	PAPACY.	SCOTLAND.	SPAIN.
Henry I.	Philip I.	Alexander II. ob. 1073.	Malcolm III.	Sancho I. ob. 1072.
		Gregory VII – 1085.		Alphonso I.
		Victor III. – 1087.		

THE most decisive victory in a civil war, and such was the war between the brothers Harold and Tostig, is not immediately productive of peace and unity. The transitory union, which had taken place against the invading foreigners, was instantly dissolved, when Harold had fallen by the hostile shaft. A vast number of Normans, not less, it is said, than fifteen thousand, fell in the first pursuit of the fleeing Anglo-Saxons, who knew how to take advantage of their knowledge of the country[1]; but the panic caused by the loss of the great battle operated on minds still influenced by old dissensions and mutual mistrust, to the bereavement of all energy and moral strength. Not the government alone, but all military command was dissolved, and the Anglo-Saxons took refuge in the nearest towns, or by their domestic hearths in the hundreds. Further measures for resistance were nowhere prepared, nor was there any one to devise them: London alone, with its walls and towers and brave citizens, armed itself for defence. There dwelt Ealdgyth, Harold's

---

[1] Ord. Vitalis, p. 501., more circumstantial than Guil. Pictav. p. 204.

.

widow ; the young Eadgar Ætheling, who, as the grandson
of king Eadmund Ironside, was the rightful heir to the crown.
Stigand and Ealdred, the archbishops of Canterbury and
York ; Wulfstan, bishop of Worcester, and other distinguished ecclesiastics, who had been the counsellors of Harold,
had also taken refuge there. The powerful earls, Eadwine
and Morkere, comely energetic young men, the favourites of
the Anglo-Saxon people, who, when too late, must have repented of forsaking their brother-in-law, Harold, at Senlac,
entered London with a military force. These sons of Ælfgar
strove, in the first instance, to obtain the guardianship of
their nephews, the sons of Harold, if not to gain for themselves the crown of their brother-in-law[1] ; but finding that
their aspirations met with no favourable reception, they united
with the other witan, who, with the approval of the citizens
of London and the butse-carles, placed the crown on the head
of Eadgar. But Eadwine and Morkere, who were bound and
had promised to afford all the aid in their power, suddenly
left London with their forces, together with their sister, the
widowed queen, whom they sent to Chester[2], filled with envy
and hatred towards the more fortunate claimant of the throne,
and probably in the hope of changing their earlship over the
north of England into an unlimited royal authority[3]. Thus
was London left almost wholly to the defence of its citizens
and soldiers[4], under the brave Ansgar[5], its chief magistrate,
and heard with apprehension of the progress of the Norman
duke and his rapacious army.

The day following the battle of Senlac, William proceeded
to Hastings, where he continued for five days, in the deceitful
hope that the Anglo-Saxons would immediately take steps to
apprize him of their subjection. On the contrary, the people

[1] W. Malm. p. 421.   [2] Flor. Wigorn. a. 1066.   [3] W. Malm. p. 421.
[4] Guil. Pictav. p. 205. " Cum solos cives habeat, copioso ac præstantia
militari famoso incolatu abundat."
[5] Wido of Amiens, v. 690.

of Romsey opposed the landing of a considerable body of Norman soldiers, who ignorant of the country attempted to disembark there; thus proving that the Anglo-Saxon power was not totally annihilated. But William no longer delayed profiting by the confusion of the moment. He hastened to Romney, to take vengeance on the inhabitants for the loss sustained by his men, and thence proceeded to Dover, within the bulwarks of which, that had been strengthened by the labours of ages, a vast mass of people had sought protection from the enemy. But here, too, a man was wanting capable of concentrating and employing the existing means; a state of things to which the circumstance probably contributed, that the castle of that place, which had previously belonged to Harold, and by him had been strongly fortified[1], must have been almost totally abandoned by its garrison, who had, no doubt, hastened to the aid of their chief. William, whose followers had regarded it as impregnable, and who must have been encouraged to the extremest exertions by the promise of a rich booty, was no less rejoiced than surprised when, before he had arrived in sight of the rocky fortress, he was met by deputies from the town, who presented him with its keys[2]. But this peaceful surrender did not satisfy the Norman army, which was by no means disposed to conquer England for the duke, but for spoil and enjoyment. The accidental delay of some of the people in leaving the

[1] "Traditurus Doveram studio atque sumptu suo (scil. ducis Heraldi) communitam." Guil. Pictav. p. 191.

[2] Guil. Pictav. lib. i. Wido vv. 599 sq. The unequivocal expressions of the contemporary writers forbid us to assume a siege of Dover: consequently no importance is to be attached to Thierry's "on ne connait point les détails du siège." The more I admire the spirit and acuteness with which this excellent work on the conquest of England is written, the more I regard myself obliged to caution against the misrepresentation of many facts, as well as the abuse of his authorities in the course of it, to which he has been seduced by sympathy for the oppressed nation. Mackintosh also allowed himself to be misled by the historian of the Conquest, when he pronounced his citations as very accurate, and also speaks of a siege of Dover.

fortress was used by the enemy as a pretext for plundering
them; for the safer accomplishment of which object, they set
fire to several of the houses. The town was almost totally
consumed, and the duke, who was unable either to prevent
the outrage, or to punish the perpetrators, could only offer
restitution and other compensations to his new subjects, for
their destroyed habitations. He spent a week in repairing some
defects in the fortress; then, leaving a strong garrison and
many sick behind, who were suffering from dysentery, caused
by the too abundant use of fresh meat and cold water, was
on the point of advancing to Canterbury, when the inhabitants
of that city also, and shortly after those of the neighbouring
towns, came and presented him with their homage, with hostages, and valuable donations. Like hungry flies, that settle
in swarms on a bleeding wound—so a Norman expresses
himself[1]—the Anglo-Saxons hurried forward to offer their services to the duke. From Canterbury he sent to the widowed
queen Eadgyth, who was residing at Winchester, which city
had been assigned to her by her consort, king Eadward, as a
jointure, and assured her the possession of that large city, in
consideration of a tribute. At Canterbury he fell seriously
sick, and was compelled to remain there, or in the neighbourhood, during a whole month[2]. A delay by which the in-
fatuated country was incapable of profiting.

William had despatched five hundred horse to lay siege to
London, to shatter its walls by battering rams and subter-
ranean passages, to force the numerous population to surrender
by fire and famine, as well as by treason and bribery; while
he himself, as soon as he had recovered, overran the adjacent
counties of Sussex, Surrey, Middlesex, Hampshire, and Hertfordshire[3], where his army abandoned itself to the most unbridled

<hr>

[1] Wido v. 617.
> " Et veluti muscæ, stimulo famis exagitatæ,
> Ulcera densatim plena cruore petunt."

[2] Fracta Turris. G. Pictav. p. 205.

[3] Flor. Wigorn. a. 1066. Edit. E. H. Soc. The old editions and Simeon
of Durham have the erroneous reading *Herefordensem.*

cruelty and licentiousness, from which a multitude of unpaid vassals, allies, and adventurers cannot be withheld. Those well-meaning Anglo-Saxons at London, who had fostered the hope of being able to defend their native country, were now convinced that resistance was vain, and that a speedy submission was the best means for obtaining favourable conditions. Archbishop Stigand, therefore, and Ægelsine, abbot of St. Augustine's at Canterbury, whose possessions were among those that had most severely suffered, went to the conqueror at Wallingford, as he was about crossing the Thames, renounced the youth whom they had crowned, and swore allegiance to the Norman duke[1]. William promised what was demanded of him; for so rich a prize as the kingdom of England there was no scruple about words, and a change in the constitution, provided the imposts were adequate to his wants, was not among the designs of a warrior astounded at his own success. Shortly after, he was met at Berkhamstead[2] by Ealdred, archbishop of York; Wulfstan, bishop of Worcester; the ætheling Eadgar himself, and the citizens of London, which last, through the false representations of an agent, bribed by the crafty William, who had

[1] Guil. Pictav. p. 205. The author here adds : " It is not improbable that they came with a body of warriors ready to fight if William had not granted to them a confirmation of their ancient rights and customs : perhaps, too, the tradition is not unfounded, that the Kentish army, advancing under the covering of branches from the trees, might have appeared to the enemy as a wood until, standing in face of them and casting down their leafy screen, they at once appeared threatening with sword and spear." For this story, which seems more at home in a note than in the text, the author cites as his authority : Chron. W. Thorne ap. Savile, col. 1768, and a ballad of the 16th century in Thierry ii.; and adds : " the story of Birnham Wood, known to every one, is to be found in Buchanan (Hist. Scot. lib. vii. c. 85.). But less known it is that a similar tradition is to be found in the history of Holstein, where it is assigned to the 14th century." See Chron. Holsat. S. Presbyter. Bremens. c. 18.—T.

[2] That Eadwine and Morkere were also present is evidently an error of the Saxon Chronicle, as they had left London and, according to the account of an eye-witness, did not appear before William till the meeting at Barking.

vainly endeavoured to shake the fidelity of Ansgar, had been seduced to deliver up the city[1]. William confirmed the rights and possessions of those who submitted to him, including even Eadgar Ætheling, to whom he gave assurance both of life and an honourable treatment. The word solemnly pledged to the Anglo-Saxons, to restrain his soldiery from pillage, he was unable to fulfil, as against the aversion of the great body of the nation, notwithstanding the submission of some of the most distinguished, which manifested itself on every occasion, the good will of his Normans was indispensable.

No conqueror understood better than William of Normandy the advantage of confirming the power and brilliancy of his sword by a specious show of right. When scarcely master of a tenth part of England, he resolved, by having himself crowned as king, to secure the whole kingdom, that had devolved on him, ostensibly by right of succession and transmission, as well as through the favour of the pope. The obsequiousness of the English prelates, who considered themselves bound to obey the court of Rome, seconded this scheme; nor was there any lack on the side of William of well-sounding proclamations[2] and assurances to the most influential Anglo-Saxons. More difficult it was to gain the consent of the Normans, whose desires were solely bent on booty, and to whom the elevation of their ducal leader might prove prejudicial.

In this conjuncture also William gave a proof of the craftiness which distinguished his character. As if perfectly aware of the weighty reasons which existed in favour of his assuming the royal dignity, he artfully set them forth in the strongest light; but, at the same time, pretended, in his love of repose and of his consort, with whom he must share the crown, should God be pleased to bestow it on him, as well as

[1] Wido, vv. 681 sqq.

[2] We probably still possess fragments of such in the first part of the Charter " De quibusdam Statutis per totam Angliam firmiter observandis." Rymer. i. p. 1.

in the uncertainty of the new conquest, to find reasons for at least postponing the coronation. But, as William fitz Osbern had acted on a former occasion[1], a foreign knight, named Aimery, of Thouars in Guienne, rendered him equally welcome service on the present occasion, fascinating and gaining over the multitude by the power of his eloquence. The leaders were won by the prospect held out to them of counties and baronies, together with lands for their younger sons. When those that had been sent forward to London had erected a strong-hold for the conqueror[2], and all things were prepared for the solemnity, William, who had been amusing himself in hunting and hawking, proceeded to the capital of the Anglo-Saxon realm, and on the first day of Christmas, in less than three months from the day of his landing, caused himself to be crowned by Ealdred, archbishop of York. The first metropolitan, Stigand, attended in the procession, in the place of honour belonging to him[3]; though it would seem either that that prelate had refused to place the crown on the head of the Norman usurper, after having, within the space of a year, acknowledged and anointed two pretenders to the Anglo-Saxon throne[4], or that to William himself a consecration at the hands of an ecclesiastic at variance with the papal and Norman clergy did not appear satisfactory[5]. While the duke was in the abbey church of Westminster, and the anthem had ceased, Geoffrey, bishop of Coutances[6], ascended the pulpit, addressed the conquerors in French, and demanded of

---

[1] See Engl. under the A. S. Kings, ii. pp. 282, 285.

[2] Guil. Pictav. p. 205. (Maseres, p. 144.)

[3] According to Wido's testimony, vv. 803, 804,

" Illius ad dextram sustentat metropolita,
Ad lævam graditur alter honore pari."

[4] Will. Newburg. lib. i. c. 1, and from him Bromton, p. 962.

[5] " Quia multa mala et horrenda crimina prædicabantur de Stigando, noluit eam ab ipso suscipere, ne maledictionem videretur inducere pro benedictione." Eadmer, Hist. Novorum, p. 6.

[6] Constantiensis, not " of Constance," as Turner and Lingard have rendered it.

them whether the king proposed were agreeable to them?
in which case he desired them to declare their consent by
a sign. With loud acclamations and clapping of hands the
lively Normans manifested their approbation. Hereupon
archbishop Ealdred applied in a similar manner to the Anglo-
Saxons[1]. A still louder cry now arose from both nations,
and a noise ensued, which the Normans assembled outside of
the church mistook, or pretended to mistake, for a tumult;
whereupon some of them hurried to London and set fire to
that city. Those in the church were soon aware of the conflagration and rushed forth, every one who possessed a house
there, or other property, considering it in peril. William remained behind, abandoned by nearly all excepting the priests;
but would hear of no delay; so with trembling and precipitation the ceremony of anointing and crowning was completed.
Exasperated at the conduct of his licentious hordes, and
trembling for his life thus exposed in the moment when he
had reached the goal of his wishes, William was hardly able
to repeat, in the French tongue, the customary oath of the
Anglo-Saxon kings. His presence soon restored order, and he
imposed on himself the duty of repressing, by the announce-
ment of severe punishments, and the appointment of rigid
judges, the disorder among the lower ranks of his army.
Nevertheless, this untoward event could not fail to increase
the hatred of the Anglo-Saxons to the Normans.

The king did not venture to take up his abode in London,
until he had constructed a new fortress there, and while that
was in progress, passed some time at Barking in Essex. Here
he soon received a proof how justly he had calculated on the
effects of a coronation. The earls Eadwine and Morkere
soon appeared before him, offering him their homage; and
Copsi[2] also, who had been Tostig's deputy in Northumber-

---

[1] Such is the account given by Wido (vv. 817, 818), who describes the
particulars of the coronation more circumstantially than William of Poitiers (pp. 205, 206).   [2] Called by the Norman writers Coxo.

land, in which relation he might easily find a motive for attaching himself to the destroyer of Harold. Here also the submission took place of Turkell of Limes, of Siward and Ealdred, sons of Æthelgar, a kinsman of the royal house, and of Eadric, surnamed the Wild, or the Forester, a grandson of the infamous Eadric Streona, and, consequently, related to the family of Godwine. Their example was followed by many rich and powerful men, actuated by the conviction, that a country defended by so few strong places must infallibly, after a decisive battle, become the reward of the victor. Each of these individuals made separate terms with the new sovereign, and every one hastened to get the start of the others, in the hope of obtaining more favourable conditions. To Eadwine the king promised the hand of one of his daughters, while Morkere was treated less leniently. Other Norman ladies were married to Anglo-Saxons, whose sisters were bestowed on Norman husbands.

Vast riches, arising from plunder and gifts, must have been collected for the king, chiefly from the monasteries[1]. All these treasures William sent to Rouen, at the same time that he neglected no measures at home, either civil or military, for the security of his newly acquired kingdom. The several lands belonging to the crown, the rich inheritances of king Eadward and the sons of Godwine, the royal treasure at Winchester, and Harold's share of the booty at Stamford bridge[2], were all taken by William as property rightfully devolving on him, from which he distributed rewards among the bravest of his followers. At Winchester, the ancient residence of the West Saxon kings, the inhabitants of which he regarded as dangerous, on account of their attachment to the old dynasty, of their wealth and courage, he caused a new castle to be

---

[1] Catalogues of these church-plunderings are to be found in the chronicles of the English monasteries, as Thomæ Hist. Eliensis; Hist. Abbatum S. Albani, and of Waltham (see Monasticon, vi. p. 56); of Worcester (Hemming, Chart. p. 393).   [2] Adam. Bremens. Schol. 66.

erected, which, together with the Isle of Wight and the government of the whole north of England, he bestowed on William fitz Osbern, whom he also created earl of Hereford [1], a dignity with which king Eadward had formerly invested his nephew, Ralf, as a possession equally honourable and lucrative, and which, at later periods, we always find in the hands of the bravest, coupled with the expressed permission to extend their domain, with the help of their good sword, beyond the Welsh border. Of all William's vassals no one had rendered him more essential services, particularly in the conquest of England, than William fitz Osbern. Here we again meet with king Eadward's Norman favourite, Richard fitz Scrob [2], who possessed lands in those parts, and, like many other so justly detested foreigners, in conjunction with his newly arrived countrymen, strove for the oppression of all those Anglo-Saxons, who struggled against the Norman tyranny. At this time, or in the years immediately following, William raised other Normans to English earldoms; Walter Giffard was created earl of Buckingham, on Roger of Montgomery [3], a sagacious, upright, and pious nobleman, was

[1] Flor. Wigorn. aa. 1067, 1070. Guil. Pictav. p. 209. Ord. Vital. pp. 506, 521.

[2] See Engl. under the A. S. Kings, ii. p. 255. His heir was his son Osbern. Doomsday, Worcester, fol. 176 b.

[3] As supplementary to my note on Norman names, in "Engl. under the A. S. Kings," ii. p. 283, it seems desirable here to remark that what is there stated relative to the prefix *fitz* (son), is equally applicable to the particle *de*, when set before local names, with which only at a later period, when made transmissible, it can be said to form a surname in the modern sense. At the period comprised in this volume the *de* was simply our *of*, its regimen varying, if required, with the individual. When the same local name was transmitted from one generation to another, then only with its prefix *de* can it be said to form a surname, and is no longer to be rendered by *of*. *Fitz*, too, signifying *son*, when, with the baptismal name of the individual's father, it was made to form a permanent surname, was applied both to sons and daughters, as Eleanor Fitz John - Eleanor Johnson. The Danish peasantry still retain the more rational, though less convenient, usage; with them the daughter of Hans would be Maria or Trina Hans *datter*, not Hansen, as in the higher grades.—T.

bestowed the city of Chichester, the castle of Arundel, and the earldom of Shrewsbury ; on Robert of Moretain, the king's uterine brother, that of Cornwall ; on Gherbod the Fleming that of Chester, which, after his return to his native country, was given to Hugh of Avranches. Odo (Eudes) of Champagne, William's brother-in-law, son of Stephen, count of Champagne, after whose death he had been driven from his rightful inheritance by his brother, Theobald III., was invested with the earldom of Holderness [1] ; Ralf of Guader, son-in-law of William fitz Osbern, with that of Norwich [2].

William was now above all things desirous to return to his French provinces as a king. The southern parts of England he intrusted to the administration of his brother Odo, bishop of Bayeux, under whom and William fitz Osbern he placed several warriors of distinction, as William of Warenne, subsequently invested with the earldom of Surrey, to whom he gave his daughter Gundrada in marriage [3] ; Hugh of Grentemaisnil, to whom was given the government of the Gewissi or West Saxons [4], and afterwards the shrievalty of Leicester ; Hugh of Montfort, to whom the custody of Dover was committed [5], together with other individuals, who, although proved in the field, were for the most part ill qualified to conduct a peaceable administration. While by these deputies he secured his dominion in England, he availed himself of his visit to Normandy to render harmless those Anglo-Saxons whose position excited his mistrust, by taking them, under the false pretence of showing them honour, but in reality as hostages, with him in his suit to Normandy. Of these the chief were: Eadgar

[1] Ord. Vital. p. 509, calls his wife a daughter of duke Robert, contrary to the usual account, viz. that she was the daughter of Harlette by a second marriage. Comp. Rom. de Rou, ii. pp. 127, 234, and M. Prevost's notes.

[2] Ord. Vital. p. 522.

[3] Ellis (Introd. to Domesd. i. p. 506.) corrects the false statement of Ordericus Vitalis, who makes Gundrada a sister of Gherbod the Fleming.

[4] Ord. Vital. pp. 512, 522.   [5] W. Gemmet. lib. vii. c. 39.

Ætheling, archbishop Stigand, the earls Eadwine and Morkere, Waltheof, son of Siward, to whom he had given his
niece Judith in marriage, together with his paternal earldom
of Northampton[1]; Ægelnoth, abbot of Glastonbury[2], and
others.

William, on his departure for England, had left the government and defence of Normandy to the duchess Matilda, aided
by certain men of experience, particularly by Roger of Beaumont. In Normandy William enjoyed a twofold triumph,
when, attended by a numerous and joyful train of knights
returning to their homes, and by his Anglo-Saxon hostages
from the conquered kingdom, he again found himself in his
patrimonial inheritance. He celebrated the Easter festival
(March 1067) at Fécamp, whither many French princes and
nobles were attracted, in honour of their former equal, now
by craft and the fortune of war exalted high above them.
Great was the wonder manifested by all on beholding the
young Anglo-Saxons with their long flowing locks, whose
almost feminine beauty excited the envy of the comeliest
among the youth of France. Nor was their admiration less
on seeing the garments of the king and his attendants, interwoven and encrusted with gold, causing all they had previously seen to appear as mean; also the almost numberless
vessels of gold and silver of surpassing elegance; for in such
cups only, or in horns of oxen, decorated at both extremities
with the same metals, the numerous guests were served with
drink. Overwhelmed with the sight of so much magnificence,
the French returned home, all, but especially the clergy,
richly gifted, and celebrated both by their words and writings
the superabundant treasures of the new region, which their

---

[1] Ord. Vital. p. 522.

[2] Sax. Chron. a. 1066. Flor. Wigorn. 1067. Ordericus Vitalis has
" Egelnodun, Cantuariensem satrapam." Lingard, though citing Guil.
Pictav. and Ordericus, calls him " Egelnoth, abbot of St. Augustine's."
By Guil. Pictav. he is not named at all.—T.

hero, greater than Cæsar, more bountiful than Titus, the lord
of the Normans in Apulia and Sicily, at Constantinople and
Babylon, had acquired without the loss of a single knight of
eminence, within a few hours, under the papal benediction.
The inhabitants of the country were liberally indemnified for
the supplies furnished by them for this visit, and also for the
burthens laid on them on account of the war.   Thus the
most wonderful of all spectacles presented itself to the contemporaries : the homes of the peasants were not plundered,
their harvests not reaped by the forager, nor trodden down
by cavalry ; even an unarmed defenceless man might ride in
all directions without fear of the soldiery[1].

The following account of the state of the wealth and arts
in England at this period, from the pen of the Conqueror's
chaplain, will no doubt both surprise and amuse some of the
readers.   " In abundance of the precious metal that country
by far surpasses the Gauls ; for while by its exuberance of
corn it may be called the granary of Ceres, from its quantity
of gold it may be termed a treasury of Arabia . . . . . . The
English women are eminently skilful with their needle, and in
the weaving of gold ; the men in every kind of artificial work-
manship.   Moreover, several Germans, most expert in such
arts, are in the habit of dwelling among them ; and merchants,
who in their ships visit distant nations, introduce curious
handiworks[2]."

But a different spectacle from that described above presented itself on the opposite side of the Channel[3].   The
oppression of new burthens, and the yet greater of foreign
pillagers, rendered more licentious by the absence of their

<hr />

[1] Guil. Pictav. pp. 211 sq. (Maseres, p. 162.)   " Provincialium tuto ar-
menta vel greges pascebantur, seu per campestria, seu per tesqua : segetes
falcem cultoris intactæ expectabant, quas nec attrivit superba equitum
effusio, nec demessuit pabulator.   Homo imbecillus aut inermis equo can-
tans, qua libuit vectabatur, turmas militum cernens, non exhorrens."— T.

[2] Guil. Pictav. p. 210 (Maseres, p. 157).—T.

[3] Six. Chron. a. 1067.

I

masters, excited repeated commotions among the sunken people, whose noblest defenders had been basely carried off, and who thus manifested a disposition which, under better guidance, and supported by the secular and ecclesiastical aristocracy, might have freed the land of the foreign intruders. Of the wealthier class many fled, some in the hope of one day returning, provided a miracle, or the energy of others, should restore them to their inheritances; some to solicit aid from the Danes against the Normans; others for ever, seeking a new home, where valour and hatred of the Normans would insure them both pay and booty. Of the first-mentioned many sought refuge in Flanders, while many turned to the home of their forefathers, the Saxon lands on the banks of the Elbe. History makes mention of a count of Stade, the son of a noble Saxon lady who had fled thither[1]. The Scottish cloisters of the Continent gave shelter to many a fugitive[2]. To the last-mentioned class belong those Anglo-Saxons who fled to Constantinople, where they found a welcome reception, and by the emperor Alexius Comnenus I., who feared their too immediate neighbourhood, were settled first at Chevetot (Kibotus near Helenopolis) on the opposite shore of the Sea of Marmora, but were afterwards employed by that prince against Robert Guiscard and the Normans of Apulia, for the deliverance of his realm from those dangerous enemies who had invaded it. The Normans recognised their bitterest foes[3], and not in vain directed their shafts against them. They were, nevertheless, forced to abandon the country, and a body of Anglo-Saxons, with some Danes and other Væringer, whom we find at an earlier period in the

[1] Frederic, who in the year 1095 possessed the county of Stade, was grandson and son of two ladies, who, departing in a vessel from England, were there driven on land. For an account of their posterity see Alberti Stadensis Chronica, edit. Reineccii. p. 153 sq.

[2] Chron. S. Martini Colon. in Monum. Hist. Germ. t. ii.

[3] Ord. Vital. p. 508. (Maseres, p. 204.) Comp. also Torfæus, P. iii. lib. vi. c. 3. Anna Comnena, v. Villehardouin, lxxxix.

Greek service, maintained, as a body-guard, under the denomination of Ingloi, with powerful arm, bright battle-axes and
harness, the Grecian emperors in that consideration and security, which the enervated race of their own subjects was
incapable of affording. While the fate of these brave Saxons
in the East, who, warring with a more than janissaries' valour
and Swiss fidelity, thus proving themselves the firmest support of the throne, claims our warmest sympathy, we cannot
forbear reflecting on the wonderful complications of worldly
affairs, through which to fugitives from a fallen state, one infinitely more vast, as well as more rotten, was indebted for its
preservation. Wonderful, too, does it appear that the last
emigration of the Anglo-Saxons was destined to protect the
brightest spot of the ancient world against a European race
which, if not the most distinguished, was high-minded and sus-
ceptible of the most refined civilization, that it might one day
fall a prey to the most obtusely barbarous of Asiatic hordes[1].

Equally fallacious were the hopes of those Anglo-Saxons
who strove to obtain foreign aid for the liberation of their
country. In France not even the faintest prospect of support presented itself; the king of France had already proved
his indifference or weakness, in tamely witnessing the aggrandizement of his most dangerous vassal. The German emperor, Henry IV., was too deeply engaged in warfare with
the Slavic nations, and still more deeply in the frivolities and
sensual pleasures of a court, to see in a conqueror, who did
not immediately endanger his own frontiers, the violator of
the peace of Europe; although those Norman adventurers,
who beset Europe at almost every point, threatened to make

[1] Some interesting particulars relating to the Anglo-Saxons at Constantinople are contained in the 'Chronicon ab Origine Mundi ad a. 1218;'
MS. in the rich and valuable collection of sir Thomas Phillipps at Middle-
hill, where it stands as N° 1880. It was formerly N° 783 of Meermann's
collection, and is the work of a Præmonstratensian born in England, from
which the editors of the Recueil des Historiens de la France (t. xvi. p. 677,
and t. xviii. p. 702), have extracted some passages relating to France.

i 2

a Normandy of all that portion of the globe. William, too, was vigilant, and indefatigable in engaging in his interest some of the most influential men at the imperial court, for which object the means, irresistible in those times, were supplied him from the wealth of his newly acquired dominion. The chief counsellor of the emperor, Adalbert, archbishop of Bremen, was, by his largesses, bribed to intrigue for the security of the munificent conqueror, and it must have proved an easy task to suppress an excitement in the imperial court against William, to him who, for the same object, did not shrink from the attempt to influence his friend, the Danish king, Svend Estrithson[1], although the inclination of that prince lay in the opposite direction. With Svend, nevertheless, the representations of the Anglo-Saxons found a favourable reception[2]. The nephew of Cnut the Great had not attempted to claim from its Anglo-Saxon rulers the kingdom of England as his inheritance; though the death of Harold brought to maturity the thought, to which the death of Eadward must have given birth, of asserting his pretension to the throne of his uncle and his deceased childless cousin. But after vainly waiting till the despair of the Anglo-Saxons and their intense hatred of the Normans should work wonders in his favour, the Danish monarch contented himself with sending one of his nobles to William, to demand his homage for *his* realm of England, the investiture of which he was not unwilling to grant him, in consideration of a yearly tribute. William, instead of angrily or scornfully refusing this demand, listened to the envoy with all the sly serenity characteristic of the Normans; nor was it enough to lull the envoy by feastings and presents; a costly embassy, composed of

[1] Adam Brem. lib. iv. c. 16. Both Turner and Lingard unaccountably call this prince Sveno Tiulfveskegg, confounding him with Svend Tveskiæg (Sveinn Tjúguskégg) the *father* of Cnut, who died in 1014. The prince here spoken of was Cnut's *nephew*, the son of his sister Estrith, married to Ulf Jarl. See Engl. under the A. S. Kings, ii. pp. 181, 208.—T.

[2] Guil. Pictav. p. 212 (Maseres, p. 163).

four men of eminence, among whom was Ægelsine, abbot of
St. Augustine's at Canterbury, on whom king Eadward had
formerly bestowed the abbey of Ramsey, embarked, as soon
as the season permitted, for Seeland, charged with an abundance of fair promises as well as valuable presents, which
could not fail of convincing king Svend and his court of the
wealth and power, and also of the good will of the possessor
of the claimed fief.   To Olaf, king of Norway, William likewise sent an embassy, in a vessel freighted by Norwegian
merchants at Grimsby, who must have found it no difficult task
to obtain from the natural foe of Harold the rejection of the
solicitations of the Anglo-Saxons, and to conclude a treaty of
friendship between the two sovereigns [1].

The Anglo-Saxons were thus left to their own resources
and to the aid of their neighbours, the Welsh.   Eadric, surnamed the Forester [2], could no longer endure the yoke of the
stranger : he attacked the garrison of Hereford, by whom
and the hated Richard fitz Scrob his lands had frequently
been ravaged, and, in conjunction with Blethgent and Rith-
walon, kings of the Welsh, having laid waste the county of
Hereford as far as the bridge of the river Lug, returned with
an immense booty [3].   An insurrection raised by Meredith
and Ithel, sons of Griffith ap Llewelyn, in North Wales, prevented the British princes from following up this advantage [4].
William was not slow to prize the valour of the bold Forester,
and preferred gaining him as a friend to overcoming him as
an enemy ; we, consequently, find the only Anglo-Saxon, who
had defeated and chastised the Normans, in possession, at a
later period, of extensive landed estates [5].

But the Anglo-Saxons found an unexpected ally in the dis-

<hr/>

[1] Knyghton, col. 2343 ; Langebek, iii. pp. 252 sq. Ellis, Introd. to
Domesd. ii. pp. 98 sqq.   Hist. Rames. c. 119. Sim. Dunelm. a. 1074.

[2] Ord. Vital. pp. 506, 514 (Maseres, pp. 195, 223), where he is called
Edricus Guilda.—T.

[3] Flor. Wigorn. a. 1067.   [4] Powel, History of Wales, p. 101.

[5] See Domesday under the name of Eadric.

content of several Norman and French nobles, whose private
interest they considered not to have been sufficiently consulted by William in his distribution of lands in England.
Of these one of the most dissatisfied was Eustace, the powerful count of Boulogne, the brother-in-law of the late king
Eadward, who, as the smallest reward for the auxiliaries he
had supplied, as well as for the personal service he had rendered to the duke in the field of Senlac, expected at least to
receive the town of Dover, which had once before slipped
through his hands[1]. A moment was chosen, when the commanders of that fortress, bishop Odo and Hugh of Montfort,
together with the best men of the garrison, had passed the
Thames, for crossing the Channel in the stillness of the night,
and with a body of French and Kentish men proceeding to
Dover. There, however, they met with more precaution and
more determined valour than they expected. Count Eustace
was indebted for his life, as he had been twenty-six years
before, to the swiftness of his horse, his knowledge of the
road, and a vessel in readiness to receive him. His grandson, a brave youth, fell into the hands of the pursuing garrison. The king caused his faithless friend and vassal to be
cited before a court composed of Normans and Anglo-Saxons,
and the heavy charge to be brought against him, which admitted of no defence. All his fiefs in William's states were,
consequently, confiscated; to whose policy, however, which
sought to gain over those who evinced the courage to oppose
him, it appeared more advisable to reconcile his hot-headed,
daring companion in arms, and propitiate him with new investitures[2].

By another tribunal, that of popular hatred, fell earl Copsi,
whose reasons for siding with the Normans were regarded by

---

[1] See Engl. under the A. S. Kings, ii. pp. 247, 249.
[2] Both his widow, Ida, and his son, Eustace, received lands in England. See Ord. Vital. p. 523 Maseres, p. 256) and Ellis, Introd. to
Domesd. i. pp. 384, 446,

his relations and vassals as disgraceful selfishness and short-sighted self-interest. Proscribed as a traitor by the unanimous voice of his people, he fell a sacrifice to rash national hate[1]. Earl Morkere had transferred the administration of Bernicia, or the northern part of Northumberland, which had been bestowed on him after the expulsion of Tostig[2], to the young Osulf, son of earl Eadulf, who had been slain by Siward, but which William restored to his devoted adherent, Copsi[3]. Such an appointment, in a province where no Norman had yet set foot, could not reckon on acknowledgment; Osulf was, consequently, expelled by violence from his office and castle. For some weeks the proscribed earl wandered about in the woods, sustaining life with difficulty, until, assured of the good will of the people, he surprised Copsi at Newburn on the Humber, while at his repast, who fled for refuge to the neighbouring church, which being set on fire, Copsi, in endeavouring to escape, was slain by Osulf at the door of the sacred edifice (March 12th, 1067). The king had just departed for Normandy, and there was no one to oppose the return of Osulf to his earldom, who, with the fatality which pursued the Anglo-Saxons, perished by the spear of a robber. Gospatric, a grandson of earl Uhtred of Northumberland, (ob. 1017,) and Ælfgifu, a daughter of king Æthelred, then laid claim to the earldom by hereditary right, which was granted him in consideration of a large sum of money[4].

In the meantime intelligence reached the king in Normandy of the disordered state of the kingdom and the unfitness for

[1] Here the instructive (notwithstanding its partiality and rhetorical garb) work of William of Poitiers terminates, as we do not possess the end in original; we have, nevertheless, a probably almost verbal extract of the last pages in Ordericus Vitalis.

[2] See Engl. under the A. S. Kings, ii. p. 271.   [3] See p. 105.

[4] Simeon Dunelm. a. 1072. ejusd. Hist. Dunelm. iii. 14. Gospatric held the earldom as early as 1067, as we are expressly informed by Simeon. The Sax. Chron. styles him 'earl' in 1067, yet Palgrave (Commonw. ii. p. cccxxii.) places his appointment under 1069.

the civil administration of the country of those to whom he
had intrusted it. The Anglo-Saxon commonalty threatened
to be more dangerous to him than the nobles. The wealthy
and well fortified city of Exeter, in which both Britons and
Saxons lived in concord and flourishing under a free civic
constitution, was little disposed to submit to a foreign domination. The presence of the nobility of Devonshire, and
more particularly of the mother of king Harold, confirmed
this adverse disposition. The citizens strengthened their
walls and towers, sent deputations to the neighbouring towns,
summoning them to a general resistance, and retained all
foreign traders residing in their city, if capable of bearing
arms. Some Norman troops, who had been driven into that
port by a storm, had been treated with scorn and cruelty;
and the king was convinced that his presence alone could
prevent an unfavourable issue. Intrusting, therefore, the
administration of his hereditary dominions to his consort
Matilda, and his eldest son Robert, assisted by experienced
ecclesiastics and valiant knights, he embarked with his late
vicegerent, Roger of Montgomery, from Arques, at the mouth
of the river Dieppe[1], for the opposite port of Winchilsea[2], on
a December evening (Dec. 6th 1067), in spite of the storms
of winter. He hastened to London, where he kept the Christmas festival, and sought by numerous proclamations, abounding in fair promises, tending to lull the Anglo-Saxons, and
by kindly giving ear to their complaints[3], to palliate not only
the misconduct of his followers, but also a heavy contribution
which he laid on the impoverished nation[4].

The citizens of Exeter[5], in answer to his message, demand-

[1] Now the Bethune.—T.
[2] Portus Wicenesium. Ord. Vital. p. 509.
[3] " Ipse omnes officioso affectu demulcebat, dulciter ad oscula invitabat,
cunctis affabilitatem ostendebat; benigne, si quid orabant concedebat," etc.
Ib. p. 509 (Maseres, p. 209).
[4] Sax. Chron. Flor. Wigorn. a. 1067.
[5] For *Eroniam* some MSS. of Malmesbury read *Oxoniam*. That the

ing their oath of allegiance, declared that they would swear no oath to him, nor would they admit him into their town; that they would only pay him tribute, according to ancient custom. William replied that he was not accustomed to have subjects on such conditions, and, without further delay, drew near to the city, the English being placed in the front of his army. On his approach he was met by a deputation of the principal inhabitants, suing for peace, assuring him that their gates stood open to receive him, and that they were ready to submit to his will. To secure their fidelity, William demanded a number of hostages, which were delivered to him. On their return to the city, it would seem that they found the bulk of the inhabitants in no wise disposed to partake of the weakness of their superiors, but resolved on defending their rights and hearths to the utmost. But they little knew the artifices of the besieger, nor were they sufficiently guarded against treachery within their walls.

William, who had encamped about four miles from the place, now approached with a body of five hundred horse, for the purpose of reconnoitering. Finding the gates closed and the works densely manned, he ordered his entire army to advance, and the eyes of one of the hostages to be put out close to one of the gates; but the inhabitants were not yet to be intimidated. After a siege of eighteen days, and when their walls had been undermined, they surrendered[1]. The citizens and clergy, bearing the sacred Scriptures, went out to meet the king, who treated them with clemency, sparing their effects, and placing a strong guard at each gate, to prevent his soldiery from plundering. Within the city he caused a strong castle to be erected, and having left a powerful

latter reading is erroneous seems hardly to admit of a doubt, yet see W. Malm. p. 421. edit. E. H. Soc. and Hardy's note; R. Wendover, ii. p. 4; and Ellis, Introd. to Domesd. i. p. 191.—T.

[1] "And hig him þa burh ageafon, for þan þa ðegenas heom geswicon hæfdon." *And they surrendered the city to him, because the thanes had deceived them.* Sax. Chron. a. 1067. T.

garrison under the command of Baldwin of Moles, a son
of count Gilbert of Brionne, he proceeded into Cornwall,
for the purpose of pacifying that county [1]. The old countess
Gytha, with many ladies of distinction and great treasure,
fled from Exeter to Steepholm, a small island in the
Bristol channel, near the mouth of the Severn, where they
continued for some time, awaiting probably the result of
an expedition from Ireland, commanded by Eadmund and
Magnus, sons of the late king Harold [2]. But seeing her
hopes frustrated, Gytha embarked for Flanders and found
an asylum at St. Omer's [3].

The king availed himself of this interval of apparent tranquillity to celebrate the Easter festival (a. 1068) at Winchester,
and to send for his consort, the countess Matilda, from Normandy, who, at the following festival of Whitsuntide, was
solemnly crowned queen at Westminster, by the hands of
archbishop Ealdred [4]. She was attended from Normandy by
a numerous train of noble knights and ladies, and, among
others, by the bishop of Amiens, Wido or Guido, to whose
muse we are indebted for a poem of no small value, in neat
hexameters and pentameters, on the battle of Senlac and the
succeeding events, to the coronation of the Conqueror [5]. The
queen, as well as the other new comers, received their share
of the spoil, and in a manner which shows manifestly the
spirit of the conquest. In her youth, Matilda had seen, at
the court of her father at Bruges, a young Anglo-Saxon of
rank named Brihtric, son of Ælfgar, to whom, it appears, she

---

[1] Ord. Vital. p. 510 (Maseres, p. 210.)

[2] Of her seven sons by earl Godwine, we have recorded the death of five:
Sweyn, Tostig, Harold, Gyrth and Leofwine. Of the two survivors, Ælfgar
became a monk at Rheims, and Wulfnoth at Salisbury. See Engl. under
the A. S. Kings. ii. pp. 255, 280, 301. Ord. Vital. p. 502 (Maseres, p. 186).

[3] Sax. Chron. Ord. Vital. p. 513 (Maseres, p. 221), who erroneously
places Gytha's flight in 1069.

[4] Sax. Chron. a. 1067.

[5] The poem is printed in the Materials for the History of Britain, under
the title of " De Bello Hastingensi Carmen."—T.

formed a warm attachment, but which was not reciprocated. While engaged in the consecration of a chapel, Brihtric was seized by the Normans, at his manor of Hanley, and dragged to Winchester, where he died in prison childless : his lands, which escheated to the crown, were bestowed partly on Robert fitz Hamon and partly on queen Matilda[1].

About this time, the Anglo-Saxon nobles, whom William had taken with him to Normandy, having returned to England, he thought he might now permit them to go from place to place without restraint. When again in their native country, they could not avoid seeing the fate that awaited it under the Norman aristocracy, and ere long Eadwine (who had received a personal injury in William's refusal to give him his daughter in marriage, according to his promise), Morkere, the nobles of Northumberland, the new earl Gospatric, Mærlesweyn[2], the sons of king Harold, Blithwallon, king of North Wales, and many others, formed a league with the

[1] The following note is from Ellis' Introd. to Domesday, ii. p. 54.— " Kelham, from Rudder's Gloucestershire, p. 739, says, ' Brihtric had the honour of Gloucester, which was a noble seigniory, and many other great estates, by inheritance from his grandfather Hailward (Ægilweard, Æthelweard ?) Snow; but having incurred the displeasure of Maud, queen to William the Conqueror, and daughter to Baldwin earl of Flanders, by refusing to marry her, when he was ambassador at her father's court, she revenged the insult by procuring his imprisonment and the confiscation of all his possessions. Illustr. p. 165'." See Monast. vi. p. 62.

"The anonymous continuator of Wace, who wrote in the reign of Henry III., and who says he translated his poem at Amesbury in Wiltshire, is perhaps the oldest authority for the story of Matilda's disappointment. He states Brictric to have died in prison at Winchester, without heir, and that his property in consequence escheated and was disposed of by the Conqueror, in part to *his Queen*[1] and in part to Robert Fitz Haimon. But the honour of Gloucester, which had been Brictric's, was really bestowed upon Robert Fitz Haimon by king William Rufus : so that Wace's continuator is guilty of at least one anachronism."

[2] This and the preceding name are by Ordericus Latinized into Caius Patricius and Marius Suevus !

[1] There is no mention of this in the extract as given by Ellis.   T.

object of expelling the Normans from the country. But the want of plan and unanimity among the Anglo-Saxons, which had so greatly contributed to their defeat at Senlac, now even to a greater degree led to the firmer establishment of the intruders. Eadwine and Morkere, when they found themselves opposed to the king in arms near Warwick, could not resolve on risking the fate of a battle, and again placed themselves at the mercy of the Conqueror[1]. Godwine, Eadmund, and Magnus, the youthful sons of Harold, who had found an asylum with Dermot, king of Leinster, landed in the mouth of the Avon, from an Irish fleet, that had been long looked for by the fugitives on Steepholm; but the people of Bristol, with an eye to their tranquillity and trifling commerce, opposed a vigorous resistance to the invaders, though Eadnoth, an Anglo-Saxon, who had been master of the horse to their father, Harold, marching forth against them, was totally defeated and slain. Seeing then, in consequence probably of the defection of Eadwine and Morkere, no prospect of support from the interior of the country, they proceeded to ravage Devonshire and Cornwall, and, loaded with booty, returned to Ireland[2]. The king now caused a castle to be built at Warwick, the custody of which he bestowed on Henry, son of Roger of Beaumont; also another castle at Nottingham, which he intrusted to the keeping of William Peverel[3].

In Northumberland, whither Eadgar Ætheling had also fled, the bitterest hatred prevailed towards the foreigners. The citizens of York, through the defection of the archbishop from the national cause, were only the more exasperated, and his authority was not of the least avail in appeasing those who dwelt in his immediate neighbourhood. Forests, marshes, towns, whatever, in short, could be so applied, were transformed into fortresses, intrenchments, and barricades.

[1] Ord. Vital. p. 511 (Maseres. pp. 214, sqq.)
[2] The Sax. Chron. places this expedition under the year 1067.
[3] Ord. Vital. p. 511 (Maseres. p. 216.)

Many swore never to sleep in a house until the enemy was driven out of the kingdom. A multitude of hardy warriors lived in tents and huts constructed in haste, whom it pleased the Normans to scoff at as savages (salvages, silvatici). The ætheling Eadgar, earl Gospatric, and Mærleswcyn fled with Agatha, Eadgar's mother, and his sisters, Margaret and Christina, to king Malcolm III., surnamed Canmore, of Scotland, who, captivated by the attractions of Margaret, who had probably been previously betrothed to him, was the more easily induced to adopt the policy of assailing the enemy who was already threatening his frontier. Nevertheless, York, the only strong bulwark of their country's defenders, yielded to the Normans. The keys of the city, and the noblest hostages, were delivered to William; and Archil[1] also, the most powerful of the Northumbrians, made his peace with the king, and gave him his son as a pledge of his fidelity. Two strong castles were erected at York, and committed to the custody of William Malet and Robert fitz Richard, with five hundred horsemen. Ægelwine also, bishop of Durham, hastened to the Conqueror, who, knowing how to value the spiritual ally, received him benignantly. Ægelwine was forthwith sent with a mission, consisting of William's son Robert, the abbot of Abingdon, and other prelates, to the camp of the king of Scotland, whom he induced to send an embassy back with him to William, for the purpose of swearing to the latter the fealty of the Scottish king, which, no doubt, comprised his homage for the lands held by him in England[2].

By this act the conquest of England may be regarded as

---

[1] Many possessions of Archil are recorded in Domesday, T. R. E. (Tempore Regis Edwardi), which are most probably referrible to this person.

[2] Ord. Vit. p. 511. (Maseres, pp. 216–218); lib. Abingd. (MS. Cott. Claud. c. ix. p. 135.) ap. Palgrave, ii. p. cccxxxi. The value of this latter unprinted authority I am unable to estimate; though the mention of Robert, to whom the king, a short time before, had committed the government of Normandy, appears hardly credible.

completed, and William now, by the right of the sword and
oaths acknowledging his authority, was in possession of the
entire dominion of the last Anglo-Saxon king.   But this
sagacious prince was fully aware how unstable is a government that has no root in the hearts of the natives, and, therefore, on his return to the south, took care to erect castles at
Lincoln, Huntingdon, and Cambridge.   It would seem that
there was a scarcity of trustworthy persons of consideration,
to whom the king might commit the keeping of so many
places of importance, and that he found himself, contrary to
his better judgment, compelled to intrust many considerable
shrievalties and garrisons to rugged, violent, and rapacious
men, who could not understand, much less carry out his
subtle, conciliatory policy.   Many of his older knights were
dissatisfied with their share of the booty, which, generally
speaking, on account either of its insignificance or supposed
insecurity, was so far from tempting, that it fell to the share
not of the first-born, but usually of the younger branches.
The greater number of the Normans did not yet venture to
send for their wives, and as, during their two years' absence
from their country, they heard only anxious complaints from
them, and but too often bad accounts of improprieties that
had taken place, many of the most distinguished men, as
Hugh of Grentemaisnil, his sister's son, Humfrey of Tellenil,
to whom the castle of Hastings had been intrusted, and
others, heedless of the threatened loss of their English fiefs,
resolved to return to Normandy.   The threats alluded to
were not, however, always carried into effect[1], particularly
as the king could not easily dispense with men like Hugh,
who, it appears, soon returned, with his wife Adeliz, to his

---

[1] Domesday refutes the erroneous assertion of Orderic. p. 512. (Maseres.
p. 217), who says : " Sed honores, quos jam nactos hac de causa relique-
runt, ipsi, vel heredes eorum, nunquam postea recuperare potuerunt."
See Ellis, Introd. i. p. 429, under " Grentemaisnil," and p. 502, under
" Uxor H. de Grentemaisnil," also p. 361.

castle at Leicester. On the other hand, in consequence of the increasing misery of the country, desolated by famine and its attendant, pestilence, by fire and plunderings, the king found it advisable to discharge and send back to their homes, richly rewarded, many of his soldiers, whose services were available only on a day of battle.

Still these praiseworthy measures, in a state of such great excitement, were not sufficient. In the beginning of the following year (1069), he sent Robert of Comines[1] to the Scottish border with seven hundred horse[2], to administer the county of Durham. Full of confidence in himself, the king, and the strong walls of the place, he rode, in spite of the warnings of the bishop, Ægelwine, with the Norman banner, into the city of Durham. He would not, even for a moment, repress the insolence of his soldiers, who treated the city as a conquered place, and even massacred many ecclesiastics. In the following night, when the gates were closed, and the Normans, defenceless and suspecting no danger, were either merry-making or sleeping, the fire-staff passed from village to village between the Tees and the Derwent, and a multitude breathing vengeance secretly beset the city. On the 28th of January, when at early morn the gates were opened, the men of the country burst in, quickly joined themselves to the townsmen, assailed the new earl (who, with his knights, valiantly defended himself in the episcopal palace, in which he had taken up his abode, and when it was set on fire, perished in the flames) and massacred the entire Norman squadron,

[1] Ancestor of the historian, Philip de Comines, and of the Scottish family of Comyn, or Cumin.

[2] So Sim. Dunelm. The Sax. Chron. (a. 1068) has 900; Orderic says 500, a number apparently used by him to signify a large body. Thierry, who has overlooked the genuine authorities, making use of their epitomizers only, Alfred of Beverley and Hemingford, speaks besides of " 1200 chevaliers complétement armés, mais on ne sait pas au juste combien de gens de service et de fantassins les accompagnaient." Such exaggerations should be banished from the province of history.

with the exception of two swift-footed fugitives, who carried the intelligence of the disaster to the king.

Nothing spreads itself more widely around than an excited popular animosity. Only a few days after the above-mentioned occurrence, Robert fitz Richard was slain with a considerable number of his followers. In the other castle, however, William Malet still maintained himself, and not only communicated to the king information of this new calamity, but also of the approach of the Anglo-Saxons from Scotland, under Eadgar Ætheling, Gospatric, and Mærlesweyn, against whom he felt himself unable to hold out. And these soon began their attack; but the king arriving suddenly at the place, dispersed the besiegers, and provided the garrison thus relieved with a reinforcement, under the command of his best general, William fitz Osbern. The king himself returned to Winchester, there to celebrate the Easter festival, according to royal custom[1]. How well William could rely on fitz Osbern appears also on this occasion. After his departure, the Anglo-Saxons lost no time in assembling and marching upon York; but were met by fitz Osbern, who, after an obstinate engagement, returned with many prisoners, leaving only corpses and despairing fugitives behind him.

Some months after, (the end of June,) either too late or too early, as it usually happened in these struggles of the Anglo-Saxons, two of Harold's sons, with the aid of Dermot, king of Leinster, again landed, from sixty-four ships, at the mouth of the Tavy in Devonshire, and from Tavistock proceeded to Exeter, ravaging all the neighbouring country. but were surprised by Brian, son of Eudes, count of Brittany, and William Gualdi, and in two battles, fought on one day, lost the greater

---

[1] A charter of donation and confirmation, dated from the monastery of St. Swithin, on the 2nd day of Easter, by William, king of England, and count (see p. 15) of Normandy and Le Maine, in the third year of his reign, in favour of the abbey of St. Denys, is still preserved among the archives at Paris. It is, perhaps, the oldest charter of William the Conqueror extant.

part of their followers. The remaining few returned in two small vessels to Ireland[1].

Tranquillity had hardly been re-established in the south, when, in the mouth of the Humber[2], arrived the formidable Danish fleet, so long hoped for by the natives, so feared by William, who, foreseeing the coming storm, had sent his queen back to Normandy. This fleet, consisting of two hundred and forty ships, was under the command of the two elder sons of king Svend Estrithson, Harald and Cnut[3], of their uncle Asbiörn[4], who had formerly been banished from England, and of the jarl Thorkell. Bishop Christian of Aarhuus, afterwards of Ribe, together with other ecclesiastics, was also with the fleet, both to fight and give counsel. They had previously made an attempt to land at Dover, which seems sufficiently to show that their object was to act in common with the sons of Harold, and that the several pretenders were at least unanimous in the intention of expelling the Normans with their combined forces. On their course northwards they landed at Sandwich, where they were

[1] Sax. Chron. Flor. Wigorn. a. 1064. W. Gemmet. lib. vii. c. 41. Ord. Vital. p. 531 (Maseres, p. 219.) Thierry errs in placing the expedition of the *three* sons of Harold, and that of the *two* sons, which was not undertaken till after Midsummer in the year following, both in last mentioned year. He has, generally speaking, paid too little attention to Florence. [William of Jumièges and Orderic give 66 as the number of ships.—T.]

[2] Sim. Dunelm. Ante Nativitatem Mariæ, (Sept. 8th). Lingard was probably thinking of the Assumption, when he made the landing of the Danes in the Humber in the beginning of August, and, consequently, at Dover in July.

[3] The Saxon Chronicle (a. 1069) makes three sons of Svend in this expedition, but without giving their names. The Chronicle in these years is very incorrect.

[4] See Engl. under the A. S. Kings, ii. p. 242. The identity of this person is undoubted, although disregarded by the older authors, while the later wholly pass over Asbiörn's share in the expedition, or disfigure his name so as to render it no longer recognisable; as Lingard, copying from Domesday, writes it 'Sbern'. [Both he and Turner have also 'Sveno' for Svend.—T.]

K

repulsed by the Normans. At Ipswich, where they next
landed, they were attacked and put to flight by the inhabitants, while engaged in ravaging and plundering the neighbourhood; but at Norwich a still worse fate befell them.
Having landed at that city, they were encountered by Ralf
of Guader, when many perished by the sword and many were
drowned, the remainder being driven to their ships. On their
arrival in the Humber, they were joined by Gospatric, Mærlesweyn, Waltheof, Archill, who had deserted the cause of
William, and other Anglo-Saxons[1]. Eadgar Ætheling was,
with some troops, gone southwards on a predatory expedition,
and was attacked by the garrison of Lincoln, who captured
all his men with the exception of two, who escaped with their
leader[2]. When archbishop Ealdred, who had so zealously
espoused the cause of the Conqueror, received intelligence of
the invasion of the Danes, he was so stricken with consternation and grief, that he fell sick, and in a few days died[3].

King William was engaged in the diversion of the chase in
the forest of Dean[4], when intelligence was brought him of the
landing of the Danes at Norwich. He instantly despatched
a messenger to York, counselling his officers there to take
their measures with caution, and to send for him, should they
deem his presence necessary. They answered, that the commanders of the garrisons would not require aid for a year, as
the number of Normans there was above three thousand.
Their precautionary measures they carried so far as to burn
those houses of the citizens that lay round the castles, the
flames from which, having caught the city, the greater part
of it, together with the minster of St. Peter, in which the

---

[1] " Elnocinus et quatuor filii Karoli." Ord. Vital. p. 513 (Maseres,
p. 223). Carl appears to have been a man of considerable property in
Yorkshire and other counties. See Ellis, Introd. ii. p. 65.

[2] Ord. Vital. p. 513. (Maseres, p. 222.)

[3] Flor. Wigorn. a. 1069.

[4] " Dana sylva." Ord. Vital. p. 513. (Maseres, p. 222.)

body of the archbishop had just been deposited, was laid in ashes (19th Sept.). The Danish fleet had in the meanwhile sailed up the Ouse, and saw from afar the blazing conflagration which, driven by a storm, within a few hours consumed the wood-constructed city[1]. On the third day the Anglo-Saxons appeared before the walls of York, and so well-planned was their attack, so unceasing their impetuosity, that on the same day they succeeded in taking the castles by storm. The garrisons, with the exception of William Malet and his family, of Gilbert of Ghent[2] and a few others, whose lives were saved for the sake of the ransom, were put to the sword[3].

The insurrection of the Anglo-Saxons had in the meantime taken a wider range, although, from lack of adequate guidance, with little result. In Somersetshire the count of Mortain and Cornwall had caused a strong castle to be erected, and named it from its position Montagut[4] (Monsacutus, Montagu). The people of the district, with those of Dorsetshire and other neighbouring parts, rose while count Robert was staying with the king his brother, for the purpose of attacking the detested structure. The men of the castle, however, repelled the assault, till Geoffrey, bishop of Coutances, came to their relief, with forces from London, Winchester, and Salisbury. The prisoners taken on this occasion were by the Normans, according to their barbarous custom, cruelly mutilated. In Shropshire the people had assembled under Eadric the Forester and other unconquered patriots, and, with the men of Cheshire and the neighbouring Welsh, united to

---

[1] Ord. Vital. *ut sup.* Sim. Dunelm. col. 198. Flor. Wigorn. a. 1069.

[2] " Dugdale has given a long account of Gilbert of Ghent in his Baronage, i. p. 400. He was son to Baldwin earl of Flanders, whose sister the Conqueror had married. He was the refounder of Bardney abbey in Lincolnshire, and is believed to have died about the year 1094. See also Kelham, p. 78, and the " Descensus de Gant," in the account of the abbey of Vaudey, in the Monast. Anglic. v. p. 491." Ellis, Introd. i. p. 422. T.

[3] Ord. Vital. p. 512 (Maseres, p. 223.) Flor. Wigorn. a. 1069.

[4] Domesday, i. fol. 93.

K 2

surprise the castle of Shrewsbury. The town was burnt, and when the counts William Gualdi and Brian, son of Eudes of Brittany, hastened to chastise the insurgents, they avoided the encounter. They durst not follow them into the mountain passes; for the men of Devonshire also, and the British population from the extremity of Cornwall, had combined together to capture the Norman barons and their followers in Exeter. But the defenders of the city, in a sudden sortie, succeeded in driving off their assailants who, in their flight, were met by the royal forces from Shrewsbury, under the two counts above mentioned, and routed with great slaughter [1].

King William had in the meanwhile hastened into Staffordshire, the inhabitants of which, like those of Cheshire, had followed the example of their earls, Eadwine and Morkere. But these movements were by his powerful arms soon quelled, and William then proceeded to Northumbria. There the Danes had spread themselves over the land south of York, and many of them had crossed the Humber to the opposite shore of the rich district of Lindesey, where, however, they were attacked by Robert, count of Mortain, and Robert of Eu, and, after suffering considerable loss, with difficulty reached their ships. The king in the meanwhile continued to march forwards. At Pontefract he found the Are so swollen, that it was not passable at any of the usual fords. In this conjuncture he was by some advised to return; to others, who would persuade him to construct a bridge, he answered, that it would not be prudent, lest the enemy should suddenly attack them while engaged on the work. For three weeks he was detained there, until a valiant soldier, named Lisois des Moustiers [2], after much labour, discovered a ford,

---

[1] W. Gemmet. lib. vii. c. 41. Ord. Vital. p. 513 (Maseres, p. 223.)

[2] Perhaps the "Lisoisus in Essex" of Domesday, fol. 496. [Ellis. ii. p. 349. "De Monasteriis," as he is named by Orderic, p. 514 (Maseres. p. 224) is, no doubt, Des Moustiers, or Des Moûtiers Latinized. See Maseres, ut sup.—T.]

where, at the head of sixty horse, he crossed the river. On the opposite shore he was assailed by a numerous body of the enemy, whom, however, he repulsed. On the following day, having returned to the camp, he showed them the ford, by which the whole army crossed without delay. They had now to pass through forests and across morasses, over mountains and through valleys, and ways where two were unable to march abreast. On reaching York they found that the Danes had abandoned it[1]. With all his rancour towards his enemies, William did not forget that he could inflict on them much greater injury by other and more effectual means than by the sword. The object of the jarl Asbiörn in engaging in the expedition was gain, and this he found in the rich presents of gold that William caused to be made to him, and for which he engaged to hold his countrymen in a state of inaction on the coast till the spring, and then return with them to Denmark. Many of them had in fact already returned, on account of want of provisions, and not a few had perished by storm. Asbiörn's return to Seeland was delayed until July of the following year. On his arrival he was met by a sentence of banishment[2]. William now gave the reins to his insatiable vengeance. He sent some of his chieftains with a

---

[1] It was probably on this occasion, if on any, that, according to Malmesbury (p. 427), Waltheof is said to have slain so many Normans with his own hand : "Siquidem Weldeofus in Eboracensi pugna plures Normannorum solus obtruncaverat, unos et unos per portem egredientes (ingredientes?) decapitans." The story, if not a fiction, strongly resembles one.—T.

In the Registrum Honoris de Richmond (edited by Gale) there is a charter of William's dated " In obsidione coram civitate Ebor." The genuineness of this document, in which William designates himself " Ego Willielmus cognomine Bastardus," is doubted by Gale. See Ellis, Introd. i. p. 366.

[2] The Peterborough MS. of the Saxon Chronicle and Hugonis Candidi Historia Cœnobii Burgensis relate that king Svend himself, in the year 1070, landed in the Humber, and afterwards concluded a peace with king William ; both which accounts are contrary to the most trustworthy authorities.

body of troops to York to restore the ruined castles, leaving
others to oppose the Danes on the banks of the Humber,
while he himself went in pursuit of the enemy, who had taken
refuge in thickly wooded and almost inaccessible places. Corn,
cattle, utensils, and every species of food he ordered to be
heaped together and burnt. The famine that had already
raged for more than a year, was by such execrable proceedings so aggravated, and so horrible was the misery, that the
wretched inhabitants were compelled to subsist on horses,
cats, and even on human flesh. Hunger forced many to sell
themselves and families into perpetual slavery to their oppressors. During this calamitous state of things, it is supposed that no less than a hundred thousand human beings
perished. Many who, with some little property, had forsaken
their country, in the hope of finding an asylum in a foreign
land, perished ere they could reach the wished-for shore.
Appalling was it in the silent houses, in the lonely streets,
and public roads, to see the corpses rotting, covered with
myriads of worms, in an atmosphere insufferably redolent of
putrefaction. For the last duty, that of burial, no one survived to perform it in the desolated land. Those whom the
sword and the famine had spared, had fled from the scene of
ruin. Even Ægelwine, the bishop of Durham, and other
innocent ecclesiastics durst not venture to remain at home ;
for the sword of the avenger knew no difference among Anglo-
Saxons. Northumbria and the parts adjacent were become
one vast desert, where no one for the next ten years would
settle, with the object of cultivating the land ; and even after
the lapse of more than half a century, tracts of above sixty
miles in extent were still in a state of desolation. On the
once frequented road from York to Durham, as far as the
eye could reach, not a single inhabited village was to be seen.
In ruins and caverns dwelt only crews of robbers and wolves,
for the destruction of the traveller[1].

[1] Simeon Dunelm. a. 1069. W. Malm. de Gest. Pont. lib. iii. Proleg.

But William was not content with having spread his fame as a warrior, or, more correctly perhaps, his infamy as a destroyer, he was also desirous of displaying his royal dignity before the eyes of his neighbours. He caused the crown and other regalia to be brought from Winchester to York, where he kept the Christmas festival. Large districts in Yorkshire, particularly the possessions of the earls Eadwine and Morkere, were now bestowed on his adherents. Alan Fergant (the Red), count of Brittany, received, in Yorkshire, the lands on which he erected the castle of Richmond[1], Gilbert of Lacy received Pontefract, a Fleming, Drogo Bruiére, Odo of Champagne, Gamel, son of Ketil of Meaux, and others received vast grants of land, but which scarcely afforded them a scanty subsistence. He then marched as far as the Tees, where he spent a fortnight, during which time earl Waltheof appeared before him, for the purpose of making his submission. Gospatric renewed his oath of fealty by proxy, and was reinstated in possession of his earldoms. Eadgar and the other Anglo-Saxon chieftains took shipping at Wearmouth for Scotland, whither also Ægelwine, bishop of Durham, who (sensible of the impossibility of intercourse with people speaking a foreign tongue and of still more foreign

[His words are : "Qui [Willielmus] urbanis [Eboraci] iratus, quod Danis adventantibus receptui et consultui fuissent, prius inedia, mox flamma civitatem confecit ; regionis etiam totius vicos et agros corrumpi, fructus et fruges igne vel aqua labefactari jubet. Ita provinciæ quondam fertilis nervi, præda, incendio, sanguine succisi. Humus per lx. et eo amplius milliaria omnifariam inculta, nudum omnium solum *ad hoc usque tempus.* Urbes olim præclaras, turres proceritate sua in cœlum minantes, agros lætos pascuis, irriguos fluviis, si quis videt modo peregrinus, ingemit ; si quis vetus incola, non agnoscit. In aliquibus tamen parietum ruinis, qui semiruti remansere, videas mira Romanorum artificia, velut est in Lugabalia civitate triclinium lapidum fornicibus concameratum, quod nulla unquam tempestatum contumelia, quinetiam nec appositis ex industria lignis et succensis valuit labefactari."

Malmesbury wrote in the middle of the twelfth century.—T.]

[1] The charters are still at Nantes. See Daru, Hist. de la Bretagne, i p. 106. Ellis, Introd. i. p. 366

ideas) had resolved on going to Cologne, was driven by a
storm. William returned to York[1], by a way until then
never trodden by an army, where, while the adjacent country
was rejoicing in vernal mildness, the mountain-tops and the
deep valleys were thickly covered with snow. But William
prosecuted his march, during an intensely hard frost, cheering
his soldiers by his alertness. During his progress a great
number of his horses perished. Every one was anxious only
for his own safety, recking little for his chief or his friend.
In this state of difficulty, the king, attended only by six
knights, lost his way, and passed a whole night without
knowing where to find his army. On his return to York, he
caused several castles to be restored, and the necessary measures to be taken for placing things on a better footing in
the city and neighbourhood. He then proceeded with his
army against the men of Cheshire and the Welsh, who, in
addition to their other offences, had laid siege to Shrewsbury.
But the army, which had already undergone so many hardships, was fearful that still more and greater awaited them in
this expedition. They dreaded the rugged ways, the severity
of the winter, the scarcity of provisions, and the terrific ferocity of the enemy. The Angevins, Bretons, and those of Le
Maine, who were in the pay of William, were, as they said,
oppressed beyond endurance by intolerable duties ; they
therefore pertinaciously demanded their dismissal. The king
did not vouchsafe to retain them either by entreaties or promises ; but boldly continued his march, commanding those
bands that were faithful to follow him, and looking with contempt on the deserters, as spiritless, cowardly, and weak.
Unwearied he pursued his march by ways never before explored by cavalry, over lofty mountains and through deep
valleys, across streams and rivers, in rain and hail. The king

---

[1] Orderic, p. 515 (Maseres, p. 226) has : " Rex Guillelmus Haugustal-
dam (Hexham) revertabatur a Tesia ; ' no doubt a mistake for Eboracum,
as is manifest from the context. See Maseres ut sup. T.

himself frequently led the way on foot, readily lending aid to those in difficulty. At length he brought his army safely to Chester, and suppressed by force every hostile movement in the province of Mercia. At Chester and also at Stafford he caused castles to be erected[1]. The county of Chester (in which that part of Lancashire which lies between the Ribble and the Mersey, as well as some adjacent Welsh districts, was comprised), which Gherbod the Fleming, preferring his inheritance in his native country[2], had resigned, was now granted to Hugh, surnamed Goz, also Lupus, or the Wolf[3], son of Richard, surnamed Goz, a man abandoned to the grossest sensuality and most unbounded extravagance. This earldom he received to be held as freely by the sword as the king held England by his crown; and even the other possessors of fiefs there did not, as in other provinces, hold them of the king, but immediately from the earl. We may here perceive the same policy which is to be found in other states

[1] Besides those mentioned in the text, William caused castles to be erected at the following places: Pevensey, Hastings, London (the Tower), in 1066; Winchester, 1067; Chichester, Arundel, Exeter, Warwick, Nottingham, York, Lincoln, Huntingdon, Cambridge, 1068; a second at York, Chester, Stafford, 1070. Maseres' note to Orderic, p. 228.—T.

[2] There does not appear to have been much preference in the case. Orderic, p. 522 (Maseres, p. 253), speaking of Gherbod, says: "Cestram et comitatum ejus Gherbodo, Flandrensi, jamdudum rex dederat, qui magna ibi et difficilia tam ab Anglis quam a Guallis adversantibus pertulerat. Deinde legatione coactus suorum, quos in Flandria dimiserat, et quibus hereditarium honorem suum commiserat, eundi citoque redeundi licentiam a rege acceperat: sed ibi adversa illaqueatus fortuna, in manus inimicorum inciderat, et in vinculis coercitus, mundanaque felicitate privatus, longæ miseriæ threnos depromere didicerat."—T.

[3] Orderic, p. 598 (Maseres, p. 253) gives a very indifferent character of Hugh Lupus: "Hic non dapsilis, sed prodigus erat: non familiam secum, sed exercitum semper ducebat. In dando vel accipiendo nullam rationem tenebat. Ipse terram suam quotidie devastabat, et plus aucupibus ac venatoribus, quam terræ cultoribus, vel cœli oratoribus applaudebat. Ventris ingluviei serviebat; unde nimiæ crassitiei pondere prægravatus, vix ire poterat. E pellicibus plurimam sobolem utriusque sexus genuit, quæ, diversis infortuniis absorpta, pene tota periit." T.

of Europe, where the Margraves frequently obtained very extensive powers, as well as the privilege of holding as their own such lands as they might win by the sword, by way of inducement to guard and extend the frontier the more vigilantly and valiantly. Hugh the Wolf availed himself of this right, and, even in his latter years, when the mass of his fat almost deprived him of the faculty of locomotion, conquered the isle of Anglesey. But the real margrave would appear to have been his lieutenant, Robert, son of Humphrey of Telleuil, who had in his youth already served his apprenticeship in the art of war in England, probably in Hereford against the Welsh [1]. To him the king gave permission to erect a castle at Rhuddlan, in Flintshire, whence he derived the designation of "de Roelent," and invested him with North Wales, in consideration of an annual payment of forty pounds of silver [2].

But a new calamity was reserved for the unhappy north of England, and from a quarter whence it was not expected. Malcolm, king of Scotland, at the head of a numerous army, marched through his province of Cumberland, then, turning eastward, laid waste and depopulated the whole of Teesdale and the adjacent country, under the pretext of aiding the cause of Eadgar Ætheling. At "Hundredeskeld," after massacreing some of the principal inhabitants, Malcolm sent back a part of his army, laden with immense booty, craftily anticipating that the miserable people, who had concealed themselves and their little remaining property, would, supposing the enemy to have departed, emerge from their hiding places, and thus fall an easy prey to the invader. And so it proved. For after partially ravaging Cleveland, he burst into "Heortnisse," whence he overran the lands of St. Cuthbert, slaughtering and plundering wherever he came. Nu-

---

[1] See Engl. under the A. S. Kings, i. p. 246, n [2].

[2] Domesday. i. fol. 269. Ellis. Introd. i. p. 479. Orderic. p. 670. repeatedly calls him Marchio, Marchisus.

merous churches, together with those who had sought refuge in them, were burnt by his soldiers, among others that of St. Peter at Wearmouth, while Malcolm himself looked on. As he was riding along the bank of the river, and from an elevated spot glutting his eyes with the desolation he had caused, intelligence was brought him that Eadgar Ætheling and his sisters, with many fugitives of distinction, had landed at Wearmouth. Malcolm received them with kindness, and promised them a safe and permanent asylum in Scotland. In the meanwhile, Gospatric, who had bought of William the earldom of Northumberland, burst with an army into Cumberland, which he laid waste with fire and sword, and returned with a rich booty to his castle of Bamborough, whence he made frequent irruptions, to the great detriment of the enemy. This retaliation served only to increase Malcolm's fury, who now gave orders not to spare one of English race, but to slay or drive into perpetual slavery the entire population. In consequence of these orders, the aged, both male and female, were mercilessly massacred; infants torn from the breast were thrown on high, and in falling received on the points of the spears. The young of both sexes, and all who appeared capable of labour, were driven bound before their enemies into perpetual bondage. Many, through the fatigue and misery of being thus driven, fell dead by the way. But Malcolm, so far from being moved by the prayers and groans of his victims, ordered them to be urged on the faster. Scotland thus became filled with English slaves of both sexes; so that long afterwards there was scarcely a farm or even a cottage, in which the posterity of these English slaves was not to be found in the condition of serfs.

When Malcolm returned to Scotland, Eadgar Ætheling and his before-mentioned relations and friends had already arrived there; also bishop Ægelwine, who, on his passage to Cologne, had, as we have seen, by adverse winds been driven to Scotland. Malcolm now made the offer of his hand to

Margaret, but met with a refusal both from herself and her
relations, it being her wish to lead a life of celibacy devoted
to the service of her Creator. But Malcolm's importunities
finally prevailed on Eadgar, who gave his consent to the
union, nor, in fact, could he well persist in refusing it; for,
as it is observed by the chronicler, " they were come into his
power." Malcolm was, and had good reason to be, contented
with his choice; and had sagacity enough to profit by his
consort's exhortations and example; so that from a bloodthirsty barbarian, he became a mild and just sovereign. By
Margaret he had six sons: Eadward, Eadmund, Eadgar,
afterwards king, Æthelred, Alexander, and David, the two
last-mentioned also kings of Scotland; and two daughters:
Matilda, married to king Henry the First, and Mary, the
consort of Eustace, count of Boulogne[1].

A loss more prejudicial than a defeat the Anglo-Saxon
cause suffered at this time, through the determination of earl
Waltheof to submit to the Conqueror. He visited William
on the bank of the Tees, and not only met with a gracious
reception, but received from him the earldoms of Northampton and Huntingdon, together with the hand of Judith, the
daughter of his half-sister by her consort, the earl of Albemarle[2]; and shortly after, the county of Northumberland,
which had been taken from Gospatric.

William's thoughts were now engrossed by the means of
firmly establishing his power in England. An ancient custom of depositing in churches and monasteries treasures and

<hr>

[1] Sim. Dunelm. col. 201. Sax. Chron. a. 1067. Flor. Wigorn. a. 1068.
Alured. Riv. 130. Vita S. Marg. ap. Pinkerton, Vitæ SS. Scotiæ.

[2] Her mother was the daughter of Arlette, by her husband, Herluin of
Conteville. W. Gemmet. viii. 37. Cf. Ord. Vital. p. 522 (Maseres, p. 254).
She was not, as Ellis (Introd. i. p. 440) supposes, the daughter of Odo of
Champagne, who married a daughter of Robert, duke of Normandy. According to another account in ' Libello de Vita Gualdevi' (Leland, Iti-
nerar. iv. 140), she was the daughter of count Lambert of Lens, and sister
of Stephen count of Albemarle.

documents of importance had, during these years of trouble, by Anglo-Saxons of wealth and rank, been much resorted to. To gratify his rapacity, and, at the same time, enfeeble his enemies, by depriving them of their pecuniary resources, William, by the advice of William fitz Osbern (A. D. 1070), ordered the churches and monasteries to be ransacked, and the booty thus found, together with many charters of immunity and much church property, not sparing even the plate for the service of the altar, to be seized and conveyed to his own treasury. The bishoprics and abbeys, which until then had been exempt from every secular service, he compelled to render military service, arbitrarily fixing the number of soldiers to be furnished by each bishopric and abbey in time of war[1]. For as he could not be otherwise than sensible that if, from the first moment of his landing, he was an object of hatred to the whole nation, the Anglo-Saxon clergy in particular must, on longer acquaintance, from day to day, entertain an increased aversion towards both himself and his martial prelates; a heavy, yet, for their past obsequiousness and flattery, not unmerited punishment was, therefore, destined for them, which had been deferred only till the king felt himself sufficiently strong to carry it into effect. Hence not satisfied with the confiscation of their treasures, William now began to depose and banish those whose hostility was known to, or only suspected by, him, supplying their places, as he had already done those of the earls and other lay officials, with Normans; a proceeding quite in accordance with existing circumstances and the policy of the Conqueror, but most pernicious in its influence on the Anglo-Saxon people. For although the Anglo-Saxon church had not risen in reputation since the death of Cnut the Great, it had, in the intermediate space, at least maintained its individual character and integrity; but by this measure its peculiar character was

[1] Sax. Chron. a. 1070. Sim. Dunelm. col. 200. Mat. Westm. p. 226. R. Wendov. ii. p. 7.

entirely destroyed, and the instruction of the people, particularly of the higher classes, which was wholly in the hands of the clergy, assumed a different nature. Such a change of language and habits in the priesthood must to the people have been almost tantamount to a suppression of the church, and have wrought a still greater disregard of all religious feelings, had not the complicated miseries of the nation served to raise its thoughts to the Supreme, and direct its hopes to His protection, and to a better future, more immediately and efficiently than the priesthood with its exotic service could accomplish. An inevitable consequence of the introduction of a clergy speaking a foreign tongue was, that the conquerors, the future nobility of the country, adhered exclusively to their native French, and the subjugated inhabitants corrupted the pure Germanic speech of their forefathers, and before many years had elapsed only imperfectly understood it. The collective fruits of the intellectual exertions and experience of the Anglo-Saxon race, deposited in a literature richer than that of any of their Germanic brethren, either in expressive prose or artificially constructed, alliterative, rhythmical poesy; the wisdom of hoar antiquity, all the learning, every animating, warning, exhilarating example in national tradition, became lost to the people. Such a loss we should with reason deplore, even had it been supplanted by something nobler and better: but that which the Normans brought with them was certainly far from being an equivalent, even in point of mere learning. Those Norman bishops, at the head of their squadrons, in a war of attack and conquest, afford us a spectacle as instructive as rare, even in the days of heathenism; and a very slight inquiry suffices to show, that the highly cultivated men, whose names, before and during the time of William, are enumerated among those of the Normans, do not belong to that people. No poem, no national historic work, no sermons, no essays, no collection of laws, from the pen of a native, have the Normans, before their military occupation of England, either transmitted to posterity, or to which they can refer. We may, therefore, fairly assume, when we see the English nation, after ages of depression, again vigorously flourishing, that this resurrection, but for the Norman conquest, would have taken place much earlier and more completely; and that the civilization of southern Europe, which the clergy of those migratory ages spread abroad, would have shed its influence more benignly over Anglo-Saxon life, without the transplanting of the court of Rouen to England. By some, indeed, the fraternizing of the English clergy with their continental brethren has been regarded as the greatest, if not the only, benefit resulting from the Conquest, as if, when casting a glance at the consequences, the too close harmony, which the Romish church strove to effect, did not manifestly appear as the chief cause of their later separation; as if, when we look at its origin, so bloody a conquest, such rugged means must not cast a suspicion over every pretended spiritual advantage.

From the burning and ravaging in the northern part of England, and the violation of sanctuaries, William, laden with church plunder, proceeded at Easter to Winchester, (oct. Easter, Apr. 4), where a great council was appointed to be holden, consisting of Norman barons and Anglo-Saxon thanes, as well as of ecclesiastics, both from this and the opposite side of the Channel, and where the legates of his great ally, pope Alexander II., Ermenfred, bishop of Sion, who had already been employed on a mission to England in the time of the Confessor [1], and the cardinals John and Peter [2], awaited him. William, on this occasion, allowed himself, by a new coronation, at the hands of the two cardinals, to receive the papal ratification of his royal dignity [3]. He was conscious

[1] Flor. Wigorn. a. 1062.

[2] So Florence, though Lanfranc (Ep. i.) names one of these cardinals Hubert.

[3] Vita S. Lanfranci, c. 6. "Coronam capiti ejus imponentes, in regem

that he enhanced the supposed value of this ceremony the
more important he himself appeared to consider it. For
nearly a year he entertained the legates in the most honourable manner; promised, and constantly appeared, to follow
their counsel, and did, in fact, follow it, as far as it had reference to the introduction of a stricter church-discipline. So
great, indeed, was his veneration for them, that he listened to
their discourse as if they were angels from heaven [1]. But however craftily he played his part in this respect, he proved
himself no less firm in maintaining the rights of his crown in
essential matters, and the pope made the discovery that he
had wasted banners, holy water, benedictions, and crowns to
no purpose, the moment he would exact from the most recent
of kings more than what every other sovereign willingly conceded to the papal chair.

The most essential object of the council of Winchester,
both for the pope and the king, was the deposition of the
stubborn archbishop of Canterbury. Stigand, in a constant
state of dissension with the Romish court, had also more and
more incensed the king by occasional compliance and subsequent opposition [2]. The accusation that, together with his
archbishopric, he unlawfully held the see of Winchester [3], not
alone appearing of sufficient importance to justify his deposi-

Anglicum confirmaverunt." Ord. Vital. p. 516 (Maseres, p. 231) " ubi
(Guentæ) cardinales Romanæ ecclesiæ coronam ei solemniter imposue-
runt." Orderic either copies from the above-mentioned Life, or the authority common to both, the Vita Herluini. It is remarkable that only
these two writers mention this second coronation.

[1] " Audiens et honorans eos tanquam angelos Dei." Ord. Vital. p. 516
(Maseres, p. 231).—T.

[2] Matt. Paris, a. 1070 (R. Wendover, ii. p. 7) relates that Stigand together with Alexander, bishop of Lincoln, fled to Scotland. [This is
evidently a mistake, as there was no bishop of Lincoln of that name
until 1153; nor was the see transferred from Dorchester to Lincoln in
1070.—T.]

[3] The Normans falsely charge him with holding two bishoprics besides
the archbishopric (Milonis Crispi Vita Lanfranci. c. 6. Rob. de Monte,

tion; not less criminal was it—adds the accusation—that he had received his pall from the anti-pope Benedict, who had been excommunicated, and, until it arrived, had celebrated mass in that of the expelled archbishop Robert. Stigand was deprived of his dignity; his wealth, at least as much as could be discovered, was confiscated; but his person, as even royal promises cannot be broken at once, was left at liberty. Walkelin, one of the royal chaplains, an ambitious man, who robbed his own church[1], and was long an object of hatred to the monks, until he conciliated them by his prodigality and love of building, received the see of Winchester. The see of East Anglia was taken from Ægelmær, the brother of Stigand, and bestowed on Herfast, another royal chaplain, whose ignorance had long been a subject of derision in Normandy, where it was doubted whether he knew his letters[2]. Many abbots also were deposed, and their rich benefices disposed of in a similar manner. Thomas, a canon of Bayeux, received the archbishopric of York[3], on the decease of archbishop Ealdred[4]. In a synod held by the two cardinals, besides many other abbots, Ægelric, a friend of Stigand's, previously a monk of Christ-church Canterbury, and for thirteen years the blameless bishop of Selsey, was degraded in defiance of the canons; and, without any proved delinquency, was by the king committed to strict custody at Marlborough, and his bishopric given to the royal chaplain Stigand. The pope took offence at this violation of the law in the person of

---

Chron. a. 1070); but he had long lost that of E. Anglia, or Elmham, and that he ever possessed the see of Sussex, or Selsey, is a gross error of Malmesbury (De Pont. p. 238), which he himself rectifies at p. 257.

[1] " Peccavit, ad trecentas libratas terras monachis auferens." Malm. de Pont. p. 246.

[2] W. Malm. ib. p. 238. See p. 148.

[3] Malmesbury is eloquent in praise of archbishop Thomas, on account of his liberality, the elegance of his manners and his mental accomplishments. De Pont. p. 238.—T.

[4] " Unus (Walkelinus) in loco depositi (Stigandi, alter defuncti Aldredi." ib.—T.

Ægelric, and demanded his immediate reinstalment, and a new investigation of the charges brought against him. It does not, however, appear, in this case, in which the accusation was probably that of high treason, that any attention was paid to the precept of the papal court[1]. Remigius, a monk of Fécamp, was rewarded with the see of Dorchester, after the death of bishop Wulfwine, in 1067, having, for his able command of the soldiers furnished by his abbey, received a promise from the king of the first bishopric that fell vacant. Such a remuneration for military service, together with glaring simony, excited general indignation, and Gregory VII., the successor of Alexander, felt it incumbent on him to cite the culprit before his tribunal; but the affair seems to have fallen to the ground, and, at a subsequent period, we find Remigius lauded as the mirror of virtues, the gem and light of the priesthood[2]!

Archbishop Stigand ended his days at Winchester. His great wealth, to which his contemporaries ascribed the real motive of his persecution, was seized by the king; much, it is said, was discovered only after his death. A small quantity of the gold left by the deposed prelate William gave to the church of Winchester[3]. For a similar reason, Ægelric, the

[1] Flor. Wigorn. aa. 1057, 1070; Rymer, Fœdera, i. p. 1.

[2] Giraldus Cambrensis de Vitis Episc. Lincoln. Proœm. and cap. i. Eadmer, Hist. p. 7. W. Malm. de Pont. lib. iv. p. 290. " Wilhelmus habuit a Romo vel Rumi, elemosinario Fescanni, postea episcopo Lincolniensi, unam navem cum xx. militibus," says the list given by Taylor. Thierry's account (ii. p. 135.) of one large and sixty small ships furnished by Remigius may be passed over without comment; but not his statement, that Remigius first had the see of Dorchester, and then that of Lincoln. He transferred the former to the latter city.

[3] W. Malm. p. 449.; De Pont. p. 205. He relates that Stigand was confined in chains; but Thomas Rudborne (Hist. major Winton. in Anglia Sacra, i. p. 250) corrects him, saying that Stigand was allowed to go at large within the walls of the castle. Even the story told by Malmesbury himself, that he carried the key of his treasures concealed in his clothes as long as he lived, renders the tale of the fetters in the highest degree improbable.

former bishop of Durham, who, on his dismissal from that see twelve years before, had secretly conveyed a treasure which he had found there to the monastery of Peterborough, was seized in that sanctuary and dragged to Westminster, where he ended his days in prison[1]. One of Ægelric's crimes was, no doubt, his being the brother of Ægelwine, his successor in the see of Durham, a man whom the king regarded with feelings of bitter hostility.

But the most important act in thus providing for the king's Norman chaplains, which has very arbitrarily been called a reform of the Anglo-Saxon clergy, was the appointment to the primacy and archbishopric of Canterbury. The choice made by the king on this occasion, with the advice of the papal legates, appeared the more happy the more it stood in contrast with his other nominations. Among the Anglo-Saxons a man fit for this exalted dignity was of course not to be looked for; though William admitted that neither any of his military prelates nor any other illiterate and sensual Norman ecclesiastic was competent to the office. The eyes of all those discerning men, who were conscious of the higher requirements of religion, were turned towards one who had resided in Normandy for the last thirty years, and was on an equally friendly footing with the courts of Rouen and of Rome —the celebrated Lanfranc, abbot of St. Stephen's at Caen.

The magister Lanfranc, of an eminent family in Pavia, and son of a magistrate of that city, had in his youth greatly distinguished himself by his profound knowledge of the law, both as a teacher and advocate, and gained a reputation, which his scholars had spread abroad far beyond the limits of his native city[2]. So great was his fame for jurisprudence, that

---

[1] Hist. Eccles. Dunelm. iii. cc. 7, 9. Simeon de Gestis Regum, a. 1056. Sax. Chron. aa. 1069-1072, where it is said that "he had been consecrated bishop of York, but that was unjustly taken from him, and the bishopric of Durham given to him."

[2] The principal source of Lanfranc's history is his biography by Milo Crispus, composed soon after the death of that prelate, extracted partly

tradition ascribes to him and the celebrated Garnerius the first scientific commentary on the then recently discovered Justinian Pandects (a. 1032)[1]. In the year 1040, for reasons unknown to us, he quitted his native country, and, accompanied by many devoted disciples, proceeded across the Alps to the northern coast of France, where, at Avranches, he for some time followed his early profession, as a teacher among the Normans. This residence he soon changed for the needy abbey of Bec, just then founded by Herluin, where for three years, by his retired life and the strictness of his manners, he ennobled, in the eyes of his contemporaries, both himself and the newly founded monastery. By his fellow monks he was persecuted from jealousy; but threatening to leave them, he availed himself of the apprehension he thereby excited to get himself chosen prior of the monastery, with the same worldly craft, which, at a later period, from being a stern opposer of duke William's marriage with Matilda of Flanders, on account of their too near relationship, transformed him into that prince's ambassador to the pope, for the purpose of procuring the necessary dispensation. The character of the man, whose shrewdness let slip no means not absolutely unlawful, and whose presence of mind never failed him, is admirably shown in the anecdote, how when banished from the court, at the instance of the duke's chaplain, Herfast, and riding towards the frontier on a lame jade, he met the irritated prince, whom in a pleasant joke he entreated to bestow on him a better horse for the journey he had ordered him to take. By which unexpected request, and through the mediation of William fitz Osbern, the duke was inclined

from the biography of Herluin, first abbot of Bec. Both are printed in D'Achery's edition of Lanfranc's works. Paris, 1648. folio.

[1] This account of Robert de Monte (Accessiones ad Sigebertum, a. 1032), (who, until the year 1054, when he became abbot of Mont St. Michel, was, like many of his predecessors, a monk of the abbey of Bec), if not true to the letter, yet, with reference to Lanfranc, is not without internal probability, and has more extrinsic credibility than half of our history.

to listen to his application, and again receive him into favour[1]. The prior Lanfranc was at this time regarded throughout christendom as one of the most learned theologians, and a support of the papal throne. An ecclesiastic of Tours, named Berengar, had orally defended the doctrine of Johannes Scotus, that in the holy eucharist the bread and wine, after consecration, were merely a symbol of, but not the real body and blood of Christ. Lanfranc not only declined the invitation of Berengar to declare in favour of his opinion, but even triumphantly, at Rome, where he at that time happened to be, defended the old faith of the church, which, at the council of Vercelli, the provincial synod of Tours, in the time of pope Victor II. (a. 1055.), and also at Rome, under Nicholas II. (a. 1059.), where Lanfranc was present, and in the great ecclesiastical warfare took an active part, received new confirmation. The dispute between Lanfranc and Berengar, which was once regarded as a brilliant point in the life of the former, forms now, since the discovery and discussion by Lessing, of Berengar's answer to the treatise of Lanfranc, "De corpore et sanguine Domini," rather a dark spot. Even if we feel disposed to consider Lanfranc as perfectly sincere in his defence of the Church's faith; if we forgive him for accusing at Rome, and persecuting, through a succession of years, one holding opinions differing from his own, who approached him cordially and respectfully, until the sagacious Gregory VII. put a stop to their hostilities; if we ascribe no malice to him, he, nevertheless, manifests in his writing a passionate precipitancy, that in so exalted a man is painful to us, and in such important questions must appear both culpable and contemptible. Lanfranc's first journey to Rome, when Berengar was only orally defending the doctrine of Johannes Scotus, took place in the year 1049; his work, still extant, against that of Berengar, after the latter's with-

[1] W. Malm. de Pont. p. 148; D'Achery, ut sup.

drawn recantation, was not composed till twenty years later, as he did not send it to pope Alexander till the year 1070[1].

During his stay at Rome in the year 1059, Lanfranc obtained for his prince the dispensation for the canonical obstacle to his marriage, through the promised erection of a monastery of monks and one of nuns. The abbatial mitre of the first of these richly endowed houses, erected at Caen, was the reward for the successful negotiation of the able theologian, the jurist, the ascetic, and man of the world, who, only after apparent resistance, allowed it to be forced upon him by the pious violence of his grateful sovereign[2]. From this time Lanfranc appears as William's most intimate and confidential counsellor in ecclesiastical affairs[3], as William fitz Osbern was in secular concerns. On the death of the archbishop of Rouen, Maurile, in September 1067, the vacant see was, it is said, offered to the abbot of Caen, and by him refused. He even sent to Rome, to the new pope, to request the pall for John, bishop of Avranches. The offer of king William and his nobles of the primacy of England, supported by queen Matilda and prince Robert, he, filled with holy indignation and pious affliction, at first rejected; whereupon the legates, bishop Ermenfrid and cardinal Hubert, passed over to Normandy

[1] See G. E. Lessing, Berengarius Turonensis, 1770, among his works, Th. xiii. This treatise of Berengar "De Sacra Cœna, adversus Lanfrancum, liber posterior," has been reprinted by A. F. and F. Th. Vischer, Berlin, 1834. 8vo. The account in the Chronicon Beccense, under 1051, of Lanfranc's treatise, appears to refer not to its date, but to the beginning of the dispute with Berengar.—Highly worthy of notice is the consideration in which the heretic Berengarius was held by his contemporaries in the latter years of his life. See W. Malm. De Gestis, pp. 462–466., and the verses there by bishop Hildebert.

[2] Robert de Monte, Access. a 1063., with whom the Vita Lanfranci, c. 5, W. Gemmet. vi. c. 9, and, from the tone of his narrative, also Guil. Pictav. p. 194 (Maseres, p. 97). The date of 1066 assigned by Orderic (p. 494) as that of Lanfranc's investiture with the abbatial dignity, we must set down among that writer's mistakes.

[3] Guil. Pictav. 194 B., whose words are in part to be found also in Lanfranc's biographer, v. c. 7.

and assembled a synod of the bishops and abbots of that duchy, in which Lanfranc, by the authority of the pope, was invited to accept the proffered dignity. In vain he alleged his infirm powers, the lowliness of his manners, his ignorance of the speech of the barbarous nation. The approval of such reasons was not to be expected, as it would have implied too severe a reproach to other foreigners in the English church. Lanfranc was, therefore, compelled to undertake an office, which—unless we regard him as an ambitious hypocrite—with a sincere inclination for solitude and tranquillity, must have been distasteful to him, or which, through impending misunderstandings with his former superiors, the bishop of Bayeux and other prelates, appeared not free from danger. Even after his acceptance of the dignity, he addressed himself to the pope, whom he implored by the Supreme Being, by his soul, by the services rendered to him, to his predecessors, to his relations and messengers, when travelling in Normandy, to free him from the bonds laid on him, and restore him to the quiet of monastic life[1]. If Lanfranc mistook his

---

[1] Lanfranci Epist. I. [More steadfast and, we suspect, more sincere was the refusal of Lanfranc's disciple, the venerable and celebrated monk Guitmond, who, when solicited by William to reside in England and await a favourable opportunity for promotion, alleged in excuse his infirmities mental and bodily, his inability to preside over those of whose barbarous tongue he was ignorant, and whose fathers and relatives had been either slain by William, or expatriated, or imprisoned, or reduced to servitude. He reminds the king that none of his forefathers had borne a royal diadem, and that he himself had not attained to that dignity by hereditary right; that Eadgar Ætheling and others were the nearer heirs to the crown. He prays him to examine the Scriptures, and see whether it be sanctioned by the law that a pastor chosen by its enemies be placed over the Lord's flock by violence; that an ecclesiastical election should be first truly made by the people, and afterwards solemnly confirmed by the fathers [of the Church]. On his return to Normandy the king offered him the archbishopric of Rouen, but which, in consequence of the hostility his frankness had raised against him, he declined, and proceeded to Rome, where he was made a cardinal, and raised to the metropolitan see of Aversa. Ord. Vital. pp. 524, sqq. (Maseres, pp. 264, sq.)—T.]

own character, his friends judged of it more correctly. He effected much ; the great name, the exalted and restless zeal of this spiritual hero, have shed a mitigating, if not a reconciling light on the Conquest in the eyes of contemporaries, among whom, not a voice, not even an Anglo-Saxon one, was heard against him ; and posterity must not condemn, but must strive to understand, that which inspired our forefathers with veneration.

On the day of the Assumption (Aug. 15th) the king solemnly invested Lanfranc with the highest dignity of his kingdom.   On St. John's day (Aug. 29th) he was consecrated by two bishops[1], who had been canonically ordained by pope Nicholas, Giso of Wells and Walter of Hereford, both natives of Lorraine.   Immediately afterwards, Thomas was by Lanfranc consecrated archbishop of York.   But Lanfranc, in consequence of the pretensions of archbishop Thomas, soon had occasion both to maintain the right of his Church to the primacy of all England[2], and to humiliate that prelate, by espousing against him the cause of bishop Wulfstan of Worcester[3] (the possessions of whose see had been appropriated by the late archbishop Ealdred, and retained by his successor, Thomas) ; as well as by a well-conducted contest with the king's uterine brother, Odo, bishop of Bayeux and earl of Kent, and other Norman nobles, for the restoration to the church of Canterbury of its secular privileges, which had been greatly abridged by those individuals : a contest rendered the more difficult by the loss of the charters of that cathedral, which had perished in a recent conflagration[4].

Lanfranc's first acts betoken at once the new spirit of disci-

---

[1] Sax. Chron., where *eight* suffragan bishops are mentioned. Flor. Wigorn. a. 1070.

[2] Lanfranci Epist. iii.   The unfavourable judgments on this affair are from the later work of Thomas Stubbs, col. 1707. Bromton, p. 976.

[3] Wil. Malm. Vita B. Wulfstani lib. ii. c. 1. in Anglia Sacra, t. ii.

[4] Eadmer, pp. 7–11. Selden in Spicel. pp. 197–199.

pline and of subjection to Rome, by which the Church was thenceforward to be governed. The see of Rochester, which, by the death of its possessor, had fallen vacant immediately after the arrival of the Normans, and in the storms of the period was greatly decayed, was bestowed on Arnost, from that house of rigid discipline, the abbey of Bec ; and, on his sudden death, on a monk named Gundulf[1], a man deeply skilled both in law and divinity. He would not allow the aged bishop of Salisbury, Heriman, to retire into an inactive monastic life, which he so ardently desired ; nor, without the command of the pope, notwithstanding the sanction of the legates, would he venture to ratify the deposition of Peter, a Norman, from the see of Lichfield, and the appointment of another in his stead; although that prelate, by his notoriously loose morals, and the circumstance of his openly having a wife and children, had brought great scandal on the Church. The pope approved of the archbishop's conduct, and both bishops continued in their sees till their death[2].

In the number of excellent men whom Lanfranc appointed to English prelacies, must be reckoned also Robert, a native of Lorraine, whom he raised to the see of Hereford, become vacant by the death of bishop Walter, who had fallen a sacrifice to his unconquerable lust[3]. Robert has claims to our respect as a man of learning, and a skilful mathematician and

---

[1] Flor. Wigorn. a. 1070. W. Malm. de Pont. lib. i.

[2] Lanfranci Epist. ii. W. Malm. lib. i. p. 249. Heriman remained in his see until his death in 1077.

[3] W. Malm. de Pont. lib. iv. "Erat in villa muliercula, quam, nescio quo infortunio, ex occursu visam, multo arsit tempore. Ignorabat illa flammas pontificis ; et si sciret, contemneret. Interea sæpe cogitans pontifex quod nihil est miserius quam senex amans, luctabatur, pro ætatis et gradus reverentia, morbum depellere. Probeque jam convaluerat, et victus furor terga dederat, cum ex occasione, quam diaboli fraus administravit, intra cubiculum illam accersiit. Subjecerat causam ut cubiculariis vestes incideret. Dicebatur enim officii perita. Illa ingressa, et operi propter quod venerat intenta, clientes secretorum conscii, agmine facto discedunt. Tum, ne multis morer, episcopo post obscœna dicta vim inferre paranti

astronomer, also as the abridger and introducer into England
of the great chronicle of Marianus Scotus; but, perhaps,
above all, for his friendship towards the Anglo-Saxon bishop
Wulfstan of Worcester, which ended only with the death of
that venerable prelate. Osmond also, the successor of Heriman in the see of Salisbury, must, with several others, be
numbered among these distinguished dignitaries. Against
those who appeared unworthy of the confidence placed in
them, Lanfranc was not backward in launching the severest
reprehension[1]. Yet not unfrequently do we meet with appointments of highly unworthy persons to abbeys; but such
nominations were usually the act of the king, who made a
sale of those dignities.

The arrival of Lanfranc in England, and his elevation to a
post which brought him into such close connection with the
king, appear the more important through the almost simultaneous loss of the most faithful and most sagacious counsellor which that prince had ever possessed, his seneschal,
William fitz Osbern, a man, whose influential character, and
prominence in all the events connected with the conquest of
England, raised him far above all the other instruments of
William. A relationship to the ducal house—Herfast, his
grandfather was a brother of count Richard the First's second
wife,—the office enjoyed by his father, who had been seneschal of Normandy[2]; vast riches, to which the founding of a
monastery at Lyre, where his wife Adeliza lies buried, and

femina forcipibus, quas tenebat, inguina suffodit. Rumor criminis et
ultionis totam pervagatus Angliam regis quoque aures attigit."—T.

Malmesbury, l. c. erroneously assigns Walter's death to the fifth year of
king William. In 1075 Walter assisted at the synod of London, and
Robert is first mentioned in 1079. Knyghton (col. 2347) calls him William;
misled by which error, Thierry (ii. p. 135) ascribes Walter's misdeed to
one of the newly arrived Normans. But Walter was the Lotharingian
chaplain of queen Eadgyth, wife of the Confessor, and made bishop of
Hereford in 1060. See Flor. Wigorn. h. a.

[1] See his letter to Robert, bishop of Chester, Epist. xxix.
[2] W. Gemmet. vii. c. 2., viii. c. 15.

another at Cormely, where he himself is interred, bear witness; his near connection with the Anglo-Saxon royal race; probably an earlier residence in England, his brother, the chaplain Osbern, having also resided at the Saxon court; intimate connections with other neighbouring princes:—all these circumstances combined tended to form of the talented youth a judicious and influential man, who more calmly than his prince could conduct and execute the ambitious schemes of the latter[1]. His youthful energies had been proved in warfare: he had mainly contributed to the capture of Domfront, and afterwards held out the newly erected castle of Breteuil against the king of France, and thence acquired his designation of "de Breteuil[2]." To his just discrimination the duke was indebted for the acquisition of the exiled Lanfranc, and thereby the friendship of the papal chair, and that alliance, in consequence of which the head of christendom leagued himself with the potentate of Rouen against the Anglo-Saxons, as he had already done with the Normans of Aversa and Capua against the Greeks and Saracens. William fitz Osbern was William's first confident in his warlike designs after the death of king Eadward, and it was he who disposed the Norman barons, against their inclination, to give a favourable ear to them. To his presence of mind the salutary words are ascribed, when the duke had shown himself over-hasty, while, at the same time, he held him aloof from the opposite fault of delay. The most important and difficult posts were intrusted to him: the conquest of the Isle of Wight, protected by rocks and fortresses, was his work. He was invested with the earldom of Hereford, and afterwards

---

[1] He is possibly first named in a charter of the year 1024, in the Monast. Anglic. v. p. 1108. " Willerinus fil. Osberni." William of Poitiers under the year 1054, calls him and Roger of Montgomery, "ambo juvenes ac strenui." [The former mention can hardly refer to our William fitz Osbern, who is denominated *juvenis* thirty years later.—T.]

[2] W. Gemmet. vii. c. 25.

with the government of the north of England, which, during
that crisis, might easily have been made instrumental to the
establishment of an independent principality. His great
liberality to the military, whereby he preserved the people
from pillage, and, at the same time, rendered them well-disposed towards him, had gained him such universal esteem,
that the king, although mistrustful and irritated against him,
yet durst not venture to counteract him ; and his laws, although at variance with those of the rest of England, were
regarded as valid after the lapse of a century. From York
the king soon removed him, and appointed him, conjointly
with queen Matilda, to the government of Normandy. We
cannot question his fidelity, nor even harbour the slightest
suspicion of it, in consequence of the acts of his relations
after his death ; although we cannot but be sensible that he
was actuated by the most dangerous ambition, which brought
his life to an untimely end. Baldwin VI., count of Flanders,
the brother of queen Matilda, had nominated William fitz
Osbern and the king of France, Philip I. as guardians of his
sons, Arnulf and Baldwin, whereby the former was seduced to
form the design of marrying Richilde, the widow of the count.
Abandoning himself to this scheme, he with a number of
knights attached himself to the king of France, and took an
active part in the war, in which the young count Arnulf was
engaged, against his paternal uncle Robert, surnamed the
Frisian, who was supported by the king of Germany, Henry
IV., and fell in an ambush laid by Robert, either shortly before or in the battle of Cassel (1071. 20th Feb.), which made
count Robert master of Flanders. The fall of the first of
their barons, whose brilliant valour, whose bounty. and lively
humour had won for him the affection of all. incensed his
countrymen to the utmost, so that it required all the energy
of the king to prevent the outbreak of a war with Flanders,
which at that moment might have been perilous to him.
William fitz Osbern's rich inheritance was. according to the

usage at that time, divided.   His eldest son, named also
William, had his father's fief in Normandy, Breteuil in Pacy,
with other possessions there and privileges; the younger son,
Roger, succeeded to the earldom of Hereford, and all that his
father had acquired in England[1].

Although the conquest of England was completed before
the death of William fitz Osbern, yet there was not wanting
a considerable number of unsubdued and valiant hearts that
had in appearance only yielded to superior force, for the
purpose of awaiting a favourable moment for the salvation of
the Anglo-Saxon name[2].   Many of these had assembled in
the Isle of Ely, in the neighbourhood of which, in consequence of the inclination of the land, many rivers collect
themselves towards the bay called the Wash, whence proceed
inundations and mists which, from want of dikes, transform
the land there into vast swamps.   In this neighbourhood,
accessible to the sea by its waters, and through the nature of
the ground hardly approachable to the Norman cavalry, the
patriots found a central point in the celebrated and valiant

---

[1] W. Gemmet. lib. vii. c.15. Ord. Vital. pp. 526 sq. (Maseres, pp. 270,
271). W. Malm. pp. 431, 432. Rom. de Rou, ii. pp. 122–126.
Thierry's account of a conspiracy directed by the three prelates,
Frederic abbot of St. Alban's, Wulfstan bishop of Worcester, and Walter
bishop of Hereford, of an insurrection of the Londoners, and the consequent proclamation of the laws of king Eadward at Berkhampstead in the
year 1071, appears to me quite groundless.   That the only authority for
such important matter should be the "Vitæ Abbatum S. Albani" must, of
itself, render the story very suspicious.   I see in it only a misunderstood
repetition of what has been related under the year 1066, when, in the
transactions at Berkhampstead, the presence of Wulfstan (who in 1070
was protected by the Normans in the rights of his see against the archbishop of York) is expressly mentioned by Florence, and where the neighbouring abbot of St. Alban's would hardly have failed to be present.
Walter, a Lorrainer, belonged, moreover, to the favoured clergy, and had
just assisted at the consecration of Lanfranc; he was also at Berkhampstead in 1066, as we learn from Rad. de Diceto, Abbrev. Chron. h. a.
What is related in the Chronicle of St. Alban's about the abbot Frederic is
matter for much doubt, as he held his abbey till the year 1077.

[2] About Hereward see Hallam Mid. Ages, ii. p. 301 note.

Hereward. This chieftain was the son of Leofric, lord of Brunne in Lincolnshire, of an ancient race[1], and of Eadgifu, a descendant of Oslac, the great earl of Northumberland in the time of king Eadgar. His father was unequal to the task of restraining the turbulent disposition of Hereward, and was himself the author of his banishment by king Eadward. The chivalrous youth then betook himself to those parts where he hoped to find the stoutest adversaries in the battle-field, Northumberland, Cornwall, Ireland. Thence he proceeded to Flanders, and within a short space acquired the character of a most fortunate and valiant warrior. The fame of his heroic deeds had already reached England, and had there become the theme of song[2]; and the hand of a noble Flemish lady, named Turfride, was reconciling him to a life of domestic tranquillity, when the news reached him of his father's death, and that his inheritance had been given by the king to a Norman, and that his mother had been exposed to insult and injury. On receipt of these tidings, Hereward, accompanied by his wife, hastened back to England, and instantly expelled the foreign intruder from his paternal estates. In the abbey of Peterborough he received, according to Anglo-Saxon usage, which required ecclesiastical consecration and ceremonies, the dignity of knight, at the hands of the abbot Brand, his paternal uncle. Placed at the head of the exiles and fugitives there assembled, he gloriously achieved,

[1] Morkar, lord of Brunne, is mentioned in 870. (Ingulf, p. 492 edit. 1596, and Chron. Petroburg.) It is one of Ingulf's gross blunders (p. 511), when he speaks of Radinus (Radulf) the great earl of Hereford, who married king Eadward's sister, Goda. Goda, as is well known, was the mother of Radulf. Ingulf was probably thinking of Leofric III., earl of Hereford and Chester, the husband of Godive (Godgifu) the daughter of a prefect of Lincoln. I must also consider it a mistake when Leofric earl of Mercia, is given as the father of Hereward (Ellis, Introd. ii. p. 146); for then Hereward must be taken for a younger brother of Ælfgar, and uncle of Eadwine and Morkere.

[2] "Cum ejus gesta fortia etiam Angliam ingressa canerentur." Ingulph. p. 67 (p. 511 b. ed. 1596).

to the detriment of the Normans, numberless bold adventures, which failed not to excite the admiration of his adversaries. But if the Normans were unable to extirpate the band of Hereward, the latter were too few to inflict any very serious injury on their adversaries. The Danes under Asbiörn had at this time betaken themselves to Ely, which they quitted after a short stay. Of this opportunity—why not earlier we are not informed—the earls Eadwine and Morkere, who for two years had been living amid the pomp of the royal court, although really in a state of durance, availed themselves to flee from that and greater evils to be apprehended. Not finding the general disposition favourable to a revolt, Morkere fled to Ely, where Hereward had constructed a fort of wood, which served as a place of refuge and a gathering spot for his adherents. Morkere found here the bishop of Durham, Ægelwine, who had returned from Scotland, probably also Frederic, abbot of St. Alban's[1], also Siward Barn and others, who had either not sworn fealty to the conqueror or, in consequence of his breach of faith, considered themselves released from their oath[2]. They prepared themselves to pass the winter here, protected by the inaccessibility of the place, when the king, perceiving the danger with which the trans-

---

[1] Hist. Abb. S. Albani. Thom. Eliens. Hist. in Anglia Sacra, i. p. 609, where, under the name of Egfridus, abbot Frederic is, no doubt, meant. In the same place it is also related, that Willelmus, Herefordensis episcopus, suggested to the king measures against Ely, where the editors emend William into Walter, whereby the foregoing statement relative to this bishop would receive a new refutation. I should, however, be more inclined to change episcopi into comitis, as Walter was not among the intimate friends of the king, while William fitz Osbern is known also as the adversary of the Anglo-Saxon monasteries.

[2] Thierry infers the presence of Stigand from Thomas of Ely. But it is hardly credible that the Anglo-Saxons would not have mentioned the circumstance with praise, and that the Normans would not have reckoned it among his transgressions. Some ground for the supposition is, indeed, afforded by the Annales Wintonienses, where it is said that Stigand was not imprisoned till the year 1072. But this is too late to be connected with Morkere's capture.

formation of an asylum of a few outlaws into a rendezvous of
the old nationality threatened him, spared neither promises,
nor threats, nor preparations to dissolve the Anglo-Saxon
confederacy. On the east of the isle he posted his "butsecarls," for the purpose of obstructing all egress on that side.
On the west he caused a large causeway to be thrown up,
two miles in length, to enable him to send his cavalry against
the insurgents. Yielding to the sapient counsel of one of his
commanders, Yvo Taillebois, from Anjou, lord of Holand,
William caused a sorceress to cast her spells over the besiegers; but who was burnt by the bold Hereward and his
men, together with the wooden tower in which she had been
drawn near to the fort. Many a daring exploit was achieved
by the brave adventurer, which afforded delight even to the
Normans themselves. Among others, it is related how Yvo
Taillebois with a numerous army, with which he boastingly
swore he would drive the banditti from their forests and
lurking places, entered their retreat on one side, while Thor-
old, the Norman successor of Brand, with several persons of
note, remained behind, all of whom Hereward, issuing forth
and coming round from the other side, captured without
difficulty, and did not release them until he had received a
ransom of three thousand marks weight of silver[1]. But the
weakness of the Anglo-Saxons soon again appeared manifest.
Morkere was seduced by the fair promises of the king to return to him. Bishop Ægelwine and the rest, with the exception of Hereward and his band, surrendered to William[2],
who, in violation of his word, ordered them to be treated as
rebels, and, only sparing their lives, to be cast into prison, or
sent home, either blinded or with the loss of hands and feet.
Bishop Ægelwine was imprisoned at Abingdon, where he died

[1] Petri Blesensis Cont. ad Ingulphi Hist. p. 125.
[2] Sax. Chron. Flor. Wigorn. a. 1071. It is singular that Orderic Vitalis, p. 521 (Maseres, p. 248), represents Morkere as less culpable, and the
king as more treacherous than the above Anglo-Saxon authorities.

the following winter. Morkere was committed to the custody
of Roger of Beaumont, in whose castle in Normandy[1] he
passed a miserable life in chains. Eadwine, bitterly exasperated by this new treachery, resolved on avenging his brother
and his people. He gathered a band of faithful Anglo-
Saxons and leagued himself with Scots and Welsh. Exalted
birth, wealth derived from his forefathers, great personal
beauty, liberality, kindness of disposition—all these combined
to render Eadwine, more than any other Anglo-Saxon, beloved by the Normans, who had been in the habit of regarding him as one of themselves: and William, since his coronation, had no other adversary to fear than this. Of this care
he was relieved by treachery. Eadwine, after having for six
months striven to find partisans, to incite, unite, and order
them, was betrayed by three brothers among his " huscarls "
to the Normans, who surprised him with twenty of his warriors on their way to Scotland, not far from the sea, when
being arrested in their progress by the swell of a rivulet at
flood-tide, they were all massacred[2]. The king confiscated the
vast estates of both earls, yet did not venture to applaud the
murder, but feigned to share in the general sympathy for the
fate of these unfortunate victims, by banishing the disap-
pointed, rapacious assassins. Of Ælfgar's race there still remained a daughter, whom the king, according to the feudal
law, bestowed, as his ward, on Yvo Taillebois, the most
detested of the foreigners, together with the family possessions of that race in Holand.

Hereward strove for some time to maintain himself in his
isolated warfare. Finding help and friends in all the country
people, he frequently succeeded in deceiving the Normans

---

[1] At Beaumont-le-Roger, dep. Lower Seine.

[2] It is a mistake that Eadwine was slain in the Isle of Ely (Palgrave,
Engl. Comm. ii. p. ccxcii.), or, as Thierry says, that he sojourned there.
We must also notice another of his errors, viz. that he places this event in
the year 1072, and in the same year makes the Danes leave England, who
took their departure in 1070.

M

and causing them sensible loss.   When Gilbert of Clare and
William of Warenne, the king's son-in-law, had made themselves masters of Ely, Hereward fled to the fens of Lincolnshire.   Fishermen conveyed him and his adherents in their
boats, concealed under heaps of straw, into a fort there occupied by the Normans.   The well-known fishermen were received with welcome by the garrison, and a repast was prepared of their capture.   But scarcely had the men of the fort
sat down to their meal, when Hereward and his followers
started up from the straw, slew their unarmed adversaries,
and mounted their ready-saddled horses[1].   Not until he felt
convinced that all his efforts were vain, did Hereward, together with Eadric the Forester and other right-minded,
valiant men, demand and obtain an honourable capitulation
from the Conqueror.   Ælfthryth, a rich Anglo-Saxon lady,
captivated by his fame, offered him her hand, and allured him
to the enjoyment of a more tranquil life[2].   But her love does
not seem to have had the influence it merited over this restless man: he fled again[3], but after a while returned to his
country, which after a lapse of many years, received his bones
in her maternal lap at Crowland[4].   His memory appears to
have been soon effaced in England, and has been preserved
chiefly in the chronicles of some monasteries in the neighbourhood of Ely[5].

The subjugation of these desultory enemies William left to

[1] Geoffroy Gaimar, in Michel, Chroniques Anglo-Normandes, t. i.
Rouen, 1836.

[2] Geof. Gaimar.   [History is silent as to the fate of his first wife.—T.]

[3] Herewardum die quæ aufugit.—Terram S. Guthlaci. . . . . . .Vichel
abbatem commendasse eam ad firmam Herewardo. . . . sed abbas resnisivit
eam antequam Herewardus de patria fugeret, eo quod conventionem non
tenuisset.   Clamores de Chetsteven in Domesday, i. fol. 376 b., 377.

[4] Ingulph. p. 511 b. edit. 1596. According to Gaimar, he was, during an
armistice or safe-conduct granted by the king, attacked while at dinner
by some Normans and slain.

[5] Crowland, Peterborough, and Ely.   An old narrative, " De Gestis
Herewardi," is mentioned by Cooper on the Public Records, ii. p. 165.

his knights and to time, while he himself strove to destroy the hotbed of every important conspiracy, the asylum of all his foes. In the following year (1072), therefore, he marched with a strong army, composed chiefly of cavalry, to Scotland[1], to the coast of which he had also despatched a fleet. He met with no considerable resistance, and when he had advanced, across the Forth, as far as Abernethy on the Tay, he was met by king Malcolm Canmore with offers of submission and hostages for his fidelity, among which was his own son[2]. On his return William passed through Durham, where he found the successor, whom he and Lanfranc had appointed to bishop Ægelwine, named Walchere, a man highly esteemed for his upright life and his knowledge, of a family of consideration, in Lorraine, though he had previously lived at Liege[3]; and for which reason was, perhaps, nominated to a see but little suited to a Norman. At Durham the king caused a new castle to be constructed, and, in the place of Gospatric, whom he banished, under the pretext, that, three years before, he had secretly instigated the murder of Robert Cumin, and taken an active part in the insurrection at York against the Normans, bestowed the earldom on Waltheof, the son of Siward, who had recently submitted to his authority. Gospatric fled to king Malcolm, who at first did not receive him; but, after he had passed some time in Flanders, bestowed on him Dunbar, with its demesne lands in Lothian. His property in England does not appear to have been all confiscated, as at a later period we find much of it as fiefs held either by himself or his sons, Dolfin and Gospatric, though not in every case immediately of the king. His other son, Waltheof

---

[1] He was accompanied by Eadric the Forester. Flor. Wigorn. h.a.

[2] Among the homages rendered by the Scottish kings, this one is particularly a subject of difference; though the chronicles, although not explicit as to the extent of the subjection, yet leave no doubt with regard to the fact itself and the other circumstances. See Lingard, ii. c. 1. Palgrave Commonw. ii. pp. 331 sq. Ann. Ulton. a. 1072; Allen, Vindic. p. 47.

[3] Sax. Chron. Flor. Wigorn. Sim. Dunelm. a. 1071.

M 2

(Gallev) was a monk at Crowland, of which abbey he became abbot [1].

The more William's attention was engaged on his kingdom, the more his adversaries sought occasion to disturb him in his hereditary states, and in his relations with France. Eadgar Ætheling had been invited by the French king, Philip I. to come to France, and take up his abode in the castle of Montreuil, from which he could easily make incessant war on the Normans. Previously Eadgar, in the hope of getting support at the court of his sister, had visited Scotland; but Malcolm, who had probably sent him an invitation, when his oath taken at Abernethy no longer allowed him to afford active aid to his brother-in-law, could only give him a friendly reception, and, with costly habits and other effects, shortly after (8th July) dismiss him.

While in France the arrival of the legitimate claimant of the Anglo-Saxon crown was expected, Le Maine had for a year or more been in a state of insurrection against William, excited chiefly by Fulk, count of Anjou, who could not forget the ancient claims of his house to that province. William was therefore under the necessity of employing his earliest leisure in subjugating the insolent Manceaux, and availed himself of this revolt to employ the warlike Anglo-Saxons, who, obeying the commands of their common oppressor, manifested no repugnance mercilessly to ravage the country of those with whom similar relations, similar hate, similar misery closely united them. To the powerful army led by the king himself the several fortresses soon surrendered. Hubert delivered up his towns of Fresnay and Beaumont [2]; Sille also

---

[1] Simeon, a. 1072. Ellis, Introd. ii. pp. 131, 331, and i. pp. 405, 428. Sir Walter Scott (History of Scotland) commits a palpable error in designating this Anglo-Saxon as Cospatric, or Comes Patricius, one of the *Norman* barons who fled to Malcolm. I suspect that the nationality of other Normans, under William the Conqueror, is not much better founded.

[2] This Hubert was son-in-law of William, count of Nivernais. See more concerning him under a. 1087., where he is styled viscount.—T.

was yielded up by its governor. The citizens of Le Mans had established among themselves one of the first of those unions called *communes*, which were half guilds, half armed fraternities, out of which has proceeded the development of free civic constitutions in the greater part of Europe. With ardent enthusiasm and the magnanimous sacrifice of much property, they had fortified their city, and ravaged the possessions of such nobles as were favourably disposed towards the Normans; yet, on the appearance of the conqueror before their gates, they presented him with the keys of the place, met with a gracious reception, and thus preserved their former rights and privileges[1]. The subjection of the other Manceaux followed shortly after; yet, nevertheless, William returned to Normandy without having revenged himself on his great foe, the count of Anjou. But an opportunity is rarely wanting to him who seeks for it. A powerful and noble Angevin, John of la Fleche, who had married Paula, a daughter of Hugh, count of Le Maine[2], revolted against count Fulk, and applied to William for support, which the latter instantly sent him, consisting of some of his bravest warriors. Fulk, aided by Hoel count of Brittany, besieged the castle of his vassal. William, thinking himself justified by the danger of his friends, moved at the head of an army, which fame has augmented to the incredible number of sixty thousand cavalry, towards the besiegers, who, however, did not flee, but crossing the Loire and burning their vessels, boldly awaited the conflict. The providential presence of a cardinal and some monks, as well as the aversion of the young count William of Evreux, Roger of Montgomery and other Normans to a war, which to them appeared unjust, led to a peace at Blancaland (La Bruere), by which William acknowledged Fulk's suzerainty over Le Maine, and the latter in-

[1] Ord. Vital. p. 532 (Maseres, p. 290); Sax. Chron. a. 1073. Acta Pontific. Cenoman. lib. i.

[2] Ord. Vital. p. 532 Maseres, p. 292.

vested William's eldest son, Robert, after having taken the customary oaths, with that province, and all the possessions and right that had been assured to him by count Heribert[1].

While affairs in France were so arranged as to give promise of a lasting peace, William was anew favoured by fortune in England. Eadgar Ætheling had with his treasures been wrecked on the coast of France. With his followers, partly wretchedly mounted and partly on foot, he again appeared at the Scottish court, where he found a favourable reception from his royal brother-in-law and sister, who again loaded him with presents, in compensation for the treasures he had lost. Malcolm, however, it would seem, now lost all hopes of a cause, for the success of which the character of the ætheling was as ill adapted as his fortune was unpropitious; he therefore persuaded him to make a voluntary submission to William, and by that act give peace and quiet to himself, his friends, and his country. Eadgar, who felt neither energy nor hope in himself, had no alternative but compliance, as soon as foreign aid was withdrawn from him. He, therefore, proceeded to the English border, and at Durham was received by the sheriff of Yorkshire, Hugh the son of Baldric[2], who, no doubt to secure him no less against his own wavering than the insolence of the Normans, accompanied him the whole way to Rouen, where he was received by William with all the outward tokens of respect due to his high birth, and was maintained for several years at the court there, receiving a daily allowance of a pound of silver[3]. A life passed in inactivity, and the most ordinary knightly recreations was highly prejudicial to him, and contributed, if not to render him contemptible, to make him sooner forgotten than if his early death had excited an unsatisfied but affectionate longing after

---

[1] See pp. 51, 52.

[2] The name occurs on another occasion in Simeon, col. 206. See also Ellis, Introd. i. p. 436.

[3] W. Malm. p. 424.

him, and, accompanied by a fair image, hallowed his name in the memory of the nation.

All these successes must have rendered the name of William the Bastard one of the most exalted and feared in Europe. To what degree he influenced the relations of the neighbouring states, of France, Flanders, Germany, is difficult to determine; although we know that at times he did influence them. Of his relations to the last mentioned country, it may be adduced, that he was most probably in an understanding with Anno, archbishop of Cologne, in consequence of which the emperor Henry IV., at that time at Ratisbon, was astounded by the report that the king of England had raised a large army for the purpose of proceeding to Aix-la-Chapelle [1]. Events, however, took place, which rendered the execution of such plans, even if they were ever entertained, impracticable.

In seven years the conquest of England was completed, and William saw his boldest wishes attained in the most brilliant manner. He was now to experience the usual lot of conquerors, the hostility of his brothers in arms and their mutual dissensions. At his court no knight considered himself more entitled to an independent position than Roger, son of William fitz Osbern, who had succeeded his father in the earldom of Hereford. In defiance of the prohibition of the king, his feudal lord, he had given his sister Emma in marriage to the earl of East Anglia, Ralf of Guader [2]. At the nuptial festivities, which were held at Ixning in Cambridgeshire, a conspiracy was formed against the king, into which both earls strove to draw earl Waltheof. Taken by surprise or compelled, Waltheof promised to join the confederacy, ac-

---

[1] Lambert Schafnaburg, a. 1074.

[2] According to the Saxon Chronicle, a. 1075, Ralf was the son of an Anglo-Saxon of the same name and of a Breton (Bryttisc) mother, and not as Matthew Paris (R. Wendover, ii. 15) renders it a Welsh woman (ex matre Wallensi). His father was probably Radulf the 'stallere,' who had large possessions in Norfolk and Suffolk, T. R. E.

cording to which one of the three was to be raised to the throne, and the two others to be the king's principal nobles[1]. But soon calling to mind the fealty he had sworn, Waltheof divulged the plans of the conspirators to archbishop Lanfranc, and by his advice hastened to Normandy, for the purpose of revealing to the king all that had taken place, and imploring his clemency. Lanfranc, too, by written representations, to which he endeavoured to add also verbal persuasions, strove to induce the Norman Roger to remain faithful to the king. When these were found of no avail, the gentler spiritual weapon of excommunication was employed against him[2]: it was deemed sufficient to hold him in check: with his Norman chivalry, therefore, Wulfstan, bishop of Worcester, opposed him on the Severn, and thus prevented him from forming a junction with his brother-in-law. More rigorous measures were taken against Ralf of Guader. He had encamped near Cambridge, towards which place Odo, bishop of Bayeux, with a numerous army, together with Geoffrey, bishop of Coutances[3], had marched to encounter him. Ralf, without risking a battle[4], fled with his newly married wife to Norwich, and thence, leaving his consort behind, to Denmark, where he found support from king Svend Estrithson. Cnut, the king's son, and the jarl Hakon[5] proceeded with two hundred ships to England, where, at least on the southern coast, they durst not venture to land; and as in the north, Bishop Walc-

---

[1] Flor. Wigorn. a. 1074. W. Malm. p. 430. Ord. Vital. p. 534 (Maseres, p. 307).

[2] Lanfranci Epist. 39–41.

[3] Ord. Vital. p. 523, (Maseres, p. 255,) styles him 'magister militum.'

[4] Flor. Wigorn. a. 1074. Lanfranci Epist. 34. " totus exercitus ejus (Radulphi traditoris) in fugam versi fuerunt et nostri cum infinita multitudine Francigenarum et Anglorum eos insequebantur."

[5] Suhm's conjecture seems by no means improbable, that this Hakon was the son of Sweyn, the brother of Harold, and grandson of earl Godwine. (Historie af Danmark, iv. 440.) See also " England under the A. S. Kings," ii. p. 267.

here, by the direction of the king and Lanfranc[1], had taken every precaution against their progress, after having plundered the cathedral of York, they betook themselves to Flanders[2]. On Hakon rests the charge that he, like Asbiörn before him, allowed himself to be bribed by William, on which account he also, after his return to Denmark, was banished from the country by king Svend[3]. The strong city of Norwich was soon forced to surrender, and the Bretons, vassals of Ralf, of whom the garrison chiefly consisted, had their lives spared only under the conditions of renouncing the fiefs they had acquired in England, and of quitting the country within forty days. The mercenaries were compelled to leave at a shorter notice. Bishop Geoffrey, William of Warenne, who with Richard of Bienfait, the son of earl Gilbert, the chief justiciary and representative of the king during the absence of the latter, Robert Malet, and three hundred men at arms with engineers[4] remained in Norwich. The king himself also now embarked for England, as the measures adopted by Lanfranc had not proved sufficient to reduce Roger to subjection. On his arrival William cited the rebellious vassal before his court. Roger hesitated not to appear, relying on his near relationship to the king, who, however, soon gave him to understand how futile had been his confidence. According to the Norman law, he was declared to have forfeited all his honours and possessions, and condemned to perpetual imprisonment. Even then his haughty spirit did not desert him, but served to exasperate the king still more against him. For when William on Easter day had sent him a rich suit of clothes, he ordered a large fire to be kindled and burnt them. He outlived the king, and died in prison and in fetters. Many of the rebels were banished, many hanged, some were blinded[5], others underwent mutila-

---

[1] Lanfranci Epist. 25.　　[2] Sax. Chron. a. 1075, erroneously for 1074.

[3] W. Malm. p. 437.

[4] " Balistarii et machinarum artifices." Lanfranci Epist. 35.

[5] Dr. Ingram, *suo more*, thus ludicrously renders the words of the Sax.

tion of their hands and feet. But of none was the fate so
deplored, and proved so lasting a reproach to the king as that
of earl Waltheof.

This individual had thrown himself on the king's mercy and
carried none of his traitorous designs into effect. His wife
Judith, the king's niece, came forth, it is said, as his accuser;
yet whatever her disclosures may have been, the accusation
can have been founded only on wishes, words, and plans, as
Waltheof had not, like the other conspirators, risen in arms
against the king immediately from the nuptial festivity. Even
the Norman nobles found no severer punishment for him than
close imprisonment and the forfeiture of his posts; a punishment certainly too rigorous, being the same as that awarded
to Roger of Hereford. But the general sympathy manifested
for Waltheof roused the mistrust of the tyrant, who was tortured by dread and anxiety, and by which he was at length
driven to the resolution, by the murder of the Anglo-Saxon,
of bringing to his fancied earthly peace and security the offering of a deed, of which a deadened conscience, savage vengeance, and blind fear caused him to overlook the consequences for his own mind, the reproach of his contemporaries,
and the indelible stain on his fame in the judgment of after
ages[1]. In the following year (1075, 31st May) Waltheof
was brought from his prison at Winchester, at early dawn, to
the spot without the city, where the church of St. Giles was
afterwards erected, where his head was struck off while he
was in the act of repeating the Lord's prayer, which indecent

---

Chron. h. a. "calle þa Bryttas þe wæron æt þam bryd-caloð æt Norðwic,
sume hy wurdon ablænde, and sume of land adrifene, and sume getawod
to scande." "All the Britons (r. Bretons) were condemned who were at
the bride-ale at Norwich. Some were punished with blindness; some
were driven from the land; *and some were towed to Scandinavia*" [*!!!*].
—L. T.

Lappenberg considers the meaning to be expressed by Matt. Paris (R.
Wendover, ii. p. 15) in the words: "nonnullos patibulo fecit suspendi."
I rather think to scande getawian means *to treat with ignominy*.—T.

[1] Comp. Ord. Vital. p. 544 (Maseres, p. 345).

hurry on the part of the executioners arose from their apprehension that the citizens might awake and rush to the rescue
of a man held in such high veneration. His body was at first
ignominiously cast into a pit and covered with turf, but after
the lapse of a fortnight, at the request of Judith and with
the king's permission, it was conveyed to Crowland by the
abbot Ulfkytel and honourably interred in the chapter house
of that monastery[1]. Judith continued in possession of the
earldoms of Huntingdon and Northampton, until she refused
obedience to the king's mandate, to give her hand to a nobleman named Simon of Senlis, whose high lineage appeared in
her estimation no idemnity for a lameness in one of his legs.
Enraged at her disobedience, the despot deprived her of the
two earldoms, which he bestowed on Simon, who afterwards
married Judith's eldest daughter[2].

At this time a measure was adopted, which, although it
proceeded from the great council held by Lanfranc at London,
yet probably originated with the king himself[3]; namely the
decree for the translation to cities of such bishops as still
resided in villages. For the letter of this decree speak the
obsolete canons of popes Damasus and Leo, but which, when
speaking of villages, could hardly have had in view such places
as were now the subject. But it was highly desirable for
William to transfer his Norman bishops to cities, where they
could be protected by the castles he had caused to be built,
and where those few Anglo-Saxon prelates, who had not been
displaced, could be more easily watched and held under control. By virtue of this decree, the see of Sherborne was
transferred to Sarum, that of Selsey to Chichester, and that
of Lichfield to Chester. Sarum—after the founding of the
neighbouring city of Salisbury, known as Old Sarum—was
little more than a fortress in a lofty situation, and well en-

---

[1] It was afterwards, by abbot Ingulf, taken thence and buried near the
high altar. Ord. Vital. p. 543 (Maseres, p. 343).—T

[2] Ingulph. p. 513 b. [3] Wilkins, Concil. i. p. 363.

compassed by walls; citizens it at that time had none[1].
Chichester had been granted by the king to Roger of Montgomery, earl of Arundel and Shrewsbury: the number of
houses there had increased, although only nine burghers
are recorded there in Domesday; whence it seems to follow
that the Anglo-Saxons had been expelled from a city lying
so conveniently for the Normans, at no great distance from
their home, and their places supplied by the new settlers.
Chester, with its Roman walls, which have been partially preserved to the present day, offered a similar asylum to the
Norman bishops. In the same spirit, bishop Remigius also
transferred his see from the old town of Dorchester to the
well-fortified Lincoln; bishop Herfast his from Elmham to
Thetford. In those places which retained their bishops,
strong, well-appointed castles had been erected by the Normans, as at Durham, Rochester, Exeter, etc. It may be here
worth remarking, that these measures seemed to have their
model in the half Normanized reign of the Confessor, when
bishop Leofric, a Lorrainer, previous to the expulsion of the
Norman favourites, in the year 1050, transferred his see from
Crediton to the strong city of Exeter.

With Waltheof's death the king's good fortune appears to
have forsaken him: irascibility, sudden outbreaks of anger,
and all those storms which insensibly tend to impair the judgment, allowed none of his later undertakings to succeed. Even
in punishing the principal culprit in the plot, on account of
which Waltheof was put to death, he signally failed. He had
followed Ralf of Guader into Brittany, where he besieged
him in the town of Dol, which he solemnly swore he would
never quit until he had taken it. But Alan Fergant count
of Brittany, and a body of troops sent by Philip king of
France[2], hastening to the relief of the place, the haughty

---

[1] " Est vice civitatis castellum locatum in edito, muro vallatum non
exiguo." Malm. de Pont. lib. ii. Domesday.
[2] Sax. Chron. a. 1076. Flor. Wigorn. a. 1075. W. Malm. p. 433. That

monarch found himself compelled to raise the siege, leaving all his tents, baggage, and treasure behind him, to the value, at that time, of fifteen thousand pounds sterling[1], and to flee before the approaching enemy. William now found that he must seek for allies, and not scorn to look for such even among the hereditary foes of his house. He accordingly made an offer of peace to the count of Brittany, together with the hand of his daughter Constance, which the count joyfully accepted. This union fulfilled its object of establishing peaceable relations between the Bretons and Normans; and, although the amiable, mediating countess died fifteen years afterwards childless, the amicable feeling established by her efforts continued to subsist both between the reigning families and the people[2].

With mortification, yet without fear, William had seen the king of France's banner in the ranks of his enemies. The intimate connection with the court of Rouen, which the weakness and policy of that of Paris had in earlier times so often sought, was broken, and the king of France discovered when too late that the acquisition of a kingdom, far from removing a formidable vassal, only augmented the danger of his liege lord. The wish to allay the natural jealousy of the latter was probably one of the reasons which induced William, a short time before the battle of Senlac, and on a subsequent occasion, to declare his eldest son Robert the heir to his paternal dominions, and cause the Norman barons to pay homage to him. For the same reason his claims on Le Maine had been secured not to the father but to the son. William was,

Florence's date is correct appears from the words of the council held at London in 1075: "regis, qui in transmarinis partibus tunc bella gerebat." Ord. Vital. p. 544. (Maseres, p. 346.)

[1] According to Baron Maseres (Monum. p. 347), equivalent to more than nine hundred thousand pounds sterling at the present day.—T.

[2] Ord. Vital. p. 544 (Maseres, p. 317). Daru represents these events very differently (T. i. pp. 107-109), but is not borne out by the authorities which he cites.

however, very far from intending to renounce either these or
any other rights to this or any other son, but, on the contrary,
held them all in such restraint, that of the vast possessions
acquired in England, not a single hide of land was granted to
one of them[1]. For the withholding of Le Maine a reason
appears in the early death of Margaret, who had been betrothed to Robert[2]. Robert, well practised in arms, valiant
and, after the manner of his nation, eloquent, yet vehement
and prodigal, had hardly reached the age of majority when
he resolved no longer to serve as a puppet in his father's
political show, but to turn the intentional deception into
reality. In the year 1074, and therefore probably not unconnected with the pretensions of the young Norman nobles
in England, dissensions arose between prince Robert and his
father which led to the most lamentable consequences. Robert
demanded Normandy and Le Maine of his father, and was
answered by long speeches and references to Absalom and
his counsellors, Ahithophel and Amasa. But the haughty
young prince replied, that he was not come to hear wise
speeches, with which he had of old been surfeited to loathing
by his pedantic teachers. He demanded the honours that
were due to him, as he would no longer serve as a mercenary
among mercenaries. The father, however, declared himself
wholly averse to renouncing any part of the dominion bestowed on him by God and confirmed to him by his earthly
vicar. The prince, who, from his preceptors, had learned
some rhetorical flowers, replied in a determined tone, that he
would then, like the Theban Polynices, go and serve in a
foreign land, there to seek the honour which his paternal
lares had denied him: may he there meet with another
Adrastus, who would one day gladly reward his fidelity[3]!

[1] Ellis, Introd. i. p. 321.

[2] Guil. Pictav. p. 190. Ord. Vital. p. 545 (Maseres, p. 349). See also
p. 55.

[3] Ord. Vital. pp. 569. *sq.* If these classical allusions are really Robert's
own, and not imagined for him by Orderic (who by the way is not in the

An accidental quarrel with his brothers, who appeared to him to be preferred by his father, while he was his mother's favourite, prompted Robert to such a forgetfulness of his duty that he attempted to make himself master of the eastle of Rouen, an attempt which was, however, frustrated by the vigilance of the castellain, Roger of Ivery, the king's cup-bearer[1]. Robert now fled from Normandy, accompanied by many of the chief of the young nobility, among whom we find the names of Robert of Belesme, son of Roger of Montgomery, earl of Shrewsbury, of Ralf of Conches, standard-bearer of Normandy, of William of Breteuil, son of William fitz Osbern and brother of Roger earl of Hereford, of Roger, son of Richard of Bienfait, of Robert of Molbray, William of Molines, William of Ruperia and others. Hugh of Neufchâtel, a brother-in-law of Robert of Belesme, received the fugitives,—whose possessions William instantly confiscated,—and opened to them his castles of Neufchâtel, Raimalast and Sorel. The king of France, too, declared in favour of Robert, and all those countries that stood in immediate connection with Normandy wavered as to whether they should side with the father or the son. But William induced the greater number to decide in his favour, by concluding a peace with Rotrou, count of Mortagne[2], and, with his aid, laying siege to the

habit of introducing such) we may suppose they were supplied him by the recollection of his school-boy days. [Robert is thus described by Orderic, p. 545 (Maseres, p. 350): "Erat loquax et prodigus, audax et in armis probissimus, fortis certusque sagittarius, voce clara et libera, lingua diserta, facie obesa, corpore pingui, brevique statura, unde vulgo *Gambaron* cognominatus est, et *Brevis-ocrea*."—T.

[1] The event Related by Orderic at the end of his fourth book (p. 570) belongs to the same period as that which he recounts in his fifth. (Maseres, p. 352.)

[2] This Rotron seems to have been a sort of freebooter. Orderic's words concerning him are: that he was in the habit of plundering the lands belonging to the church of Chartres, and though frequently reprehended by the bishop and clergy, was at length excommunicated, and as a Divine punishment became deaf, and so continued till his death. William bought his services. Ord. Vital. p. 546 (Maseres, p. 353). T.

castle of Raimalast[1]. After Hugh's violent death[2], the castle
was surrendered by his son Gulfer, and Robert with his
friends fled to his mother's brother, Robert the Frisian, count
of Flanders. Thence he proceeded to Udo, archbishop of
Treves[3], and from him to other dukes, counts, and castellains
in Lorraine, Alamannia, Guienne, and Gascony, everywhere
uttering bitter complaints against his father, and seeking aid.
He received many valuable presents, which he squandered on
parasites, jugglers, and harlots, and was consequently soon
reduced to beggary, and compelled to contract debts. At
length, the king of France resolved on giving him an asylum.
He granted him half the castle of Gerberoi in the Beauvoisis,
from which he made frequent irruptions into his father's territory, ravaging the country. William besieged him for some
weeks in this castle. In a sally of the garrison, the horse on
which the king rode was killed under him, and Tokig, the
son of Wiggod, who brought him another, was slain by an
arrow[1]. By a knight from the opposite ranks he was assailed,
wounded in the arm, and thrown from his horse. An ex-

[1] At this time (Aug. 14th) London was so burnt as it had never been
before, says the Sax. Chron. a. 1077.—T.

[2] The text of Orderic is by no means clear on this point, viz. "Interea,
dum quadam die Aimericus de Vilereio dapiferum regis Francorum, qui ad
eum diverterat, deduxisset, et cum tribus militibus ad castrum suum, ubi
hostes regis tutabantur, remearet, forte de regia phalange quatuor equites
exierunt, eique obviantes aditum jam proximæ munitionis suæ obturave-
runt, ipsumque percutientes illico peremerunt." If for *Aimericus* we read
Aimericum, which, indeed, the context seems to require, the verbs *diverterat*
and *deduxisset* will naturally and aptly refer to Hugh of Neufchâtel, and
that is he who was slain on his return from conducting back his guest,
Aimeric of Villeroy, the French king's steward, and not Aimeric, who was
slain on his return from conducting the *dapifer*.—T.

[3] Orderic, p. 570 (Maseres, p. 270) errs in making this Udo, who was a
son of count Eberhard *ex gente Alemannorum* (See Gesta Trevirorum, c.
58), a brother of Robert count of Flanders.

[4] Sax. Chron. a. 1079. According to Orderic, (p. 570,) " per extera
regna ferme quinque annis pervagatus est." He must, therefore, have
fled in 1074 or the beginning of 1075.

clamation of pain and for aid escaped him, which his anta-
gonist hearing, leaped from his horse and offered it to his too
late recognized father. William raised the siege and returned
to Rouen, where Roger earl of Shrewsbury and other Norman
barons, whose sons and relations were among the followers of
the prince, prevailed on him to make over to his son the long-
promised duchy of Normandy. After a short interval, during
which Robert was sent on an expedition against Scotland[1],
the father and son were again at variance, and the latter returned to France, where he continued until his father sent to
him earl Aubrey with the renewed offer of Normandy[2].

A more instructive example can hardly be given for the
purpose of showing the condition of the European states than
the reign of William the Conqueror. A foreign nation by
which he was held in abhorrence; his nobles in rebellion
against him; his eldest son for years at the head of a party
striving to deprive him of his continental possessions; hardly
a powerful neighbour, who was not ready at every moment to
take up arms against him; one war and insurrection after
another—such were the adverse circumstances of his reign in
England, and yet were they all so unconnected and so void of
a common object, that the king had no cause for apprehension, lest he should sink under such general hate and enmity.
How fiercely this hatred continued to boil in the breasts of
the Anglo-Saxons is manifest from the events which about this
time took place in Northumberland. Since the death of Waltheof the earldom had been bestowed on the bishop of Durham,
Walchere, who had, in great measure, committed the administration of temporal matters to a relation named Gilbert, while
at the same time he acted chiefly by the advice of Leobwine,
the dean of Durham. Both these functionaries abused the
power thus placed in their hands, to the great injury of the
natives, whom they mercilessly oppressed, and the principal
men among whom they persecuted and not unfrequently caused

[1] Flor. Wigorn. a. 1079.   [2] Ord. Vital. pp. 572. 573.

N

to be murdered[1]. It happened that a noble Saxon named
Liulf, a relation of the earls Ealdred and Waltheof, had been
driven from the possessions which he held in many parts of
England, by the injustice and tyranny of the Norman officials,
and taken refuge at Durham, where he gained the esteem of
the bishop, who frequently had recourse to his advice. Leobwine, highly exasperated at this connection so prejudicial to
his avarice and tyranny, prevailed on Gilbert to effect the
murder of Liulf.   This deed was soon noised abroad and
engendered the bitterest rage in the yet unsubdued minds of
the Northumbrians.   The bishop was aware of the danger
which threatened himself and all the Normans there, especially Leobwine the cause of it. He banished Gilbert and his
associates, and with this sentence, at the same time caused it
to be declared throughout the country that he was ready to
clear himself, according to the ecclesiastical law, of suspicion
of complicity in the murder. The ferment in the minds of
the people was thus in a certain degree allayed, and it became
possible to grant a safe-conduct to Gilbert, that he might
arrange in the county court respecting a pecuniary atonement
with the relations of his victim. But the familiarity constantly displayed by Walchere towards Leobwine, together
with the welcome reception which he gave to Gilbert on his
return, again excited the indignation of the people, which
soon showed itself in so significant a manner, that Walchere,
not daring to preside at a tribunal in the open air, decided
on transferring the proceedings to the neighbouring church of
Gateshead (1080, May 14th). But Liulf's relations and other
Northumbrians led by Eadulf Rus, of the family of the former
earl Uhtred, being convinced of Gilbert's guilt and of the
bishop's injustice, would listen to no composition, and slew
the messengers of the latter, together with all the bishop's
men whom they found standing before the church, with the
exception of some Anglo-Saxons. Walchere now prevailed on

_____
[1] Hist. Episc. Dunelm. in Anglia Sacra, i. p. 703.

Gilbert to present himself, escorted by the bishop's body guard, to the multitude; but no sooner had they issued from the gate than the whole party fell under the spears and swords of the assembled people. The enraged multitude now called for Leobwine, whom Walchere had vainly endeavoured to prevail on to leave the church. The bishop himself then stept to the threshold to beg for his own life, which he found to be very insecure. Trusting to the sanctity of his office, and wrapping his head in the episcopal mantle, he imprudently quitted the sacred asylum, and strove to make his way through the multitude; but when only a few paces from the church he was stricken down by the swords of the exasperated people. Yet even now no one ventured to enter the sacred edifice for the purpose of slaying Leobwine, when on a sudden the roof of the church burst out in flames above his head, caused by torches that had been hurled upon it. The fire soon reached the walls[1]. Nevertheless, Leobwine there stood firm in the consecrated place, until half burnt and stupified with agony, he rushed without the churchyard's pale on to the naked swords of his enemies, and fell hewed into a thousand pieces[2]. The Anglo-Saxons then hastened to Dur-

---

[1] The church was probably built of wood with a roof of shingles.—T.

[2] In the above narrative I have followed Simeon (aa. 1080, 1072) as the most authentic in all matters relating to Durham. With him W. Malm. (De Gestis, p. 451, and De Pont. lib. iii.) agrees in the main. Lingard mixes up parts from another account, but without referring to it, which Thierry has adopted, giving, however, his authority, viz. the much later Matthew Paris, who places the murder of Walter[!], bishop of Durham in the year 1075[!!]. [Lingard's prejudice has in this instance (by no means a solitary one) prompted him to treat the character of an ecclesiastic of his church with a tenderness not justified by the authorities. He says of him: "The bishop was of a mild and easy disposition: his humanity revolted from the idea of oppressing the inhabitants himself; but indolence prevented him from seeing or from restraining the oppressions of his officers." Let us see what Wendover (ii. p. 17) says of Walchere: "Walcherus.... contra dignitatem pontificalem curis se immiscens secularibus, a Willelmo emit Northanhumbriæ comitatum; et, viccomitis agens vices, ad laica se recedit judicia atque ab omnibus provincialibus,

ham, for the purpose of massacreing the Norman garrison
there, and rendering themselves masters of the city. But the
Normans were beforehand, and behind their recently fortified
walls were well able to defend themselves, until relieved,
against an unorganized and inexperienced multitude[1]. The
looked-for relief and with it the royal vengeance were soon at
hand, and the unhappy province must again atone for the
very natural lawless spirit that prevailed among the cruelly
injured inhabitants. Another earl, bishop Odo, now proceeded to Durham, not to hold a court of justice, but to lay
waste and slay with fire and sword wherever the wretched
people could not instantly pay their ransom and the contributions laid on them. A friend of Odo, William, abbot of
St. Karileph's, and afterwards of St. Vincent's, received the
vacant see[2], a man, who, like the other Norman ecclesiastics,
attained to power in the church, not through his spiritual
endowments, but through the talents of the courtier, of the
attorney, of the soldier. But such men were indispensable
to the Conqueror, who saw, even in the monk, only a military
tool to prevent the dismembering of England into several

tam nobilibus quam servis, insolenter retorsit pecuniam infinitam. Popu-
lus tandem, assiduis episcopi ac ministrorum ejus exactionibus ad extre-
mam perductus inopiam, indignabatur valde sese ad tam gravem redem-
ptionem sine intermissione compelli...... Cumque paulo post ad placita
consueta omnes comprovinciales, ut prælocutum fuerat, satis animose ad-
venissent, et de diversis injuriis sibi justitiam fieri exegissent, episcopus
nimis crudeliter respondit, quod de nulla injuria vel calumnia ipsis justitiam exhiberet antequam sibi libras quadringentas monetæ optimæ nume-
rassent." Malmesbury's words (p. 451) on the same subject are : " Fusus
ibi non paucus numerus Lotharingorum, quod præsul ipse nationis ejus
erat. Causa cædis hæc fuit : erat episcopus, præter pontificatum, custos
totius comitatus ; præfeceratque rebus forensibus Gislebertum cognatum,
interioribus Leobinum clericum, ambos in rebus commissis strenuos sed
effrænes. Tolerabat episcopus eorum immodestiam, gratia strenuitatis
inductus ; et, quia eos elevarat, cumulum benignitatis augebat. Indulget
enim natura sibi, placidoque favore suis arridet ipsa muneribus."—T.}

[1] Simeon Dunelm. a. 1072. Ejusd. Hist. Dunelm. iii. 24.

[2] He established monks at Durham. W. Malm. pp. 451, 452. Flor.
Wigorn. a. 1080.

states. Thenceforth, however, the earldom continued separate from the bishopric, and was, in the first instance, committed to Aubrey, a Norman, but of whose name there is no further mention; and afterwards to Robert of Molbray[1]. King Malcolm did not fail to profit by this state of things on his frontier, but the marching of a Norman army under duke Robert sufficed to quell all further hostilities[2].

After the last victories gained by William over his enemies in the subjugated land, as well as over his own barons, he found leisure for an expedition to Wales (1081). The Welsh, although embroiled in unceasing contests, on account of the succession of their princely houses, yet, protected by their mountains, made repeated incursions into England, where, in the county of Gloucester, they left behind them lamentable traces of their ravages[3], though frequently compelled to retire before Hugh, the Norman palatine of Chester, and other Norman knights. William, fully aware that this enemy, too securely protected by nature, was only to be gradually humbled by incursions, had, with this object, not merely invested the earldom of Chester with such great power[4], but granted also to other knights on the borders of Wales—as to William of Ogy, at Wollerton in Shropshire and Tuderham—the liberty of wresting, with their good swords, whatever they could from the Welsh[5]. Robert of Avranches, a valiant, active, and eloquent knight, of old Danish lineage, who had already had experience in those wars[6], in the time of king Eadward, surnamed, from his castle, Robert of Rhuddlan (Roclent), first officer of earl Hugh Lupus, had put to flight (ob. circa 1073), the most considerable prince of Wales, Blethyn ap Confyn, and whose successor, Trahaern ap Caradoc, together with the

[1] Sim. Hist. Dunelm. col. 52.

[2] Idem, de Gestis Regum Angliæ, a. 1080.

[3] Domesday ascribes them to Caradoc, probably Trahaern ap Caradoc is meant.

[4] See page 137.   [5] Monasticon Anglicanum.

[6] Ord. Vital. p. 669.

kings, Hoel and Griffith, had fallen into his hands[1]. At a subsequent period, Trahaern appears as related to Norman knights, whom as allies he repeatedly conducted into South Wales, as far as Dyved and Cardigan (a. 1071), though that prince's early death interrupted these relations, and king William had the satisfaction of extorting from the kinsmen of the hated Britons both the oath of homage and hostages. Not without a smile can we read in the Welsh writers, that the king of England made at this time a pilgrimage to St. David's, for the sake of praying at the relics of that holy bishop; but that he was attended by thousands of armed men, and many hundreds fell of both nations[2]. The English chroniclers scarcely notice this expedition[3]; it is, therefore, probable, as earl Hugh and Robert of Rhuddlan vigorously and vigilantly attended to their office in North Wales, that it was confined to the southern Welsh states.

[1] Ord. Vital. p. 671.　　　　　　　[2] Powell, p. 110.

[3] The chief authority is the Sax. Chron. a. 1081 : "Se cyng lædde fyrde into Wealan. and þær gefreode fela hund manna :" *The king led an army into Wales, and there freed many hundred men.* Neither Florence nor Simeon have adopted this passage. H. Huntingdon merely says : "Rex W. duxit exercitum in Walliam et eam sibi subdidit ;" and from him word for word Radulf. de Diceto, a. 1080. ap. Twysden, p. 487. Likewise Bromton, a. 1080. Annal. Waverl. a. 1080, adds : "et multi ex utraque parte perierunt." Matt. Paris (R. Wendover, ii. 20), a. 1079: "W. duxit in Walliam exercitum copiosum, et eam sibi subjugavit, et a regulis illius ditionis homagia et fidelitates accepit :" with which his namesake of Westminster almost verbally agrees ; a. 1079. [To the above may be added, in corroboration, the following : Sax. Chron. a. 1087, "Brytland him wæs on gewealde, and he þarinne casteles gewrohte, and þet mancynn mid-ealle gewealde :" *Brytland* (Wales) *was in his power, and he wrought castles therein, and completely subdued that nation.* Ingram prints 'Mancynn' and *suo more* translates : *and ruled Anglesey withal*[?]—T.] The Annal. Waverl. have correctly : "Habuit etiam Britanniam in potestate sua, et in ea castella fecit, et gentem illam sibi acclivem fecit." H. Huntingdon, who seems in doubt as to the meaning of Brytland, translates : "Britanniam sibi acclivem fecerat...... Walliamque rebellantem in suam acceperat ditionem ;" for so, (from Bromton's excerpt, p. 981) Savile's senseless reading : "Walliamque *reverendus* in suam acceperat," etc. seems to require emendation.

William, it appears, thought it either more advisable or more agreeable to abide in Normandy, while his brother, bishop Odo, conducted the government of England in his stead. As the latter appeared true to his trust, and the Anglo-Saxons became more enduring from year to year, William let him follow his own course in extorting vast treasures as booty, imposts, and judicial fees. Still his extensive power and almost fabulous wealth, which he well knew how to augment by parsimony, did not content this ambitious man. The raising of Lanfranc to the primacy he regarded, it would seem, as a slight to himself, and the wish of attaining to higher ecclesiastical dignities displayed itself in him more manifestly every day. If we call to mind the relations of the Normans in the south of Italy, and their multifarious connections with their kinsmen in Normandy and England, it will appear to us less striking, that Odo should cherish the hope, by dint of craft, money, and power, of one day obtaining the papal chair. If we cast a glance at the position of Gregory VII., who, although allied with the Normans of Apulia, had with difficulty been able to withstand the second siege of Rome by the German king, Henry IV., and through his agents was incessantly seeking aid in every land of Europe, it will appear far from improbable, that the crafty pontiff would, through his emissaries, secretly strive to allure to him, as a condottiere, for the defence of Rome against the Germans, the powerful bishop, who had contributed to the subjugation of the despicable Anglo-Saxons, even by holding out the prospect of one day succeeding to the papal throne. In Rome, too, a prophecy was abroad, that Hildebrand's successor would be an Odo, and which was, in fact fulfilled, as the bishop of Ostia of that name, soon after the death of Gregory and the short reign of Victor III., received, as Urban II., the ring of the fisherman. But the bishop of Bayeux applying the prophecy to himself, caused a palace to be bought for him at Rome, which he decorated with astonish-

ing magnificence, and, by means of costly presents, gained the
good will and voice of many Roman senators. He prevailed
on Hugh of Avranches, the powerful earl of Chester, and
many other knights, to attend him across the Apennine.
Thus did insatiable thirst after gain and glory, and an un-
quenchable love of adventure combine together a band of
valiant men under the leadership of Odo, who, without the
king's permission, resolved on leaving England. They had
already embarked for the expedition, and reached the Isle of
Wight, when William, who had received intelligence of their
plan, came unexpectedly upon them. To his clear-sighted-
ness the project of his brother must have appeared impracticable, and even its success he probably thought hardly to
be desired ; the threatened misunderstanding with the German king must by William, already surrounded by enemies,
have been regarded as perilous ; but the manner in which
Odo deserted the land committed to his guardianship was
high treason. The king brought this accusation of his brother
before his barons, and when no one else seemed disposed to
arrest him, he was the first to lay hands on him, not, as he
said, on the bishop of Bayeux, but on the earl of Kent[1]. Odo
was laid in fetters, deprived of his dignities and possessions
in England, and remained until William's death a prisoner in
the tower of Rouen. His immense treasures, which in part
were found in sacks hidden in the bed of the river, were confiscated for the benefit of the crown. Gregory did not fail to
complain of a proceeding so deeply injurious to the spiritual
authority, and, after the deliverance of Rome, in the year
1084, by duke Robert Guiscard, demanded, in very mild

---

[1] The distinction, as we are informed by Malmesbury (p. 487), was suggested by Lanfranc, which seems highly probable.—His words are : " Cum
olim Willelmus senior apud Lanfrancum quereretur se a fratri deseri, 'Tu'
inquit, 'prende eum et vinci.' 'Et quid,' respondit ille, 'quia clericus
est?' Tunc archiepiscopus lepida hilaritate, 'Non,' dixit, 'episcopum
Baiocarum capies, sed comitem Cantiæ custodies.' "—T.

terms, the liberation of the imprisoned bishop, which, however, he did not obtain[1].

In all cases affecting the doctrines of the church and the customary rights of the papal court, William had ever proved himself an obedient son, and to pope Gregory personally continued so faithful, that he refused to receive the delegates of the antipope Guibert. His compliance, however, suffered a great diminution after he found himself firm in his possession of England; even Lanfranc had no influence over him, when Gregory demanded of him what appeared detrimental to his secular authority. As during the king's long absence in France, his representatives in England had allowed the collection of the Peter-pence from the impoverished Anglo-Saxons and the avaricious Norman barons to be much neglected, Gregory sent his legate named Hubert. The cause of complaint with regard to the Peter-pence was speedily and readily removed[2]; but when Hubert made the extraordinary

---

[1] W. Malm. p. 457. Ord. Vital. p. 647. Flor. Wigorn. a. 1082. Registrum Gregorii VII. lib. xi. ep. 2, and a fragment of a letter of Gregory to his friend Hugo, archbishop of Lyons. Wace knows nothing of Odo's designs on the papacy, but represents him as aiming at the kingly power, as others, overlooking their relation to the contemporary events in Italy, have also supposed. Nor have they called to mind that earl Hugh, if those plans had been directed against the crown, could not have continued in possession of his honours. [Wace says of Odo :

En l'isle de Wic l'aveit pris,
Et à Roem en prison mis ;
Malicios ert, ço diseit,
E coveitos plus ne poeit.
Pose out esté ses seneschals,
A totes genz cruels è mals ;
Tote Engleterre se plaigneit,
Povres è riches raenmeit.
Privéement aveit enquiz
E demandé à ses amis,
Se jà Eveske Reis sereit,
Ne se jà estre Reis porreit ;
Reis esperout k'il devendreit,
Se li Reis ainz de li morreit. vv. 14302–14315.—T.]

[2] In foreign countries William had thereby gained great fame: " Wil-

demand that the king should swear the oath of homage to
the proud ecclesiastical sovereign and his successors, he refused it in the most decided terms[1]. Even the representations, which the pope did not disdain to make through queen
Matilda, and his application to duke Robert, for the purpose
of effecting a restoration of amicable feeling towards his father, brought him no nearer to his chief object. Equally
fruitless was a letter, which Gregory, in the zenith of his
power, (24 April 1080) addressed to William, when he had a
second time sent forth the ban of excommunication against
the king Henry IV, and yet was striving to raise secular aid
against him, in which, after acceding to many of his wishes,
he reminds him of the great services which, even before his
elevation to the tiara, he had rendered him in acquiring his
kingly crown; and, with boundless promises and flatteries,
endeavoured to prevail on him to show obedience to the papal chair[2].

William's conduct to the rest of the clergy was perfectly
consistent with that which he had observed towards its head.
In the nomination to vacant abbeys he acted very arbitrarily,
rather following the counsel of his barons than that of the
heads of the church[3]. The praise bestowed on him by Gregory, that he never sold such appointments, must, if not
ironical, have been given in the hope of exciting the wish and
the endeavour to deserve it. From the Norman cloisters he
took the most unfitting monks, to intrust to them the richest
Anglo-Saxon abbeys. Among numerous instances, we may
cite that of Thurstan, a monk of Caen, whom the king raised

---

lelmus Rex, qui totam Anglorum terram Romano pontifici tributariam fecit, nec aliquem in sua potestate aliquid emere vel vendere permisit quem
apostolicæ sedi inobedientem deprehendit." Bertholdi Constantiensis Chron.
a. 1084.

[1] Lanfranci Epist. 7, 8.

[2] Registrum Gregorii VII. lib. vii. ep. 23, 26, 27.

[3] See the letter of the abbot of Fécamp to the king, in Mabillon, Anal.
i. p. 228.

to the headship of the old abbey of Glastonbury. This man with his countrymen squandered the accumulated wealth of the monastery, while, not content with holding the monks to the strictest observance of the rule of their order, he even let them suffer privation. An arbitrary change of the old Gregorian chant, in place of which he strove to introduce one composed by John, abbot of Fécamp, gave occasion, together with his profane violences, to a disastrous conflict in the church, at the altar of which some of the monks were slain and many wounded. As a punishment, Thurstan merely forfeited his abbey, and was sent back to his Norman cloister. To archbishop Lanfranc even this penalty seemed too severe, and he counselled the abbot to offer a pecuniary atonement to the king, and not to be disheartened, even should it be rejected. The result was, that Thurstan immediately recovered the abbey of Glastonbury from William's successor, for five hundred pounds of silver [1].

Occurrences of this kind frequently took place, although with their details but seldom recorded. One merit only is wont to be ascribed to the greater number of these prelates of Norman origin, that of having employed great exertions and much care in the erection and restoration of abbeys, churches, and other structures connected with them. This merit belongs unquestionably to the Normans, to whose love of architecture we are indebted for many grand and beautiful monuments, that will long bid defiance to the destroying hand of time, and continue to excite our admiration. Yet, in appreciating their founders, it must be borne in mind, that this, like other styles of architecture, rose out of given and imperative circumstances [2], and the wonder-exciting, castle-like abbey was no other than the fortress, in which the war-

---

[1] Sax. Chron. Flor. Wigorn. a. 1083, Lanfranci Epist. 53.

[2] Lappenberg here is of course speaking of the massive Norman architecture, which is evidently a barbarous imitation of the Roman, and closely resembling the Anglo-Saxon. though somewhat less rude.—T.

like abbots were compelled to defend themselves against the violence of the neighbouring hostile laity. But here, as in the rest of Europe, not one of the larger and more splendid structures is wholly the work of its first founder, though the almost lightless, strong walls of hewn stone, with few and narrow entrances, may still be easily traced, and which, even without ditch and rampart, protected the spiritual castellain and his monks.

Nearly twenty years had now passed since the conquest of England, and the children of Harold had saved themselves by flight to the neighbouring kingdoms. William's tranquil possession of the country seemed no longer endangered by any commotion, when, on a sudden, intelligence was received that the Danish king, Cnut, afterwards distinguished as " the Saint," the second son of king Svend Estrithson, either to avenge his expelled kinsmen's or his own former failure, or to make good his pretensions to the crown, was preparing for an expedition against England (1085). He had, as we are informed, assembled a fleet of more than a thousand vessels in the Limfiord (a firth on the north-west of Jutland[2]); and his father-in-law, Robert the Frisian, count of Flanders, was ready to support him with six hundred sail. The Norwegian king, too, Olaf Kyrre, who had to avenge on England the death of his father, Harald Hardráda, at Stamford Bridge[3], sent him sixty ships completely equipped[4].

William, who had never placed any trust in the good disposition of the Anglo-Saxons, and much less than formerly in that of the Normans in England, assembled numerous bands of mercenaries from Normandy, Le Maine, and the rest of

[1] See page 129.

[2] Lingard forgets to make mention of the thousand or more Danish ships, merely saying that " he obtained a fleet of sixty ships from Olave, king of Norway, and a promise of another six hundred sail from his father-in-law, Robert, earl of Flanders."—T.

[3] See Engl. under the A. S. kings, ii. p. 280.

[4] W. Malm. Flor. Wigorn. a. 1084. Snorri, Olaf Kyrri's Saga, cap. 8.

France, and even from Spain. Many noble knights, too, and among them Hugh, the king of France's second brother, joined him, and accompanied him to England, where, dispersed over the country, they were a heavy burden to the inhabitants, who were charged with their maintenance [1]. Besides this, the old tax of Dane-gelt, at the rate of six shillings the hide [2], was re-imposed, to defray the expenses of the preparations, but which the Norman lords again extorted from their Anglo-Saxon vassals [3]. All the land on the coast, where a landing might be expected, was laid waste, that nothing might be left to the enemy whereon to seize [4]. The inhabitants were even forbidden to wear their native garb, that their Danish friends might not so easily recognize them; and were, moreover, commanded to shave off their long beards; though few, it is said, complied with this mandate [5]. It was probably the great and efficient measures adopted by William for the defence of the country, which inclined Cnut to deliberate before venturing further; and, in the following year, when a rebellious spirit had spread itself among his followers, and his army was tired of the long delay, induced him to abandon the enterprise [6]. His brother, Olaf, who was the instigator of the rebellion, he caused to be arrested, ignominiously bound, and sent to his father-in-law, the count of Flanders. Here again, the golden missiles, which William never spared, together with those of steel, most probably fulfilled their mission; and of the Dane-gelt, no inconsiderable portion found its ultimate destination at king Cnut's court in Haithaby (Sleswig). The murder of the Danish king, which took place shortly after,

---

[1] Ingulphus, p. 516.

[2] We still have notices respecting the produce of these exactions in the Inquisitio Geldi, in the Exeter Domesday.

[3] Sax. Chron. a. 1085. Flor. Wigorn. a. 1084.

[4] Sax. Chron. a. 1085.

[5] Ælnothi Vita Canuti, cap. 12 sq. apud Langebek, SS. Rer. Dan. iii.

[6] Ælnoth. l. c. Saxo Gram. edit. Müller. p. 585.

assured William against any future attempts on his kingdom from that quarter.

Of William's civil acts, after the conquest of England, the most prominent is the introduction of the Feudal System. This was the natural and necessary consequence of a revolution, by which all the landed property of the country was wrested from its native holders, and bestowed on those foreign chieftains, who had aided in the subjugation of the land, who naturally looked for a share of the spoil, and were to constitute its aristocracy; while these, in like manner, had to provide for their followers, by a subdivision of the estates conferred on them by the crown. Hence the distinctions of *tenants in chief*, (*tenentes in capite*), and *under tenants ;* the former being those who held their lands immediately of the king; the latter those who held of the great immediate holders, or tenants in chief.

The lands thus bestowed by the king consisted at first either in the demesne lands of the crown, or of those native proprietors, who had fallen in battle, or had preferred voluntary exile to submission ; but gradually, in consequence of forfeitures, (the penalty of resistance to a foreign yoke), and other causes, nearly the whole landed property of the kingdom passed into the hands of the Normans.

Although these landed possessions were bestowed for past services, they were, nevertheless, subject to certain obligations to the lord paramount, of whom they were held ; to the king, in the case of tenants in chief; and to the tenant in chief, in that of an under tenant. Of these obligations, the most honourable was that of *knight-service*, or the obligation to furnish a certain number of cavaliers completely armed for the king's service, and to maintain them in the field for forty days. This service was extended to all tenants in chief, both lay and ecclesiastical, including monasteries and other religious foundations, with the sole exception of those who held by *frankalmoign*, or *free alms*.

Thus all the landed property of the kingdom was held either by the sovereign, or by a tenant in chief, holding immediately under him. In the distribution of lands, each of such feudal possessions was divided into two parts, one of which was doled out to the under-tenants, consisting of Norman officials and others, military and civil, or of such Anglo-Saxons as had been ousted from the possession of the estate, and were now reduced, from the degree of thane, to the condition of simple freeholders, or franklins. The other portion the Norman lord retained in his own hands, under the denomination of his *demesne lands*, which he either farmed out to the cultivators of the soil, or cultivated for his own benefit, by the hands of his villeins, or serfs.

Besides military service, the great tenants of the crown were required to attend the king's court at the three grand festivals, of Christmas, Easter, and Whitsuntide; and at all other times when summoned. They constituted the great legislative body of the kingdom[1].

On succeeding to a fief at the death of the possessor, the heir was required to pay a certain sum to the lord of whom he held. In the Norman times this was called a *relief*, and originally, like the heriot of the Anglo-Saxons, consisted of certain chattels, as horses, hauberks, helmets, lances, etc.; but which was afterwards commuted into a pecuniary fine[2]. In addition to the relief, payments (*aids*) were exacted from the tenant; 1. when the lord paid the relief of his fief to his superior lord; 2. when his eldest son was made a knight; 3. on the marriage of his eldest daughter; 4. when he was captured by an enemy[3].

A fief could not be devised by will, or otherwise alienated by its holder; but must descend to the legal heir, subject to the same burthens, on payment of the customary relief.

---

[1] Lingard, ii. p. 46. edit. 1837.

[2] Anc. Laws and Inst. p. 204, fol. edit. and (pp. 72, 73) Cnut's laws 'Be Hergeate,' of which William's is only a modification.

[3] Hallam, Middle Ages, i. p. 178, edit. 1855.

With the descent of fiefs in England were connected *wardships* and *marriages*. When the heir was a minor, he was considered incompetent to hold the fief, being incapable of military service; in which case the lord entered into possession, and either appropriated the revenues to his own use, or let them out to farm. The heir he took under his own charge, for the purpose of having him educated in a manner qualifying him for military service. All the expenses of the ward devolved on the lord, who was bound to deliver over the estate, without a relief, when the ward had completed his twenty-first year.

When the heirs were females, and, consequently, incapable of military service, they might not be disposed of in marriage without the lord's sanction; for the refusal of which he was, however, bound to assign a valid reason. On the death of a tenant, the fief descended to the daughter, or, if more than one, to the daughters in common. Like the heirs male, these were under the wardship of the lord. On completing the age of fourteen, the lord could compel his female ward to marry any man he might select; and if, after that age, he allowed her to remain single, she could not marry without the consent of the lord and guardian. The husband of an heiress entered on all the rights of a male heir, and performed all the services due to the lord[1].

Besides the profits accruing to the lord from the beforementioned sources, there was that derived from *escheats*, of which there are two cases, viz. 1. a fief escheated, or fell back to the lord when the holder died, leaving no heirs; and, 2. if the holder was convicted of treason or felony[2].

The confirming of a fief was accompanied by three forms or ceremonies, viz. 1. *homage*; 2. *the oath of fealty*; 3. *investiture*.

1. Homage (hominium, homagium) was the form, according to which the homager became the vassal, or man (homo) of

---

[1] Lingard, *ut sup.* p. 51. [1] Blackstone, ii. p. 72, edit. 1830.

his lord. In doing homage, the vassal's head was uncovered, his belt ungirt, his sword and spurs laid aside; then kneeling he placed his hands between those of the lord, and promised to become his man from thenceforward; to serve him with life and limb and worldly honour, faithfully and loyally, in consideration of the lands which he held under him. None but the lord in person could accept homage, which was usually concluded with a kiss.

2. The oath of fealty, though indispensable, was taken with less formality than the performance of homage, and might be received by proxy.

3. Investiture, or the actual conveyance of feudal lands, was of two sorts, proper and improper. The first was an actual putting in possession on the ground, either by the lord or his deputy, which is called in our law *livery of seizin*. The second was symbolical, and consisted in the delivery of a turf, a stone, a wand, a branch, or whatever else might have been made usual by the caprice of local custom[1]. Upon investiture the duties of the man or vassal commenced[2].

A knight's fee was fixed in England at the annual value of £20. Every estate supposed to be of this value, and entered as such in the rolls of the exchequer, was bound to contribute the service of a soldier, or pay an *escuage*, or *scutage*, to the amount assessed upon a knight's fee.

Under the Anglo-Saxon kings, the oath of a man to his hlaford, or lord, contained no reservation of fealty or obedience to the king: and the question naturally occurs, what was the duty of a man, who had contracted that obligation, when a quarrel arose between the king and his immediate lord? When such cases occurred, and in those remote times they were not unfrequent, it is probable that in England, as on the Continent, the men ranged themselves on one side or the other, as interest, fear, or affection dictated. The law of England appears to have continued in this unsettled state

[1] See Grimm, Rechtsalterthümer.   [2] Hallam, ut sup. pp. 169 sq.

o

till the Norman conquest was completely established. One of the Conqueror's laws obliges every freeman in his dominions to take an oath of fealty to his person, without reserve or qualification ; and in the latter part of his life, he assembled all the landholders of any account throughout England, whose men soever they were, and compelled them to become his men, and to swear fealty to him against all persons whatever, without any exception [1].

Besides the tenure of knight-service properly so called, there were other species, such as the tenure by *grand serjeanty* (*per magnum servitium*), whereby the tenant was bound, instead of serving the king *generally* in his wars, to do some special honorary service to the king in person ; as to carry his banner, his sword, or the like ; or to be his butler, champion, or other officer, at his coronation. It was in most other respects like knight-service, only he was not bound to pay aid or escuage ; and when tenant by knight-service paid five pounds for a relief on every knight's fee, tenant by grand serjeanty paid one year's value of his land, were it much or little. Tenure by *cornage*, which was to wind a horn. when the Scots or other enemies entered the land, in order to warn the king's subjects, was (like other services of the same nature) a species of grand serjeanty [2].

Lands were also given by the king to persons for meaner services ; as to his woodwards, foresters, huntsmen, falconers, cooks, chamberlains, goldsmiths, bailiffs of manors in his own hands, and many other officers, which in Domesday-book are called " terræ thanorum regis," and sometimes " servientium regis." Such tenures were held by *petit serjeanty ;* and whatever the notion of petit serjeanty now is, I doubt not, says Tyrrell, that this holding of lands was the true tenure ; not but presenting the lord with a bow and arrow, a pair of spurs every year, etc. might also be called petit sergeanty. though

<hr/>

[1] Allen on the Royal Prerogative, pp. 69, 70, edit. 1849.

[2] Blackstone, ii. pp. 72, 73.

not so properly as the other. Tenants in petit serjeanty were subject to wardship, marriage (maritagium), and relief[1].

Socage, in its most general and extensive signification, seems to denote a tenure by any certain and determinate service, in which sense it is by our ancient writers constantly put in opposition to chivalry or knight-service, where the render (service) was precarious and uncertain. Thus Bracton: "if a man hold by rent in money, without any escuage or serjeanty, "id tenementum dici potest socagium." But if you add thereto any royal service or escuage, to any, the smallest amount, "illud dici poterit feodum militare." Socage was of two sorts: *free socage*, where the services are not only certain, but honourable; and *villein socage*, where the services, though certain, are of a baser nature[2].

Another important enactment of William's was the separation of the ecclesiastical court from that of the hundred[3].

Great as was the revolution produced in the country by the introduction of the feudal system, whereby almost every native landholder was either wholly despoiled of his possessions, or reduced to hold them, or a part of them, as the *man* of some powerful or favoured Norman; yet were the kingly and legislative functions less changed in form than in spirit. The oath taken by the king was the oath of the Anglo-Saxon kings. The Witena-gemôt, or grand national assembly, under the ancient dynasty, may be said to have been continued by the Conqueror and his sons under the name of the Great Council. The twelf-hynd and six-hynd-men, the ealdormen, eorls, and thanes had, it is true, disappeared, but their places were occupied by Norman prelates and the great vassals or *tenentes in capite*; though a few of the highest class of Anglo-Saxon nobles might, in the early part of the Conqueror's reign, have been among the members of this supreme council.

[1] Tyrrell, Bibl. Politica, p. 318, edit. 1727.   [2] Blackstone, ii. p. 79.
[3] See the document in Anc. Laws and Inst. p. 213.

For the guidance of these and other Norman legal functionaries, an edition of the Confessor's laws was issued, both
in Latin and French, with such modifications as in the new
state of things were deemed desirable. This, it is evident,
was a measure of necessity, as the judges in a court composed
solely, or with very few exceptions, of Normans, could hardly
be familiar with the language of the natives. That the plead-
ings were in French, follows as a matter of course. The old
scîr-môt (shire-moot) still continued under its synonymous
Normanized denomination of County-court; although its pre-
sident and chief assessors were, no doubt, Normans. In the
Hundred-court the judges were most probably English, and
its proceedings must naturally and necessarily have been conducted in the vernacular tongue.

Among the legal innovations introduced[1] by the Conqueror
may be mentioned the trial by battle, or judicial combat, as
being more congenial to the martial spirit of his followers
than the ordeal of the Anglo-Saxons. By William it was
enacted, that if an Englishman challenged a Frenchman to
the " ornest," or battle, for theft, homicide, or anything for
which a battle ought to take place, he was at full liberty so
to do. Should the Englishman refuse the ornest, let the
Frenchman clear himself with his witnesses by oath, according to Norman law. If a Frenchman challenged an Englishman to battle for the like charges, the latter was at liberty to
defend himself by battle, or, if he preferred it, by the iron
ordeal. If, on account of infirmity or other causes, he declined the combat, he might choose a legal substitute to do
battle for him. If a Frenchman accused an Englishman of

---

[1] "The trial by battle does not seem to have been usual in England before the Conquest, though, without doubt, originating in the kingdoms of
the North, where it was practised under the name of *holmgang*, from the
custom of fighting duels on a *holm*, or small island." Anc. LL. &. Inst.
Glossary, *v.* Ordeal. The word *cornest* or *ornest*, signifying this kind of
combat (Ohg. ernust, Mhg. ernest, *battle*) though undoubtedly Anglo-
Saxon, is not extant in any A. S. work hitherto printed.—T.

perjury, murder[1], theft, homicide, etc., the latter might defend himself either by ordeal or ornest. In all cases involving outlawry, an Englishman might clear himself by ordeal; but if an Englishman preferred a like charge against a Frenchman, which he was ready to make good, the Frenchman might defend himself by battle. If the Englishman declined the battle, the Frenchman was to clear himself by oath.

For the security of his power in England, a strong military force seemed to William now no longer necessary; the foreign mercenaries were, therefore, dismissed. Shortly after (1086) Eadgar Ætheling having received permission to leave Normandy, with two hundred warriors proceeded to Apulia[2]. In this year, when keeping Whitsuntide with his court at Westminster, William solemnly dubbed his son Henry a knight, and, for the first of August following, commanded an assembly of the estates of the realm to be holden at Salisbury. This, from the number of summonses issued, was, in fact, a grand review, at which his warriors still remaining in England were estimated at sixty thousand[3]. William, at this time caused his vassals to take the oath of allegiance, which, during the period of conquest, must have been frequently neglected, and confirmed to them their possessions in England. For this object it is probable that Domesday-book[4], which was completed in this year (1086), was first called into requisition. By this name is designated a detailed register, drawn up in the several counties, by juries impa-

---

[1] "Murdritus homo dicebatur antiquitus cujus interfector nesciebatur, ubicunque vel quomodocunque esset inventus; nunc adjectum est, licet sciatur quis murdrum fecerit, si non habeatur intra VII. dies." LL. Hen. I. xcii. §. 5.

[2] So Flor. Wigorn. a. 1086. The words of the Saxon Chronicle, 'beah fram him,' are wrongly rendered by Ingram, *revolted from him*.

[3] Ord. Vital. p. 649.

[4] In consequence of an address of the Upper House, king George III. caused an edition of this most important and ancient national monument to be undertaken, which, in the year 1783, issued from the press in 2 volumes folio. A volume of very useful commentaries upon it was composed

nelled by royal commissioners, showing the extent, division, and nature of the landed property in each, the tenants holding immediately of the king, or tenants in chief (tenentes in capite); the under-tenants, the freeholders and serfs, the nature of the tenure, the revenues, and their amount previous to and at the time of the Conquest, and the possibility of in-

by Kelham (Domesday Book illustrated). Alphabetical indexes of the local and personal names contained in it were formed by (Sir) Henry Ellis, who, at the same time, under the authority of the Record Commission, composed a highly meritorious dissertation on it, by way of introduction (first printed in folio, 1813). This work, with notices of individuals named in the document, and much augmented, was again published in the year 1833, in 2 vols. 8vo. In the opinion expressed by its editor we most sincerely participate: "A patient comparison of Domesday Book with the Registers of our earliest Abbeys is the surest way to accomplish its thorough illustration: and this is to be effected, not merely by the examination of charters and partial surveys, but by the scattered details of an historical kind with which many of them abound. No archives but those of our ancient ecclesiastical establishments throw light to any great extent upon the Domesday survey." Pref. pp. xv. xix. The said Commission published also the Exeter Domesday, the Inquisitio Eliensis, the Liber Wintoniensis and the Boldon Book, in the year 1810, of which the first two appear to be more copious original inventories of the royal commissioners than those given in the great collective Domesday-book. In these, too, the cattle are registered, which in Domesday are noticed only in East Anglia, from the mention of which in the Saxon Chronicle (a. 1085) we may perhaps infer that its author was a resident at Peterborough in that province. The third of the above-mentioned works is a Winchester Domesday-book (a. 1107–1128), the last, of the county of Durham of the year 1183. Later extracts from Domesday exist in manuscripts in the King's Remembrancer's office, also one in the Chapter House at Westminster, where the original is also deposited. [Domesday-book consists of 2 volumes, the first "is a large folio of vellum, and in 382 double pages, written in a small character, contains thirty-one counties, beginning with Kent, and ending with Lincolnshire. The other is a quarto volume of 450 double pages in a large character, but contains only the counties of Essex, Norfolk, and Sussex. There is no description of the four northern counties, but the West Riding of Yorkshire is made to comprehend that part of Lancashire which lies to the north of the Ribble, with some districts in Westmoreland and Cumberland: while the southern portion of Lancashire is included in Cheshire. Rutland is similarly divided between Nottinghamshire and Lincolnshire." Lingard. –T.]

creasing the income ; the property in cattle, woods and forests, fisheries, mines, and, in general, everything that was deemed requisite for an accurate cadastre and rental of the kingdom. The idea of this work was borrowed from no preceding one ; the tradition of a similar one having been composed by Ælf-red, being void of proof, and is, moreover, not mentioned in the Domesday-book of William ; nor does it appear to have found a model in any of the then existing states. It would rather seem that while until then only isolated rentrolls of royal monastic and other possessions, terriers of cities and towns, and lists of a similar kind were in existence, the defects of which were supplied by tradition or public know-ledge, the need felt by the Conqueror of possessing trust-worthy and accurate information on the state of property in a foreign land gave the original impulse to an undertaking, which the improvements, however slow, that domestic policy was making in other states, also rendered highly desirable. The security of the king's revenue and the administration of justice were the objects chiefly in view, as the confiscation of the property of the Anglo-Saxons, the desolation of whole counties, the flight of the native landowners, the contentions between the rapacious Normans and the cloisters under them, the uncertainty of inheritance even among the Normans them-selves, whose kin lived dispersed in Britain, France, and Italy, together with other circumstances, arising from the violent change of proprietorship, through the Conquest, greatly aug-mented the insecurity of possession. Domesday-book was with other treasures preserved at Winchester, whence it is sometimes called ' Rotulus Wintoniæ ;' though it occasionally accompanied the king or his justiciaries on their judicial pro-gresses. The northern counties, Northumberland, Lancaster, Cumberland, Westmoreland, and Durham are not comprised in it, on account probably of their desolate condition, though some southern tracts of those counties are included in Cheshire and Yorkshire. London, Winchester, and other cities of im-

portance are also omitted, possibly because all the information
required regarding them, as far as the king was interested,
was already to be found in the royal chancery or treasury.
Many of the returns are partially composed in favour of Norman cloisters; other inaccuracies may be assigned to the
shortness of the time allowed for the completion of the work.
Hence, in the times immediately following, we find many
similar works commenced, though always for particular districts only, yet not one superior in value to the great Domesday-book of king William. This will ever be found an inexhaustible source of information respecting the Anglo-Saxon
and Norman constitutions, particularly the rights and revenues of the kings and their vassals, the relations of cities
and towns, statistic accounts of various kinds, families and
their landed members, together with innumerable matters
highly interesting to inquiring posterity, but unnoticed by
the chroniclers of those times, either as too well known or as
worthless. An intimate acquaintance with Domesday should
supply the basis of every historical account of England,
particularly of its special history during the middle age.
Such a portraiture, consisting in great part of figures, will
not admit of a reduced sketch of the whole, but serves us
rather as a voucher for and illustration of the law-books and
chronicles. Still it will not be out of place here from this (notwithstanding its defects and imperfections) rich description
of the political condition of England before the end of the
reign of William the Conqueror, to give in a collected shape
some essential statistic and political notices, which may afford
us an insight into the misery of the country and the relations
of its oppressors.

In every county we meet with frequent mention of lands
usurped by Normans, although the king or earlier Norman
possessors laid claim to them (clamores et invasiones). Often
too, even when the property was not disputed, the commissioners had to remark, that the new possessor had neither

charter nor seal to show for his assumed fee, and that he had not been legally inducted into it by the sheriff.

The vassals holding immediately of the king (tenentes in capite) together with the ecclesiastical corporations, amounted scarcely to fourteen hundred. Of these the majority were holders of one fee, while others, as the brothers of the king, had vast possessions in almost every part of England: those of the bishop of Bayeux lay in seventeen, of Robert of Mortain in nineteen counties, and also in Wales. Eudes, the steward or sewer (dapifer) had fees in twelve counties; Hugh of Avranches, surnamed Lupus, or the Wolf, had considerable possessions, exclusive of those in his own county of Chester, in twenty-one shires.

Of mesne lords, or under tenants, the number was about eight thousand, though exactness with regard to these is not attainable, so many of them being registered only by their Christian names, without the addition either of patronymic or any locality whereby to distinguish them. The number of other tenants recorded in Domesday was about two hundred and fifty thousand[1]. The serfs were twenty-five thousand. The monks in the cloisters, the garrisons of the fortresses, and the burghers of the cities, where the royal commissioners did not set foot, are not specified. Among these there are about a thousand priests (presbyteri), and eight thousand burgesses. Above ten thousand are mentioned as free men (liberi homines); above two thousand are named as free men under patronage or protection (commendati), though neither of these classes are to be regarded as consisting solely of absolutely free proprietors[2]. Both of them are found almost exclusively in the old East Anglia, or the counties of Norfolk and Suffolk; about three hundred in Essex, and about fifty

---

[1] See England under the A. S. Kings (ii. p. 320) respecting the slaves in England.

[2] " In dominio sunt......III. liberi homines cum III. carucis ——— unus liber homo cum una caruca et II. bordariis." Domesd. i. fol. 183 b.

in Cheshire and Staffordshire: a circumstance that may perhaps be explained by the numerous Danish population that were settled in the ancient kingdom of Guthrum.

Next in degree to the free were the Socmen (Sochemanni), who, in consideration for a holding heritable by their sons, who were considered in their majority at the age of fifteen, and which the lord could not resume at will, took the oaths of fealty and of homage (homagium), and thereby bound themselves to military service, to a relief on the inheritance, and to certain stipulated services and imposts[1]. That they were not on a level with the above-mentioned Free, is manifest from the circumstance that socmen are named also in Norfolk and Suffolk, in the first-mentioned county as many as 4600, being a fifth part of the whole number (23,072) of persons included under that denomination in the record. But it is very striking to find no free men mentioned in the neighbouring county of Lincoln, nor even in Kent, where they would seem proverbially to belong; but, on the other hand, the half of all the socmen in England. In Suffolk we find above 1000, and as many in Northamptonshire; above 1500 in Nottinghamshire, above 1900 in Leicestershire, in Essex 520, in the desolated extensive Yorkshire not quite 450. The remaining socmen are found in very small numbers in the counties like those just mentioned, lying to the north of the Watling Street, excepting Cheshire and Staffordshire. South of this great road there is no mention of socmen[2].

---

[1] Fleta, lib. i. c. 8. Britton, c. 66. A proof may be found in the Rotul. Magn. Pipæ Henrici I. a. 31.: "decem marcæ argenti de Sochemannis de Oswardesbec."

[2] As an exception, perhaps, may be regarded 44 socmen in Kent and 20 in Buckinghamshire; though these counties, lying partly to the north of the Watling Street, were possibly comprised in the northern district of the commissioners. But another exception, as it would seem by the list in Ellis (Introd. ii. p. 445), appears to be groundless, viz. that of six socmen in Gloucestershire. The words of Domesday (fol. 169 b.) unus homo reddit vi. sochs. cannot surely mean that there were six socmen. More probable, it seems, that for sochs. we should read sorcos. In corrobora-

In the western counties we meet with a class of men called COLIBERTI; the number of whom in Wiltshire, where they are most numerous, amounts to 260; but their whole number to 858. This class would seem identical with that of the socmen, as the two denominations never occur together in the same county[1]; and as their name is not to be met with in any unquestionably genuine Latin document of any Anglo-Saxon cloister prior to the Conquest, it seems not unreasonable to suppose it to have been applied to the socmen by some of the Norman commissioners, as more usual in their native country[2]. This supposition is rendered still more probable by the circumstance that coliberti are never named in Anglo-Saxon law authorities.

In these mention occurs of a class called GEBURAS or BURES (Boors). Of which we meet with 64 only in Domesday, and those in six counties south of the Watling Street, viz. Buckingham, Oxford, Hereford, Berks, Worcester, and Devon. Co-existent with the socmen they are found in no county excepting that of Buckingham, their common boundary; but to regard them as identical with these and the coliberti is not tenable, from their occurrence with the latter in the counties of Berks, Devon, Hereford, and Worcester[3]. They belong to the class of which the greater and freer portion are de-

tion of this conjecture may be cited the following: Fol. 139 b. De pastura et silva II. solidos et III. soccos; Fol. 167b. In Gloucestre I. burgensis reddit IV. soccos; Fol. 179 b. Ad Hereford sunt IV. burgenses huic manerio reddentes XVIII. socos (pro) carucis.

[1] The small number of these coliberti compared with that of the socmen renders this ingenious hypothesis of the author somewhat doubtful. In the twelve counties where coliberti occur the total number is only 858, giving on an average about 72 to each county; while 23,066, the number of socmen in the sixteen counties where they occur gives an average of 1048 to each; a difference that could hardly exist if the classes were identical.—T.

[2] See Du Cange, Glossarium.

[3] A gloss in Domesday, fol. 38, under Hamptonshire, of "vel bures" written over the word coliberti, can hardly be cited against the many places in the text.

signated as Villani, amounting in all to about 109,000[1], of whom those in Kent alone are estimated at 6597, or above the half of all the classes mentioned in that shire. In Lincolnshire, out of a total of 25,305, are 7723 villeins ; and in Devonshire, out of a total of 17,434 are 8070 villeins together with 3294 serfs (servi). The class of the rural population distinguished by the Norman name of villeins, was probably at an earlier period comprised in the Anglo-Saxon one of ceorls, although, together with the other peasantry, in general, they may probably be considered as posterity of the old Roman-British population, while the slaves are found in the provinces conquered at a later period by the Anglo-Saxons. It does not appear that the Normans made any change in the legal position of this class so burthened with divers imposts and services ; but rather that their previous condition, through the harsh coercion and unfeeling orders of their new masters, assumed a more unhappy character.

Distinguished from the villeins we find, 1749, COTSETLAN, COSCETS (Coscez, Cozets, Cozez). These, with the exception of 9 in Shropshire, are met with only among the West Saxon races of the Wilsætas (among whom there are no fewer than 1418), the Defensætas, the Dorsætas, and the Sumorsætas. They were less free than the villeins, but bound to fewer services than the geburas.

A more numerous class is that of the COTARII, of whom there are 5054. Their Anglo-Saxon name nowhere appears. They are met with in almost all the counties south of the Watling Street, also in those where no coliberti are mentioned, as, for instance, 765 in Sussex. Among these counties, they are wanting in Cornwall, Gloucester, Hants, and Oxford, but not in those bordering on the Watling Street, Berks, Hertford (in which are 837), and Middlesex. Beside these

---

[1] In the Rectitudines Singularum Personarum (Anc. Laws and Instit.) the term of Villanus is made to correspond with the A. S. Geneât.—T.

there are 736 in Cambridgeshire, and 16 at Tateshale in York-shire.

The RADCHENISTRI, under which denomination we find 196, and under that of RADMANNI 369, are, with the exception of 5 of the first mentioned in Hampshire, all found in the counties bordering on Wales, as 137 radchenistri in Gloucestershire, 47 in Herefordshire; 167 radmen in Shropshire, 145 in Che-shire, 24 in Herefordshire, 33 in Worcestershire; consequently collectively in the districts of the Magesætas, or the Hecanas and Hwiccas. Their relative position seems to be between the free and the villeins.

As a peculiarity of Cheshire, dating no doubt from the conquests of the Danes, we find in that county a class of DRENGHS, a name originally applied to sons, but afterwards given to servants. Mention of them occurs occasionally for some centuries later, and on the Scottish border[1] they corre-spond to the radchenistri on the marches of Wales.

Passing over some classes of minor importance[2], we have yet to notice 82,609 BORDARII (including 490 BORDARII PAU-PERES[3]), whom we meet with in all the counties contained in the Domesday survey, in a tolerably equal proportion to the sum total of the inhabitants recorded in that document. They form a class usually named after the villeins and before

---

[1] Domesday, i. fol. 269 b. Before the Conquest there were forty-nine of them there. See Grimm, D. R. A. p. 305. Jamieson, Scottish Dic-tionary; also Rotulus Magn. Pipæ, 31 Hen. I. pp. 28, 132. In the year 1292 we find them at Tyndal. See Rot. orig. in Curia Scaccar. Abbrev. i. 70. The *Dingi* dwelling in the house of Gamel, a vassal (homo) at York, do not appear to have been drenghs, but subordinate servants like the *pardingi* in Legg. Henr. I. 29.

[2] On this subject, see "Engl. under the A. S. Kings." ii. p. 357, *sq.* and "Rectitudines Singularum Personarum" in Anc. Laws and Instit.

[3] With the exception of ten in Herefordshire, the bordarii pauperes ("qui propter pauperiem nullam reddunt consuetudinem"), all in Norwich, which had severely suffered, "partim propter foris facturas Rogerii comi-tis, partim propter arsuram, partim propter geltum regis, partim propter Waleranum." Domesday, ii. fol. 117 b.

the slaves. Their name, if explained by the hut, provided
with a small garden or kale-yard, in which they dwelt, would
agree with that of the cotsetlan and the cotarii; but in
Domesday all the three classes are distinguished one from
another. This denomination does not seem to occur in
any ancient, unquestionable Anglo-Saxon document, while in
France it was common. Hence we may assume that this
appellation was transferred to the Anglo-Saxons by the Normans, or that the bordarii were themselves Normans, that
had stood in the same relation in their own country, and
lived on the estate and in the hall of their lord, and originally
fed at his table or *bord*[1]. In favour of this opinion, we may
mention, that it does not appear how the shoals of Normans
of the lower classes, that came over to England, were disposed
of, while the number of bordarii well corresponds to that of
the army of sixty thousand men, after deducting the slain,
and doubling the remainder, in consequence of the masses
that flocked over in the following years. In some places we
find them in round numbers, which seems corroborative of
the opinion that they were but recently established there[2].
It is, moreover, obvious that the Anglo-Saxon ceorls could
not always be displaced by the herd of Normans and followers,
particularly as these must constantly be under arms, and,
consequently, incapacitated from devoting much time to field
labour. Still a conclusive opinion on this subject is not
possible, as, even under the Anglo-Saxon rulers, in consequence of the increase of an indigent population and the incessant wars with the Danes, similar relations could easily
exist.

[1] Bord, Dan. and Anglo-Sax. Engl. *bourd*. The bordarii are not mentioned in the "Rectitudines S. P."; but borda, signifying *hut*, is found in
a questionable charter of king Eadgar, in Monast. Angl. i. p. 209. Cod.
Diplom. iii. p. 179.

[2] Extra burgum (Warwick) C. bordarii cum hortulis suis reddunt L.
solidos. Domesd. i. fol. 238. Sub eis (civibus Huntingdon) sunt C. bordarii. Ib. fol. 203. In Norwich there were 480, in Thetford 20 bordarii.

The total number of persons registered in Domesday-book, after allowing for the repetition of numerous tenants in several counties and hundreds, amounts to about two hundred and eighty-three thousand, which, with the addition of the counties and cities omitted in Domesday, will form a total of at least three hundred thousand heads of families. That other taxable classes have been omitted must appear highly improbable, when we call to mind that the grand object of the composition of Domesday was the benefit of the royal treasury. That church property was exempt from all imposts, appears only as a rare exception. Monks, on the other hand, because not personally taxable, are only incidentally mentioned. It has been supposed that frequently whole classes of the lower rural population have not been registered, because in several counties, in which the rearing of swine was an object of industry, no mention is made of swineherds. But these were, no doubt, frequently taken from the serfs. If then we would estimate the total number of inhabitants of England at that time, two millions might seem a number rather too great than too little.

The extent of the forests in England was very considerable, enormous tracts were waste, and others of great magnitude had latterly been desolated or abandoned. The villages were very small, on which account several, at a later period, were united into one. Yorkshire was desolated more than any other part; in four hundred and eleven manors in that county, there were found only thirty-five villeins and eight bordarii. The cities and towns had few and only very small houses. Previous to the Conquest, London and York alone numbered above ten thousand resident inhabitants, and only the former many above that number. The greater number of the towns had severely suffered, partly by plundering and fire, partly through the construction of fortresses, for which purpose many houses were demolished. In Exeter, of 463 houses existing at the time of the Confessor, above 50 were destroyed; in Dorchester, of 172, and in the wealthy city of Norwich, (the burgesses of which possessed 43 chapels,) of 1320, the half. In Lincoln, of 1150 houses, 166 were sacrificed to the erection of the castle, and 100 others no longer inhabited. In Cambridge 27 houses were destroyed to make room for the castle; in Chester, of 487 houses, 205 were destroyed; in Derby, of 243, no fewer than 103; the remainder were inhabited by 100 great and 40 small burgesses. In Stafford, of 131 houses, 38 were destroyed; in York, of 1800, or thereabouts, 800 were probably no longer standing. But no city suffered more than Oxford, where geld was paid by 243 houses, while 478 were so ruined that they could no longer pay it. One town only, Dunwich, showed any sign of increase after the Conquest, where the number of burgesses, in the time of the Confessor, 120, was, at the time of the survey, augmented to 236; a phenomenon easily explained by the decay of the neighbouring city of Norwich.

The total amount of the yearly revenue of the king of England, as enjoyed by Eadward the Confessor, has, at a later period, been estimated at sixty thousand marks of silver; but by donations to the church and other gifts, this amount, according to the expressions of the discontented eldest son and immediate successor of the Conqueror, was diminished to the half. A century after the Conqueror, it is said to have amounted to a fifth only, or twelve thousand marks, the trifling value of which will appear the more striking, on calling to mind that the revenue of the German emperor, at the last-mentioned time, was estimated at three hundred thousand marks[1].

While the power of William in England was every year becoming more firmly established (1087), the state of things in France was a source to him of unceasing trouble, which claimed his constant attention, and finally led to the cause of

[1] Giraldus Cambrensis, De Institutione Principis, Distinct. iii. c. 28, in Recueil des Historiens Français, tom. xviii.

his death.   After the decease of queen Matilda, who had by
her prudence contributed to the better government of Normandy, as well as to the calming of the differences with the
neighbouring states, the turbulent nobles of Le Maine again
rose in arms against William.   Among these his most dangerous adversary was the viscount Hubert, son-in-law of
William, count of Nivernais.   This individual, leaving his
castles of Beaumont and Frenay, fortified himself, on the
boundary of Le Maine and Anjou, in the castle of St[e] Susanne,
situated on a steep rock, where, at the head of the malcontents and many knights, collected from Guienne and Burgundy,
he for three years plundered and captured the Normans and
the inhabitants of Le Mans, and slew them, if they resisted
him with arms; until the king, at length, after fruitless sieges
and the loss of many of his most distinguished warriors,
listening to the representations of the Normans, agreed to a
reconciliation with the fortunate rebel, on terms prescribed
by himself.

William's chief motive for this concession lay in the dissensions with the king of France, which had at that time broken
out afresh.   The vassals of Mantes on the Seine, Hugh, surnamed Stavelus, Ralf Mauvoisin and others had entered the
Norman territory and committed great depredations in the
diocese of Evreux.   William availed himself of this opportunity to demand the restoration of the Vexin, which, after
the death of the count Drogo of Mantes, had been re-united
to the crown of France, together with the towns of Pont
Ysère, Chaumont, and Mantes, and supported this frivolous
demand, in contravention of the feudal law and in contempt
of a possession confirmed through the course of half a century,
by the most violent threats[1].

A joke of the French monarch reported to William served
as fuel to the anger that was burning within him.   Alluding
both to William's corpulency and to his delay in carrying his

[1] Ord. Vital. p. 661 q.

threats into effect, Philip, as we are told, observed, that the
king of England was lying-in at Rouen. On hearing this,
the latter swore by God's splendour, that, when he went to
mass after his delivery, he would offer a hundred thousand
candles in the kingdom of France. The new flight of his
eldest son added to his exasperation, and shortly after, he
made an inroad into the Vexin, and surprised Mantes, which,
together with its churches, he reduced to ashes. While, exulting in his vengeance, he was riding over the ruins, his
horse trod on some of the burning materials, and plunging
cast its rider on the pommel. A dangerous rupture was the
consequence. William was conveyed to Rouen; but afterwards, on account of the noise in so populous a city, he desired to be removed to the church of St. Gervais in one of the
suburbs [1]. The danger he was in was not concealed from
him, and he strove to overcome the fear of death by tranquillizing his conscience. Great donations were without delay
sent for the restoration of the ruined churches of Mantes;
by a last testament, drawn up by notaries, he distributed
treasures to cloisters, churches, ecclesiastics, and the poor.
The unfortunate Anglo-Saxons, Morkere, Siward Barn, and
king Harold's brother Wulfnoth, who had long been languish-
ing in prison, also Roger, the son of his friend, William of
Breteuil, he ordered to be restored to liberty [2]. To the valiant
knight Balderic fitz Nicholas, whose estates he had confiscated, because he had, without permission, deserted the king's
service for the sake of fighting against the Mohammedans in
Spain, he restored his fee and inheritance [3]. Last of all, and
not without much opposition, and yielding only to the conviction that, after his death, it would be done by others, he
also liberated his brother, bishop Odo, from confinement.
To his eldest son Robert, who was at that time sojourning

---

[1] Rom. de Rou, vv. 14181 *sqq.* Bromton, col. 979.

[2] According to Malmesbury (p. 430) the order was not obeyed.—T.

[3] Ord. Vital. p. 660. Of the feats of individual Normans in Spain, see
more at p. 44.

in the dominions of the king of France, even if he was not
in arms against his native country [1], he left his paternal inheritance of Normandy, with his other possessions and rights
in France.   To William, his second son, he bequeathed his
realm of England.   Henry, his youngest son, had only a
legacy of five thousand pounds of silver [2]; but, on the prince
complaining that he had received no land, his father, as we
are told, assured him that, on the death of his brothers, he
would inherit the dominions of both.   Both were at the time
childless.   According to Orderic, William's revenue amounted
to no less than the incredible sum of a thousand and sixty-
one pounds, ten shillings and three half-pence sterling per
day, exclusive of royal gifts, fines, or commutations, etc. ;
" which, as in the Conqueror's reign the pound sterling was a
pound weight of silver, contained more than thrice as much
as a pound sterling at this day.   Therefore the king's revenue
must have been 365 times £3185, or £1,162,525 [3]."

William died early in the morning of the 9th September,
1087, while his physicians were regarding the tranquil night

[1] Flor. Wigorn. a. 1087.   Ord. Vital. p. 659.   W. Malm. p. 460.

[2] Of William's rapacity the chronicle makes repeated mention, as,
a. 1086 : " According to his custom, he collected a very large sum from
his people, either justly or otherwise, if he could find any pretext."   And
a. 1087 : " The king and the head men loved much and over much covetousness in gold and in silver, and recked not how sinfully it was gotten,
provided it came to them.   The king sold his land as dearly as he possibly
could.   Then would a second come and bid more than the other had
before given, and the king let him have it who had bidden more.   Then
would a third come and bid yet more, and the king would let him have it
who bade most of all."—T.

[3] See Baron Maseres's note, p. 258, who adds : " If we suppose the
value of money at this time to have been only about 20 times as great as
it is in the present year 1787, so that an ounce of silver would have bought
only twenty times as much bread, or corn, or meat, as it will at this day
(which I take to be a very reasonable and moderate supposition, and
rather under than over the true difference of the value of money then and
now,) this revenue will have been equivalent to a revenue of 20 times
£1,162,525, or £23,250,500 a year at this day," exclusive of that arising
from escheats, forfeitures, mulcts, wardships, &c.—T.

P 2

he had passed as a sign of his recovery. On hearing the
sound of a bell, he inquired the occasion of it, and on being
informed that it was tolling the hour of prime, he said,
stretching forth his arms, "Then I commend my soul to my
Lady, the mother of God, that by her holy prayers she may
reconcile me to her Son, my Lord Jesus Christ," and immediately expired. The treatment of his corpse aids us in forming a striking picture of the social condition of the time, and
a still more striking and more instructive one, for all times,
of the vanity of earthly greatness. The bishops, physicians,
and others belonging to the court, on hearing of his unexpected death, lost all self-command : those among them who
possessed any property, instantly throwing themselves on
their horses, hastened to their habitations, for the purpose
of protecting or concealing themselves and all belonging to
them. Those of a lower grade, finding themselves relieved
from all restraint, rushed to the palace, and plundered it of
all they could find of clothing, vessels, and royal furniture.
The body of the king, the mightiest commander of his age,
when scarcely cold, was left for many hours on the floor
almost in a state of nakedness. The citizens of Rouen, apprehensive of a general pillage, hurried in all directions in
the utmost confusion ; of William's sons not one was on the
spot to take charge of the government, or pay the last duties
to their parent. The eldest was still among his father's
adversaries ; of the two younger one had already hastened to
England, to assume the government, the other was gone to
get possession of his treasure. At length, some considerate
monks assembled together to form a procession, for the purpose of performing a mass, in the church of St. Gervais, for
the soul of the departed ; and the archbishop of Rouen gave
orders for the removal of the body to the abbey of St. Stephen,
that had been founded by the king. But no one appeared on
whom this duty should devolve. Of the brothers, the relatives, the courtiers of the king, even of his body guard, not

one was to be seen. At last, a simple knight, dwelling in the neighbourhood, named Herluin, for the honour of God and the Norman name, resolved to provide for the costs of the conveyance, hired a carriage and the requisite people, had the body borne to the Seine, put on board a vessel, and then accompanied it himself by land to Caen. There the clergy of the abbey were prepared to give it an honourable reception; but the funeral service had scarcely begun, when a fire broke out in one of the houses of the city, and both clergy and laity hurried away to extinguish the wide-spreading flames. Thus was this solemnity, like that of his coronation at Westminster, attended with a conflagration, and brought to a conclusion by a few monks. When at length the interment of the body in the abbey-church was about to take place, many ecclesiastics of distinction had there assembled, the stone coffin was already sunk in the earth, and the corpse lying on the bier was ready to be placed in it, Gilbert, bishop of Evreux, held a funeral discourse, which, after extolling the virtues of the deceased monarch, he closed by beseeching those present to pray for the soul of the departed, and if he had done injury to any one among them, to grant him forgiveness. At this moment a vavassor, named Ascelin fitz Arthur, pressed forward and declared that the ground on which the assembled multitude was standing had been the property of his father, of which he had been robbed by the king, that he solemnly demanded its restitution, and forbade, in the name of God, the interment of the king in that place. The justice of this charge was so incontestably proved by the neighbours, that the prelates assembled resolved to pay immediately to Ascelin sixty shillings for the burial spot, and to guarantee him a sufficient indemnity for the land[1]. The

[1] According to Malmesbury (p. 461), prince Henry, who was present at the funeral, was content to pay the claimant a hundred pounds of silver. His words are: "Quocirca volente Henrico filio, qui solus ex liberis aderat, centum libræ argenti litigatori persolutæ audacem calumniam compescuere."—T.

corpse was now lifted, for the purpose of being deposited in
the vault; but another mishap was to follow. The grave,
lined with masonry, was too narrow to admit the corpse,
which, in the act of pressing it, burst and filled the bystanders
with the most insupportable exhalation of corruption : the
officiating priests could with difficulty perform their duty to
its conclusion[1].

William possessed an extraordinary degree of bodily
strength. His bow, which no other could bend on foot, he
was able to draw while riding at full speed. For the savage
diversion of the chase his passion knew no bounds, and his
recklessness and barbarity in its gratification were as boundless. The numerous forests of Normandy and England were
insufficient for him. A district of seventeen thousand acres,
comprising above sixty parishes, in the most thriving part of
England, lying between Winchester and the coast, he assigned for the enlargement of the ancient forest of Ytene, and
the formation of the *New Forest*; and the royal hunter mercilessly caused churches and villages to be burnt down within
its circuit[2]. He also enlarged Windsor Forest[3]. His chase-
and forest-laws were barbarous to an extreme. If any one
slew a hart or hind, his eyes were put out. He forbade the
killing of even wild boars and hares. " He loved the high
game," said his contemporaries, " as if he were their father[4]."

What distinguishes William from all similar characters, is
the security in which he placed his acquisitions, although the
means employed by him for that end always created him new
enemies among both his nobles and the people. The severity

---

[1] Ord. Vital. pp. 660 *sq.* Eadmer, p. 13.

[2] Flor. Wigorn. a. 1099. W. Gemmet. viii. c. 9. Ellis, Introd. i. pp.
105–110, who has, however, overlooked Ord. Vital. p. 781.

[3] MS. apud Ellis, Introd. p. 107.

[4] Sax. Chron. a. 1087. [This year the cathedral of St. Paul, with many
monasteries and the greater and best part of London, were destroyed by
fire. Sax. Chron. Flor. Wigorn. —T.]

he exercised towards his barons and nearest connections, must not unfrequently have caused him to appear in their eyes as hateful as he must ever have done to the subjugated people.

His consort, Matilda, died a few years before him (3rd Nov. 1083) at Caen. She had borne him four sons, Robert, Richard, William, and Henry. Of his daughters, we know of Cecilia, an abbess at Caen; Constance, married to Alan Fergant, count of Brittany and earl of Richmond, who died childless; Agatha, first betrothed to the Anglo-Saxon king Harold, and afterwards to Alphonso king of Gallicia, but died before her marriage; Adela, married to Stephen count of Blois, whose third son, named after his father, afterwards made a conspicuous figure in the annals of England; Adeliza, who died a nun [1]; and Gundrada, married to William of Warenne, earl of Surrey [2]. One praise, and a rare one among

---

[1] W. Malm. pp. 455, *sq.* W. Gemmet. viii. c. 34. Ord. Vital. pp. 512, 573. [In Domesday i. fol. 49, mention occurs of a daughter of William named Matilda—" Goisfredus, filie regis camerarius, tenet de rege Heche ...... Goisfredus vero tenet eam de rege, pro servitio quod fecit Mathildi ejus filie." Of a daughter thus named we find no trace in the chronicles; but Mr. Blaauw (Archæolog. xxxii. p. 119.) suggests, that Gundrada and Matilda may be the Dano-Norman and Flemish names of the same individual; an identity of which I hardly entertain a doubt, the components of either name being synonymous with those of the other, though in inverse order, viz. Goth. gunþs, Ohg. kund, O. Nor. gunnr, *bellum ;* O. Nor. rád, *vires, might ;* and Goth. mahts, Ohg. maht, *might ;* Goth. hilds, A. S. hild, *bellum.* In corroboration of this supposition, I will remind the reader, that the Norman Emma assumed the name of Ælfgifu, on her marriage with Æthelred; and Eadgyth that of Matilda, on her marriage with Henry I. Gundrada (O. Nor. masc. Gunnráðr) is in fact a translation of Matilda.

[2] In a charter (Monast. V. p. 12. Rymer, i. p. 3) William calls her his daughter; and William of Warenne, on the occasion of founding the priory at Lewes, names queen Matilda as her mother. A document of the pair, from a chartulary of the abbey of Cluny, is cited in C. G. Hoffmann, Nova Scriptorum ac Monumentorum Collectio, tom. i. Lips. 1731. The chroniclers ignore her, except Orderic, who calls her a sister of Gherbod the Fleming. See Orderic, p. 522. (Maseres, p. 254.) Documentary

the princes of his family, is due to William—that of conti-
nence. Even the voice of slander has been unable to utter

evidence of their posterity exists in the charter of Castleacre Priory in
Norfolk. See Monast. Angl. v. pp. 49, *sq.* [The following notes, chiefly
from Ellis's Introduction to Domesday, (vol. i. p. 507) will, it is hoped,
be thought of sufficient interest to justify their insertion. "Gundreda was
really a daughter of the Conqueror. William de Warren's second charter
of foundation, granted to Lewes priory, in the reign of Rufus, states this
fact distinctly: 'Volo ergo quod sciant qui sunt et qui futuri sunt, quod
ego Willielmus de Warrena, Surreiæ comes, donavi et confirmavi Deo et
Sancto Pancratio et monachis Cluniacensibus, quicunque in ipsa ecclesia
Sancti Pancratii Deo servient imperpetuum, donavi pro salute animæ
meæ et animæ Gundredæ uxoris meæ et pro anima domini mei Willielmi
regis, qui me in Anglicam terram adduxit, et per cujus licentiam monachos
venire feci, et qui meam priorem donationem confirmavit, et pro salute
dominæ meæ Matildis reginæ, *matris* uxoris meæ, et pro salute domini mei
Willelmi regis, filii sui, post cujus adventum in Anglicam terram hanc
cartam feci, et qui me comitem Surregiæ fecit.'
   "Gundreda is also acknowledged by the Conqueror himself as his
daughter, in the charter, by which he gave to the monks of St. Pancras
the manor of Walton in Norfolk, the original of which is preserved in the
Cott. MS. Vesp. F. III. fol. 1. He gives it 'pro anima domini et ante-
cessoris mei regis Edwardi . . . . . . et pro anima Gulielmi de Warenna, et
uxoris suæ Gundredæ, *filiæ meæ,* et heredibus suis.'
   "Gundreda died in child-bed at Castle Acre in Norfolk, May 27th 1085,
and was interred in the chapter-house of Lewes priory. Her tomb was
found in 1775 in Isfield church in Sussex, (forming the upper slab of the
monument of Edward Shirley, cofferer to Henry VIII.) whither it was
supposed to have been taken at the dissolution of Lewes priory. It was
removed in that year to the church of Southover. It was ornamented in
the Norman taste, and the inscription was obscure and mutilated; the
names of Gundreda and St. Pancras, however, appeared upon it. See
Sir William Burrell's Collections for the History of the Rape of Lewes in
Sussex, MS. Donat. Brit. Mus.
   "William de Warren himself died June 24th 1088. The Register of
Lewes priory, MS. Cott. Vesp. A. IIV. preserves the epitaph which was
formerly upon his tomb, also at Lewes."
   The following is from the Athenæum, No. 940. "On Tuesday morn-
ing, as the workmen employed by the Brighton, Lewes, and Hastings
Railway Company were removing the earth in the priory grounds at
Lewes, their progress was arrested by a stone, on the removal of which
they discovered two cists, or coffers, side by side. On the lid of one was
the word 'Gundreda,' perfectly legible; and on the lid of the other,

more than one ill-founded reproach against him[1]. At all events, we know of no illegitimate offspring left by him.

'Will'us.' On removing the lids, the remains appeared to be quite perfect, and the lower jaw of William, earl de Warren, in extraordinary preservation. The cists in which the bodies were deposited were not more than three feet in length, and about two feet wide, and there is no doubt that they had been removed from some other place, and re-interred; and, according to tradition, the bodies of William de Warren and Gundreda his wife were re-interred two hundred years after their decease. These interesting and ancient relics were removed to Southover church, in which there is a very ancient tablet to the memory of 'Gundreda,' and it is intended to place the remains near this tablet."

" It is obvious," writes Mr. Blaauw, (Archæolog. xxxi. p. 439,) " that the bodies have been transferred from their original sepultures to these cists at some period not recorded, but probably on their being found decayed, when, in the progress of the buildings of the priory, the chapter-house, in which they were buried, was completed." For an interesting account of Gundrada, the reader is recommended to consult the two valuable papers by Mr. Blaauw, above referred to.—T.

[1] Will. Malm. p. 453. [" Non desunt qui ganniant eum ...... volutatum cum cujusdam presbyteri filia, quam per satellitem, succiso poplite, Matildis sustulerit, quapropter illum exhæredatum, illam ad mortem fræno equi cæsam."—T.]

A

HISTORY OF ENGLAND

UNDER THE

NORMAN KINGS.

WILLIAM THE SECOND,

SURNAMED RUFUS.

CONTEMPORARY SOVEREIGNS.

GERMANY.	FRANCE.	SCOTLAND.	SPAIN.
Henry IV.	Philip I.	Malcolm III. ob. 1093.	Alphonso VI.
		Donald Bane, dep. 1094.	
		Duncan ob. 1094.	
		Donald Bane 1097.	
		Edgar 1097.	

POPES.
Urban II. ob. 1099. | Paschal II.

IN nothing did the complete triumph of William the Conqueror more manifestly display itself than in the succession to the English throne established solely in conformity with his wish. So entirely broken was the power of the Anglo-Saxons, that neither the claims of the royal race, represented by Eadgar Ætheling, and not denied by the Normans themselves, were of any avail; nor was any regard paid to the sons of Harold, at that time sojourning beyond sea. Neither the right nor the semblance of an election was conceded to the Norman and Anglo-Saxon chieftains, and even that of primogeniture was violated. The bequest of Normandy to the eldest son was in accordance with the feudal law of France, to violate which the Conqueror would, at the same time, have scrupled as little as any of the other French princes, who entertained consideration for their suzerain only when it suited them. The assignment of England to the second son may have appeared illegal to the Anglo-Saxons[1], yet not so to the Normans, as we have already remarked,

[1] Eadmer, p. 13.

that among them the paternal inheritance in Normandy
descended to the eldest son, while the frequently greater,
though less secure, acquisitions by conquest in Apulia, Brittany, and other provinces, fell to the share of the younger[1].
More probable, however, than reasons founded on right, are
those deducible from William's knowledge of the characters
and capabilities of his sons; and even if he judged too favourably of his second son, and had constantly preferred him to
his elder brother, it was, at the same time, but too evident,
that Robert, weak-minded, wavering, fondly priding himself
in eloquence, valour, and other knightly accomplishments, was
unequal to the task of ruling England, and to the struggle
with its inhabitants.

The younger son, William, who, at his father's death, had
not attained his twenty-fifth year, had been educated and
knighted[2] by Lanfranc, and had distinguished himself by his
courage and bodily activity. The alacrity with which he attended to every intimation of a wish on the part of his father,
combined with the qualities just mentioned, gained him the
affection of that dark and suspicious prince. On his deathbed, William gave him a letter to the archbishop of Canterbury, in which he conferred on that prelate the office of
crowning his son William king of England. Even before the
prince could embark at Witsand, the intelligence of his father's death overtook him. To the most influential and intimate friend of the Conqueror, this his last wish could be no
matter of surprise. He caused his royal pupil to promise,
that as king he would ever practise justice, equity, and mercy;
defendt he Church, and ever follow his precepts and counsel.
Whereupon, preventing all discussions about an election,
after a lapse of eighteen days only from the death of the

1 Examples: the sons of William fitz Osbern (see p. 156); of Roger of
Montgomery, whose eldest had Belesme and Alençon; the second, Hugh,
the earldom of Shrewsbury.

2 The ceremony of knighting at that time is thus described by Orderic,
p. 665: " Eum lorica induit, et galeam capiti ejus imposuit, eique militiæ
cingulum in nomine Domini cinxit."—T.

Conqueror, Lanfranc consecrated and crowned him, in the abbey-church of Westminster, as king William the Second. The Normans settled in England, and the Anglo-Saxons, to whom the establishment of England as a separate kingdom, independent of the duke of Normandy, must appear in the highest degree welcome, submitted to the anointed of the Church, and swore to him the oath of allegiance. The young king then proceeded to Winchester, where the well-filled treasury of the Conqueror was opened, and, in compliance with his last wishes, for the benefit of his soul; gifts, some amounting to ten marks of gold, were bestowed on every cloister and church in England, and to every shire a hundred pounds in gold were given for their respective poor[1]; a sum which must call to mind how considerably the number of poor must have increased since the Conquest, but, at the same time, seems to show that a secular provision for them still continued[2]. Precious stones, gold and silver, were also taken from the hoard, to be applied by Otto the goldsmith in the erection of a costly mausoleum to the memory of the deceased[3].

William brought with him to England the captives, earl Morkere and Wulfnoth, the brother of Harold, but who only exchanged one prison for another, as they were committed to close custody immediately on their arrival at Winchester; though it seems that Wulfnoth afterwards recovered his liberty, as we are told he died a monk at Salisbury. Ulf, a son of king Harold, and Duncan, son of Malcolm king of Scotland, also received their liberty and the honour of knighthood from duke Robert[4].

While the winter was well employed by the king in establishing himself on the throne and in the minds of the people, under the guidance of his older and more experienced coun-

---

[1] Saxon Chron. a. 1087.

[2] See England under the Anglo-Saxon kings, i. pp. 198 sq.

[3] Ord. Vital. lib. viii. init. This Otto aurifaber was a tenant in chief of lands in Essex. See Ellis, i. p. 462.

[4] Flor. Wigorn. a. 1087. Ord. Vital. ed. Maseres, p. 186. Engl. under the A. S. Kings, ii. p. 267. See also p. 163.

sellors, the great vassals of Normandy, availing themselves of the weakness of his elder brother, expelled the garrisons that had been placed in their castles by the Conqueror, and, at the same time, extorted new enfeoffments from his less formidable successor. If similar attempts were made in England, they speedily miscarried, though the Norman barons were in want only of a leader, (who soon presented himself in the paternal uncle of their prince, bishop Odo (1088)), to rise up with words and deeds against the separation of the country conquered with their blood from the smaller hereditary state, a separation in many respects so prejudicial to their interests. Duke Robert allowed himself to be flattered with the prospect of dominion over the whole of his father's territories. With bishop Odo, who had again received the palatinate of Kent, were combined two other bishops, Geoffrey of Coutances and William of Durham, together with the brother of Odo, Robert count of Mortain and earl of Cornwall; Roger of Montgomery, earl of Shrewsbury; his eldest son, Robert of Belesme, together with two younger ones; Hugo of Grentemaisnil, earl of Leicester, his nephew, Robert of Rhuddlan; Eustace the younger, count of Boulogne; Osbern, son of Richard Scrope, and others of illustrious name. For the king declared themselves his brother-in-law William of Warenne, Hugh earl of Chester; Robert of Molbray, earl of Northumberland[1], and Robert fitz Hamon. But the best protection the king had to look for was in the Anglo-Saxon population. Of this he was fully aware, and caused his men to be summoned, particularly the Anglo-Saxons. To these he promised just and mild laws, such as had never been known to their forefathers, and the abolition of all unjust imposts; even the immunities of the chase and forest, of which they had been deprived under

---

[1] Orderic (p. 667) names him, for whom also speaks the silence of the Saxon Chronicle and even of Simeon of Durham; while Florence and William of Malmesbury name him among the accomplices of Odo, which is hardly probable, as we find him, several years after, in possession of his extensive earldom.

his father, he restored to the inhabitants. The Anglo-Saxons, to the number of thirty thousand, assembled under Norman leaders, marched straightways to Rochester, where the earl-bishop Odo had strongly fortified himself, and whence he had plundered the possessions of his bitter enemy, archbishop Lanfranc, as well as those of the citizens of London. The war was, however, carried on more with words than with swords and missiles. Roger of Montgomery who, feigning treachery, had come to the king, was, partly by William's seeming submission to the old counsellors of his father, and the promises of presents, partly by the consideration, that those who denied the rights of the king attacked, at the same time, the validity of all the Norman possessions in England that were the grant of the Conqueror, seduced to follow the banner of William [1]. He nevertheless, did not prove faithful, but secretly favoured the conspirators [2]. On receiving intelligence that Odo had withdrawn to the castle of Pevensey, which was held by Robert of Mortain, the king himself proceeded thither, of which, as also that of Tun-bridge, he made himself master, though stoutly defended by its owner, Gilbert fitz Richard, grandson of the count of Brionne, Gilbert Crespin. After a long siege, impelled by hunger, and vainly looking for the arrival of his confederates from Normandy, many of whom had been slain by the English on the coast or, bereft of their ships, driven back into the waves of the ocean, Odo appeared ready to deliver Rochester to the king. After agreeing on the conditions in the royal camp, Odo accompanied the king's knights into the castle, for the avowed purpose of carrying the surrender into effect, when count Eustace and the other conspirators, who had adroitly availed themselves of the time spent in negotiating, in

---

[1] W. Malm. p. 488. ["Nec minori astutia Rogerium de Monte Gome-rico, secum dissimulata perfidia equitantem, circumvenit. Seorsum enim ducto magnam ingessit invidiam, dicens: Libenter se imperio cessurum, si illi et aliis videatur quos pater tutores reliquerat."—T.]

[2] Ord. Vital. p. 667.

gaining intelligence and procuring supplies, caused the drawbridge to be raised, making captives of the royal delegates
and, for the sake of appearance, of the treacherous bishop
himself. It was therefore necessary to renew the siege, and
as his adversaries had also gained possession of some other
strong places, the king issued another general summons, for
the purpose of reinforcing his army. The threat, that who-
ever remained behind should be held as a " nithing[1]," proves
that an appeal to the feelings of the Anglo-Saxons was deemed
desirable. Nor in other parts of England did the conspirators
find any support. Bishop Geoffrey saw his operations limited
to predatory incursions from Bristol to Bath and into Wiltshire; his followers had been repulsed from Ilchester. At
Worcester bishop Wulfstan directed the defence of the adjacent provinces, which Bernard of Neumarch, Roger of Lacy,
and Ralph of Mortimer, had attempted to lay waste. William
of Eu had ravaged the royal possessions at Berkeley, and the
plains and vineyards of Gloucestershire. Roger Bigot had
made himself master of the castle at Norwich, yet found no
adherents, but only an opportunity for predatory excursions[2].
Earl Roger, finding his treachery no longer a secret, deserting
the royal camp, hastened not to any settled place of meeting,
but to his own castle at Arundel, there to await the coming
of duke Robert. But that prince, occupied with the enjoyment of his new dignities and treasures, found the road in
England too rough for a triumphal procession to Westminster
abbey, and shrank from the difficulty and uncertainty of a
struggle, which bade fair to be a civil, a national, and fraternal contest. In the beginning of the summer, bishop Odo,
sensible that Rochester could no longer hold out, surrendered

---

[1] Sax. Chron. a. 1088. ["He (Willelm) "sende ofer call Engla lande,
and bæd hæt ælc man þe wære unniðing sceolde cuman to him"—*He
(William) sent over all England, and bade that every man who was 'unnithing'
should come to him.*" W. Malm. p. 489. "jubet ut compatriotas advocent
ad obsidionem venire, nisi si qui velint sub nomine 'niðing,' quod *nequam*
sonat, remanere."—T.

[2] Flor. Wigorn. Sim. Dun. a. 1088

it to the king, on the condition of a free passage to Bayeux.
It was with difficulty that William consented to spare the
lives of the garrison ; but the request of Odo, that at his
departure the besiegers should abstain from every demonstra-
tion of triumph, was contemptuously refused. The moment
he appeared, the trumpets were ordered to sound : and as he
passed through the ranks, the English cried out : "Halter and
gallows." He slunk away, muttering threats of vengeance.
This decisive step was soon followed by the termination of
the whole war. Earl Roger was not tardy in making his
peace with his sovereign, who, on his part, was sensible that
leniency towards the old vassals of his father was the wisest
policy. A powerful army was sent to Durham, which city
bishop William, likewise on condition of leaving England
under a safe escort, surrendered to the royal forces (Sept. 11).
The remaining French adversaries of the king fled, leaving
their lands and castles as a reward to his adherents [1].

With prince Henry, to whom his brother Robert, urged by
his necessities, had pledged or sold the Cotentin for three
thousand pounds, but who was now in England endeavouring
to make good his claims to a share of the lands that had been
possessed by his mother, but which after her death his father
had not divided among her children, the king too found means
of compromise; the lands in question having been granted
to Robert fitz Hamon [2], and, consequently, no longer at the
king's disposal. This agreement between his two pupils, a
work dictated by the best judgment, seems to have been the
last act of archbishop Lanfranc, who died in the May following
(24 May 1089), and with him the only man who was able to
exercise a wholesome influence over the king, and to curb his
ever more and more unbridled, brutal passions. Into Lanfranc's place in the king's confidence insinuated himself an

[1] Sax. Chron. a. 1088. Ord. Vital. pp. 667-669. Sim. Dunelm. col. 215.
W. Malm. pp. 489, 490. Alur. Bev. 137.
[2] Ord. Vital. pp. 665 *sq.* According to Ellis, Introd. i. p. 432, who,
however, cites no authority, the king gave him the Honour of Gloucester.

ecclesiastic named Ranulf Flambard[1], who served him especially as a tool whereby to enrich the royal treasury out of the
possessions of the Church.   Pernicious as his influence over
his master unquestionably was, yet in his instance traces of
the calumny of his contemporaries are visible, particularly of
the monkish chroniclers, whose fraternity he had so sensibly
injured. These, among other reproaches, revile him with being
of most abject birth, the son of Turstin, a low-born priest of
Bayeux, and with having acquired the surname of Flambard
(Flambeau) in consequence of his early manifested covetousness[2]. Under this name, however, we find him not only repeatedly mentioned among both the mesne and immediate tenants
of the Conqueror, and on the road to some influence at court,
but also noticed as a proprietor in Hampshire, under king
Eadward the Confessor[3]. As his plan, and which is said to
have excited great hatred towards its author, is mentioned
that of causing a more accurate measurement by the line of
the hides throughout England; the Anglo-Saxon measure
being, it was alleged, too incorrect, thereby to gain for the
king either land or an increase of revenue; a proceeding
which could infringe the rights of no one. This statement,
however, may not improbably originate in a substitution for
the survey according to the Winchester Domesday of the
Conqueror of one of the many special and more accurate
surveys; for, if such a re-measurement of the whole country

[1] The Sax. Chron. (a. 1128) and Flor. Wigorn. (a. 1094) call him
Passeflambard.

[2] W. Malm. p. 497 : "Accessit regiæ menti fomes cupiditatum, Ran-
nulfus clericus, ex infimo genere hominum lingua et calliditate provectus
ad summum." See also ejusd. de Pont. lib. iii. Ord. Vital. p. 678. Thierry,
T. ii. lib. 1. " Renouf Flambard, évêque de Lincoln, autrefois valet de pied
chez le duc de Normandie. He had merely the administration of the
church property of the vacant see of Lincoln. [It is not easy to conceive
how the sobriquet of *Flambeau* could be given to an individual on account
of his covetousness.—T.]

[3] Domesday, i. p. 51. Ord. Vital. p. 678. As royal chaplain, see docum.
of a. 1088, in Monast. ii. p. 266.

Q

had taken place, we should unquestionably be in possession
of some further notices of the transaction, which must necessarily invalidate the original Domesday as a legal authority [1].
The office held by Flambard at the court of the youthful
king we are unable accurately to designate; that of chancellor, sometimes assigned to him, we find in the hands of
another royal chaplain, Robert Bloet, and, at a later period,
of William Giffard [2]; and are therefore rather disposed to
regard him as filling the very comprehensive one of chief
justiciary [3].

The history of England is at this time so intimately interwoven with that of Normandy, the hereditary land of the
royal house and the nobility, that it is often requisite to cast
a glance at that country, even when no immediate connection

---

[1] Ord. Vital. p. 678, a. 1089 is the only authority for this account, who,
on the other hand, instead of the real Domesday survey of the elder
William, mentions only the number of men able to bear arms, but nothing
of the more accurate subsequent measurement of the hides. Palgrave
(Origin and Progress, ii. p. 449) believes in an old Lieger Book of Evesham
abbey to have discovered, in a fragment relative to Gloucestershire, a portion of Flambard's record. I have no more doubt than he has that the
era of its compilation is between 1096 and 1112, though there seems but
little ground for the opinion that it is a part of the very comprehensive
work in question. [The fragment is in MS. Cott. Vesp. B. xxiv. pp.
53–60.—T.]

[2] Sax. Chron. Flor. Wigorn. a. 1093. Ord. Vital. p. 783.

[3] Flor. Wigorn. a. 1099: "negotiorum totius regni *exactor*." Alured.
Beverl. p. 144: "*placitor* et totius regni *exactor*." W. Malm. de Pont.
"totius regni *procurator*." Petri Blesensis Hist. p. 110: "*exactor* cru-
delissimus, regis consiliarius præcipuus." Eadmer, p. 20: "quidam nomine
Ranulphus, regiæ voluntatis *maximus executor*." Hen. Hunt. a. 1099:
"placitator sed perversor, exactor sed exustor totius Angliæ." Orderic,
p. 786: summus regiarum opum procurator et *justiliarius*. That this
Ranulf composed a work de legibus Angliæ may, as long as we have no
more trustworthy testimony than the Chronicon Johannis de Sci Petri
Burgo (a. 1099), be regarded as a mistake for the work of Ranulf de
Glanvile; but that he was the king's justiciary is also evident from the
Sax. Chron. a. 1099; "þe æror calle his gemôt ofer eall Engleland draf
and bewiste," *who previously had conducted and directed all his councils
over all England.*

between it and England is apparent. Thus, when prince Henry with Robert of Belesme, who had also made his peace with king William, returned to Normandy, certain evil-disposed persons deluded duke Robert with the false representation, that both had entered into an engagement with William for his ruin, who thereupon taking council of bishop Odo, caused the prince and his companion to be arrested, as soon as they trod the Norman shore, and sent the latter to Bayeux and the former to Neuilly in strict custody. The father of Robert, however, arriving shortly after from England, for the purpose of securing the several castles that belonged to his house, the duke found himself compelled to summon the nobility of Le Maine to his aid, with the object of reducing those castles under his own power. Yet, although the aid was not denied him, and the castles began gradually to fall into his hands, the slothful prince dismissed the army and, at Roger's solicitation, released his son from prison, and, on the representations of his nobles, his brother Henry also[1].

The king of England did not neglect the favourable opportunity offered him by the weakness of Robert (1090), whose vassals, Walter of St. Valery and Odo of Albemarle (Aumale), or his son Stephen[2], delivered to him their castles, in which he stationed forces, for the purpose of reducing to subjection the neighbouring country as well as other castles on the right bank of the Seine. William scrupled not to enter into a compact with a wealthy citizen of Rouen, named Conan, son of Gilbert the Hairy, for the traitorous delivery of the city. Conan persuaded the majority of his fellow-citizens that their privileges and commerce would be more secure and thriving under the more powerful prince than under one who only demanded taxes, without the ability to afford them protection and free activity; that they should, therefore, admit the

[1] Ord. Vital. pp. 672. 673 sqq.

[2] Florence (a. 1090) says the former, William of Jumieges viii. 3 the latter.

forces of the king from the neighbouring town of Gournay, and make him master of the metropolis of Normandy. The preparations for this plan under the eyes of the duke, then dwelling in the castle of Rouen, were not unobserved, who thereupon lost no time in conciliating his brother Henry and his disaffected vassals, William count of Evreux, Robert of Belesme, William of Breteuil and Gilbert of L'Aigle. Henry hastened to the aid of his brother, and (Nov. 3d) Gilbert likewise led a body of men to his relief, approaching the city on the south side, while from another direction Reginald of Warenne appeared at the Cauchois gate; whereupon one portion of the citizens ran to oppose Gilbert, while another strove to open the west gate, to admit Reginald and his force. Some of the royal troops had already found entrance, and were impatiently awaiting the issue of the insurrection. While this military and civic contest was taking place, the duke with his brother Henry sallied from the castle for the purpose of succouring his friends; but seeing the tumult and confusion, and unable to distinguish friend from foe, he was persuaded to take flight and seek shelter in a suburban village; then, crossing the Seine, he proceeded to the church of St. Marie aux Champs, and there awaited the result of the contest. When Gilbert, supported by Henry and the loyal portion of the townsmen, had obtained possession of the south gate, a fearful slaughter ensued within the city, and Conan was soon captured, when all resistance was at an end. Many of the richest traders were taken by the ducal knights and cast into the castle dungeons, until they redeemed themselves with immense sums extorted from them in every possible way. From one wealthy individual, William son of Ansgar, William of Breteuil extorted three thousand pounds. On that same day Conan was conducted to the top of the tower, whence prince Henry showed him in derision the beautiful fields, the fortresses, the Seine abounding in fish and covered with shipping, the wealthy city with its castles and churches,

in short, the land he had wished to conquer. Conan, who
was well aware to what the bitter mockery tended, offered all
that he and his family possessed as an atonement. But
Henry, apprehending the dangerous lenity of his brother,
that merciless mercy[1], which was the ruin of his country,
swore by the soul of his mother, that nothing should save
the traitor, and without granting the suppliant the last spiritual consolation, he grasped him with both hands and pre-
cipitated him through the window into the depth below. The
corpse, bound to a horse's tail, was afterwards dragged through
the city and the neighbouring villages[2].

Although William's intrigues with the citizens had thus
failed, it was, nevertheless, no difficult task to continue them,
to the injury of his brother, with the vassals of the latter.
Hugh of Grentemaisnil and Richard of Curci, both barons
possessed of large estates also in England, commenced
hostilities against Robert of Belesme, in whose cause the
duke took up arms. But he failed in his endeavours to
subdue these and other rebellious vassals, who had delivered
up their castles to the king. In his state of helplessness
Robert then had recourse to his superior lord, the French
king, Philip I., who at first made some preparations for besieging one of the castles ; but certain purses of English gold
arriving soon after, the short-sighted monarch returned to
his sensual enjoyments, and suffered the castles of his feeble
vassal to fall into the hands of a stronger and most dangerous
adversary. In the beginning of the following year (1091)
king William in person embarked for Normandy, where he
commenced the siege of Eu, but soon, under the personal
mediation of the king of France, he concluded at Caen a

[1] Ralf of Caen says of him : " Misericordiam ejus immisericordem
sensit Normannia, dum eo consule per impunitatem rapinarum nec homini
parceret nec Deo licentia raptorum." Radulphi Cadom. Gesta Tancredi,
ap. Muratori SS. Rerum. Ital. T. vi.

[2] Ord. Vital. pp. 689, 690. W. Malm. p. 618.

highly advantageous treaty of peace with the duke, by which
he acquired the county of Eu, Fécamp, the country about
Gournay and Conches, the abbey of Mont St. Michel, and
Cherbourg. On the other hand, William engaged to conquer
Le Maine for Robert, and the towns that had revolted from
him, also to restore to the Normans banished from England
their fiefs in that country. Whichever of the two brothers
should die first without legitimate issue should be succeeded
by the other in all his states. This convention was sworn
to by twelve barons on the part of the king, and the like
number on that of duke Robert[1].

By some of the above-mentioned cessions the rights of the
youngest brother were grossly prejudiced, and they were opposed by him accordingly; but being forsaken by the greater
number of his former adherents, on account of his poverty,
and supported only by a few Bretons, he withdrew to Mont
St. Michel, where he was besieged by his brothers, now for
the first time acting in concert. Connected with this siege
some stories are related of the two elder brothers too graphi-
cally descriptive of times and character to be passed wholly
in silence. In a skirmish the girths of the king's saddle burst
asunder and he fell to the ground. His adversaries vigorously pressed on him, but springing up he seized the saddle
and defended himself with his sword, until his faithful knights,
Normans and Anglo-Saxons, whom he had summoned to his
aid, had with great difficulty rescued him. On his return homeward his knights jested with him on the danger to which he
had exposed himself for his saddle. " By the holy face of
Lucca[2] !" answered he, " one must be able to defend one's

[1] Sax. Chron. Flor. Wigorn. a. 1091.

[2] Upon this oath M. Pluquet has added the following notes (Rom.
de Rou, ii. p. 328). " C'était son jurement habituel, comme celui de
Guillaume-le-Conquérant était : Par la resplendor Dé (par la splendeur de
Dieu). Le savant auteur de l'Histoire des Anglo-Saxons, M. Sharon
Turner, a cru qu'il s'agissait ici de saint Luc, et a constamment traduit
cette formule, si souvent répétée dans Guillaume de Malmesbury, par ces

own! It would be shameful to lose it as long as one could defend it. The Bretons would have bragged prettily with my saddle[1]." In another encounter there, the king, mounted on a horse he had just purchased, rushed alone against a multitude of enemies, when his horse, mortally wounded by an arrow, threw him to the ground, and he was dragged by the foot a considerable distance, yet, owing to the goodness of his armour, sustained no injury. When the soldier who had unhorsed him was preparing to strike, the king exclaimed: "Stop, rascal, I am the king of England!" The soldiers around trembled at the well-known voice, and, respectfully raising him from the ground, brought him another horse. Waiting for no aid, the monarch leaped into the saddle, and casting a sharp glance at those about him, "Which of you," cried he, "struck me down?" All were silent, when a warrior stept forward, saying: "It was I: I took you for a knight, not for the king." Whereupon William with a placid coun-

mots: *By the face of St. Luke.* Voyez *Hist. of Engl. during the Middle Ages,* i. ch. v." (A Le Prevost).

" On entend ordinairement par un *Saint-Voult,* une effigie représentant la face du Christ, couronné d'épines et baignée de larmes et de sang, telle enfin qu'elle était représentée sur le voile de sainte Véronique ou Bérénice; mais le Saint-Voult de Lucques est un Christ revêtu d'habits précieux et couronné de pierreries. On en trouve une gravure dans le *Voyage de Misson en Italie,* ii. p. 321 (E. H. Langlois)."

To the above may be added Mr. Hardy's note to W. of Malmesbury (p. 492) relating to the same oath.

Per vultum de Luca.] These words have been frequently mistranslated into ' By St. Luke's face!' whereas it means 'By the face at Lucca!' Lord Lyttleton says, 'There is at Lucca in Tuscany an ancient figure of Christ, brought there miraculously, as they pretend. They call it "Il santo volto di Lucca:" it is stamped on their coins with this legend, "Sanctus vultus de Luca."' In an Italian book, called ' Il Forestiere informato delle cose di Lucca,' this legend is given in great detail. The author states that it was the work of Nicodemus of the Gospel. See further on this subject in the Rev. J. F. Tyler's interesting volume entitled ' Oaths, their Origin, Nature, and History;' London, 8vo. pp. 289-296.—T.

[1] Rom. de Rou, vv. 14670, sqq.

tenance exclaimed : " By the holy face of Lucca ! thou shalt
henceforth be mine, and, entered on my roll, shalt receive the
recompense of praiseworthy bravery[1]."

Of duke Robert's goodness of heart there is only one though
striking instance recorded. The besieged suffered from want
of water, and on Henry's representation, that the element
which was common to all ought not to be denied them, and
that a contest should not so be decided, but by the arm of
the most valiant, Robert commanded his soldiers to be less
strict, that his brother might not suffer from want of water.
When this was reported to the king, he reproached his soft-
hearted brother, saying : " Truly a fitting one art thou to
conduct a war, who allowest thy enemies an abundance of
water. How are we to overcome them, if we indulge them
with victuals and drink ?" But he gently answered : " What !
shall we allow our brother to die of thirst ? and where shall
we find another, if we lose him[2] ?" But William was made of
sterner stuff, and not to be attuned to such soft measures.
He, therefore, took care that the besieged should obtain no
further supply of water, and prince Henry found himself
compelled to surrender the fortress together with his other
possessions, on condition of a free departure. He fled to
Brittany, there to return thanks to his generous friend, the
count, and thence to France, where he found no aid. For
two years the future powerful monarch of England lived in
the Vexin, attended only by one knight, a priest, and three
esquires, and, in this school of privation. learnt the first of
kingly virtues, self-command, as well as the true wants of
men, and to know their hearts far better than in the sensual
habitations and riotous banquetings of his brothers. Some
time after, the inhabitants of Domfront placed themselves

---

[1] W. Malm. p. 491. [Wace gives a verson of the occurrence totally
different from the above as related by Malmesbury. See Rom. de Rou, vv.
14670, *sqq.*—T.]

[2] W. Malm. p. 492. Rom. de Rou, vv. 14672, *sqq.*

under his government, on condition that he would not change
their laws and customs, and that he would never surrender
his claims to Domfront to any one[1].

For his liberty Henry was less indebted to the good will
of his royal brother than to an inroad of the Scots, whose
king, Malcolm Canmore, had entered the country as early as
May. It was probably in his anger at this hostility that
William caused Eadgar Ætheling, Malcolm's brother-in-law,
to be deprived of his fiefs in Normandy, that had been granted
him by Robert, and driven from the duchy. In August
William returned to England and proceeded northwards, with
the intention of punishing the Scots. At Durham, in consequence of negotiations at Caen, he re-established the expelled bishop William. But he had not yet crossed the
border, when intelligence reached him, just before Michaelmas, that in the first of those storms, for which that year
was distinguished, nearly his whole fleet had perished. Many
also of his cavalry had died of hunger in those desert regions,
that had so recently been harried by the Scots, and not a few,
probably French, had fallen victims to the intense cold.
When, therefore, Malcolm came to meet him in the county
of Lothian with an army of Gaels better provided than his
own, inured to the northern air and soil, William was not
sorry to find a mediator in his brother Robert. For the
lands held by him in England Malcolm engaged to render
homage to William, as he had before rendered it to his
father; while William, on the other hand, promised to restore to him the twelve manors in England which he had
held under his father, and to give him twelve marks of gold
annually[2].

---

[1] Ord. Vital. pp. 696, 698. Rom. de Rou, 14708, *sqq*.

[2] Flor. Wigorn. a. 1091. The details concerning these manors (villæ)
and the payment in gold are unfortunately wanting. As there is no mention of these vills in Domesday, we ought not probably with Lingard
(ii. 2) to regard them as habitations for the kings of Scotland, while on
their way to their superior lord, as granted by king Eadgar to Kenneth of

While on this expedition, the king could not fail to observe
how cruelly the northern parts of his realm had suffered
through the previous devastations, and that even as a defence
against enemies a prosperous population is better than barren
heaths and deserts. He proceeded with a strong force to
Carlisle, and having expelled the nominal under-tenant probably of the king of Scotland, Dolfin, a son perhaps of Gospatric, the former earl of Northumberland[1], whose Anglo-
Saxon lineage but ill fitted him for the wardenship of the
marches, he restored that city, which had been laid in ruins
by the Danes two hundred years before, built a castle there,
and divided the wasted lands among a large number of
peasants who had been sent thither with their wives and
cattle[2], consisting probably, for the greater part, of those who,

Scotland. Matthew of Westminster (a. 975), on whose words alone the
supposition is founded, speaks merely of certain "mansiones in itinere,"
which were possessed by the kings of Scotland to the time of Henry II.
[With regard to this very obscure point, I confess I am by no means
adverse to the opinion of Lingard, which appears at least countenanced by
the words of Matthew of Westminster, that seem worth quoting: " Eodem quoque tempore, Ælfsius episcopus, et comes Eadulfus Kinedum,
regem Scotorum, ad regem Eadgarum conduxerunt. Quem cum per-
duxissent ad regem, multa donaria a regia largitate suscepit, inter quæ
contulit ei centum uncias auri purissimi, cum multis sericis ornamentis et
annulis, cum lapidibus præciosis. Dedit præterea eidem regi terram totam,
quæ Laudian (Lothian) patria lingua nuncupatur, hac conditione, ut annis
singulis, in festivitatibus præcipuis, quando rex et ejus successores dia-
dema portarent, venirent ad curiam, et cum cæteris regni principibus
festum cum lætitia celebrarent. Dedit insuper ei rex mansiones in itinere
plurimas, ut ipse et ejus successores ad festum venientes, ac denuo rever-
tentes, hospitari valuissent, quæ usque in tempora regis Henrici Secundi
in potestate regum Scotiæ remanserunt."—T.]

   [1] See page 150. A son of earl Gospatric, the father, or of the brother of
Dolfin of the same name, Waltheof, and also his son, Alan, are frequently
mentioned in documents relating to Cumberland and York. See Monast.
iii. pp. 583 sq. vi. p. 144.

   [2] Sax. Chron. Sim. Dunelm. a. 1092. We must here call attention to
the apparently erroneous statement of Matthew of Westminster, a. 1072,
as Palgrave, i. p. 449 receives it as true, viz. that the Conqueror (a. 1072)
had created an earl of Cumberland in the person of Ranulf of Meschines.

in consequence of the destruction of the villages around Winchester, were made houseless. Whether William intrusted this castle to the keeping of Ranulf of Meschines, whom, according to spurious traditions, the Conqueror is said to have already placed at Carlisle, or whether this appointment only took place under his successor, must remain undecided. It is, however, of importance here to notice, that William Rufus, and not his father, first made Cumberland a complete province of Norman England.

In this Normanizing, as it were, of Cumberland the English king had left unheeded the rights and claims which the Scottish monarchs had till then possessed over that county. For the adjustment of the complaints preferred by Malcolm, that prince accepted the invitation of William, after the delivery of hostages, and accompanied by Eadgar Ætheling, to attend the court at Gloucester. He arrived there on the 8th of August, but William refused to see his royal vassal until, according to the judgment of the Norman barons, he would consent to " do him right." This Malcolm refused to do, contending, that by ancient custom he was not bound to " do right" to the king of England, except on the frontiers of the two kingdoms, and by judgment of the nobility of both[1]. Without having been admitted to the presence of William,

But if we remark that Matthew represents Ranulf as earl of Carlisle, which city the Conqueror then ordered to be fortified, and that, having deprived Ranulf of Carlisle, he gave him the earldom of Chester (which is known to have been held by Hugh of Avranches), it seems highly probable that the above-mentioned chronicler has confounded the seizure of the fortress of Carlisle by William Rufus, and its fortifying under Henry I. in 1122, and the appointment of the viscount of Bayeux, Ranulf, as earl of Chester in 1122, with the events of 1072, in consequence possibly of one of those frequent clerical errors of C for L (MLXXII for MCXXII). [This year (1092) a considerable part of London was destroyed by fire. Flor. Wigorn.—T.]

[1] Sax. Chron. Flor. Wigorn. a. 1093. The precise meaning of the expression "rectitudinem facere" seems far from certain. Lingard understands by it "to answer for any alleged failure in the performance of feudal service." Allen (Vindication, p. 45) leaves it unexplained. —T.

Malcolm in indignation left the English court, collected a large army in his own kingdom, and burst into England. Scarcely, however, had he advanced as far as Alnwick when, in an ambuscade laid for him by Robert of Moubray, earl of Northumberland, he was treacherously slain by a pretended deserter, who feigned to deliver to him the keys of that castle (13th Nov. 1093). With him also perished, in the confusion which ensued, his eldest son, Edward[1]. The death of both these princes by treachery was lamented and blamed even by their adversaries. The name of Morel of Bamborough, the nephew and steward of earl Robert, and by spiritual ties connected with Malcolm, is preserved as that of the perpetrator. The good queen Margaret, the Anglo-Saxon, Malcolm's consort, died shortly after of grief, and his brother, Dufenald (Donald Bane) expelled all the English employed in the court from his kingdom. Duncan, an illegitimate son of Malcolm, who was at that time residing as a hostage at the English court, having been knighted by William and sworn to him the fealty required, was by that prince enabled to proceed to Scotland with a considerable body of Anglo-Saxons and French[2], and succeeded in expelling his uncle from that kingdom, which William might now flatter himself with having reduced to the condition of a Norman province. But those short-sighted supporters of the young king, the foreign knights who had accompanied him, excited so much discontent among the people, that they were nearly all slain by them, and Duncan himself was permitted to remain on the throne only under the promise that he would bring no more Anglo-Saxons nor Normans into the kingdom. But Duncan could not wholly detach himself from the Norman court, and in the following year was slain by the Scots, and Donald replaced on the throne[3]. A few years after, William, availing himself of a favourable juncture, sent Eadgar Æthel-

---

[1] Sax. Chron. Flor. Wigorn. a. 1093. Forduni Scoti-Chron. v. 20.
[2] Sim. Dunelm. a. 1093.　　　　[3] Ibid. a. 1094.

ing with an army into Scotland, who having expelled Donald, who was subsequently captured and died of grief in prison, caused Eadgar, a third son of Malcolm, to be crowned king in vassalage to the English monarch[1].

After these advances in the northern parts of his kingdom, the wish must naturally be excited in the mind of William to reduce the Welsh also completely under the yoke of his domination. No disquietude in the interior of the realm, no war on the other frontier ever took place of which the Welsh did not avail themselves for the purpose of assailing the Normans. During Odo's rebellion, Robert of Rhuddlan had been recalled to his march, in consequence of the inroads of the North Welsh into the earldom of Chester, under their king Griffith ap Conan. Too great precipitation, however, led the ardent warrior unarmed into the proximity of his foes, by whose missiles he perished[2]. Through his death the Welsh enjoyed some repose on their border, though internal dissensions soon arose. Llewelyn and Eineon from Dyfed had excited Jestyn ap Gurgant, lord of Morgannwg, to rise in arms against Rhys ap Tewdor, king of South Wales, and invited Robert fitz Hamon and twelve other Norman knights, by tempting promises, to their aid. King Rhys fell, by the treachery of his people, in a battle near Brecknock, and in him perished the last king of South Wales of the ancient royal stock[3]. A considerable portion of the country then fell into the hands of Norman barons, though the old princely families were neither extirpated nor expelled, and were in general much more gently treated than the Anglo-Saxons of rank. The Normans left them, both then and afterwards, always a part of their old honours and revenues, as they were indispensable to them as mediators with a people of foreign tongue. Hence they strove gradually, by marriages of Nor-

---

[1] Sim. Dunelm. a. 1097. Ethelred. col. 344.
[2] Ord. Vital. pp. 670, sq.
[3] Flor. Wigorn. a. 1093. Giraldi Cambrens. Itin. lib. i. c. 12.

mans with Welsh heiresses, and other successive acquisitions,
to bring every possession into the hands of the Norman aristocracy. Robert fitz Hamon retained the lordship of Gla-
morgan, and of the eighteen castles, thirty-six knight's fees,
and other smaller lordships belonging to the greater one, distributed some among his companions in arms[1]. The lordship
of Brecknock was conquered by Bernard of Neumarch, who,
by his marriage with Nesta, of an ancient Welsh princely
house, gained the good will of his new dependents. But his
son, Mahael, did not succeed to his father's fief, his mother,
through hatred, having denounced him to the king as unlawfully born[2]. Henry of Newburgh, son of Robert of Beaumont, conquered the district of Gower. These acquisitions
were not, however, cheaply bought; for, after the death of
Rhys, the Welsh formed a combination against their false
friends, demolished the castles that had been erected in West
Wales, and made repeated destructive inroads into the counties of Chester, Hereford, and Salop. Even in Anglesey
they succeeded in wresting from the Normans the castle and
the power over the isle. And although Hugh of Montgomery,
earl of Shrewsbury, was able to annihilate some bands of
Welsh, others still remained protected by the nature of the
country, as well as by their skill in availing themselves of it;
and king William, in the year 1095, believed it incumbent on
him personally to undertake a campaign against the Welsh[3].

Here again it was made manifest that against mountaineers
it is seldom productive of glory to contend with a large force.
After a great loss both of men and horses, the king made a
speedy retreat. The Welsh, emboldened by this success as
well as by the dissensions then prevailing among the Norman
nobility, assaulted the castle of Montgomery and put Hugh's

---

[1] For their names and acquisitions see the essay of Gryffith ap Conan
prefixed to Powell's History of Wales.

[2] Ord. Vital. p. 606. Giraldi Cambrens. Itin. lib. i. c. 2.

[3] Sax. Chron. Flor. Wigorn. a. 1094.

garrison to the sword. This outrage embittered the king yet more, who, highly incensed, again marched against the Welsh after the Michaelmas festival, but only in the same year to be twice scorned and beaten by a little band of despised ancient Britons[1]. The incursions which the barons incessantly made on the border, though less discreditable, were unattended by any lasting results, and cost much blood and treasure. Cadogan, son of Blethyn, and nearly related to king Griffith, had brought the Welsh to a state of unity, which to a defensive warfare is indispensable, and, consequently, in the year 1097, they again succeeded, after a campaign of more than four months, in repelling king William Rufus. Instead, therefore, as he had promised, of massacreing every man in Wales, he discovered that the reduction of the country must be left solely to the guerilla warfare of the border barons, and accordingly sought to stimulate the noblest and bravest of his vassals, to the conquest of that country by the grant of districts on the border. Roger of Montgomery, consequently, did homage for Powys, where he had won the castle, afterwards from his family name, called Baldwin, so also for Cardigan; and his son, Arnulf, for Dyfed, where some years after he built the castle of Pembroke, at first of trunks of trees and earth-works[2]; so Hugh of Lacy for the small district of Ewias; Eustace of St. Omer's and Ralph of Mortimer, (who, besides other rich possessions, had the castle of Wigmore; together with other knights of illustrious name) for other districts, which they were partly to defend partly to conquer[3]. Earl Hugh, after several years of exertion (a. 1098), recovered Anglesey, and exercised on his prisoners a more cruel vengeance than was usual even in those times; after the

---

[1] Sax. Chron. Flor. Wigorn. a. 1095. The latter, as also Simeon of Durham, mention two campaigns by the king against the Welsh in 1095, the Saxon Chronicle one only.

[2] Giraldi Cambrens. Itin. lib. i. c. 12.

[3] Powell, p. 117, who in this section errs in the chronology only.

amputation of their hands and feet, they were emasculated
and blinded.

But now, unforeseen, like the lightning's flash, there suddenly rose up to the Welsh a helper and avenger, yet also,
like the lightning, without further influence on the course of
events.   King Magnus III. of Norway, surnamed Barfod,
was in several ways connected with the British islands.   He
had married a noble Anglo-Saxon lady, a captive, by whom
he had the future king Sigurd, surnamed Jorsalafar, so famed
for his exploits against the infidels in Palestine and elsewhere[1].   Magnus had given a hospitable reception to many
fugitive Anglo-Saxons; the Orkneys, the Hebrides, the Isle
of Man were subject to him.   His marriage with the daughter
of an Irish king had been a source of dissension, which the
restless Norwegian had resolved on settling with the sword
in Dublin itself.   On his way thither the crews of some of his
ships landed at Anglesey, where their appearance caused the
greatest consternation among the Normans there, although the
red shield suspended on the mast ought to have convinced them
of the friendly disposition of the strangers.   The intelligence
also that Harold, the son of the last Anglo-Saxon king, was
in the Norwegian fleet[2], caused them to be regarded as more
than ordinary pirates.   The Norman earls speedily collected
their people, and, while both parties were mistrustfully regarding each other, it happened that Hugh of Montgomery,
for the purpose of checking some of his cavalry, who had
advanced too far, rode to the summit of a rock on the sea,
and in the proximity of the Norwegians ; when Magnus, in

[1] The nickname of Barfod or Barbeen (Barefoot, Bareleg) was given to
Magnus in consequence of his having adopted the costume of the Scottish
Highlanders. The mother of king Sigurd Jorsalafar was named Thora, and
therefore not likely to have been an Anglo-Saxon. See their Sagas in
Snorri. The narrative given in the text is from Orderic, p. 767, and
differs in many other points from Snorri's.—T.

[2] W. Malm. p. 506, [who considers Magnus to have intended an invasion of England.—T.]

a viking's wanton mood, aimed an arrow at the steel-cased knight, and struck him in the right eye [1]. He sank down and fell into the sea. The Norwegian insulted the fallen. "Let him run," cried he; yet was shocked on learning whom his arrow had struck, it not having been his desire to slay a friend of the English king. He therefore instantly gave assurances to Hugh the Fat, earl of Chester, of peace and protection. This event, however, was of no small importance with reference to its influence on the people there, and was, moreover, the last collision with the Northmen. The Britons long maintained themselves in Mona against the Normans [2]. Hugh of Montgomery's earldom was bought of the king, for the large sum of three thousand pounds, by his elder brother, Robert of Belesme, whose unheard-of cruelty, avarice, and pride not only sorely afflicted the Anglo-Saxons and Welsh, but rendered him an object of detestation to the Normans themselves. Wales was now more and more hemmed in by Norman castles, which the Conqueror had begun to erect of large hewn stones and after a uniform model. Of forty-nine castles mentioned in Domesday, nearly a sixth part lay in Herefordshire, viz. Wigmore, Monmouth (which afterwards gave name to the county taken from the Welsh), Clifford, Caerleon (Monmouthsh.), Ewias, etc. In Shropshire also may be noticed a similar strong permanent encampment against the Welsh, in the castles of Shrewsbury, Luvre, Stanton, and that erected by earl Roger, and named after his paternal dwelling, Montgomery, whose walls harboured a valiant garrison, which gradually took from the Welsh the

[1] According to Snorri, both Magnus and a Norwegian standing by him aimed at Hugh; the latter struck the nasal of his helmet and forced it on one side.

[2] Sax. Chron. Flor. Wigorn. a. 1098. Ord. Vital. pp. 767 sq. Chron. Mannize, h. a. Giraldi Cambrens. Itin. lib. ii. c. 7. Theodor. Monach. de Reg. Norveg. c. 31. This last mentioned errs, however, in placing the occurrence in Cornwall, as well as in mistaking Hugh the Fat for the earl shot by Magnus. Comp. also Th. Torfæi Hist. Norveg. vii. 4.

R

country that subsequently formed the district known thenceforward as Montgomeryshire.

The military reign of William Rufus was also fated to
be the starting-point, as it were, of the ecclesiastical quarrels,
which were destined long to influence the fortunes of England. The dissensions on the subject of the investiture of
bishops and abbots, provoked by Gregory VII., and carried
on with the German emperor, Henry IV., to the great scandal
of Christianity, were in England, under the mighty Conqueror
and the prudent pope, through the mediation of the expert
Lanfranc, productive of no rupture. Distance from Rome,
the complete separation, through its insular position, from
the temporal interests of Italy, and the heterogeneous culture
more Germanic than Roman, gave a character to the contest
between the crown and the church of England widely different
from that which it assumed on the Continent. It began
later, but was, by some English ecclesiastics, maintained
with perhaps greater zeal than even in Rome itself. Royalty
in England hardly ever appeared to greater disadvantage
than in this warfare, while the belligerent prelates not unfrequently contended with the abnegation of all earthly, selfish
interests and with exalted constancy. The dissensions between pope Gregory VII. and the emperor Henry IV., as
well as the election caused in 1080 by the latter of the anti-
pope Guibert, under the name of Clement III., appear to have
been unheeded in England, and to have had no influence on
the relations subsisting between that pontiff and the Conqueror. Even in the last year of his life, we find Gregory in
friendly connection with William. That after the death of
Gregory (a. 1085) a change in the king's sentiments took
place in favour of Guibert, is improbable. Of the short reign
of Victor III. all accounts of interest are wanting; but of
Urban II. (1088–1099) we know that he was acknowledged
by Normandy; while, on the other hand, Guibert was persecuted by the Italians. During the life of Lanfranc, it is

highly probable that Urban II. was at least tacitly acknowledged in England. But with the contempt in which the clergy were held by William Rufus, as well as with his avarice, it was in perfect keeping to take advantage of the division in the Church, for the sake of acknowledging neither of the popes, and, under pretext of that dissension, to plunder it without restraint. The filling of the vacant bishoprics and abbacies had been long delayed, and the large produce of their revenues paid to the royal treasury. The king frequently expressed his indignation, that the crown had lost half its revenues through the Church, and we know of but two religious establishments founded anew by him, viz. St. Mary's abbey at York, and a convent of nuns at Armathwaite[1], both in the first year of his reign, while he was endeavouring to conciliate friends. Even the primacy of England, after the death of Lanfranc, was not filled up, and the revenues of his well-endowed see, which had been expended by him in the erection of some of the most considerable monuments of middle-age architecture, the cathedral church of Canterbury, the abbey of St. Alban's, and many hospitals, were now destined to supply the deficiencies caused by a most deplorable administration, unnecessary wars, and a dissolute court. Four years had passed, during which the spiritual government of England became more and more lax; no pope was acknowledged; on the contrary, it was maintained, that it was a privilege of the king of England, over that of all other kings, to acknowledge the pope or not, according as it might seem good to him[2]. No correspondence with the Roman court was permitted, no vacant ecclesiastical benefice of value filled, when the king, in the beginning of the year 1093, was seized at Gloucester with a malady that every one considered mortal. The resolve was now wrung from him to supply the vacancies in the Church. For the see of Lincoln, however, no better choice was made than of his friend and

[1] Monast. Angl. [2] Eadmer, p. 9.

R 2

chancellor, Robert Bloet. For the archbishopric the selection was less easy.

A man for his profound learning honoured by the clergy, through his humility and exemption from all pretension not unwelcome to the higher classes, through a long sojourn among them enjoying the confidence of the Normans—such a man, in short, as there seemed to be in Anselm, the celebrated abbot of Bec, appeared to William a most fitting subject for filling the vacant dignity. But he little knew the character of the Piedmontese—Anselm was a native of Aosta. —and still less the power which spiritual superiority, even when obscured by an over-valued dialectic and display of book-learning, can exercise over contemporaries. Anselm, born in 1033, was the son of Gundulfo, a Lombard of consideration, (who, having squandered all his wealth, became a monk,) and of Ermenburg, who trained up her beloved son to piety and study[1]. After his mother's death the youth was inspired with a craving after secular things, which when his father sternly strove to suppress, he forsook both father and country. He first travelled to Avranches, where Lanfranc had formerly taught, and shortly after proceeded to that distinguished man himself, at that time prior of the abbey of Bec. Fascinating in an extraordinary degree must have been the talents and character of the individual, who in a land, which at that period, like no other in all Europe, resounded with the clash of arms and warlike deeds. where to every knightly sword its conquest seemed promised, where even the dignitaries of the Church gave an example of a secular and

---

[1] See the work "De Vita S. Anselmi libri duo," by Eadmer, a monk of Canterbury, who has also given his political life in his Historia Novorum. Both are printed at the end of Gerberon's edition of Anselm's works (Paris 1675, 2nd edit. 1721. folio), the last-mentioned work was also published at London in 1624, with illustrations by John Selden. The Vita S. Anselmi by John of Salisbury. as well as what is related of Anselm by William of Malmesbury and others. is composed almost wholly of literal extracts from Eadmer's writings.

military life, which could confer no honour on the laical order and brought disgrace on their own—who, under such circumstances, was able, in those days and in that land, to create an unrivalled seat of science and piety. The young and energetic Anselm among others was smitten with the brilliancy and depth of Lanfranc and his doctrines: in his twenty-seventh year he renounced the world, entered the Benedictine order, and became a member of the community at Bec, of which he was elected prior after Lanfranc's removal to Caen, and abbot after the death of Herluin in 1078.

Not less distinguished by solid mental endowments, the scientific cultivation of which has entitled him to a high rank among the profoundest doctors of the scholastic philosophy, than by ardour and kindness of disposition, Anselm enjoyed, in a remarkable degree, the esteem and veneration of the most eminent of the laity and the clergy. His counsel was repeatedly sought on the occasion of erecting monasteries and the restoration of discipline in them. The great, whether French, Norman, or English, even the haughty, reserved Conqueror himself evinced towards him the most flattering courtesy. So also the sick, prostrate earl of Chester, Hugh the Fat, when engaged in the transformation of the monastery in that city, formerly founded by king Eadgar to the honour of St. Werburg, into a Benedictine abbey, invited him to come over to England, to which country he was no stranger, having visited it on former occasions, and to bring with him some monks from Bec, to abide in his new foundation. But the real object of the earl and of other Normans of rank was, through Anselm to put a stop to the system of Church plunder carried on by the king, and obtain his nomination to the primacy that had been for four years vacant. For a long time Anselm refused to come over; for he suspected the latter object, and sincerely wished to avoid its fulfilment. Anselm we believe, in this instance, to have been thoroughly sincere, as well as in his subsequent refusals to accept the arch-

bishopric. However erroneous the views of the Romish
court, which he defended, may appear to us, he, no doubt,
believed in their soundness, and defended them without
thrusting himself forward in their defence, or from motives of
self-interest. Anselm was one of those heroes of love and
humility which Christianity has produced in every age, and
which only the narrow views of a time sunk in selfishness, or
occupied in contemptible speculations, can mistake. How
greatly the weight of years—he was already a sexagenarian—
and a just estimation of the great difficulties which the character of the king and court opposed to all his better exertions, how far a habit of three and thirty years of successful
labour in his sacred avocation and in scientific pursuits may
have operated on him — for the ascertaining of all this
more exact details are required; but how he knew and estimated all the difficulties of his later position, may be understood from the presence of mind and firmness with which he
encountered and defied them. If we must expose the weak
point in the conduct of Anselm, it does not appear to us to
lie in an ostentatious humility before the acceptance of his
high dignity, but in his acceptance of it contrary to his own
higher views, founded on a not altogether sincere submission
to the wishes of his many friends and reverers.

It was only after a resolution of the monks of Bec, charging
him with the management of their conventual affairs at the
royal court, that Anselm was induced to cross over to England[1]. The king received him with distinction; but the

---

[1] On the 7th Sept. 1092 he was at Canterbury. The chronology, and
therefore the whole course of events, is to be ascertained only by careful
comparison of the Vita S. Anselmi with the Historia Novorum, the former
having been written by Eadmer as a supplement to the latter. Alford
therefore (Annales Eccles. Anglic. iv. p. 114) errs in referring Anselm's
letter (Epist. i. ii. c. 18.) wherein he speaks of his arrival in England in
the middle of Lent to the journey above mentioned. Eadmer previously
speaks of his earlier journeys in the time of Lanfranc : " Anglia, prout
diversitas causarum ferebat, ab eo frequentata."

abbot availed himself of an opportunity of seeing him alone to represent to him the many loudly expressed reproaches of his subjects against him [1]. Their parting seems not to have been friendly, as the affairs of the abbey of Bec were not discussed. Anselm hastened to Chester, where he found earl Hugh already recovered, and passed the following winter in the erection of the new convent. At the court held at Christmas, the nobles of the realm took into consideration the destitute condition of the Church, and unanimously adopted the extraordinary resolution, humbly to beseech the king to permit prayers to be addressed to God in the churches of England, that He would fill the king with his grace, so that after the appointment of a worthy shepherd, the Church might rise from her depressed state. William listened to this petition with displeasure, yet granted it. Anselm, in spite of his reluctance to encroach on the office of some one of the bishops, was compelled, at the entreaty of the English prelates, to draw up a form of supplication, which, after the dissolution of the court, was read in all the churches of the realm. But all this was, on the part of William, only a profane mockery both of that which is most sacred and of his people. When one of his nobles praised the abbot Anselm, as a man loving God alone, and desirous of nothing transitory, he answered sarcastically : " Nothing, except only the archbishopric of Canterbury. He will come running to me rejoicing with hands and feet, and clasp me round the neck, if I give him the faintest hope of it. But, by the holy face of Lucca, neither he nor any other shall be archbishop besides myself." Shortly after this utterance, the king, who daily abandoned himself more and more to the grossest passions, was seized with a malady which inspired him with thoughts of death and indescribable mental anguish. He now promised sincere amendment and penitence. but above all, clemency

---

[1] Vita S. Anselm. lib. u.

and justice. His bishops, as his sureties, were compelled to make this vow for him before the high altar at Gloucester. A proclamation sealed with the royal seal announced that "captives should be freed, debts forgiven, all offences against his person pardoned and for ever forgotten. Good, holy laws, such as were in the golden days of king Eadward, were anew promised to the people; offenders and oppressors of the inferior people should, without consideration of nation or rank, be punished with inflexible severity." How the well-meaning people rejoiced at the unexpected conversion, exulted in the joyous future, and thronged to the churches, to pray for the recovery of the excellent father of his country! The king was moreover induced to give a shepherd again to the bereft Church, and, contrary to the expectation of every one, he named Anselm, a choice that was confirmed by universal approbation. At this intelligence Anselm turned pale; he represented to the importunate bishops how unfitting, it would be for the abbot of a state, where he was bound by allegiance to its prince, to accept such a dignity in a foreign country: that he, an old man of sixty, who, after he had entered a cloister, had shunned all worldly concerns, and felt a true joy in that vocation, was in the highest degree unqualified for an office in which he knew not how to be useful. Even the king's entreaties failed to prevail on him. When, at William's command, all present knelt before Anselm, he himself fell on his knees before them, and prayed them to spare him that cup, declaring, at the same time, that he would rather die than yield to their prayer. When conducted to the king's bedside, he refused to receive the episcopal staff, and when the bishops endeavoured to force him to take it, he held his hand so clenched that they could only place it near him. He was dragged into the cathedral, where, notwithstanding his refusal to both king and clergy, thanks were given to the Most High for the election that had taken place. With a clearness and self-denial, which can proceed only from true humility, he continued to represent to his friends his view of their desire: "Consider, ye imprudent men," said he, "what it is ye are striving for.   England's plough is drawn by two supereminent oxen, the king and the archbishop of Canterbury, the one by secular justice and authority, the other by divine doctrine and instruction.   Of these oxen one is dead, and the other, fierce as a savage bull is yoked young to the plough ; and in place of the dead ox, ye would yoke me, an old feeble sheep, with the wild bull.   I tell you that, if ye desist not from your purpose, I, from whom some might have wool, and the milk of God's word, and lambs, shall sink under royal ferocity, and your joy shall be turned to sorrow."   The king now commanded everything that had been possessed by Lanfranc, namely, the city of Canterbury and the abbey of St. Alban's, to be transferred to Anselm, and immediately caused application to be made to duke Robert, the archbishop of Rouen, and the monks of Bec, for Anselm's discharge.   When, after a long delay, Anselm's release from his Norman connection arrived in England, the king was recovered and had relapsed into all his old vices.   The given promises were unfulfilled, the released prisoners again confined, the remitted debts again exacted, the courts served only for oppression and greedy extortion. When Gundulf, bishop of Rochester, exhorted him to live more in conformity to the will of God, he answered : " Hear, bishop, by the holy face of Lucca, the Lord shall find no good one in me for all the evil he has inflicted on me."   Such being the king's state of mind, Anselm might well expect a release from the dignity conferred on him, when he demanded that, when all the lands had been restored to the see of Canterbury, which it possessed in the time of Lanfranc, a judicial inquiry and decision should take place, with regard to others, of which it had been deprived at an earlier period.   He, moreover, informed the king that he had already acknowledged pope Urban, and should ever yield him obedience, although still unacknowledged by William.   On both these points he desired a declaration from the king, who, after having summoned his council together, informed him that all the lands possessed by the Church under Lanfranc should, as before said, be restored to it ; but, with regard to those which it did not possess under him, no agreement could then be made ; but that both this and other matters should soon be settled.   The king afterwards strove to induce Anselm to confirm to his barons many lands that he had granted them after the death of Lanfranc [1], though in this instance he was compelled to yield ; and Anselm, in an assembly of the nobles at Winchester, and, after the example of his predecessor, became, according to usage, the king's vassal, and was directed to take possession of the archbishopric as it was in the time of Lanfranc (25th Sept.).   When he at length reached Canterbury, his solemn reception was disturbed by the arrival of Ranulf Flambard, who, in the king's name, commenced a process regarding certain claims of the Church; and not until some months had passed was Anselm, in the presence of all the bishops of the realm at Canterbury, consecrated as archbishop (4th Dec.). He afterwards proceeded to the royal court, where he was joyfully received.   As the king, through his efforts to obtain possession of Normandy, was in a state of the greatest pecuniary embarrassment, the new archbishop, following the counsel of his friends, offered him a present of five hundred pounds of silver.   The king required the double of that sum, but Anselm, who " would not bargain for the king's favour as for a horse or an ass," refused it, gave the intended present to the poor, and thereby exasperated the king to the utmost, who, when too late, declared his willingness to accept it.

If in Anselm we have hitherto revered the pious, learned, and modest monk, and if the worth of such a man is rendered the more prominent by contrast with a tyrant brutal almost

<hr>

[1] Epist. lib. iii. c. 24. Anselm's letters are of less value than almost any other similar authority, Eadmer having evidently most carefully availed himself of them. Eadmer, pp. 15, sqq.

to frenzy, it greatly increases our reverence to see him, under
the most trying self-denial, faithful to his duty, indefatigably,
heroically administering the charge he had undertaken, while
a king and son of a king, who had dispossessed his elder brother
of a throne, was reckless of every princely duty and of every
promise. While Anselm, in every direction, with the approval
and advice of the elder clergy of England, was defending the
rights of his Church, he set his colleagues an example of
resistance to the pervading luxury and effeminacy of the
court. We may well imagine that an acute thinker and calm
observer, like Anselm, would not have regarded the long hair
of the courtiers, or their long-beaked shoes, at that time in
vogue, as soul-destructive[1], but he saw how these manners, in
the new generation, engendered among the sons of the heroes
of the Conquest an effeminate, trifling disposition, which but
too clearly manifested itself in the increasing passion for
show. With the object of repressing transgressions of deeper
die, especially one of the deepest, which unhappily prevailed
among the Normans in England, he applied to the king, before
his departure for Normandy (1094 Feb.) for the assembling of
a synod, but who harshly refused not only this request, but
also one relative to the filling of the vacant abbacies[2].

The present temper of the king, as well as his journey to
Normandy, must necessarily cause a suspension of all applica-
tions to him on the subject of obtaining the pall for the new
primate. Scarcely, however, at the close of the year, had

[1] See W. Malm. p. 498, and *note.*—T.

[2] W. Malm. p. 498. " Enerves, emolliti, quod nati fuerant inviti mane-
bant; expugnatores alienæ pudicitiæ, prodigi suæ. Sequebantur curiam
effœminatorum manus et ganearum greges." Eadmer. p. 24. " Nefandis-
simum Sodomæ scelus, (ut illicita consanguineorum connubia, et alia
multa rerum detestandarum facinorosa negotia taceam,) scelus, inquam,
Sodomæ noviter in hac terra divulgatum jam plurimum pullulavit, multosque sua immanitate fœdavit. Cui fateor nisi districtius a te prodiens
sententia judicii, et ecclesiasticæ vigor disciplinæ celerius obviet, tota terra
non multo post Sodoma fiet." The above are Anselm's words to the
king. - T.

William returned to England, when Anselm applied to him
for permission to solicit the pontiff, namely Urban, for his
pall, to whom, as the king well knew, he had done homage
before his call to England. But William maintained that
neither his father nor himself had allowed any one of their
bishops to choose a pope for himself; that such an attempt
would be tantamount to endeavouring to deprive him of his
crown. It was only in the preceding year that the king had
taken from Herbert of Losinga the episcopal staff, that he had
bought of him for a thousand pounds of silver, because he was
desirous of proceeding to Rome, for the purpose of getting
absolution from the pope for the crime of simony[1].

That England continued for nearly ten years without acknowledging any pope, is a circumstance that deserves some
consideration, though it will no more be found that England
was a gainer by this separation from the universal regimen,
than that the motives for such a procedure are to be sought
for in a purer view of Christianity operating, though indirectly,
on the court. The best excuse for the delay in this matter can
be sought for only in the distance from Rome, and the lack
thence arising of trustworthy accounts respecting the legitimate
possessor of the ring of the fisherman. The king, however,
could not avoid submitting the demands of Anselm to the court
which he summoned to assemble at Rockingham[2] (March
1095). On this occasion William displayed even more than
his usual violence, being excited by Flambard, who had hoped
to obtain the archbishopric for himself. The other bishops

[1] Sax. Chron. a. 1094. More fully in Simeon, h. a. Florence makes
no mention of the taking away of the staff by the king, but says (also
Malmesbury p. 517,) that Herbert resigned it at Rome, and that it was
there restored to him.—T.

[2] Eadmer, p. 26. Anselm, Epist. lib. iii. 35, speaks without doubt of
the same place, although the printed text reads Notingeham. Wilkins,
Concil. t. i., Lingard and others place the assembly at Nottingham in
1094; but from Eadmer's narrative it clearly follows that it was not held
until after the king's return from France. The day of his return (29th
Nov. 1094) are given both by the Saxon Chronicle and Florence.

declared that Anselm could not be deposed, but that at the
king's command they were ready to renounce all obedience
to and friendly intercourse with him. On this compliance
of a set of dastardly priests and courtiers, the king resolved
to withdraw from Anselm his protection and confidence, and
to treat him no longer as archbishop or his spiritual father.
The lay nobles, at whose head stood the most excellent and
eminent man of the English court, Robert count of Meulan[1],
acted far more honourably: they declared, that while they
lived they would not abandon Anselm, their archbishop, the
director of all religious concerns, as he had rendered himself
guilty of no crime. It was Anselm's wish to be relieved from
the burthen of his office, but the principal laity mediated a
delay of any determination on either side. The archbishop
then received instructions not to leave the county of Kent,
ostensibly for the purpose of keeping watch, that the coast
might not be infested by enemies roaming about the sea[2].
The king availed himself of this interval partly in annoying
the archbishop, by driving some of his faithful clergy from
England, and partly in awaiting the return of two of his
chaplains, William of Warlewast and Girard, whom in the
preceding year he had secretly sent to Rome for the purpose
of ascertaining the state of papal affairs and of prevailing on
the pope to send to him the pall for the archbishop of Canterbury, without mention of his name, so that there might be
no restriction on any arbitrary measure he might resolve on.
Urban acquiesced in this plan, and sent over Walter, bishop
of Albano, to England with the desired pall. The legate
rode unnoticed through Canterbury to the king, who was
holding a court at Windsor, and who was desirous of surpris-
ing Anselm into an acceptance of the pall from his hands.
But the primate proved himself a stouter champion for the

---

[1] Eadmer, p. 30, names, as mouthpiece of the "principes, Robertus
quidam, ipsi regi valde familiaris." That it was the above-mentioned
count whom we again meet with under William's successor, is hardly to
be doubted. [2] Epist. lib. iii. 35, 37.

rights of the Church than the pope, and on his refusal to receive the pall from the secular power, the expedient was adopted, that the legate should lay it on the high altar at Canterbury, and Anselm take it thence, as it were, from the hands of St. Peter[1].

By this act the Church for some time seemed restored to its old order. Some of the bishops, who had previously spoken against Anselm, stricken with remorse, caused themselves to be absolved by him ; and the king bestowed the sees of Worcester and Hereford, rendered vacant by the death of Wulfstan and Robert, on his chaplain before mentioned, Girard, and Samson, and his episcopal staff was restored to Herbert of Thetford. The bishops of Wales and Ireland acknowledged Anselm as their primate, and the papal legate made himself so beloved, that he collected an abundant Peter-pence, such as Rome had not for a length of time received from England[2].

Anselm now found confirmed, what he had long foreseen, that with the means he possessed, calm wisdom, profound scientific knowledge, and purity of life, the struggle with the tyrant was too unequal. A dispute respecting the alleged insufficient equipment, both as to arms and provisions, of the men supplied by the archbishop for an expedition against the Welsh, brought Anselm's resolve to maturity, to leave England at any cost, and go to the pope, with the object of enlightening the pontiff on the real state of things, of which he had received an account not over faithful from the king's agents, and, at the same time, of obtaining peace and quiet for himself, and for his Church protection against plunder, blasphemy, and every kind of outrage. It was only by the greatest firmness that Anselm obtained permission for his journey to Rome from the king (1097. 15th Oct.), who immediately seized on the revenues of the archbishopric. In obedience to the mandate of Him whom he confessed, he

<hr>

[1] Eadmer, p. 34.   [2] Sax. Chron. a. 1095.

offered to the king, at his departure, as primate of the realm, God's and his own blessing. William received him with surprise, yet declined not his benediction ; but, nevertheless, caused the venerable man to be persecuted to the last moment of his stay in England. Two monks only, Baldwin, who afterwards followed him in the primacy, and Eadmer, his faithful biographer [1], accompanied him in his voluntary exile. On the Continent Anselm's journey was a triumphal procession; both clergy and laity rejoicing, and with flags waving received the revered philosopher and divine, now hallowed by an unheard-of martyrdom. He was obliged to avoid Normandy. From Witsand he proceeded to the abbey of St. Bertin (St. Omer's), where he again enjoyed the exhilarating feeling of being able to serve only the Lord. Odo, the pious duke of Burgundy, with Hugh, archbishop of Lyons, then engaged, at the instance of St. Robert, in founding the abbey of Citeaux, received him with the greatest joy. He visited the monks of Cluny and sojourned at Lyons, until a message from the pope summoned him to Rome. The favourable reception which he found there, as well as from Roger duke of Apulia, proves that king William Rufus, even in those parts, notwithstanding new deputations to Urban, was held in just estimation. Anselm employed his leisure in completing some theological and philosophical works. He also assisted at the council of Bari (1st Oct. 1098), where he had the happiness of acting a distinguished part in the discussions on a point at that time of vital importance, whether the Holy Ghost proceeded solely from the Father. In a council held shortly after at Rome (25th April 1099) the affairs of the English Church were discussed, and a general anathema was pronounced on those laymen who conferred or received ecclesiastical investitures, as well as on those who for ecclesiastical offices became

---

[1] " Eramus quippe tres monachi...... dominus videlicet et pater Anselmus, Baldvinus, et ego qui hæc scribo, frater Eadmerus." Eadmer, p. 45.—T.

the vassals of laymen, and on others offending against the views of the Church. Urban, however, did not deem it advisable to accuse king William of these transgressions, but appears rather to have restrained the zealous partisans of the archbishop from the adoption of any violent measures. Anselm, too, himself, on his knees, implored the council not to pass a sentence of excommunication against the king. Some months after, Urban died, and shortly after the accession of Paschal to the papal chair, accounts arrived of the death of William, which caused Anselm to return to England[1].

During these dissensions, the king was engaged in many more weighty secular affairs, chiefly in consequence of his incessant craving after the possession of Normandy and the neighbouring provinces. Notwithstanding his compact with duke Robert, he strove to gain over the vassals of Normandy, and, by means of great presents and promises, succeeded in seducing from his allegiance William count of Eu[2]. Robert now found himself compelled to declare to the king, that he neither could nor would abide by so partial and ill-observed a compact. On this occasion William deemed it expedient to cross over to Normandy and have a conference with his brother, but which ended in no concord. The sureties of the compact were then summoned to decide with reference to its violation, and their decision was against William, who, highly exasperated, refused to submit to it; but proceeding to Eu, he thence directed the intrigues of the Norman nobles against his brother, and captured the castle of Bures. Duke Robert had in the meantime obtained the support of the French king Philip, with which, by stratagem, he took the castle of Argences, though defended by Roger of Poitou with seven hundred knights; and although king Philip, bribed by English gold[3], soon returned to his own dominions, Robert,

---

[1] Eadmer, pp. 15 sqq. Ord. Vital. pp. 682, 773. Anselmi Epist.

[2] Flor. Wigorn. a. 1093.

[3] Robert de Monte, a. 1091. W. of Malmesbury, the Norman writers,

nevertheless, succeeded in taking the castle of La Houlme defended by William Peverel. William had ordered twenty thousand foot soldiers from England, but when they were on the point of embarking, he caused the ten shillings that had been given to each for his subsistence to be taken away, through his tool, Ranulf Flambard, and all of them to be sent home. The money thus obtained he employed in buying off the French, who threatened Eu with a siege, and had already advanced as far as Longuevile[1]. Hugh earl of Chester, was then despatched to fetch prince Henry from Domfront, who accompanied him, but, instead of coming to Eu, they both crossed over to Southampton, and celebrated the Christmas festival at London. William, too, not feeling at ease in his position, returned, and sent prince Henry to prosecute the war against his brother.

More dangerous for William than the disgraceful contest with his brother, or his rash quarrel with Anselm, was a rebellion now raised by some of his most considerable barons. Robert, son of Roger of Molbray, earl of Northumberland, was one of the most valiant but proudest knights, harsh towards his dependents, cold and reserved towards his associates, arrogant to his superiors. After the death of his uncle, Geoffrey bishop of Coutances, William had confirmed to him two hundred and eighty villages, which that prelate, chiefly on account of his military services, had received from the Conqueror[2]. Robert, probably because the transactions with Scotland after the death of Malcolm, were not to his satisfaction, entered into a conspiracy against the king's crown and life with the count of Eu, who but a short time before had passed over to the side of William. Their pro-

and even Orderic himself, make no mention of this campaign, and appear to confound it with the earlier. The last-mentioned is very confused in the chronology of the years 1091–1095.

[1] Near Vernon in Normandy, not Luneville, as Ingram supposes.

[2] Ord. Vital. pp. 523, 703. These possessions must have lain for the most part in the shires of England not included in Domesday.

fessed object was to place on the throne Stephen of Albemarle, a cousin of the king, who had previously been a faithful adherent to him[1]. Stephen was the son of a half-sister
of the Conqueror, married to Odo count of Champagne, to
whom she had borne this count Stephen[2], Judith, the consort
of the unfortunate earl Waltheof, and William of Alderi,
the king's steward or sewer[3]. The paternal uncle of Stephen
and many other barons of consideration joined in the conspiracy. The cause of its premature outbreak was the refusal of earl Robert to appear before the king's court at
Windsor, without the delivery of hostages or other pledge
for his security, to answer a charge against himself and his
nephew, Morel, of having detained and plundered four Norwegian merchantmen[4]. William thereupon assembled an
army, and had already nearly reached the county of his refractory vassal, when Gilbert of Tonbridge fell at his feet,
praying him not to enter the forest, where there was an
ambush stationed, and to pardon him, an accomplice in the
conspiracy[5]. William then laid siege to Tynemouth, which
the brother of earl Robert bravely held out against him for
two months. Earl Robert himself was shut up in Bamborough castle, opposite to which the king had caused a
fortress to be constructed, to which he gave the appropriate
name of Malveisin (the bad neighbour). The king's perseverance was overcome by the obstinacy of the besieged; but
while he was gone on an expedition against the Welsh,

---

[1] Ord. Vital. p. 681, a. 1089.

[2] For this relationship see W. Gemmet. lib. viii. c. 3. Orderic (p. 522)
calls the mother "filiam Roberti ducis;" W. Gemmet. (lib. viii. c. 37)
"Comitissa de Albemarla, soror uterina Wilhelmi regis Anglorum." This
is correct; she was full sister of bishop Odo; her name seems to have
been Adeliza.

[3] Sax. Chron. Flor. Wigorn. a. 1096. Ingram renders modrie, *maternal
aunt* (though here in the Chronicle used erroneously for *paternal aunt*) by
step-mother; thus making Odo of Champagne the king's son-in-law.

[4] "Quatuor naves magnae, quas canardos vocant." Ord. Vital. p.703.—T.

[5] Ord. Vital. p. 703.

Robert was tempted to leave his strong-hold, the garrison of
Newcastle having falsely promised that they would open their
gates to him. Issuing then from Bamborough in the dead of
the night, accompanied by only thirty horsemen, he was immediately followed by the garrison of Malveisin, and on
reaching Newcastle found the gates closed. Finding himself
thus deceived, the earl fled to the monastery of St. Oswine
at Tynemouth, that had been richly endowed by him, in which
he defended himself for six days, when he received a severe
wound in the leg, and fell into the hands of his enemies.
William ordered him to be led before the walls of Bamborough, which was still stoutly defended by Matilda, the
young wife of Robert, and Morel. Being invited to a parley,
the countess saw her consort in bonds with an executioner
at his side ready to put out his eyes, if the castle were not
forthwith surrendered. This threat had the desired effect.
Morel purchased his life by revealing to the king all the
details of the conspiracy; he was, nevertheless, banished,
and died abroad in penury and detestation. Earl Robert
languished for thirty years a captive at Windsor; but his
countess, having procured a papal dispensation, became the
wife of Nigel of Albini (Aubigni), whom she afterwards faithlessly abandoned. When the crisis was over, many of the
most eminent barons were betrayed to the king as accomplices in the plot. The count of Eu denied his guilt, but
being vanquished in judicial combat by Geoffrey Bainard,
though chiefly, perhaps, because he had Hugh earl of Chester
for an enemy, was sentenced to the loss of his eyes and mutilation[1]. The royal sewer, William of Alderi, who was likewise the king's relation and godfather, after having confessed
to bishop Osmund and been scourged in all the churches of
Salisbury, underwent the ignominious death of hanging,
although he strongly protested his innocence of the conspiracy

[1] Sax. Chron. Flor. Wigorn. a. 1095. 1096. Ord. Vital. p. 704. W.
Malm. p. 501. " Willehmus de Ou cæcatus et extesticulatus est."

to the last[1]. Roger of Lacy was declared to have forfeited
his large estates to the benefit of his brother Hugh, and
banished[2]. The king's uncle, the aged Odo of Champagne,
and Philip, son of Roger earl of Shrewsbury, were thrown
into prison[3]. Even Hugh earl of Shrewsbury could not clear
himself of the charge of complicity; but, like others whom
William, on account of their connections in Normandy,
deemed it prudent to treat with lenity, was permitted to redeem himself with a large sum of money[1]. With greater
moderation than we are accustomed to find in William, he
confirmed the donations made by Robert of Molbray to pious
foundations[5].

An unlooked-for and, we may be allowed to say, unmerited,
turn of fortune brought William from the brink of ruin to
the consummation of the wish for which he had, during the
whole term of his rule, striven with every exertion, every injustice, every prodigality to attain. With every year duke
Robert found himself deprived of a portion of his paternal
inheritance. Domfront, his strongest town, was in the possession of prince Henry, who from that fortress had extended
his territory by dint of arms, and gained many adherents
among Robert's followers. King William also held more
than twenty castles in Normandy, and the most influential
nobles were bound to him, partly by reason of possessions
held by them in England, partly by other obligations. Robert
was, in fact, deprived of all power, of the greater part of his
revenues, and, in consequence of the weakness of his character, of all means and prospect of ever recovering them.
At this juncture the trump of the holy war resounded on a
sudden from Clermont, and among the many whom unpropitious circumstances impelled to obey the inspiring call was
duke Robert. What still remained to him of Normandy he

---

[1] Flor. Wigorn. a. 1096.   [2] Ord. Vital. p. 704.
[3] Flor. Wigorn. a. 1096.   [4] Ord. Vital. p. 704.
            [5] Monast. Anglic. iii. p. 313.

transferred, for five years, to his brother William, in consideration of a loan of ten thousand marks of silver[1]. The raising of this money was in all haste recommended to the chief persons of England. Bishops and other Church dignitaries were compelled to break up the church plate, and melt it for coining money. Barons plundered their vassals and peasantry, to take gold and silver to the king. In September William embarked for Normandy, made peace with his brother, and paid him the sum required of 6666½ pounds of silver, in consideration of a pledge of tenfold greater value[2].

This possession was employed by William in several attempts to secure and extend the acquisitions of his house in France. In the following years we find him occupied with the French and Bretons, and also with the Flemings[3], though of these disputes and transactions few accounts or traces are extant. The count of Flanders, Robert II., in the year 1093, came to a conference with William at Dover, the object of which was probably the restoration of the old feudal relations, according to which the counts of Flanders received for military service a yearly revenue from England of three hundred marks of silver, which settlement having been revoked, in consequence of the hostilities of count Robert the Frisian, was renewed with his son by king William, in consideration of their relationship[4]. The Bretons, under count Alan Fergant, who was related to duke Robert, probably assisted the king, as they previously had his brother[5], in his war with the county of Le Maine. Duke Robert had laid claim to Le Maine, though founded merely on his betrothal to the second daughter of count Hugh, but who died before marriage[6]. This frivolous pretension was opposed by Hélie, the son of John of la Flèche,

[1] Ord. Vital. pp. 723, 724.

[2] Sax. Chron. Flor. Wigorn. a. 1096. Ord. Vital. pp. 713, 764. W. Malm. p. 500. Al. Bev. p. 142. W. Hemingb. p. 30. ed. E. H. S.

[3] Ord. Vital. p. 769.   [4] Eadmer, p. 19. W. Malm. p. 573.

Daru, Histoire de la Bretagne, T. i.   [6] See page 55.

who had married Paula, the third or youngest daughter of
Hugh, and sister of Heribert, the last count, and who, subsequently to the year 1090, had bought from the son of the
eldest, by Azo marquis of Liguria, his claims on Le Maino
for ten thousand shillings[1]. Notwithstanding the support of
Fulk count of Anjou, Robert had never been able to keep
possession of Le Maine; and William either would not or
could not proceed more vigorously, yet he for some months
harboured Hoel, the bishop of Le Mans, who had fled to
England, in consequence of some dissensions at home. But
when Hélie, previously to the departure of duke Robert, came
to William, for the purpose of obtaining from him an assurance
of peace during his intended absence on the crusade, he refused it scornfully. saying: Hélie might go whithersoever he
would: he would not fight against crusaders, but would recover the province taken from his father with a hundred
thousand lances, swords, and innumerable engines; and would
soon settle matters with the cowherds of Le Maine[2]. Notwithstanding these and similar vaunts, and although the
Manceaux had recently put to flight Robert of Belesme, from
his grandfather likewise surnamed Talevas, who had erected
castles in their territory, and had captured other Normans
of consideration, William was unable immediately to take the
field against Le Maine[3]. Not until February 1098, at the
instigation of Robert of Belesme, was he induced to proceed
against Hélie, who at Dangeuil had erected a castle against
him. But the severity of the season came to the aid of the
Manceaux, and the king was compelled to retire to Rouen,
and for the moment content himself with reinforcing his
vassals and soldiers and other means for the security of his
castles. Hélie, however, fell shortly after into his hands. He

[1] Acta Episcoporum Cenom. ap. Mabillon. Vet. Anal. iii. pp. 290 299.
[2] Ord. Vital. p. 769.
[3] " Differens per biennium." Ord. Vital. p. 770. Only under the successor of bishop Hoel, who died in July 1097.

had entered a wood accompanied by only seven knights, and was there made prisoner by Robert Talevas. He was conducted to Rouen, where the king commanded that he should be treated as a knight, but detained him as a prisoner. William then convoked and deliberated with the barons of Normandy, and as the proposed undertaking met with their approval, he proceeded with a numerous force against Le Mans. But that city was so stoutly defended by the inhabitants under the command of Fulk IV. surnamed Rechin (Morose), count of Anjou, and his valiant son, Geoffroy, surnamed Martel, that William returned to Rouen, but through the mediation of Hildebert, the bishop of Le Mans, obtained the surrender of the city, in consideration of the liberation of Hélie, who was apprehensive lest Fulk might enter into some compact with William to his detriment. Hélie now endeavoured by pliancy to the conqueror to recover a portion of what he had lost, and offered to become his vassal. The king was inclined to grant his request, but Robert count of Meulan, who ever appears as a far-sighted counsellor of his sovereign[1], dissuaded him from so hazardous a step. Thereupon Hélie could not refrain from declaring that, as he was so despised, he would strive in every way to recover his inheritance. "Go now," answered William, "do what thou canst; if thou overcomest me, thou shalt not be punished for it[2]." Le Mans was then committed to a very strong garrison, under the command of William count of Evreux, Gilbert of L'Aigle, and other warriors, who soon, by their oppressions and severity caused the citizens doubly to regret the loss of their

---

[1] Ord. Vital. p. 773. Comp. Eadmer, pp. 20–40. See also p. 218.

[2] Ord. Vital. p. 773. [What Malmesbury (p. 503) reports as William's words is at least highly characteristic: on Hélie saying: "Fortuitu me cepisti, sed si possem evadere, novi quid facerem," he answered: "Tu, nebulo! tu, quid faceres? Discede, abi, fuge! concedo tibi ut facias quicquid poteris: et, per vultum de Luca' nihil, si me viceris, pro hac venia tecum paciscar."—T.]

former lords. In the following year (1099) Hélie succeeded
in raising a considerable force, in defeating his enemies in
Le Maine, and in driving them into the fortress of Le Mans,
the inhabitants of which town had joyfully joined his followers. But the Normans one evening, taking advantage of
a strong gale, set fire to the houses lying nearest to them,
which communicating itself to others, the greater part of the
city was soon a prey to the flames. The besieging engines
raised by Hélie produced no effect, and the inhabitants, who
had already sustained great damage and were threatened with
still greater calamity, lost all courage. Soon, too, intelligence
was brought, that William, while hunting in the New Forest,
had, on receiving information by a messenger of what had
taken place at Le Mans, instantly ridden to the sea-shore,
and in a presumptuous vaunt that a king could not be drowned,
cast himself into a miserable vessel he found lying there, crossed
over, and, notwithstanding the tempestuous weather, arrived
safe at Touques, and was the first to announce his arrival to
the astonished Normans[1]. Hélie now deemed it advisable
to abandon the unfortunate city, and not expose himself and
people to the anger of the king. The inhabitants had been so
cruelly oppressed, that only the king's arrival could check the
most unbridled licentiousness and prevent their total destruction. The tower of the cathedral, which had been used
to good purpose by the citizens during the struggle, he ordered
to be demolished, and took with him to England the refractory bishop Hildebert[2], whom he even required to clear himself from the suspicion of treason by the ordeal of hot iron[3].
Of the warfare of this time some idea may be formed from the

[1] Ord. Vital. p. 775. W. Malm. p. 502.

[2] Acta Episcop. Cenom. Sax. Chron. a. 1099, the Rom. de Rou is very
circumstantial though inaccurate on this war with Le Maine; Wace, and
Malmesbury, who often agrees with him, make the capture of Hélie only
after the conquest of Le Mans.

[3] Ivonis Carnot. Ep. 74, Hildebert. Ep. lib. ii. 8.

circumstance, that it was found impracticable to take all Hélie's castles, and that the king himself was obliged to raise the siege of Mayet[1], derided by the besieged and almost deserted by his army[2].

Equally fruitless, yet, on account of the higher interests involved in them, worthy of some notice, were the wars which William, as mortgagee of Normandy, commenced with the king of France. The demand made by the Conqueror in the last year of his life for the restoration of the Vexin, which had been taken from him, during his youth, by king Henry, had not been persevered in by duke Robert; but William did not delay reclaiming not only that province, but also the towns, of Pontoise, Chaumont, and Mantes, and meeting with a refusal from Philip (1097) forthwith assembled an army from his dominions on both sides of the Channel. Of the French, many who held fiefs also in Normandy did not dare to oppose him, while others who were imprisoned were induced to enter the English service, and many were bought by English gold. The French prince Lewis, afterwards king Lewis VI., frequently fought valiantly and successfully against the English[3]; but William, with William VIII. duke of

---

[1] A castle in the arrondissement of La Flèche. M. Le Prevost, note to Rom. de Rou, v. 15027.—T.

[2] The following particulars of this siege are interesting. They are from Orderic, translated by M. Le Prevost (Rom. de Rou, ii. p. 336): "Le roi après avoir accordé aux assiégés une espèce de trève de Dieu, depuis le samedi jusqu'au lundi, voyant qu'ils avaient passé ce temps à palissader leurs murailles, pour amortir les coups qu'on voudrait leur porter, chercha à combler les fossés avec des fascines; mais on réussit toujours à s'en débarrasser par le moyen du feu. Au moment où il se désespérait du peu de succès de ses mesures, une pierre lancée des remparts vient fracasser la tête d'un guerrier placé près de lui. Alors les assiégés s'écrièrent: 'Voila de la viande fraiche pour le roi; qu'on la porte à la cuisine, et qu'on l'apprête pour son souper.' Guillaume découragé renonça au siége, fit aux vignes, aux vergers et aux maisons une guerre d'extirpation, et s'en revint triomphant, dit l'historien au Mans, où il licencia son armée. Ces événemens se passèrent dans le mois de juillet." T.

[3] Suger Vita Ludovici Grossi, c. i. Historiæ Franciæ Fragm. ap. Bouquet, xii. p. 5.

Guienne and count of Poitiers, with whom he had formed an
alliance, advanced slowly but surely, and was not till the
following year (1098), probably alarmed by the defection of
Nivard of Septeuil, to be prevailed on to accede to a truce[1].
William was on the eve of gaining an extension of influence
as far as the banks of the Garonne, in consequence of the
intention of the duke above-mentioned to pledge to him his
rich dominions and proceed to the Holy Land[2]. In France
the apprehension prevailed that William, whose ambition
knew no bounds, was aiming at the French crown, and
collecting suffrages and support in case of the death of Lewis,
the only legitimate heir of Philip, whose sons by Bertrade, the
seduced countess of Anjou, could not be acknowledged as such[3].

The ever more and more complicated plans, the incessant
striving after aggrandizement, the important successes of king
William were destined to a sudden end. The chase in those
days was followed so passionately, that it not unfrequently
exacted a bloody sacrifice. In the New Forest, which had
been enlarged by the Conqueror with such glaring cruelty
towards the numerous inhabitants of those parts, Richard, an
elder brother of William Rufus, and, shortly after, a son of
duke Robert, named also Richard, had already fallen. On
the 2nd August 1100 the king rode into the forest to hunt,
his attendants were gradually dispersed, and about sunset he
was found lying dead on the earth and pierced with an arrow.
Many authorities concur in stating, that Walter Tirel, a
French knight, to whom William was much attached, had,
with the intention of striking a boar that rushed past them,
inflicted the fatal wound, with an arrow given him by
the king himself, as being the better marksman. His in-
stantaneous flight to France, and a pilgrimage to the holy
grave, undertaken by him at a later period certainly countenance this narrative[4]. Yet Tirel, whom we find mentioned

[1] Ivon. Carnot. Ep. 71. Ord. Vital. p. 767.
[2] Ord. Vital. p. 780.   [3] Suger, lib. i.
[4] Ord. Vital. p. 782. W. Malm. p. 509. Flor. Wigorn. a. 1100. Hugo

as a venerator of Anselm[1], declared to Suger, the celebrated abbot of St. Denys, and offered to confirm it on oath, that the rumour was false, and that he had not even entered the forest on that day[2]. But who can say that it was not an Anglo-Saxon arrow that pierced the tyrant? or that one of so many that he had injured, stimulated possibly by a higher direction, was not the perpetrator? The warnings given to the king by Robert fitz Hamon, in consequence of the counsel of a monk, that he should not go to the chase on that day, and the prophecy imparted to prince Henry, declaring his speedy accession to the throne, together with the complete desertion of his attendants, greatly strengthen the suspicion of a premeditated plan[3]. But there is also another story worthy of notice : that the king, in stooping to take up an arrow lying on the ground, stumbled, and thus forced the arrow into his breast. This belief appears to have been very current in in England shortly after the king's death[4], though that implicating Walter Tirel found most favour with the multitude. At a later period it was also said, that it was not Tirel, but

Floriac. De Modernis Francorum Regibus, xii. p. 798. Petri Blesens. Cont. Huntend. p. 378. W. Gemmet. lib. vii. c. 9. Gaimar entertains greater suspicion against Tirel.

[1] Eadmer, Vita Anselmi, p. 6.

[2] Suger, lib. i. Joh. Salisbur. Vita Anselmi, c. 12. Hist. Franciæ Fragm. ap. Bouquet, xii. p. 5. Walter Tirel was one of ten children that Fulco of Guarlemville, dean of Evreux, had with the beautiful Orielde sprung from a distinguished race. Ord. Vital. p. 574. Tirel was lord of Poix in Picardy. The warriors of Poix were at Hastings, Rom. de Rou, v. 12793.

[3] Sax. Chron. a. 1100 may be cited for this view of the case, which relates that the king was shot while at the chase by an arrow from one of his own people, without any allusion to an accident : so likewise Acta Episc. Cenom.

[4] Eadmer (Hist. Nov. p. 54.) says : " plures affirmant." Wace (vv. 15180, sqq.) also mentions this belief :

[Plusors dient k'il tresbucha,
En sa cote (robe) s'empéescha,
E la saete (flècke) trestorna,
Et b acier el rei cola, (coula vers le roi.) T.]

Ralf of Aix, to whom William, against the counsel of the abbot of Dunstable, handed five arrows, with one of which he shot him [1].

Never did a ruler die less regretted than William Rufus, although still young, being little above forty, not a usurper, bold, and successful in his undertakings. He was never married, and besides the crafty and officious tools of his power, was surrounded only by a few Normans of quality and harlots. In his last struggle with the clergy, the most shameless rapacity is especially prominent, and so glaring, that, notwithstanding some exaggerations and errors that may be pointed out in the chronicles, he still appears in the same light [2]. Effeminacy, drunkenness, gluttony, dissoluteness, and unnatural crimes, were the distinguishing characteristics of his court [3]. He was himself an example of incontinence. Kindness towards valiant knights, even the conquered, and trust in a knightly word, as is related of him, are less proofs of good feeling than of a knowledge of the character of his time. The warlike talents displayed by him in his youth, in which bodily strength and valour founded on it were chiefly conspicuous, have been over-valued; and at a later period, his successes were usually obtained without his personal co-operation, while he shone chiefly through the rich rewards he bestowed on his faithful followers, and the still more profuse

[1] Giraldus Cambrens. De Instructione Principis, c. 30. ap. Scriptt. Rer. Gall. xviii.

[2] Thus Peter of Blois appears to be in error when he asserts that at the king's death one archbishopric and four bishoprics were vacant. The archbishoprics were filled, and of the bishoprics, Winchester only from 1098, and Salisbury from December 1099, appear to have been vacant. See Sax. Chron. and Flor. Wigorn. a. 1100.

[3] See the unanimous testimonies of Orderic, pp. 763, 782; Malmesbury. p. 510; Eadmer, p. 94; Will. Newburg. lib. i. c. 2: Huntingdon. Hugo Floriac. (De Modernis Francorum Regibus, lib. i.) a contemporary, says: "armis quidem strenuus atque munificens, sed nimis lascivus et flagitiosus."

bribes on his adversaries[1]. His ambition as well as his course of life required great resources, and both clergy and people were oppressed with a rigour as offensive as it was senseless. His officials durst not flinch from any expedient to supply the royal treasury; the delinquent could always redeem himself from the cord that entwined him, if he could but show thereby a gain to the exchequer[2]. To the people he usually appeared with repulsive coldness and affected indifference, threatening looks, and a fierce tone of voice[3].

Among the memorials of his reign, some architectural works could hardly be wanting, in an age so devoted to and skilled in the art of building. At London he built a new bridge across the Thames, surrounded the Tower by a wall[4], the strength of which tradition ascribes to the cement used for the purpose being mixed with the blood of animals, and the great hall at Westminster, in which, the year before his death, he held a numerous court[5].

His ecclesiastical foundations are, as we have already ob-

[1] Suger, lib. i. "Ille opulentus Anglorum thesaurorum mercator et solidator."

[2] Ibid. lib. i. "Pauperum intolerabilis oppressor." H. Hunt. aa. 1098, 1099, "Nihil recti rex pravus in regno suo fieri permittebat, sed provincias intolerabiliter vexavit in tributis, quæ nunquam cessabant. . . . tributis et exactionibus pessimis populos Anglorum non abradens, sed excorians." And from him, Robert de Monte and Chron. Beccense: "pauperes incolas regni sui omnes opprimebat, et illis violenter auferebat, quæ prodigus advenis tribuebat." Ord. Vital. p. 763. Sax. Chron. a. 1100.

[3] In such descriptions Malmesbury (p. 495) is particularly happy; he says: "Erat is (Willelmus) foris et in conventu hominum tumido vultu erectus, minaci oculo astantem defigens, et affectato rigore feroci voce colloquentem reverberans." The beau ideal of a baron of many lands and times!

[4] H. Hunt. a. 1098, "in opere muri circa turrim Londoniæ."

[5] Sax. Chron. a. 1099. "To Pentecosten forman siðe his hired innan his niwan gebyttlan æt Westmynstre heold." H. Hunt. a. 1098. "in opere aulæ regalis apud Westminster." To this also Malmesbury (p. 504) undoubtedly refers: "Unum ædificium, et ipsum per maximum, domum in Londonia incepit et perfecit, non parcens expensis, dummodo liberalitatis suæ magnificentiam exhiberet."

served, but few, and belong to the early part of his reign. In his time occurs the donation of the city of Bath to the bishop of Somerset. At a later period, the only good deeds recorded of him are the founding of some hospitals at York and Thetford. Any patronage of science and art, notwithstanding his pretended education by Lanfranc, is hardly to be expected from William Rufus. Hence, in his dissensions with Anselm, he has found no defender; no panegyrist, rife as they were in those days; no biographer; probably not even one to dedicate a book to him [1].

[1] The medical work, Schola Salernitana, is said to be dedicated to him; though the editor, Z. Sylvius, has shown that, if not a later king, William's brother, duke Robert, is intended.

A

HISTORY OF ENGLAND

UNDER THE

NORMAN KINGS.

HENRY THE FIRST,

SURNAMED BEAUCLERC.

CONTEMPORARY SOVEREIGNS.

GERMANY.	FRANCE.	SCOTLAND.	SPAIN.
Henry IV. 1106.	Philip I. 1108.	Edgar 1107.	Alphonso VI. 1109.
Henry V. 1125.	Lewis VI.	Alexander I. 1124.	Alphonso VII. 1134.
Lothair II.		David I.	Alphonso VIII.

POPES.

Paschal II. 1118. | Gelasius II. 1119. | Calixtus II. 1124.
Honorius II. 1130. | Innocent II.

THE Red King, with other tall deer, had fallen on a Thursday, and his carcase, as a wild boar's, only covered with miserable rags, was conveyed in a cart to Winchester, where, on the following day, attended by a few monks, townsfolk, and beggars, he received the little that was granted of last honours and offices to the king of the preceding day, in his royal residence. He was interred in the cathedral, but the solemn knell, which was wont to express or supply the last lament of the survivors, was, on this occasion, silent in almost every church. No one was there who thought of distributing the customary alms for the repose of his soul, out of the vast treasures of the departed. On the other hand, there resounded from every side a loud, stern, damnatory judgment, on the dead. No priest ventured to absolve or reconcile the worthless tyrant, whom God had thus suddenly summoned before him[1].

[1] Ord. Vital. p. 782.

Prince Henry, who was present at that hunting in the New Forest, (or Ytene wald), was no sooner apprized of his brother's death, than, clapping spurs to his horse, he rode at full speed to the castle of Winchester, to demand the keys as next heir to the throne. But William of Breteuil, who had outridden him, opposed the delivery of them, on behalf of duke Robert, the first-born son of the Conqueror, to whom, by right of primogeniture and by treaty, the crown of England belonged, to whom all had sworn fealty, and to whom, on his return from his glorious warfare for Christ, God would give the crown to which he was born. Henry had already drawn his sword against the unwished-for champion of strict legality; but the friends of both, and the counsellors of the late king, who had hastened to the spot, declared themselves unanimous in favour of the younger and more energetic brother, who must be considered as the next heir, if Robert's exclusion by his father were to be regarded as valid, and the legality of William the Second's reign acknowledged, to deny which would be to sow the seeds of irremediable confusion.

On the Sunday immediately following his brother's death, Henry, at that time in his thirtieth year, was crowned at Westminster by Maurice, bishop of London (5th Aug. 1100[1].) The prompt services of his party he did not, however, obtain without considerable donations, and gained over the more intelligent and well-disposed by promises and concessions, which, as far as they concerned the general interest, he swore, previously to being anointed, to observe, before God and the whole people, at the altar at Westminster. William Giffard, the chancellor of his predecessor, was immediately appointed to the see of Winchester. The archbishopric of York was bestowed on Girard, bishop of Hereford; the va-

[1] The surname of 'Beauclerc,' bestowed on him, on account either of his superior education or beautiful handwriting, occurs first in Grafton. The epithet of 'Le Clerc,' applied to him, is not mentioned earlier than Bromton.

cant abbacies were filled by the sons of the Norman aristocracy, or by other ecclesiastics of that province. With the
object of conciliating the clergy, William's great opponent,
and Henry's early instructor, Anselm, was immediately and
reverently summoned back to England. But infinitely more
important, both for the present and the future, was a proclamation issued by the new king, in which he pledged himself
to remedy the abuses of the preceding government, and to
maintain the old Anglo-Saxon constitution, or, according to
the phraseology of the time, the laws of king Eadward. This
compact (for so, on consideration of the circumstances under
which it was called forth, it may justly be termed, and as
being only the written record of what he had sworn to only a
few days before,) was by Henry's successors always confirmed
anew, and became thereby the fundamental law of the state,
until, after the lapse of more than a century, it was found
necessary to check new encroachments on the part of the successors of the Conqueror, by the exaction of further concessions, as embodied in the Great Charter, when a rude constitutional structure was raised on this foundation-stone [1].

The provisions of this charter, by which Henry purchased
his right to the throne and the good will of his subjects, are
the following : Through the mercy of God and with the common advice and consent of the Barons of England (who are
here mentioned for the first time in place of the old ' Witan'),
being crowned king, he will, as the realm was oppressed by
illegal exactions, before all things liberate God's Church, so
that he will neither sell nor farm, nor on the death of an
archbishop or bishop or abbot, accept anything from the
possessions of the Church, or its tenants, until the entrance
of a successor. And will abolish all oppressive imposts (make
consuetudines), so that if any of his barons, earls, or other
person dies, who holds immediately of him, his heir shall not
redeem his land as in the time of his brother, but with a law-

[1] Sax. Chron. a. 1100. Eadmer, p. 55.

T

ful and just relief. In like manner, the tenants of his barons
shall redeem their lands from their lords. And if any one of
his barons or vassals wishes to give his daughter, niece, etc.
in marriage, he shall speak with him (the king); who will,
however, accept nothing for the permission, nor forbid the
marriage, unless he wishes to bestow her on his (the king's)
enemy. And on the death of a baron or other vassal of the
king, if he leaves an heiress, he (the king) will give her in
marriage, together with her land, with the advice of his
barons. If a widow is left childless, she shall possess her
dowry and "maritatio"[1], and not be given in marriage, except with her consent. If she is left with children, she shall
possess her dowry and "maritatio" as long as she leads a
spotless life, and shall not be given in marriage but with her
own consent; and the wife, or other relation of upright character, shall be the guardian of the land and children. And
the king's barons shall act in like manner towards the sons,
or daughters, or wives of their tenants. And the common
mintage (monetagium[2]), which was levied in the cities and
counties, and which did not exist in the time of king Eadward,
is thenceforth prohibited. If any moneyer or other be taken
with false money, he shall be brought to justice. All fines
(placita) and all debts owing to his brother he remits, excepting his just farms, and those that were settled for other
inheritances or for those things which more justly affected
others. And if any one has stipulated anything for his inheritance, he remits it, as well as all reliefs that have been
stipulated for just inheritances. And if any of his barons or
tenants falls sick, as he shall give or be disposed to give his
money, he grants that it be so given. But if, prevented by

---

[1] In what this consisted is by no means certain: it was probably the
foster-leán of the Anglo-Saxon Laws.—T.

[2] "Id quod monetarii, seu monetæ fabricatores, domino, cujus est
moneta, exsolvunt ex monetarii fusionis et signaturæ proventibus." Du
Cange.—T.

arms or infirmity, he shall neither have so given nor disposed
of his money, then his wife, or children, or relatives, or vassals
legally authorized shall distribute it for the good of his soul
as to them shall seem good. If any of his barons or vassals
incurs a penalty, he shall not give a surety to the amount of
all his money, as in the time of his father and brother ; but,
according to the amount of the penalty, let him be amerced,
as he would have been before the time of his father and brother, in the time of his other predecessors. But if he be
convicted of perfidy or crime, let him make such compensation as is just. " Murders"[1] also he pardons up to the day
of his coronation, and for those committed from that time
just reparation shall be made, according to the law of king
Eadward. The forests, with the consent of his barons, he
retains in his own hands, as his father held them. To knights
holding their lands by military service (per loricas) he grants
exemption from all payments and all works. Finally he restores the laws of king Eadward, with those emendations
which they received from his father, with the consent of his
barons[2].

While the king was thus endeavouring to conciliate not
only the great and inferior vassals, but also the lower orders
of burghers and peasants, he, nevertheless, reserved to himself
all the rights of the chase and forest, as they had existed
under his father and brother, thereby manifesting that passion for hunting, which induced William of Warenne, who

[1] The crime of 'murdrum' is not to be taken in the modern sense of
murder. In Legg. Henrici I. xcii. §. 5. it is said : "Murdritus homo
dicebatur antiquitus cujus interfector nesciebatur, ubicumque vel quomodo-
cumque esset inventus ; nunc adjectum est, licet sciatur quis murdrum
fecerit, si non habeatur intra vii. dies."

[2] The several readings of this document are very varying. The copy in
the Statutes of the Realm has many variations. It is to be found also in
Matt. Paris (R. Wendover) and Ric. Hagustald. a. 1100, and the Textus
Roffensis, edit. Hearne, p. 51. The copy here given is from Legg. Hen. I.
ap. "Ancient Laws and Institutes of England."

T 2

was never well disposed towards him, to bestow on him the nick-name of 'Pied de Cerf'[1]. Copies of this charter were sent into all the counties, and deposited in the several abbeys[2].

A step taken by Henry of perhaps even greater moment for its immediate effect, was his marriage with the granddaughter of prince Eadward, son of Eadmund Ironside, the niece of Eadgar Ætheling, and daughter of his sister Margaret and her consort, king Malcolm Canmore. By this connection he not only formed a friendly relation with her brothers, the kings of Scotland, and restored a better state of morals and greater decorum to the court, but also established a joyful association, as it were, with the greater, or Anglo-Saxon, portion of the people, who saw the crown revert to their beloved royal race, and awaited the realization of a beautiful picture, conjured up in their imagination, of golden days, in the supposed return of the good old times of their forefathers. We would fain ascribe to the excellent Anselm, who, in consequence of a summons of the king and his barons, had hastened back to England, a considerable share in all these measures of liberality and wise policy; but the happy idea of the marriage cannot have originated with that prelate, who, on the contrary, opposed it on the ground that Matilda[3], to escape from the violence of the Normans, had formerly taken refuge with her aunt Christina in the abbey of Wilton, and had, moreover, worn the veil, to avoid a marriage with Alan earl of Richmond. He yielded, however, to

---

[1] Li quens Willame le gabout;

Pié de cers par gab l'apelout.—Rom. de Rou, v. 15650.
which see for other curious particulars, illustrative of the time, relative to Henry.

[2] Matt. Paris (R. Wendover, ii. p. 164). Henry also granted a charter to the citizens of London, which is printed in Rymer, and at the beginning of his Laws (Anc. Laws and Institt. of Engl.).

[3] Her baptismal name was Eadgyth, which on her marriage was changed to Matilda. Ord. Vital. lib. viii. Ann. Waverl. p. 133.

the explanations given [1], and the marriage was solemnized in the same year. Characteristic of the time, in which minstrelsy was coming into vogue, and love, with valour and piety, formed the chief materials for the poet, is the contemporary tradition, that Henry had long loved the Anglo-Saxon daughter of kings, and, regardless of her scanty portion, desired her before all the richly endowed daughters of princes [2]. The good-natured Anglo-Saxon, while enjoying with his family the fire on his hearth, which under the two preceding kings he had been compelled to quench at nightfall, readily gave credit to the tale, which proved more beneficial to the Norman king than the possession of many strong castles; while on the Normans the event produced a contrary effect. Popular wit is always ready, and among those people was chiefly distinguished by its aptitude in the invention of nicknames and epithets, and so the king and queen were called by the Normans by the Anglo-Saxon names of Goderic and Godithe, in allusion probably to some lost love story ; which appellations drew from the king himself peals of laughter.

Yet neither by the offensive wit nor the dangerous malice of many of his vassals was the king to be diverted from the course on which he had entered, but persisted in following the counsels of the faithful friend of his youth, Henry earl of Warwick [3], son of Robert of Beaumont, whose name appears as first lay witness to the charter granted to the English. Simultaneously with the publication of this charter, the individual, whose oppressions it chiefly put an end to, Ranulf Flambard, bishop of Durham, was arrested, conveyed to the Tower of London, and committed to the custody of William of Manneville. Here he lived in luxury on the allowance made him from the exchequer and the liberality of friends; by his wit and pleasantry conciliating the good will, and lulling the vigilance of his keepers. In the beginning of

[1] Eadmer, Hist. Nov. p. 56.   [2] W. Malm. p. 649.
[3] Ibid. p. 648.

February (1101) his sewer contrived to convey to him a rope
concealed in a vessel of wine, by means of which the corpu-
lent prelate, while his guards, after their potations, were sunk
in sleep, glided down from the window of his prison and, with
hands sorely flayed, effected his escape to Normandy[1], where
Robert bestowed on him the bishopric of Lisieux[2].

Duke Robert had now returned to his paternal inheritance.
The crusade with its rapid succession of strange spectacles,
important events, pleasing and exalting sensations, had on
Robert, as on the other participators, shed a lustre which he
previously had not possessed and never afterwards sustained[4].
His high birth greatly increased the impression which the
courage and bodily strength of the short and somewhat cor-
pulent hero had made[4]. But his renown was shared by
many of his countrymen, whose influence in the origin and
success of the crusade neither the duke knew how to turn to
advantage, nor posterity justly to appreciate. Among no
other contemporary people do we perceive so strong an inclination for pilgrimages, arising partly from enthusiasm,
partly from love of travel; nor among any other that successful thirst after conquests. As early as the beginning of the
century, a pilgrim knight of Normandy had delivered the
chair of the successor of St. Peter from the power of the
Saracens, and acquired, as a kingdom for his posterity, some
of the fairest lands of Europe. Between Rouen and Jerusalem reciprocal intercourse, both through priests and laymen never ceased. And they were Normans, who first in
the spring of the year 1096, with Peter de Acheris[5] (com-
monly called of Amiens) the hermit, went forth on the cru-

---

[1] Sim. Dunelm. a. 1100. W. Malm. p. 620. Ord. Vital. p. 786.

[2] At which the good Yvo of Chartres expresses his indignation.

[3] Guibert. Gestor. Dei per Francos, lib. ii. c. 7.

[4] W. Malm. p. 607.

[5] The family name of this individual has hitherto been overlooked,
though preserved by Orderic (p. 723), while the locality of his cell has
been sought in vain.

sade, through Germany and Hungary. Among these were
Walter of Pacy[1] and his four nephews, Walter Saunzaveir,
William, Simon, and Matthew. That among the fifteen
thousand pedestrians led by them there were many Normans,
can hardly be doubted. Duke Robert, who left Normandy
in September, was joined by Hugh the Great, count of Vermandois and brother of the king of France; Hugh count of
St. Pol; his brother-in-law, Stephen count of Blois and
Chartres[2]; his cousin, Stephen count of Aumale (Albemarle),
who had formerly aspired to the English crown; his uncle,
Odo, the notorious bishop of Bayeux, who died on his way at
Palermo; Philip le Clerc, son of the count Roger of Montgomery; Rotrou, son of Geoffrey count of Mortain; Walter
of St. Valery, a descendant of Richard II. duke of Normandy,
with his son Bernard; Girard of Gournay; the Breton Ralf
of Guader, who twenty years before had planned the conspiracy against the Conqueror at Norwich, and his son Alan;
Yvo and Aubrey, sons of Hugh of Grentemaisnil[3]; Roger of
Barnevile; William of Ferrières; Alan Fergant; Conan,
son of count Geoffrey of Brittany, and others, whose deeds
have shed the most glorious splendour on their names[4].
Duke Robert proceeded with his forces, through France and
Lombardy, to Lucca, where he met with pope Urban, and
received his blessing[5]. In Apulia, whether compelled by the

[1] De Pexeio. Ord. Vital. p. 723. Paxeium, Pacy on the Eure was a fief
of the lord of Breteuil. Ord. Vital. pp. 527, 655, 705. The identity of
Pexeium and Paceium is maintained by the editors of the Recueil des
Hist. de la France, xii. p. 814. A sire de Pacie fought at Hastings. See
Rom. de Rou, v. 13655. [Pacy seems at the Conquest to have belonged
to William fitz Osbern; but there certainly was a William de Pacy in 1080,
who possibly held under him. See Taylor, ' Master Wace,' p. 230.—T.]

[2] He died in the East in 1102. Fulcher. Carnot. p. 414.

[3] Their brother William, who married the daughter of Robert Guiscard,
we no longer count among the followers of duke Robert.

[4] Ord. Vital. p. 724.

[5] For Robert's journey comp. Fulcher. Carnot., who accompanied his
count, and, consequently, duke Robert.

storms of winter, or seduced by indolence and frivolity, we
are unable to decide, Robert and Stephen of Blois made
some stay, although count Robert of Flanders had found
means to embark from Bari without delay. By the duke of
Apulia, Roger Borsat[1], the son of Robert Guiscard, and
brother-in-law of William of Grentemaisnil, the first-born of
his old princely house, was received as his native sovereign,
and these exalted personages, forgetful of their vow, passed
the time in a round of revelry, while of the lower orders many
resolved to return home ; and this state of things continued
till the following year (1097), when, in the month of April,
Robert embarked at Brindisi. He landed at Durazzo, and
proceeded, through Bulgaria and Macedonia, to Constantinople, before the walls of which the crusaders had to content
themselves with good cheer and permission to enter the city
one by one.

The princes, Robert and Stephen, like most of those who
had preceded them, having performed the required homage
to the emperor Alexius Comnenus I. for the conquests they
were to make in Asia, were supplied with money (of which
Robert, notwithstanding his frugality at the outset, was now
greatly in need[2]), and other necessaries, and forthwith despatched to Nicæa. Already, under the walls of that city, a
successful battle had been fought by the princes Godfrey and
Hugh (who had been joined by the count of Flanders, Raymond count of Toulouse, Baldwin of Mons[3] and others) with

---

[1] 'Borsat,' Lat. *Marsupium*, a sobriquet given him by his father, on
account of his love of money. W. Malm. p. 598. " Rogerius cognomento
Bursa." Ord. Vital. p. 724.—T.

[2] Radulf. Cadom. lib. i.

[3] " Baldwinus de Monte castello, Hannicorum comes et princeps, vir
illustrissimus in omni militari actione." Albert. Aquens. lib. ii. c. 22.
Petrus Tudebod. p. 1. He had accompanied Godfrey. Balderic. p. 91.
Wilken overlooks him entirely until his return (i. p. 230), when he does
not recognise in him the count of Hainaut or Mons. Gesch. der Kreuzzüge, i. p. 70 ; he seems to confound him with the much later Baldwin of
Rames, and this latter again with Baldwin de Bourg (of Mons), the son of

the Seljuk sultan, Kilidsh Arslan (or the Lion); yet Robert with his band arrived, in the beginning of June, early enough to take a glorious share in the capture of the city. He afterwards joined the body of the army, in which were Boemund of Tarentum, his nephew Tancred, and Richard del Principato[1]. In the attack which this force sustained from the Turks at Dorylæum (1st July), the salvation of the Christians is chiefly to be ascribed to the presence of mind, the valour, and eloquence of Robert. Early in the battle Boemund resigned the command to him, and it was he, who, seizing the golden standard with his right hand, placed himself in front of the fleeing Christians, showed them the impossibility of safety by flight; and, in the hope of falling gloriously and in fulfilment of his duty, once again raised the inspiring cry of " Deus le volt," and led them to a victorious resistance[2]. On their onward march Robert remained with the grand army, to which the Armenians submitted without resistance, and, with the consent of the other princes, bestowed the town of Alfia on a knight named Simeon, a native of those parts, that from thence he might preserve the country in faith to God, the holy sepulchre, and the army of the cross[3].

When the host arrived in the neighbourhood of Antioch, the vanguard was placed under the command of duke Robert, who valiantly sustained a conflict at the bridge of Ifrin, until

Hugh of Rethel. Baldwin of Rames, of unknown origin, appears to have received his surname from the town in Galilee.

[1] Erroneously in Wilken called 'de Principaute.' He was a grandson of Tancred of Hauteville, by his second marriage, and son of William. See Malaterra, lib. i. cc. 12, 15.

[2] Radulf. Cadom. lib. i. cc. 20-22. Henry of Huntingdon's account of this crusade has been overlooked by its historians, while they make use of the meagre extract from it by Robert de Monte. Comp. Petr. Tudebod. Rob. Monach. lib. iii. p. 41. W. Malm.

[3] The duke of Normandy is named as the donor by H. of Huntingdon. Balderic (lib. ii.) supplies the name of the place, and Orderic from him. Both they and Guibert supply the name of Simeon. The rest is found in Petr. Tudebod. and Robert. Monachus.

the advance of fresh troops to his aid [1]. At the siege of the city (from Oct. 18th 1097) he displayed at first his wonted courage, and often with a very small force [2]; but on the appearance of famine in the camp, the prince, accustomed to sensual enjoyments, was missing [3]. It is to us particularly interesting to receive from a contemporary and subject of Robert the account that, from dread of advancing enemies, those Anglo-Saxons, who had formerly fled from his father, and whom the Greek emperor had sent to the defence of Laodicea, had summoned the Norman duke to their help and guidance. Robert was so delighted with the abundance of the necessaries and luxuries of life, and the wines, with which that city was supplied from the isle of Cyprus, that in the enjoyment of them he sank into a state of complete inactivity, and it was only after a thrice-repeated threat of the anathema from the representative of the holy father, Ademar bishop of Puy, that he could be prevailed on to return [4]. Although in this instance he had suffered himself to be seduced by his unconquerable addiction to sensuality, yet did his inborn valour again shine forth, when the Turks from Aleppo, Emesa, and Hamah, had assembled at the castle of Harem, for the purpose of relieving Antioch. On one day he, with Eustace of Boulogne, defended the camp of the crusaders against a sally of the besieged; on the day following (9th Feb. 1098) he led six bodies of troops against the new enemies [5]. The capture of Antioch took place at length (3rd June), after a siege of more than seven months, through treachery, yet were valiant men required for the execution of the plan, and here also is Robert's name recorded as that of the second who ascended the hostile wall [6]. Antioch was now acquired, and with it a

---

[1] Alb. Aquens. lib. ii. c. 83.   [2] Raimund. de Agilis, p. 143.

[3] Ib. p. 144. Will. Tyr. lib. iv. c. 18.   [4] Rad. Cadom. lib. i. c. 58.

[5] Petr. Tudebod. p. 13. H. of Hunt.

[6] Wilken, i. p. 200. According to Raimund (p. 151), this second was Robert's namesake, the count of Flanders; according to Albert. Aquensis (lib. iv. c. 19), it was his men.

new Christian principality in the East; though the immediate consequence of its capture was only by new hardships to steel the pilgrims for further deeds of valour.　After a few days, the prince of Mousul, Kerboga Cavem ed Daula, appeared before the walls of the city.　Roger of Barnevile, a Norman knight, was the first victim of the attack of the Moslem besiegers[1].　Many knights fled, clandestinely leaving the city, by letting themselves down from the wall by ropes, whence, even in their home, the opprobrious epithet of *rope-dancers* was for ever attached to them.　Among these were even the brothers of Grentemaisnil, and William viscount of Melun[2], noted alike for faithlessness and strength of arm, whereby he was able to cleave iron as it were soft wood, and thence acquired the appellation of William the Carpenter.　But duke Robert, on the other hand, saved the city from the first assault of Kerboga by his obstinate defence of the castle at the bridge gate.　He was one of the princes, who mutually bound themselves by oath, never to the last gasp of breath, in any case, to abandon the defence of the city[3].　His perseverance found a glorious reward in the defeat and dispersion of the besiegers (28th June).　Although he had lost his last warhorse, he borrowed that of count Raymond, then confined by sickness, and, with Philip le Clerc of Montgomery and Warin of Taneye, pursued the enemy until he had slain one of the leaders[4].　After the relief of Antioch, Robert, who was among those princes who, true to their oath, had originally refused to bestow the city on Boemund, would deliver it up to the Greek emperor.

[1] Petr. Tudebod. Alb. Aquens. lib. iv. c. 37. Guibert. lib. v. c. 15.

[2] "De regali prosapia et vicecomes cujusdam regii castelli, quod Milidunum dicitur, olim extitit." Rob. Monach. lib. iv. c. 48. This formidable hewer of iron had previously fled from the leaguer before Antioch, and was noted in Spain on account of similar treachery. Guibert. lib. iv. c. 4.

[3] Guibert. lib. v. c. 18.

[4] Malmesbury (p. 608) takes this for Kerboga himself, but he had fled to Aleppo. See Kemaleddin ap. Wilken, ii. Beilagen. p. 41.

During the time that the other princes had separated until the beginning of winter, either for the sake of refreshing their soldiers, or making foraging excursions, we lose sight of the Norman duke. Probably he had returned to Laodicea, where Winemar of Boulogne[1], a notorious pirate during the last eight years, had previously with his followers landed from ships pretending to be from Antwerp, Thiel, and Friesland, combined with some Provençals, under the pretext of a pilgrimage[2]. With these was also Eadgar Ætheling, to whom the defence of Laodicea had been intrusted, which he afterwards delivered up to duke Robert; who subsequently lost it through an insurrection of the inhabitants, who, exasperated at the exactions of the prodigal duke, drove out his people, and even prohibited the money of Rouen from passing current in their markets[3]. When the march of the crusading army to Jerusalem was resolved on (24th Nov.), duke Robert, while the others hesitated, joined Raymond of St. Giles, and with him besieged and captured the city of Marra (12th Dec.). Raymond offered Robert ten thousand shillings (solidi), if, united with him, he would proceed to Jerusalem[1]; an offer, which Robert, who was ever in need of money, hardly refused. He accompanied Raymond's army to Kafertabad (1099[5]), and thence to the siege of Arka. In the dissensions which here

---

[1] "De terra Bulonæ et de domo comitis Eustachii, magnifici principis ejusdem terræ." Alb. Aquens. lib. iii. c. 14. lib. vi. c. 55. Therefore not of Bologna, as Wilken (i. p. 254) supposes; but is identical with him, whom (i. p. 163) he calls Guinemer aus Bouillon, misled by William of Tyre's Guinerus Boloniensis. lib. vii. c. 15.

[2] Ord. Vital. p. 778. It seems to me not improbable that these ships are the thirty which Raimond de Agilis (p. 173) calls English. He relates of the English what the older writers do of Winemar; and the time and place of landing agree. Albert of Aix (lib. vi. c. 55) places the services of the squadron of Winemar along with those of the Genoese and Pisans, as Raimond does of those whom he calls English.

[3] Guibert. lib. vii. c. 35.

[4] Raim. de Agilis, p. 161. Balderic. lib. iv. c. 1. Guibert. lib. vi. c. 8.

[5] Petr. Tudebod. c. 34.

arose between Raymond and Tancred, Robert sided with the
latter, and it was his chaplain, Arnulf,who convinced the army
of the spuriousness of the lance found by Raymond at Antioch[1]. Robert, after the example of duke Godfrey, having
burnt his tents before Arka, detached himself from the southern French, and continued as before, and as both natural
and spiritual affinity seemed to point out, more closely united
with the northern French and the Italian Normans. At this
time Robert found a companion in arms in Hugh Budvel, son
of Robert de la Roche d'Igé (de Rupe Jalgeii), a Norman, for
many years resident in the East, having been exiled from his
country on account of the murder of the barbarous and tyrannical countess Mabil of Montgomery, who, through his
knowledge of the manners and habits of the Mohammedans,
proved of great utility[2]. At the siege of Jerusalem, Robert
had joined his camp with that of the count of Flanders, before the gate of St. Stephen; had, together with that prince,
engaged in many a glorious conflict; and both had succeeded,
by means of their military engines, in breaking through the
walls of the city. Deeply impressed with those religious feelings which constituted the peculiar ornament of those warriors, they humbly implored the favour of victory, and were

---

[1] "Domini Normannorum comitis familiaris et capellanus, vir quidem
literatus, sed immundæ conversationis et scandalorum procurator." Will.
Tyr. lib. vii. c. 18. He had formerly been the friend and heir of bishop
Odo. Guibert. lib. viii. c. 1.

[2] "Justus arbiter, qui peccatoribus pie parcit et impœnitentes districte
percutit, crudelem feminam, quæ multo sanguine madebat, multosque
nobiles violenter exheredatos per externa mendicare coegerat, permisit per-
ire gladio Hugonis, cui castrum quod in rupe Ialgeii situm est abstulerat,
et sic eum injuste paterna hereditate privaverat. Ille nimirum mœrens
audaciam vehementem arripuit, junctis sibi tribus fratribus suis, qui militari probitate pollebant, noctu ad cameram comitissæ accessit, ipsamque
in municipio super Divam quod Buris dicitur, in lecto post balneum deli-
ciantem, pro recompensatione sui, ense detruncavit." Ord. Vital. pp. 578,
753.—T.

soon so fortunate as to be among the foremost who from duke
Godfrey's tower rushed into the holy city[1] (15th July).

On the election of a king for the new state, we are told
that the crown was offered to Robert, as being the son of a
king[2]. But he was too self-indulgent, and probably reckoned
too much on the prospect of one day obtaining secure possession of both Normandy and England, to accept this fair,
though thorny, diadem. Robert's influence in the army and
the council is apparent from the circumstance, that his chaplain and companion, Arnulf, attained to the high dignity of
chancellor, and, at a later period, to that of patriarch of Jerusalem[3]; and, at an earlier period, the first episcopal see
founded by the crusaders at Lidda was bestowed on a Norman named Robert. Here also, as in every place where he
felt at ease, he was very well disposed to stay, and from that

---

[1] Fulcher. p. 398. Balderic. p. 131. Guibert. lib. vii. c. 6.

[2] Will. Malm. p. 608. H. Hunt. pp. 377—379. See also "Continuation du Brut," and "Chronique de P. Langtoft," ap. Michel, pp. 100, *sq.*
and 160, *sq.* Gervas. Tilb., Otia Imper. ii. 20, has the erroneous account
that Robert was already informed of his brother's death. His character,
as drawn by Ralf of Caen (lib. i. c. 15), may here find a place :—" Robertus, Normanniæ comes, Wilhelmi regis et expugnatoris Angliæ filius, genere, divitiis, facundia quoque non secundus duci (Godofredo), sed superior; par in his quæ Cæsaris sunt, quæ Dei, minor; cujus pietas largitas-
que valde fuissent mirabiles, sed quia in neutra modum tenuit, in utraque
erravit. Siquidem misericordiam ejus immisericordem sensit Normannia,
dum eo consule per impunitatem rapinarum nec homini parceret, nec Deo
licentia raptorum. Nam sicarii manibus, latronum gutturi, mœchorum
caudæ salaci, eandem quam suis se reverentiam debere consul arbitraba-
tur. Quapropter nullus ad eum vinctus in lacrymis trahebatur, quin so-
lutus mutuas ab eo lacrymas continuo impetraret. Ideo, ut dixi, nullis
sceleribus frænum, imo omnibus additum calcar ea tempestate Normannia
querebatur. Hujus autem pietatis sororculam eam fuisse patet largitatem.
quæ accipitrem sive canem argenti qualibet summa comparabat. Cum
interim mensa consularis unicum haberet refugium rapinam civium, atque
hæc tamen intra patriam, verum fines patrios egressus, magna ex parte
luxum domuit, cui ante per magnarum opum affluentiam succubuerat."

[3] Albert. Aquens. lib. vi. c. 39 *sq.*

cause even again attached himself to his old rival Raymond[1]. But having yielded to the representations of king Godfrey, he fought with his wonted and oft-proved valour in the battle of Ascalon (14th August). All the chroniclers of the time unanimously celebrate a deed which long shed lustre on Robert's name, both in the east and west. On catching a glimpse of the enemy's silver standard, adorned with a golden knob, he instantly rushed towards it, and sorely wounded the banner-bearer. He could not, however, seize the standard himself, but rewarded one of his warriors, who had gained possession of it, in a manner befitting his usual munificence, with a donation of twenty silver marks, for the purpose of offering it at the holy grave[2].

Shortly after this battle, duke Robert, the counts of Flanders, Boulogne, and Toulouse, Cuno of Montagu[3], and other knights, announced to Godfrey, in the camp at Cæsarea, their intention, having fulfilled their vow, of returning to their several states. Those faithful brothers in arms parted from each other with tears; the noble-hearted, pious king remained behind, to defend the land of his faith against the ferocity of the infidels. The duke and count Robert made a pilgrimage to the Jordan, bathed in its sacred waters, and gathered palm branches in Abraham's garden at Jericho. With twenty thousand pilgrims they proceeded to Laodicea, whence the two princes embarked for Constantinople[4]. From that city

[1] Balderic. p. 136. Guibert. lib. vii. c. 17.

[2] Guibert. lib. vii. c. 18 *sq.* Balderic. p. 136. Raimond. p. 183. Albert. Aquens. lib. vi. c. 50. Among the glass paintings, representing the principal events of the first crusade, which the contemporary abbot Suger caused to be executed for the church of St. Denys, there is one representing either this or some similar feat of Robert's. It is given in Montfaucon, Monumens de la Monarchie Françoise, tom. i.

[3] This Cuno of Montagu (de Monte acuto) had accompanied duke Godfrey (Albert. Aquens. lib. ii. c. 11), and belonged probably to the Norman families of that name, whom we find in Domesday among the tenants in chief of the Conqueror.

[4] Fulcher. p. 100. Albert. Aquens. lib. vi. c. 54.

the duke passed to Apulia, where he continued the greater
part of the year; there he espoused Sibylla, the beautiful and
accomplished daughter of Geoffrey count of Conversana, a
near relation of duke Robert Guiscard. The rich count by
the dowry, and other friends by loans, supplied Robert with
a considerable sum of money, with which he hoped to redeem
his dukedom out of the hands of his brother[1]. In the intoxi-
cation of a happiness almost unutterable, he returned home,
the lord and heir of powerful states, in the prime of manhood,
covered with fresh, well-earned laurels, supplied with the treasure that he so greatly needed, gifted with the hand of exqui-
site beauty, combined with rare judgment.—Who could have
predicted how, in a few short years, so much happiness passed
away from this most thoughtless of mortals?

While on his homeward journey, the intelligence reached
him of the death of William, and of the treachery of his brother Henry[2]. The news affected him but slightly. Received
with festivities by the Normans, the money he had brought
with him was in a few weeks squandered away in so culpable
and frivolous a manner, that at times, because his clothes
had been stolen from him by harlots and other rabble, he was
unable to leave his bed[3]. Besides the pecuniary aid he had
brought with him, he had also lost the respect and good-will
of the Normans, when Ranulf Flambard and other Anglo-
Normans, discontented with Henry's severe measures, instigated him to wrench England from his brother by arms. A
year was spent in the mere preparations for war. Le Maine
in the meanwhile fell again into the hands of the expelled
count Hélie, and Robert in his indolence even treated with
contempt the opportunity offered him by the faithful vassals

[1] W. Gemmet. lib. vii. c. 4. Ord. Vital. p. 780. W. Malm. p. 609. Rom.
de Rou, vv. 15419 sqq.

[2] As he arrived in Normandy in August 1100 (according to Rob. de
Monte in September, according to Orderic, p. 784), that intelligence cannot have induced him to leave Apulia.

[3] Ord. Vital. p. 786. W. Malm. p. 609.

of holding the castle of Le Mans [1]. While the most distinguished Normans, Robert fitz Hamon, Richard of Reviers, Roger Bigot, the influential count of Meulan, and his brother Henry, seceded from the duke, there joined him of the nobles in England Robert of Belesme, his brothers Roger of Poitiers and Arnulf, William of Warenne, earl of Surrey, whom the king disliked on account of his witticisms; Walter Giffard, Robert of Pontefract, son of Ilbert of Lacy; Robert Malet, and the duke's former companion in arms, Ivo of Grentemaisnil [2]. Of these, Robert of Belesme had already fought for duke Robert in his wars with his father; the house of Grentemaisnil had declared for him on the usurpation of the throne by William Rufus; the count of Warenne and Robert fitz Hamon were at that time disaffected towards him [3]. In the summer of the following year (20th July 1101) the duke embarked at Tréport for Portsmouth. The "butsecarls" sent by Henry—who with his army awaited his brother in the neighbourhood of Hastings—to watch the coast, went over to Robert, who found many Normans well disposed towards him at Winchester. For Henry, however, was the whole Anglo-Saxon population, which adhered faithfully to the consort of their Godithe. But the most effectual support Henry found in Robert of Meulan, son of Roger of Beaumont, shortly afterwards earl of Leicester. This highly distinguished and illustrious knight had in his youth signalized himself by his deeds at Hastings; and subsequently, by the political sagacity displayed by him as counsellor to William Rufus, had acquired the reputation of being the wisest statesman between London and Jerusalem, and arbiter of peace or war between England and France. His counsels allayed the dissensions between the laity and clergy. By the latter he was held in the highest consideration, while the former regarded him as their oracle in all secular affairs, and even as a pattern for imitation in habits,

[1] Ord. Vital. p. 784. Acta Cenoman. p. 309.
[2] Ord. Vital. pp. 785 sq., 801. W. Malm. p. 620.   [3] See p. 221.

clothing, entertainments, and, in short, the entire business of
life[1]. Hence it was almost decisive against duke Robert, who
had once detained him as a prisoner, and, at a later period,
was unable to protect him against the injustice of his enemies, that the count of Meulan was ill-disposed towards him.
It was to his address and eloquence that Henry was chiefly
indebted for the preservation of his throne, the chief support
of which, Robert of Meulan,—who was to the sons what William fitz Osbern had been to the father,—continued to be
until his death in the year 1118. With a feeling not unusual
in that chivalric age, Robert refused to take possession of
Winchester, thereby risking his chance of a kingly crown,
that he might not cause annoyance to his sister-in-law,
Henry's consort, at that time on the eve of her accouche-
ment[2]. Shortly after, without a battle, at an interview with
his brother, Robert, awed by the threat of excommunication
from archbishop Anselm, allowed himself to be persuaded to
release Henry from the oath he had taken to him with reference to the crown, in consideration of the cession of the
Cotentin, possessed by Henry, and of his other possessions in
Normandy, with the exception of Domfront, and of a yearly
pension of three thousand marks, or two thousand pounds
sterling. The vassals of one brother were mutually absolved

---

[1] Guil. Pictav. p. 202. Ord. Vital. pp. 686 *sq.*, 709, 784. See also pp.
253, 263. Hen. Hunt. de Contemptu Mundi, apud Wharton, Angl. Sac.
ii. p. 697. W. Malm. p. 636. John of Salisbury also mentions of the
"Comes Legestriæ Robertus, modeste proconsulatum gerens apud Bri-
tannias," an expression which bears witness to his kindly disposition,
"that true majesty is of God alone, and that the crimen læsæ majestatis
is so called only because the king is God's image on earth." The scanty
notices existing of such men cannot be too carefully collected, as showing
that every country, even in the darkest and most troubled times, if it be
not hastening to its downfall, has possessed wise and benevolent states-
men.

[2] Roman de Rou, vv. 15456 *sq.*

　　　　Et il dist ke vilain sereit,
　　　　Ki dame en gésine assaldreit.

from all crimination on account of the aid they had afforded
to the other, and the confiscated estates were restored. The
article also, as usual, was added, that in the event of one
brother dying without lawful issue, the survivor should succeed to his states on both sides of the Channel. Twelve of
the most influential barons on each side swore to enforce the
fulfilment of this compact[1]. Robert with his army continued
for some months in England, to the great hardship of the inhabitants of those parts.

The duke had hardly left England, when Henry, reckless
of the promised amnesty, summoned before his court and
severely punished those barons, who, by their desertion to
Robert, had most offended him. Among these was that Ivo
of Grentemaisnil, who had acquired for himself the unenvia-
ble sobriquet of *the rope-dancer of Antioch*[2], and now, apprehensive of the implacable vengeance of the king, had pledged
to the crafty, overreaching count of Meulan, his share of the
earldom of Leicester, and, with his wife, departed on a new
pilgrimage, on which they both died. Among the other opponents of the king, Robert of Belesme had been yet more
dangerous and hateful to him, as, in addition to his earldoms
of Alençon and Shrewsbury[3], he had, by the death of his
father-in-law, Guy count of Ponthieu, acquired that county,
and had, moreover, from duke Robert, received the possessions of his father in Normandy. Henry also deprived his
own brother-in-law, William of Warenne, of the earldom of
Surrey, who thereupon hastened to Robert, whom he seduced
very imprudently to cross over to England, in the hope of
persuading Henry to other measures. But Henry soon gave
his brother to understand, that, by such a step, he exposed
his liberty, and even life, to no small peril; and, under the
deceitful mask of kind feeling, remonstrated with him for harbouring traitors, in contravention of their agreement. Robert

1 Sax. Chron. Flor. Wigorn. a. 1101. Ord. Vital. p. 788. Eadmer, p. 49.
2 See p. 283. 3 See page 241.

u 2

was now fully aware of the net in which he had entangled
himself by his visit to England, and it was from apprehension,
rendered yet stronger by the insidious mediation of the count
of Meulan, rather than in a fit of perverted, prodigal gal-
lantry, that he was induced, at the request of the young
queen, to relinquish the pension promised him in consideration of his renunciation of the throne.   At this price assurances of royal favour were readily given him by his brother,
and he received not only a safe-conduct for his return home,
but also the restoration of the earldom of Surrey to their
common brother-in-law[1].

In the meanwhile Robert of Belesme, who imagined himself powerful enough to contend single-handed with the king,
caused his castles in various parts of England, as Shrewsbury,
his newly-erected one at Bridgenorth, Arundel, and Tickhill,
to be strongly fortified.   This nobleman, although he had
generally attached himself to the vanquished side, had, by
availing himself of extraordinary events, as well as through
the fear which he knew how to inspire, and by skilful working
on the selfishness of those in power, succeeded in acquiring
vast influence.   His contemporaries are unanimous in describing him as one of the most detestable characters known
in history, to whom the most unheard-of barbarities were not
merely a means, not merely acts of revenge, but an insatiable enjoyment.   In Le Maine the memory of this monster
still lives, where the ramparts erected by him are yet shown
as those of Robert the devil.   Justly, it is said, did he bear
his grandfather's surname of Talevas[2] (man-crusher).   He
scorned the rich ransoms offered by his numerous captives,

---

[1] W. Malm. pp. 609, 621. Ord. Vital. p. 804. Wace (vv. 15680 *sqq.*)
is very circumstantial here. According to him, Robert's visit took place
in 1102, which is rendered probable by the circumstance that William of
Warenne does not appear among the later opponents of the king. According to the Saxon Chronicle and its translation it took place in 1103.

[2] Talevas signifies a shield that covers the whole man. See Roquefort,
in voce.

that, like another Phalaris, he might torture them by new-invented instruments. The mutilation of hands and feet, and putting out of eyes, usual in those times, he disdained, but found delight in seeing men and women empaled and struggling in the agonies of death. Of a little boy, to whom he was godfather, he thrust out the eyes, while pretending to play with him under his mantle, because the father of the child had given him some trivial offence and escaped from his vengeance. As talents in which he excelled, were his arts of dissimulation, by which he often deceived his victims, and his knowledge of the art of war, which he promoted by the invention of many military engines[1]. Against this vassal, a like object of abhorrence, both to those of his own rank and those of an inferior degree, whose preparations had been long regarded with suspicion, the king had caused forty-five articles of accusation to be drawn up, all founded on his actions during the last year, and summoned him to appear before his court. Probably not aware of this preliminary step, he appeared before the king with his wonted case and affected submission; but no sooner had he heard the well-supported charges, than, under the pretext of consulting his friends, according to the usage of that time, he withdrew, flung himself on a horse, and fled with all speed to his castle of Bridgenorth. He was now declared contumacious, and a convicted traitor. The king assembled an army, and proceeded in person against Arundel, which, after a siege of three months, capitulated with the sanction of its lord. Tickhill was taken by Robert, the warlike bishop of Lincoln. From Arundel, Henry passed into Nottinghamshire, where the castle of Blythe, which, as well as Tickhill, Robert, as heir of Roger of Busli, had recovered from William Rufus, gladly surren-

---

[1] W. Gemmet. lib. viii. c. 35. Ord. Vital. pp. 675, 707, 768. W. Malm. p. 621. Roman de Rou. vv. 15012-15050. H. Hunt., de Contemptu Mundi, ap. Wharton. p. 698.

dered to him[1]. The king now disbanded a part of his troops during the harvest, after which he marched against Bridgenorth, with the object of subduing Robert himself, together with the Welsh, under their princes Caducan and Gervatus, the sons of Rhys, on whose aid he chiefly relied. Here, however, the contest was very easy, as the ranks of the Welsh gave ground, not so much from the arrows, as through the influence of English silver[2]; so that at the end of thirty days, that strong and curiously constructed fortress, which was regarded as impregnable, was delivered into the hands of the king[3].

But Henry's most important victory was that which he wrested from his aristocracy. When the barons saw how their dreaded chief had been forced to yield before the power of the king, the thought seized them that he might soon annihilate them also as so many feeble women. Hereupon they formed a combination, with the object of laying before their liege lord all the reasons which spoke in favour of lenity towards his enemy. Henry was wavering, when three thousand peasant soldiery[4] assembled, disclosed to him what to their unprejudiced judgment appeared manifest, the treason of his nobility, and promised to shed the last drop of their blood in overthrowing the detested magnates. Henry obeyed the voice of the good people, and had no cause to repent of having done so.

In this struggle no one was more useful to him than William Pantolf, a Norman of rank, immediately holding of the king, whom Roger of Montgomery had placed over the earldom of Shrewsbury, but afterwards, on account of suspected participation in the murder of his countess, Mabil of Belesme[5], had persecuted. Notwithstanding his proved innocence, Robert

---

[1] Domesday,   Ord. Vital. pp. 768, 806.
[2] Ord. Vital. pp. 806, 807. Flor. Wigorn. a. 1102.
[3] Domesday,   Ord. Vital. pp. 583 *sq.* p. 807.
[4] Pagenses milites. Ord. Vital. p. 807.—T.   [5] See page 285.

had subsequently deprived him of the fief he held of him, who, thereby exasperated and imbued with feelings of the bitterest revenge, found, for the general good, the means of wreaking it in his increased loyalty to the king. Robert had fled to Shrewsbury, where he considered himself the more secure, as the only approach to it for the king's troops seemed to be a narrow pass strongly occupied by his followers. But the royal army cleared itself a way through the dense forest, felling its aged trees with the sharp axe, and by its unlooked for arrival struck terror into the furious count. The townsmen then caused the keys of their gates to be delivered to the king by the hands of Ralf abbot of Séez, and shortly after, the count also submitted, on condition of a free departure from England for himself and his brother, Arnulf of Montgomery—who, through his marriage with the daughter of the king of Ireland, hoped to obtain the crown of that realm—and Roger of Poitou, so designated from his wife[1].

The king could now be regarded as the real master of his realm: he had also demanded of his brother the observance of the compact between them, a strict adherence to which could alone ensure the tranquillity of both states, by the one not harbouring exiles from the dominions of the other. But, although the duke had successfully fought against the vassals of Robert of Belesme, although the whole of Normandy had risen against the detested count, and even his brother Arnulf, with many followers, had passed over to the duke, yet, nevertheless, through that prince's inactivity, the dread in which count Robert was held by the people, the discord that prevailed among the nobles, and, finally, through the good fortune that so often attends the worst of men, and which now

[1] For these events Orderic (pp. 806 sq.) is the most circumstantial and, through his family connections, our most trustworthy informant. The Sax. Chron. and Florence (a. 1102) speak as if Robert surrendered at Bridgenorth. Malmesbury (p. 622) relates that from Bridgenorth Robert went to Arundel, and from thence crossed over to Normandy. See also Langtoft, apud Michel, pp. 156—158.

placed in his hands, as prisoners, William of Conversana, the
duke's brother-in-law, with other Normans of rank, he at
length succeeded in effecting a treaty with the duke, by which
he was restored to all his father's possessions in Normandy [1].
A most unfortunate occurrence both for the country and its
prince was the death of his consort, Sibylla, who had borne
him an heir, count William, and through her prudence, had
been able to preserve many friends to him. It was asserted
that poison was the cause of her death, and suspicion ascribed
it to Agnes, the widow of the recently deceased earl of Buckingham, Walter Giffard, and a sister of Robert's companion
in arms, Anselm of Ribemont [2], who had received the duke's
promise, that after Sibylla's death, he would make her his
duchess [3]. That promise, however, was never fulfilled, as
Robert's difficulties, which were now thickening upon him,
forbade all thoughts of such a connection and of a new
household.

Shortly after, Henry, enraged at the treaty made with
Robert of Belesme, sent troops over to Normandy, for the
purpose of taking possession of certain castles, as well as of
occupying Domfront, which belonged to him, and of strengthening himself in the Cotentin, to which, it was said, Robert
had raised pretensions [4]. He also banished from England,

---

[1] Ord. Vital. p. 811. a. 1103. Sax. Chron. a. 1104.

[2] " De Ribode Monte," " Riburgis Monte." There is by him an account of the first crusade extant, in which he himself fell a sacrifice at the
siege of Arka, at the foot of Lebanon, in the year 1099. He was the
founder of the monastery of Anchin, near St. Quentin. Ribemont is in
the department of L'Aisne, between St. Quentin and Laon.

[3] Ord. Vital. pp. 809 sq. W. Malm. (p. 609), ascribes her death to improper treatment in her confinement : [" deceptam, ut dicunt, obstetricis
consilio, quæ pro affluentis lactis copia, puerperæ mammas stricta præce-
perat illigari fascia."—T.]

[4] Sax. Chron. a. 1104. According to Orderic (p. 813), Henry himself
went to Domfront. M. Le Prevost must have overlooked this passage,
when he regards as pure invention what Wace (vv. 15846 sqq.) relates on
this occasion.

Robert count of Mortain and earl of Cornwall, who, on his
mother's side, a nephew of Robert of Belesme, had laid claim
to the earldom of Kent, which had been held by bishop Odo,
the brother of his father, Robert[1]. In the following spring
Henry himself crossed the sea, and with little difficulty took
Bayeux and Caen, two of his brother's best cities. The latter
had closed its gates against the duke, who had already appeared there as a levier of contributions, from whom they
had to conceal their property in the church, but now only as a
crafty borrower and beggar[2]. There seems, therefore, to have
been hardly any need of the bribery and treachery, by which
the city fell into the power of Henry[3]. The siege of Bayeux
required greater exertions, the castle being valiantly defended
by Gunther of Aunay (de Alneio). The single combat of a
brave ducal knight, Robert of Argouges, with one of the
king's named Brun, who fell in the contest, is one of the
memorable incidents of the siege. It was only with the aid
of Hélie count of Le Maine, and the count of Anjou, that
Henry attained his object, and that not without a great
sacrifice of religious feeling and of humanity, by the burning
of the cathedral and churches and those houses to which the
besieged had fled for safety[4]. In the autumn the king again

---

[1] His father was, consequently, a half-brother of William the Conqueror and son of Herluin. The county of Mortain (Moritolium, Mori-
tonium, Moretoign, Moretun), in the south of the department of La
Manche, is frequently confounded with the also Norman county of Mortagne (Mauritania, Moritonia), in the south of the department of L'Orne.
William the Conqueror had given the former to Robert, after the expulsion of William, surnamed Werleng, the son of Mauger; while the latter
(better known at a later period under the name of Perche), belonged at
that time to count Geoffrey, his son Rotrou, and their successors of like
name.

[2] Rom. de Rou, vv. 16000 *sqq.* W. Malm. p. 610.

[3] H. Hunt. a. 1105. Ord. Vital. p. 818 d. Rom. de Rou, vv. 16270 *sqq.*

[4] Rom. de Rou, vv. 16042–16238. H. Hunt. Ord. Vital. p. 818. By
Serlo, the bishop of Séez expelled by Robert of Belesme (ob. 1124) there
are extant 538 Leonine verses: De capta Baiocensium Civitate, which are
printed in Notices et Extraits des Manuscrits de la Bibliothèque du Roi

embarked for Normandy, and compelled his brother to cede
to him one of his chief vassals, William count of Evreux,
with his county and all his tenants. The count, although
mortified at being treated as a horse or an ox, yet soon became reconciled to his lot by the simplifying of his former
double services, and served his new lord firmly and faithfully.
That by these measures Henry conferred real benefit on the
country, and materially promoted its tranquillity, although
he omitted the most important one of all, namely to place his
brother under a guardianship, is apparent from the attempts
made by Robert of Belesme to enter again into his favour
(1106), though he failed in effecting a reconciliation. Equally
fruitless was an attempt by duke Robert, in a visit to his
brother's court at Northampton, to obtain from him the restitution of his possessions. In the same year the king made
an attempt to repress the rebellious vassals. He laid siege
to Tinchebray, a fortress belonging to the count of Mortain;
whereupon the troops in the neighbourhood of the counts of
Mortain and Belesme, of Robert of Estouteville, William of
Ferrières, William Crespin, and, at length, of duke Robert,
which had also been joined by the queen's uncle, Eadgar
Ætheling, who had returned from Palestine later than
Robert[1], formed a junction; and against them the royal
forces, among which those of the count Hélie of Le Maine,
of the counts of Evreux, Warenne, and Meulan, and others of
high rank are mentioned by name. Men of right feeling were
desirous of avoiding the scandal of a conflict, and Henry
himself went so far as to offer his brother the revenues of
half Normandy, and a compensation, in the shape of an an-
nuity, for the other half, if he would resign the government

t. xi; also in Recueil des Historiens, t. xix. A W. de Brun appears in
Domesday. Suffolk, fol. 377.

[1] His valiant friend and companion, Robert, son of Godwine, was taken
prisoner by the Mohammedans in king Baldwin's flight from Rama, in
May 1102, and, refusing to renounce his faith, was shot to death with
arrows. W. Malm. p. 425.

of the duchy, of his incapacity for which he must be fully
aware[1]. Those about the duke were but too successful in
prevailing on him to refuse these conditions, and the fraternal
conflict took place on the day, on which, forty years before,
the battle of Hastings was fought by their father (28th Sept.).
Victory soon declared itself in the king's favour; a great
number fell by the sword, and about four hundred knights
were taken; of the leaders, Robert of Belesme was the only
one that escaped; the duke himself was made prisoner by
Galdric, one of the king's chaplains; the count of Mortain
by some Bretons[2]. This noble and some other barons were
condemned to perpetual imprisonment. Eadgar Ætheling
and Robert of Estouteville were set at liberty. The former,
who, from love of his native land, had declined the invitations
of the German and Greek emperors to pass the remainder of
his days at their court, retired to some remote corner of
England, where he lived solitary and unheeded, and, it is
supposed, died at an advanced age in the latter years of
Henry's reign[3]. Flambard was restored to his see on re-
signing that of Lisieux, conferred on him by duke Robert.
Duke Robert's lot seems to claim our commiseration, on
calling to mind how much fortune had seemed willing to bestow on him; though it can hardly be pronounced lamentable, if we take into consideration the welfare of his subjects
and his own imbecility. At first he was held in captivity at
Falaise, and afterwards in England, though treated as a

---

[1] Ord. Vital. p. 820.

[2] A letter on this battle from the king to archbishop Anselm is given
in Malm. de Pont. lib. i. and Eadmer, p. 90. [The chaplain, Galderic, was
rewarded with the bishopric of Llandaff. Having incurred the hatred of
the townsmen, he, with five of his prebendaries, was murdered in a field.
Ord. Vital. p. 821.—T.]

[3] Malmesbury (p. 425) speaks of him as still living: ["Eadgarus,
fatua cupidine illusus, Angliam rediit, unde, ut superius dixi, diverso
fortunæ ludicro rotatus, nunc remotus et tacitus canos suos in agro con-
sumit." T.]

prince, and in full enjoyment of every luxury[1]. He lived in
indolence twenty-eight years, and died at Cardiff[2]. Henry
now, as his father is said to have foretold, added the dominion
of Normandy to that of England; although it would seem
that, notwithstanding his having received the investiture from
the king of France[3], he observed the forms of etiquette towards his brother so far that, while Robert lived, he never
assumed the title of duke of Normandy[4].

It seems remarkable that these wars, regarding a fief of
the French crown, were carried on by two of its vassals, without any interposition on the part of the king of France. We
find, indeed, intimations of negotiations between that monarch and Henry[5], yet no traces worthy of notice of any act
or expression of will on the part of the powerless suzerain.
A very different spirit of foresight and activity prevailed in
the council of Henry. No prince could be more useful to
England than the count of Flanders, who also possessed the
power, by his proximity to Normandy, of being a troublesome
and dangerous neighbour, and, in consequence of his double
vassalage, to the king of France and the German emperor,
was the better able to maintain his independence. Henry,
under many more defined conditions, renewed with count Robert an old treaty, based originally on the relations subsisting between the Conqueror and his father-in-law, count Baldwin V., by which, in consideration of a yearly stipend of four
hundred marks of silver, that prince engaged, as far as his
feudal obligations to the Roman and French realms permitted,
to supply the king of England, at his desire, within forty days,

---

[1] Ord. Vital. p. 823. "Omnibus deliciis abundanter pavit." W. Malm.
p. 611. Also Joh. Saresbur. Polycrat. lib. v. c. 18. "captum in custodia
publica, habita tamen æstimatione dignitatis sanguinis."

[2] Ord. Vital. p. 893. Flor. Wigorn. Cont. a. 1134.

[3] Suger. lib. i. p. 28.

[4] I do not find the title in any document of Henry's; for that in Rymer
of the year 1132 belongs evidently to Henry III. and to the year 1248.

[5] Ord. Vital. p. 816, a. 1105.

with a thousand horse soldiers, each with three horses, in England, with an equal number in Normandy, and five hundred in Le Maine. Should count Robert be bound, with king Philip of France, to make an attack on England, he promised with the smallest number, ten knights only, to proceed against Normandy. He moreover bound himself to the king to aid him not only against foreign enemies, but also against rebels. The further, more circumstantial provisions of this treaty, in which the count of Flanders appears half as an independent prince, and half as a mercenary of England, conclude with the engagement of twelve of the highest Flemish barons, viz. Robert of Bethune, the constable Amauri, Hugo of Aubigny, the castellains of Bruges, Mons, Lisle, etc., who, in case the count should not fulfil his obligations to king Henry, promise to pay that sovereign twelve hundred marks of silver, under the penalty of confinement in the Tower of London. On the other part, the king gave eight sureties for the payment of the annual stipend promised by him[1]. After the death of king Philip, this treaty was renewed, with some modifications, and with express reference to any hostilities that might take place between Henry and the successor of Philip, Lewis VI[2].

Less definite was the relation in which the county of Le Maine stood to England. At the intelligence of king Wil-

---

[1] Rymer, Fœd. i. p. 7. The treaty is placed in the beginning of March 1103. It was concluded at Dover. Eadmer (p. 69) mentions the meeting. See also England under the A. S. Kings, ii. p. 287, and this volume, p. 261.

[2] Rymer, i. p. 6, under the date 1101, erroneously, as king Lewis is named; therefore between 1108, when that prince succeeded to the throne, and 1111, when count Robert died. The first of these years is probable, not only from all the circumstances, but is almost confirmed by the fact, that Robert of Belesme appears as one of the deputies and sureties for the king, which seems imaginable only, in the brief space between his reconciliation with Henry and his new defection in favour of the son of duke Robert. A similar treaty of the year 1163 is given in the Fœdera, lib. i. p. 22.

liam's death, count Hélie instantly hastened to Le Mans, the
inhabitants of which came joyfully to meet him. With these
and those knights who had faithfully adhered to him in his
exile, together with the auxiliaries he had demanded from
Fulk count of Anjou, as his feudal lord, he laid siege to the
castle, which was stoutly defended by two Norman knights,
Haimeric of Moria and Walter fitz Ausger, of Rouen. But
the besieged, who could not be ignorant of the perplexed
condition of their prince, entered into an armistice, for the
object of obtaining, from the princely brothers, through the
medium of deputies, instructions for their future measures.
Duke Robert, just returned from Palestine, and called upon
to strive for the crown of England, thanked his knights for
their willingness to preserve Le Maine for him, but, at the
same time, declared that, for the present moment, he was
compelled to leave them to their fate. From the English
monarch, who had still greater reason not to divide his forces,
they received a similar answer[1]. At the end of three months
the place was surrendered to Hélie, who from that time kept
undisturbed possession of the county of Le Maine until his
death eight years afterwards. While drawing the bond of
union with Anjou still more closely, by marrying his daughter
Erenburg to count Fulk, he entered into more intimate relations with king Henry, to whom he afforded aid in his wars
in Normandy. The circumstances, under which the feudal
relation of Le Maine to England was renewed under Hélie,
are unknown; it might possibly have been in virtue of a treaty
similar to that before mentioned with Flanders[2]. That after
Hélie's death no feudal relationship existed is beyond all
doubt[3].

---

[1] Ord. Vital. pp. 784 sqq. Acta Cenoman. p. 309.

[2] Ord. Vital. p. 818. a. 1106.

[3] It is the Sax. Chron. only (a. 1110) which states that Hélie held Le
Maine of K. Henry. [I add the passage: " Ðises geares forðferde Elias
eorl, þe þa Mannie of þam cynge Heanri geheold, and on cweow." The
last word has sadly puzzled the translators: Bp. Gibson says: " Lectio

Henry's relations with France were, in the beginning of his reign, on a most friendly footing, as on his part the power, on the other both the power and the inclination, to enter on a border-warfare were wanting. Prince Lewis, the heir to the French crown, even visited Henry at London. Soon after his arrival Henry received a letter, written, in the name of king Philip, by the countess Bertrade of Anjou, in which he is requested to consign the prince, her step-son, to perpetual imprisonment. A proposition of such importance could not be decided on without the consent of the barons, who were instantly called together. But hospitality prevailed over the delusions of self-interest, and a companion of the prince, William of Buschely, who, suspecting something of what was in agitation, had, as it were in joke, thrust himself into the meeting of the nobles, was commissioned to disclose the proposed treachery to his master. Henry dismissed the prince with rich presents, who vainly demanded vengeance at the hands of his father, and was even exposed to murderous machinations on the part of the royal harlot[1]. To appease his resentment, his father conferred on him Pontoise and the Vexin, by which act the design of bringing him

fortasse vitiosa: certe vocabuli significatio me latet." Ingram adds: "The territory was not a *fee simple*, but subject to *taillage* or taxation; and that particular species is probably here intended which is called in old French *en queuage*, an expression not very different from that in the text above." Perhaps without rendering myself liable to the charge of over-rashness, I may venture on reading oncneow, *agnovit*, in place of the no-meaning on cweow. That is, *he held of, and acknowledged, Henry (as his feudal lord).*—T.]

[1] Sim. Dunelm. a. 1101. Ord. Vital. p. 813. [After his return Bertrade attempted his destruction by secret arts, and for that purpose employed three sorcerers (malefici de numero clericorum), one of whom divulged the plot and rendered it abortive. She then suborned poisoners, and the prince, taking to his bed, for some days could neither eat nor sleep. When the French physicians had exerted their skill in vain, a shaggy individual from a barbarous land (hirsutus de Barbarie) came, and, by his medicaments, saved the patient's life, but who remained an invalid ever after.—T.]

into hostile collision with the Normans and king Henry is not to be mistaken. Nor was it long after the acquisition of Normandy by Henry and the accession of Lewis VI. to the throne of France, that an old dissension respecting Gisors again burst out, (1109). Notwithstanding the treaty, that this town, lying on the Epte and on the boundary of the two states, should not be occupied by the troops of either king, Henry had contrived to seduce it from its possessor, Payen of Gisors. A war of two years' duration was the consequence of this step, and king Lewis, attended by his most powerful vassals, among whom was count Robert of Flanders, at the head of four thousand men, took the field in person against the king of England. Their armies met at Neaufle, where a very ruinous bridge led across the river. Lewis at first had recourse to negotiation, and offered to prove the justice of his pretensions by the encounter of a certain number of their barons, among whom appeared count Robert himself. This proposal was rejected by the Normans, who professed a preference for a judicial decision. Lewis afterwards offered to engage with Henry in single combat ; but the position of the two armies on each side of the river rendered their meeting with safety impracticable. A proposal made in jest that the kings should fight in the middle of the ruinous bridge, was thoughtlessly and rashly entertained by Lewis, but declined by Henry, who said that he was not to be moved by such idle talk to run the risk of losing a noble and strong town. If Lewis should meet him where he must defend himself, he would not flinch from him. Hereupon all flew to arms, though the river prevented a conflict. On the following day the armies met at Gisors, when the English and Normans were driven back into the town, with considerable loss on both sides.

While the reign of Lewis evinces an earnest endeavour to correct the mischiefs that had arisen from his father's negligence, and, as far as it was practicable, to hold his proud

Norman vassal within the bounds of duty, and both kings were, consequently, keeping a jealous watch over their ancient or pretended rights, the exertions of both to curb the insolence of their own vassals, and, with powerful hand to punish their disobedience, supplied an inexhaustible source of dissension between them. Le Maine, Evreux, the Vexin, Blois, Belesme, Alençon, and other frontier districts were subject to a constant change of lords and claims; and the faithless vassal could with confidence rely on the protection of that king, who, for the moment, did not happen to be his feudal superior. From this cause blood flowed in streams, countless treasure was squandered, a more useful application of which was never dreamed of by the political economy of those days. It was in this year particularly that Theobald, the young count of Blois, son of count Stephen, who had fallen before Ramla, and Adela, a daughter of William the Conqueror, maintained a constant warfare against king Lewis, in which he was supported by his uncle Henry. A battle near Meaux, (1108), which took place not long after the engagement before mentioned at Gisors, was followed by an immediate cessation of hostilities in that neighbourhood [1].

Since the battle of Tinchebray Henry had resided in England, and repeatedly held splendid courts there. To Winchester he was less attached than his predecessors, as the proximity to the daily increasing and flourishing London offered greater facilities for the gratification of luxury. The Whitsuntide of the year 1110 was solemnized in the new palace of the ancient royal residence of Windsor. But here the king did not live solely for the pleasure of the chase and other diversions. The insolence and revolting spirit of his barons he repressed instantly and severely; and, in this year, Philip of Braiose, William Malet, and William Bainard, although all men of noble blood and of approved fidelity to the royal house, were sentenced to banishment. To the first one alone,

---

[1] Suger, p. 36. Ord. Vital. p. 837. W. Malm. p. 633.

x

after a lapse of some years, was permission to return granted[1]. The name of the last-mentioned disappeared from that time from among the noble races of England, and his memory is preserved only in the name of one of the wards of London, where, on the river's bank, stood Bainard's castle, until swept away by the great conflagration of 1666.

A new cause for apprehensions, both immediate and remote, had in the meantime arisen on the opposite side of the Channel. After the defeat of Robert, William, a child of five years, the only son of that unhappy prince by Sibylla of Conversana, was brought to him. Henry caressed the weeping boy, and that no evil suspicion might attach itself to him, should any mischance befal the child in his tender infancy, he assigned him to the guardianship of Hélie of St. Saens, who had married an illegitimate daughter of Robert, and to whom that prince had already intrusted the education of a son born before his marriage, and bestowed on him the county of Archies[2]. Soon, however, on the warning of his counsellors, Henry was sensible that the choice he had made was not a prudent one, and he endeavoured to have the boy conveyed to England. But Hélie fled with his charge, and soon succeeded in exciting the sympathy of his Norman friends for the fair child of their captive prince. To no one was this occurrence more welcome than to Robert of Belesme, who clearly saw what a weapon was placed in his hands, in the person of the legitimate successor of the Conqueror. All means were soon attempted, by letters, agents, and visits, to excite the king of France, the dukes, William of Guienne, Henry of Burgundy, Alan of Brittany, and other powerful princes to active intervention in favour of the young pretender[3].

Henry soon found a pressing occasion again to cross the

---

[1] Sax. Chron. aa. 1110, 1120. Rotul. magn. Pipæ, 31 Hen. I.

[2] Ord. Vital. p. 821. Mackintosh's account, that Henry seems to have struggled with murderous thoughts, is picturesque, but quite unhistorical.

[3] Ord. Vital. p. 838.

sea, in the refusal of count Fulk of Anjou, son-in-law of the
deceased count Hélie of la Flèche, instigated chiefly by his
uncle, Amauri of Montfort, to acknowledge the king of England
and duke of Normandy as superior lord of Le Maine (1111[1]).
Other vassals, also, had committed acts of rebellion. Henry's
contemporaries remarked in him the art, which they often
erroneously ascribed to cowardice, of sparing the lives of his
faithful vassals and warriors[2]. External enemies he was said
to overcome oftener with silver than with steel; but his own
subjects, more frequently than either of his predecessors,
to bring, without warfare, before his courts, and pay attention to their demands. Count William of Evreux, whom his
beautiful and ambitious wife, Helvise of Nivernais, had instigated to transgression against the king, was banished,
with some others (1112). At the end of the year Henry was
so fortunate as to capture Robert of Belesme at Bonneville,
where, although he had never obeyed the repeated citation of
the court, yet, trusting to a commission undertaken for king
Lewis to Henry, he ventured to appear before him. It was
no violation of the law of nations, when Henry refused to
extend to his rebellious subject the inviolability of an envoy
from a foreign prince; yet, in consideration of the occasion
of his coming, he granted him his life. In the following year,
Robert was conveyed to the castle of Wareham, where, in
gravelike stillness and frantic despair, forgotten by those
who did not execrate his detested memory, he passed many
years[3].

While Henry was thus engaged in quelling his rebellious
vassals, count Theobald was so fortunate as to put Lewis to
flight at Puysac. Henry, too, himself took the town of Alen-

---

[1] Sax. Chron. Flor. Wigorn. h. a. Ord. Vital. p. 840, a. 1113.

[2] Ord. Vital. p. 840d. "ipsis sine eorum sanguine deculcatis." W. Malm.
p 642: "libentius bellabat consilio quam gladio: vincebat, si poterat,
sanguine nullo, si aliter non poterat, pauco."

[3] Ord. Vital. pp. 841, 858. H. Hunt. 'De Contemptu Mundi.'

x 2

çon (1113), and skilful negotiators prevailed on the count of
Anjou to swear fealty to him for Le Maine, and betroth his
daughter to the young prince William, who was wont to be
designated by the Anglo-Saxon title of *ætheling*. William of
Evreux, Amauri of Montfort, and his nephew, William Crespin, all fugitives to the court of Angers, were pardoned by
the king. In a few weeks after, peace took place with France,
which, on terms very favourable to Henry, was concluded and
sworn to at a meeting of both kings at Gisors, (end of Mar.)
Lewis resigned to Henry the rights he had till then reserved
to himself over Le Maine, Belesme, and the whole of Brittany.
This last concession was the more desirable to Henry, as he
had destined his own daughter in marriage to Conan, son of
the prince Alan Fergant[1]. Of Robert's son no mention is
made. Thus did peace, through these alliances, seem for a
long time established, and the garrison of Belesme, which had
refused to deliver that fortress to the king, was compelled to
surrender to the now united forces of Le Maine, Blois, and
Normandy. In the summer the king was enabled to return to
England.

Five years of Henry's reign now succeeded, which, although
not in perfect, yet in almost unbroken tranquillity, with regard to foreign countries, were passed by him in England.
In the year immediately following (1114. 7 Jan.), the marriage of his daughter Adelaide — who afterwards bore the
then more loved name of Matilda[2] — with the German emperor
Henry V. was solemnized at Mentz. The match had been
settled as far back as 1109, and a marriage contract concluded at Westminster, whereby Henry assigned to his

[1] The English historians have either omitted to mention, or very slightly
noticed, this treaty of peace, so important, at least in a political point of
view. Lingard places it by two years too late. See Suger, p. 21. Ord.
Vital. p. 841, who also notes the date, which accurately agrees with what
the English chroniclers relate of Henry's abode in Normandy.

[2] In the Sax. Chron. a. 1127 she is still called Æthelic, and also by
the North English chronicler, Joh. Hagustald. aa. 1139. 1142.

daughter a portion of ten thousand marks of silver. In the following spring, the young princess, who had scarcely attained her seventh year, was conducted to Utrecht by Burchard, bishop of Cambrai, where the emperor saw her, and was solemnly betrothed to her. Shortly after, she was, at Mentz, consecrated queen of the Germans. A swarm of Norman knights, ever ready to migrate, accompanied her, deluded probably with the hope of rising to be lords in the land of their young princess, like their forefathers in the suite of Emma in England, or of Sichelgauda in Apulia[1]. Among these was the valiant and expert Roger of Bienfaite, son of Richard of Tonbridge, who was himself a son of count Gilbert, and, consequently, a relative of the king[2]. But the emperor was not slow in discovering the object of his guests, whose services, in his contests with Rome, must appear to him of a very dubious character. Loading them, therefore, with honourable presents, he lost no time in dismissing them.

During the wars in Normandy, England was suffering under an ecclesiastical warfare, which was probably more deplorable on account of the disorders and laxity of the clergy, to which it indirectly led, than important with reference to its object, still less to its result. The religious excitement which the first crusade had called forth in Europe, and the favourable accounts which resounded from the East, were highly serviceable to the Roman court in its plans for strengthening and extending its power. The pope Urban II., as well as his successor, Paschal II, renewed, in most of the states under subjection to their Church, the dissension respecting the investiture of bishops and abbots with the ring and crosier. In England, as in other states, the usage for the prelates to receive this investiture at the hands of the king

---

[1] Sax. Chron. aa.1109, 1110. Ann. Hildeshem. a.1110. Ord.Vital. p.838. W. Gemmet. viii. 11. Rom. de Rou, v.13366. [Sichelgauda was a daughter of Gaimar, prince of Salerno, and second wife of Robert Guiscard.—T.]

[2] W. Gemmet. viii. 15, 37. Ord. Vital. p. 686.

was so decided, that Anselm, known to him as the opinions
were so fiercely maintained by Gregory VII., offered no objection to it at his nomination. His last sojourn in Italy had,
however, instilled into him other views, and he considered
himself bound to give validity in England to the decrees of
the council of Rome, and, consequently, to abolish for ever
the investiture with staff and ring by the king, as well as
what was then regarded as inseparable from it, the homage
and oath of fealty, performed, and sworn on their part by
the prelates. The position of Henry at that time, who saw a
war with his brother impending, was particularly favourable
for the extorting from him of promises and compacts; yet,
even among the Anglo-Norman clergy, Anselm found but
little sympathy, and from the king's counsellors strong opposition, especially from Robert of Meulan, who would not
suffer that the half of the realm, which was in the hands of
the bishops and abbots, should be entirely withdrawn from
the crown. But as Henry had confirmed to the Church of
Canterbury all the lands, revenues, and privileges it had possessed at his father's death, and with the honest object not to
aggravate the existing uncertain state of the kingdom, the
archbishop gave his consent to the proposal of applying to the
pope for the repeal of the decrees on the subject of investiture,
with regard to England. Before the return of the deputation,
the attempt of Robert on England (a. 1101), had taken place,
on which occasion Anselm gave effectual support to his sovereign by summoning the men of Kent, by negotiating with
the wavering barons, and even by the threat of excommunicating the pretender, a step not easily to be justified, when
taken against one who, as a valiant crusader, had defended
the interests of the pope[1]; thus incontrovertibly showing that,
by the sincerest attachment to Henry's cause, he would secure
both the tranquillity of the country and the interests of the

---

[1] See a letter on the occasion of the pope to Anselm. Anselmi Epist.
lib. iii. 42.

Church. Shortly after, the king received an answer to his message from the then pope Paschal II., in which that pontiff expressed himself very bitterly against the claim of investiture by laymen. In his letter many reasons and authorities are adduced, among the latter—what was not likely to appear of much weight to Henry—that of the emperors Constantine and Justinian[1]; chiefly for the purpose of proving that spiritual jurisdiction did not belong to the laity, and, consequently, could not be conferred by them, nor ecclesiastics be nominated by them. These principles were, however, at the time, in general, either not or only partially contested, while the principal point, the fealty of the bishops and abbots for the lands of their churches, was left untouched. The letters of the king have not, as those of the ecclesiastics, been preserved, we can, therefore, only surmise that, with reference to the fealty of the prelates, he expressed himself in a manner to render all opposition fruitless. As Paschal also did not mention the subject, and seemed tacitly to acquiesce in that point, Henry summoned the archbishop to take the oath of fealty to him, and to consecrate those on whom he had conferred bishoprics and abbeys ; or, in case of his refusal, to leave England. After new negotiations between the ecclesiastical and secular chiefs and the king, a deputation was again sent to the pope, of three bishops on the part of Henry, and two ecclesiastics on that of Anselm, to make known the king's determination. The verbal answer brought back by the bishops it was difficult to reconcile with the letter to the archbishop, in which he was pressingly urged to perseverance ; while the prelates unanimously declared that the pope had charged them to announce to the king, that so long as in other respects he conducted himself as a good prince, he would not be adverse to him on account of the investiture, and not excommunicate him for that reason, provided he

---

[1] The words of the latter are from the Novella vi. c. 1, 3, though so as they appear in Julian's Epitome Constitut. xxiv, xxvi.

bestowed the spiritual staff on pious men ; but that he could not give this promise in writing, lest it should be used against him by other princes. While some declared themselves in favour of the written document, or for the declarations of the monks, others rejected the latter, because monks, after they had renounced the world, were incapacitated from bearing witness in secular concerns; and the former, because a sheep-skin blackened with ink and loaded with a lump of lead was not to be put in competition with the declaration of three bishops and living witnesses. Anselm's representatives had nothing better to answer than that the affair was not a secular one, and that the Gospels were also written on sheepskins. Anselm was plunged into the greatest embarrassment by this ambiguous conduct of the pope, who evidently wished to throw all responsibility on the bishops, and avoid coming to a rupture with the king; he probably saw through the conduct of the pontiff, and, consequently, durst not question the veracity of the bishops, which was. moreover, hardly advisable, in order not to cause a still greater scandal in the Church. Therefore, after the before-mentioned deputations, there remained for him no alternative but to undertake a journey to Rome, for the purpose of coming to a better understanding with the pope, and to leave the king to act in ecclesiastical affairs according to his own views, though without any sanction on his part.

But before this resolution was carried into effect, Anselm presided at a synod at Westminster (1102), to which, by his desire, the chief persons of the realm were also summoned, to assure the execution of its decrees. From these we perceive but too evidently how seriously the cause of religion had suffered amid the quarrels of the Church. Three abbots, convicted of simony, were deposed, three for other crimes deprived, and three not yet consecrated turned out of their abbeys. It was again enacted, that priests and other ecclesiastics should not have wives ; that the sons of priests should not inherit their churches; that ecclesiastics should not addict themselves to drinking, nor clothe themselves in an unseemly manner; that bishops should not hold secular courts; that new chapels be not erected without the bishop's consent; that churches be not consecrated till all necessaries be provided for both priest and church; that no one attribute reverence or sanctity to a dead body, or a fountain, or other thing (as it sometimes is), without the bishop's authority; that no one exercise the wicked trade, then usual in England, of selling men like beasts. In this synod profligate, obstinate sodomites, both lay and clerical, were stricken with anathema[1]. These and other decrees of the same synod bear honourable testimony to Anselm's fitness for the practical duties of his office. The firmness with which he refused to consecrate those bishops who had allowed themselves to receive the ring and crosier from the king, could not fail of gaining to him many partisans among both clergy and laity. Roger bishop of Hereford, when on his death-bed, sent to implore consecration at his hands, a request which supposed an inconsequence in Anselm, and could, therefore, only raise a smile in him[2]. William Giffard, the new bishop of Winchester, declared that he could receive the pastoral staff only from the archbishop of Canterbury; but the king would not permit his consecration, and strove to procure consecration for all the bishops nominated by him through Gerard archbishop of York. One of these, Reinhelm, the newly invested bishop of Hereford, who had previously been chancellor to the queen, shrank from these ulterior steps to which his compliance had led him, and brought back to the king the insignia he had received from him, whereupon he was punished with banishment from the court. William, who had consented to receive consecration from the archbishop of York, declared at the

[1] Spelman. Conc. ii. p. 23. Wilkins, i. p. 382. Johnson, Ecclesiastical Laws, ii. p. 24. edit. Baron.—T.

[2] W. Malm. de Pont. lib. iv.

moment of the solemn act, that he would never lend himself
to such a desecration of the mystery of the episcopal succession.   He was banished from the realm, but returned shortly
after.

This seems a fitting place to mention the erection of the
see of Ely, although strictly belonging to an earlier period.
The plan of raising the abbey there to a bishopric, and of in-
demnifying the bishop of Lincoln for the cession of a portion
of his diocese was not new, though only carried into effect,
through the exertions of Anselm, on the death of the abbot
in 1101[1]. The measure is chiefly interesting because it seems
to have originated in political considerations, namely, by the
establishment there of a higher official, to maintain a stricter
watch over the refractory inhabitants of the fens.   With this
object, therefore, the bishop was invested with royal privileges, or regalities, within the isle of Ely.   Although the
bishopric of Ely does not appear, like that of Durham, to
have been a palatinate, it, nevertheless, possessed unlimited
jurisdiction in criminal and civil causes.   Henry, it is probable, did not contemplate the great extension of their privileges which, at a later period, the crafty policy of the bishops
contrived to effect.   Among the privileges granted by Henry,
that alone seems extraordinary, that in the castle and isle of
Ely, the bishop, by his soldiers, should keep watch and ward.
The privilege of having his own soldiers could very soon lead
to the exclusion of the king's, and so of all the royal rights.

Anselm resolved with reluctance to proceed to Rome, and
having embarked at Witsand, stayed several months at Bec
with the celebrated jurist, bishop Yvo of Chartres.   On his
arrival at Rome he found there the emissary of the English
court, William of Warlewast, bishop elect of Exeter, to
whose representations on the subject of investitures the pope
did not yield, although he granted the king certain immuni-

---

[1] See Monasticon, i. p. 483, Eadmer, p. 96, and Selden's notes.

ties which are not more particularly specified[1], and even promised him support against Anselm, if, on his return to England, he should proceed to too great lengths[2]. Anselm, on
the other hand, that his journey might not appear wholly
fruitless, received a general confirmation of the privileges of
his Church; and thus, ill supported, if not faithlessly abandoned, by the court for which he had contended with all his
energies, he tarried, in his state of helplessness, with his friend
Hugh, archbishop of Lyons.   On the arrival of William of
Warlewast from Rome, Henry appropriated to himself all
the revenues of the province of Canterbury, the collection of
which he intrusted to two of the archbishop's vassals.   Some
time after, Anselm received a letter from the king, forbidding
him to return to England, unless he would promise faithfully
to comply with all the usages observed under his father and
brother.   Anselm rejected the condition, and, despoiled of his
resources, prolonged his stay for a year and four months with
his venerable friend the archbishop[3]. He, however, succeeded
in extorting from the pope some more vigorous measures, as
the excommunication, in the council of the Lateran, of the
count of Meulan (1105), and of the counsellors who defended
the investiture by the king, as well as of those who had received investiture from him.   But as no excommunication
was known to have been pronounced against the king, and
the pope rather let it appear that he was expecting an envoy
from him, Anselm resolved to employ the moment in an attempt to bring about a settlement of the dispute.   On the
road to Cluny he learned that the countess Adela of Blois,
the king's sister, lay sick at her castle of Blois.   Like others

---

[1] " Romanorum consilio papa nonnullos paternos usus regi concessit."
Eadmer, p. 73.

[2] Paschal wrote to the king: " Revoca pastorem tuum, revoca patrem
tuum; et si quid, quod non opinamur, adversus te gravius gesserit, siquidem investituras aversatus fueris, nos juxta voluntatem, quantum cum
Deo possumus, moderabimur." Eadmer, p. 74.

[3] Eadmer, p. 76. R. Wendover, ii. p. 176.

of his profession, Anselm loved to exercise influence over the
female mind[1], and, therefore, hastening to her, succeeded in
prevailing on her to accompany him to the king, who, at that
time, engaged in triumphant warfare against his brother, a
short time before the capture of the latter, was sojourning at
L'Aigle. As Anselm now no longer refused to return to England, the king did not hesitate to assure him the possession
of the archiepiscopal property, if he would only hold intercourse with the bishops and abbots who had received investiture
from him. After many messengers had been sent across the
Alps[2], on account of the negotiations then pending, a settlement
rather, perhaps, through the mediation than with the consent
of the pope, was effected in the following year (25th Aug. 1106)
at Bec, between the king and the archbishop, whereby the
former consented to renounce, as insignificant, the investiture
with ring and staff, having no desire to impair the ecclesiastical tribunals, but that the essential oaths of fealty and
homage should be taken to him, as they had formerly been
to his father[3]. Every one now hastened to remove the remaining points in dispute. The king abandoned the iniquitous
taxation of the churches, to which his predecessor had had
recourse, and of which Henry himself, in consequence of the
expenses of his Norman wars, had once availed himself[4]; the
archbishop of York performed the usual obligations to his
brother of Canterbury; consecration was bestowed on the
bishops nominated in the last years, including Anselm's old
opponent at the Roman court, William of Warlewast, to
whom the king had given the bishopric of Exeter. The dispute
between the crown and the national Church in England was

---

[1] See his letters to queen Matilda, the countess Clementia of Flanders,
and others.

[2] See a letter of the pope to Anselm, of the 23rd March, in Eadmer,
p. 87. Many letters relating to these matters are inserted under wrong
dates in Wilkins, Concil. They are all to be found in Eadmer.

[3] Eadmer, p. 91.

[4] Ibid. p. 83. who is very partial in his representation of this matter.

now settled for a long time, sixteen years earlier than it was afterwards at Worms, on similar principles, yet less favourable to the crown, between Henry's son-in-law and pope Calixtus II. But Anselm did not long enjoy the re-established peace. In less than three years after the compromise at Bec, in the seventy-sixth year of his pious life, and in the sixteenth of his anxious administration of the Church, Anselm was removed to the higher community of spirits, by few of his contemporaries so serenely contemplated as by him (21st April 1109).

Together with the dispute about investitures, there was also another subject of contention between England and Rome, which very nearly concerned the archbishop personally. In the eleventh century the popes had been in the habit of sending legates more frequently than previously into the several countries of Europe, for the purpose of remedying by means of councils and synods, the errors of doctrine and defects of discipline that had crept in. To the remote realm of England, however, few legates had been sent[1], probably because the popes, in the peculiar circumstances of that country, thought that such supervision might be intrusted to the archbishops of Canterbury; so that the opinion became firmly rooted, that since the days of Augustine there had been no legate in Britain, because the legatine power in the country had been exclusively appropriated to him and his successors in the see of Canterbury. It excited, consequently,

---

[1] About the year 678 a legate was sent by pope Agatho. Beda, lib. iv. c. 18. Nevertheless, in 785 the two legates sent by pope Adrian to the council of Cealchythe write to that pontiff: " Quia, ut scitis, a tempore S. Augustini pontificis, sacerdos Romanus nullus illuc missus est, nisi nos." Wilkins, Concil. i. p. 146. But this ought not to excite wonder, since more than three centuries later they, in their turn, were also forgotten in England, especially by the Norman clergy. Eadmer (p. 58) writes : " Inauditum scilicet in Britannia cuncti scientes, quemlibet hominum super se vices apostolicas gerere, nisi solum archiepiscopum Cantuariæ."

as much sensation as dissatisfaction, when, immediately after Henry's accession, Guido archbishop of Vienne, a son of William Tête-hardie, duke of Burgundy, and a relative of the dukes of Normandy[1], landed and announced that the legatine authority over this district had been conferred on him. Notwithstanding the dissensions that had already arisen between the king and Anselm, neither of them were disposed to seek an ally in the person of the legate, who, unacknowledged, recrossed the Channel. Anselm, personally offended, applied to the pope, who deemed it advisable for the moment to confirm the primate in all his rights, and also to promise, that during his life no legate should be placed over him. There was, in fact, no legate again sent to England by the papal court for many years after the death of Anselm, when his nephew, named like himself, who had numerous friends in England, and possessed accurate knowledge of the state of things there, and who a short time before had brought over the pall to archbishop Ralf[2], appearing particularly well adapted to make the attempt, was employed for the purpose accordingly. Nevertheless, although loaded with costly presents, his mission was regarded with such universal displeasure, that both laity and clergy prevailed on the primate Ralf to obtain permission of the king to proceed to Rome, for the purpose of explaining and establishing the rights of the English Church[3]. These attempts of the papal court were the more to be looked on with distrust, as a legate had already entered France, and excommunicated the bishops of Normandy, for their non-appearance at a council appointed by him; whereupon the king sent to Rome his old agent William of Warlewast, now bishop of Exeter, who was already well known to the pope[4]. Ralf, who had been detained by illness, arrived in Italy at an unfortunate moment (1117),

[1] William was a son of duke Rainald and Adeliza, a daughter of Richard II. of Normandy.   Ord. Vital. p. 848.
[2] Eadmer, p. 112.   [3] Ib. p. 118.   [4] Ib. p. 116.

when the emperor, Henry V, was there with his army ; yet
obtained from Paschal, both for himself and the king, new
bulls respecting the preservation of the ancient rights of the
Church of Canterbury, in terms as plain as the provident
papal chancery is in the habit of employing on such occasions. Under the immediate successor of Paschal, then recently deceased, Gelasius, who did not long enjoy an uncon-
tested sway, the ecclesiastical affairs of England made no
progress ; yet, when archbishop Guido, who as legate to
England had formerly been disavowed and dismissed, ascended the papal chair under the name of Calixtus II (Jan. 1119),
they were again vehemently agitated. Calixtus, both with
address and firmness, followed up the plan of depriving the
primate of England of his too extensive privileges, which
were obstructive to the papal authority. To this end he supported Thurstan, the archbishop of York, in his endeavours
to withdraw himself from obedience to Canterbury, and scrupled not to consecrate Thurstan archbishop, notwithstanding
his breach of promise to the king, not to do anything prejudicial to the dignity of the see of Canterbury, (Nov.) ; and,
in an interview which took place at Gisors, even to make an
abortive attempt on the more upright nature of the latter to
induce him also to a breach of faith. " But who would," said
Henry, " ever place faith in the word of man, if I, the king,
should allow myself to be released from my promise by the
pope[1] !" Although Calixtus, on this occasion, assured the
king that he would never permit a legate to pass to England,
excepting at the king's own request, he, nevertheless, a few
years after, conferred the legatine authority over France,
England, Ireland, and the Orkneys, on the cardinal Peter,
the grandson of Leo[2], a rich Jew, and Roman proselyte,

[1] Eadmer, pp. 124, 125, 126. W. Malm. de Pont. lib. iv.

[2] Ibid. p. 137. Of this pope, Gibbon (c. lxix.) says : " In the time of
Leo IX., a wealthy and learned Jew was converted to Christianity ; and
honoured at his baptism with the name of his godfather, the reigning

known afterwards as the antipope Anaclet II., as was his
fellow-legate, Gregory of St. Angelo, as pope, under the
name of Innocent II. Peter found the same opposition as
his predecessors, but consoled himself with an honourable
reception and liberal presents. Calixtus, nevertheless, appointed a new legate in the person of the cardinal of Crema,
who, on the death of Calixtus, which happened shortly after,
was confirmed by his successor, Honorius II. The dissolution
of the marriage, so distasteful to Henry, of Robert's son
William, with Sibylla of Anjou[1], effected through this legate,
could not fail to secure him a friendly reception at the English court, though the yet unabated dissension between the
archbishops must, in a yet greater degree, tend to nourish
the hope of realizing the schemes of the papal court, which
for his own interest were supported by Thurstan. He required a council, under the presidency of the legate, to be
held at Roxburgh, of those Scottish bishops who were partially subjected to his diocese; and the archbishop of Canterbury, at a similar synod held in London (1126), did not
deem it advisable to refuse his sanction. Among its decrees[2],
the old prohibitions of simony and the pretensions by the

pope. The zeal and courage of Peter, the son of Leo, were signalised in
the cause of Gregory VII., who intrusted his faithful adherent with the
government of Adrian's mole, the tower of Crescentius, or, as it is now
called, the castle of St. Angelo. Both the father and the son were the
parents of a numerous progeny; their riches, the fruits of usury, were
shared with the noblest families of the city; and so extensive was their
alliance, that the grandson of the proselyte was exalted by the weight of
his kindred to the throne of St. Peter."

"The origin and adventures of this Jewish family are noticed by Pagi
(Critica, tom. iv. p. 435. A. D. 1124. N°. 3, 4), who draws his information
from the Chronographus Maurigniacensis, and Arnulphus Sagiensis de
Schismate (in Muratori, Script. Ital. tom. iii. p. i. p. 423–432.). The fact
must, in some degree, be true." See also " Recueil des Historiens,"
t. xii. *passim.*—T.

[1] Epist. Calixti, a. 1124, Aug. 26th. Simeon Dunelm. col. 251.

[2] Wilkins, Concil. i. p. 408.

sons of priests to their fathers' churches were, for the most part, repeated ; the plurality of benefices forbidden ; the prohibition of marriage extended to kinship in the seventh degree. But this mission of the cardinal rendered him an object of dislike in England [1], and we must in justice hesitate to believe all that the tongue of calumny, envenomed by the strict inculcation of celibacy, relates of the profligate conduct of the legate [2].

Shortly afterwards Honorius conferred on the archbishop of Canterbury, William, the legatine authority in England and Scotland [3], which was, at a later period, (1132) confirmed by Innocent II. [4], the principal ground for which step may probably be found in Henry's firm position on the throne during the latter years of his reign. In fact, the Church had in Henry, if not a warm friend, yet a well-disposed ally, as long as it made no attack on the inherited rights, which to his electors and defenders he had sworn to maintain. On the death of a prelate, he sometimes applied to his own use the demesnes of the see for some years ; yet the zealous adherent of his Church, Eadmer, who had scorned to accept the bishopric of St. Andrew's, through his abhorrence of royal investiture [5], bears testimony, that neither the government of

---

[1] Gervasii Acta Pontif. Cantuar. col. 1663.

[2] Hen. Hunt. [" Cum igitur in concilio severissime de uxoribus sacerdotum tractasset, dicens summum scelus esse a latere meretricis ad corpus Christi conficiendum surgere : cum eadem die corpus Christi confecisset, cum meretrice post vesperam interceptus est. Res apertissima negari non potuit, celari non decuit. Summus honor ubique habitus in summum dedecus versus est. Repedavit igitur in sua, Dei judicio confusus et inglorius." R. Hoveden, Matt. Westmon. and others, repeat the story.—T.]

[3] See the bull, 25 Jan. in Wharton, Anglia Sac. i. p. 792.

[4] W. Malm. Hist. Nov. p. 699.

[5] Eadmer, p. 138. [The vacant sees of which Henry appropriated the revenues to his own use, were : Canterbury, Durham, and Hereford, for five, and Norwich and Ely for three years. From William Giffard, his chancellor, whom he had promoted to the see of Winchester, he extorted eight hundred marks ; from Roger, three thousand marks, before he would nominate him to Lichfield.   In a

Y

the Church nor the administration of other Church property
had thereby suffered, but that both had been in the hands of
respectable ecclesiastics, and indirectly intimates, that the
churches during that interval might have been enlarged by
the monks[1]. Even the ecclesiastical chroniclers hardly complain of these vacancies, and we should, perhaps, do well to
consider, whether those prelates might not sometimes have
been indebted to the king for undischarged feudal obligations, as well as the reasons and pretexts which, through the
schisms in the papacy, the contests between the English
archbishops, and their as well as the king's frequent absence
from England, at a time when modern financial expedients
were unknown, might but too easily and temptingly present
themselves.

The circumstance most prejudicial to the internal happiness,
although perhaps not to the external glory, of Henry's government, was his oft-repeated and protracted residence in France.

In a council held at Westminster by archbishop Anselm, in 1102, it was
enacted, *that no archdeacon, priest, or deacon, should take a wife, or, if
taken, retain her; but a subdeacon, who was not a canon, if he married after
having made profession of chastity, should be bound by the same rule.* During
Anselm's exile, this rule was violated by many, who resumed their wives,
thereby affording the king a pretext for extorting money, and who accordingly ordered his ministers to implead the offenders, and to receive money
as an atonement for the crime ; but as a great number were proved to be
innocent, the sum so obtained fell far beneath expectation, whereupon a
certain sum was exacted from every parish priest, whether guilty or not.
Hence arose much trouble, some being unable, others unwilling to pay so
unjust a demand. The consequence was, that they were incarcerated and
tortured. Henry being at that time in London was met, on his way to
the palace, by about two hundred priests barefooted in their albs and
stoles, who, casting themselves at his feet, with one voice implored his
mercy; but he was deaf to their prayers, and ordered them to be driven
from his sight. They then betook themselves to the queen, praying for
her intercession. She, it is said, was moved to tears, but withheld by fear
from intervening in their favour. Eadmer, pp. 67, 83, 84.—T.]

[1] Eadmer, p. 109. Simeon Dunelm. col. 62. The abbot of St. Denys
calls him "ecclesiarum liberalis ditator et eleemosynarum dapsilis dispen-
sator." Suger, lib. i. 44.

Of the thirty-five years of his reign, he passed not less than the half in that kingdom. The English in general were of opinion that this arose from an aversion to their country; while others accused the count of Meulan of imparting to the king his hatred towards them[1]. But it cannot be denied that the critical condition of Normandy, as well as the hostile neighbours by whom it was so constantly threatened, rendered the presence of the sovereign in his newly acquired province indispensable.

After the peace of Gisors it was Henry's earnest endeavour to secure for his son William an undisputed succession to the throne. For this object, as soon as a war with the Welsh permitted him, he crossed over to Normandy, (Sept. 1115,) and prevailed on the chief persons of the duchy to do homage in the following year to his son then scarcely twelve years old[2]. It seems not improbable that king Lewis had previously received the young prince's homage for the French provinces of the kings of England, on which occasion the French monarch ceded to him the often disputed town of Gisors. After acknowledgment in the hereditary states of his grandfather, William had no difficulty, in the following year[3], in obtaining the oaths of homage and fealty of the barons of England, which they performed on a great court-day held at Salisbury (19th Mar. 1116).

A few weeks afterwards Henry again embarked for Nor-

---

[1] According to the respectable authority of Eadmer (p. 110), the English had good reason for entertaining such an opinion; he says: "Si Anglus erat, nulla virtus, ut honore aliquo dignus judicaretur, eum poterat adjuvare. Si alienigena, solummodo quæ alicujus boni speciem, amicorum testimonio prætenderent, illi adscriberentur, honore præcipuo illico dignus judicabatur."—T.

[2] Sax. Chron. a. 1115. His age appears from a letter of the pope in Eadmer, p. 74.

[3] Suger, p. 29. Recueil des Hist. Malmesbury (pp. 634, 652) places William's homage to Lewis later; but he is notoriously unworthy of trust in such details, and the homage of the Norman barons to William would have been of no force if not preceded by the other.

y 2

mandy, where he remained nearly five years. The dissensions
between his nephew Theobald count of Blois and the king of
France claimed his immediate attention, and led to an incessant border warfare between the two kings. Lewis himself,
with the count of Flanders, appeared at one time at the head
of a body of French warriors not far from Rouen [1]. On his
side fought the count Fulk of Anjou, on that of Henry his
nephew, the brother of Theobald, Stephen of Blois, who by
his valour in those wars earned his later pretensions to
the throne of England. Henry's adversaries combined in
a plan for recovering his paternal inheritance for William,
the son of duke Robert; but throughout a number of years
their wars consisted more in a series of adventures than
of results. King Lewis himself had, on one occasion, disguised as a monk, together with some warriors muffled in
black cloaks, taken by surprise the town of Le Gué Nicaise,
on the Epte, and, in the cell of St. Ouen, erected a strong
castle there [2]. In this neighbourhood there was much contention both with the sword and with wit, and Henry constructed many new castles, which retained the nicknames of

[1] Sax. Chron. aa. 1116, 1117. W. Malm. p. 634. Orderic, in passing
from the 11th to the 12th book, omits the events of the years 1113—1118
with the extraordinary remark, that in these five years, profound peace
took place with Henry's neighbours.

[2] Ord. Vital. p. 842. Suger, p. 43. [According to Suger, Lewis only
sent forward a body of men, disguised as travellers to occupy the place.
In the Chroniques de St. Denis, it is said that the king "envoia avant soi
de ses genz, les hauberz vestus desoz les chapes et les espées ceintes, et
descendirent ou comun chemin ausi comme se ce fusent païsanz, vers une
vile qui a non li Guez-Nicaise." p. 175. In the Chronica Regum Francorum (p. 211) they are described as vine-dressers: "in habitu viticolarum
fecit capi villam." It is to Orderic alone that we owe the more romantic,
though probably less veracious, account adopted in the text: "Porro Lu-
dovicus Vadum Nigasii, quod *Vani* vulgo vocatur, fraudulenter adiit, ac
veluti monachus cum sociis militibus, qui nigris cappis amicti erant, ex
insperato intravit; ibique in cella monachorum S. Audoeni castrum muni-
vit, et in domo Domini, ubi solummodo preces offerri Deo debent, speluncam
latronum turpiter effecit."—T.]

' Mal-assis[1],' 'Gîte de lièvre[2],' and the like. On a sudden, however, many losses rendered this war extremely critical for
Henry. Within a few weeks died count William of Evreux,
whose county Amauri of Montfort, having failed to obtain it
at his request, sought to acquire by arms, and contrived to
alienate many Norman barons from the king. Queen Matilda
also died at this time, who had inclined the hearts of many,
particularly English, towards her consort; and, lastly, he
whose loss was the most sensibly felt by the state, the sagacious minister of the king, Robert of Meulan, who by his
counsel and influence appeared as the chief support of the
throne. King Henry was also at this time forsaken by many
of his most powerful barons: by Henry count of Eu, Stephen
count of Aumale, Hugh of Gournay, and Eustace of Pacy, a
natural son of William of Breteuil, who was married to Juliana, a natural daughter of the king[3]. Eustace had obtained
from the king a grant of the castle of Ivry, belonging to the
ducal demesne; but Henry having some doubts of his fidelity,
had received from him, as a pledge of his allegiance, his two
daughters by Juliana, while the son of Ralf Harenc, the
governor of the castle, was given as a hostage to Eustace,
who, at the instigation of Amauri of Montfort, barbarously
deprived the boy of sight; whereupon the king, whose anger
had by the unhappy father been raised to fury, allowed Harenc
to put out the eyes and amputate the noses of the innocent
daughters of Eustace, his own grandchildren, and, moreover,
loaded him with presents. Juliana's agony and thirst of vengeance naturally knew no bounds. At a parley granted her
by her father she endeavoured to kill him by a projectile.
This first attempt failed. With an arrow also that she aimed
at him she was equally unsuccessful. When at length compelled to surrender Ivry to her father—Eustace had previously escaped—he allowed his daughter no other means of

---

[1] Ill-placed.   [2] Hare's form.—T.
[3] W. Gemmet. vii. c. 15. Ord. Vital. p. 810.

departure than to wade through the ditch of the fortress, at that time—it was the month of February—filled with ice, into which, as he had caused the drawbridge to be removed, she was compelled to let herself down from the rampart, exposed to the gaze and mockery of the soldiery[1]. In this excited state of the passions of hate, rage, and vengeance, the king's life was not safe in his own palace ; he durst no longer trust his chamberlains, frequently changed his bed, having his sword and shield constantly at his side. A chamberlain named Henry, son of one of his treasurers, sprung from a plebeian race, whom the king's partiality had greatly favoured and promoted, was convicted of a plot to assassinate him. The king spared his life, but, as an appalling example, caused him to be blinded and emasculated[2].

Henry was now so pressed on all sides, that the moment appeared not far distant when he should be compelled to renounce his favourite Normandy, and withdraw to the foggy northern island, when an unexpected occurrence and skilful negotiations restored to him his ancient good fortune. The count of Flanders, who had been foremost among the protectors of the young William of Normandy, had in an attack on the town of Eu, been stricken with an arrow by a Breton (Sept. 1118), the wound from which, owing to his intemperance, laid him on a bed of sickness, and, in the following midsummer, caused his death[3]. Of still greater importance was it, that Fulk of Anjou, whom the king of France imagined he had just bound to his interest by the office of seneschal of the kingdom, and who had promised the county of Le Maine, together with his daughter Matilda, to the son of duke Robert, deserted to the enemy, and, seduced by English gold, affianced the bride to Henry's son William (June 1119), transferred Le

---

[1] " Nudis natibus usque in profundum fossati cum ignominia descendit." Ord. Vital. p. 849.—T.

[2] W. Malm. p. 642. Suger, p. 44. Ord. Vital. p. 848.

[3] Ord. Vital. p. 843. Suger. p. 45. W. Malm. p. 630.

Maine to him and, in the event of his not returning from his intended pilgrimage to Jerusalem, which at a later period gained him the crown of that kingdom, also the county of Anjou itself [1].

In the state of things then prevailing, an engagement between very small bodies, yet consisting of knights of renown, was decisive. The king with five hundred of his most distinguished knights was riding in the vicinity of Noyon (20th Aug.), where he had attended mass, when his scouts descried the king of France with four hundred chosen knights, and among them William of Normandy, approaching from Andely by way of Brenneville. Neither king would listen to his counsellors, dissuading from a conflict, which threatened much personal danger without the prospect of any important result. Only a hundred Norman knights, under Richard, an illegitimate son of Henry, had mounted their horses, the king himself with the rest of the company fought on foot. The first onset of Burchard of Montmorency and Guy of Clermont with eighty knights shook the ranks of the Normans and English, and William Crespin with the men of the Vexin appeared at first to force them to give ground; but by a skilful movement of Henry they were soon surrounded. William Crespin, perceiving the king, brake rashly through those around him, and struck him violently on the head, but the goodness of his helmet effectually protected him. A hundred and forty French knights fled, the bravest were taken, three only were slain, which small number is to be explained rather by the personal consideration entertained by the opponents for each other, than by the hope of ransom for the prisoners. The remaining French fled towards Andely; some escaped by mingling among the conquerors, where, joining in the cry of victory, they passed for brothers in arms. King Lewis himself wandered long about the forest alone, until he was

[1] Suger, p. 45. Ord. Vital. p. 851. Sax. Chron. a. 1119. W. Malm. p. 634.

guided to Andely by a Norman peasant who, fortunately for
the king, little thought what a price Henry would have paid
him for the wanderer. His banner fell into the hands of
Henry, his saddled charger also, which the king of England
sent him back, as his son William did his also to his cousin William of Normandy. Even some prisoners, who were vassals of
both kings, were dismissed by Henry without ransom[1].

After this engagement some inconsiderable attempts only
were made to carry on the war. The king of France had
recourse rather to pope Calixtus, for the purpose of settling
the quarrel with England, while the pontiff was at Rheims,
on account of the council summoned to meet in that city
(October). Lewis, who was not deficient in eloquence, preferred his complaints in person against the king of England,
and set in a prominent light that prince's treatment of his
brother Robert, who had been left unprotected by king Philip.
The flight of the young William of Normandy was represented
as a banishment, the imprisonment of the execrable Robert
of Belesme as a violation of the ambassadorial privileges;
and other occurrences in a similar fashion, as adversaries,
with more or less consciousness, are apt to sin against im-
partiality and truth. This harangue found so much favour
with the assembly, that it was impossible for the archbishop
of Rouen to conduct the defence of the king of England[2].

Henry had in the meanwhile been engaged in terminating
some of the misunderstandings with his vassals. To Amauri
of Montfort he had ceded the county of Evreux, had become
reconciled with Eustace of Bretenil and Juliana, received the
submission of Hugh of Gournay, Stephen of Aumale, and
other rebels. When therefore Henry and the pope afterwards met at Gisors, it was not difficult for the former to

---

[1] Ord. Vital. p. 853. Suger, p. 45. In Camden's Remains are some
Latin verses on this battle (apud Nugentum) which are erroneously assigned to an earlier one.

[2] Ord. Vital. p. 858.

place in a totally different light, if not completely refute, the charges brought against him at Rheims, and, at the same time, adduce many circumstances in his own favour, which turned the mind of the pope to his advantage; and also to conclude a peace with France on the easiest conditions, viz. the restoration of his possessions to each of the kings, and the liberation of the prisoners. The interest of William of Normandy was completely abandoned: he neither received his father's land nor the earldoms that Henry had formerly promised him in England. With the count of Flanders, Charles the Good, a friendly intercourse was soon restored. William Talevas, son of Robert of Belesme, received, through the mediation of Fulk of Anjou, confirmation of the county of Ponthieu [1].

Thus was Henry's grand object attained. After twenty years of strife he saw all his adversaries overcome, himself in firm possession of all the lands over which his father had ruled, and his son acknowledged as his successor. Exulting in his prosperity Henry embarked at Barfleur (25 Nov. 1120.) and returned to England. His son William, attended by numbers of the young nobility, followed with the royal treasure in another vessel named the White Ship, for the purpose of giving satisfaction to one Thomas the son of Stephen, its owner, who claimed the conveyance of the king as an hereditary right, his father having conveyed the Conqueror on his expedition against Harold. All who loved pleasure and merriment rushed on board this vessel, which at the same time, promised the greatest security, and in which nearly three hundred persons were collected. Among them were Richard, a natural son of the king, distinguished for his valour; the king's natural daughter Matilda, the consort of Rotrou count of Perche; Richard the young earl of Chester, with his countess and his brother; Otuel the tutor of the

---

[1] Sax. Chron. a. 1120. Ord. Vital. p. 848.

young prince; the daughter of the count Theobald of Blois; Theodric, a nephew of the emperor Henry V.; with many young nobles, for the purpose of receiving investiture of their estates in England; besides a hundred and forty knights, and eighteen ladies, nearly related to the king or the chief nobility. The ship was so heavily laden that count Stephen of Blois left it and returned to land, and his example was followed by some monks and several more prudent elderly persons. In the exuberance of his gaiety, prince William caused three barrels of wine to be distributed among the fifty rowers. Thomas, the master, in a state of drunkenness, and, unconscious of the helplessness of his crew, in the evening made the signal for departure, and now all exerted themselves to the utmost to overtake the other vessel. Suddenly those on board the king's ship and those on shore heard a cry which, as they learned on the following day, proceeded from the White Ship. This vessel, owing to the haste with which it was rowed, and the drunken condition of the steersman, was, notwithstanding the bright moonlight, driven on the rocks of the Catteraze, wrecked and quickly filled with the rushing water. There was scarcely time to put out a boat, into which the prince was lowered, when, hearing the cries of his beloved sister, the countess of Perche, from the fast-sinking ship, he could not resist her supplications to receive her. Together with her rushed a multitude of despairing beings from the vessel into the boat, which, borne down by the weight, instantly disappeared in the mass of waters. Of all who were on board the White Ship only two still held by the mast, the young Geoffrey of L'Aigle and Berold, a poor butcher of Rouen. Thomas, the master, rose once from the water and inquired after the prince. On hearing that he and all the others had perished with the vessel, he cried; "Then it is of no use for me to live longer!" and sank into the abyss. Geoffrey, stiffened with the cold, sank soon after him, Berold alone, the obscure, humble individual, with whom not one of those on board would have changed condition, survived the dreadful night, protected from the cold by raw sheepskins. On the following morning he was found by some fishermen, to whom he related the appalling catastrophe. The royal treasure was afterwards recovered; of the corpses very few were found.

The sad intelligence was soon spread on the English coast, but there was no one venturous enough to announce it to the king, who believed at first that his son had landed at some other port, yet with increasing anxiety made hourly inquiries after him. There was hardly one at the court who had not lost some friend or relative through this disaster; all were stricken most poignantly, and could with difficulty refrain from tears. On the second day a youth, the son of count Theobald of Blois, was commissioned to cast himself at the king's feet and disclose to him the cause of the general sorrow, the loss of the White Ship. Henry, convulsed with the acutest pain at the destruction of all his hopes, fell speechless to the earth; nor until he was conveyed to his chamber did he recover his consciousness, only to burst forth in the most mournful wailings. Though with a faculty characteristic of the Normans he was able to repress his feelings and conceal them beneath an assumed austerity, he was never seen to laugh afterwards[1]. In the general loss of the Anglo-Norman nobility, no one's death was more painfully felt than that of William the Ætheling; for he had assumed that title to give pleasure to the native population. The sudden bereavement of the father could kindle no hope in the Anglo-Saxons, who had now served their conquerors above half a century, of recovering their ancient independence; both races, as the duration of Henry's life could not be ascertained, must only dread the uncertainty of the succession to the throne; since no one would accept of duke Robert, and a few only of his

[1] Ord. Vital. p. 867. W. Malm. p. 653. Flor. Cont. a. 1120. Sim. Dunelm. h. a.

son; the empress Matilda had no heir, and the miraculously
saved Stephen of Blois was little thought of. The clergy
profited by an event which so impressively called to mind the
instability of all things earthly, while even the possibility of
earthly repentance and atonement was cut off; nor did the
pride of princes and the vices of the court escape without
animadversion [1].

The queen Matilda had, as we have already stated, died
two years before her son. Not alone on the gravestone in
the royal burial place at Westminster, but also in the hearts
of the people was engraved the name of the good queen
Molde [2]. After the birth of her second and last child, and
while the king was engaged in war and knightly pursuits in
Normandy, she had retired to Westminster. Here, yielding
to the impressions of her early cloister-days, she devoted
herself to pious meditations and works of charity. Clad in
hair-cloth under the garb of royalty, she would, during the
days of Lent, visit the churches bare-footed; she would also
wash the feet of the sick, and shrank not from touching their
ulcers; would imprint kisses on their hands, and set meat
before them [3]. A monument of the industry of herself and
maidens we probably possess in the tapestry belonging to the
cathedral of Bayeux. But her cell ever continued a palace.
Her kindness and liberality attracted ecclesiastics and
strangers from all countries. Poets, who recited before her

---

[1] Henry of Huntingdon (a. 1120) speaks of them as a loathsome set;
and of prince William, Bromton, col. 1013 (as he says from Malmesbury)
says: "quod ille Willielmus, regis primogenitus, palam Anglis fuerat
comminatus, quod si aliquando super eos regnaret, faceret eos ad aratrum
trahere quasi boves." The passage does not appear in Malmesbury.—T.

[2] Rudborne, Hist. major Winton. p. 276.

[3] For this excess of humility, or its opposite, she was, as we are told by
Robert of Gloucester (p. 435), one day reproved by one of her knights:

　　"Madame, he seyde, vor Gode's loue, ys bys wel ydo,
　　þat þou þys unclene lymes handlest and cust so?
　　Vyl wolde myn louerd þe kyng telle, wan he þy mouþ cust.
　　þat so vylyche yuyled ys, me þyngþ, gyf he yt wuste."—T.

any new works in the language of the court, were nobly rewarded; even yet more lavish was she towards those melodious minstrels who charmed her well-practised ear with their
songs. Yet the good intention of her prodigality did not
screen her from its natural consequences, nor hallow the
means of satisfying it. She was ever in debt, and the peasants on her lands groaned under the most intolerable exactions of her agents, and uttered maledictions on their lady,
who, although their countrywoman, appeared to them inex-
orable; while the French poet, clad in new silk and costly
furs, gently lisped his tender valedictory lay, and the well-fed
singer, in joyful, jeering mood, carried off the heavy, easily
earned bag of sterling money[1]. Henry had not entered into
a second marriage; though after this loss it appeared advisable, without delay, to form an engagement, which might
insure the future stability of his kingdom. His choice fell
on Adela, the young and beautiful daughter of Godfrey VII.
count of Louvain[2], by favour of the emperor Henry V. also
duke of Lower Lorraine and marquis of Antwerp, who afterwards became and died duke of Brabant. But this marriage
was unproductive of the fruits for the sake of which it was
contracted, and, with the exception of some not very important relations of foreign policy, of no influence on England[3].

The return of count Fulk of Anjou from the Holy Land
soon gave occasion to new wars. This ambitious prince was

[1] W. Malm. p. 650.

[2] Eadmer, p. 136. Flor. Cont. a. 1121. W. Gemmet. viii. c. 29. It is
perhaps to more than monkish simplicity we may ascribe what the monk
of Worcester says of the object of this marriage, viz. "ne quid ulterius
inhonestum committeret." [After Henry's death, Adela married William
of Albini, the first earl of Arundel. *Carte.*—T.

[3] We must here call attention to the erroneous chronology of Orderic,
who places the prince's shipwreck in 1119, and Henry's second marriage
in 1120, both a year too early; but, on the other hand, the death of the
archbishop, Ralf of Canterbury, in 1123, a year too late. Conf. Sax. Chron.
aa. 1120, 1122. Flor. Cont., whose accuracy is confirmed both by an
eclipse of the moon and other accounts.

as fully sensible as Henry of the importance to each of an
alliance between their respective states; though in such alliance each consulted only his own selfishness and ambition.
Henry had retained his intended daughter-in-law in England
and, on the return of her father, refused to relinquish her
dowry[1]. The princess herself, spontaneously renouncing the
world and its treasures, at the age of twelve years, devoted
herself to a life of piety, and ten years after took the veil in
the convent of Fontevrauld, where her tender frame soon
sank under the strict ecclesiastical discipline of the place[2].
But her father, now on terms of hostility with Henry, sought
to increase the future power of his race by the marriage of
his second daughter Sibylla, with the young William of Normandy, instigated chiefly by his uncle, the old enemy of
Henry, Amauri of Montfort, count of Evreux, with whom
other Norman nobles of high rank were associated in favour
of William.   Among these were Hugh of Montfort, Hugh,
son of Gervase of Neuchâtel, and even their uncle Walcram,
son of Robert of Meulan. The names of these men disclose
to us the character of this combination against the king, of
which the real object was simply to exchange a rigid and
powerful lord for one more docile and indulgent.

The intrigues of his Norman barons could not long remain
unknown to Henry, who, after an absence of some years, had
returned to Normandy, where, while passing his time at
Rouen, apparently in perfect security, he prepared measures
for the suppression of the rebellion (Whitsuntide 1123). He
collected forces from all quarters, and commanded Hugh of
Montfort to his presence, whom, without betraying his anger,
he ordered to deliver up the castle whence he derived his
name. But Hugh outwitted the king, who had expected to
obtain the castle without striking a blow. He promised im-

---

[1] Sax. Chron. a. 1121. W. Malm. p. 654. Ord. Vital. p. 875. Sim.
Dunelm. a. 1123.

[2] Ord. Vital. p. 875.

mediate compliance with the will of his sovereign, and rode
away with the knights appointed by the king to receive the
fortress. He soon, however, contrived to withdraw from
them by a side way, which led him to Montfort before the
arrival of those who followed the high road. Here he committed the defence of the castle to his wife, Adeline, a
daughter of Robert of Meulan, and to his brother, while he
himself hastened to Brienne, to his brother-in-law, count
Waleram, for the purpose of beginning open warfare against
his sovereign. To the children of his former friend, Robert
of Meulan, Henry offered unconditional pardon for the past,
provided they would return to their duty, and also lead back
Hugh as a faithful friend and vassal. But the petulant young
man was not to be moved to submission, and the king found
himself compelled to sacrifice both time and force in besieging
the several castles of the insurgents. Before the end of the
year he had gained Pont-Audemer from Waleram, a strong
fortress defended by a hundred and forty knights; but a
tower of wood, twenty-four feet higher than the walls, being
raised before it, the archers from its summit so galled the
garrison, that, after a siege of seven weeks, it was compelled
to surrender. Nevertheless, the war threatened to become
more serious, as the king of France was beginning to take an
active part against Henry, on behalf of William and his adherents[1]. Henry hereupon prevailed on the emperor, his
son-in-law, over whom, in concerns of state, he exercised no
inconsiderable influence, to undertake an expedition against
France, to which he had long borne a grudge[2]. This attack
compelled Lewis to hold himself at a distance from Nor-

---

[1] Ord. Vital. p. 879. " Fœdus inter reges ruptum et rediviva guerra
feraliter inordescens utrobique exorta est." Also Sax. Chron. a. 1124.

[2] Conf. Stenzel, Fränkische Kaiser, b. i. p. 716. Suger, lib. i. p. 50.
Otto Frising. Chron. Ursperg. h. a. To the king of England is ascribed
a plan of his son-in-law to make the German empire tributary. See Otto.
ut sup.

mandy, where, even before the emperor had crossed the
frontier, Henry, while residing at Caen, had the unhoped-for
good fortune to get into his power his chief adversary, count
Waleram, the two Hughs, and twenty-five other knights, who
on an incautious march were attacked by Ralf of Bayeux
and William of Tancarvile[1]. The battle was gained chiefly
by the aid of forty English archers, by whom the foremost
horses of their opponents were slain, those following falling
over them, so that eighty knights lay prostrate, and among
them the leaders of the rebellion (26th Mar. 1124). Five
years after, these were set at liberty; Waleram, probably
less through respect for his father than from inclination for
his sister, who had yielded to Henry's embraces and borne him
a daughter, received back all his possessions, with the exception of his castle, and was afterwards restored to Henry's full
confidence[2]. Hugh of Montfort, however, even during the
succeeding reign, continued sunk in his miserable lot. The
prisoners were punished with revolting cruelty, chiefly by
mutilation. Among them Luke of Barré, a knight and poet,
who, more than through his fierce valour, had by his gift of satire, oftentimes so fatal to its possessor, and by his lampoons
against Henry, so embittered that merciless prince against
him, that, giving no ear to intercession, he sentenced him to
the loss of his eyes. In his agony the poet, breaking from
the hands of his tormentors, dashed out his brains against a
wall[3].

In the intended advance against France, the king was still
opposed by count Amauri, and in the following year the unexpected death of the emperor (23 May a. 1125) put an end
to a contest reluctantly and inertly conducted on both sides[1].

---

[1] Ord. Vital. p. 880. Sax. Chron. a. 1124. H. Hunt. Rob. de Monte.
a. 1124.

[2] Sax. Chron. a. 1129.   [3] Ord. Vital. p. 880.

[4] From his union with the daughter of the king of England may have
originated the Chester tradition, that the emperor tortured by remorse on

William of Normandy was abandoned by the count of Anjou
and his other French adherents, and the dissolution of his
engagement with Sibylla, on the pretended plea of too near
consanguinity, through the intrigues of Henry at Rome and
in Anjou, confirmed[1]; the good understanding between the
two kings restored; and we soon after find English troops,
under the banner of France, in an expedition against the
rebels in Auvergne[2].

William of Normandy was in the meanwhile wandering
from monastery to monastery and among his adherents, to
whom, through his pretensions and claims, he had become
extremely burthensome. But king Lewis soon found it politic
to patronise him, and not suffer so formidable a weapon against
Henry to slip from his hands. He therefore gave him in
marriage the countess Jane, a daughter of Giselas, the queen's
mother, by her second marriage with Regnier count of Mont-
ferrat, at the same time investing him with the territory of
the Vexin and the towns of Pontoise, Chaumont, and Mantes
(Jan. 1127)[3]. After some weeks William's lot became changed
in a most unexpected manner. The count of Flanders, Charles
the Good, had been assassinated while at his devotions in the
church of St. Donatus at Bruges. William, burgrave of
Ypres, was probably the instigator of this barbarous murder,
of which he was fully capable, and his motive for which may
be found in his pretensions to the Flemish throne. He was a
natural son of Philip, son of Robert II., and, consequently, a
nephew of Baldwin VII, on whose death he had endeavoured
to make good his claim to Flanders. After the death of

account of the imprisonment of pope Paschal, became a voluntary exile
and ended his days in a wilderness there. Such is the story told sixty
years after the emperor's death by Giraldus Cambrensis (Itiner. lib. ii. c.
11.) from an impostor, who assumed the emperor's name, and died as a
monk at Cluny. See Ricardi Pictav. Chron. Turon. a. 1139.

[1] Sax. Chron. a. 1128. Bulls of popes Calixtus II. and Honorius II.,
relating to this affair, may be seen in D'Achery. Spicileg. iii. p. 119.

[2] Suger. p. 53.   [3] Ord. Vital. p. 884.

z

Charles he immediately assumed the title of count of Flanders, for which, however, he had many competitors, among whom it may suffice to mention the king of England, his nephew William of Normandy—both on account of their descent from Matilda, the wife of the Conqueror—and Diederik count of Alsace, who was the son of the sister of the last count's mother, and undoubtedly the nearest heir[1]. But the sudden resolution of the king of France, the superior lord of the greater part of Flanders, who instantly proceeded to Arras, induced the Flemish burgraves and cities to declare in favour of William; an occurrence which plunged Henry into a state of the greatest anxiety. His attempt, by sending a force under Stephen count of Blois and Mortain, who by his marriage was also count of Boulogne, a Flemish fief, proved a failure. But Henry would most willingly have renounced all claim to Flanders for himself, could he only have set aside his nephew[2]. He now lost no time in completing the measures we shall presently relate for securing his daughter's succession and inheritance; when death, which had so cruelly bereft him of his greatest joy, now as unexpectedly relieved him from his formidable youthful rival[3]. William, who in consequence of the rigour with which he pursued the murderers of Charles and their adherents, as well as through the firmness with which—herein resembling his uncle—he strove to maintain the public tranquillity, had raised up many enemies among his new subjects, was forsaken by a vast number of them, while count Stephen persisted in refusing his homage for his fief of Boulogne. Count Diederik, supported by king Henry, was called in by the Flemings, who even made an inroad into France, and near Epernon (dep. Eure and Loire) for some time detained king Lewis himself; when William, although victorious

[1] Warnkönig, Flandrische Rechts- und Staatsgeschichte, i. p. 138.
[2] Helinand, in Chron. Alberici, a. 1127. Gualteri Vita Caroli, c. 66.
[3] Hen. Hunt. a. 1128. Guil. de Nangis, aa. 1127, 1128. Chronica, c. 32, in " Flandria Generosa."

against him in a battle, died of the consequences of a slight
wound in the hand, before Alost, which he was besieging in
conjunction with his new ally, Godfrey of Louvain[1]. From
his death-bed in the abbey of St. Bertin at St. Omer's, whither
he had been conveyed (24 July 1128), he sent a conciliatory
letter to his uncle, commending to his clemency those Normans who had been faithful followers of their lawful prince.
Having nothing more to fear from the claims of his nephew,
Henry complied with his request, and granted an amnesty to
his adherents, with permission to return to Normandy, whereby he cheaply gained the good will of the Normans. Henry
still continued to support count Diederik both by counsel and
deeds[2], compelling his own nephew, Stephen of Boulogne, and
other Normans, holding possessions in Flanders, to submit to
him. He, moreover, induced the count to take to wife Sibylla
of Anjou, who had been betrothed to his predecessor, and
neglected nothing that might conduce to bind him firmly to
his interest; while Diederik, although to obtain the investiture of Flanders, he must necessarily subject himself to
France, entered into a secret league with Henry[3].

The king had long been firmly resolved that his nephew
should not be his heir, a resolution, in which we can recognise
only the caprice of an exasperated relative rendered yet more
obdurate by the consciousness of the illegality of his own possession[1]. His daughter, the empress, had passed her year of
mourning in Germany, and then, by her father's desire, proceeded to Normandy, where he at that time was residing.
William's marriage (1126) had rendered a speedy execution
of Henry's plans in the highest degree necessary. In the
autumn, therefore, accompanied by his daughter, he crossed
over to England, whither also the king of Scotland had been

[1] Ord. Vital. p. 886. Sax. Chron. Sim. Dunelm. Anselm. Gemblac. Alberic. a. 1128.

[2] Simeon of Durham (col. 256) asserts, that Henry had received Flanders from the king of France.

Ord. Vital. p. 886.   [3] Hen. Hunt. Epist. lib. i. ap. Wharton

z 2

invited. At the Christmas festival, a numerous assemblage of clergy and laity met at the royal court at Windsor. These, after a long opposition to the proposed departure from the ancient usage of the land, and chiefly out of regard, most strongly dwelt on, for the descent of his daughter Adelaide or Æthelie—such, as we have seen, was her original name—from the old royal stock of the island, as well as by the promise that she should not again marry a stranger, he prevailed on to engage that, in the event of his death without male offspring, they would acknowledge her as queen of England and duchess of Normandy. William archbishop of Canterbury, and after him all the prelates present down to the lowest abbot, swore to this effect; in like manner the laity, at whose head stood the king of Scotland; him followed Stephen of Mortain, the king's nephew, after a dispute respecting precedence with Robert earl of Gloucester, a natural son of the king. Stephen and many others took the oath with seeming alacrity, as they had no belief in its fulfilment. But far more was all trust in it shaken, when Matilda, attended by earl Robert and Brian fitz Count, son of the count of Brittany, embarked for Normandy, whither her father soon followed (26 Aug. 1127), and was there betrothed to Geoffrey the young count of Anjou, son of Fulk, who, as the count his father was on the eve of marriage with the daughter of the queen of Baldwin II. king of Jerusalem, and for the prospect of whose crown had renounced his hereditary states, was virtually their ruler [1]. Thus was the king's long-cherished wish attained, of seeing Anjou and England united; a project at the time universally blamed, it being thought derogatory to the rank of the empress to marry a young count of fifteen; but chiefly because

[1] Sax. Chron. a. 1127. Sim. Dunelm. h. a. Ord. Vital. a. 1129. Of the courtship, knighthood and betrothal many particulars are given in Johannis Monachi Majoris Monasterii Historia Gaufredi Ducis Normannorum, lib. i. The chronology is apparent from the birth-day of Geoffrey, 24th Aug. 1113., and the account of his age (in his sixteenth year) at his marriage.

such a union could hardly, or rather impossibly be of long duration. But Henry and his ministers, and also many of his contemporaries, were sensible that this connection with Anjou not merely secured to the English crown the possession of certain provinces, but they well comprehended what an influential position with regard to France and, consequently, to the whole political system of Europe, England might through them obtain. But Henry had soon to experience that the realization of great ideas only too easily miscarries through the personality of those concerned in executing them. Scarcely had Henry reached England after the termination of the Flemish dissensions and the settlement of matters in Normandy connected with them, when, shortly after the marriage which had taken place at Whitsuntide (15 July 1129) he received intelligence that his daughter had been contumeliously put away by her young consort, and had returned to Rouen[1]. The uncertainty of Matilda's succession, which was generally acknowledged, must, no doubt, have tended to aggravate the misunderstanding between them. In the following year (8 Sept. 1130) Henry summoned a great council of the nobles to attend him at Northampton, for the purpose of deliberating on the request made by count Geoffrey for the return of his consort. This was agreed to, and, at the same time, the oath, which assured to Matilda the succession to the crown, was renewed, and also taken by those who had not sworn on the former occasion. Henry thereupon proceeded with his daughter to Normandy, where count Geoffrey received his wife in an honourable manner[2]. In the following years, the birth of two children was for some time a source of domestic pleasure, and brought Henry repeatedly and at length for several years back to Normandy. But Geoffrey's demands for certain castles in Normandy, promised to him on his marriage, but which the king refused to deliver to him, his wars against the king's relations, and lastly, his demand,

[1] Sim. Dunelm. a. 1129.   [2] Hen. Hunt. a. 1130. W. Malm. p. 698.

in the name of his children, as heirs to Henry, of valid security for the possession of the English and Norman castles, produced so violent a quarrel—which the ambition of Matilda tended greatly to aggravate—that Henry had resolved on bringing her back with him to England, when death surprised him in the midst of his plans [1].

The connection with count Fulk very soon brought the English into closer intercourse with the settlements of the crusaders in the East. After the return of his brother from Palestine, Henry had striven to check the journeys of his knights to that land, that he might not be bereft of those forces which were necessary for the support of his own power. On this account he had kept at a distance from England Boemund of Antioch, who, after his liberation from captivity among the Saracens, was desirous of visiting the king, and even crossed over to Normandy for the purpose of seeing him there. Individual knights only were not to be hindered, or, on account of their restless spirit, were permitted. Yearly sendings of arms and other munitions he liberally allowed, and granted lands in Avranches to the Templars, with many privileges [2]. But after tranquillity had been restored in Normandy, and peace concluded with the neighbouring states, Henry appears to have seen with pleasure the arrival of the grand master of the Templars, Hugh of Payens. In Normandy he loaded him with rich presents, and allowed him to proceed to England, where he likewise collected many donations. A considerable number of warriors was permitted to accompany the grand master to Jerusalem [3],

[1] Ord. Vital. p. 900. Hen. Hunt. aa. 1128, 1129.

[2] W. Gemmet. lib. viii. c. 32. The tradition that the Templars in Henry the First's time had built a church in England, in which the king wished to be buried, is a mistake. See Wilken, Gesch. der Kreuzzüge. ii. Beilage VIII.; where, however, the bishop of Chichester is mistaken for him of Chester.

[3] Sax. Chron. a. 1128. Hen. Hunt. aa. 1128, 1129.

whose turbulent spirits and military ardour must in times of peace have appeared to the king somewhat dangerous.

The death of pope Honorius II., which happened in this year (1130), plunged Europe, both secular and ecclesiastical, into a state of excitement. The majority of the cardinals, together with the Romans and the Normans of Italy, declared for Peter Leonis, who assumed the tiara under the name of Anaclet II.[1]; while the clergy of France, to whom king Lewis had left the decision, were in favour of his opponent Gregory, who styled himself Innocent II. The French ecclesiastics had been influenced in their choice by St. Bernard, the celebrated abbot of Clairvaux. This powerful supporter of Innocent proceeded also to Normandy, where Henry was then residing, and whom the English prelates, many of whom had been gained over to Peter Leonis during his stay in England, had predisposed in his favour. But Bernard's eloquence prevailed, and Henry was induced to accompany the abbot to Chartres, where he cast himself at the feet of Innocent, as the supreme head of Christendom, and presented him with royal gifts (13th Jan. 1131[2]). Some months later, the pontiff visited the king at Rouen, where he found a most honourable reception[3], and it is probable that the solicitations for aid, made by St. Bernard to Henry, were not needless, as the emperor Lothair had not been able to effect the acknowledgment of Innocent at Rome[4].

It is now incumbent upon us to cast a glance at the state of things in Wales during the reign of Henry. From a nationality as vivid and tenacious as that possessed by the natives of the principality at the present day, it was hardly to

[1] See p. 319, note 2.

[2] Ord. Vital. p. 895. Suger, lib. i. p. 58. Guillelmi Vita Bernardi in Opp. S. Bernardi Clarvall. edit. Mabillon, t. ii. Neander, Der H. Bernhard, p. 72. Arnulf Sagiens. De Schismate, c. vi. apud Muratori Scriptt. iii. p. 430.

W. Gemmet. vii. c. 30, confirmed by a document issued by Innocent from Rouen, dated May 9th 1131.

S. Bernardi Epist. 136.

be expected that, even weakened as they were by the settlement of Norman barons in the midst of their country, they
would, during so long a reign, continue either peaceful subjects or neighbours. Already in the insurrection of Robert
of Belesme they took part with the rebels. Availing himself
therefore of a year when he was not engaged in foreign warfare, Henry adopted an apparently peaceful, although in the
execution perhaps, severe method of confirming the subjection
of the Welsh, and, at the same time, rendering harmless an
enemy of the public tranquillity that he was harbouring in
the midst of his realm. His father, the Conqueror, had been
followed to England by many Flemings, the greater number
of whom sojourned in the northern counties, as most congenial both to their habits and native climate. Many of these
also dwelt dispersed over all the other parts of England, and
were very vexatious to the inhabitants [1]. Other bodies of
Flemings had been driven from their country by inundations
(1106), the greater number of whom had sought shelter in
Germany, while others had betaken themselves to England [2].
To these Henry had at first assigned the desolated lands on
and beyond the Tweed. It is not improbable that it was
owing to his connection with the emperor Henry, that the
thought occurred to him of planting Flemish colonies among
the Welsh, after the example set him in Germany of employing them to curb the Slavish nations and in the culture of the
land [3]. Henry collected all those Flemings settled in England,
who had not previously acquired more considerable possessions, and sent them to the western parts of Wales, to the
land of Rhos, and the neighbourhood of Haverford and

[1] W. Malm. p. 628.

[2] The account of this second immigration of Flemings has by Bromton
been assigned to the year 1106, and from him by Knyghton, p. 2377, and
by Powel, History of Wales, p. 128.

[3] In the year 1106 the "privilegium" of the Flemish colonists was
granted by the archbishop Adelbero of Hamburg. See Lindenbrog.
Scriptt. Rer. Septent.

Tenby[1]. Antiquaries have imagined that the posterity of these colonists may, both by their manners and language, be recognised down to the latest times[2]. They were advantageous to the kingdom, if not, as elsewhere, for the construction of dikes, yet through the weaving of wool and their knowledge of husbandry, though at first chiefly as military mercenaries. The land ceded to them was the western point of Wales, where Milford-haven afforded the best place for embarkation to England, and where Arnold of Shrewsbury had already availed himself of his acquired territory in an attempt on the royal crown of Ireland. After his expulsion from England, his constable, Gerald of Windsor, defended the castle of Pembroke, which was assailed by the Welsh, with as much valour as artifice, and caused them to retire at the moment when his provisions failed, by casting to them, on the preceding day, as a present over the wall, the small portion still remaining, accompanied by vaunting words, and by a letter which he had caused to fall into their hands, in which it was stated that he could well hold out for four months longer. He afterwards espoused Nesta, the daughter of Rhys ap Theodor, the last king of South Wales, sister of prince Griffith, and one of the numerous mistresses of king Henry, to whom she had borne two sons, one named after his father, and Robert earl of Gloucester[3]. A grandson of Gerald and Nesta was the noted Gerald, to whose numerous writings we are indebted for the best accounts of the ancient state of Wales.

Notwithstanding the valour of his vassals and colonists in Wales, Henry was unable to secure peace and tranquillity in that country. Dissensions among the several tribes never ceased, through whose mutual support of each other violent

---

[1] Flor. Wigorn. a. 1111. W. Malm. p. 493. Bromton, col. 1003.

[2] Giraldi Cambrens. Itiner. lib. i. c. 11. and H. Lluyd on Powell's note; also Rot. Magn. Pipæ 31 Hen. I. pp. 136 sq. contains mention of the Flemings in Pembrokeshire.

Giraldi Cambrens. Itiner. lib. ii. c. 7.

wars sometimes burst forth, which not unfrequently required
the armed interposition of the king. A short time before the
planting of the Flemish colony in Rhos, Henry had been
compelled to enter the country, on which occasion even the
aid of king Alexander of Scotland is said to have been demanded (1111[1]). But still more serious was the appearance
of Griffith, son of that Rhys, who had been slain twenty
years previously. Griffith, who had been reared in Ireland,
excited by his return to his native country the minds of all
the South Welsh. He succeeded in taking Caermarthen from
the Normans, and found considerable support in Cardigan,
the castle of which was held by Gilbert Strongbow, earl of
Strigul. Gerald of Windsor and the Flemings were thereby
completely cut off from the rest of the English, and Henry
found it necessary, for the safety of his barons there, to lead
his warriors to Wales in person (1114). Under his direction
his brave son, Robert of Gloucester, suppressed the insurrection, and a number of new castles and forts were erected,
and distributed among the Normans and Flemings[2], of whom
many of the latter had been sent to Cardigan, which was held
by Richard of Clare[3]. In two years after this a new rebellion
was raised[4]. The noble-hearted Griffith retained only a small
part of the cantref Mawr, in Caermarthenshire, in his possession; yet did the natives of the ancient Deheubarth pay him
the respect due to the old princes of their country, a respect
allowed even by Henry himself. In the summer following the
king's second marriage, a new expedition against Wales was
found necessary (1122), during which, in Powys, he was
stricken with an arrow, but which was fortunately arrested

---

[1] Powell, pp. 139 sq. The English chroniclers make no mention of the
king's presence in Wales in this year.

[2] Sax. Chron. h. a. Powell, lib. i., who does not, however, mention the
king's presence.

[3] Giraldus. lib. i. c. 4.

[4] Flor. Wigorn. a. 1116.

by his chain-armour [1]. For a series of years we hear of no
further disturbances of magnitude; the natives were held
down by the iron hand of foreigners, who, like the Flemings
in Germany, may have been followed by numbers of their
wandering and adventurous countrymen. By these strangers
the Welsh were expelled from one possession after another,
and those who resisted stricken down like dogs. The people,
thus provoked beyond endurance, again rose in the latter
years of Henry's reign (1134), burned Caus, a castle of Payne
fitz John, sheriff of Hereford and Shrewsbury, one of the
king's most distinguished counsellors and scribes, and wreaked most barbarous vengeance on their captives. Henry hereupon resolved to leave his beloved Normandy, for the purpose
of proceeding once more against the never totally subdued
ancient Britons; but thrice did the wind drive him back on
the coast of his paternal home, which death, that overtook
him shortly after, did not permit him again to leave [2].

By dissensions with his son-in-law, Henry found himself
detained still for some months in Normandy. At Lions, near
Rouen, he had been enjoying his favourite diversion of the
chase, on his return from which he was suddenly seized with
illness, the consequence, it is said, of a surfeit of lampreys,
which, in a few days, terminated in death (1st Dec. 1135).
Time and quiet were afforded him for the adoption of many
measures of mercy and beneficence. He recalled the exiled,
remitted pecuniary mulcts, restored to their paternal inheritance those who had been displaced; sixty thousand pounds
of silver he caused to be distributed among his servants, his
mercenaries, and the poor. His body, according to his desire,

[1] Sax. Chron. h. a. Giraldus, lib. i. c. 2. W. Malm. p. 628. Eadmer,
p. 138. Powell, p. 152, who erroneously places this expedition in the year
1118.

[2] Ord. Vital. p. 900. Gesta Stephani, edit. E. H. S. p. 9. Payne was
lord of Ewias. [A. D. 1132 a considerable part of London, together with
St. Paul's cathedral, was consumed by fire. Fl. Wigorn. T.]

was conveyed to England, and interred in the abbey of Reading, which he had founded[1].

His daughter Matilda did not see him again before his death. Of his numerous natural children, Robert of Glocester[2] alone was present, whom he had married to Mabil, a daughter of the distinguished knight, Robert fitz Hamon. Of his other children, we know of Richard, the son of Amice, a daughter of Ralf of Guader[3], whose early death by shipwreck, as also his sister's, Matilda, the wife of Rotrou, count of Perche, has been already noticed; Reginald of Dunstanvile, afterwards earl of Cornwall[4]; a second Robert, borne to him by Eda[5]; Gilbert; William of Tracy[6], who died soon after his father; and Henry, also born of the Welsh princess Nesta; also another Matilda, married to Conan III. count of Brittany[7]; Juliana, already mentioned as the wife of Eustace of Pacy. There were also four other daughters married: one born to him by Elizabeth, sister of Waleram count of Meulan, to Alexander, king of Scotland[8]; one named Constance, to

[1] Ord. Vital. p. 901.

[2] Giraldus tells a singular story respecting the paternity of Robert of Gloucester, making him the son of Nesta by one Stephen: his words are: " Fuerunt autem duo nobiles viri, ut ejus qui scripsit hæc avunculi, Henricus scilicet, regis Henrici Primi filius, et Secundi avunculus, ex nobili Nesta, Resi filia, in australi Cambria Demetiæ finibus oriundus, et *Robertus Stephani filius*, Henrici frater non germanus sed uterinus.—T.

[3] According to Carte, Richard's mother was the widow of Anschil, a nobleman near Abingdon.—T.

[4] His mother was Sibylle, a daughter of sir Robert Corbet of Alcester in Warwickshire.—*Carte.*—T.

[5] Joh. Hagust. a. 1142, col. 270. [" Eda, or Edith, was a daughter of Forne, a great baron in the north. She afterwards married Robert of Oily, baron of Hokenorton in Oxfordshire. There is still preserved a charter of this Robert, being a grant of the manor of Porlock to Hugh de Ralegh, and another of lands beyond the Exe to Richard Floyer, among the writings of the families of Chichester and Floyer; and in the tenth box in the Duchy office is a charter likewise of his wife Maud, under her seal."—*Carte.*—T.

[6] Probably by the same mother as Reginald, being in the Red Book of the Exchequer styled his brother.—*Carte.*—T.

[7] Ord. Vital. p. 514.   [8] Ib. p. 702.

Roscelin, viscount of Beaumont in Le Maine; a third, named Aline, to Matthew, a son of Bourcard of Montmorency; a fourth, named Eustacia, to William of Gouet, a Norman baron[1].

Henry was of middling stature, strong-breasted and of great muscular power; black hair overshadowed his forehead, beneath which beamed eyes expressive of serenity. He always appeared joyous, even when engaged in affairs of importance. Less a warrior than a leader, he reminded his contemporaries of the saying of Scipio Africanus: " Imperatorem me mea mater, non bellatorem peperit." His moderation in all enjoyments, except in that of the chase, has been celebrated by the chroniclers; though not with strict regard to truth, as is manifest from his numerous illegitimate offspring[2].

Besides the exertions made by Henry to quell the open rebellions of his barons, we find him incessantly engaged in endeavours to break their power. While he maintained all the old royal castles in good and strong condition, with trustworthy garrisons, he allowed those of his barons, which through death or other accidents had fallen into his hands, to go to ruin. His strict administration of the law, which procured for him the appellation of the " lion of justice," described in the prophecies of Merlin, is the more deserving of notice, as it was rigorously exercised against the nobility[3]. The crime of debasing, or diminishing the weight of, the public money he punished with the utmost severity, the penalty affixed to

[1] Other illegitimate children are ascribed to Henry, particularly a daughter married to William of Chaumont. Ord. Vital. p. 856.—T.

[2] Henry's praise is nowhere more loudly sounded than in the Acta Cenoman. p. 345; but the testimony of the abbot Suger is weightier: " prudentissimus Henricus, cujus tam admiranda quam prædicanda animi corporis strenuitas quam scientia," etc. Cf. also H. Huntingd. l. viii. init. ejusdem epistola ' De Contemptu Mundi. Sim. Dunelm. a. 1135. Ricard. p. 310.

[3] W. Gemmet. lib. viii. c. 13. Bromton, p. 998. Joh. Sarisb. Polyc. vi. 16. Galfr. Monom. Ord. Vital. p. 888.

which being the loss of the right hand, or the eyes, and castration. This crime had become so general, that it was found necessary to summon all the moneyers of the realm to appear before the chancellor, the bishop of Salisbury, at Winchester, when not less than fifty were condemned to undergo the penalty prescribed by the law[1].

One great benefit he conferred on the oppressed people, by an ordinance relative to the royal claim of purveyance, by which he set bounds to the avidity and outrages of the royal officers, when the king was on a progress in the country. On these occasions, the court followers were supplied gratis by the inhabitants of the places through which they passed, when the disgusting atrocities perpetrated by those miscreants exceed all belief. The consequence was that, whenever it became known in a place that the king was coming, the inhabitants fled from their dwellings, and took refuge in the woods and forests, or wherever they could find shelter. To remedy this crying evil, Henry decreed to those found guilty of such outrages, the loss of hands, or feet, or other members. By this severity, those who valued their bodily integrity were, on seeing these examples, deterred from injury to others. By the same ordinance it was stated how much was to be supplied by the peasantry gratis, and how much at a fixed rate. He also prohibited the false ell in use among traders, fixing the length of his own arm as a standard throughout England[2].

---

[1] Sax. Chron. a. 1125. Flor. Wigorn. aa. 1108. 1124. W. Malm. p. 641. H. Hunt. a. 1125. Sim. Dunelm. b. a. W. Gemmet. lib. viii. c. 23. [H. Hoved. a. 1108. "Et quoniam sæpissime dum denarii eligebantur, flectebantur, rumpebantur, respuebantur. statuit ut nullus denarius vel obolus, quos et rotundos esse jussit, aut etiam quadrans, si integer esset, respueretur."—T.]

[2] W. Malm. p. 641. Eadmer, p. 94. ["Tempore siquidem fratris sui regis hunc morem multitudo eorum qui curiam ejus sequebantur habebat, ut quæque pessundarent, diriperent, et nulla eos cohibente disciplina, totam terram, per quam rex ibat, devastarent. Accedebat his aliud malum ; plurimi namque eorum, sua malitia debriati [inebriati], dum reperta

Sometimes, indeed, his zeal for the strict administration of the law was carried to too great an extreme, as was the case with a number of robbers at Huncot, in Leicestershire, forty-four of whom the justiciar, Ralf Basset, condemned to death, and six to the loss of eyes and castration; although it was the general belief that some of them suffered unjustly[1]. These severities, however, prevailed chiefly in the earlier part of his reign, and latterly gave way to pecuniary mulcts[2].

But he attained his great object, the tranquillity and security of the country. Even the Anglo-Saxons must have prized a state of things which enabled a traveller, laden with gold and silver, to pass through the land in safety[3]. It must not, however, be imagined that it was the severity of the punishments and the inflexibility of the judge alone that in those days reproduced this wonder of the golden age; it was the strict police, grafted by the Normans on the Anglo-Saxon institutions.

In the times immediately succeeding the Conquest, the kings received the rents of the crown lands in kind, from which source the royal household was supplied with necessaries; and such was the usage till the time of Henry I. But latterly, when that king was much engaged abroad, he had need of payments in ready money: in consequence of which querulous multitudes assembled at the court, or, what was yet more serious, were frequently to be met on the ways, offering their ploughs, in token of their ruined husbandry; for they were overwhelmed with difficulties on account of

in hospitiis quæ invadebant, penitus absumere non valebant, ea aut ad forum, per eosdem ipsos quorum erant, pro suo lucro ferre ac vendere, aut supposito igne cremare, aut, si potus esset, lotis exinde equorum suorum pedibus, residuum illius per terram effundere, aut certe aliquo alio modo disperdere solebant. Quæ vero in patresfamilias crudelia, quæ in uxores ac filias eorum indecentia fecerint, reminisci pudet." From this burthen of purveyance (A. S. feorm-fultum), which had existed under the Anglo-Saxon kings, the people were relieved by Cnut. See his Secular Laws, tit. 70. in "Ancient Laws and Institutes." T.]

S: x. Chron. a. 1124   [2] W. Malm. p. 641   [3] Ib. a. 1145

their produce, which had now to be conveyed for sale from their homes to many destinations. Whereupon the king appointed certain officials to visit the several lands, for the purpose of valuing the produce payable by each, and reducing the amount into money; the sum total of the several payments in each county to be paid by the sheriff into the exchequer[1].

But notwithstanding these measures, adopted for the relief of his own tenantry, the miseries of the people, during his reign continued with little mitigation. "It is not easy," says the chronicler, "to relate the miseries of this land, which it was suffering at this time through various and manifold wrongs and imposts, that were never intermitted or ceased; and ever, when the king journeyed, there was plunder and destruction by his followers of the wretched people, and but too often burnings and murders." And again: "First they (the wretched people) are bereft of their property, and then they are slain." The tax of Danegelt was continued during the whole of Henry's reign, at the rate of twelve pence the hide; and an aid of three shillings the hide was demanded on the marriage of his daughter with the emperor. "What and what grievous oppressions the whole of England suffered is difficult to narrate. In raising money to complete the subjugation of Normandy, no mercy was shown by the collectors. Those who had nothing to give were driven from their humble dwellings, or the doors being torn down and carried off, their habitations were left open to be plundered; or their miserable chattels being taken away, they were reduced to the extreme of poverty, or in other ways afflicted and tormented: while against those who were thought to possess something, certain new and imaginary offences were alleged, when, not daring to defend themselves in a plea against the king, they were stript of their property and plunged into misery[2]."

[1] Selden, Spicel. ad Eadmer, p. 216, from the Dialogus de Scaccario.—T.
[2] Sax. Chron. aa. 1104, 1124. H. Hunt. a. 1108. Eadmer, p. 83. Bromton p. 1001.

Less content must the people have been with the system of taxation. The numerous wars required much money. Of the endeavours after order in the management of accounts we possess no mean example in the book yet extant of receipts and disbursements by the royal exchequer[1]. The existing traces also of renewals and completions of the Domesday-book are a proof of such endeavours. Moreover, if we consider the collection bearing the title of the Laws of Henry I.[2], we may, perhaps, recognize that England, even at that early period, availed itself of its insular position and the peculiar relation of the conqueror to the conquered, for the obtaining of a more regular administration and regard of justice than had been possessed by any people since the migration of nations.

That Henry not only frequently bestowed rich donations on many monasteries and churches, but also founded several, is the worthier of notice, as this tendency in him proceeded from no slavish subjection to the clergy, but from a well-founded sense of their relation to the state, and of respect for higher spiritual interests. The noble abbey of St. Mary at Reading, was founded by him for monks of the order of Cluny[3]; for regular canons of the Augustine order he founded a monastery and a church dedicated to St. John, at Cirencester, and a monastery at Dunstable; he also founded an abbey at Wellaw near Grimsby, and one at Anglesey in Cambridgeshire[4]; also a religious house at Creke in Norfolk; to

[1] The Magnus Rotulus Scaccarii sive Pipæ, edited by the Rev. Jos. Hunter for the late Record Commission, 1833.

[2] The best edition of this collection is that in the "Ancient Laws and Institutes of England," published by authority of the late Record Commission.

[3] The dotation is dated 1121. Monast. Anglic. iv. p. 28.

[4] W. Gemmet. lib. viii. c. 32. The deed of foundation of Reading abbey see in Monast. vi. p. 175. Joh. Hagust. col. 258. R. Hagust. col. 310. R. de Diceto. col. 505. Knyghton, col. 2384. Chron. de Dunstap. col. 677. [All the chronicles agree in the reading of Cirecestra (Circestra?). Anglesey abbey is in the hundred of Stane.—T.]

\ :1

the monks of Bec he gave an alien priory at Steventon near
Abingdon; to the abbey of St. Valory one at Takely in
Essex. He also appears as a joint founder of the priories
of Augustine canons at Carlisle, and at Merton in Surrey;
and, finally, as the founder of many large hospitals[1]. The
founding of the majority of these appears to have taken place
in the last fifteen years of his reign, after the loss of his son.
That Normandy, in this respect, was not neglected by him
needs hardly be mentioned. We will here notice only the
beautiful church at Evreux as his foundation. Towards
foreign churches and hospitals he was frequently not less munificent; the church at Cluny he almost entirely built, and
bestowed on it large possessions in England, also the church
of St. Martin aux Champs at Paris. The rich possessions of
the monks of the abbey of St. Remy at Rheims he not only
religiously protected, but also augmented[2]. The hospital for
the sick at Chartres, at that time distinguished both for its
extent and as a work of art, was completed through his
liberality. His numerous donations to the cloisters that lay
on the road of pilgrims to Rome, facilitated the way over the
Alps and Appenine to the metropolis of Christendom.

One who so munificently favoured monasteries operated
also indirectly on the promotion of knowledge and civilization; but on the part of Henry Beauclerc a more direct influence may be traced. If his consort Matilda rewarded
minstrels and melodious songsters, he gave proofs of his munificence to men like the Benedictine Æthelhard of Bath[3],
a distinguished philosopher and investigator of nature, who
translated the Elements of Euclid from the Arabic version

[1] Monast vi. *passim*.

[2] Monast. vi. p. 1099. Domesday. Rot. magn. pipæ, p. 74. W. Gemmet.
lib. VIII. c. 32. For other donations by the first Norman kings to the
abbey of Cluny, see C. G. Hoffmann, Nova Scriptorum Monumentorum
Collectio. i. pp. 340 *sq.*

[3] Rot. magn. pipæ. p. 22. His "Quæstiones naturales perdifficiles" are
in the Cottonian Library, Galba E. IV.

into Latin. Mediæval Latinity, both prose and verse, as well as familiarity with the Roman classics, reached in his time a height from which, in England, they shortly afterwards fell. During his reign flourished and wrote Eadmer, Ingulf, Jeffrey of Monmouth, William of Malmesbury, William of Jumièges, Florence of Worcester, Simeon of Durham. Henry of Huntingdon's earlier days fall also within this period. Of the epigrams of the excellent Godfrey, prior of St. Swithin's at Winchester[1], a native of Cambray, many are preserved. The poems of Radulfus Tortarius[2] and of Serlo bishop of Séez, which are known to us, excite the wish to possess those still hidden from us. The earliest traces of dramatic representations in northern Europe are met with, under the reign of Henry, in the monastic school of Dunstable[3], where he sometimes held his court[4]. Geoffrey, the master of the school there, was the director of these spiritual plays or miracles, the model of which he borrowed from his former residence, Paris, but which were known in Germany some centuries earlier in the Latin poems of the nun Hroswithe.

Henry took great delight in wild beasts from distant regions, as lions, leopards, lynxes, camels, etc., among which particular mention is made of a porcupine. These were kept in the park which he had enclosed at Woodstock, one of his favourite places of abode[5]. He had also a similar establishment at Caen, in which were placed beasts from all the known parts of the world[6].

At this period the Anglo-Saxon tongue began rapidly to decline, being expelled from the halls of the noble and power-

---

[1] He died in 1107. See W. Malm. p. 678. Camden's Remains, p. 421, edit. 1674. Warton, H. E. P. p. cxi. edit. 1840. Camden has preserved several of his epigrams.

[2] Histoire de l'Académie des Inscriptions, xxi. pp. 511 sq.

[3] Matt. Paris, Hist. Abbat. p. 56. Warton ut sup. p. cxii.

[4] Sax. Chron. a. 1122.

[5] "Wodestoc, regis Henrici familiarem privati secreti recessum." Gesta Stephani," p. 87.

[6] W. Malm. p. 638. Radulf Tortarius. A rivarium regis at Brichestoc mentioned in the Rotul. magn. pipæ. p. 88. probably at Bristol.

V a 2

ful, and corrupted among the people by an influx of Norman-
French. This latter was the language of the law and of the
court, and was also cultivated by the poets; of whom we will
here make mention, on account of their particular relation to
England, only of Philip of Thaun[1] and Geoffrey Gaimar[2].

Of educational establishments there was no lack, either in
England or Normandy. The abbatial school of Bec was attended by students from all parts of Europe. The schools
of Canterbury, York, Oxford, Abingdon, where king Henry
is said to have been educated, Winchester, Peterborough,
and others enjoyed a high reputation. But many English
also visited the learned foundations of other lands, and we
find them not only at Paris, Pavia, and Salerno, but also in
the lecture halls of the Arabians at Cordova and Salamanca,
imbibing, at the same time, copious draughts from the wells
of knowledge and of the errors of scholastic logic. The
system of the foreigner also found admission into the acade-
mic institutions of England. Thus Joffrid, abbot of Crowland, formerly prior of St. Evroult in Normandy, invited
teachers from Orléans, where he had been educated, and
established them at Cotenham, a manor belonging to his
abbey, by whose aid a school arose in the neighbouring town
of Cambridge, from which the university of that place may
probably date its origin. Priscian's grammar with the commentary of Remigius, Aristotle's logic, the rhetorical works of
Cicero and Quinctilian, together with theology, engrossed the
attention of scholars both then and many centuries later[3].

[1] There are several manuscripts extant of this writer, the most ancient
of which Mr. Wright states to be that in the Cotton Library (Nero A.V.).
See Popular Treatises on Science, by T. Wright. London 1841, pref.
pp. ix. seq.—T.

[2] See England under the A. S. Kings i. Liter. Introd. p. lvi. and the
epilogue to his Estorie des Engles, where he speaks of Robert, earl of
Gloucester, Walter Espec, and other contemporaries. Cf. (F. Wolf) Wiener
Jahrbücher, 1836.

[3] Petrus Blesens. Contin. p. 111. The mention of Averroes (ob. 1206)
shows, however, that this passage is not free from interpolation.

A

HISTORY OF ENGLAND

UNDER THE

NORMAN KINGS.

STEPHEN.

CONTEMPORARY SOVEREIGNS.

GERMANY.	FRANCE.	SCOTLAND.	SPAIN.
Lothair II. 1138.	Lewis VI. 1137.	David I. 1153.	Alphonso VIII.
Conrad III. 1152.	Lewis VII.	Malcolm IV.	
Frederic I.			

POPES.

Innocent II. 1143. | Celestine II. 1144. | Lucius II. 1145.
Eugenius III. 1153 | Anastatius IV.

THE death of Henry was productive of great disorder in his states. It was the opinion of almost every one, that the oaths which the late king had caused to be taken, with the object of securing the throne to his daughter Matilda, were not binding. Royalty was still too near its origin in Europe, to admit of its being forgotten that its most prominent attribute was the supreme command in war, which could not be held by a woman. Neither among the Anglo-Saxons, with one very unfavourable exception, had queens, nor among the Normans countesses or duchesses, ever ruled the land. By the violation too of the assurance given by the king, that his daughter should marry no Frenchman, the obligation was cancelled also on his part. Count Geoffrey was, moreover, held in great aversion by the Normans, which his incessant contentions with his father-in-law did not tend to mitigate. It is, indeed, far from improbable, that Henry himself in his anger may have harboured the thought of excluding his daughter from the promised succession to the throne ; and Hugh Bigot asserted on oath, that Henry, in his last moments, in his presence, released the chiefs of the realm from the oath they had taken in favour of Matilda, while others at least affirmed that he had heartily repented of it[1]. The son of Matilda was little more than two years old, and to acknowledge him as successor to the throne would have been equivalent to delivering the kingdom over to his parents under the name of a regency. The next male heir was Theobald, son of Stephen, count of Blois and Chartres, and Adela, a daughter of William the Conqueror, a valiant prince, who had ever proved himself a faithful ally of Henry against the king of France, and for his piety and beneficence was highly esteemed by all[2]. Many Normans, consequently, flocked together at Neubourg, with the object of raising him to the vacant dignity ; but while they were discussing the subject, a messenger arrived from England with the intelligence, that Theobald's younger brother, Stephen, had been there elected king, and was already crowned. This prince had constantly enjoyed the favour of Henry, had been educated by him, and about thirty years previously received knighthood at his hands, and afterwards been invested with the county of Mor-

[1] Gesta Stephani, p. 7. [" Ad ipsam hæredandam imperioso illo, cui nullus obsistebat, oris tonitruo, summos totius regni jurare compulit potius quam præcepit. Et quanquam eosdem invite jurare, juramentumque haud ratum fore prænosceret, voluit tamen, more Ezechielis, in diebus pacem reformare, perque unius mulieris conjugium multa hominum millia ad concordiæ adsciscere glutinum. Utque patenter agnosceremus, quod ei in vita certa de causa complacuit, post mortem ut fixum foret displicuisse, supremo eum agitante mortis articulo, cum et plurimi astarent, et veram suorum erratuum confessionem audirent, de jurejurando violenter baronibus suis injuncto apertissime pœnituit."—T.] H. Hunt. a. 6 Steph., where the assertion of the release from the oath by Henry is virtually refuted by the partisans of Matilda. Gervasius, a. 1135. Rad. de Diceto. Abbrev. Chron. col. 505.

[2] W. Gemmet. viii. c. 34. Ord. Vital. pp. 902-905. Girald. Cambrens. de Instr. Prin. in Recueil des Historiens. t. xviii. Anselmi Gemblac.. Chron. a. 1134.

tain. His marriage with the daughter and heiress of count Eustace of Boulogne had, after the death of that prince, put him in possession not only of that county, but also of vast estates in England[1]. From Boulogne he had frequently interfered in the Flemish dissensions, as he never let slip an opportunity for gratifying his love of arms and increasing his military renown. But yet more was he distinguished for kindness, courtly manners, an amiable serenity of character, and a condescension which had long gained him the hearts of many among all conditions of people[2]. On the other hand, he often proved himself imprudent, rash, and on his fairest promises no reliance could be placed. In short, he exhibited, in all its traits, a complete specimen of the accomplished French knight of those days, who, although capable of enacting many parts excellently well, was, nevertheless, but ill qualified to rule over a kingdom. On the news of his uncle's death, Stephen, with a few followers, set sail from Witsand, and landed on the coast of Kent, whence, without loss of time, he proceeded to London. His pretensions to the crown of England were favoured by the general aversion of the people towards Anjou, but more particularly by the influence of his brother Henry bishop of Winchester. Roger bishop of Salisbury also, and William of Pont-de-l'Arche, both of whom had held the important office of royal treasurer, declared in his favour, and delivered to his reckless extravagance the money accumulated during Henry's administration, amounting to a hundred thousand pounds of silver, together with innumerable precious things[3]. The scruples of William

---

[1] W. Gemmet. lib. i. Ord. Vital. p. 811. Wil. Newburg. lib. i. c. 4.

[2] Even his enemies confirm this account of Stephen. W. Malm. p. 709. "Homo mansuetissimus, ... qui, si legitime regnum ingressus fuisset, et in eo administrando credulas aures malevolorum susurris non exhibuisset, parum ei profecto ad regiæ personæ decorem defuisset." R. Hagust. a. 1136. Sax. Chron. a. 1137. [Da he suikes undergæton þ he milde man was.] softe.] gód," etc. *When the traitors understood that he was a mild man, and soft, and good*, etc.—T.]

W. Malm. p. 703. Gesta Stephani. p. 5.

archbishop of Canterbury were overcome by the declaration, already mentioned, of Hugh Bigot, the seneschal of the deceased sovereign. The slight opposition, which some faithful friends of Henry endeavoured to set up against the pretensions of Stephen, was soon crushed, and the wealthy citizens of London and Winchester declared in favour of the chivalrous aspirant. Scarcely three weeks after the death of Henry, and before his corpse was conveyed to England, Stephen was crowned, on the 22nd Dec.[1], by the archbishop of Canterbury, William Corboil, in the presence of a few ecclesiastics and laymen of rank, but who were quickly followed by many others, who hastened to solemnize the Christmas festival at the court of the newly crowned sovereign at London, from whence he issued a missive, addressed to the judges of the land, the sheriffs, barons, and vassals, both French and English, in which he confirmed to his English subjects all the immunities and good laws that his uncle king Henry had granted them, as well as the good laws and good customs which they possessed in the time of king Eadward[2]; and, accordingly, strictly forbade every violation of the same.

The mortal remains of the late king, who had desired to be interred in the abbey founded by him at Reading, had not yet arrived in England. They were detained at Rouen and Caen, where they had been rudely embalmed or rather salted, to the annoyance, and even deadly injury of those who approached them[3]. In the first days of January (1136), Ste-

---

[1] Malmesbury (p. 704) and Gervase (col. 1340) give the precise date. The Saxon Chronicle: "on mide wintre dæi," would seem also to signify the shortest day. The Annal. Waverl. give St. Thomas' day, the 21st Dec.; John of Hexham, the 1st Jan., probably an error of the MS.; Richard of Hexham, Christmas day; Orderic the 15th Dec.

[2] Printed in the Charters of Liberties, p. 4. without date, though, without doubt, earlier than the ampler charter placed before it, issued at Oxford.

[3] In his account of this event we recognise in Henry of Huntingdon the author of the treatise De Contemptu Mundi. [His words are worth transcribing: "Rex Henricus prima die Decembris obierat, cujus corpus

phen, attended by the ecclesiastical and secular dignitaries of the kingdom, received the body of his uncle on the English shore, with every sign of external veneration, and, as it is said, assisted in conveying it to Reading.

From this scene Stephen hastened to the northern frontier of his kingdom, where the Scots had made a hostile inroad, from whom, however, as we shall hereafter have occasion to mention, he, by considerable cessions to their king David, purchased both acknowledgment and homage. But this appeared to him not too dearly bought, as his position with respect to his own subjects was not yet firmly established. After having celebrated the Easter festival with great pomp at London, Stephen proceeded to Oxford, where, in the meanwhile, many English and Norman prelates and barons had assembled. Here he was so fortunate as to be able to produce a letter from the pope, Innocent II., in which the pontiff expressed his approval of Stephen's election, referring to the declaration and mediation of the English prelates, of the king

allatum est Rotomagum, et ibi viscera ejus, et cerebrum, et occuli consepulta sunt; reliquum autem corpus cultellis circumquaque desecatum, et multo sale aspersum, coriis taurinis reconditum est causa fœtoris evitandi, qui multus et infinitus jam circumstantes inficiebat, unde et ipse, qui magno pretio conductus, securi caput ejus diffiderat, ut fœtidissimum cerebrum extraheret, quamvis linteaminibus caput suum obvoluisset, mortuus tamen ea causa pretio male gavisus est. Hic est ultimus e multis, quem rex Henricus occidit. Inde vero corpus regium Cadonum sui deportaverunt; ubi diu in ecclesia positum, in qua pater ejus sepultus fuerat, quamvis multo sale repletum esset, et multis coriis reconditum, tamen continue ex corpore jugitur humor et horribilis scoria pertransiens decurrebat, et vasis sub feretro susceptus, a ministris fœtore et horrore fatiscentibus abjiciebatur. Vide igitur quicunque legis, quomodo regis potentissimi corpus, cujus cervix diadematizata auro et gemmis electissimis, quasi Dei splendore vernaverat; cujus utraque manus sceptris præradiaverat, cujus reliqua superficies auro textili tota rutilaverat, cujus os tam deliciosissimis et exquisitis pasci solebat cibis, cui omnes assurgere, omnes expavescere, omnes congaudere, omnes admirari solebant; vide, inquam, quo corpus illud devenerit, quam horribiliter delituerit, quam miserabiliter abjectum fuerit. Vide rerum eventum, ex quo semper pendet judicium, et disce contemnere quicquid sic disterminatur, quicquid sic annihilatur." T.]

of France, and the count Theobald of Blois[1]. To the French king, Lewis VI., nothing, indeed, could be more unwelcome than to see his vassal of Anjou raised at once to be lord of both Normandy and England. After long deliberation[2], the document or charter was framed, by which the ancient privileges of the ecclesiastics, the barons, and the people were confirmed, and which, by some of its provisions, removed certain, though to us not always apparent, causes of complaint against the administration of Henry. The king of the English, by the grace of God, with the consent of the clergy and people elected, by the archbishop of Canterbury, legate of the holy Roman Church, consecrated, and by Innocent, bishop of the Roman see confirmed, was, in the first place, not sparing of promises to the Church. What it possessed at the death of William I., that is about fifty years before, it might claim as its property. But, if the Church shall demand anything it held or possessed prior to the death of that king, of which it is now deprived, he reserves to his own indulgence and dispensation either to refuse or restore it. All later acquisitions of the Church were confirmed; he promises in all things to maintain peace and justice. The forests made by William I. and William II. he reserves for himself; but those added by Henry he restores to the Church and realm. If any bishop, or abbot, or other ecclesiastic makes a reasonable distribution of his property, he confirms such distribution; but if prevented in such distribution by death, let it be made by the advice of the Church, for the good of his soul. Vacant sees and their possessions he orders to be committed to the custody of the clergy and other upright men of such see, until a pastor be canonically appointed. All exactions and extortions[3] wickedly introduced by sheriffs and others he totally

[1] See the letter in Ricard. Hagust. col. 313.

[2] " Angli, diu habita deliberatione, quem sublimarent regis nomine et honore," etc. Auctarium Anselmi Gemblac. a. 1136.

[3] " Meschenningas." See Glossary to Anc. Laws and Inst. v. 'Miskenning.'—T.

abolished, and promised to observe and cause to be observed good laws and the ancient and just customs in cases of *murdrum* and other pleas[1]. The discontent caused by the numerous enclosures, and by the severe laws for the protection of the beasts of the forests, was wide-spread over England, and on the intelligence of Henry's death had manifested itself in the destruction of the enclosures and slaughter of the hateful game[2]; so that of the many thousand animals with which the country had, as it were, been overrun, it was now a rare sight to see two together. The numerous witnesses of high consideration to this document forbid us to harbour a doubt of its containing the real substance of the concessions demanded from and granted by Stephen. Its several transcripts, all of the same tenour, are a guarantee that we possess it in its genuine form. Among those witnesses we find the archbishops of Canterbury and Rouen; the bishops of Winchester, Salisbury, Lincoln, Evreux, Avranches, Hereford, and Rochester; the chancellor Roger; Henry, the king's nephew[3]; the earls, Robert of Gloucester, William of Wa-

---

[1] Gesta Stephani p. 2. W. Malm. p. 708.

[2] Charters, p. 3. W. Malm. p. 708. R. Hagust. col. 311.

[3] Probably the eldest son of Theobald, who was his heir in the counties of Champagne and Brie, while the younger, Theobald V., received Blois and Chartres. His presence was of importance as proving the good understanding between the king and his elder brother. The former was present also at Easter, at the investing of bishop Robert with the see of Bath, the document relative to which stands in the new Rymer (p. 16), without date, after the year 1153. The printed text of this document abounds in blunders, by which the entire work is rendered as much a monument of the ignorance of its editors as of English history: e. g. Safarus for Sefridus, Adelardus for Adelulfus, Willelmus de Pont for W. de Pontarci, R. de Fered for R. de Ferrariis, Albert de Laci for Ilbert de Laci —all well-known names of bishops and barons. But there are yet worse blunders than the above, as at p. 9., where several documents of Henry II., with his titles, dux Aquitanie et comes Andegavie, are placed under the reign of Henry I.! Compare p. 259, note. Hence it hardly will excite our wonder when, at p. 91, we find a document in which mention is made of Dominicans and Franciscans, assigned to the year 1201, and to pope Innocent III. (at Lyons').

renne, Ranulf of Chester, Robert of Warwick ; the constables, Robert of Vere, Milo of Gloucester, Brian fitz Count[1] and Robert of Oily ; the sewers, William Martel, Hugh Bigot, Humphrey of Bohun and Simon of Beauchamp ; the cup-bearers, William of Aubigny, and Eudes Martel ; also the barons of high rank, Robert of Ferrières, William Peverel of Nottingham, Simon of Senlis, Payne fitz John, Hamon of St. Clair, William of Albemarle, Ilbert of Lacy[2]—all names of note under the preceding monarchs, or destined to become so in the present reign. The more striking, therefore, and in-credible is it that among the chroniclers hostile to Stephen, one asserts that he also promised to abolish Danegelt for ever[3].

The names of the witnesses to this charter are here ad-duced for the purpose also of drawing attention to the eccle-astics and vassals of Normandy appearing among them. Im-mediately on receipt of the news of Henry's death, count Geoffrey and his consort, the empress, had with little diffi-culty, and with the aid of the viscount there, Guiganalgaso, who from a low condition had raised himself to eminence, taken possession of several towns on the southern frontier of

[1] Who his father was we learn from the Sax. Chron. a.1127. See p. 340.

[2] Ilbert forthwith received back from the new sovereign the lands which had been taken from his father Robert by Henry. Ric. Hagust. a. 1135. But that the old Ilbert of Lacy, at the time of Domesday, possessed Ponti-fract, as Ellis (Introd. i. p. 221) and Hunter (Rot. magn. pipæ, p. xxii.) assume, appears, from the above-mentioned chronicler very doubtful, ac-cording to whom it belonged to William Travers (Transversus).

[3] Henry of Huntingdon. While William of Malmesbury, whom Hume cites as his authority for the assertion, makes no mention of it. Lin-gard speaks of two assemblies at Oxford, in the latter of which the letter of the pope was read, but it escapes his notice that Malmesbury, whom he adduces as his authority for the first, likewise makes mention of the papal confirmation in his transcript of the document there sworn to by the king. Henry of Huntingdon, on the other hand, speaks of the docu-ment from treacherous memory, and while placing its emission in the be-ginning of January, omits all notice of the documentary proof of its publi-cation after Easter.

Normandy, as Domfront, Argentan, Hiesmes, Ambrières, and others, but of which he delivered over some to Joel of Mayenne; all the strong places, too, were opened to him, which the exiled count of Ponthieu, William Talevas, had recovered from the late king. Nevertheless, in the greater part of Normandy no favourable disposition displayed itself to the pretensions of Matilda; even Robert of Gloucester, at a conference with count Theobald, the elder brother of Stephen, delivered Falaise to the friends of the king, though not until he had carried off the greater portion of a treasure that had a short time previously been brought thither by Henry from England[1]. One of the most illustrious of the Norman nobles, Waleram count of Meulan, Stephen sought to attach to his fortunes, by the betrothal to him of his daughter of two years old. When, therefore, the Norman barons, probably on receipt of the intelligence of king David's homage, and of the part taken both by the pope and the king of France, had formed the resolution to acknowledge Stephen, there appeared no urgent personal necessity for him to cross the Channel, greatly as the duchy had suffered, after the death of Henry, by feuds and private revenge. Nevertheless, such was the anarchical state of the country since Henry's decease, that Stephen deemed it advisable at least to manifest a disposition to listen to the calls made on him from that quarter. At midsummer, therefore, he hastened to one of the southern ports, but found the wind unfavourable for the perilous summer passage to France. After a delay of some time, a messenger arrived with intelligence of the death of Roger bishop of Salisbury, to whom he had intrusted the administration of the kingdom. Roger was, however, as it proved, in perfect health, yet the king availed

---

[1] Robert. de Monte, a. 1135. Ord. Vital. p. 903. In the Rotul. magn. pipæ we find frequent mention of two men of this name, one of whom is designated *Brito*. The above-mentioned cupbearer is also therein named, whence we see that even court-offices, in the tranquil beginning of this reign, retained their old occupants. Martel, Henry's cupbearer, was now promoted to the post of sewer.

himself of the false report to postpone his departure till the following spring. The numerous disturbances, that had broken out in England, rendered his presence necessary in many parts of the country, and it seems not improbable that he intentionally cast a veil of obscurity over his place of residence, as, in the north of England, it was believed, that in August he had actually passed over to Normandy [1].

Stephen's reign of almost twenty years is scarcely other than an ever-repeated tale of petty border wars, internal feuds, and deeds of violence. Nevertheless, a state of things, that could exist for so long a time, will not appear indifferent to the student of history, but, while an enumeration of every individual event can have no value for the history of the country, demands a more exact consideration than it has hitherto met with, in order to elucidate their mutual connection; to comprehend how such a state of things could so long continue; to form a judgment how far it accorded with similar phenomena in the history of Europe, or whether it was of a peculiar character; in order finally to be able to set forth whatever may present itself in isolated events, either illustrative of the past, or capable of developing future occurrences and principles.

The means chiefly adopted by Stephen for the maintenance of his power in England, but by which he, at the same time, laid the foundation of its decline, had, though with a greater degree of caution, been already resorted to by his predecessor —the hire of foreign mercenaries. As long as the treasure accumulated by Henry lasted, he was enabled to maintain a standing army, whereby his barons were partially relieved of the burdens of warfare, and whose chief incitement was Stephen's gold. The greater part of this force consisted of Flemings, led, for the most part, by turbulent and impover-

---

[1] Joh. Hagust. col. 258. Ric. Hagust. col. 312. All the other chroniclers agree in stating that Stephen's visit to Normandy was not till 1137. The above account rests on circumstances related by Orderic, p. 904.

ished knights, who, driven from their possessions through the ascendency of the towns, or by the violence of destructive floods, sought to retrieve their fortunes in the game of war, while their more peaceful peasants and townsfolk, migrating to the east of Europe, found a livelihood in the arts of embanking, husbandry, and traffic. The most influential of these Flemings was William of Ypres, who had formerly raised pretensions to the Flemish crown, but had been recently driven from the port of Sluys, which he had till then possessed, by the reigning count, Diederik[1]. Around him and others of a similar character were gathered many warriors of the lower class, as townsmen and artizans, to whom, as their looms were too laborious for them, some leader of such bands guaranteed either pay or other means of subsistence. Among these were also numerous Bretons[2], whom Henry had frequently employed as mercenaries, as their poverty compelled them to fight under any banner, and obey every command of the chief that supported them[3]. Among the Bretons, whom we find in the pay of Stephen, are many whose rank and position in England forbid us to place them on a level with the Flemish mercenary leaders, although it was their lineage and connections in their native land which attracted to them their needy countrymen. Among these may be reckoned count Stephen of Penthièvre, probably a younger son of

[1] See concerning him p. 296, and Warnkönig, Flandrische Geschichte, i. p. 144. That he was in England in the time of Henry I. seems uncertain, although the Willelmus Flandrensis in the Rotul. magn. pipæ, p. 83, may allude to him; but that he either then or later held the rank of earl in England is not proved. He governed the county of Kent; but in no genuine document does it appear that he bore the title of earl. See Palgrave, Rise and Progress, ii. p. lxv.

[2] W. Malm. p. 706. "Currebatur ad eum ab omnium generum militibus, et a levis armaturæ hominibus, maximeque ex Flandria et Brittannia. Erat genus hominum rapacissimum et violentissimum." Ib. p. 731. "Sub Stephano plures ex Flandria et Brittannia, rapto vivere assueti, spe magnarum prædarum Angliam involabant."

[3] W. Malm. p. 629.

Alan Fergant (the Red), and, consequently, a grandson of the Conqueror. He enjoyed the vast possessions of his father in England, consisting of the barony of Richmond in Yorkshire, with many estates in Lincolnshire and other counties, which, after his death, in the early part of Stephen's reign, fell to his second son, Alan II., surnamed the Black[1]. In his youth he had borne the character of a valiant, but rugged and cruel warrior; at a later period he chiefly distinguished himself by the ambitious endeavour to raise Brittany again to a kingdom. Not far behind him for illustrious birth, and still less for haughty arrogance, stood Hervé, viscount of Leon[2], who, at the request of Henry, would never condescend to visit England, though with Stephen, whose daughter he had espoused, he resided for some years, and very little to that prince's advantage. To a distinguished Breton race belonged also Alan of Dinan, son of Oliver, who, during the reign of Henry, had received large possessions in England, and served Stephen on both sides of the Channel[3], as did likewise Geoffrey Botarel, count of Lamballe and Penthièvre, the elder brother of the before-mentioned Alan[4].

[1] Domesday, *passim*. In Rotul. magn. pipæ the latter is constantly called "Stephanus, comes de Britannia." Chron. Britan. a. 1146. "Obiit Alanus comes, in Anglia atque in Britannia strenuissimus." [See Ellis, Introd. i. p. 366.—T.]

[2] "Herveius de Leions (Liuns), tantæ nobilitatis, tanti supercilii, ut nunquam regi Henrico petenti animum indulserit in Angliam venire." W. Malm. p. 721. "Leon, pagus Lehonensis." Of him and his race, see Daru, Histoire de la Bretagne, i. p. 109. That he was a son-in-law of Stephen, appears from the Gesta Stephani, p. 68, "Herveio Britoni .... genero regis." Ib. p. 74. "Comes Herveius, gener regis."

[3] In Rotul. magn. pipæ, pp. 16, 39, etc. it is written "Dinam." In the Chron. Britan. his father's death is noticed under the year 1150; his own under 1157.

[4] "Boterellus quidam, comes Britanniæ." Gesta Steph. p. 81. Comp. Joh. Hagust. a. 1146. He is probably the Gaufridus Bucherel of the Rot. magn. pipæ, where a Willelmus Boterel and Bucherel, also a "Thomas, filius Odonis Bucherel" occur. We know of an elder Breton, Galfrid Botherel, son of Odo of Penthièvre, who died in 1092.

It is not to be supposed that the number of foreigners in England consisted solely of Bretons and Flemings; although the presence of others is rather to be conjectured than proved. Here we will merely mention Faramus, a nephew of the queen, the daughter of Eustace III., count of Boulogne, as it was he, with William of Ypres, who for some time swayed the royal court [1].

The death of Henry had caused great excitement in Wales, to subdue which he had resolved to pass over to England. The united bands of the natives invaded the well-cultivated district of Gower, lying on the southern coast, and on the banks of the Tawy, which they ravaged, and surrounded and put to the sword a body of five hundred and sixteen [2] Normans (1st Jan. 1136). The mercenaries sent against them by the king were unable to gain any lasting advantage over them, and were compelled to make an inglorious retreat. The renowned and dreaded adversary of the Welsh, Richard fitz Gilbert of Clare, whose influence in South Wales was almost as great as that of his wife's brother, Ranulf earl of Chester, in the northern parts of the realm, a man highly esteemed and beloved by his people, having by alliances and hostages secured himself against his neighbours, now hastened back from England. Irritated apparently by the king's refusal to comply with some of his wishes, he appears to have harboured the design of rebelling against him, and of uniting himself with the Welsh; when, having sent back the companion of his journey, Brian, son of the count Alan Fergant and baron of Wallingford, more usually styled fitz Count [3], with his numerous band of armed followers, and riding through a dense forest, to the sound of song and bagpipe, the music soon

[1] " Pharamus, nepos reginæ Mathildæ, et iste Bononiensis." Joh. Hagust. a. 1142. " Faramus, filius Willelmi de Boloniæ . . . ut haberet terram suam (in Sudreia), quam noverca sua tenet." Rot. magn. p. p. 50. Cf. further on, under 1153.

[2] The Gesta Steph. p. 10, and Flor. Cont. p. 97, agree in this number. Sax. Chron. a. 1147.

roused the attention of the Welsh, of whom Jorwerth of
Caerleon made a deadly onslaught on the Normans, and massacred him and his attendants[1] (15th April). This catastrophe kindled new hopes in the minds of the Welsh.
Three thousand marched to Cardigan (October), sparing no
foreigner, not even the women and children, to the fortress
of which, where resided the wife of the slain Richard, they
laid siege. After a long resistance, the place was relieved
by Milo of Gloucester[2]. Baldwin, the brother of Richard
fitz Gilbert, although aided by the royal treasures, did not
advance beyond Brecknock, and there wasted both time and
the gold intrusted to him. Nor was Robert fitz Harold more
fortunate, although he proved himself not lacking in energy,
and Stephen himself felt convinced that against the tenacious
love of country cherished by that excited people, the oppressor had no better weapon than patience, in the expectation that internal dissensions and famine would eventually
effect their ruin (1137). The Flemings had in particular
suffered under their arms, and one of the bravest barons,
Payne fitz John, fell in the pursuit of some Welsh, stricken
by a hostile spear[3].

Immediately after the homage at Oxford, Stephen summoned the high clergy and most distinguished of the laity to
meet at London, for the purpose of hearing the complaints of
the former against the abuses that had crept into the Church
during the reign of his predecessor. They complained of simony; of the voluntary gifts demanded of them, which threatened gradually to become a compulsive impost; of the viola-

[1] Gesta Steph. p. 10. Flor. Cont. p. 97. Giraldi Itiner. Cambriæ, lib. i.
c. 4.

[2] "Qui castellum ejusdem urbis (Gloccstriæ) sub comite habebat tempore regis Henrici, dato ei homagio et fidelitatis sacramento; nam eadem
civitas caput est comitatus." W. Malm. p. 725.

[3] Flor. Cont. p. 98. Gesta Steph. p. 16. Cf. p. 305. Joh. and Ric. Hagust. (coll. 258, 313), [who mention two barons as slain, viz. Payne fitz
John and Richard fitz Roger.—T.]

tion of the ecclesiastical immunities; in short, of everything, on account of which the clergy of those days were ever quarrelling with princes, who had to protect the interest of their governments; also of the facility with which marriages were dissolved, on which occasion it was not difficult bitterly to censure the life of the departed monarch, highly as only a few months previously he had been extolled. Stephen promised most readily to maintain the rights of the Church unimpaired, and to remedy the abuses that had crept in; but the vicissitudes of his reign permitted him neither to fulfil this promise, nor earnestly and vigorously to manifest an opposite disposition, in a strife implicating the substance and extent of his rights.

But it was necessary for Stephen to preserve the friendship of the clergy, as it early appeared but too evident, that, by his easiness of disposition and prodigality, he had lost the esteem of his Norman barons, without having succeeded in satisfying their insatiable desires.

In this year, shortly after Easter, the king was attacked with lethargy, when Roger Bigot, availing himself of a report of his death, seized on the castle of Norwich, which he refused to surrender, except to the king himself, and very reluctantly to him. It seems, however, to have been conferred on him at a later period, as we find him styled earl of Norwich and East Anglia [1].

At this time there lived a knight of noble lineage and extensive possessions, named Robert of Bathenton [2], whose life had been chiefly passed in gluttony and drunkenness; but who, after the death of Henry, forsaking his former habits,

---

[1] H. Hunt. lib. viii. aa. 1136, 1141. R. Hoved. a. 1136. Charter of 1153 ap. Rymer.: "Norwic . . . . tertium denarium, unde Hugo Bygotus comes est."

[2] The Badentone (Baentone) of Domesday, foll. 100ᵇ, 101, in Devonshire. "Robertus de Baentone," in that county, occurs in the Rotul. magn. pipæ, pp. 153, 154.

n b 2

had gathered round him a band of lawless followers, and was become the terror of the neighbouring country. When at length, having done homage to Stephen, it was expected that he would desist from his depredations, he became only more cruel and hostile. Being cited before the king's court, to answer for his misdeeds, he appeared sad, as one conscious of his perjury and perfidy. When accused by those whose property he had plundered, he was found guilty, and sentenced to deliver up his castle, and place all his possessions at the king's disposal. In the king's resolution to send an armed force, accompanied by Robert himself, to take possession of the castle, the wily knight, with a cheerful, smiling countenance, expressed his concurrence, while in his mind he was devising how he might deceive the soldiers, and retain possession of his castle. On reaching a country dwelling belonging to him, he gave orders for a sumptuous refection, with wine in abundance, to be served to his escort; and when all after their good cheer were buried in sleep, Robert quietly mounted his horse and made his escape. Having strongly fortified his castle, he wandered from place to place, at times lurking in concealment. at others joining the king's enemies, and at last died a miserable death among strangers. On being apprized that the retainers of Robert were continuing the game of plunder and destruction, the king proceeded without delay to Bathenton, to which he laid close siege. One night during the siege, a wretched man, in an attempt at flight, by letting himself down from the wall, was captured by the watch, and conducted to the king, who commanded him to be hanged in sight of the whole garrison, declaring that all should undergo a similar punishment, unless the castle were forthwith surrendered. It was surrendered accordingly. Having thus got possession of the place, Stephen banished its defenders from the realm, who, it is said, found an asylum with the king of Scotland [1].

[1] Gesta Stephani, p. 18.

The rebellion of Robert of Bathenton had hardly been quelled, when intelligence was brought to the king, that Baldwin of Redvers, a powerful baron of illustrious family in the west of England, had entered Exeter with an armed force, seized on the castle, and threatened with destruction by fire and sword all who did not appear favourable to his views. In compliance with the prayer of the citizens, the king immediately despatched two hundred horse to their aid, who were speedily followed by the king himself, at the head of a body of troops, who fortunately arrived at the moment when the insurgents, irritated with the citizens for having applied to the king, had issued from the castle, for the purpose of plundering and burning the city. Baldwin now, with his family and adherents, retired to the castle, which he had strongly garrisoned, and whence he made frequent sallies on the royal forces, while the king, on the other hand, left unemployed no means of annoying his adversary, and forcing him to surrender. In the meantime the castle of Plympton, belonging to Baldwin, was treacherously delivered to the king by its garrison, and levelled to the earth. The rest also of the rebels, seeing the desperate state of things, submitted, in the guise of suppliants, to the royal mercy, with the solitary exception of Alfred fitz Joel[1], a man of note, and the intimate friend of Baldwin. Finding his castle too extended and weak, and unprovided with a sufficient garrison, this faithful adherent abandoned it, and his brother, with a strong band, proceeded to Exeter, where he and his followers, pretending to come in aid of the king, dispersed themselves among the royal forces. Here he soon found means to apprize Baldwin's people of his arrival, who, sallying forth, exultingly conducted him and his followers back with them into the castle, in the sight of the king and his army.

But, fortunately for Stephen, water now failed the garrison, their wells were dried up. So great was the extremity, to

[1] Twice mentioned in Rotul. magn. pipæ, under Devonshire, pp. 153, 158.

which they were thereby reduced, that in making bread, and
for culinary purposes, they were obliged to use wine; even
the torches and other fires, cast by the besiegers into the
place, for the purpose of destroying their enginery and habitations, they had no means of quenching but by wine, until
at length not a drop remained either of wine or water. In
this their sad necessity, the besieged offered terms of capitulation, but which Stephen, by the advice of his brother
Henry, bishop of Winchester, refused, who, seeing the at-
tenuated condition of the two deputies, felt convinced that in
a very short time the garrison must surrender at discretion.
The wife of Baldwin also. bare-footed, with disheveled hair,
and bathed in tears, appeared before the king, but with no
better success. At last, at the intercession of his barons,
Stephen allowed the besieged to march out with their effects.
and to attach themselves to any lord they might choose. But
Baldwin himself fled to the Isle of Wight, where he possessed
a beautiful and strong castle, whence, having manned a large
vessel with pirates, he hoped to make booty of the merchant-
ships trading between England and Normandy, and otherwise
cause every annoyance in his power. Stephen, however, being
apprized of his designs, was speedily in pursuit of him, and,
on his arrival at Southampton, where he had ordered a fleet
to be equipped, Baldwin, taken by surprise at the rapidity of
the king, appeared as a suppliant before him. He had, it appears, ascertained that the supply of water in his castle was
insufficient for the number of its inmates. Failing to obtain
the restoration of his possessions in England, he sought and
found an asylum with the count of Anjou, from whom he of
course met with a most welcome reception, whence he ceased
not from intriguing against the king by exciting dissensions
in Normandy, to which he was in great measure instigated
by the countess Matilda, the daughter of Henry [1].

[1] Gesta Stephani. pp. 20 *sqq.* Flor. Cont. a. 1135. Joh. and Ric. Hagust. a. 1136.

The autumn of this year, which the king passed at the royal residence of Brampton in Huntingdonshire, for the sake of amusing himself, like his predecessors, with the pleasures of the chase, and the following year, which he began at Dunstable[1], and concluded with a residence of nine months in France[2], were, with the exception of his latter years, for England the only tranquil periods of his unhappy reign. In March (1137) the long-delayed visit to Normandy was carried into effect, which duchy, in consequence of the disunion existing under Stephen, had, to the prejudice of the reigning sovereign, entirely lost the character of the chief and hereditary state, which in after times, unquestionably to the great advantage of England, it never recovered. Count Geoffrey of Anjou, in alliance with the counts of Poitiers, Ponthieu, and others, had, in the preceding year, made an inroad into Normandy, but met with no favourable disposition towards him. The atrocities perpetrated by his army, on which was bestowed the opprobrious appellation of *Hilibccs*, or *Guiribccs*, excited the most intense hatred, and so universal a rising of the Normans against the intruders, that they soon found themselves compelled to abandon the country[3].

In May Stephen had an interview with the king of France, who invested him with the duchy of Normandy, on conditions similar to those on which it had been held by Henry, and was content with the homage of Stephen's son, Eustace[4]. Yet in no public document does Stephen bear the title of Duke of Normandy, a circumstance which, in conjunction

---

[1] H. Hunt. aa. 1136, 1121. Rotul. magn. pipæ, mention these royal residences, also those at Hallingbury in Essex, Woodstock, and Windsor. See pp. 44, 100, 57, 58, etc. 128, 122, 126, etc.

[2] Flor. Cont. aa. 1137 and 1138.

[3] Ord. Vital. pp. 905 *sq.* This appellation adhered to the troops of Anjou till a later period. Vita B. Ulfrici ap. Bollandi Acta Sanct. Feb. 20. "Ingressus est Angliam Henricus, Normanniæ dux, cum exercitu hominum, quos vulgus appellat Hirebellos."

[4] Ord. Vital. p. 909. H. Hunt. a. 1137.

with the unquestionable investiture, appears inexplicable[1]. Some rebellious barons were quelled by the potent arm of Stephen, new investitures were bestowed; yet was the king unable completely to humble Geoffrey of Anjou. The insolent presumption and violences of the Flemings in the king's service, particularly of William of Ypres, who ventured on an attempt to get possession of the person of the earl of Gloucester[2], who had followed the king to Normandy, exasperated the Normans, and led to the most serious dissensions among Stephen's adherents and army. Forsaken by a portion of his troops, when, full of ardour, he was eager to give battle to his adversary, he found himself necessitated to conclude a truce with him for three years, and to pay him annually three thousand marks[3].

Hardly had Stephen celebrated in tranquil splendour his Chistmas festival in England, when a rebellion and, shortly after, a storm, that had long been gathering, burst forth, which, had unity prevailed in the councils of those who raised it, must inevitably have proved his ruin. The rebellion was in its origin local, and wholly unconnected with the wars by which it was soon followed. Stephen's predecessors had been very sparing in the conferring of earldoms, and Henry more

---

[1] The want of this title does not appear to have been observed: Sir Harris Nicolas even adduces: "Stephanus, Dei gratia Dux Normannorum;" yet neither in Rymer nor the Monasticon is such a designation to be found. [The authors of the Nouveau Traité de Diplomatique produce an instance of his having denominated himself "Duke of Normandy." In the legend on his great seal, Stephen certainly styled himself "Dux Normannorum." The legend on the reverse of his seal was, "Stephanus, Dei gratia Dux Normannorum." Nicolas, Chron. of Hist. edit. 1838. p. 367. —T.] It appears also that Henry I. styled himself "Dux Normannorum" only in some documents relating to the duchy.

[2] Ord. Vital. p. 909. W. Malm. p. 710.

[3] So Robert de Monte; but Ord. Vital. p. 910. Rich. and Joh. Hagust. (coll. 259, 315) say that the truce was for two years only. [According to Richard of Hexham, Stephen received a large sum: "Stephano regi redeunti de Normannia, postquam data magna pecunia a comite Andegarensi, biennii inducias acceperat."—T.]

especially had exerted himself to bring into the royal hand both the revenues connected with them and the military command. In the place of those deceased earls who had been appointed by his father and brother, he seldom nominated a new one; so that, with the exception of his son Robert, earl of Gloucester, we find, in the year 1131, only the earls of Chester and Leicester, the latter of whom, it seems, died shortly after. This wise policy, to which England owed so much of its peculiar character and prosperity, was not imitated by Stephen, who bestowed the privileges of earl as well as other rewards on his adherents. When he created the earldom of Pembroke for Gilbert of Clare, it may be supposed that the state of things in those parts required a military dignity, which, at the same time, might serve as a counterpoise to the earls of Chester in the north and east of Wales. The dignity of earl of Derby, conferred at a later period on Robert of Ferrières (Ferrars), was the recompense of most important military services. But it is less obvious what induced Stephen to bestow the title of earl of Bedford on Hugh surnamed the Poor, of whom all that we know is, that he was a younger son of the once powerful Robert of Beaumont, count of Meulan[1]. At the same time, he bestowed on him the hand of the daughter of the deceased Simon of Beauchamp. Milo and his brother, sons of the deceased Robert of Beauchamp, who were in possession of the castle of Bedford, which they must surrender to the new earl, apprehensive of losing all their hereditary property, resisted the commands of the king. Whereupon Stephen, contrary to the advice of his brother, the bishop of Winchester, undertook the siege of Bedford, which occupied him a considerable time, until, through the bishop's mediation, the lords of Beauchamp surrendered the fortress. Hugh the Poor received the earldom, but held it for a short time only, and to hear the words parodied which St. Bernard wrote of the elder count Theo-

[1] Ord. Vital. p. 506.

bald of Blois, who had taken the cross against the infidels, and afterwards became a templar; that from a count he had become a knight, and from a knight a pauper[1].

Stephen did not remain till the end of the siege, being compelled to direct his attention to the Scots, whose king, David, the son of Malcolm Canmore and brother of Matilda, Henry's first wife, and of Maria, the wife of Eustace count of Boulogne, was uncle both to the empress and to Matilda, the consort of Stephen. By his mother, Margaret, the daughter of prince Eadward and granddaughter of king Eadmund, David himself represented the eldest line of the Anglo-Saxon house. If we therefore admit that the empress, by her marriage with a Frenchman, had forfeited her claim to the crown of England, it naturally fell to David, an opinion which did not lack supporters[2]. But David declared himself faithful to the oath, in favour of his niece, the empress, which he had taken to her father, and only demanded for his son Henry the renewal of the old customary investiture of the Scottish heir apparent with Cumberland[3], and for himself the inheritance of his queen, the daughter of earl Waltheof, in the counties of Northumberland and Huntingdon. With a double army he attacked Carlisle and the towns on the border of Northumberland, Carham and Norham, and, after a fruitless attempt to take Bamborough, he gained the towns of Alnwick and

---

[1] Gesta Stephani, p. 30. Ord. Vital. p. 915. Flor. Wigorn., H. Hunt. a. 1138. My interpretation of the saying assumes that for the senseless "Rogerium de comite" of the 'Gesta,' we should read Hugonem de comite. [Lappenberg's emendation is certainly very plausible; though he omits mentioning that, according to the 'Gesta,' the castle was retaken: "Sed quanto tunc humiliores et depressiores, tanto, aliquantillo elapso tempore, elatiores et acerbiores, ad ipsum castellum redeuntes, non solum illud recuperarunt, verum ipsum Rogerium de comite militem, de milite pauperem, Deo judice, ordine mirabiliter transverso, effecerunt." The passage is very obscure, and no doubt corrupt. The text of the 'Gesta' in this part is imperfect and evidently very fragmentary.—T.]

[2] Palgrave, Rise and Progress, i. p. 611.

[3] "Cum consulatu patris sui." Ric. Hagust. a. 1136. col. 312.

Newcastle, in the beginning of the year 1136. From the
principal inhabitants he exacted an oath of fealty to Matilda
and hostages. Before, however, he could advance to Durham,
Stephen, with a strong army, had already arrived at that city
(5th Feb.)[1], and David considered the event of a battle so
doubtful, and Stephen's readiness to acknowledge the specific
Scottish interests was so strong, that, in the course of a few
weeks, an agreement was concluded between the two kings,
by which David's son Henry should do homage to Stephen
for the county of Cumberland, and the towns of Carlisle,
Doncaster, and Huntingdon, with all their privileges, be delivered to him[2]. Stephen would not grant him Northumberland, but promised, as it is said, to bestow it on no other,
without investigating Henry's claims in the royal court. The
Scottish prince accompanied the king of England to London,
where we find him partaking in the festivities of Easter. But
the attentions shown him excited the displeasure of the archbishop of Canterbury and other English of rank, whereby
Stephen's desire of a friendly intercourse was so frustrated,
that David, deeply offended, recalled his son from the royal
court. No sooner had the latter, in the following year, embarked for Normandy than the Scots renewed their attempt
to get possession of Northumberland; but, at the king's summons, the Norman barons assembled in such numbers at Newcastle, that when the aged Thurstan, archbishop of York,
appeared at Roxburgh, as a mediator with king David, the
Scots entered into an armistice until Advent, at which time
Stephen returned home.

In this interval it seems not improbable that the Scots
entertained a deep-laid plan. The party of the old patriots,

---

[1] Ingram makes the Scots advance to Wessington in Derbyshire. But
the words of the Sax. Chron. a. 1135: " Dauid toc to wessien him," signify, David began to disquiet him. Wessien is an error or Semi-Saxon
for wessian, to vex.

[2] Ric. and John Hagust. (coll. 258, 342.) H. Hunt. a. 1136.

or of the subjugated Anglo-Saxon population, had, during the family dissension among the Normans, and in the absence of Stephen, greatly gained both in courage and numbers. Among these a conspiracy was formed to murder all the Normans, and transfer the crown of England to the royal house of Scotland. The clergy, who, through daily intercourse with all classes, knew far better the perilous ground on which the race of the conquerors stood than did the Norman barons, (among whom the cold contempt and rugged repulsiveness towards those subject to them, which had rendered the past generation objects of hate, were but ill glossed over by the levity, debauchery, and prodigality of the present,) obtained knowledge of the secret wishes and hidden impulses of the dejected, alien-tongued Saxons. The bishop of Ely, who also conducted the temporal administration of his diocese, durst not delay communicating to the clergy and secular lords of the land the plot that had been revealed to him. As many of the conspirators as could be discovered and taken were delivered to the hangman for degrading and painful punishments. Many others, either not known or not betrayed, secretly left their goods and possessions, to seek an asylum in Germany; or in Scotland and Wales, probably also in Denmark, help for the restoration of the golden age of Anglo-Saxon liberty, or the laws of king Eadward[1].

Stephen had hardly returned to England when David's ambassadors appeared before him, again to demand the cession of Northumberland, if he wished the truce not to be ended. They had scarcely been dismissed with a refusal, when William, son of Duncan, David's nephew, marched into England, for the purpose of besieging Carham, on the north border of Durham, where he was joined by David and his son. His army was composed of Scots, Picts, or inhabitants

---

[1] Ord. Vital. pp. 912–915. It may seem remarkable that only a monk residing in Normandy should supply us with information on these important events.

of Galloway, of the people of Lothian and Teviotdale, Cumbrians, Northumbrian deserters, fugitive Anglo-Saxons, discontented Normans, even Germans, under which denomination are probably to be understood Dutch and Flemings. The little border fortress, commanded by the brave Jordan of Busli, nephew of the famed general, Walter Espec, defended itself so well against the strong but undisciplined army of David with all its battering enginery, that, after the loss of his banner-bearer and many of his warriors, he was compelled to abandon the place, and, leaving behind a portion of his troops, to proceed to Northumberland. The cruelties here perpetrated by his army on women, old men, and infants, rival the most revolting and disgraceful recorded in history of the most savage barbarians[1], and appear almost incredible, if prince Henry really had for object the investiture of Northumberland, and David fostered hopes of the crown of England. The Scots had already crossed the Tyne, when Stephen, at the head of a numerous army, hastened to encounter them. David's forces rapidly retired and left England, passing again by Carham, with the object of awaiting Stephen in an ambuscade by Roxburgh, in reliance on the treachery of some Normans of rank. Stephen crossed the Tweed, but marched in another direction, laid waste a portion of the Scottish Lowlands, and, as David declined a battle, and provisions failed the English army in the wasted lands, many of which, on account of the near approach of Easter, refused to continue hostilities, he retired southwards; impelled probably to this step by the unfavourable accounts which he had received from England, and which induced him to intrust the further conduct of this war to his valiant and faithful barons.

No sooner had king David celebrated the Easter festival than he again marched into England, and this time proceeded

---

[1] Joh. and Ric. Hagust. (coll. 260, 316.) H. Hunt. Flor. Cont. a. 1138.

along the sea coast as far as Newcastle. Detachments from
his army were sent, for the purpose of taking Norham, a
castle belonging to the bishop of Durham, and of laying waste
the country around it.   Another considerable detachment,
under prince William, son of Duncan, had advanced into the
middle of Lancashire, where at Clithero on the Ribble, they
were met by the first division of the English army in four
bodies.   These William assailed with such impetuosity that
he soon broke their ranks, and put them to flight, many being
slain and many captured, as well as a great booty taken.
(10th June)[1].

The king of Scotland himself had meanwhile advanced into
Yorkshire. He had gained a powerful associate in Eustace
fitz John, who, under king Henry, had maintained a high
position, but had been estranged from Stephen for having
deprived him of Bamborough; though he still possessed
Alnwick in Northumberland and Malton in the East Riding
of Yorkshire[2]. The Scots now obtained possession of Bamborough, which was played into their hands, through the
thoughtless wantonness of its youthful defenders. Imperious
necessity now awakened all the Normans in Yorkshire to a
combined and bold resistance. The aged, feeble archbishop
of York, Thurstan, caused himself to be borne about on a
litter, that, by his harangues, he might kindle the courage
and thirst for vengeance of every one, and operate in effecting
the necessary order, without which so much power only wasted
itself in vain.   Here were also assembled count William of
Albemarle, Walter of Ghent, a pious old man near the verge
of the grave; the youthful Roger of Molbrai (Moubray)[3], the
aged Walter Espec, who, after the loss of his only son, had

[1] Joh. Hagust. a. 1138. col. 261.

[2] Ibid.   Ailred de Bello Standardii, col. 343.

[3] This rich baron was a son of Nigel of Aubigny (de Albini), who had
received from Henry I. the vast estates of the deposed Robert of Molbrai,
earl of Northumberland, who ended his days in prison. W. Gemmet.
viii. c. 8.   Among his castles he numbered Thyrsk in Yorkshire, Burton

founded Kirkham priory and, at a later period, the noble
Cistercian abbey of Rievaux, both in Yorkshire, also that of
Wardon in Bedfordshire[1]; William of Perci, Richard of Curci,
William Fossard, Ilbert of Lacy, Robert of Brus, Bernard of
Balliol—noble names, but which clearly prove to us that, even
in those northern provinces, the population of which, down to
the present day, show many traces of Anglo-Saxon or Anglo-
Danish descent, the lords were purely Norman. These were
joined by William Peverel from Nottinghamshire, and from
Derbyshire, by Robert of Ferrières and Geoffrey Alselin. A
general review and deliberation confirmed the confidence of
all, and reciprocal oaths were taken of immutable constancy
and inviolable faith. Every one confessed to the holy fathers
present, the holy eucharist was distributed, and, after a fast of
three days and many works of piety, the archbishop confirmed
the hearts of all, by bestowing on them his reconciliation and
his blessing. Thereupon the Norman chivalry, under the
protection of the Lord, to whom they had sought wholly to
consecrate themselves, advanced as far as Thyrsk. Here the
noble barons, Robert of Brus and Bernard of Balliol, both
connected by feudal obligations with the king of Scotland,
went to that prince, in the hope, by respectful but firm representations, of inducing him to desist from so unholy a war,
in which case they, in the name of king Stephen, promised
his son the earldom of Northumberland, which was the pretext for engaging in hostilities[2]. But as the Scots scornfully
refused to listen to their arguments and offers, Robert of Brus

in Kendal (Lonsdale, Westmoreland), Brichlawe (Brughlaw, Northumberland), Malessart. See Rotul. magn. pipæ, pp. 137, 138.

[1] Monast. Anglic. v. pp. 274, 369; vi. p. 207.

[2] Robert's speech is given by Ailred, abbot of Rievaux, Bellum Standardii, ap. Twysden, col. 343. [The local name of Brus (Bruis) is supposed
to be from Brix, near Valognes. In John's Itinerary (Arch. xxiv.) it is
written Brus, and Brucius in the Latin legend mentioned by M. de Ger-
ville (Mem. Ant. Nor. v. 318). See Taylor's "Master Wace," pp. 228,
131, and Capt. Williams' note in Gesta Henrici v. p. 120.—T.]

solemnly renounced his feudal oath to the Scottish monarch
for his barony in Galloway, as did Bernard of Balliol[1] a similar
obligation, and, as free masters of their sword, returned to
their own people. The army of Stephen then marched to
Cutcenmoor[2], near Northallerton, where they raised a tall
mast on a carriage, on which were displayed the banners of
the three patron saints of the north, St. Peter of York, St.
John of Beverley, and St. Wilfrid of Ripon. On the summit
of the mast was a cross, in the centre of which was fixed a
silver pyx, containing the consecrated wafer, the personally
present body of Christ, who should lead them to victory.
This carriage, in the sequel, had great influence on the issue
of the battle, which thence ever after bore the name of the
Battle of the Standard. As the Scots approached the English camp, Ralf Novellus, bishop of the Orkneys (22nd Aug.),
the representative of Thurstan, who was suffering from sickness, mounting an eminence, addressed an inspiring speech to
the warriors pressing around him. But yet more impressive
were the words uttered by the aged leader, Walter Espec,
a man of gigantic stature, with long, flowing, black locks
and beard, broad, lofty forehead, all-seeing, deeply-penetrating,
yet friendly eyes, in a voice betraying emotion, but clear and
piercing as a trumpet[3].

In marshalling his army, David, with the approbation of
his chief nobles, had intended to place his men at arms and
archers in front, but this disposition was opposed by the Galwegians, who claimed, as their right, to form the van. "Why,
king," said they, "do you dread those iron tunics which you
see yonder? We have sides of iron, breasts of brass, minds
void of fear, whose feet know not what it is to flee, or backs
to feel a wound. Of what good to the French at Clithero
were their mail corslets?" Seeing the king inclined to follow

[1] Written also Balliol, now Bailleul, in the dep. du Nord.—T.
[2] Chron. Mailros.
[3] See it in H. Hunt. a. 1183. Ailred, Coll. 337, *sqq*.

the advice of his nobles, Malise, earl of Strathern, indignantly exclaimed, "Why, king, do you yield to the wishes of these Frenchmen, not one of whom, with their armour, will go beyond me, though unarmed, in the battle to-day." Galled by these words, the bastard Alan of Perci, a valiant soldier, turning to the earl, said, "You have spoken bold words, which, for your life you cannot make good." To end the altercation, David granted the place of honour to the men of Galloway, while the second body, consisting of the men at arms and the archers, with whom were joined the men of Cumberland and Teviotdale, was led by the king's son, with whom was associated Eustace fitz John. The third body was formed of the men of Lothian and the isles. As a guard, the king retained with himself the Scots and natives of Murray, together with some English and French cavalry[1].

The great superiority in number of the Scottish army rendered it a point of vital importance to withstand their first violent, wild onset. The Normans, therefore, for the most part, dismounting from their horses, which at the savage howl of the Galwegians might become restive, joined themselves with the archers of the first body; the rest assembled round the holy banner. The Picts of Galloway now advanced with an appalling howl, vociferating thrice their war-cry, 'Albancigh,' and succeeded, by their numberless, well-directed arrows, in breaking the first line of the English armed with spears[2]. The latter, however, soon recovered their order, the

[1] Ailred, col. 342.

[2] Ailred Riev. col. 345. Bromton, col. 1027. [The following lofty lines, describing the discomfiture of the Scots, are highly graphic:

"Scotti vero dum grassando efferant immaniter,
Ad congressum belli primum terga vertunt pariter;
Truces quoque Gawedenses tremebundi fugiunt,
Et quas prius extulerunt caudis nates comprimunt.

*   *   *   *   *

Verum Angli fugientes ut amentes barbaros
Insequuntur, atque sternunt ut canes lepusculos.
Tunc abjecta manticarum mole cum viatico,

c c

413

weak arrows of the almost naked Picts were broken on the strong armour of the Normans, and when the latter fell among them with the sword, great havoc ensued, and the English archers made them safe objects for their missiles. But the valiant Prince Henry soon reunited them, and with a lion's courage rushed through the affrighted body of English, until he reached the spot, behind the order of the battle, where the horses were stationed. A feeling of dejection now began to spread itself among the Normans, when one of them raising on high the head of a slain enemy, declared it to be that of the king of Scotland, and by this device inspired his fellows with fresh courage and led them against the Picts, who were soon overthrown. The men also of Lothian, whose leader, in the first onslaught, had been slain by an arrow, now fled in consternation. King David still endeavoured to advance, but succeeded in gathering round him only so many of his men as to enable him, in firm order, and defending himself against the pursuing English, to reach Carlisle. Prince Henry, who, through his violent onset had fallen in the midst of the English, with great presence of mind mingled with the host of the pursuing victors, and thus contrived to escape unnoticed. Eleven thousand Scots are said to have fallen on the field of battle, besides those who were afterwards slain in the flight, in conflict with the Picts and peasantry [1], and through divers mistakes by their own fellows or, in the woods and fields were massacred by the English. The Normans lost no knight of eminence, excepting a brother of Ilbert

> Plus timore sunt repleti quam pane vel caseo.
> Seminantur hinc per agros panes atque casei,
> Crudæ carnes et illotæ velut canis usui.
> Utrum enim crudam carnem sive coctam comedant,
> Nil differre sed utramque licitam existimant.
> Nec equina carne vesci minus ducunt licitum,
> Quam eorum quæ mugitum præbent animalium."
>
> Serlo Monachus, ap. Twysden, col. 331.—T.]

[1] Ricard. Hagust. col. 323.

of Lacy. Some of them took Malton, the castle of the traitor
Eustace fitz John. The army then speedily dissolved itself,
and a vast booty was carried home by individuals, consisting
of armour, habits, etc. The banners taken were consecrated
to the saints in various churches. Stephen, greatly rejoiced
at the intelligence of this victory, appointed William of Albemarle to be earl in Yorkshire, and Robert of Ferrières to be
earl in Derbyshire. King David, not yet weary of war, resumed, though in vain, the siege of Carham. The papal
legate Alberic, bishop of Ostia, who had been an eyewitness
of the havoc made by the Scots in the north of England, was
so. shocked at the scene, that on his knees he implored the
Scottish monarch to listen to terms of peace; but David, who
clearly saw that, notwithstanding his recent defeat, his cause
was stronger than that of Stephen now pressed on all sides,
would only consent to a truce of two months, promising, however, that all the captured females, who had been sent as
slaves into Scotland, should be released and conducted to
Carlisle; also that churches should thenceforth be respected.
After the departure of the legate, in the following year (9th
April 1138), a peace was concluded at Durham, the conditions of which were to Stephen as unfavourable as if the
battle of the Standard had never been fought. Prince Henry
received Northumberland, and the barons of the earldom took
the oath of homage to him. For the towns of Bamborough
and Newcastle, which Stephen retained, an ample compensation was promised to the Scottish prince in a southern county.
The laws promulgated by king Henry for Northumberland
were to be held inviolate, and five sons of Scottish earls delivered to Stephen as hostages for peace and fidelity, during
life, on the part of king David and his son. The latter then
proceeded to the residence of Stephen, where he passed the
summer in all the splendour he could command[1].

[1] According to the Auctarium Gemblac. a. 1138, Stephen, in the beginning
of his war with the Scots, had also another enemy to encounter. The

c c 2

At the same time, Stephen had also many minor contests with his rebellious subjects in the southern and western parts of his kingdom. From a council held at Northampton he proceeded to Gloucester, by the joyful inhabitants of which he was met at a distance of five miles, and where his constable Milo, towards whom the king must naturally entertain considerable mistrust, on the following day conducted him to the public hall, where the citizens swore to him the oath of fealty. From Gloucester, Stephen marched against Geoffrey Talbot, who with deadly hate towards him, headed an insurrection of many of the barons of those parts[1]. Talbot had strongly fortified the castle of Hereford, of which the king, only after a considerable loss of time, obtained possession. He next attacked Geoffrey himself in his castle at Weobley, which he captured, although Geoffrey effected his escape, and which, as well as Hereford, was soon strongly garrisoned with royal forces[2]. While the king was thus engaged, a Norman herald appeared in his camp, who announced to him that Robert earl of Gloucester, renounced his friendship and allegiance, and declared void the oath of homage he had taken to him; since Stephen had violated all his earlier oaths in favour of his sister, the widowed empress. Stephen could hardly be surprised at this proceeding on the part of earl Robert, whom,

Danish king, Eric Lamb, had been inspired with the belief that he had juster pretensions to the crown of England, that had been worn by Cnut and his sons, than those Frenchified Normans, pretensions which he himself must have regarded as weak, when he deemed it necessary to support them by the extraordinary and unheard of argument, that the common washing of his own and the English coast by the German ocean gave him the preferable right. Stephen did not instantly attack the Danes who had landed, but allowing them to disperse in search of booty, fell upon their isolated parties, and thus succeeded in breaking their power, and driving them back.

It is striking that no Danish nor English writer makes mention of this expedition; at the same time we should hardly be justified in wholly omitting the account of the Belgian contemporary.

[1] Flor. Wigorn. Contin. a. 1138. Ord. Vital. p. 917.   [2] Ibid.

as his deadliest foe, he had endeavoured to remove through
the murderous hand of William of Ypres[1]; he was, nevertheless, bitterly indignant and declared the earl to have forfeited
all his possessions in England. Many of his castles were
accordingly demolished, Bristol and Slede castle alone being
left to the earl, or could not immediately be taken[2]. The
rebellious barons had garrisoned and fortified many castles.
Walkelin Maminot was at Dover, which was soon taken possession of by the queen[3]; Robert, son of Alured of Lincoln,
held the castles of Wareham and Morguan[4]; Walkelin held
that of Oakham[5], and William of Moiun (Mohun), Dunster
castle in Somersetshire[6]; William Peverel was in possession
of the towns of Brunam, Ellesmere, Obreton (Overton?), and
Wintenton[7]; William Louvel of Castle Cary in Somersetshire[8]; William fitz John of Harptree in Somersetshire[9];

[1] W. Malm. p. 710.

[2] R. Wendover, ii. p. 222. [who calls it Leedes castle. H. Hunt. a. 1138.
—T.] It leads to a very erroneous representation of events, when Lingard,
under the year 1140, names Gloucester, Canterbury, and Dover, as places
in which the standard of Matilda was first raised.

[3] H. Hunt. R. Wend. Ord. Vital. p. 917.

[4] H. Hunt. R. Wend. Ord. Vital. Qu. Margam?

[5] Ord. Vital. [This was Walkelin, or Vauquelin, of Ferrières, near Bernay. "On voit encore l'emplacement du château de cette famille, entouré
d'énormes fossés. Sa mouvance était très étendue. Les seigneurs de
Ferrières prenaient, probablement à cause de l'ancienneté et de l'importance primitive de leurs forges, le titre de premiers barons fossiers de Normandie." Note of M. Prevost. "Walcheline held Oakham." Lib. Rub.
Scacc. tit. Rotel. (Rutland).—T.]

[6] H. Hunt. R. Wend. Ord. Vital. "Will. de Moiont." Rot. magn.
pipæ, p. 108. His grandfather of the same name fought at Hastings,
Rom. de Rou, v. 13620. Gesta Steph. p. 52. Ellis, Introd. ii. p. 355.

[7] Ord. Vital. [Brunn in Cambridgeshire was given by Henry I. to the
father of Wm. Peverel. Wintenton is, no doubt, Whittenton, near Oswestre.
Here was a castle of the fitz Warines, but before them, a possession of
Peverel. Dugdale, Baronage, i. 432, 443.—T.

[8] Flor. Cont. a. 1138. Ord. Vital. R. Wend. ii. p. 222.

[9] Flor. Cont. a. 1138. Ord. Vital. Gesta Steph. p. 43. Rot. magn. pipæ,
pp. 13, 15.

William fitz Alan had garrisoned the castle of Shrewsbury[1];
Paganel held Ludlow, and Eustace fitz John, Melton[2].

But the head quarters of Stephen's enemies were at Bristol,
which earl Robert had caused to be strongly fortified and
stored with provisions. From this city the Norman knights
made frequent inroads on the peaceful and innocent inhabitants, and, with barbarous violence and horrible engines of
torture, wrung from them their money and other property.
A kinsman of the earl of Gloucester, named Philip Gai, is
branded as the inventor of those instruments with which, in a
short time, the castle of every one of these knightly robbers
was provided[3]. According to a contemporary account, "some
of the victims were suspended by the feet and smoked with a
foul smoke, others by the thumbs or the head, while burning
was applied to their feet; about the heads of others knotted
cords were bound so that they penetrated to the brain. Some
were cast into prisons, in which were adders, snakes, and toads,
and thus destroyed; some were placed in a "crucet-hûs,"
that is, a short, narrow, shallow chest, in which sharp stones
were laid : into this the man was pressed so that all his limbs
were broken. In many of these castles were instruments of
torture called a "laδ and grim," which were a sort of collars
for the neck, so heavy that it was not without difficulty two
or three men could bear one. This was thus applied : being
fastened to a beam, the sharp iron was placed round the
man's throat and neck, so that he could neither sit, nor lie,
nor sleep, but must bear all the weight of the iron[1]. These

[1] H. Hunt. R. Wend.   [2] Ibid.   [3] Flor. Wigorn. a. 1138.
[4] Sax. Chron. a. 1137. The entire passage, with all its corruptions, is as
follows : "Me henged up bi þe fet an smoked heom mid ful smoke; me
henged bi þe þumbes, oþer bi þe hefed, and henged bryniges on her fet.
Me dide cnotted strenges abuton here hæued, and þuryδen to þat it gæde
to þe hærnes. Hi diden heom in quarterne þar nadres and snakes and
pades wæron inne, and drapen heom swa. Sume hi diden in crucethus,
þat is in an ceste þat was scort and nareu and undep, and dide scærpe
stanes þer inne, and þrengde þe man þær inne, þat hi bræcon alle þe limes.
In mani of þe castles wæron lof and grim, þat wæron sachenteges þat twa

miscreants caused also many thousands to perish by hunger ; and this appalling state of things continued for nineteen years. They levied contributions on the villages, and when the wretched people had no more to give, they plundered and burned all the villages, so that a man might travel for a whole day without finding a human being in a village or the land tilled. A dearth naturally followed ; many perished of hunger, many went a begging who had previously been rich

oðer þre men hadden onoh to bæron onne; þat wæs swa maced, þat is fæstned to an beom, and diden an scærp iren abuton þa mannes þrote and his hals, þat he ne mihte nowiderwardes ne sitten, ne lien, ne slepen, oc bæron al þat iren."

Although not without diffidence, I will venture to suggest that, by substituting laðð for lof, and rachenteges (correctly racenteagas) for the unmeaning sachenteges, blunders may be removed from the above which have puzzled and misled Bp. Gibson, Sharon Turner, and the Drs. Ingram, Lingard, and Lappenberg, who have imagined an instrument of torture called a *sachentege*. " Láð and grim" (hateful and grim), I understand to be a nickname, by which the iron collar was usually called by the Saxon population. Racenteagas (sing. racenteah), I take to be a compound of raca (hraca) *neck* and teah, pret. of teón, *to draw, drag ;* the compound may therefore be rendered a *drag-neck*, and not as the name of an engine of torture, which, as I have stated, was called a "láð and grim." The similitude between the A. S. ſ and þ renders the emendation all but certain. In the A. S. Gospels we find : Mar. v. 3. "hine nán man mid racenteagum ne mihte gebindan," and Luc. viii. 29. "he wæs mid racenteagum gebunden."

A typographical error in the Edinburgh Review, closely resembling the above, was also attended with like consequences. It was there said : "The Hindoos have some very savage customs, which it would be desirable to abolish. Some swing on hooks, some run *kimes* through their hands, and widows burn themselves, etc. In a work entitled " Strictures on two critiques in the Edin. Rev." etc. the author, John Styles, is particularly severe on the reviewer for not being more shocked at the Hindoos for piercing their hands with *kimes*. "This," says Sydney Smith, "is rather an unfair mode of alarming his readers with the idea of some unknown instrument." But, to the great dismay of Mr. Styles, "a *kime* is neither more nor less than a false print in the E. Review for a knife, and from this blunder of the printer has Mr. S. manufactured this Dædalian instrument of torture called a kime ! We were at first nearly persuaded by his arguments against kimes.........but we looked in the errata, and found Mr. Styles to be always Mr. Styles." Sydney Smith's works 1854, vol. 1. p. 252.—T.

men, others fled from the land.   Neither church nor churchyard was spared by these plunderers.   So great, in fact, was
the general misery that men said publicly that Christ and his
saints were asleep[1]."

The adherents of Matilda in Bristol deeming it desirable
to gain possession also of Bath, a body of them marched forth
one day at early dawn, provided with ladders and other things
necessary for scaling the wall.   On reaching a certain valley
they halted, awaiting the return of their chiefs who had preceded the others, for the purpose of reconnoitering the place.
These, consisting of Geoffrey Talbot, his kinsman Gilbert of
Lacy, and William Hoset, while cautiously, as they thought,
making the circuit of the city, were suddenly met by a body
of the bishop's soldiers.   Gilbert, through his greater energy
and presence of mind, effected his escape, but Geoffrey was
captured, loaded with fetters and cast into a dungeon.   On
his return, Gilbert related to his comrades what had taken
place, who thereupon unanimously resolved to proceed forthwith to Bath, where they sent for the bishop, engaging themselves by oath for his safe egress and return ; though no
sooner was the prelate in their power than, laying hands on
him, they threatened to hang him, unless Geoffrey were instantly restored to them.   In this dilemma the bishop had no
alternative but to release his captive[2].

The outrages perpetrated at this time by the inhabitants of
Bristol were such as to call forth the immediate attention of
the king.   Not only was the neighbouring country a prey to
their depredations, but even distant parts of the kingdom
were not exempt from their plunderings and abductions.   On
being apprized of this state of things, Stephen summoned a
force and forthwith proceeded to Bath, where he was met

---

[1] Sax. Chron. a. 1137. Gesta Stephani, p. 41.

[2] Gesta Steph. p. 39. Flor. Wigorn. Contin. a. 1138. [I have given the
account of Talbot's capture chiefly from the Gesta, in preference to any
other authority, as being more circumstantial, and is, moreover, that of a
contemporary.—T.

without the city by the bishop, who, on being severely reproved by the king for having released his enemy Talbot, succeeded in appeasing the angry monarch, by representing to him the risk he incurred of perishing at the gallows, had he persisted in retaining his captive in custody. Stephen thereupon proceeded to survey the city, the walls of which he ordered to be heightened, and forts to be erected on the declivity, supplied with a sufficient force, as a check to the marauders of Bristol, to which city, with the intention of besieging it, he then directed his march. He here consulted with his barons as to the most effectual means of gaining possession of the place, when some advised the obstruction to the entrance of the port, where it was narrowest, by casting in vast masses of stone, turf, and timber, so that the course of the two rivers being stopped, their waters might form a lake and inundate the city. Others recommended the erection of forts on two sides of the place, thereby hindering all egress and ingress ; while those who, although in Stephen's army, secretly favoured the earl of Gloucester, expressed as their opinion, that such labours would prove futile, and that the masses thus thrown into the water would be carried away by the violence of the stream.

Listening to this last opinion, Stephen abandoned the siege of Bristol, after plundering and devastating the surrounding country, and directed his course towards Castle Cary and Harptree, of which the one, as we have seen, was held by Ralf Louvel, the other by William fitz John. Both these barons were united to the earl by ties of friendship and by the oath of vassalage, so that no sooner were they apprized of his intention to take arms against the king than they were ready to join him. In the belief that Stephen was engaged in a tedious siege, they laid waste and plundered all the neighbouring country; but the king soon appeared before Castle Cary, to which he laid close siege, casting fire and incessant showers of stones from his balistas into the place, till

at length, their provisions also beginning to fail, the castle
was compelled to surrender. From Castle Cary Stephen
proceeded to Harptree, before which he caused a fort to be
erected, and which he manned from the garrison at Bath.
Some time after, when passing by the castle, with the intention of laying siege to Bristol, the garrison issued forth and
attacked his rear; whereupon Stephen making a rapid retro-
grade movement with his cavalry, found the place nearly
deserted. Commanding then fire to be applied to the gates,
and scaling ladders and other engines to the walls, he soon
reduced the remainder of the garrison to deliver up the
castle [1]. Thence he proceeded to the siege of Dudley castle,
which Ralf Paganel had fortified against him, where having
laid waste all around him, he directed his march to Shrewsbury, the castle of which was held by William fitz Alan, who,
when apprized of the king's approach, clandestinely fled with
his wife and children, leaving those behind him who had
bound themselves by oath not to surrender the castle. Having
besieged it for many days in vain, Stephen caused a vast pile
of wood to be raised in the castle ditch and set on fire, the
smoke from which nearly stifled those within the place. The
gate at the same time being forced, the garrison, miserably
crawling or falling from the castle wall, took to flight, but
were pursued and put to the sword by the king's order;
Arnulf of Hesdin, the uncle of fitz Alan, and four of the
nobler among them he ordered to be hanged. From Shrewsbury Stephen returned to Wareham. On a mutual exchange
of promises, a pacific arrangement was, for a time, entered
into with Ralf Paganel [2]. Walkelin Maminot, whom the
queen with an army had vainly besieged in Dover, while her
friends from Boulogne endeavoured to cut off all supplies by

---

[1] Gesta Steph. pp. 42 *sqq.*

[2] Flor. Wigorn. Contin. a. 1138. H. Hunt. Ord. Vital. p. 917. Ern.
of Esding held Chivelai (Cheveley?) in Wiltshire. Rot. magn. pipæ.
p. 18.

sea, on hearing what had taken place at Shrewsbury, resolved on surrendering this key of England[1].

These successes and the yet more fortunate events in Northumberland seem to have lulled the zeal of Stephen in prosecuting the war against the rebels. We hear, however, of the capture, about Christmas, of the castle of Slede[2]. After the peace concluded at Durham, Stephen, accompanied by the Scottish prince Henry, proceeded against Ludlow, where the prince was dragged from his horse by an iron hook, and would have been taken, had not the king nobly rescued him from the enemy. Abandoning the siege of Ludlow, after leaving garrisons well supplied with provisions in two forts that had been erected against the place, Stephen directed his march towards London, having with difficulty succeeded in repressing sanguinary feuds among the besiegers[3].

A worse presage for the stability of Stephen's reign than the open hostility of those barons, to whose natural condition of existence, in the absence of a war, such an excitement seemed indispensable, while the work of quelling them gained for the king military fame together with a new and, as it were, a conqueror's right to the crown, was the equivocal conduct of Roger bishop of Salisbury and his nephews, Alexander bishop of Lincoln, and Nigel bishop of Ely. As Henry's chancellor, bishop Roger had accumulated vast riches, and, although enjoying under Stephen some of the highest offices in the state, was, nevertheless, supplying the castles of Devizes, Sherborne, Malmesbury, and Salisbury[5], which he

---

[1] Ord. Vital. p. 917. H. Hunt. a. 1138.

[2] H. Hunt. a. 1139.   [3] Flor. Wigorn. Contin. a. 1139.

[4] Alexander had also built a castle at Newark on Trent, "ad tutamen, ut dicebat, et dignitatem episcopii." W. Malm. p. 715.—T.

[5] "Rogerius, qui ædificiorum constructione magnanimum se videri vellet, plura apud Scireburnam, et apud Divisas multum terrarum ædificiis amplexus, turritas moles erexerat. Apud Malmesbiriam in ipso cœmeterio, ab ecclesia principali vix jactu lapidis, castellum inchoaverat. Castellum Salesbiriæ, quod cum regii juris proprium esset, ab Henrico rege impetratum, muro cinctum custodiæ suæ attraxerat." W. Malm. p. 715.—T.

had erected, with provisions and warlike munitions for the
service of Matilda, whose cause he had clandestinely espoused,
and with whom he was in secret correspondence. In daily expectation of the arrival of Matilda and the earl of Gloucester
from Normandy, Roger never went abroad, not even to court,
unattended by a numerous body of knights and friends, thus
holding himself ever in readiness to succour the enemies of
Stephen. Following the example of their uncle, the bishops
of Lincoln and Ely, who are described as proud men, regardless of the pure and simple dictates of Christianity, and wholly
given to secular pomp, never attended the court without exciting the admiration of the multitude by the splendour of the
armed train which accompanied them.

This dazzling and martial display on the part of the three
prelates raised the indignation of the count of Meulan and
other friends and adherents of the king. They accused them
of enjoying their preeminence in the realm, their wealth and
power for their own vainglory and gratification, not for the
honour of the sovereign ; of raising splendid castles and
towers, not to secure the kingdom to the king, but to deprive
him of his royal dignity ; it would therefore be advisable and
expedient to order their arrest, that they might be compelled
to surrender into the hands of the sovereign their castles and
every other source of discord ; for if the king would consent
to deliver them into custody, as violators of his peace, until
they had delivered up their fortresses, and rendered to Cæsar
the things that were Cæsar's, both he himself would be more
secure and the realm more tranquil. To these representations, from time to time renewed, Stephen was at length
induced to yield.

On the 24th June (1139) an assembly of the magnates of
the kingdom was held at Oxford, which was attended by the
three bishops in their usual state[1]. Here a quarrel, insti-

---

[1] Malmesbury (p. 716), who heard the bishop of Sarum's words on the
occasion, informs us that that prelate obeyed the summons to attend with

gated by the count of Meulan and other adherents of Stephen, broke out between the retainers of the king and those belonging to the bishops, in which many of the latter were killed and the rest dispersed. The bishops themselves, being apprized of what had taken place, were, it is said, meditating flight, when a band of armed satellites appearing, arrested the bishops of Salisbury and Lincoln and hurried them into the presence of the king. But the bishop of Ely, having intelligence of what was passing, succeeded in effecting his escape, and took refuge in his uncle's castle of Devizes, where he prepared for a vigorous resistance [1].

On receipt of this intelligence the king immediately adopted measures for gaining possession of the castles of the three bishops. Taking with him, therefore, the two other prelates under strict custody, he proceeded to Devizes, the castle of which is described as a structure of extraordinary strength and beauty. By the king's order, the captive bishops were confined apart from each other in loathsome places, and rigidly kept from food, the one in the stall of a cowhouse, the other in a vile hovel. His chancellor, a son of the bishop of Salisbury, he commanded to be led forth, with a halter round his neck, threatening to hang him before the gates of the castle, unless the bishop of Ely would forthwith surrender

great reluctance: he says: "Invitus valde Salesbiriensis hanc expeditionem incepit. Audivi etenim cum dicentem verba in hanc sententiam: ' Per dominam meam Sanctam Mariam, nescio quo pacto, reluctatur mens mea huic itineri. Hoc scio, quod ejus utilitatis ero in curia, cujus est equinus pullus in pugna.'"—T.

[1] With the above account from the Gesta, that given by the continuator of Florence (erroneously under 1138) nearly agrees: "On seeing which (their military parade), the king suspecting treason, ordered his people to arm themselves and, if necessary, to hold themselves ready to defend him. While he was treating on various matters with the bishops, a great tumult arose, on the subject of lodging, between the retainers of the two parties, when the royal retainers rushing to arms, the episcopal ones took to flight, leaving their equipage behind them. The bishops of Salisbury and Lincoln were taken, together with the son of bp. Roger, surnamed ' de Paupere censu.' "—T.

the place and admit the royal forces. The bishops now overwhelmed with the most torturing anxiety, seeing the imminent
peril to which their lives were exposed, surrendered into the
king's hands the castles they had erected with so much care
and at so vast a cost.

The castle of Devizes and the others belonging to the three
prelates, together with all the munitions and treasures contained in them, being thus delivered to the king, the bishops,
humbled, and stript of all their pomp and vainglory, descended
to the administration of their ecclesiastical functions[1].

[1] Gesta Steph. pp. 46 *sqq*. According to Malmesbury the quarrel between the retainers in the king's court was attended with a different result; I will, therefore, give his account of the seizure of the bishops,
which varies also in other particulars from that in the Gesta, which is
adopted in the text:—

"Then, as if fortune would seem to favour the wishes of the king, a
disturbance arose, about their lodging, between the retainers of the bishops
and those of Alan count of Brittany, in which the followers of Alan were
put to flight and his nephew nearly killed; many also of the bishops' men
being wounded and one slain. The king, influenced by the instigators,
commanded the bishops to attend and give satisfaction for the breach of
his peace by their followers, by delivering up the keys of their castles as
a pledge of their fidelity. The prelates, although willing to give satisfaction, demurred to the surrender of their castles; whereupon the king placed
them under close restraint. He thus conducted bp. Roger without chains,
and his chancellor, who was nephew, or, as it was said, more than nephew
of the bishop, in fetters to Devizes, for the purpose of getting possession
of the castle, which had been erected at an almost boundless cost, not, as
the bishop himself stated, for ornament, but in truth to the injury of the
Church. This expedition was attended with the surrender of the castles
of Salisbury, Sherborne, and Malmesbury, and, at the expiration of three
days, that of Devizes also; the bishop having imposed on himself a fast,
for the purpose of thereby moving the heart of the bishop of Ely who held
it. Nor was the bishop of Lincoln more obstinate, but purchased his
liberty by the surrender of Newark and Sleaford."

According to Henry of Huntingdon (a writer not remarkable for accuracy) the fasting was not voluntary on the bishop's part, but enforced
by the king, who had recourse to the same method of compulsion in the
case of the bp. of Lincoln. His words are: "Angarians eum jejunii tor-
mento."......"Rex inde rediens Alexandrum episcopum Lincoliensem,
quem dimiserat in captione apud Oxinefordiam, duxit secum ad Newer-

STEPHEN.   399

This bold measure on the part of Stephen was viewed in diametrically opposite lights. By some it was said that the bishops were justly deprived of the castles, which they had erected in defiance of the prohibition of the canons; that they ought to be preachers of peace, not builders of structures that might serve as asylums to criminals. Such was the opinion entertained and eloquently defended by Stephen's firm friend, Hugh archbishop of Rouen. Others, on the contrary, among whom was the king's brother, Henry bishop of Winchester, maintained, that if bishops swerved from the path of right, judgment on them was not of the king but of the canons; that without a public ecclesiastical council, they ought not to be deprived of any possession; that the king had not acted from any love of right, but solely for his own advantage, by not restoring the castles to the churches, at whose cost and on whose lands they were erected, but granting them to laymen, who made little account of religion. Finding that his words were unheeded by the king, he summoned him to answer for his conduct before a council, which he appointed to be held on the 29th August.

On that day, Theobald archbishop of Canterbury and almost all the bishops assembled at Winchester, where, after reading the decree of pope Innocent II., conferring on him the legatine authority, the bishop of Winchester addressed the meeting in a Latin speech, in which he expressed his indignation at the seizure of the bishops of Salisbury and Lincoln, the former of whom had been arrested in an apart-

cam. Ibique construxerat episcopus super flumen Trente, in loco amœnissimo, vernantissimum florida compositione castellum. Vix igitur episcopus lachrymis et precibus a suis obtinere potuit ut castrum suum a jure suo in extraneorum custodiam deponerent. Similiter redditum est castellum aliud ejus, quod vocatur Slaforde, neque forma neque situ a prædicto secundum."

According to Orderic (p. 919), the castle of Devizes was occupied by Maud of Ramsbury, the bishop's concubine and mother of Roger the chancellor. T.

ment of the king, the latter in his inn, while the bishop of Ely, fearing a similar fate, had saved himself only by a precipitate flight to Devizes; and terminating his harangue by informing them that Stephen, after his repeated exhortations to atone for the outrage, had manifested no objection to the summoning of a council. He therefore called on the archbishop and others to deliberate as to the steps necessary to be taken, adding that, although brother to the king, yet neither from fraternal affection, nor for the loss of his possessions, nor even of his life, would he fail in the execution of their decree.

While the legate was thus speaking the king sent some of his earls into the assembly, to inquire why he had been cited? They were answered by the legate, that it ill beseemed any one, who remembered he was a follower of the faith of Christ, to be indignant if summoned by the ministers of Christ to atone for a crime such as the age had never witnessed; that the king would act wisely if he would either justify his deed, or submit to a canonical sentence; that it was his duty to show favour to the Church, by whose support, and not with the aid of an army, he had been raised to the kingdom. The earls thereupon departed, and shortly after returned, accompanied by Aubrey of Vere[1], a man well skilled in legal knowledge. He reported the king's answer, and with his utmost power, yet abstaining from all violence of language, aggravated the cause of bishop Roger. The king, he said, had suffered numberless injuries at the hands of that bishop, who rarely came to court, but his followers, presuming on his power, raised a tumult; as recently at Oxford they had assailed the men and even the nephew of count Alan of

[1] Rot. magn. pipæ, passim. He founded the priory of Hatfield Regis about a. 1135. Monast. Angl. iv. p. 432. As chamberlain he appears in a charter a. 1136, ap. Rymer, i. p. 16. He was slain in London in an insurrection of the people. See Chron. Joh. de Burgo, a. 1141, ap Sparke, Hist. Angl. Scriptt.

Brittany, also the retainers of Hervé of Leon, a man of such high nobility and pride, that he had never gratified the wish expressed by king Henry, that he would visit England; that the violence thus offered to him tended greatly to the prejudice of king Stephen, through regard for whom he had visited England; that, on account of an old grudge, the bishop of Lincoln had excited his followers against count Alan; that the bishop of Salisbury secretly favoured the king's enemies, though for a time he had succeeded in dissembling his treachery, a fact of which the king had certain knowledge from many quarters; though more especially from his refusal to permit Roger of Mortimer, with the king's soldiers under his command, although standing in great peril from the garrison of Bristol, to remain one night in Malmesbury. It was, moreover, the talk of every one, that, as soon as the empress landed, he and his nephews and castles would be at her disposal; that Roger was not arrested as a bishop, but as a servant of the king, who had the administration of his affairs and received his pay[1]; that the king had not seized the castles by violence, but that both bishops had gladly surrendered them, to escape from the consequences of having excited a riot in the king's court; that the money found by the king in the castles was lawfully his own, as bishop Roger, in the time of king Henry, had amassed it from the returns of the royal revenue; both that and his castles he had delivered up from fear of the consequences of his acts against the king.

At these words of Aubrey, bishop Roger loudly exclaimed: that he had never been an official of king Stephen nor received his wages, and, moreover, threatened, that if in that council justice were not done him, with respect to what had been taken from him, he would seek it in a higher court. On this the legate mildly observed: that it would have been

[1] "Ut regis serviens, qui et procurationes ejus administraret et solidatas acciperet." W. Malm. p. 722.

D d

more decent to have inquired whether the charges against the bishops were true than, in contravention of the canons, to pronounce sentence on the innocent. Let the king, therefore, do that which is the usage in legal cases; let him restore their property to the bishops ; as by the law of the land, persons disseized are under no obligation to plead.

At the king's request, the proceedings were now postponed till the morrow, and then again till the arrival of the archbishop of Rouen on the day following. That prelate expressed his readiness to grant that bishops might possess castles, if only it could be shown that, according to the canons, they might lawfully possess them ; but as that was impossible, it was the extreme of impiety to act contrary to the canons. "And," added he, "even supposing it lawful to possess them ; yet in such perilous times, following the usage in other nations, the magnates of the realm ought to deliver up the keys of their fortresses to the king, whose duty it is to strive for the peace of all. Thus is the entire plea of the bishops quashed ; for either according to the decrees of the canons, it is illegal for them to hold castles, or, if by the indulgence of the prince such illegality is tolerated, they ought to yield to the necessity of the times and deliver up the keys." Aubrey then concluded by saying : it had reached the ears of the king that the bishops were holding out threats and preparing to send some of their number to Rome, to plead against him. "And this," added he, "the king advises you not to do ; because if any one, contrary to his will and the dignity of the realm, departs from England, he may, perhaps, find it difficult to return. Moreover the king feeling himself aggrieved, spontaneously appeals against you to Rome."

The council was then dissolved, the king refusing to submit to the censure prescribed by the canons, and the bishops not deeming it prudent to pronounce any judgment on him, either because they thought it hazardous to excommunicate a prince without the papal sanction, or because they had heard, and some also had seen, that swords were being drawn around them. Nevertheless, the legate and archbishop Theobald, making a last effort in fulfilment of what they deemed their duty, cast themselves at the king's feet, and implored him to have pity on the Church, on his own soul and reputation, nor suffer dissension between the sovereignty and priesthood. Their attempt was fruitless [1].

It would seem, however, that, to appease the clergy, Stephen submitted to a sort of penance, by divesting himself of the royal habit and expressing his contrition for the violence of which he had been guilty [2].

At this time, William of Mohun, a man of noble lineage, raised a powerful opposition to the authority of Stephen, and from the fair and strong castle of Dunster, which he had erected on the coast of the Bristol channel, in Somersetshire, in which he had assembled a considerable body of knights and soldiers, laid waste and plundered the surrounding country far and near, putting to the sword, carrying off, and burning all and everything offering resistance, and inflicting tortures on those who were suspected of possessing wealth ; in fact, renewing those horrors, of which so appalling a recital has been already given.

When intelligence of these enormities reached the ears of the king, he speedily raised a large force for their repression ; but on arriving before the castle, and viewing its formidable defences, it being on one side washed by the sea, on the others guarded by its walls and towers, by outworks and intrenchments, he despaired of taking it by assault, and, listening to the advice of others, caused a fort to be erected

---

[1] W. Malm. pp. 719, *sqq*.

[2] Gesta Steph. p. 51. "Sed quia ab omni clero juste provisum, et discrete fuit dijudicatum, nulla ratione in christos Domini manus posse immittere, ecclesiastici rigoris duritiam humilitatis subjectione mollivit, habitumque regalem exutus, gemensque animo, et contritus spiritu, commissa sententiam humiliter suscepit."—T.

d d 2

in face of the fortress, whence he could hold it in check and give greater security to the surrounding country. Being then summoned to other parts, he delegated his authority to Henry of Tracy, a soldier of approved valour and experience, enjoining him vigorously and incessantly to assail the enemy. Nor, in the absence of the king, was Tracy backward in fulfilling the orders he had received, but from his town of Barnstaple carried on the warfare with such energy, that not alone did he repress the predatory excursions of the garrison, but on one occasion captured a hundred and four knights, in an encounter of cavalry, and reduced Mohun himself to such straits, and so humbled him, that he ceased from further hostilities against him, and restored to the land a comparative degree of tranquillity, and immunity from all cause of disquietude[1].

But William of Mohun was not the only one whom the vigour of Tracy reduced to obedience; other disturbers also of the public peace, among whom William fitz Odo was especially conspicuous, he forced to submit to the king's authority. After having in various conflicts weakened the power of this turbulent noble, Henry of Tracy received intelligence from his spies that the castle of his adversary was deserted by its defenders, who had sallied forth on a plundering expedition. Proceeding then to the castle in the silence of the night, and eluding the watch, he caused lighted torches to be cast through the windows of a tower, whereby the interior habitations were soon wrapped in flames, and its lord, half burnt, together with all his treasure was carried off by Tracy, who also, on other occasions, gave proofs of his zealous attachment to the cause of Stephen[2].

During this state of disquietude into which the country was plunged, Baldwin of Redvers, who, as we have seen, had been passing his life in exile, landed with a considerable body of followers at Wareham, whence he proceeded to Corfe

---

[1] Gesta Stephani, p. 52.   [2] Ib. p. 53.

castle, where he prepared to oppose a stout resistance to the king, of whose speedy approach he had received reports. These reports were well founded, for the king was no sooner apprized of his landing than, summoning his friends, he at once proceeded to lay siege to the castle, where after passing a considerable time, in expectation of overcoming his enemy, either by means of his military engines or by hunger, he at length, yielding to the advice of his followers, raised the siege, and allowed Baldwin to withdraw unmolested. What prompted Stephen to this apparently imprudent step was the intelligence that the earl of Gloucester and his sister, the countess of Anjou, having united their forces, were on the eve of invading England, against a sudden surprise from whom he commanded the entrance of all the ports to be closely watched, both by day and night, deeming it more prudent and at the same time more desirable to frustrate with all his might the designs of his principal enemies, than, by directing his efforts solely against Baldwin, to run the risk of being circumvented by others[1].

While the king's attention was thus distracted, the whole country was plunged into a state of consternation, by the intelligence that, on the 30th Sept., the earl of Gloucester and his sister, accompanied by Guy of Sableuil and a body of a hundred and forty knights, had landed on the coast of Sussex[2], and had found an asylum in the castle of Arundel, belonging to William of Aubigny (Albini), who had married Adela, the queen dowager, and step-mother of the empress[3].

[1] Gesta Stephani, p. 54.

[2] Flor. Contin. a. 1139, asserts that she landed at Portsmouth on the 1st Aug., while the king was besieging Marlborough. Robert de Monte also says: mense Augusto transierunt in Angliam. H. Hunt. also says: in autumno, and John of Hexham speaks of the landing at the close of the year 1139.

[3] Robert de Monte. Ord. Vital. p. 920. [Arundel castle was possessed by William of Aubigny in right of his wife, on whom, together with the earldom, it had been bestowed, "pro dote" by Henry I. R. Wendover, ii p. 227. — T.

At this intelligence, the minds of men were impelled in opposite directions, those who favoured the cause of Matilda appearing more alert, and more eager to embarrass the king,
while those of his party were depressed and thunderstricken.
The king alone stood unshaken amid all the wars and dissensions in which he was involved, and without a moment's delay,
placing himself at the head of a body of tried veterans, unexpectedly appeared before the castle of Arundel, where, on
receiving intelligence from his scouts that the earl with his
followers[1] had, in the silence of the night, withdrawn from
the castle, and was gone in the direction of Bristol, there to
place himself at the head of ten thousand Welsh and other
adversaries of the king[2], but that Matilda with her Angevin
followers was still in the castle, leaving a portion of his force
to prevent her escape, he directed all his efforts to the capture
of the earl.   In this design, however, he was frustrated, as
Robert, avoiding the beaten road and following a devious
course, succeeded with his friends in reaching Bristol safely.
Stephen thereupon hastened back to resume the siege of the
castle.   By the chronicler of Stephen's acts we are told, that
the bishop of Winchester, on hearing of the arrival of the
earl and his sister, caused all the by-ways to be occupied by
soldiers, and having by this means met with the earl, he
entered into a compact of peace and amity with him, and
allowed him to depart without let or injury.   Such was the
common report, though as the chronicler adds, it must appear
not only doubtful but incredible to every thinking person,
that a brother should meet with the kiss of peace the invader
of his brother's kingdom.   The bishop then, as if he had not
met with the earl, and accompanied by a numerous body of
knights, joined the king.   On finding that his brother was
resolved on prosecuting the siege with vigour, he pronounced
that resolution both useless to the king and not grateful to

[1] Not more than twelve knights. W. Malm. p. 725.
[2] Ord. Vital. p. 920.

the kingdom; for if he undertook to besiege the countess in one part of England, her brother would forthwith raise an insurrection in another; it would, consequently, be more advisable, both for himself and the realm, to permit her without molestation to join her brother, so that the forces of both being confined in one spot, he could the more easily direct all his efforts to their destruction, and would be the better enabled to pursue them with his whole power. Stephen imprudently followed this advice, and, pledges being given and received, permitted the countess to join her brother. The shortness of Matilda's sojourn at Arundel may, however, partly at least, have been caused by the unwillingness of her step-mother to afford her longer entertainment, notwithstanding the repeated promises transmitted to her while residing in Normandy[1]. Besides the permission so imprudently granted, Stephen, with equal, if not greater imprudence, assigned to the countess, as an escort, his brother Henry with Waleram count of Meulan[2]. By the latter she was not attended beyond Calne, but the bishop accompanied her until she was met by her brother with an armed force, who conducted her to Bristol. On reaching Bristol she gave notice of her arrival to all the barons of the realm, imploring their aid, to some promising gifts, to others an augmentation of their lands. All those, therefore, who had only feigned adherence to the royal cause, breaking their oaths of homage and fealty, hastened to her standard. She afterwards withdrew to Gloucester, the castle of which was held, under earl Robert, by Milo the constable, from the time of king Henry[3].

To recount all the vicissitudes, as far as any memorials of them have been preserved, of the petty warfare which from

---

[1] " Noverca fœminea levitate fidem, toties etiam missis in Normanniam nunciis promissam, fefellerat." W. Malm. p. 725. See also Flor. Contin. p. 117.

[2] According to Malmesbury (p. 725), it was not the custom of praiseworthy knights to refuse an escort even to their bitterest enemy.

[3] Gesta Stephani, p. 56, and antea p. 323 note.

this time to nearly the close of Stephen's reign never ceased, would be neither interesting nor instructive; we will, therefore, limit ourselves to a brief notice of the principal occurrences that took place in the course of it.

Among the foremost who declared in favour of Matilda was Brian fitz Count[1], of whom slight mention has been already made. On receiving intelligence of her arrival, he forthwith supplied his strong castle of Wallingford with a numerous garrison, and rose in open and zealous rebellion against the king Milo of Gloucester, also, in violation of his oath to Stephen, rose in open rebellion against him, and giving an asylum to all the enemies of the king who flocked to him, desolated the surrounding counties. But Stephen, rising above the torrents of adversity which threatened to overwhelm him, collected his forces with the resolution of attacking his foes in detail; in prosecution of which, his first intention was to blockade the castle of Wallingford. but from which he was diverted by the counsel of his barons, founded on the vast strength of the place and its stores both of warlike munitions and all the necessaries of life. Far more advisable, added they, would it be to erect two forts before it, placing in them a number of men sufficient to continue the blockade, and proceed immediately to the suppression of other adversaries.

Following this counsel, Stephen caused two forts to be erected before the place, and with all speed proceeded to Trowbridge, which Humphrey of Bohun[2], the late king's constable, had, by the advice and at the instigation of Milo, rendered almost impregnable. On his march thither he was

---

[1] See pp. 364, 369.

[2] E de Bohon li vieil Onfrei. Rom. de Rou, v. 13584.

"*Onfroi, seigneur de Bohon*, à deux lieues au midi de Carentan. On y voit encore la motte du château de cette famille, qui après la conquête posséda long temps le titre de connétable héréditaire d'Angleterre, et fournit plusieurs comtes de Hereford, d'Essex et de Northampton." Note of M. Prevost.—T.

so fortunate as to take by assault the castle of Cerney, which
Milo, for rebellious purposes, had erected against him; and
also gained by surrender the strong castle of Malmesbury, in
which he captured, together with his followers, Robert fitz
Hubert, a Fleming, and kinsman of William of Ypres, notorious for his cruelty and unequalled atrocities[1]. But now for
a season his good fortune forsook him; for while on his
march to Trowbridge, Milo with a chosen band made an
attack by night on the forts erected by Stephen at Wallingford, and forced the garrisons to surrender. In the opinion
of his chronicler, Stephen drew down this disaster on himself,
for having desecrated a church, by converting it into one of
his forts.

In prosecution of his success against the royal forces, Milo
now gathered around him at Gloucester all those whose possessions had been laid waste by, or from other causes were
hostile to, the king (a. 1140)[2], whence he committed the most
horrible devastations over the surrounding country. But his
only deeds worthy of remembrance were the capture of those
castles which the king had erected in Gloucestershire and
Herefordshire, the garrisons of which perpetrated unheard-of
outrages on the peaceful inhabitants. Of these, some he over-
threw, as at Cerney and Hereford; others he committed to
the keeping of his partisans, as at Winchcombe. To the
praise of Milo be it however spoken, that his fidelity to the
daughter of Henry was unshaken; with him both herself and
friends found an hospitable asylum; nor did he cease from
acting towards her as a father and counsellor until, by the
capture of Stephen, he had made her queen of England. In

[1] Robert fitz Hubert had gained possession of the castle by nightly
surprise, at the same time setting fire to the town. He enjoyed his acquisition for a fortnight only. W. Malm. p. 726. " Captivos melle litos
flagrantissimo sole nudos sub divo exponebat, muscas et id genus animalia
ad eos compungendum irritans." Ib. p. 733.—T.

[2] Dr. Lingard passes from the year 1139 to 1141, thus unaccountably
omitting all the events of 1140.—T.

the meantime the king had arrived before Trowbridge, where
finding the fortifications of the most formidable character, he
toiled on the construction of vast and powerful machines for
the capture of the place; but the garrison withstood his
efforts, while his barons grew weary of the siege, being under
constant apprehension of the approach of the earl of Gloucester.   Stephen thereupon resolved on returning to London,
leaving a military force at Devizes, to hold the garrison of
Trowbridge in check, by whose incursions and mutual hostilities the whole surrounding country was soon converted into
a miserable desert [1].   Stephen next proceeded to Worcester,
which had sustained considerable damage from the army at
Gloucester, where he deprived Milo of the office of constable,
and bestowed it on William, the sheriff of Worcester, son of
Walter of Beauchamp [2].

The death of the bishop of Salisbury, which took place in
the preceding year (Dec. 11th, 1139), was, no doubt, a fortunate event for Stephen, as thereby many causes of dissension might more easily be removed, and the never wholly
alienated favourable disposition of the clergy towards him
rendered more available.   Bishop Roger commenced his
career by gaining the favour of prince Henry, whose scanty
finances he administered with so much prudence and frugality,
that, on ascending the throne, there seemed nothing, or very
little that Henry could deny him.   Lands, churches, prebends,
abbeys were bestowed on him; he was raised to the dignity
of chancellor and, lastly, to the see of Salisbury.   It was now
that his real character began more manifestly to display itself.
If any land lay contiguous to his own, which he was desirous
of adding to his possessions, he obtained it, if not by entreaty
or money, by violence.   He gloried in the erection of splendid
edifices in all his possessions.   In his latter years, however, as

---

[1] Gesta Stephani, pp. 58, *sq.*

[2] Flor. Wigorn. Contin. a. 1139, where it is said that Stephen went from
Oxford to Worcester.—T.

we have seen, misfortunes thickened upon him; he saw the plunder of his treasures, himself overwhelmed with reproaches before the council at Winchester, and the remnant of his money and plate, which he had laid on the altar for the purpose of completing his church, carried off against his will [1].

From Worcester the king proceeded to Oxford, and thence, with his court, to Salisbury, there to celebrate Christmas and wear his crown, according to royal custom. Here the canons presented him with two thousand pounds of silver, in return for which he granted them an exemption from all imposts on their lands, besides twenty marks for their own use, and forty for the covering of their church, moreover promising them that, if he obtained peace, he would restore what they had given him [2].

When the bishop of Ely received intelligence of his uncle's death, he resolved on executing that which he had long meditated—vengeance on the king for the injury he had inflicted on his relative, by aiding to the utmost of his power the daughter of Henry in her struggle for the throne. Casting

---

[1] As Malmesbury (p. 727) appears to speak very impartially and in no flattering strain of his bishop, I have preferred his account to that of the author of the Gesta, who (p. 62) says of Roger: "qui sicut divitiarum gloria, prudentisque animi ingenio omnes regni magnates superavit, ita a luxuria fractus, et prorsus enervatus, quicquid in se virtutis continuit sola sorduit immunditia. Reliquit autem in ecclesia Salesbiriæ infinitam nummorum quantitatem, sed et vasa plurima ductili aurificum opere, ista ex argento, illa ex auro artiste et gloriose cælata; quæ omnia in usus regis cesserunt....... Rex vero partem pecuniæ ad ecclesiam cooperiendam, partem ad canonicorum relevandam necessitatem indulsit, terrasque ecclesiarum et possessiones, quas episcopus in proprios usus redegerat, deque dominabus, sublatis pastoribus, ancillas effecerat, libere et ecclesiastice ipsis ecclesiis reddidit, pastoribusque canonice inthronizatis, duas ecclesias, Malmesbiriensem et Abbesbiriensem, ut fuerant antiquitus, splendide restauravit." According to the Continuator of Florence (p. 113) the bishop's wealth that fell to Stephen consisted of 40,000 marks of silver, besides a large quantity of gold and ornaments, which Roger "thesaurizavit, et ignoravit cui congregavit ca."--T.

[2] Flor. Wigorn. Contin. a. 1140.

away, therefore, all evangelical weapons, and abandoning the
warfare of ecclesiastical discipline, he put on the man of blood,
and having hired soldiers in Ely inured to deeds of violence,
became the terror of all around him.   When informed of the
rebellion of the bishop, the king immediately hastened to Ely,
at the head of a considerable force, when, seeing the extraordinary natural strength of the place, he held anxious council
with his followers, as to the best method of attack.   It was
finally resolved to join a number of boats together in a part
where the water, which surrounded the isle, appeared shallow,
and form a bridge across them composed of hurdles.   This
plan was executed, and the army reached the margin of the
isle, consisting of muddy fens, over which a ford was pointed
out to them by, it is said, a monk of Ely, who for that service
was made abbot of Ramsey.   The king then advancing into
the interior of the isle, permitted his soldiery to disperse
themselves and plunder in all directions.   Of the bishop's men
some were taken, together with much valuable spoil.   A small
castle also at the entrance of the isle, to which some soldiers
of the bishop had retired, was captured.   The bishop himself with difficulty escaped to Gloucester[1]; but the monks
were treated by Stephen with that unalterable kindness of
feeling which, in the midst of all his troubles, he ever preserved[2].   Hence his contemporaries and even tradition[3] have
justly separated Stephen's individuality from the cruelties
committed during his reign, which, moreover, were for the
most part perpetrated by his enemies.

   It was at this moment so critical for Stephen's stability
that the young king of France, Lewis VII., who could not
regard with satisfaction the advancement of the house of

---

[1] Gesta Stephani, p. 63.

[2] Gesta Steph. p. 64.   Ricardi Hist. Eliens. ap. Wharton, Anglia Sacra.
ii. p. 620.

[3] As in the old ballad: "King Stephen was a worthy peere." See
Percy's Reliques, and Shakspere. Othello, Act II. sc. 3.

Anjou, did not hesitate (Feb. 1140) to betroth his sister Constance to Stephen's son Eustace [1]. While the queen, with a numerous assemblage of the barons of both realms, was in France, enjoying the festivities consequent on this occasion, Stephen wholly unexpected appeared in Cornwall, where William fitz Richard, on whom he had conferred the government of that province, had, in traitorous violation of his oath, received into one of the royal castles Reginald of Dunstanvile, an illegitimate son of the late king, had given him his daughter in marriage [2], and delivered the entire county into his hands. But no sooner did Reginald find himself possessed of power than he began to bend all things to his will, to strengthen the castles throughout the county, and grievously to oppress the adherents of the king in his proximity, sparing neither churches nor church property, whereby he drew on himself the penalty of excommunication by the bishop of Exeter.

When apprized of this state of things in Cornwall, Stephen, as we have said, unexpectedly appeared in that province, where, having recovered the castles that had been seized by Reginald, he improvidently committed them to the keeping of count Alan of Brittany, a man notorious for craft and cruelty, charging him to prosecute the contest with Reginald, until he had driven him from the county. On receipt of the intelligence that Stephen had entered Cornwall, great was the joy of earl Robert and his adherents at Gloucester, founded on the persuasion that, shut up in that remote county, and separated from the main body of his army, it would be no difficult task to attack and overcome him. Having, there-

[1] Flor. Wigorn. Cont. a. 1140. H. Hunt. a. 1139. After the death of Eustace she gave her hand to Raimond V. count of Toulouse. Eustace had in his early days been betrothed to a daughter of Diederik count of Flanders; so at least we are informed by Orderic, p. 916.

[2] She afterwards lost her reason: " Uxor illius furiis agitata, non simplicem in ejus amplexus sexum, sed dirum et horrendum offerebat dæmonum." Gesta Steph. p. 65.—T.

fore, collected a numerous body of soldiers, Robert was hastening towards Cornwall, when the unexpected and unwelcome intelligence reached him, that the king had not only quelled the rebellion, but was close at hand, on his return, at the head of a most powerful force. The fact was, that Stephen, apprized of Robert's movements, had summoned to his aid all the barons of Devonshire, and made preparations to join in battle with his adversary on that same day. And a battle would have ensued, had not Robert, yielding to the advice of his friends, made a speedy retreat towards Bristol. On his return from Cornwall, the king destroyed many lawless castles, thus completely clearing and tranquillizing those parts that had long suffered under the tyranny of their possessors[1].

But isolated deeds of valour and military prowess were at this time of little avail, as a spirit of anarchy was predominant, which defied and threatened to destroy the leaders of both parties. To what insecurity in the law, to what extravagant projects and wild undertakings such a revolutionary state of things gave birth, may be conceived from the following example. Robert fitz Hubert, a mercenary of the earl of Gloucester, whose exploit at Malmesbury has been already noticed[2], having with some of his countrymen clandestinely withdrawn from the earl's army, succeeded by the aid of ladders made of leather, in scaling the walls of the strong castle of Devizes (Mar. 26, 1140), then garrisoned by the royal forces. Having eluded the watch, he surprised and captured the sleeping garrison, with the exception of a few who, on hearing the tumult, sought refuge in a lofty tower; but being without sustenance or succour, were, in a few days, compelled to surrender.

When the intelligence of this event reached the earl of Gloucester, he sent his son, at the head of a large force, in support of Robert's daring enterprise; but the Fleming received him with insult, drove him from the gates, and con-

[1] Gesta Stephani, p. 66. "adulterina castella." [2] See p. 409.

temptuously sent him back to his father, saying, that as he
had won the castle so he would hold it. In fact, he here
carried into effect what he had failed to accomplish at Malmesbury, not only maintaining himself in the place, but gradually
reducing all the neighbouring country under his power, in
furtherance of which purpose he sent for soldiers from Flanders. At this time the neighbouring castle of Marlborough
was held against the king by a certain John fitz Gilbert, a
man as crafty and unscrupulous as Robert himself. To this
person Robert sent messengers, proposing a friendly league
between them : the proposal was accepted, and Robert
invited to visit his new ally at Marlborough. No sooner,
however, had he entered the castle than the gates were
closed upon him, and he was cast into a dungeon, there to
perish by hunger and torture. Of his followers some were
taken and thrown into the same dungeon with their lord ;
the others were ignominiously driven to the gates of Devizes.

When apprized of what had taken place, the earl of Gloucester, accompanied by the ex-constable Milo, proceeded to
Marlborough and promised five hundred marks for the delivery of Robert into his hands, engaging to render him back
within a fortnight. To this proposal John acceded, and the
earl, with Robert in his custody, returned to Gloucester.
When required to surrender the castle of Devizes, Robert
refused, on the plea of the oath he and his associates had
sworn, never to deliver up the place ; but on being threatened
with the gallows, he promised compliance, provided his life
were spared. On the day fixed, he was conducted back to
Marlborough, when the earl, having related all that had
passed between them, proposed to proceed with Robert to
Devizes, promising that if the castle were surrendered, to
place it under John's authority. To this proposal John
assented ; but in the meanwhile sent letters secretly to
Robert's friends at Devizes, in which he swore that neither
himself nor the earl meditated injury to Robert ; and, at the

same time, exhorted them to keep their oath by holding out to the last extremity. Leaving Milo and others before Devizes, earl Robert then returned to Gloucester, previously, however, commanding them to hang Robert, if he refused to surrender the castle. As was to be expected, Robert and his followers refused, and the end of the affair was, that his two nephews first and himself afterwards forfeited their lives at the gallows. The adherents of Robert, notwithstanding their oath, finally consented to deliver up the place to the king, for a considerable sum of money, who intrusted the custody of it to his son-in-law, Hervé the Breton[1].

Although in these wars the chief and immediate sufferers were generally the combatants themselves, there were, nevertheless, occurrences that fell heavily on the rising burgher class. The rich town of Nottingham, which had been spared from harm in every preceding civil strife since the Conquest, and in which industry and commerce preeminently flourished, was, at the suggestion of Ralf Paganel, attacked and plundered by the earl of Gloucester, the inhabitants fleeing to the churches for refuge. While the work of plunder was in progress, one of its most opulent inhabitants was seized and led strongly bound to his dwelling, where he was compelled to deliver up his treasures. Conducting the plunderers into a vault, in which his wealth was deposited, he clandestinely withdrew from them, closing all the doors and every means of egress, and then set fire to the dwelling. More than thirty persons are said to have perished in the vault; it was even asserted that from that house the fire spread until the whole town became a prey to the devouring element. Of the inhabitants those who were without the churches were carried away captives; those who had sought shelter within the sacred structures, men, women, and children, perished in the general conflagration[2].

[1] Gesta. Steph. p. 66. Flor. Wigorn. Cont. a. 1140.
[2] Flor. Wigorn. Cont. a. 1140.

While weak was the feeling of consideration and good-will which the party of the empress had been able to excite, the court of Stephen exhibited a series of ever increasing dissensions, throughout which the king allowed himself to be guided more by personal favour than by higher aspirations for the unity and quiet of his realm. The choice of a new bishop of Salisbury gave birth to acrimonious disputes. The legate bishop of Winchester demanded the vacant see for his young nephew, Henry of Sully, but, failing to obtain it, withdrew from the court highly exasperated. Stephen strove to pacify him, by bestowing on the nephew the rich abbey of Fécamp; but, at the instance of count Waleram of Meulan, he desired the bishopric for his chancellor, Philip of Harulfcour, archdeacon of Bayeux, an appointment to which the legate and clergy in general offered so strong an opposition, that the see of Bayeux was at length bestowed on Philip, while that of Salisbury for some years continued vacant, until it was given to Joscelyn of Bailleul[1].

This transaction so alienated the hearts of the clergy from Stephen, that when he celebrated the festival of Whitsuntide in the Tower of London, one prelate only, the bishop of Séez, appeared at his court[2].

A negotiation for peace (May 26) was now set on foot at Bath, conducted on the part of the empress by her brother, the earl of Gloucester, while Stephen was represented by his untrustworthy brother, with whom the queen and archbishop were associated, for the sake probably of keeping a watch over him. The legate, in the following September, went to France, where he passed the months of October and November, with the object of gaining over to his views the French monarch Lewis, Theobald count of Blois, and a number of the clergy. The proposals he brought back were, as was to be

[1] Ord. Vital. p. 920. Flor. Cont. a. 1140.
[2] W. Malm. p. 734. "cæteri vel fastidierunt vel timuerunt venire."

I. e

foreseen, such as the empress readily accepted, but which the king could not but totally reject [1].

Stephen was now no longer blind to the difficulties of his position, and spared no means of confirming the attachment of those barons who remained faithful to him. With great consideration he treated the earl Ranulf of Chester, who had married a daughter of Robert of Gloucester, as well as his brother, William of Roumare [2]. Ranulf had shown an inclination to take advantage of the king's difficulties by endeavouring to establish claims on Carlisle and the south of Cumberland, and thereby excited the indignation of the generally kindly disposed prince, to a degree that it was through the queen's mediation alone that he escaped with life [3]. Stephen readily forgave, and, at Christmas, had left his deeply indebted and, as he imagined, well-disposed vassal quiet at Lincoln [4]. After a few days, however, while the garrison of the castle were diverting themselves without the walls, the wives of the two earls went to pay a visit to a lady who dwelt within it. In a short time the earl of Chester appeared, but without weapons or armour, under the pretext of escorting them home. Three of his soldiers likewise stole after him into the castle. They then speedily possessed themselves of some weapons, drove out the few of the garrison that were left, and gave admission to William of Roumare and the rest of their associates, and from the fortress easily rendered themselves masters of the city. The bishop and citizens, dreading the new lord of the castle, instantly communicated intelligence of what had taken place to the king [5]. who with his usual, though by the earl little looked-for, celerity appeared and captured seventeen of his adversary's

---

[1] Ibid. [2] Ord. Vital. p. 922.

[3] Joh. Hagust. a. 1140. col. 268. [4] W. Malm. p. 739.

[5] Ord. Vital. p. 921. Malmesbury (p. 739) is so disingenuous that he omits all mention of the treachery of the two earls, and accuses the citizens of having betrayed them.

knights; but the castle was too strong to be speedily taken, however considerable the number of men brought against it. Under cover of the darkness, earl Ranulf, with some companions, escaped from the castle, for the purpose of seeking aid from Chester, and of having an interview with earl Robert. The latter not only lent a willing ear to earl Ranulf, who swore fealty to the empress, but resolved, on this occasion, to effect a decision of the contest, and put an end to the lamentable state of the country[1]. Without disclosing his intention, he caused the Welsh, the outlaws, and malcontents from all sides to march to the Trent, which, in consequence of the heavy rains, they crossed with difficulty, and, in the beginning of February, appeared unexpectedly with a considerable army before Lincoln, in front of the king. By his barons Stephen was advised to withdraw into the interior of the country; for the purpose of reinforcing his army, but heedless even of the feast of the Purification (Feb. 2. 1141), he rashly resolved on a battle. He divided his army in three bodies, the first of which consisted of the Flemings, under William of Ypres, and the Bretons, under count Alan of Dinan. Opposed to these stood the Welsh, under two princely brothers, Meredith and Cadwalader, with the first division under earl Ranulf. Speeches are preserved which, as we are told, were made before the battle, by the leaders of the two armies. Those of the earls Ranulf and Robert abound in vaunt, and vehement, if not coarse, outbreaks against the most distinguished of their adversaries, which with equal justice might have been applied to themselves[2]. That of Baldwin fitz Gilbert, who

---

[1] W. Malm. p. 740.

[2] Of all of them John of Salisbury (Polycrat. viii. 21.) says: "Gaufridus (de Magnavilla), Milo, Ranulphus, Alanus, Simon (de Senlis), Gillebertus (de Clara), non tam comitis regni quam hostes publici." [It appears that Stephen had many traitors in his army, from the words of Orderic (p. 922). "In illo conflictu perfidia nequiter debacchata est. Nam quidam magnatorum cum paucis suorum regi comitati sunt, suorumque satellitum turmam adversariis ut prævalerent præmiserunt."—T.]

E e 2

had undertaken to harangue the royal army, instead of the king, who was suffering from hoarseness[1], enlarged judiciously and with dignity on the justice of Stephen's cause, the sufficiency of their force, and the valour of his fellow warriors[2].

The first onset was given by the royal forces with their missiles; but the body of outlaws pressed so irresistibly on the foremost ranks with their swords, that the former quickly dismounted and had recourse also to their swords. But almost instantaneously their first line was broken through in many places, and the most distinguished warriors, who were too closely crowded together, were compelled to flee. Among them, after a short resistance, were count Alan and William of Ypres; but with disgraceful precipitation and cowardice, Waleram of Meulan and his brother, William of Warenne, William earl of York and Gilbert of Clare. Earl Alan of Richmond, who in latter times had, by his depredations on the possessions of the bishop of Durham and the recently deceased archbishop Thurstan of York, proved himself one of the greatest and most licentious enemies of law and order, renounced, together with his followers, before the beginning of the battle, both the king and the contest[3]. Only a few valiant knights, Baldwin of Clare, Richard fitz Urse, Engelram of Sai, and Ilbert of Lacy, flinched not from the side of the king. Stephen himself fought with a lion's courage; with a Norwegian battle-axe, with which a young man of Lincoln had supplied him, he prostrated every foe that approached him[4]; he smashed the helmet of earl Ranulf, but without slaying him; at length he was struck by a stone which brought him to the ground[5]. With only three com-

<hr>

[1] "Quia rex festiva voce carebat." H. Hunt. Gervas. col. 1352.—T.
[2] H. Hunt. a. 1141.
[3] Joh. Hagust. a. 1142 (1141). [Alan earl of Richmond is, it would seem, a distinct person from the count Alan who, with William of Ypres, commanded the first body.—T.]
[4] Ord. Vital. p. 922.   [5] W. Malm. p. 742.

panions by his side, he found himself compelled to retire before the pressing enemy. A valiant knight, William of Cahaines, seized him by the helmet, and with a loud voice announced the prize he had taken. Stephen had now no alternative but to yield himself a prisoner to the earl of Gloucester. With the king were likewise taken Baldwin fitz Gilbert and Richard fitz Urse. The earl conducted his royal captive to the empress, whereupon he was consigned to durance in Bristol castle, lenient at first, but afterwards more rigorous, and was even loaded with chains, in consequence, it is said, of his repeated attempts to escape[1]. In the speedily decided conflict few were the fallen, the number of corpses found not exceeding a hundred. A greater booty did the angel of death find among the unfortunate citizens of Lincoln. On the calamitous issue of the battle, they had to expect that the vengeance of the earl of Chester and the rapacity of his followers would be glutted to the utmost. Many consequently fled by means of the small vessels on the river, escaping from murder by voluntary exile. Owing to the pressure of the crowd, the boats, being too heavily laden, sank with their freight, and about five hundred of the citizens thus found a watery grave. Those who remained in the city and were taken fell a sacrifice to the barbarity of earl Ranulf and his well-practised myrmidons in the hangman's art[2].

The consequences of the king's captivity were, however, not so important as they would have shown themselves, had a universally favourable disposition towards the empress prevailed in the nation. The earls, Waleram of Meulan, William of Warenne, and Simon of Northampton, with William of Ypres, hastened to the queen who had found a safe asylum among the faithful men of Kent. Earl Ranulf gained possession of some castles and treasures not belonging to him, partly

[1] Ibid. Sax. Chron. a. 1141.
[2] Ord. Vital. p. 922. W. Malm. p. 742. H. Hunt. a. 1141. Gervas. coll. 1350 *sqq.*

by treachery, through which he got count Alan into his power,
whom, by hunger and other acts of violence, he compelled to
become his vassal, and to deliver up his castles. The county
of Cornwall Stephen also lost, now that Reginald's party was
in the ascendant. Count Hervé also, his son-in-law, after
being long besieged in the castle of Devizes by a multitude
of the peasantry, who had risen in a body against him, was
at length compelled to surrender that fortress to the empress,
and, with a few followers, to flee precipitately from England.
And Hugh, surnamed the Poor, whom, on the expulsion of
Milo of Beauchamp, the king had created earl of Bedford, a
negligent and effeminate man, was now forced to restore that
castle to Milo [1]. Among the foremost who joined the party
of Matilda were Robert of Oilli and the earl of Warwick [2].
The town of Nottingham was by the empress taken from
William Peverel and given to William Paganel. From the
knights captured vast ransoms were extorted, and in general
nothing was done by the victors to conciliate esteem and good
will [3].

To Matilda it now appeared desirable to gain the legate
bishop of Winchester to her interests, who, in foresight and
sagacity, was thought to excel all the nobles of the kingdom,
while his courage and riches rendered him the most powerful.
If he, she declared, would attach himself to her party, honours
should await him; if, on the other hand, he proved adverse
and rebellious, the whole armed force of England should be
directed against him. The legate's position was a difficult
one; on the one hand, to defend the cause of the king
seemed an almost hopeless task, while on the other, it was
painful to himself, and must appear indecent and unnatural
to others, to declare in favour of Matilda, while his brother

---

[1] Gesta Steph. p. 73. See p. 377.

[2] Gesta Steph. p. 74. [where they are described as " viri molles, et deliciis magis quam animi fortitudine affluentes."—T.]

[3] Joh. Hagust. col. 269.

was yet living. In this dilemma he resolved to temporize, and enter on terms of peace and friendship with the enemy, thus waiting the event of things, in the hope, when an opportunity presented itself, of coming forward in support of his brother[1].

With the legate the majority of the prelates were gained over to the party of the empress, whose indecent exultation and unbridled arrogance were alike prejudicial to her adherents and her own interest. From Gloucester, where she had been so long entertained by Milo, she hastened, accompanied by the bishop of Ely and other prelates, together with many barons, to Cirencester, and thence to Winchester, where the most distinguished ecclesiastics, the nobles of her party, the mercenaries and others had assembled. The meeting took place on the 2nd of March, on the open plain near the city; the day was wet and foggy, as if the fates foreshowed a sad vicissitude of affairs[2]. Here Matilda swore to the legate, that all the most important concerns of the realm, particularly the disposal of vacant bishoprics and abbacies, should be according to his will, if he and the holy Church would receive her as their sovereign lady and ever observe fealty to her. The same swore and vouched for her the earl of Gloucester, Brian fitz Count marquis[3] of Wallingford, Milo of Gloucester, afterwards earl of Hereford, and some others. On his part, the legate did not hesitate to acknowledge her for lady of England, and with some of his friends to engage that, so long as she held the compact inviolate, he would be faithful to her. On the following day, attended by the legate and

[1] Gesta Stephani, p. 74. [This is a lenient view of the legate's case, though perhaps not altogether an unjust one, and is, moreover, from the pen of one well disposed towards Stephen, and therefore hardly inclined to favour his brother, at the expense of truth. As an ecclesiastic and representative of the holy see, the legate was naturally exasperated against his brother, for his treatment of the bishops of Salisbury, Lincoln, and Ely, a consideration which, if borne in mind, may serve to explain and even palliate much of his conduct.—T.]

[2] W. Malm. p. 743. " mœstam causæ vicissitudem." [3] " marchio." ib.

other prelates, she went in procession to the cathedral, where the crown and the scanty treasure left there by Stephen being delivered to her, she was proclaimed queen of England, the legate cursing those who cursed her, and blessing those who blessed her. From Winchester she proceeded to Wilton, where the archbishop Theobald swore allegiance to her, which he had till then withheld, deeming it derogatory to his office and character to take that step until he had consulted and obtained a release from the king. His example was followed by the majority of the prelates and some of the laity[1].

A few days after (April 7th), a council of the archbishop Theobald, and all the bishops of England, with many abbots and archdeacons, was held at Winchester, at which the legate presided. With each of these orders the legate held a private conference, at which he explained to them his views and intentions[2]. On the following day he addressed them in a speech in which there was no lack of shallow sophistry, though admirably adapted to his audience. He reminded them of the peaceful state of the country under the late king; how some years before his death he had caused all the bishops and barons of England and Normandy to swear fealty to his sole surviving offspring, should no male successor be borne to him by his second consort. "This was not granted to him, and he died in Normandy without male issue. To await the coming of a lady, whose departure from Normandy was delayed from various causes, seemed tedious, and the peace of the country was provided for by allowing my brother to reign. Alas!" continued he, "although I became his surety before God, that he would honour and exalt the holy Church, maintain good laws, and abrogate bad ones, it grieves me to call to mind, I feel shame in uttering it, how he

---

[1] W. Malm. p. 743. Flor. Wigorn. Cont. a. 1141.

[2] Malmesbury, the substance of whose narrative is here given at full, was present at the council. He says: "Cujus concilii actioni, quia interfui, integram rerum veritatem posteris non negabo."—T.

has conducted himself in the kingdom, how he has neglected
to execute justice on the contumacious, how all peace, from
the very beginning of his reign, has been at an end; bishops
being held in captivity and compelled to deliver up their possessions, abbacies sold, churches despoiled of their treasures,
the counsels of the wicked listened to, those of the good
either delayed, or treated with scorn. You know how often
I have addressed him, both directly and through the medium
of bishops; more particularly at the council lately held, and
that I have thereby gained nothing but odium. To all who
rightly think it will be manifest, that while it is my duty to
love my brother, of far greater moment is the cause of our
everlasting Father. Therefore, since God has pronounced
judgment on my brother, and allowed him to fall into the
hands of his adversaries, lest the realm be convulsed if it lack
a ruler, I have, in virtue of my legatine authority, summoned
you all to meet me here. Yesterday the subject was discussed
in private before a considerable number of the clergy of
England, whose province it especially is to elect and ordain
princes; therefore, in the first place, invoking the divine
assistance, as is meet, we choose the daughter of our late
glorious king for our sovereign lady, and promise her our
fealty and support." When all present had, either by tem-
perate acclamations testified their approval of the legate's
harangue, or, by holding silence, not objected to it, he added:
"The citizens of London—who are, as it were, nobles, by
reason of the magnitude of the city—we have summoned by
our messengers, and sent them a safe-conduct, and I trust
they will not defer their coming beyond this day."

On the following day the Londoners arrived, and being introduced, announced that they were deputed by the city of
London, not in a spirit of hostility, but to pray that their lord
the king might be released from his captivity. Those barons
also, who had long been members of their body, but had been
captured with their liege lord, earnestly besought the legate

and the archbishop, with all the clergy present, to obtain for them their liberty. Their petition the legate answered at length, repeating the substance of his speech of the preceding day, and adding: That it ill became the Londoners, who were regarded as nobles in England, to espouse the cause of those who had forsaken their lord in battle, at whose instigation, too, he had dishonoured the holy Church, and who made a show of favouring the Londoners, merely that they might wheedle them out of their money.

When the legate had ceased speaking, a certain clerk stood forward, a chaplain, it is said, of the queen's, named Christian, and presented a letter to him, which, having read it in silence, he returned, saying aloud, that it was not genuine, nor ought it to be read before an assemblage of such exalted and religious persons; for, in addition to the objectionable matter contained in it, there was the name of a witness attached to it, who a year or two ago had, in the very chapter in which they were then sitting, applied the most opprobrious language to the venerable bishops[1]. The clerk was not, however, so to be daunted, but with admirable confidence read the letter to the council, the substance of which was: "The queen earnestly entreats the clergy assembled in general, and the bishop of Winchester, the brother of her lord, in particular, to restore her said lord to his kingdom, whom wicked men, his own liege subjects, have cast into bonds." To this letter the legate returned an answer similar in tenour to that which he had given to the Londoners, who, after having deliberated together, said they would communicate the decree of the council to their fellow-citizens, and, as far as they were able, be answerable for their good-will. On the following day, the council was dissolved, after it had excommunicated many adherents to the royal cause, among whom was William Martel, who had formerly been cupbearer to king Henry, but was

---

[1] The individual here alluded to was, no doubt, Aubrey of Vere. See pp. 400 *sq*—T.

then sewer to Stephen. Against him the legate was bitterly incensed, for having intercepted and plundered many of his chattels[1].

From Wilton, where she had celebrated the Easter festival (Mar. 30)[2], the empress proceeded to Reading (May 4th), where she was received with great honour. Here Robert of Oilli agreed to deliver to her the castle of Oxford, of which, by the appointment of Stephen, he was constable. From Oxford, after having received the homage of that city and the circumjacent country, she directed her course with great joy and exultation to St. Alban's, where she was met by a deputation of the citizens of London, with whom she entered into a compact for the delivery of the metropolis, whither, with great military pomp, she hastened, and at Westminster was received with a solemn procession.

The greater part of England now acknowledged her authority ; her brother, the earl of Gloucester, was, by every honourable means, strenuously exerting himself to promote her interest ; the legate also appeared faithfully attached to her cause, but while all things seemed to promise the speedy reduction of the whole kingdom to her rule, all became changed, a storm was ready to burst over her head. For no sooner had she been proclaimed queen than her haughty and tyrannical spirit began to display itself. Those who had submitted to the authority of the king, but now deemed it advisable to acknowledge hers, she treated with contumely, driving them with threats and insult from her presence. The lands of the few who still adhered to Stephen she distributed among her partisans, and, in general, revoked all his grants. When the king of Scotland, the legate, or the earl of Gloucester approached her with bended knees to solicit some object, she would not rise to receive them, and would most frequently

---

[1] W. Malm. pp. 744. sqq. Flor. Wigorn. Cont. a. 1141.

[2] According to Malmesbury, who is, no doubt, wrong, she passed the Easter-tide at Oxford.—T.

dismiss them with a harsh denial[1]. By the queen she had
been solicited for the release of her captive consort; many of
the nobility had likewise interceded with her for the same
object, engaging to deliver into her hands not only numerous
hostages, but castles and other possessions, for the mere release of the king, pledging themselves that, if restored to freedom, he should renounce the crown and, as a monk or pilgrim,
devote himself to the service of God alone. To these solicitations, as also to the prayer of the bishop of Winchester, that
Stephen's earldoms of Boulogne and Mortain might be conferred on his son Eustace, Matilda turned a deaf ear. When,
too, the citizens of London had lulled themselves into the
belief that peaceful and happier days awaited them, the empress, to their dismay, in an imperious tone, exacted from the
more opulent among them an immense sum of money. And
when they urged that, in consequence of the dissensions in
the state, in alleviating the miseries of famine which pervaded
the land, and in supplying the wants of the king, they had
lost a large portion of their wealth, and were in a state of
impending pauperism; therefore, humbly prayed that she
would have pity on their reduced condition, and not impose
this onerous tax on them, but wait till more tranquil and
better times should render them more able to comply with
her demands, her rage knew no bounds. The Londoners, she
said, had repeatedly and largely supplied the wants of the
king; they had lavishly spent their money for his benefit and
to her prejudice, and had conspired with her enemies; therefore they had no right to expect that she would spare them,
or make the slightest abatement of her demand[2]. Nor did
the petition of the citizens for the restoration of the laws of
king Eadward, in the stead of those of her father, which
were found too oppressive, meet with a more favourable reception[3].

[1] Flor. Wigorn. Cont. a. 1141. W. Malm. p. 749. Gesta Steph. p. 76.
[2] Gesta Stephani, pp. 76, 77. W. Malm. p. 750.
[3] Flor. Wigorn. Cont. a. 1141.

When Matilda's consort, Geoffrey of Anjou, was apprized of the victory over Stephen at Lincoln, he marched an armed force into Normandy, and summoned the holders of the royal castles there to surrender. These, however, among whom were the earls of Leicester and Meulan, as well as other Anglo-Norman nobles, had, with the king's ancient friend, Hugh, the archbishop of Rouen, at their head, betaken themselves to Stephen's brother Theobald, count of Blois, for the purpose of offering him not only the dukedom of Normandy, but also the kingdom of England. But this wise and pious prince, again declining the realm that had been a second time offered to him[1], advised them to transfer the one and the other to Geoffrey, provided that prince would restore to his brother Stephen his liberty and the counties he had formerly possessed, and to himself the city of Tours which appertained to his fief[2].

The queen now finding that the petitions of herself and others for the release of her consort and the grant of his counties to their son were rejected with insult, resolved on attempting to gain by force that which had been denied to her solicitations. In pursuance of this resolve, she sent a considerable military force to the south side of the river, opposite to London, with orders to harry and burn in every direction. Panic-stricken on seeing themselves thus exposed, as it were, to the horrors of war, and irritated by the tyrannic and unfeeling conduct of the empress towards them, the citizens unanimously resolved to enter into a confederation for the restoration of the king to his liberty[3].

While the empress was awaiting in security the answer of the Londoners to her demand, and fully confident of their compliance with her will, all the city bells at once rang out, summoning the inhabitants to rise, who thereupon rushing to arms, and inspired to a man with the bitterest animosity towards that princess, poured forth from the several gates.

[1] See p. 358. [2] Ord. Vital. p. 923. [3] Gesta Stephani, p. 77.

The empress was at the moment just sitting down to table,
when, hearing the tumult, and being secretly warned that
treason was plotting against her, she and those about her instantly sought safety in flight.   Hardly had their horses left
the suburban dwellings behind them, when an almost countless multitude of people arrived at their hostels, and destroyed
or carried off all that had been left by the fugitives in their
hurry to escape.   The barons, who had accompanied the
empress in her flight, gradually forsook her on the way, departing in various directions.   The bishop of Winchester
who, according to report, was both the accomplice and instigator of the insurrection, and others, bishops and knights,
who had assembled at London, for the purpose of solemnly
inthroning the empress, lost no time in seeking various hiding-
places.   Matilda herself, attended by the earl of Gloucester
and a very few barons, proceeded with all speed to Oxford.

The adherents of the king, thus inspired with new courage,
rose in all parts against the empress.   The queen, too, now
in possession of London, scorning the gentleness of her sex,
nobly exerted herself in gathering the partisans of the royal
cause.   The legate, with whom the queen had had an interview at Guildford, moved by her supplications, and perhaps
commiserating his brother's unhappy lot, manifested also his
anxiety to devise the means of rescuing him from the miseries
of a prison.   But the empress shrewdly anticipating the fruits
of his schemes, proceeded with a well-appointed force to
Winchester (Aug. 1st), in the hope of laying hands on him.
While she, however, with her followers, was entering the city
by one gate, the bishop, mounted on a fleet horse, passed out
by another, and with all speed fled to his castle[1].   Having
taken possession of the royal castle, Matilda sent to the bishop, saying, that as she was in Winchester, she trusted he

[1] "Castella sua." Gesta Steph. p. 80.   Hence and from what follows
it appears that the bishop had one castle within, and another without the
city, to the latter of which he fled on the arrival of Matilda.—T.

would not delay coming to her. Consulting his own safety, the bishop answered ambiguously : "I will make myself ready [1];" and immediately adopted measures to gain supporters. On her part the empress, by an edict published throughout the realm, assembled a considerable army, and commanded the castle of the bishop which, according to a most beautiful plan, he had erected in the heart of the city, and also his mansion, which he had rendered as strong and impregnable as a castle, to be invested by a strict blockade[2].

On reading the names of those who supported the cause of Matilda and attended her on this occasion, it must excite our wonder how a force such as those names imply could have been so soon and so completely overcome and scattered as we shall presently see it was doomed to be. There was David, king of Scotland, who had already been twice driven out of England ; there were Robert earl of Gloucester, Ranulf earl of Chester, Baldwin of Redvers earl of Exeter, Reginald earl of Cornwall, Milo of Gloucester, on whom the empress had recently conferred the earldom of Hereford[3] ; Roger earl of Warwick, William of Mohun, whom she had created earl of Dorset, and a Breton count named Boterel[4]. Of barons there were : Brian fitz Count, John Mareschal, Roger of Oilli, Roger of Nunant, William fitz Alan and others too numerous to mention, all of whom with a powerful army, collected from every quarter, and animated by the same spirit, marched to besiege the castle of the bishop[5].

The bishop, on his side, having assembled from all parts of England those barons who acknowledged the authority of the king, together with a numerous body of soldiery, marched with the utmost speed to the relief of Winchester. The queen, also, with a large force, including a band of nearly a thousand

[1] "Ego parabo me." W. Malm. p. 751.

[2] Gesta Steph. pp. 78–80. W. Malm. pp. 748–750.

[3] See the patent, dated July 25th 1141, the oldest on record, in Rymer. i. 19.   [4] See p. 322.   [5] Gesta Steph. p. 80.

Londoners, armed with helmets and breast-plates, hastened vigorously to besiege the besiegers. Others, too, intimate and faithful friends of the king, among whom are named Roger of Chastenay[1] and his brother William, with a well-appointed body of foot soldiers and archers, pressed hardly on one quarter of the place. Hence arose a siege of a most extraordinary kind : those engaged in assailing the episcopal castle being themselves closely besieged by the royal army. In the almost daily encounters which took place many were slain, and from the fires projected by the defenders of the castle, the greater part of the city, together with above forty churches and two abbeys[2], was reduced to ashes. To add to the calamities of the inhabitants, famine soon began to prevail, bodies of armed men being posted on all the ways leading to the city, cutting off all supplies. As a remedy for this evil, it was resolved to erect a fort at Wherwell, about six miles distant from Winchester, whence they might annoy their adversaries, and at the same time obtain the necessary supplies. But the royalists, aware of what was in progress, made a desperate onslaught on the enemy, of whom many being slain and many captured, the rest sought safety within the walls of the abbey, where they defended themselves as in a castle, until the place being set on fire by firebrands thrown into it, the half-burnt defenders were compelled to issue forth and submit to the mercy of their assailants. The abbey was sacked and burnt, it is said, by William of Ypres, and its inmates subjected to all the atrocities consequent on such events.

[1] Or Chesney (Cheney). The Latinized name is De Casneto.—T.

[2] One was a house of nuns within, the other was Hide abbey, without the walls, dedicated to Ælfred's friend, St. Grimbald, in which was a celebrated cross, adorned with gold, silver, and precious stones, the gift of king Cnut. For a miracle performed by this cross, see W. Malm. p. 752, Flor.Wigorn. Cont. p.133. Andover was also burnt by the royalists in the course of these conflicts. The continuator of Florence and others say that the conflagration of the city was by command of the bishop, forgetting, it seems, that he was not in the place.—T.

The position of the earl of Gloucester and the other adherents of Matilda being rendered thus desperate by fire and
famine, they resolved on raising the now hopeless siege of
the castle, and seeking safety in a precipitate flight (Sept.
14th)[1]. In prosecution of this design, the earl sent his sister
forward, escorted by Reginald earl of Cornwall with the van
of his army, while himself with a few of his boldest followers
formed the rear-guard. But hardly had they issued from the
gates when they were attacked and dispersed by a strong detachment of the royal army. In this encounter, the earl of
Gloucester with all those about him fell into the hands of the
enemy, being captured at Stockbridge by the Flemings under
William of Ypres. The rout was complete; the face of all
the country around bore manifest signs of the havoc made
among the followers of Matilda: horses without riders were
to be seen on every side, the earth was strewed with shields
and corselets and every kind of weapon, together with costly
robes and other articles of value. Barons and knights appeared fleeing in all directions, to escape from the rage and
violence of the peasantry. The king of Scotland, after having
been thrice captured, and as many times released by bribery,
with difficulty reached his own territories. The archbishop
of Canterbury, with some bishops and nobles, despoiled of
their horses and garments, effected their escape with the
utmost difficulty. The empress herself, with her beloved Brian
fitz Count[2], and a few attendants, fled first to Ludgershall,
and thence to Devizes; from which town, not considering her-

---

[1] According to the continuator of Florence, the siege was raised by the
bishop, who, tired of the war, ordered the gates to be thrown open and
peace proclaimed throughout the city. But hardly had the empress
mounted her horse, when he ordered his troops to attack the retiring
enemy. It must, however, be borne in mind, that the continuator was a
friend of Milo, the supporter of Matilda, and that his testimony is not
supported either by the author of the Gesta or by Malmesbury.—T.

[2] "ut sicut sese antea mutuo et indivise dilexerant, ita nec in adversis,
plurimo impediente periculo, aliquatenus separarentur." Gesta Steph. p. 85.

F f

self in security there, she continued her flight to Gloucester[1]. Milo, the newly created earl of Hereford, also escaped to Gloucester, in a state almost of nudity[2].

While these works of plunder, conflagration, and bloodshed were being enacted in various other places, the Londoners, in concert with a large body of the royal army, sacked what still remained unscathed of the unfortunate city of Winchester, breaking open and destroying not only the private dwellings of the inhabitants, but also the sacred edifices, and bearing off to their homes vast spoil, both in treasures and captives. So great was the devastation, that no one, however aged, could call to memory its parallel[3].

On his capture the earl of Gloucester was presented to the queen, and, by her command, consigned to the keeping of William of Ypres in the castle of Rochester. Thus were the leaders of the hostile parties each in the power of his adversary, and the object now of highest interest both to Matilda and the friends of Stephen was, to effect their mutual liberation. After some negotiation it was settled that, on leaving the queen with her son and two nobles in Bristol as hostages, the king should proceed to Winchester (Nov. 1st), whither the earl had been conducted from Rochester, and that a mutual release should there take place, leaving each to act as freely as if neither had been captured[4].

The liberation of his brother must have been a source of considerable embarrassment to the bishop, who, on the octaves of St. Andrew (Dec. 7th), in virtue of his legatine authority convened a council at Westminster, at which he read a letter from the pope, who blamed him for having

---

[1] The continuator of Florence (p. 134) says, that she was bound like a corpse and conveyed on a bier from Devizes to Gloucester; but the story is unsupported by the other chroniclers.—T.

[2] Gesta Steph. pp. 80-85. W. Malm. pp. 750-753. Flor. Wigorn. Cont. a. 1141.

[3] Gesta Steph. p. 85.   [4] W. Malm. p. 754. Gesta Steph. p. 85.

neglected the release of his brother, and urged him to employ every means possible for the attainment of that object. The king, then, who was present at the council, complained bitterly that he had been captured by his own lieges, and nearly succumbed under their harsh treatment, to whom he never had denied justice. Thereupon the legate rose, and strove to mitigate the odium his conduct had excited. He had, he said, acknowledged the empress, not from good-will, but necessity, when, shortly after his brother's misfortune, and at a time when all his adherents were either driven away or, with minds full of suspicion, were awaiting the event, she appeared before the walls of Winchester[1]; that all the engagements she had made regarding the right of churches she had violated; that he had been informed by trust-worthy authority, that she had plotted to deprive him not only of his dignity but his life; but that God in his mercy had turned events contrary to her hopes, so that himself had escaped from peril, and been able to free his brother from his bonds. He therefore commanded them, on the part of God and the pope, that they would with their utmost power aid a king anointed by the will of the people and the consent of the holy see; but to cite for excommunication those disturbers of the peace, who favoured the countess of Anjou, all excepting the lady of the Angevins herself[2].

"I do not," writes the old chronicler, "say that this speech was received with favour by all, though certainly no one controverted it; fear or respect bridled the tongues of the clergy present." But there was one among them, a layman, an envoy from the empress, who publicly forbade the legate, by the faith he had engaged to her, to resolve anything in that council that should be prejudicial to her honour. He more-

---

[1] Here the text of Malmesbury seems defective.—T.

[2] W. Malm, p. 755. "Jubere se turbatores pacis, qui comitissæ Andegavensi faverent, ad excommunicationem vocandos, præter eam quæ Andegavorum domina esset."—T.

over asserted that the legate had pledged himself to the empress not to afford any aid to his brother beyond sending him twenty knights; that she had come to England in consequence of his repeated letters; that having captured the king, she had held him in captivity chiefly with his connivance. Although he said all this and much besides with great severity of tone, the weight of his words failed to move the bishop to betray the slightest sign of anger. Before the termination of the sitting the sentence of excommunication was pronounced against all who should erect new castles, invade the rights of the Church, or do violence to the poor and helpless [1].

An interval of inaction seems at this time to have succeeded the late period of violence and bloodshed, each party being apparently more intent on holding what it possessed than on invading the possessions of its adversary. The king with his consort had gone to York, for the purpose of quelling some feuds among his vassals, and of retaining the people of the north of England in their favourable disposition towards him, when a severe illness, with which he was seized shortly after Easter (1142), at Northampton, threatened the speedy termination of his newly recovered power and his life [2].

The empress had fixed her temporary abode at Devizes, where, at a council, it was resolved to send for her husband, the count of Anjou, to defend and prosecute the rights of his wife and son in England. On the return of the envoys, they reported that the count was not unfavourable to the object of their mission, and that if the earl of Gloucester, whose great qualities were known to him, and who was the only one on whom he could implicitly rely, would come over to him, he would, if in his power, comply with their wishes; otherwise, in going to and fro they would spend their time and labour in vain. At the earnest solicitation of his friends, the earl undertook

[1] W. Malm. p. 756. Gervasius, col. 1357.
[2] W. Malm. p. 763. Joh. Hagust, col. 271.

the commission and proceeded to Normandy, accompanied by hostages from among the nobles, as pledges to the count for his security, and to the empress, that during his absence they would unite as one man in defending her from all injury. On arriving at Caen the earl was met by the count, who alleged a multitude of reasons for declining to cross over to England, among others, the rebellion of several places in Normandy; and when, with the earl's assistance, those places were subdued, he was prepared with other excuses equally cogent. He readily, however, allowed his son Henry to accompany his uncle to England[1].

From Devizes the empress had transferred her abode to Oxford[2], in the neighbourhood of which she had stationed bodies of troops and strengthened several castles, as at Woodstock, Bensington, and other places, even as far as Cirencester[3]. It was to the last mentioned place that Stephen, after his recovery, directed his march, whence, having burned the castle, he proceeded to Oxford, where the empress with a strong force was dwelling in perfect security, when, on the opposite side of the river, Stephen, at the head of his army, made his appearance, who on seeing the enemy issuing from the city in considerable numbers, while others were galling them with arrows, the river's breadth only being between them, resolved on crossing at a known ford, but where the water was of considerable depth. Among the foremost to plunge into the stream was the king himself; having crossed it rather by swimming than wading, he rushed

---

[1] W. Malm. pp. 673–775. Gervas. a. 1142.

[2] The author of the Gesta describes Oxford as "Civitas tutissime munita, aquis maximæ profundidatis undique proluentibus inaccessa; hinc vallis antemuralis intentissime circumcincta, inde inexpugnabili castello et *turri eminentissima* pulcre et fortissime roborata." The tower here mentioned is probably the massive one yet standing, a memorial of fallen greatness.—T.

[3] Malmesbury makes Stephen sack and burn Wareham, but is it not an error for Cirencester?—T.

on the enemy, drove them back into the city, which he entered with them, and set it on fire in several places; in consequence of which disaster, the empress retired for safety to the castle (Sept. 26th). Exulting in his success, the king resolved on laying close siege to the castle, in the hope, by capturing the empress, the cause of all his difficulties, to restore tranquillity to his kingdom. In prosecution of this design, he posted guards to prevent all access and egress, and after a close blockade of three months, succeeded in reducing the garrison to great straits. In this state of things, the escape of the empress appears little short of miraculous. Their provisions were nearly exhausted, the castle, as we have seen, was beset and assailed on all sides; yet, attended only by three faithful knights, and all clad in white, she went forth in the silence of the night, passed through the posts of the enemy, by the aid of a sentinel, who had been previously bribed; and on foot through the snow, with which the country was covered, crossed the Thames on the ice, and succeeded in reaching Abingdon, whence, on horseback, she continued her flight to Wallingford, held by Brian fitz Count[1].

When the king found that the prey, which he had been so long in hope of seizing, had thus eluded his grasp, he prudently listened to the advice of his friends, and took possession of the castle of Oxford, by allowing the garrison to capitulate. To this concession he was, however, in great measure prompted by the return of earl Robert from Normandy, who, when apprized of the critical position in which his sister was placed, had landed with a force at Wareham, and the castle of which place having besieged and taken, was vigorously preparing to attack him. Stephen, now, in his turn, proceeded with a body of troops to Wareham, when, on finding that the place had been strongly fortified by the earl, he laid waste the

---

[1] Gesta Stephani, p. 88. W. Malm. p. 766. Gervas. col. 1358. R.Wend. ii. 232. [In the Sax. Chron. a. 1140, it is said, that *she was let down by night from the tower with ropes.*—T.]

surrounding country with fire and sword, and then marched on to Wilton, where, as a check to the progress of his adversary, he strengthened the fortifications of the castle. Here he was joined by the bishop of Winchester and many barons with a strong body of men from all parts of England. On learning that reinforcements were daily hastening to join the standard of the king, the earl resolved to advance to Wilton, there to give him battle. A battle ensued (1143, July 1st), which ended in the total discomfiture of the royal army, the king himself and his brother escaping captivity only by a precipitate and ignominious flight. In this conflict Stephen's brave and faithful friend and sewer, William Martel, was made prisoner, and committed to the temporary keeping of Brian fitz Count at Wallingford. The fugitive royalists were pursued by the earl into the town of Wilton, which was made to suffer all the horrors but too common on such occasions, rapine, slaughter, and conflagration.

After his victory at Wilton earl Robert proceeded to Bristol, loaded with spoil and taking with him numerous prisoners, among others William Martel, whom he held in strict confinement, until, for his release, he had paid three hundred marks and surrendered his castle of Sherborne, which was regarded as a principal key of the kingdom. The earl afterwards followed up his success, gradually reducing the realm under his control, destroying the castles of the royalists, and erecting others, until he had subjected to the empress nearly the entire western part from sea to sea. In this portion of the kingdom, the only resistance he found was from Henry of Tracy, who maintained a harassing warfare against the partisans of Matilda, until the cause of the king was again predominant in those parts[1].

At this time the state of England was deplorable in the extreme; on the one part torn and oppressed by the king and his adherents, on the other, by the earl of Gloucester and

[1] Gesta Stephani, p. 95.

the partisans of the empress. Of the wretched inhabitants some, finding the sweetness of home turned to bitterness, sought an asylum in foreign lands; others, in the hope of protection, constructing lowly huts around the churches, passed a life of fear and misery; others lacking other food —for famine had spread itself over the country—fed on the flesh of dogs and horses, or barely sustained life by the poor sustenance afforded by raw herbs and roots. Men died in multitudes; entire large villages might be seen without an inhabitant, and a man might travel for a whole day without meeting with a living human being. Fields of yellow corn stood without one to reap it, all the husbandmen being swept away. To this accumulation of miseries is to be added the influx of foreign mercenaries, who void of pity and reckless of the calamities of the people, from the castles perpetrated all kinds of atrocities, and who, when the barons had summoned them to their aid from the most remote parts, unable either to get their stipends or satisfy their rapacity by plunder, nothing to plunder being longer left, pillaged the possessions of the Church. If a priest or monk ventured to expostulate with them, he was treated with contumely, if not with blows. The bishops, who ought to have been the bulwarks of the Church, were as reeds shaken by the wind: while some through fear yielded to the storm, others, regardless of their sacred calling, supplied their castles with provisions, arms, and sufficient garrisons, and, under the plea of driving away the robbers of Church property, proved themselves more cruel and merciless than they. Many, too, of these bishops, cased in iron, completely armed, and mounted on fiery steeds, shared the spoil with the plunderers of the country, and subjected to bonds and tortures those knights or wealthy individuals that unfortunately fell into their hands; and while they themselves were the principal agents in such atrocities, would lay the blame on their military followers. Among these worthies the most conspicuous were the bishops of Winchester, Lincoln, and Chester. One honourable exception, however, there was in Roger bishop of Hereford, a pious and courageous man, who swerved not from the path of right, but with weapons befitting a Christian soldier, boldly opposed the enemies of the Church and realm. For when Milo earl of Hereford was in need of a large sum of money for the pay of those soldiers whom he had raised to oppose the king, and would compel the churches under his power to pay a heavy contribution for that object, he was resisted by the bishop, who asserted that ecclesiastical property being the offerings of pious individuals, transferred in perpetuity to the service of the Church, no secular person had the right to exercise any control over it; the earl and his followers must therefore abstain from seizing it, or expect instantly to be stricken with the sword of excommunication. Enraged at this resistance to his demand, Milo sent his myrmidons to ravage and plunder the lands of the bishop, who, thereupon, calling together his clergy, pronounced the awful sentence on him and his agents, the effect of which was, that all divine service was suspended, that no corpse might be laid in the earth, or consumed by fire, or immersed in water, or removed from the spot where it ceased to live, until the perpetrator of the sacrilege should have made compensation to the last farthing, for what he had taken or destroyed. In the same year, on the 24th Dec., when engaged in the chase, Milo was slain by an arrow, incautiously aimed at a deer, and died without repentance[1].

About the same time, other adherents of the empress were removed by death from the scene of violence, in retribution, says the chronicler, for the violation and pillage, by earl Robert's command, of the convent of St. Mary and St. Æthelthryth at Wilton: among these are named the earl's eldest son, a youth of great promise; William, the "preceptor" of

---

[1] Gesta Stephani, pp. 96 101. Joh. Hagust. a. 1144 (1143). Also the Chron. of Lanthony abbey, which house was greatly befriended by him, in Monast. Angl. vi. p. 134.

Salisbury, and Robert fitz Hildebrand, who is described as a man of the meanest extraction and basest character: being sent by the empress to the assistance of William of Pont-de-l'Arche, in a quarrel between him and the bishop of Winchester, he seduced his wife, with whom he afterwards lived in adultery, threw William himself into prison, turned traitor to Matilda, and entered into a compact with the king and his brother, the bishop. His death was the consequence of a dreadful disease[1].

In this year, at Midlent, a council was held at London by the legate, at which the king assisted, in which it was enacted, that, whereas no honour or reverence is shown to the Church of God or its priests by impious depredators, but that clerks are captured, redeemed, and cast into prison like laymen, it is therefore ordained and decreed that, if any one violate a church or cemetery, or lay violent hands on a clergyman, he shall receive absolution from no one but the pope himself, and in his presence[2].

Among the partisans of Stephen was Geoffrey of Mannevile[3], a man of great sagacity and valour, and the wealthiest and most powerful of all the nobility, being, as constable, in possession of the Tower of London, besides other castles of

---

[1] "Vermis quidam inter vitalia illius innatus irrepsit, lentoque morsu interiora exedens, paulatim sceleratum depavit, multisque tandem vexatum questubus, multis etiam et horrendis tortum cruciatibus, dignissimo supplicio ad extrema deduxit." Gesta Stephani, pp. 96–101. H. Hunt. a. 1143. R. Wendov. ii. p. 231.—T.

[2] H. Hunt. a. 1143. R. Wendov. ii. p. 232.

[3] [This name is usually written " Mandeville;" I adopt the orthography of Domesday. In the Latin chroniclers it is rendered " Magna villa."—T.] He had been created earl of Essex by Stephen. See Rymer, i. p. 18. In 1136 he founded the Benedictine priory at Walden in Essex, afterwards made an abbey. See Monast. Angl. iv. pp. 133 sq., where a copious account is given of him and his race. Both he and his wife Roheisa were great benefactors to the priory of Hurley in Berkshire, and the latter to that of Chicksand in Bedfordshire. See Monast. iii. p. 431, vi. p. 950.

great strength, as at Walden and Pleshey[1] in the neighbouring counties, and was more implicitly obeyed than the king himself. By this plenitude of power having naturally excited the jealousy of those more immediately about the king, they availed themselves of a report that was rife among the people, that Geoffrey was meditating the delivery of the kingdom to the countess of Anjou, and thus prevailed on the king to order his arrest for treason, and demand the surrender of his castles[2]. Stephen was long reluctant to adopt any measures against him, lest he should incur the charge of treachery; but a quarrel having suddenly arisen between Geoffrey and certain barons, there were among them some who boldly accused him of treason; and when, instead of rebutting the charge, he treated the whole as a joke, the king no longer hesitated to arrest him and his followers. This event took place at St. Alban's.

Being brought to London in strict custody, the king ordered him to be hanged, unless he delivered up the Tower and his other castles. To avoid an ignominious death, Geoffrey yielded to necessity, and having delivered them, he assembled around him all his friends and vassals, together with a band of soldiery and robbers, who flocked to him from all quarters, and laid waste and plundered the country in every direction, sparing none who were attached to the king's party, regardless of age or calling, and practising unheard-of cruelties. Cambridge he took by surprise and delivered up to pillage, hewing down the church doors with axes; and with like ferocity destroyed the churches and monasteries, and laid waste in all the neighbouring country. Having sacked the abbey of St. Benedict in Ramsey, stript its altars of their treasures and relics, and expelled the monks, he placed in it a body of soldiers and turned it into a fortress. On hearing

---

[1] For an account of this celebrated castle in Essex, see Gough's History of Pleshey.—T.

[2] H. Hunt. a. 1143. Gesta Steph. p. 102.

of these outrages, Stephen marched against him with a strong force; but Geoffrey eluded him, by betaking himself to the marshes which abounded in those parts, whence he would issue to carry on the work of devastation in other quarters. Finding it impracticable to end this desultory warfare by an engagement, Stephen, having ordered the erection of fortresses in well selected places, and supplied them with troops sufficient to repress the insurgents, withdrew from the undertaking, and returned to the administration of public affairs. After the king's departure, Geoffrey assembled a numerous body of malcontents from all parts, and was, moreover, joined by Hugh Bigot, a man of illustrious birth and great power in the eastern parts of the kingdom. Following the example set by Geoffrey of Mannevile, Robert Marmiun, a warlike baron, who had distinguished himself in Normandy against the forces of Anjou, also rose against the royal authority, and transformed the cathedral of Coventry into a fortress. But both he and Geoffrey, being at length surrounded by the king's troops, were slain, the former before the holy structure which he had desecrated (1144 Aug.), and Geoffrey in the midst of his followers, each by an arrow from an unknown hand. Lying under the ban of the Church, to both were denied the rites of Christian burial[1].

The fate of these rebellious barons appears to have served rather as an incentive than a check to similar attempts by other adherents of Matilda. In the northern parts the earl of Chester maintained an incessant warfare against those barons who were well inclined to Stephen, laying waste their lands with fire and sword. John fitz Gilbert, who, as we have seen, had obtained possession of the castle of Marlborough, ceased not from oppressing the country around him, by the erection of forts in well-adapted places, seizing on the property of the Church, and compelling its ministers to attend

[1] Robert de Monte, a. 1139. Gesta Stephani, p. 104. H. Hunt. a. 1144. Wil. Newburg. lib. i. c. 12.

at his castle to pay him tribute. The sons of earl Robert carried on hostilities in the southern parts, plundering the people and devastating the land; while Stephen of Mannevile (no doubt a kinsman of Geoffrey), was prosecuting the work of destruction in the west, where he had repaired many decayed castles, from which he tyrannized over those who were well affected to the royal cause. At this time, too, one William of Dover [1], a bold and skilful soldier and client of the earl of Gloucester, proceeding to Cricklade, there, in a spot encircled by water and marshes, erected an inaccessible and impregnable fortress, the garrison of which, consisting of mercenaries and archers, spread rapine and misery around, subjecting to their depredations the country on both banks of the Thames, as far as Oxford and Malmesbury. With the object of relieving his adherents in Malmesbury, Stephen assembled an army, and succeeded in throwing a considerable supply of necessaries into the place; then, after ravaging the country around three forts erected by earl Robert not far from the town, he fixed his camp at Tetbury, and directed his efforts to the capture of one of these forts, only three miles distant from Malmesbury. He had already gained the outer works, killed and wounded many of the garrison, and was about to apply his enginery to the inner walls, when the earl of Gloucester approached, at the head of a large army raised in the neighbourhood of Bristol, and consisting besides of many Welsh and others. These were joined by a strong body under Roger, the new earl of Hereford, Milo's son. Seeing the overwhelming force opposed to him, Stephen yielded to the advice of his barons, hastily withdrew from his position, and marched on Winchcombe, where Roger had erected a fort, which, although of impregnable strength, yet being abandoned by the greater part of its defenders, who had fled at Stephen's approach, he succeeded in carrying by storm,

[1] Probably the William Peverel de Dovora mentioned in Rot. magn. pipæ.

and followed up his success by marching against Hugh Bigot, for the purpose of putting an end to his depredations. In this undertaking he was equally successful; for taking him by surprise, he slew or captured the greater number of his followers, and dispersed the rest.

About this time, a Norman of poor and obscure parentage, named Turgis[1], was tempted to resist the royal authority. To this man, whom he had overloaded with benefits, and intrusted with the most important secrets of state, Stephen had given the custody of the castle of Walden, together with the government of the surrounding district, a trust which he grossly abused, so that when the king, his benefactor, would enter the castle, he found the gates closed against him, as Turgis, fearing he might be superseded in his office, held himself and followers in strict seclusion, refusing access to all. But it one day happened that Turgis, for the purpose of partaking in the pleasures of the chase, left the castle and, winding his horn, was joyfully following the hounds, when the king with a body of soldiers unexpectedly arrived hard by, who, on being informed that his refractory servant was without the castle, caused him to be seized and bound, and commanded him to be forthwith hanged at the castle gate, if he demurred to the surrender of his charge. Turgis, after a short deliberation, preferred the latter alternative[2].

While these transactions were in progress in various parts of the kingdom, the followers of earl Robert, particularly William of Dover and his men, were carrying an incessant and sanguinary warfare from Cricklade against the royalists, now against those whom the king had left to defend Oxford, now against the garrison of Malmesbury, the commander of which, named Walter[3], he captured through an ambuscade, and delivered into the hands of the empress. At length,

---

[1] In the Gesta (p. 110) he is styled "Normannus de Aurentia," of *Arranches*, though the correct Latin of which is Abrincæ.—T.

[2] Gesta Steph. p. 110.   [3] Ibid. p. 111.

stricken with remorse for the miseries he had inflicted on so
many of his fellow creatures, William, in expiation of his
crimes, sought Jerusalem and the holy places, and fell valiantly fighting against the foes of Christ. The empress having
now in her power one who was more hateful to her than any
other of her adversaries, at first attempted by blandishments,
then by threats, to prevail on him to deliver up the castle of
Malmesbury. But Walter was not only deaf to her promises
and threats, but alleged that, even if he were disposed to surrender the castle, the king's soldiers would never allow him
to do so. Stephen, on hearing of Walter's capture immediately proceeded to Malmesbury, reinforced the garrison, and
supplied it with an abundant stock of provisions. Thus dis-
appointed, Matilda wreaked her vengeance on Walter, whom,
heavily chained, she commanded to be cast into a loathsome
dungeon [1].

After William of Dover's departure from Cricklade, that
place was consigned to the charge of Philip, a son of the
earl of Gloucester. This young man, as bloodthirsty and
tyrannical as his predecessor, carried fire and sword into the
possessions of the adherents of Stephen in every direction.
When Philip found himself in secure possession of Cricklade,
he proposed to his father, the earl of Gloucester, to draw his
forces nearer to Oxford and, by erecting forts around that
city, prevent the partisans of the king from sallying forth.
With this proposal the earl was not slow to comply, and accordingly erected a strong fort at Faringdon with rampart
and towers, and supplied it with a garrison chosen from the
flower of his army. The garrison at Oxford, finding itself
thus shut up, implored the king, by messengers and letters,
to march to its succour. On learning the state of things
there, Stephen, laying aside all other affairs, hastened to the
relief of his friends, and, at the head of a numerous and formidable army, composed chiefly of Londoners, encamped at

[1] Gesta Stephani, p. 112.

Faringdon, where he strongly intrenched himself, within a rampart strengthened with towers, against any sudden irruption from the fort. He then erected against the fort engines of an elaborate construction, posted archers thickly around it, who cruelly annoyed those within; so that, while on the one hand stones, or whatever else might be hurled from the engines, crushed those on whom they fell; on the other, a deadly shower of arrows, ever flying in their sight, cruelly harassed them. Sometimes a missile or heavy mass projected from a distance would throw them into disorder, sometimes a body of daring youth, mounting on the rampart's summit, would engage with the foe in fight, the palisade[1] alone separating the combatants. At length some of the chiefs among the besieged sent clandestinely to the king, offering terms of capitulation, which being accepted, the fortress was delivered up. Among the partisans of Matilda great was the consternation caused by this event, by which not only a large number of prisoners, arms, and other booty fell into the hands of the king, enabling him to bestow liberal rewards on his soldiery, but which struck a terror into his adversaries that was highly advantageous to him. The earl of Chester, who by force of arms occupied nearly a third of the kingdom, now humbly submitted to him at Stamford[2], expressing his contrition for the treachery and cruelty of which he had been guilty towards his royal master after the battle of Lincoln, and for the violent seizure of the king's demesnes (1146). Matters being thus amicably settled between them, the earl was restored to favour.

Conjointly with the earl of Chester, Stephen now took the town of Bedford[3], whence they proceeded to the attack of Wallingford castle, to which the earl brought three hundred chosen soldiers. Against the town they erected a fort, by

[1] So I have ventured to render the Lat. *paxillus*. The passage in the Gesta (p. 114) is: "paxillis tantum utrosque dirimentibus."—T.

[2] Sax. Chron. a. 1140.   [3] See page 330.

which the depredations of the garrison were materially checked[1].

Worthier of notice than the return of the earl of Chester to his allegiance is the transition of Philip, the son of earl Robert, to the cause of Stephen, after the confirmation of an agreement concluded between them, according to which he performed homage to Stephen, receiving from him lands and castles and numerous presents, so that the ambition and extravagance of the young man were more likely to be satisfied than under the control of a father growing stricter and more parsimonious with years. Without mercy the young political renegade ravaged the possessions of his former friends, and even those of his father, while his thoughtless arrogance and violence rendered him extremely burthensome to his new allies.

After the loss of so many men, and so many towns, and other material means, the chiefs of the Angevin party found it desirable to think of peace, by which they hoped to gain more than they had acquired by arms; Reginald of Dunstanvile was therefore commissioned to negotiate. Yet on both sides feelings soon manifested themselves which rendered every chance of an accommodation hopeless. Philip of Gloucester had even had the audacity to capture his uncle Reginald on his way to the king, in defiance of the royal safe-conduct which he bore; while the empress, on the other side, would not renounce the royal dignity in England. The spirit of hostility, which was with difficulty repressed during the negotiations, burst forth shortly after, and it availed little that the new crusade, to which the inspiring words of Bernard of Clairvaux had roused the nations of the West, removed from England the earls William of Warenne, Waleram and Geoffrey of Meulan, Philip of Gloucester, with many other young and warlike knights, in this and the following year[2]. Their

[1] Gesta Steph. p. 115.
[2] Ib. p. 117. H. Hunt. Joh. Hagust. a. 1147. Rob. de Monte, a. 1145.

G g

deeds in the East this is not the place to celebrate; though short mention must be made of the glorious crusade undertaken by Anglo-Norman and Flemish knights against the Saracens in Portugal.

The Flemish fleet, under count Arnulf of Arschot, had arrived at Dartmouth[1] (1147), where, it seems, they joined the English fleet, then about to sail for Syria, with which, after being scattered by a violent storm, they reached the coasts of Galicia and Portugal. To the pressing instances of king Alphonso, to begin their warfare with the infidels in that country, they gave ear, and in four months succeeded in rescuing from the Mohammedans the even at that time considerable city of Lisbon. Long they luxuriated in rich Saracenic spoil, and not till the following year continued their course eastwards[2].

But, notwithstanding their apparent reconciliation, the earl of Chester continued to be Stephen's most dangerous enemy. It had often excited doubts in the minds of the king and his friends that the earl always delayed the restoration of the royal castles and revenues of which he had forcibly possessed himself, as also the delivery of hostages and securities, which, under such circumstances, it was, in those times, customary to require, and which the fickleness of his character rendered indispensable; so that when he made the attempt to persuade the unsuspecting king to undertake an expedition against Wales, with the view probably of effecting his destruction

[1] So I venture to render the "Derchnede" of Dedekin and the "Tredemunde" of Arnulf. See their narrative in P. W. Gerken, Reisen durch Schwaben, th. iv. pp. 386 sq. Martene and Durand, Collect. ampliss. t. i. pp. 800 sq.

[2] Wilken, Gesch. der Kreuzzüge, b. iii. c. 12. Chron. Reg. S. Pantaleonis. H. Hunt. a. 1148. Joh. Hagust. a. 1149, but which must be corrected to 1148; so Rob. de Monte, where 1148 is throughout to be corrected to 1147. The Auct. Gemblac. has the right date, 1147. A MS. "Expeditio Francorum, Anglorum et variarum nationum ad obsidendum Ulissipona in Portugallia tempore Hildefonsi regis (1147) per Osbernum," is cited in Cooper on the Public Records, ii. p. 166.

amid the valleys and defiles of that not far distant yet strange
and hostile land, the resolve ripened in the breast of the king
to assure himself, at a fitting opportunity, of the person of
Ranulf, as he had formerly of Geoffrey of Mannevile's. This
opportunity soon presented itself at Northampton; Ranulf
was there arrested and compelled to surrender Lincoln and all
his other usurpations, to give hostages for his future fidelity
to the king, and engage to be content with his earldom and
lawful fief[1].

Stephen solemnized the Christmas festival this year at
Lincoln, wearing his crown, into which city, it is said, no
king ever durst enter (such was the current superstition);
thereby evincing a strength of mind which makes a deeper
impression on the hearts of the contemporary generation than
a battle won. After his departure thence, Ranulf, burning
with anger, attempted to make himself master of Lincoln,
Coventry, and other places; but in an attack on the first
named city, he lost many of his best men, escaping from death
or capture only by a shameful flight[2].

The empress, weary at length of these endless wars and of
a most anxious life, returned to France, in the beginning of
the year 1147[3], in the hope, however, of inspiring her party
with new zeal, if she introduced upon the scene her son
Henry, now grown up, that he might himself contend for the
crown to which he had rightful pretensions. Gilbert, son of
Richard of Clare, a nephew of the earl of Chester, and one
of his hostages, incensed at the loss of his castles, which, in
consequence of his uncle's late rebellion, were forfeited to the
crown, was the individual by whom the young prince Henry's
second crossing over to England was chiefly concerted[4]. But

[1] Gesta Steph. pp. 115, 121–123. N. Trivet, p. 20, edit. E. H. S.
[2] H. Hunt. a. 1147. It is remarkable that none of the numerous
charters of Henry I. and the earlier kings, relating to the church of Lincoln, are issued in that city.   [3] Gervas. a. 1147.
[4] Gesta Steph. pp. 125–128. Joh. Hagust. a. 1151 (instead of 1147).
Gervas. a. 1146.

g g 2

Henry's appearance failed in making the expected impression, as he was unaccompanied, contrary to the hopes of his friends, by any large body of French, and his first undertakings against Cricklade and Burton fell short of their object. Pecuniary embarrassment, too, had so increased at the court of the empress, that he was reduced to the necessity of applying for aid to his magnanimous and good-natured rival; nor did he apply in vain[1].

At this time also Stephen introduced his son Eustace on the theatre of contention. This youth was for valour, affability, and liberality the exact resemblance of his father. More fortunate than his young rival, he had succeeded in taking Lidley and other castles[2] held by the enemy. To add to the embarrassment, under which the party of the empress was suffering, the earl of Gloucester died unexpectedly in the midst of his exertions to bring all the forces of his party to bear upon the king. His death was hastened by grief for the failure of so many plans, and the desertion of faithless and indifferent friends[3].

We have, and his contemporaries also had, a most incontrovertible proof of Stephen's inability to satisfy the difficult conditions of his life, in the fact that, notwithstanding the late favourable events, he was unable to recover his sway over the whole of England. It is also remarkable, that for the year 1148, with the exception of some uninteresting matter relating to ecclesiastical affairs, we are without any account of what took place in England.

[1] Gesta Stephani, pp. 128, 129.

[2] "Castrum quod dicebatur de Silva." Gesta Steph. p. 130. [The character here given of Eustace, from the Gesta, is widely different from what we read of him in the Saxon Chronicle, a. 1140, where he is described as "an evil man, who did more evil than good; he robbed the lands and laid great imposts on them. He brought his wife to England and put her in the castle of * * *. A good woman she was, but had little bliss with him."—T.]

[3] Gesta Steph. p. 132. Joh. Hagnst. a. 1147. For the bright side of earl Robert's character, see W. Malm. pp. 757 sqq.

The eyes of Stephen's adversaries were now directed towards Scotland, whither prince Henry, now a youth of sixteen, had been sent to conciliate the good will of his great uncle, king David. He visited the king at Carlisle, where he was celebrating the Whitsun festival (1149), and was received with all honour and great cost, wherein the acknowledgment of his claims was implied : he, at the same time, received the honour of knighthood at the hands of his great uncle; David's son, prince Henry, and the earl of Chester, both of whom had renounced their allegiance to Stephen, being his sponsors on this solemn occasion. Ranulf had surrendered his former pretensions to Carlisle and received Lancaster as an equivalent, together with the promise that his son should marry a daughter of prince Henry. By this meeting of his enemies on the frontier of his kingdom, Stephen was, in the month of August, summoned to the north, and more particularly through the prayers and presents of the burghers of York, who were in great apprehensions of a hostile inroad. Prince Eustace here received the honour of knighthood from his father, the cost of the festival on the occasion being defrayed by bishop Henry. The two youthful princes, full of ambition and military ardour, now made frequent incursions on the territory of their rival; but David was compelled to renounce his plan of attacking the English king, because Ranulf had failed to appear at Lancaster with the auxiliary troops he had promised[1]. Both armies were disbanded before the winter, as Stephen also found himself too weak to act on the offensive, and Henry returned to Normandy. In consequence of the want of pecuniary means, the war now no longer proceeded with vigour. The city of Worcester was this year (1150) taken by Stephen, and a considerable part of it burnt; but the castle held out against him. This city had been bestowed by the king, to his own detriment, on Waleram count of Meulan. Loaded with spoil, the royal forces re-

[1] Joh. Hagust. a. 1150 (1149). H. Hunt. a. 1149.

turned from this enterprise through the lands of their adversaries, whence they also bore off much booty. In the following year (1151) the king resumed the siege of the castle of Worcester, and erected two forts against it, then left it to be conducted by his nobles. The place was defended by the brother of the count, Robert earl of Leicester, who succeeded in demolishing the two forts and causing the siege to be raised [1].

More important for England was that which at this time took place in France. No sooner had king Lewis VII. returned from the crusade than count Geoffrey hastened to him, for the purpose of preferring his complaints against Stephen. He renounced for himself the further government of Normandy, and the king of France conferred it on his son Henry, as the rightful heir, reserving, however, the Norman Vexin, between the Epte and the Andelle, for the crown of France, an act which soon led to hostilities between the king and the young duke, whereby prince Eustace found an opportunity of attaching himself more closely to his brother-in-law, the king of France, and even of rendering him effectual aid at the siege of Pont-de-l'Arche [2]. Hardly was peace restored at a meeting of the princes there, in which Bernard of Clairvaux acted as a mediator, to the no small advantage of the apparently compliant but politic Henry, when disease carried off his father, the stout and practised warrior; by which event the county of Anjou and his pretensions to the English crown devolved on his eldest son. Shortly after, fortune's favour brought to duke Henry a new and great accession to his power. Eleanor, a daughter of William X., count of Poitiers and duke of Guienne, had since the year 1137 been married to king Lewis VII. and had borne him two daughters. She had accompanied him on the crusade, her levities during

---

[1] H. Hunt. aa. 1150, 1151.

[2] Historia Regis Ludovici VII. ap. Bouquet, xiii. p. 127. Rob. de Monte. aa. 1150, 1151.

which gave rise to dissensions between her and her consort, which, after a union of fifteen years, led to a sentence of divorce pronounced at the council of Baugency (1152, March 18th), on the plea of too near consanguinity. Hardly was Eleanor—who retained Poitou and Guienne—separated from the king, when her hand was sought by the highest princes of France. From the importunate suit of the young count Theobald V. of Blois she was obliged to escape by night, and in a similar manner from an attempt at abduction by Geoffrey Plantagenet, second son of the recently deceased count of Anjou[1]. More fortunate was his elder brother Henry, on whom Eleanor, only six weeks after her divorce, bestowed her hand with her rich possessions (May 18th), thereby making him master of a half of France. Great were the surprise and indignation of the French monarch on this occasion, who was now sensible of the impolicy of his divorce. Nor was the consternation less which pervaded the court of Stephen, when it became known how Henry, only a short time before, the youngest and poorest knight, whose greatest pride was a successful chase, or an insignificant border war, had at once become one of the most considerable and powerful princes of Europe. King Lewis and Eustace now invaded Normandy at the head of a numerous French army, to whom Henry offered a stout resistance, yet lost the castle of Neufmarché, till then regarded as impregnable, which king Lewis gave over to Eustace[2].

While these youthful forms were entering upon the world's stage, and the eyes of all were directed towards them, more and more of those who constituted the historic matter, as it were, of Stephen's reign were retiring from it. His brother, the excellent count Theobald of Blois, had died in the beginning of this year; and a few weeks later (March 3rd) the

[1] Chron. Turon. a. 1152.
[2] H. Hunt. a. 1151 (1152). Robert de Monte, a. 1152, gives details of this war.

no less excellent queen Matilda. Of Stephen's adversaries there died about the same time prince Henry, son of king David, a valiant, and in the milder virtues, well-approved prince, who, in the next year, was followed by his royal father and, shortly after, by many of the rebellious barons[1].

It was a great error on the part of Stephen to alienate the good will of the Church, and this may be ascribed in a great degree, if not solely, to his brother Henry, who had exercised his legatine authority in a very questionable, if not arbitrary, manner. But his patron Innocent II. dying (1144) was, in the short space of two years, succeeded by two popes, one of whom, Celestine II., at the instance of archbishop Theobald, deprived Henry of his legatine office. Mortified at his disgrace, the bishop prevailed on his brother to forbid the archbishop to assist at the council of Rheims[2] (1148); but Theobald slighted the prohibition, and at his return was driven into exile. He landed in France, passed over from thence to Framlingham, where, under the protection of Bigot, earl of Norfolk, he published a sentence of interdict on all the royal demesnes, which was forthwith put in execution, when Stephen's friends, alarmed at the cessation of divine service, compelled him to seek a reconciliation with the primate[3].

There was, in fact, an internal warfare, which never ceased, between the secular and the ecclesiastical powers. The introduction of appeals to the pope, which had until then been unknown in England, but which, as papal legate, the bishop of Winchester had introduced among the clergy, gave rise to many dissensions[4]. After the death of Innocent II., and of his two short-lived successors (Celestine II. and Lucius II.), Eugenius III. had followed a hostile policy towards Stephen

---

[1] Joh. Hagust. a. 1153 (1152). Rob. de Monte, h. a.

[2] On the death of abp. William, the predecessor of Theobald, Henry had endeavoured to obtain the primacy, but was thwarted by both the king and queen. Gervas. col. 1348.—T.

[3] Gervas. coll. 1348, 1363 sq. 1665.

[4] H. Hunt. a. 1151. W. Malm. p. 723.

and bishop Henry. A new legate, the presbyter cardinal John, was sent to Ireland (1150), but was by Stephen forbidden a free passage into England, unless he engaged that his mission had for its object nothing prejudicial to the realm. Some years after, on the return of the legate, the king strove to make good his former ill-advised step[1]. He had, in the meantime, become reconciled with the archbishop of York, Henry Murdac, who, contrary to his will, had been elected by the clergy, and consecrated by the pope, and with whom Eustace had had many quarrels, but which had also been settled amicably[2].

At Midlent, in the following year (1154), a council was convoked at London, at which the king and his son Eustace were present. When an overwhelming number of appeals had been heard, Stephen demanded of the prelates that they should crown his son. From archbishop Theobald he met with a refusal, the pope, he asserted, having by his letter prohibited him from raising the king's son to the throne, because Stephen himself, in violation of his oath, had seized on the kingdom by force. This letter, it is said, was obtained of the pope, and brought to England by Thomas, son of Gilbert Becket, a priest of London, the future archbishop of Canterbury, celebrated for his disputes with Henry II. and his tragic end. When the king attempted to extort compliance from the prelates by shutting them up in a house, the archbishop found means to escape, and crossed over to Normandy. Stephen confiscated their temporalities, but Henry gained the primate of all England for a declared adherent[3].

In this year Stephen succeeded in capturing the castle of Newbury, and thence proceeded to renew the siege of Wallingford, where, at the end of the bridge at Crowmarsh, he caused a fort to be erected, to cut off all supplies from the

---

[1] Joh. Hagust. aa. 1152 (1151), 1153 (1152).

[2] Ibid. aa. 1147, 1150, 1151.

[3] H. Hunt. a. 1152. Gervas. coll. 1369, 1372, 1668.

garrison. Thus reduced to an extremity, they besought the duke of Normandy either to send them succour, or consent to the surrender of the castle to the king[1].

After a long contest, a truce was this year (1153) concluded between king Lewis and Henry, but which the former seemed disposed to violate. Nevertheless, early in January, Henry sailed with thirty-six ships and an army, consisting of a hundred and forty horse and three thousand foot, to England. Shortly after his arrival, his army being greatly increased, he laid siege to and captured the town of Malmesbury (Jan. 13th), with the exception of one tower, which could only be reduced by famine. The defence of this tower had been intrusted by the king to one Jordan, who hastened to him and announced the state of things. Stephen hereupon marched to attack the duke, and the armies met near Malmesbury, where the unfavourable position of the royal troops, who had the snow, rain, and wind storming in their faces, while those of the duke were naturally free from those annoyances, decided the fate of the day in favour of Henry[2]. Depressed in spirit Stephen hurried back to London, and many of the English nobility began to declare for Henry. Gundred countess of Warwick expelled the garrison placed by the king in her castle, which she delivered to the duke[3]. Robert earl of Leicester supplied him with everything he needed, and, by his representations, induced nearly thirty holders of castles to join him[4]. The tower of Malmesbury having surrendered, Henry hastened to the relief of Wallingford, but which he only partially effected. To prevent the garrison at Crowmarsh from acting on the offensive, Henry caused a deep trench to be dug round the fort, whereby those in Wallingford were enabled to open their gates. On hearing what was taking place, Stephen marched to the relief of his fort, and both armies again stood in front of each other; but many of the most distinguished men,

[1] H. Hunt. a, 1152. Gervas. h. a.   [2] H. Hunt. a. 1153.
[3] Rob. de Monte, h. a. R. Wendov. ii. p. 254.   [4] Gervasius, h. a.

either from the conviction how great and general was the
desire of peace, or, as some supposed, fearing lest Stephen
should be the victor, caused negotiations to be set on foot[1].
The leaders themselves held a verbal communication on the
opposite banks of the Thames, standing far distant from their
attendants. Although nothing was on this occasion finally
settled, Eustace, bitterly incensed, left his father's court and
mercilessly ravaged the neighbourhood of Cambridge and the
monastery of St. Edmund there, when death, the consequence
of violent excitement, suddenly arrested his course (Aug.10th)[2].
About this time also died, in a somewhat similar manner,
Simon of Senlis, the young earl of Northampton. Ranulf
earl of Chester, likewise died suddenly, as it was said, by
poison administered to him by William Peverel[3]. Ranulf had
obtained from Henry a grant of Peverel's possessions, according to a deed issued at Devizes, by which may be seen what a
high price the prince was willing to pay for the sake of
attaching that faithless earl to his interests[4]. By this document Henry confirms to the earl all his possessions in Normandy, and adds many others; from a viscount he raises him
to be count of Avranches; gives him the entire inheritance
of Roger count of Poitiers; in England, bestows on him Ely,

[1] The prominent part which Lyttelton makes the earl of Arundel act on
this occasion is void of historic foundation. [Gervase (col. 1373) gives a
short speech made by the earl, in favour of peace, which has been ampli-
fied by Lyttelton.—T.]

[2] What is here related of Eustace tallies well with the character given of
him in the Saxon Chronicle. (See p. 402, note). Henry of Huntingdon
says of him: "Sepultus est filius regis in abbatia, quam mater ejus funda-
verat, apud Feveresham, militia quidem probatus, sed in ea quæ Dei sunt
obstinatus, rectoribus ecclesiarum durissimus, persequentibus eam [sic]
devotissimus." Faversham abbey was the joint foundation of Stephen and
Matilda. Gerv. col. 1372.—T.

[3] H. Hunt. Gervasius, h. a. Joh. Sarisb. Polycrat. lib. v. c. 18., viii. 21.

[4] The deed in Rymer is erroneously dated 1152, instead of 1153, and
Adrinchin is there written for Abrincensi. For another document of the
duke, of this time, which is interesting on account of the witnesses, in
favour of the abbey of Trouarn, See Monast. Angl. vi. p. 1105.

the county and town of Stafford, the castle of Nottingham, and the possessions of certain distinguished knights, whose names are recited in the document. Besides all this, he engages to each of six of his vassal barons, to be nominated by Ranulf himself, a considerable portion of land [1], from the lands to be taken from the enemy, to be holden immediately of him as king. A vassal like this was hardly less powerful than his sovereign, and more dangerous than a neighbouring prince, and his death must, without doubt, have been regarded as a lucky event for the country.

At the head of a well-appointed army the duke now laid siege to Stamford, of which he speedily gained possession, and on hearing that the king was besieging the castle of Ipswich, the possessor of which, Hugh Bigot, had declared himself in his favour, he hastened to its relief; but learning that it had already surrendered, he directed his march to Nottingham, which he captured and stripped of its wealth, but declined to waste time in attempting to take its naturally impregnable castle. The town itself was set on fire by the garrison of the castle [2]. Hence those to whom the highest concerns of the country were an object of interest had no lack of an incentive to an attempt at effecting a peace between the rival princes, and thereby basing the tranquillity of the nation on the unity and stability of the supreme authority, a task rendered comparatively easy by the early death of Eustace. These mediators were Theobald archbishop of Canterbury, and Henry bishop of Winchester. On the 7th November they had the satisfaction of concluding at Winchester a treaty of pacification, the chief conditions of which were the following :—

That Stephen, during his life, should be acknowledged as king of England by Henry and his barons; while Henry should be received as his son and heir by Stephen and his

---

[1] " Centum libratas terrae."
[2] H. Hunt. N. Trivet. p. 28, edit. E. H. S.

subjects.—That Stephen's son William should perform homage to the duke, and retain all possessions in England, Normandy, and elsewhere which Stephen had held before his occupation of the throne; also all that he had acquired by his marriage with the heiress of the earl of Warenne, together with the earldom of Norwich, conferred on him by his father, and the castles, towns, and landed possessions of Pevensey, with the feudal superiority over Faramus of Boulogne [1], Dover, etc., which had been given him by Henry. Reciprocal oaths were sworn by the barons and burghers of both parties to the two princes. With respect to the numerous castles several provisions were agreed to, having for object the securing of them to Henry after the death of Stephen. The still unsubdued garrison of Wallingford had to swear fealty to the king.—The tower of London and the castle (mota) of Windsor were committed to Richard of Lucy, that of Oxford to Roger of Lucy, and the fastness (firmitas) of Lincoln to Jordan of Bussy. All these must swear to the duke or the archbishop, and give hostages to the latter for the contingent delivery of the fortresses to Henry. The bishop of Winchester also gave a contingent assurance to archbishop Theobald.—The archbishop, bishops, and abbots of England, by command of the king, swore fealty to the duke.—If either of the contracting princes should violate the compact, the archbishops and bishops were by both empowered to bind him to its observance by ecclesiastical penalties.—The mother, wife, and other relations of the duke guaranteed the observance of the compact.—Stephen further engaged, in all affairs of state, to act in concert with the duke's council, saving his royal rights in all parts of England.

Besides these provisions of the compact, which we know only from a proclamation of Stephen, there were others, it is said, which he either did not or could not carry into effect.

---

[1] Rymer i. p. 18. "villam Pevenselli et servitium Faramosi." See p. 369. The date of the instrument appears from Rob. de Monte. Bromton, col. 1038.

Of such were his engagement. that the several castles, which. since the days of his predecessor, had fallen into illegal hands, should be restored to their rightful owners; and that all castles which had been erected since his accession (the number of which is by some estimated at three hundred and seventy-five, by others at eleven hundred and fifteen) should be demolished [1].

At the end of November was the solemn day, on which the king with the duke met together in Winchester, to celebrate their pacification, when the former adopted the latter, and declared him heir to the throne, before all the assembled nobles and people. From Winchester both princes proceeded together to London, where, amid new festivities, a solemn confirmation of their reconciliation took place. Shortly after the beginning of the following year (1154, Jan. 13th), a numerous assemblage from all parts of the kingdom was convoked at Oxford, where the usual oath of fealty was taken and homage performed to the duke, by the chief persons of the realm. At a subsequent meeting of the two princes at Dunstable, some misunderstanding arose between them, on account of the delay in demolishing the castles, according to the compact; for although many had been destroyed, many, through the king's easy nature or policy, were suffered to remain. But the duke, when made sensible of the difficulty attending the execution of a work to which so much powerful opposition was raised. at length acquiesced in the delay. The consolidation of his power in Normandy, where many ducal possessions had been lost to the crown, and were now to be recovered, summoned him at Easter back to that duchy, whence he was shortly after called to suppress a rebellion in Guienne. Count William of Boulogne, Stephen's son, had resolved on accompanying him, but having been thrown from his horse and severely hurt, was brought to Canterbury and placed under surgical care [2].

---

[1] Rob. de Monte. Radulf. de Diceto, col. 525.
[2] H. Hunt. Bromton, Chron. col. 1040.

Stephen now visited the northern provinces, with the object of restoring tranquillity in those parts, of demolishing the illegal fortresses, and to provide for the filling up of the archiepiscopal see of York, that had fallen vacant by the death of Henry Murdac. This was conferred on a relation of the king, William, son of earl Herbert[1]. In the neighbourhood of York, Stephen had to encounter the hostility of Philip of Colvile, who refused to surrender the castle of Drax, · but which he took and demolished, together with many others[2]; then hastened to London, to assist at a council convened for Michaelmas, at which final measures were agreed on relative to the newly nominated archbishop. From London Stephen proceeded to Canterbury, for the purpose of having an interview with Philip count of Flanders, probably on the subject of the large number of Flemings in the country, who could no longer continue in his pay, their dismissal having been already ordered by a royal decree[3], and they themselves being, no doubt, desirous, after the conclusion of peace, to return to their country. Of these the most distinguished was William of Ypres, who, in the preceding year, far advanced in life, and blind, had retired to Loo, where he enriched the abbey with English booty[4]. Stephen here fell sick, and, after a

[1] For details concerning this prelate see Alford, Ann. Eccl. Angl. iv. a. 1143, *sq.* and from him Lyttelton. ["St. William was a son of earl Herbert and Emma, sister of king Stephen, and was canonized cir. 1280. For his penitent life and edifying death, see Stubbes, Actus Pont. Ebor. col. 1721; Bromton and Gervase ad annum; and Acta SS. Papebrochii, ii. 136, June 8th." N. Trivet, Ann. p. 22, Mr. Hog's note.

Archbishop William died by poison. "Proditione clericorum suorum, post perceptionem Eucharistiæ, infra ablutiones, liquore lethali infectas, extinctus est." R. Hoved. a. 1154. Wendover's account differs from the foregoing: "cum divina celebraret mysteria, hausto in ipso calice, ut aiunt, veneno obiit." ii. p. 272. See Gervas. col. 1375. Stubbes, coll. 1721, 1722. W. Newburg. i. p. 86.—T.

[2] Bromton, col. 1373. H. Hunt. a. 1154. R. Hoved. h. a.

[3] Joh. Hagust. a. 1154 (1153). col. 252. Rad. de Diceto, a. 1153. Matt. Paris, *ib.*

[4] Warnkönig, l. c. p. 145.

short illness, died, after a reign of nineteen years, distinguished above all others for its turbulence and numerous
calamities.   His body was buried near to those of his wife
and son, in the abbey founded by him at Faversham[1].

William, king Stephen's second son, continued, until his
death in the year 1160, in possession of the county of Boulogne[2]. Of his daughters, one of whom was married to Hervé
the Breton, the other betrothed to Waleram count of Meulan,
mention has already been made.   Another daughter, Maria,
succeeded her brother William in his county, after having
quitted the abbey of Rumsey, of which she was abbess, and
been married to count Matthew, son of Diederik count of
Flanders[3].

[1] Monast. Angl. iv. pp. 568, *sq.* [At the dissolution his remains were
disinterred and thrown into the Swale, for the sake of the leaden coffin.—T.]

[2] See some charters of his in Monast. Angl. iv. pp. 382, 574.

[1] Auctarium Affligemense, a. 1160. Rad. de Diceto, Imagines Historia-
rum, a. 1160. Auctar. Aquicinct. a. 1182. Monast. Angl. ii. p. 507.

See England under the Anglo-Saxon kings, ii. p. 217.
Wil. Gemmet. viii. 36.
Monast. Anglic. vi. p. 1063. Chron. Reg. Franc. ap. Bouquet, x. p. 303. Roman de Rou, v. 7447. Guil. Gemmet. vi. 2.
See p. 369. Wil. Gemmet. viii. cc. 29, 30, 38.
Rot. Magn. Pipæ, 31 Hen. 1

H. Hunt. a. 1141. William of Jumièges (viii. 29) makes no mention of Baldwin.
30 Chron. S. Stephani Cadom. h. a.
31 Wil. Gemmet. viii. 40.
32 Ib. v. 13, 16. Radulf. Glaber. iii. 2.
33 See Engl. under the Anglo-Saxon kings, ii. p. 296

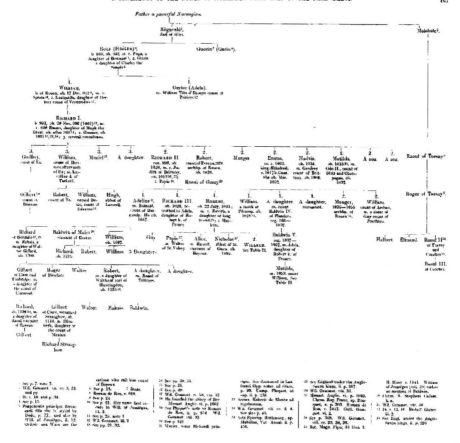

494

W
born 1027,
53 m. Matilda, daught
She

delaide[9],
a nun.

m. 1
ob. 1
vain,

Gundrada[11],
m. William of
Warenne. She ob.
27 May 1085.

3.
[13], Reginald of
. Dunstanvilels.

3.
Reline[13],
Matthew
of Burc-
of Mont-
rency.

3.
Hedwig,
daughter of
Elizabeth,
countess of
Meulan.

3.
No name[13].
m. Alexander
king of Scotland.
He ob. 1125.
s. p.

p[17].
Richard[19],
1134 bishop
of Bayeux.
ob. 1142.

bel or Hawise,
89, m. John, earl
loucester, son and
:essor of Henry II.
She ob. 1201.

. p. 884.
met. viii. 34. W.
. 455. Ord. Vital.
See p. 173.

Vital. p. 897. Rob. de
te, aa. 1134, 1142.
at. Anglic. ii. p. 60.
369.

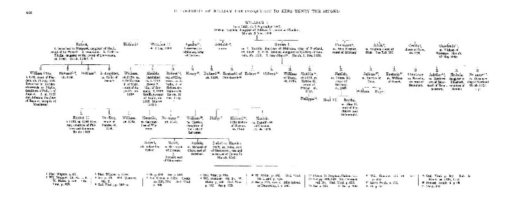

ADELA[1],
daughter of king William I.
m. 1081 Stephen, count of Blois and Chartres. ob. 1137

Agès,
m. Miles, count
of Bray.

Eleanor,
m. Raoul I. count
of Vermandois.

William[2],
m. a daughter of
Giles of Sully[4].

THEOBALD IV[1].
count of Blois, Chartres, and
Troyes, m. Matilda, daughter
of duke Ingelbert. He
ob. Jan. 1152.

Henry[3].
bishop of Win-
chester, ob. 1171.

STEPHEN[1].
king of England, ob. 25 Oct.
1154. m. Matilda, daughter
of Eustace, count of Boulogne.
She ob. 3 May 1152.

Humbert,
ob. young.

Matilda[1, 3],
m. Richard, earl of
Chester. both ob 1120.

Emma,
m. count Herbert.

Odo[4].

Raher[4].

A daughter[1],
m. Henry, count
of Eu.
3 sons and
1 daughter.

Henry[4].
1130 abbot
of Fécamp.

Henry[4],
count of
Troyes,
ob. 1180.

THEOBALD V[1].
count of Blois
and Chartres,
ob. 1191.

Stephen[2].
count of
Sancerre,
ob. 1191.

William
archbp. of
Rheims.

6 daughters.

Eustace,
m. Constance,
daughter of Lewis VI.
king of France.
He ob. 1153.

William,
count of
Boulogne,
ob. 1160.

Maria[4],
m. 1160,
Matthew,
son of the count
of Flanders.
She ob. 1182.

No name,
m. Hervé of
Leon.

No name,
betrothed to
Waleran, count
of Meulan.

William,
abp. of York.
ob. 1154

Ida.

Matilda.

[1] W. Gemmet. lib. viii. c. 34.
[2] D. c. 36.
[3] Rob. de Monte. a. 1151.
[4] Ord. Vital. pp. 810 sq.

[5] Rob. de Monte, a. 1130.
[6] See p. 464.
[7] T. Stubbes, act. Pont. Ebor.
col. 1722.

EMENDATIONS AND ADDITIONS

TO

"A HISTORY OF ENGLAND UNDER THE ANGLO-SAXON KINGS."

VOLUME I.

Preface, p xiii. l. 12. *dele* chiefly

Lit. Introd. p. xxvii. l. 28. *dele* a scholar . . . . . . Bangor.

xxxv. l. 31. *after* because *add* in some manuscripts.

xxxvi. l. 10. *dele* by a judicial sentence.

18. *dele* The old . . . . churches.

lii. l. 2. *for* relations of Thurketul *read* cousins of Æthelstân.

P. 2. l. 11. *for* Phocians *read* Phocæans.

9. n.[1] *dele* An appeal . . . . customs.

41. l. 9. *for* Whiterne *read* Dumbarton.

51. l. 21. *after* Fenny Stratford *read* Towcester, Weedon, South Lilbourne, Atheriston, Gilbert's Hill (now the Wreken), Wroxeter, Stretton, Cardigan.

— l. 24. *after* Cornwall *read* through Devonshire and Somersetshire, by Tetbury, Coventry, Leicester, and Newark, to Lincoln.

55. l. 7. *for* eastern *read* north-eastern.

83. l. 15. *for* which . . . . to the same, *read* to express any whole numbers and a half, they subtract from the following whole number, while in other tongues the half is added to the number itself, as half four *for* three and a half.

90. n.[2] l. 1. *for* two *read* a, *and dele* the poem ·. . eighth century.

— — l. 4. *dele* probably corrupt.

93. l. 18. *dele* The disproportion . . . . to proportion.

99. l. 3. *for* exists *read* exist.

— n.[1] l. 5. *for* seventy-two *read* sixty-two.

103. l. 15. *for* Camel *read* Camlan.

— l. 21. *dele* Had the . . . . occasion

P. 106. l. 6. *dele* though if . . . . conflicts.

    110. l. 3. *for* Wiltsætas *read* Wilsætas.

    — l. 8. *for* already observed *read* it seems.

    114. n.3 *after* Offa *add* It seems pretty evident that this genealogy, though given as Danish in the Danish chronicles, is that of the Anglian kings of Sleswig, the ancestors of the kings of Mercia.

    117. l. 20. *dele from* According to . . . . *to* south.

    118. *dele* notes [1] and [2].

    120. l. 11. *for* Thornsætas and Wiltsætas, *read* Dornsætas *and* Wilsætas.

    128. l. 16. *to* election *append the following note :* [2] When engaged on the first edition of the present work, I felt strongly tempted to suppress, or, at least, to modify, a part of what Dr. Lappenberg had written on the subject of the Bretwaldaship, but was withheld by the consideration, that in every question on which opinions are divided, and more particularly one on which I had myself arrived at no decision, I had no right either to omit or tamper with the words of the original : I therefore faithfully translated them without comment. Since then I have read the observations of Mr. Hallam and Mr. Kemble on the same subject, with which in the main I am inclined to coincide. —(See Archæol. xxxii. p. 245. Hallam, Middle Ages, ii. p. 350. Kemble, Saxons in England, ii. p. 8.).

      The sole source, whence all our information regarding these paramount kings is derived, is Beda, (H. E. lib. ii. 5.), who supplies us with a list of seven. The Saxon Chronicle, after copying Beda (a. 827), adds Ecgberht, as an eighth. The first of them is Ælle, who landed in Sussex from three ships ; and, five or six years after, having received considerable reinforcements from Germany, crushed the Britons and destroyed their stronghold Anderida ; in consequence of which success he appears to have obtained a preponderance that either prompted him to assume, or his followers, or the contemporary chieftains, to confer on him, the title of Brytenwalda, or Bretwalda (lord over the Britons). Ceawlin, king of Wessex, the second in the list, obtained the title, according to all probability, in like manner, by his successes against the Britons. How Æthelberht, king of Kent, the third on the list, acquired it, history omits to inform us ; though Beda tells us, that he held sway over all the country as far as the Humber, and might, therefore, well be " walda," or ruler, over a considerable British population; as the Germanic state of Mercia was then in its early infancy. Equally unknown to us is the way in which Rædwald, king of East Anglia, obtained the title. He possibly assumed it on the defeat of Æthelfrith of Northumbria, and, if an evidently corrupt passage in Beda (lib. ii. 5.) may be so interpreted ("qui etiam, vivente Ædilbercto, eidem (eundem?) suæ genti ducatum præbebat.") during the lifetime of Rædwald. The three Northumbrian kings, Eadwine, Oswald, and Oswiu, either assumed, or had the title of Brytenwalda conferred on them by their people, as one denoting supremacy, without regard to its primitive signification, as is the case at the present day among ourselves; for who now in an usher (huissier, from old Fr. huis, *door*), whether of the black or the birchen rod, sees a door-keeper? or in a marshal (Ohg. marah, *horse*, and scalh, schalk, *servant*), whether city- or field-, a horse-boy?[1] And does not the protestant sovereign of England still retain the title of Defender of the [Roman catholic] faith, conferred by the pope on Henry VIII., for having written against the protestant faith? and until recently that of king of France? and are there not still kings of Cyprus and Jerusalem? From the foregoing it will be seen that I do not place implicit confidence in the words of Beda, whose information regarding the southern states of the "Heptarchy" was far from perfect, but rather incline to the supposition, that the title in question was either assumed by its bearer, or conferred on him by his army or people, without regard to its primitive import. Whether he bore the name of Brytenwalda, or Bretwalda, seems doubtful.

Mr. J. M. Kemble (Saxons in England, ii. p. 20.) would render Brytenwalda by "an extensive, powerful king," deriving its first component from the verb breôtan, *to distribute, divide;* but this interpretation I think hardly applicable to the case, although I admit that it seems countenanced by Ethelweard, who, translating the Saxon Chronicle, renders the word by *pollens potestate.* But is bryten, in the sense of *extensive*, etc. ever found in prose? I believe not. Against this rendering is also Mr. Kemble's own citation from the Codex Diplomaticus (V. pp. 217, 218), viz. "Ego Æthelstanus, Angul-Saxonum necnon et totius *Britanniæ rex*," which is afterwards expressed in Saxon by "Ic Æthelstân, Ongol-Saxna cyning and *brytænwalda* eallæs ðyses iglandæs. Mr. K. (ib. p. 22.) says: "I am not prepared to admit the probability of a territorial title, at a time when kings were kings of the people, not of the land." But what is "totius Britanniæ rex?" not to notice numerous similar instances in the Codex Diplomaticus. The word Bretwalda occurs but once (Sax. Chron. a. 827.), and Brytenwalda only in the charter of Æthelstân just quoted.

[1] The French, in the word *maréchal* (a farrier), have retained something of the primitive signification.

P. 135. l. 15. *for* nevertheless *read* indeed.

154. l. 13. *for* brother *read* step-father.

155. l. 14. *for* brother *read* kinsman.

— n.[2]   *for* 22 *read* 20.

157. n.[1]   *for* iii. 2. *read* iii. 1.

159. l. 27. *dele* Though . . . . Gewissas.

160. l. 16. *dele* the northern boundary of Wessex.

161. l. 7. *for* that kingdom *read* England.

— l. 11. *for* his landing *read* reaching Wessex.

169. l. 22. *for* the king of Kent *read* Eadwine.

178. l. 9. *dele* under their king Birdei.

185. l. 16. *for* his adherents *read* Æbbe, the sister of king Oswiu, and abbess of Coldingham.

189. l. 4. *for* English clergy *read* agents of the archbishop.

— l. 27. *after* year, *add* at Oundle in Northamptonshire.

191. l. 22. *after* Saxons *add* with the sole exception, perhaps, of the church of St. Martin, near Canterbury.

192. l. 23. *for* former *read* latter.

199. n.[1]   *add at the end* [Perhaps the sense might be made clearer by altering the punctuation, thus : semper decimam mansionem ; ubi minimum sit, tamen, etc. *always the tenth manse; where it* [*the possession*] *is very small, still the tenth part,* etc.

206. l. 9. *dele* the.

219. n. 5. *after* 320 *add* and Thorpe's Beowulf, p. 217.

221. l. 24. *for* the British . . . . Bretwaldaship *read* a supremacy over them.

225. l. 13. *dele* in Oxfordshire.

228. n. l. 11. *dele* Higelac (Icel.) all.

231. l. 2. *for* this side *read* the English side.

241. l. 4. *dele* as . . . . recorded.

252. l. 4. *after* Bampton *read* in Devonshire.

286. l. 15. *under* Cwichelm *add* Cuthred ob. 661.

291. l. 14. *dele* Mercelin.

VOLUME II.

P. 4. l. 6. *dele* and jealousy . . . . successors.

6. l. 7. *dele* and we . . . . Wessex.

7. l. 12. *after* monarch *add* Wigláf was succeeded by Beorht-wulf, who, after a reign of thirteen years, was driven beyond sea by the Northern pirates[2].

P. 7. l. 12. *add note* [2]. Flor. Wigorn. a. 838. W. Malm. p. 133.

14. l. 17. *dele* Even . . . . of England.

19. l. 7. *note* [1] *dele* see vol. i. p. 218.

39. l. 23. *for* principal *read* middle.

41. l. 20. *after* Winburne *add:* Having died in warfare with · pagans, the Catholic Church has enrolled him among her martyrs.

69. l. 6. *for* the *read* a great.

84. l. 25. *dele* No . . . . oppressed.

— l. 30. *dele* and they . . . . tithes.

94. l. 17. *for* Britons *read* Bretons.

99. l. 4. } *for* Æthelweard *read* Ælfweard.
101. l. 25. }

106. l. 11. *after* mistake *add* of Guthorm in Denmark.

112. note [1]. *for* Æthelthryth, *read* Cynethryth.

116. l. 21. *dele* by the fair Hewa.

117. l. 6. *for* -second *read* -seventh.

142. l. 4. *dele* already.

156. l. 16. *for* Æthelstan *read* Æthelred.

179. l. 9. *dele* It . . . . people. *and dele note* [1].

187. l. 6. *dele* but . . . . martyrs.

189. note [1]. l. 4. *for* Burton *read* Bampton.

190. l. 25. *after* Arewe *read* Orwell, *and dele* note [4].

210. l. 17. *after* you *read* like dogs.

218. l. 9. *for* Alan *read* him.

222. *dele* note [2].

238. *dele* note [1].

242. l. 2. *for* Biörn *read* Sweyn.

246. l. 19. *after* of *add* a noble lady named.

250. l. 12. *dele* younger, *and after* brother *add* Leofwine.

302. l. 12. *after* foundations *add* On receiving intelligence of Harold's fall, the earls Eadwine and Morkere proceeded to London, and sent their sister, queen Ealdgyth, to Chester.

— — *add note* [1]. Fl. Wigorn. a. 1066.

— — note [2]. l. 3. *dele* For . . . . wife of Harold.

369. l. 18. *for* Æthelweard *read* Ælfweard.

THE END.

PUBLICATIONS BY THE SAME EDITOR.

A HISTORY OF ENGLAND UNDER THE ANGLO-SAXON KINGS, from the German of DR. J. M. LAPPENBERG, with additions and corrections. 2 vols. 8vo. Pub. £1. 1s. Reduced to 12s.

THE ANGLO-SAXON POEMS OF BEOWULF, THE SCÔP or GLEEMAN'S TALE, and the FIGHT AT FINNESBURG, with an English Translation, Notes, Glossary, etc. 15s. cloth.

ANALECTA ANGLO-SAXONICA. A selection in prose and verse from Anglo-Saxon Authors, with a Glossary. Designed chiefly as a first book for Students. Pub. 12s. Reduced to 8s.

THE ANGLO-SAXON VERSION of the HOLY GOSPELS, edited from the original MSS. Pub. 12s. Reduced to 8s.

THE ANGLO-SAXON VERSION of the STORY OF APOLLO-NIUS OF TYRE, from a MS. in the Library of C. C. Coll. Camb. upon which is founded the Play of Pericles, ascribed to Shakspeare, with a literal translation, etc. Pub. 5s. Reduced to 3s.

Valuable and Interesting Books,

PUBLISHED OR SOLD BY

JOHN RUSSELL SMITH,

36, SOHO SQUARE, LONDON.

BIOGRAPHIA BRITANNICA LITERARIA, or Biography of Literary Characters of Great Britain and Ireland. ANGLO-SAXON PERIOD. By THOMAS WRIGHT, M.A., F.S.A., &c., Membre de l'Institute de France. Thick 8vo, *cloth*. 6s. (*original price 12s.*)

———THE ANGLO-NORMAN PERIOD. Thick 8vo, *cloth*. 6s. (*original price 12s.*)

Published under the superintendence of the Council of the Royal Society of Literature.
There is no work in the English Language which gives the reader such a comprehensive and connected History of the Literature of these periods.

LITERATURE OF THE TROUBADOURS. Histoire de la Poésie Provençale, par M. FAURIEL, publié par J. MOHL, Membre de l'Institut de France. 3 vols, 8vo, *new, sewed*. 14s. (*original price £1. 4s.*)

A valuable work, and forms a fit companion to the Literary Histories of Hallam, Ticknor, and Ginguene.
J. R. S. is the only agent in London for the sale of it, at the above moderate price.

JUNIUS. The Authorship of the Letters of Junius elucidated, including a Biographical Memoir of Lieut.-Col. Barré, M.P. By JOHN BRITTON, F.S.A., &c. Royal 8vo, *with portraits of Lord Shelburne, John Dunning, and Barré, from Sir Joshua Reynolds's picture, cloth*. 6s. LARGE PAPER, in 4to, *cloth*. 9s.

An exceedingly interesting book, giving many particulars of the American War, and the state of parties during that period.

WORTHIES OF WESTMORELAND, or Biographies of Notable Persons born in that County since the Reformation. By GEORGE ATKINSON, Esq., Barrister-at-Law. 2 vols, post 8vo, *cloth*. 6s. (*original price 16s.*)

BARKER.—Literary Anecdotes and Contemporary Reminiscences of Professor Porson, and others, from the Manuscript Papers of the late E. H. BARKER, Esq., of Thetford, Norfolk, with an Original Memoir of the Author. 2 vols. 8vo, *cloth*. 12s.

MILTON.—Considerations on Milton's Early Reading, and the *prima stamina* of his "Paradise Lost," together with Extracts from a Poet of the XVIth Century, (*Joshua Sylvester*,) by CHAS. DUNSTER, M.A. 12mo, *cloth*. 2s. 6d. (*original price 5s.*)

MILTON.—A Sheaf of Gleanings, after his Biographers and Annotators. By the Rev. JOSEPH HUNTER. Post 8vo, *sewed*. 2s. 6d.

LIFE, PROGRESSES, and REBELLION of JAMES, DUKE OF MONMOUTH, etc. to his Capture and Execution, with a full account of the Bloody Assize, and copious Biographical Notices, by GEORGE ROBERTS, 2 vols. post 8vo, *plates and cuts, new, extra cloth*. 9s. (*original price £1. 4s.*)

Two very interesting volumes, particularly so to those connected with the West of England.

SHAKESPERIANA, a Catalogue of the Early Editions of Shakespeare's Plays, and of the Commentaries and other Publications illustrative of his Works. By J. O. HALLIWELL. 8vo, *cloth*. 3s

"Indispensable to everybody who wishes to carry on any inquiries connected with Shakespeare, or who may have a fancy for Shakesperian Bibliography"—*Spectator*.

MORLAND.—Account of the Life, Writings, and Inventions of Sir Samuel Morland, Master of Mechanics to Charles II. By J. O. HALLIWELL. 8vo, *sewed.* 1s.

COLLECTION OF LETTERS on Scientific Subjects, illustrative of the Progress of Science in England. Temp. Elizabeth to Charles II. Edited by J. O. HALLIWELL. 8vo, *cloth.* 3s.

Comprising letters of Digges, Dee, Tycho Brahe, Lower, Harriott, Lydyatt, Sir W. Petty, Sir C. Cavendish, Brancker, Pell, &c.; also the autobiography of Sir Samuel Morland, from a MS. in Lambeth Palace Nat. Tarpoley's Corrector Analyticus, &c. Cost the Subscribers £1.

ST. DUNSTAN.—The Life and Miracles of St. Dunstan. By W. ROBINSON, LL.D. 8vo, *plate.* 1s.

SIDNEY.—Brief Memoir of the Life of the Hon. Algernon Sidney (the Patriot); with his Trial in 1683. By R. C. SIDNEY. *With outline plate from Stephanoff's well known picture.* 8vo, sewed. 1s. 6d.

LOVE LETTERS OF MRS. PIOZZI, *(formerly Mrs. Thrale, the friend of Dr. Johnson,)* written when she was Eighty, to the handsome actor, William Augustus Conway, aged Twenty-seven. 8vo, *sewed.* 2s.

"—— written at three, four, and five o'clock (in the morning) by an Octogenary pen, a heart (as Mrs. Lee says) twenty-six years old, and as H. L. P. feels it to be, *all your own.*"—*Letter V, 3d Feb.* 1820.
"This is one of the most extraordinary collections of love epistles we have ever chanced to meet with, and the well known literary reputation of the lady—the Mrs. Thrale, of Dr. Johnson and Miss Burney

celebrity—considerably enhances their interest. The letters themselves it is not easy to characterise; nor shall we venture to decide whether they more bespeak the drivelling of dotage, or the folly of love; in either case they present human nature to us under a new aspect, and furnish one of those riddles which nothing yet dreamt of in our philosophy can satisfactorily solve."—*Polytechnic Review.*

Philology and Early English Literature.

COMPENDIOUS ANGLO-SAXON AND ENGLISH DICTIONARY. By the Rev. JOSEPH BOSWORTH, D.D., F.R.S., &c. 8vo, *closely printed in treble Columns.* 12s.

——— LARGE PAPER. Royal 8vo. *(to match the next article),* cloth, £1.

"This is not a mere abridgment of the large Dictionary, but almost an entirely new work. In this compendious one will be found, at a very moderate price, all that is most practical and valuable in the former expensive edition, with a great accession of new words and matter."—*Author's Preface.*

ON THE ORIGIN OF THE ENGLISH, Germanic, and Scandinavian Languages and Nations, with Chronological Specimens of their Languages. By J. BOSWORTH, D.D. Royal 8vo, *bds.* £1.

A new and enlarged edition of what was formerly the Preface to the First Edition of the Anglo-Saxon Dictionary, and now published separately.

ANGLO-SAXON DELECTUS; serving as a first Class-Book to the Language. By the Rev. W. BARNES, B.D., of St. John's Coll. Camb. 12mo, *cloth,* 2s. 6d.

"To those who wish to possess a critical knowledge of their own Native English, some acquaintance with Anglo-Saxon is indispensable; and we have never seen an introduction better calculated than the present to supply the wants of a beginner in a short space of time. The declensions and conjugations are well stated, and illustrated by references to Greek, the Latin, French, and other languages. A philosophical spirit pervades every part. The Delectus consists of short pieces on various subjects, with extracts from Anglo-Saxon History and the Saxon Chronicle. There is a good Glossary at the end."—*Athenæum, Oct.* 20, 1549.

GUIDE TO THE ANGLO-SAXON TONGUE : on the Basis of Professor Rask's Grammar ; to which are added, Reading Lessons in Verse and Prose, with Notes for the use of Learners. By E. J. VERNON, B.A., Oxon. 12mo, *cloth,* 5s. 6d.

"The author of this Guide seems to have made one step in the right direction, by compiling what may be pronounced the best work on the subject hitherto published in England."—*Athenæum.*
"Mr. Vernon has, we think, acted wisely in taking Rask for his Model ; but let no one suppose from the title that the book is merely a compilation from the work of that philologist. The accidence is abridged from Rask, with constant revision, correction, and modification; but the syntax, a most important portion of the book, is original, and is compiled with great care and skill; and the latter half of the volume consists of a well-chosen selection of extracts from Anglo-Saxon writers, in prose and verse, for the practice of the student, who will find great assistance in reading them from the grammatical notes with they are accompanied, and from the glossary which follows them. This volume, well studied, will enable any one to read with ease the generality of Anglo-Saxon writers; and its cheapness places it within the reach of every class. It has our hearty recommendation."—*Literary Gazette.*

ANALECTA ANGLO-SAXONICA.—Selections, in Prose and Verse, from Anglo-Saxon Literature, with an Introductory Ethnological Essay, and Notes, Critical and Explanatory. By LOUIS F. KLIPSTEIN, of the University of Giessen. 2 thick vols, post 8vo, *cloth.* 12s. (*original price* 18s.)

Containing an immense body of information on a language which is now becoming more fully appreciated, and which contains fifteen-twentieths of what we daily think, and speak, and write. No Englishman, therefore, altogether ignorant of Anglo-Saxon, can have a thorough knowledge of his own mother-tongue; while the language itself, to say nothing of the many valuable and interesting works preserved in it, may, in copiousness of words, strength of expression, and grammatical precision, vie with the modern German.

INTRODUCTION TO ANGLO-SAXON READING; comprising Ælfric's Homily on the Birthday of St. Gregory, with a copious Glossary, &c. By L. LANGLEY, F.L.S. 12mo, *cloth,* 2s. 6d.

Ælfric's Homily is remarkable for beauty of composition, and interesting as setting forth Augustine's mission to the "Land of the Angles."

ANGLO-SAXON VERSION OF THE LIFE OF ST. GUTHLAC, Hermit of Croyland. Printed, for the first time, from a MS. in the Cottonian Library, with a Translation and Notes. By CHARLES WYCLIFFE GOODWIN, M.A., Fellow of Catharine Hall, Cambridge. 12mo, *cloth,* 5s.

ANGLO-SAXON LEGENDS OF ST. ANDREW AND ST. VERONICA, now first printed, with English translations on the opposite page. By C. W. GOODWIN, M.A. 8vo, *sewed.* 2s. 6d.

ANGLO-SAXON VERSION OF THE HEXAMERON OF ST. BASIL, and the Anglo-Saxon Remains of St. Basil's Admonitio ad Filium Spiritualem ; now first printed from MSS. in the Bodleian Library, with a Translation and Notes. By the Rev. H. W. NORMAN. 8vo, SECOND EDITION, *enlarged, sewed.* 4s.

ANGLO-SAXON VERSION OF THE HOLY GOSPELS. Edited from the original MSS. By BENJAMIN THORPE, F.S.A. Post 8vo, *cloth.* 8s. (*original price* 12s.)

ANGLO-SAXON VERSION OF THE STORY OF APOLLO-NIUS OF TYRE;—upon which is founded the Play of Pericles, attributed to Shakespeare ;—from a MS., with a Translation and Glossary. By BENJAMIN THORPE. 12mo, *cloth.* 4s. 6d. (*original price* 6s.)

ANALECTA ANGLO-SAXONICA.—A Selection in Prose and Verse, from Anglo-Saxon Authors of various ages, with a Glossary. By BENJAMIN THORPE, F.S.A. *A new edition, with corrections and improvements.* Post 8vo, *cloth.* 8s. (*original price* 12s.)

POPULAR TREATISES ON SCIENCE, written during the Middle Ages, in Anglo-Saxon, Anglo-Norman, and English. Edited by THOS. WRIGHT, M.A. 8vo, *cloth,* 3s.

Contents:—An Anglo-Saxon Treatise on Astronomy of the TENTH CENTURY, *now first published from a MS. in the British Museum, with a Translation;* Livre des Creatures, by Phillippe de Thaun, *now first printed with a translation,* (*extremely valuable to Philologists, as being the earliest specimens of Anglo-Norman re*maining, *and explanatory of all the symbolical signs in early sculpture and painting); the Bestiary of Phil-*lippe de Thaun, *with a translation;* Fragments on Popular Science from the Early English Metrical Lives of the Saints, (*the earliest piece of the kind in the English Language.*)

FRAGMENT OF ÆLFRIC'S ANGLO-SAXON GRAMMAR, Ælfric's Glossary, and a Poem on the Soul and Body of the XIIth Century, discovered among the Archives of Worcester Cathedral. By Sir THOMAS PHILLIPS, Bart. Fol., PRIVATELY PRINTED, *sewed.* 1s. 6d.

SKELTON'S (John, *Poet Laureat to Henry VIII*) Poetical Works : the Bowge of Court, Colin Clout, Why come ye not to Court? (his celebrated Satire on Wolsey), Phillip Sparrow, Elinour Rumming, &c.; with Notes and Life. By the Rev. A. DYCE. 2 vols, 8vo, *cloth.* 14s. (*original price* £1. 12s.)

"The power, the strangeness, the volubility of his language, the audacity of his satire, and the perfect originality of his manner, made Skelton one of the most extraordinary writers of any age or country."—*Southey.*

"Skelton is a curious, able, and remarkable writer, with strong sense, a vein of humour, and some imagination; he had a wonderful command of the English language, and one who was styled, in his turn, by as great a scholar as ever lived (Erasmus), 'the light and ornament of Britain.' He indulged very freely in his writings in censures on monks and Dominicans; and, moreover, had the hardihood to reflect, in no very mild terms, on the manners and life of Cardinal Wolsey. We cannot help considering Skelton as an ornament of his own time, and a benefactor to those who come after him."

SEMI-SAXON.—The Departing Soul's Address to the Body, a Fragment of a Semi-Saxon Poem, discovered among the Archives of Worcester Cathedral, by Sir THOMAS PHILLIPPS, Bart., with an English Translation by S. W. SINGER. 8vo, *only* 100 PRIVATELY PRINTED. 2s.

DICTIONARY OF ARCHAIC AND PROVINCIAL WORDS, Obsolete Phrases, Proverbs, and Ancient Customs, from the Reign of Edward I. By JAMES ORCHARD HALLIWELL, F.R.S., F.S.A., &c. 2 vols, 8vo, containing upwards of 1000 pages, *closely printed in double columns, cloth, a new and cheaper edition.* £1. 1s.

It contains above 50,000 words (embodying all the known scattered glossaries of the English language), forming a complete key for the reader of our old Poets, Dramatists, Theologians, and other authors, whose works abound with allusions, of which explanations are not to be found in ordinary Dictionaries and books of reference. Most of the principal Archaisms are illustrated by examples selected from early inedited MSS. and rare books, and by far the greater portion will be found to be original authorities.

ESSAYS ON THE LITERATURE, POPULAR SUPERSTI- TIONS, and History of England in the Middle Ages. By THOMAS WRIGHT, M.A., F.R.S. 2 vols. post 8vo, *elegantly printed, cloth.* 16s.

Contents.—Essay I. Anglo-Saxon Poetry. II. Anglo-Norman Poetry. III. Chansons de Geste, or Historical Romances of the Middle Ages. IV. On Proverbs and Popular Sayings. V. On the Anglo-Latin Poets of the Twelfth Century. VI. Abelard and the Scholastic Philosophy. VII. On Dr. Grimm's German Mythology. VIII. On the National Fairy Mythology of England. IX. On the Popular Superstitions of Modern Greece, and their Connexion with the English. X. On Friar Rush, and the Frolicsome Elves. XI. On Dunlop's History of Fiction. XII. On the History and transmission of Popular Stories. XIII. On the Poetry of History. XIV. Adventures of Hereward the Saxon. XV. The Story of Eustace the Monk. XVI. The History of Fulke Fitzwarine. XVII. On the Popular Cycle of Robin-Hood Ballads. XVIII. On the Conquest of Ireland by the Anglo-Normans. XIX. On Old English Political Songs. XX. On the Scottish Poet, Dunbar.

EARLY HISTORY OF FREEMASONRY IN ENGLAND. Illustrated by an English Poem of the XIVth Century, with Notes. By J. O. HALLIWELL, Post 8vo, SECOND EDITION, *with a facsimile of the original MS. in the British Museum, cloth.* 2s. 6d.

"The interest which the curious poem, of which this publication is chiefly composed, has excited, is proved by the fact of its having been translated into German, and of its having reached a second edition, which is not common with such publications. Mr. Halliwell has carefully revised the new edition, and increased its utility by the addition of a complete and correct glossary."—*Literary Gazette.*

TORRENT OF PORTUGAL; an English Metrical Romance, now first published, from an unique MS. of the XVth Century, preserved in the Chetham Library at Manchester. Edited by J. O. HALLIWELL, &c. Post 8vo, *cloth, uniform with Ritson, Weber, and Ellis's publications.* 5s.

"This is a valuable and interesting addition to our list of early English metrical romances, and an indispensable companion to the collections of Ritson, Weber, and Ellis."—*Literary Gazette.*
"A literary curiosity, and one both welcome and serviceable to the lover of black-lettered lore. Though the obsoleteness of the style may occasion sad stumbling to a modern reader, yet the class to which it rightly belongs will value it accordingly; both because it is curious in its details, and possesses philological importance. To the general reader it presents one feature, viz., the reference to Wayland Smith, whom Sir W. Scott has invested with so much interest."—*Metropolitan Magazine.*

HARROWING OF HELL; a Miracle Play, written in the Reign of Edward II, now first published from the Original in the British Museum, with a Modern Reading, Introduction, and Notes. By JAMES ORCHARD HALLIWELL, Esq., F.R.S., F.S.A., &c. 8vo, *sewed.* 2s.

This curious piece is supposed to be the earliest specimen of dramatic composition in the English language; *vide* Hallam's Literature of Europe, Vol. I; Strutt's Manners and Customs, Vol. II; Warton's English Poetry; Sharon Turner's England; Collier's History of English Dramatic Poetry, Vol. II, p. 213. *All these writers refer to the Manuscript.*

NUGÆ POETICA; Select Pieces of Old English Popular Poetry, illustrating the Manners and Arts of the XVth Century. Edited by J. O. HALLIWELL. Post 8vo, *only 100 copies printed, cloth.* 5s.

Contents:—Colyn Blowbol's Testament; the Debate of the Carpenter's Tools; the Merchant and his Son; the Maid and the Magpie; Elegy on Lobe, Henry VIIIth's Fool; Romance of Robert of Sicily; *and five other curious pieces of the same kind*

ANECDOTA LITERARIA: a Collection of Short Poems in English, Latin, and French, illustrative of the Literature and History of England in the XIIIth Century; and more especially of the Condition and Manners of the different Classes of Society. By T. WRIGHT, M.A., F.S.A., &c. 8vo, *cloth, only 250 printed.* 7s. 6d.

POPULAR ERRORS IN ENGLISH GRAMMAR, particularly in Pronunciation, familiarly pointed out. By GEORGE JACKSON. 12mo, THIRD EDITION, *with a coloured frontispiece of the " Sedes Busbeiana."* 6d.

EARLY MYSTERIES, and other Latin Poems of the XIIth and XIIIth centuries. Edited, from original MSS. in the British Museum, and the Libraries of Oxford, Cambridge, Paris, and Vienna, by THOS. WRIGHT, M.A., F.S.A. 8vo, *bds.* 4s. 6d.

"Besides the curious specimens of the dramatic style of Middle-Age Latinity, Mr. Wright has given two compositions in the Narrative Elegiac Verse (a favourite measure at that period), in the Comœdia Babionis and the Geta of Vitalis Blesensis, which form a link of connection between the Classical and Middle-age Literature; some remarkable Satyrical Rhymes on the people of Norfolk, written by a Monk of Peterborough, and answered in the same style by John of St. Omer; and, lastly, some sprightly and often graceful songs from a MS. in the Arundel Collection, which afford a very favourable idea of the lyric poetry of our clerical forefathers."—*Gentleman's Magazine.*

RARA MATHEMATICA; or a Collection of Treatises on the Mathematics and Subjects connected with them, from ancient inedited MSS. By J. O. HALLIWELL. 8vo, SECOND EDITION, *cloth.* 3s.

Contents:—Johannis de Sacro-Bosco Tractatus de Arte Numerandi; Method used in England in the Fifteenth Century for taking the Altitude of a Steeple; Treatise on the Numeration of Algorism; Treatise on Glasses for Optical Purposes, by W. Bourne; Johannis Robyns de Cometis Commentaria; Two Tables showing the time of High Water at London Bridge, and the Duration of Moonlight, from a MS. of the Thirteenth Century; on the Mensuration of Heights and Distances; Alexandri de Villa Dei Carmen de Algorismo; Preface to a Calendar or Almanack for 1430; Johannis Norfolk in Artem progressionis summula; Notes on Early Almanacks, by the Editor, &c. &c.

PHILOLOGICAL PROOFS of the Original Unity and Recent Origin of the Human Race, derived from a Comparison of the Languages of Europe, Asia, Africa, and America. By A. J. JOHNES. 8vo, *cloth.* 6s. (original price 12s. 6d.)

Printed at the suggestion of Dr. Prichard, to whose works it will be found a useful supplement.

AMERICANISMS.—A Dictionary of Americanisms. A Glossary of Words and Phrases colloquially used in the United States. By J. R. BARTLETT. Thick 8vo, *cloth.* 12s.

PHILOLOGICAL GRAMMAR, founded upon English, and framed from a comparison of more than Sixty Languages, being an Introduction to the Science of Grammar, and a help to Grammars of all Languages, especially English, Latin, and Greek. By the Rev. W. BARNES, B.D., author of the "Anglo-Saxon Delectus," "Dorset Dialect," &c. Post 8vo, *in the press.*

Provincial Dialects of England.

BIBLIOGRAPHICAL LIST of all the Works which have been published towards illustrating the Provincial Dialects of England. By JOHN RUSSELL SMITH. Post 8vo. 1s.

"Very serviceable to such as prosecute the study of our provincial dialects, or are collecting works on that curious subject. We very cordially recommend it to notice."—*Metropolitan.*

HALLIWELL'S HISTORICAL SKETCH OF THE PROVINCIAL DIALECTS OF ENGLAND. Illustrated by numerous Examples, (*extracted from the Introduction to the Dictionary of Archaic and Provincial Words.*) 8vo. 2s.

GLOSSARY OF PROVINCIAL AND LOCAL WORDS USED IN ENGLAND; by F. GROSE, F.S.A.; with which is now incorporated the SUPPLEMENT, by SAMUEL PEGGE, F.S.A. Post 8vo, *cloth.* 4s. 6d.

The utility of a Provincial Glossary to all persons desirous of understanding our ancient poets, is so universally acknowledged, that to enter into a proof of it would be entirely a work of supererogation. Grose and Pegge are constantly referred to in Todd's "Johnson's Dictionary."

CORNWALL.—Specimens of Cornish Provincial Dialect, collected and arranged by UNCLE JAN TREENOODLE, with some Introductory Remarks and a Glossary by an Antiquarian Friend, also a Selection of Songs and other Pieces connected with Cornwall. Post 8vo. *With curious portrait of Dolly Pentreath. Cloth.* 4s.

CHESHIRE.—Attempt at a Glossary of some words used in Cheshire. By ROGER WILBRAHAM, F.A.S., &c. 12mo, *bds.* 2s. 6d. (original price 5s.)

DEVONSHIRE.—A Devonshire Dialogue in Four Parts, (*by Mrs.* PALMER, *sister to Sir Joshua Reynolds,*) with Glossary by the Rev. J. PHILLIPPS, of Membury, Devon. 12mo, *cloth.* 2s. 6d.

DORSET.—Poems of Rural Life, in the Dorset Dialect, with a Dissertation and Glossary. By the Rev. WILLIAM BARNES, B.D. SECOND EDITION, *enlarged and corrected,* royal 12mo, *cloth.* 10s.

A fine poetic feeling is displayed through the various pieces in this volume; according to some critics nothing has appeared equal to it since the time of Burns; the "Gentleman's Magazine" for December, 1844, gave a review of the First Edition some pages in length.

511

DURHAM.—A Glossary of Words used in Teesdale, in the County of Durham. Post 8vo, *with a Map of the District, cloth.* 6s.

"Contains about two thousand words ... It is believed the first and only collection of words and phrases peculiar to this district, and we hail it therefore as a valuable contribution to the history of language and literature ... the author has evidently brought to bear an extensive personal acquaintance with the common language." — *Darlington Times.*

ESSEX.—John Noakes and Mary Styles: a Poem; exhibiting some of the most striking lingual localisms peculiar to Essex; with a Glossary. By CHARLES CLARK, Esq., of Great Totham Hall, Essex. Post 8vo, *cloth.* 2s.

"The poem possesses considerable humour.—*Tait's Magazine.*
"A very pleasant trifle "—*Literary Gazette.*
"A very clever production."—*Essex Lit. Journal.*
"Full of rich humour."—*Essex Mercury.*
"Very droll."—*Metropolitan.*

"Exhibits the dialect of Essex perfectly."—*Eclectic Review.*
"Full of quaint wit and humour." — *Gent.'s Mag.,* May, 1841.
"A very clever and amusing piece of local description."—*Archæologist.*

KENT.—Dick and Sal, or Jack and Joan's Fair: a Doggrel Poem, in the Kentish Dialect. Third Edition. 12mo. 6d.

LANCASHIRE.—Dialect of South Lancashire, or Tim Bobbin's Tummus and Meary; revised and corrected, with his Rhymes, and AN ENLARGED GLOSSARY of Words and Phrases, chiefly used by the rural population of the manufacturing Districts of South Lancashire. By SAMUEL BAMFORD. 12mo, *cloth.* 3s. 6d.

LEICESTERSHIRE Words, Phrases, and Proverbs. By A. B. EVANS, D.D., *Head Master of Market-Bosworth Grammar School.* 12mo, *cloth.* 5s.

NORTHAMPTONSHIRE.—The Dialect and Folk-Lore of Northamptonshire: a Glossary of Northamptonshire Provincialisms, Collection of Fairy Legends, Popular Superstitions, Ancient Customs, Proverbs, &c. By THOMAS STERNBERG. 12mo, *cloth.* 5s.

SUSSEX.—A Glossary of the Provincialisms of the County of Sussex. By W. DURRANT COOPER, F.S.A. Post 8vo, SECOND EDITION, ENLARGED, *cloth.* 5s.

SUSSEX.—Jan Cladpole's Trip to 'Merricur in Search for Dollar Trees, and how he got rich enough to beg his way home! Written in Sussex Doggerel. 12mo. 6d.

WESTMORELAND AND CUMBERLAND.—Dialogues, Poems, Songs, and Ballads, by various Writers, in the Westmoreland and Cumberland Dialects, now first collected; to which is added, a copious Glossary of Words peculiar to those Counties. Post 8vo, pp. 408, *cloth.* 9s.

This collection comprises, in the *Westmoreland Dialect,* Mrs. Ann Wheeler's Four Familiar Dialogues, with Poems, &c.; and in the *Cumberland Dialect,* I. Poems and Pastorals by the Rev. Josiah Ralph; II. Pastorals, &c., by Ewan Clark; III. Letters from Dublin, by a young Borrowdale Shepherd, by Isaac Ritson; IV. Poems by John Stagg; V. Poems by Mark Lonsdale; VI. Ballads and Songs by Robert Anderson, the Cumbrian Bard (including *some now first printed*); VII. Songs by Miss Blamire and Miss Gilpin; VIII. Songs by John Rayson, IX. An Extensive Glossary of Westmoreland and Cumberland Words.

All the poetical quotations in "Mr. and Mrs. Sandboy's Visit to the Great Exhibition," are to be found in this volume.

WILTSHIRE.—A Glossary of Provincial Words and Phrases in use in Wiltshire, showing their Derivation in numerous instances from the Language of the Anglo-Saxons. By JOHN YONGE AKERMAN, Esq., F.S.A. 12mo, *cloth.* 3s.

YORKSHIRE.—The Yorkshire Dialect, exemplified in various Dialogues, Tales, and Songs, applicable to the County; with a Glossary. Post 8vo. 1s.

"A shilling book worth its money; most of the pieces of composition are not only harmless, but good and pretty. The eclogue on the death of 'Awd Daisy,' an outworn horse, is an outpouring of some of the best feelings of the rustic mind; and the addresses to Riches and Poverty have much of the freedom and spirit of Burns." — *Gentleman's Magazine, May* 1841.

YORKSHIRE.—The Hallamshire (*district of Sheffield*) Glossary. By the Rev. JOSEPH HUNTER, author of the History of "Hallamshire," "South Yorkshire," &c. Post 8vo, *cloth.* 4s. (original price 8s.)

YORKSHIRE.—Bairnsla Foak's Annual, on onny body els as beside fort 'y years 1842 and 1843, be TOM TREDDLEHOYLE; to which is added the Barnsley and Village Record, or the Book of Facts and Fancies, by NED NUT. 12mo, pp. 100. 1s.

YORKSHIRE.—Sum Thowts abaght Ben Bunt's Weddin;—Tom Treddlehoyle's Thowts abaght Nan Bunt's Chrcsmas Tea Party, &c. Two Pieces, (*Barnsley Dialect.*) 12mo. 6d.

Archaeology.

ARCHÆOLOGICAL INDEX to Remains of Antiquity of the Celtic, Romano-British, and Anglo-Saxon Periods, by JOHN YONGE AKERMAN, *Fellow and Secretary of the Society of Antiquaries.* 8vo, *illustrated with numerous engravings, comprising upwards of five hundred objects, cloth.* 15s.

This work, though intended as an introduction and a guide to the study of our early antiquities, will, it is hoped, also prove of service as a book of reference to the practised Archæologist. The contents are as follows:

PART I. CELTIC PERIOD. — Tumuli, or Barrows and Cairns—Cromlechs—Sepulchral Caves—Rocking Stones—Stone Circles, &c. &c.—Objects discovered in Celtic Sepulchres—Urns—Beads—Weapons—Implements, &c.

PART II. ROMANO-BRITISH PERIOD.—Tumuli of the Romano-British Period—Burial places of the Romans — Pavements — Camps — Villas — Sepulchral Monuments—Sepulchral Inscriptions—Dedicatory Inscriptions—Commemorative Inscriptions — Altars — Urns — Glass Vessels — Fibulæ — Armillæ — Coins—Coin-moulds, &c. &c.

PART III. ANGLO-SAXON PERIOD.—Tumuli —Detailed List of Objects discovered in Anglo-Saxon Barrows—Urns—Swords—Spears—Knives—Umbones of Shields — Buckles — Fibulæ — Bullæ — Hair Pins — Beads, &c. &c. &c. &c.

The ITINERARY of ANTONINUS (as far as relates to Britain). The Geographical Tables of PTOLEMY, the NOTITIA, and the ITINERARY of RICHARD of CIRENCESTER, together with a classified Index of the contents of the ARCHÆOLOGIA (Vols. i to xxxi) are given in an Appendix.

"One of the first wants of an incipient Antiquary, is the facility of comparison, and here it is furnished him at one glance. The plates, indeed, form the most valuable part of the book, both by their number and the judicious selection of types and examples which they contain. It is a book which we can, on this account, safely and warmly recommend to all who are interested in the antiquities of their native land."—*Literary Gazette.*

REMAINS OF PAGAN SAXONDOM, principally from Tumuli in England, drawn from the originals. Described and Illustrated by J. Y. AKERMAN, F.S.A. 4to, PUBLISHING IN PARTS at 2s. 6d. each.

DIRECTIONS FOR THE PRESERVATION OF ENGLISH ANTIQUITIES, especially those of the Three First Periods; or Hints for the Inexperienced. By J. Y. AKERMAN.

A small tract for distribution, at one shilling per dozen, useful to give to excavators, ploughmen, &c., who are apt to destroy articles they find if not of precious metal.

ARCHÆOLOGICAL ASSOCIATION JOURNAL. 8vo, vols. 2, 3, 4, 5, 6. £1. 1s. each; and vol. 7 *just completed, with an extra quantity of letter-press and plates.* £1. 11s. 6d.

J. R. Smith having been appointed Publisher to the Archæological Association, their Publications may be had of him in future.

BRITISH ARCHÆOLOGICAL ASSOCIATION.—A Report of the Proceedings of the British Archæological Association, at the Worcester Session, August, 1848. By A. J. DUNKIN. Thick 8vo, *with engravings, cloth.* £1. 1s.

VERBATIM REPORT of the Proceedings at a Special General Meeting of the British Archæological Association, held at the Theatre of the Western Literary Institution, 5th March, 1845, T. J. Pettigrew, Esq., in the Chair. With an Introduction by THOMAS WRIGHT. 8vo, sewed. 1s. 6d.

A succinct history of the division between the Archæological Association and Institute.

ANTIQUARIAN ETCHING CLUB.—The Publications of the Antiquarian Etching Club, for the year 1849, *consisting of 54 plates of Churches, Fonts, Castles, and other Antiquarian objects.* 4to, *boards.* 8s.

———— for the year 1850, *containing 66 plates.* 4to, *bds.* 10s.

———— for the year 1851, *containing 70 plates.* 4to, *bds.* 10s.

VESTIGES OF THE ANTIQUITIES OF DERBYSHIRE, and the Sepulchral Usages of its Inhabitants, from the most Remote Ages to the Reformation. By THOMAS BATEMAN, Esq., of Yolgrave, Derbyshire. *In one handsome vol.* 8vo, *with numerous woodcuts of Tumuli and their contents, Crosses, Tombs, &c., cloth.* 15s. 1848

AN ESSAY ON THE ROMAN VILLAS of the Augustan Age, their Architectural Disposition and Enrichments, and on the remains of Roman Domestic Edifices discovered in Great Britain. By THOMAS MOULE. 8vo, 2 *plates, cloth.* 1s. 6d. (*original price 8s.*)

RELIQUIÆ ANTIQUIÆ EBORACENSIS, or Relics of Antiquity, relat. ing to the County of York. By W. BOWMAN, of Leeds, assisted by several eminent Antiquaries, 4to, *with engravings, publishing in Quarterly Parts.* 2s. 6d. each.

THE ROMAN WALL: an Historical, Topographical, and Descriptive Account of the Barrier of the Lower Isthmus, extending from the Tyne to the Solway, deduced from numerous personal surveys. By the Rev. JOHN COLLINGWOOD BRUCE, F.S.A., Thick 8vo, SECOND AND ENLARGED EDITION, *with* 40 *plates and* 200 *woodcuts, a hand some volume, half morocco.* £1. 1s.—A few Copies on LARGE PAPER, 4to, £2. 2s.

" Following the impulse of a fresh interest in remains of the Roman age, recently excited amongst English Archæologists, Mr. Bruce has now supplied a desideratum in Antiquarian literature, by producing a Treatise, in which he has happily combined much of the information gathered by previous writers, with a mass of original and personal observations."—*Journal of the Archæological Institute,* Vol viii, p. 105.

"The Roman Wall is a very elaborate and painstaking work, one of the most interesting of British antiquities. Mr. Bruce is a man of learning, whether as regards Roman history, in connection with Britain,

or the works of Archæologists upon our Roman re mains, especially those which relate to his immediate subject."—*Spectator.*

" In taking leave of Mr. Bruce's work, we may express a hope that our brief notice of some of its attractions may promote its circulation. The author's style renders it highly readable, the facts he has collected will make it useful for reference, and its portability, and the clear arrangement of the subject-matter, should introduce it as a companion to all who may desire to study fully one of the noblest monuments of our country."—*Gentleman's Magazine.*

RELIQUIÆ ISURIANÆ: the Remains of the Roman Isurium, now Aldborough, near Boroughbridge, Yorkshire, illustrated and described. By HENRY ECROYD SMITH. Royal 4to, *with* 37 *plates, cloth.* £1. 5s.

——— The Same, WITH THE MOSAIC PAVEMENTS COLOURED, *cloth.* £2. 2s.
The most highly illustrated work ever published on a Roman Station in England.

DESCRIPTION OF A ROMAN BUILDING, and other Remains, discovered at CAERLEON, in Monmouthshire. By J. E. LEE. Imperial 8vo, *with* 20 *interesting Etchings by the Author, sewed.* 5s.

NOTITIA BRITANNIÆ, or an Inquiry concerning the Localities, Habits, Condition, and Progressive Civilization of the Aborigines of Britain; to which is appended a brief Retrospect of the Results of their Intercourse with the Romans. By W. D. SAULL, F.S.A., F.G.S., &c. 8vo, *engravings.* 3s. 6d.

ARCHÆOLOGIST AND JOURNAL OF ANTIQUARIAN SCIENCE. Edited by J. O. HALLIWELL. 8vo, Nos. I to X, COMPLETE, with Index, pp. 420, *with* 19 *engravings, cloth, reduced from* 10s. 6d. to 5s. 6d.

Containing original articles on Architecture, Historical Literature, Round Towers of Ireland, Philology, Bibliography, Topography, Proceedings of the

various Antiquarian Societies, Retrospective Reviews, and Reviews of recent Antiquarian Works &c.

Numismatics.

INTRODUCTION TO THE STUDY OF ANCIENT AND MODERN COINS. By J. Y. AKERMAN, *Secretary of the Society of Antiquaries.* Foolscap 8vo, *with numerous Wood Engravings from the original coins,* (an excellent introductory book,) *cloth.* 6s. 6d.

CONTENTS: SECT. 1.—Origin of Coinage.—Greek Regal Coins. 2. Greek Civic Coins. 3. Greek Imperial Coins. 4. Origin of Roman Coinage—Consular Coins. 5. Roman Imperial Coins. 6. Roman British Coins. 7. Ancient British Coinage. 8. Anglo-Saxon Coinage. 9. English Coinage from the Conquest. 10.

Scotch Coinage. 11 Coinage of Ireland. 12. Anglo Gallic Coins. 13. Continental Money in the Middle Ages. 14. Various representatives of Coinage. 15. Forgeries in Ancient and Modern Times. 16. Table of Prices of English Coins realized at Public Sales.

TRADESMEN'S TOKENS struck in London and its Vicinity, from 1648 to 1671, described from the originals in the British Museum, &c. By J. Y. AKERMAN, F.S.A. 8vo, *with* 8 *plates of numerous examples, cloth.* 15s.—LARGE PAPER, in 4to, *cloth.* £1. 1s.

This work comprises a list of nearly three thousand Tokens, and contains occasional illustrative topographical and antiquarian notes on persons, places,

streets, old tavern and coffee-house signs, &c. &c. with an introductory account of the causes which led to the adoption of such a currency.

ANCIENT COINS OF CITIES AND PRINCES, Geographically Arranged and Described, HISPANIA, GALLIA, BRITANNIA. By J. Y. AKERMAN, F.S.A. 8vo, *with engravings of many hundred coins from actual examples, cloth,* 18s.

514

COINS OF THE ROMANS RELATING TO BRITAIN, Described and Illustrated. By J. Y. AKERMAN, F.S.A. SECOND EDITION, greatly enlarged, 8vo, *with plates and woodcuts.* 10s. 6d.

The "Prix de Numismatique" was awarded by the French Institute to the author for this work. "Mr. Akerman's volume contains a notice of every known variety, with copious illustrations, and is published at a very moderate price; it should be consulted, not merely for these particular coins, but also for facts most valuable to all who are interested in the Romano-British History."—*Archæological Journal.*

NUMISMATIC ILLUSTRATIONS of the Narrative Portions of the NEW TESTAMENT. By J. Y. AKERMAN. 8vo, *numerous woodcuts from the original coins in various public and private collections, cloth.* 5s.

"Archæology is under a peculiar obligation to Mr. Akerman. To him more than to any other living man, is due the praise of having converted multitudes to the love of antiquarian research. To him we all owe the pleasant debt of an instructive acquaintance, not only with the beautiful money of Ancient Greece and Rome, but with the once barbarous, though not less interesting, coins of our earliest history. And to him now especially, the cause of religion can bring its tribute of commendation for light thrown upon Holy Writ, through the medium of "the unrighteous Mammon." The New Testament has, it appears, in the compass of the Gospels and Acts, no less than 32 allusions to the coinage of Greece, Rome, and Judæa; and these beautifully engraved, and learnedly described, give Mr. Akerman an opportunity of serving the good cause of truth in the way of his peculiar avocation."—*Church of England Journal.*

NUMISMATIC CHRONICLE AND JOURNAL OF THE NUMISMATIC SOCIETY. Edited by J. Y. AKERMAN. Published Quarterly at 3s. 6d. per Number.

This is the only repertory of Numismatic intelligence ever published in England. It contains papers on coins and medals, of all ages and countries, by the first Numismatists of the day, both English and Foreign. Odd parts to complete sets.

LIST OF TOKENS ISSUED BY WILTSHIRE TRADESMEN, in the Seventeenth Century. By J. Y. AKERMAN. 8vo, *plates, sewed.* 1s. 6d.

LECTURES ON THE COINAGE OF THE GREEKS AND ROMANS, Delivered in the University of Oxford. By EDWARD CARDWELL, D.D., Principal of St. Alban's Hall, and Professor of Ancient History. 8vo, *cloth.* 4s. (*original price* 8s. 6d.)

A very interesting historical volume, and written in a pleasing and popular manner.

AN OLLA PODRIDA, or Scraps Numismatic, Antiquarian, and Literary. By RICHARD SAINTHILL, Esq., of Cork. Royal 8vo, *many plates and portraits, a handsome volume,* PRIVATELY PRINTED, *cloth.* £1. 11s. 6d.

Containing Letters on the coinage of 1816; Memoir of Thomas Wyon jun.; on the Coronation and Guildhall Medals; Russian Medals; Coins found at Beaworth; Short and Long-Cross Pennies of Henry VII; Dublin Groats; Three Crowns, the ancient Arms of Ireland; Coins of the Mint of Exeter; Coins of Henry III; Saxon and Anglo-Norman Coins; attempt to locate Coins unappropriated by Ruding; and other papers on Coins and Topographical and Genealogical subjects.

OBSERVATIONS ON A UNIQUE CUFIC GOLD COIN of the Fatimite Dynasty. By L. LOEWE. 8vo, *engraving, sewed.* 1s.

HAND-BOOK OF ENGLISH COINS, from the Conquest to Victoria. By L. JEWITT. 12mo, 11 *plates, cloth.* 1s.

HISTORY OF THE COINS OF CUNOBELINE and of the ANCIENT BRITONS. By the Rev. BEALE POSTE. 8vo, *with numerous plates and woodcuts, cloth. In the Press.*

Topography.

JOURNEY TO BERESFORD HALL, IN DERBYSHIRE, the Seat of CHARLES COTTON, Esq., the celebrated Author and Angler. By W. ALEXANDER, F.S.A., F.L.S., late Keeper of the Prints in the British Museum, Crown 4to, *printed on tinted paper, with a spirited frontispiece, representing Walton and his adopted Son Cotton in the Fishing-house, and vignette title page, cloth.* 6s.

Dedicated to the Anglers of Great Britain and the various Walton and Cotton Clubs; only 100 printed.

GRAPHIC AND HISTORICAL SKETCH of the Antiquities of Totnes, Devon. By W. COTTON, F.S.A. Small 4to, *fine woodcuts, cloth.* 6s. (*original price* 10s. 6d.)

CAMBRIDGE.—Historia Collegii Jesu Cantabrigiensis à J. SHERMANNO, olim præs. ejusdem Collegii. Edita J. O. HALLIWELL. 8vo, *cloth.* 2s.

HISTORY AND ANTIQUITIES of the County of Hereford. By the Rev. JOHN DUNCOMB. 2 vols, 4to, *portraits and plates, bds.* £1. 4s. (*original price* £5. 5s.)

HELPS TO HEREFORD HISTORY, Civil and Legendary, in an Ancient Account of the Ancient-Cordwainers' Company of the City, the Mordiford Dragon, and other Subjects. By J. D. DEVLIN. 12mo, *cloth* (*a curious volume*). 3s. 6d.
" A series of very clever papers."—*Spectator.*
" A little work full of Antiquarian information, presented in a pleasing and popular form."—*Nonconformist.*

HISTORY OF PORTSMOUTH, PORTSEA, LANDPORT, SOUTHSEA, and GOSPORT. By HENRY SLIGHT, Esq. 8vo, Third Edition, *sbd.* 4s.

NOTES ON THE CHURCHES in the Counties of KENT, SUSSEX, and SURREY, mentioned in Domesday Book, and those of more recent date, with some Account of the Sepulchral Memorials and other Antiquities. By the Rev. ARTHUR HUSSEY. Thick 8vo, FINE PLATES, *cloth.* 18s.

KENTISH CUSTOMS.—Consuetudines Kanciæ. A History of GAVELKIND, and other Remarkable Customs, in the County of KENT. By CHARLES SANDYS, Esq., F.S.A. (*Cantianus*). *Illustrated with facimilies, a very handsome volume, cloth.* 15s.

HISTORY AND ANTIQUITIES OF RICHBOROUGH, RECULVER, AND LYMNE, in Kent. By C. R. ROACH SMITH, Esq., F.S.A., Small 4to, *with many engravings on wood and copper,* by F. W. FAIRHOLT, *cloth.* £1. 1s.
" No antiquarian volume could display a trio of names more zealous, successful, and intelligent, on the subject of Romano-British remains, than the three here represented—Roach Smith, the ardent explorer; Fairholt, the excellent illustrator; and Rolfe, the indefatigable collector."—*Literary Gazette.*

HISTORY AND ANTIQUITIES OF DARTFORD, in Kent with incidental Notices of Places in its Neighbourhood. By J. DUNKIN, Author of the " History of the Hundreds of Bullington and Ploughley, in Oxfordshire;" " History of Bicester;" " History of Bromley," &c. 8vo, 17 *plates, cloth. Only* 150 *printed.* 21s.

HISTORY OF THE TOWN OF GRAVESEND, in Kent, and of the Port of London. By R. P. CRUDEN, late Mayor of Gravesend. Royal 8vo, 37 *fine plates and woodcuts, a very handsome volume, cloth.* 10s. (*original price* £1. 8s.)

ACCOUNT OF THE ROMAN AND OTHER ANTIQUITIES discovered at Springhead, near Gravesend, Kent. By A. J. DUNKIN. 8vo, *plates,* (*only* 100 *printed,*) *cloth.* 6s. 6d.

HISTORY OF ROMNEY MARSH, in Kent, from the time of the Romans to 1833, with a Dissertation on the original Site of the Ancient Anderida. By W. HOLLOWAY, Esq., author of the "History of Rye." 8vo, *with Maps and plates, cloth.* 12s.

CRITICAL DISSERTATION on Professor Willis's " Architectural History of Canterbury Cathedral." By C. SANDYS, of Canterbury. 8vo. 2s. 6d.
" Written in no quarrelsome or captious spirit; the highest compliment is paid to Professor Willis, where it is due. But the author has made out a clear case, in some very important instances, of inaccuracies that have led the learned Professor into the construction of serious errors throughout. It may be considered as an indispensable companion to his volume, containing a great deal of extra information of a very curious kind."—*Art-Union.*

FOLKESTONE FIERY SERPENT, together with the Humours of the Dover MAYOR; being an Ancient Ballad, full of Mystery and pleasant Conceit, now first collected and printed from the various MS. copies in possession of the inhabitants of the South-east coast of Kent; with Notes. 12mo. 1s.

HAND-BOOK OF LEICESTER. By JAMES THOMPSON. 12mo, Second Edition, *woodcuts, bds.* 2s.

HISTORY AND ANTIQUITIES OF THE ISLE OF AXHOLME, in Lincolnshire. By the Venerable ARCHDEACON STONEHOUSE. Thick 4to, FINE PLATES 18s. (*original price* £3. 3s.)

HISTORY AND ANTIQUITIES OF GAINSBOROUGH, in Lincolnshire. By ADAM STARK. Thick 8vo, SECOND EDITION, GREATLY ENLARGED, *cloth.* 9s. *(original price £1. 1s.)*—LARGE PAPER, royal 8vo, *cloth.* 14s.

HISTORY AND ANTIQUITIES OF THE TOWN OF LANCASTER. Compiled from Authentic Sources. By the Rev. ROBERT SIMPSON. 8vo, *cloth.* 8s.

MEMORIALS OF THE VICARAGE HOUSE AND GARDEN OF ALL SAINTS, King's-Lynn; with a List of the Vicars, and a quantity of other useful information. By J. N. CHADWICK. 8vo, *four engravings, sewed.* 2s. 6d.

DESCRIPTIVE ACCOUNT OF THE RUINS OF LIVEDEN, near Oundle, Northamptonshire; with Historical Notices of the Family of Tresham, and its connection with the Gunpowder Plot. By THOMAS BELL. *Four plates and Tresham Pedigree.* 4to. 6s.

REPRINTS OF RARE TRACTS, and Imprints of Ancient Manuscripts, &c., chiefly illustrative of the History and Biography of the Northern Counties. BEAUTIFULLY PRINTED *on thick paper, with facsimile titles, initial letters in colours, &c.,* FORMING 7 VOLS., post 8vo, COMPLETE, *with general titles and contents, bds.* £5. 5s. *(original price £7. 7s.)*

This Collection comprises no less than 62 Tracts of the most interesting kind, edited by M. A. Richardson, assisted by several antiquaries in the northern counties. Only 100 copies of the Collection were printed, which are all sold by the printer.

RIVER TYNE.—Plea and Defence of the Mayor and Burgesses of Newcastle against the Malevolent accusations of Gardiner, (author of "England's Grievance on the Coal Trade,") 1653; with Appendix of Unpublished Documents respecting the River Tyne. By M. A. RICHARDSON. 8vo, *(only 150 printed.)* 2s.

TOPOGRAPHICAL MEMORANDUMS for the County of Oxford. By Sir GREGORY PAGE TURNER, Bart. 8vo, *bds.* 2s.

NOTICES OF THE HISTORY AND ANTIQUITIES OF ISLIP, Oxon. By J. O. HALLIWELL. 8vo, *(only 50 printed,) sewed.* 1s.

HISTORY OF BANBURY, in Oxfordshire; including Copious Historical and Antiquarian Notices of the Neighbourhood. By ALFRED BEESLEY. Thick 8vo, 684 *closely printed pages, with 60 woodcuts, engraved in the first style of art, by O. Jewett, of Oxford.* 14s. *(original price £1. 5s.)*

"The neighbourhood of Banbury is equally rich in British, Roman, Saxon, Norman, and English Antiquities, of all which Mr. Beesley has given regularly cleared accounts. Banbury holds an important place in the history of the Parliamentary War of the Seventeenth Century, and was the scene of the great Battle of Edgehill, and of the important fight of Cropredy Bridge. Relating to the events of that period, the author has collected a great body of local information of the most interesting kind. By no means the least valuable part of Mr. Beesley's work, is his account of the numerous interesting early churches, which characterize the Banbury district."—*The Archæologist.*

Odd Parts to complete copies, 1s. 6d. instead of 2s. 6d.

HISTORY OF WITNEY, with Notices of the Neighbouring Parishes and Hamlets in Oxfordshire. By the Rev. Dr. GILES, formerly Fellow of C. C., Oxford. 8vo, *plates, cloth, (only 150 printed.)* 6s.

HISTORY OF THE PARISH AND TOWN OF BAMPTON, in Oxfordshire, with the District and Hamlets belonging to it. By the Rev. Dr. GILES. 8vo, *plates,* SECOND EDITION, *cloth.* 7s. 6d.

FAUCONBERGE MEMORIAL.—An Account of Henry Fauconberge, LL.D., of Beccles, in Suffolk, and of the endowment provided by his will to encourage Learning and the Instruction of Youth; with Notes and Incidental Biographical Sketches. By S. W. RIX. Pot 4to, *very nicely got up, with 30 engravings of Old Houses, Seals, Autographs, Arms, &c., bds.* 5s.—LARGE PAPER, 7s. 6d. (VERY FEW COPIES PRINTED.)

Contents.—Fauconberges of Olden Time. II. Fauconberge of Beccles. III. Fauconberge Endowment. IV. Fauconberge and Leman. V. Appendix, Pedigrees, Memoir of Robert Sparrow, Esq. Memoir of Dr. Joseph Arnold (by Dawson Turner, of Yarmouth), Particulars of the Fauconberge Trust Estate, &c. &c.

SUSSEX ARCHÆOLOGICAL COLLECTIONS, illustrating the History and Antiquities of the County, published by the Sussex Archæological Society. 8vo, *plates and woodcuts, cloth.* Vol. I, 10s.; Vol. II, 15s.; Vol. III, 10s.; Vol. IV, 14s.; Vol. V, 14s.

SUSSEX GARLAND; a Collection of Ballads, Sonnets, Tales, Elegies, Songs, Epitaphs, &c., illustrative of the County f Sussex, with Notices, Historical, Biographical and Descriptive. By JAMES TAYLOR, Post 8vo, *Engravings, cloth.* 12s.

SUSSEX MARTYRS: their Examinations and Cruel Burnings in the time of Queen Mary; comprising the interesting Personal Narrative of Richard Woodman, extracted from "Foxe's Monuments;" with Notes. By M. A. LOWER, M.A. 12mo, *sewed.* 1s.

CHURCHES OF SUSSEX, drawn by R. H. NIBBS, with Descriptions. 84 *plates, 4to, a handsome volume, cloth.* £2. 2s.

HISTORY AND ANTIQUITIES OF THE ANCIENT PORT AND TOWN OF RYE, in Sussex, compiled from Original Documents. By WILLIAM HOLLOWAY, Esq. Thick 8vo, (ONLY 200 PRINTED,) *cloth.* £1. 1s.

HISTORY OF WINCHELSEA, in Sussex. By W. DURRANT COOPER, F.S.A. 8vo. *fine plates and woodcuts.* 7s. 6d.

CHRONICLE OF BATTEL ABBEY, in Sussex; originally compiled in Latin by a Monk of the Establishment, and now first translated, with Notes, and an Abstract of the subsequent History of the Abbey. By MARK ANTONY LOWER, M.A. 8vo, *with illustrations, cloth.* 9s.

"It will be found to contain a real and living picture of the manners and customs, the modes of thought and speech prevalent in the times of which it is the record. Mr. Lower has well discharged his office of translator and editor."—*Guardian.*

"In no respect less interesting than Jocelin de Brakelond's famous Chronicle of Bury St. Edmund's Abbey."—*Lit. Gaz.*

"Mr. Lower has added to the completeness of the book by a summary sketch of the History of the Abbey, and its succession of Abbots from the time when the Chronicle terminates to the period of the dissolution. Various intelligent notes, as well as the general style of the translation, are highly creditable to his care and skill as editor."—*Gentleman's Magazine.*

DESCRIPTIVE CATALOGUE OF THE ORIGINAL CHARTERS, GRANTS, DONATIONS, &c., constituting the Muniments of Battel Abbey, also the Papers of the Montagus, Sidneys, and Websters, embodying many highly interesting and valuable Records of Lands in Sussex, Kent, and Essex, with Preliminary Memoranda of the Abbey of Battel, and Historical Particulars of the Abbots. 8vo, 234 PAGES, *cloth.* ONLY 1s. 6d.

HAND-BOOK TO LEWES, in Sussex, Historical and Descriptive; with Notices of the Recent Discoveries at the Priory. By MARK ANTONY LOWER. 12mo, *many engravings, cloth.* 1s. 6d.

CHRONICLES OF PEVENSEY, in Sussex. By M. A. LOWER, 12mo, *woodcuts.* 1s.

HURSTMONCEUX CASTLE AND ITS LORDS. By the Rev. E. VENABLES. (Reprinted foom Vol. IV of the Sussex Archæological Collections.) 8vo, *many engravings, sewed,* 3s. ; *cloth* 4s.

NOTES ON THE ANTIQUITIES OF TREVES, MAYENCE, WEISBADEN, NEIDERBIEBER, BONN, and COLOGNE. By CHARLES ROACH SMITH, F.S.A. (Reprinted from Vol. II of the "Collectanea Antiqua.") 8vo, *with many engravings.* 7s. 6d.

ANNALS AND LEGENDS OF CALAIS; with Sketches of Emigré Notabilities, and Memoir of Lady Hamilton. By ROBERT BELL CALTON, author of "Rambles in Sweden and Gottland," &c. &c. Post 8vo, *with frontispiece and vignette, cloth.* 5s.

Principal Contents:—History of the Siege by Edward III. in 1346-7, with a Roll of the Commanders and their Followers present, from a contemporary MS. in the British Museum; The Allotment of Lands and Houses to Edward's Barons; Calais as an English Borough; List of the Streets and Householders of the same; Henry VIIIth's Court there; Cardinal Wolsey and his Expenses; the English Pale, with the Names of Roads, Farmsteads, and Villages in the English Era; the Siege of Therouenne and Tournai; the Pier of Calais; Pros and Cons of the Place; the Hôtel Dessin; Sterne's Chamber; Churches of Notre Dame and St. Nicholas; the Hôtel de Ville; Ancient Staple Hall; The Château and Murder of the Duke of Glou-

cester; the Courgain; the Field of the Cloth of Gold; Notice of the Town and Castle of Guisnes, and its surprise by John de Lancaster; the town and Seigneurie of Ardres, the Sands and Duelling; Villages and Château of Sangatte, Coulonge, Mark, Eschalles and Hammes; Review of the English Occupation of Calais; its Re-capture by the Duke de Guise; the lower Town and its Lace Trade; our Commercial Relations with France; Emigré Notabilities; Charles and Harry Tufton, Capt. Dormer and Edith Jacquemont, Beau Brummell, Jemmy Urquhart and his friend Fauntleroy, "Nimrod," Berkeley Craven, Mytton, Duchess of Kingston; a new Memoir of Lady Hamilton, &c. &c.

MONT SAINT-MICHEL.—Histoire et Description de Mont St. Michel en Normandie, texte, par Hericher, dessins par Bouet publiés par Bourdon. Folio, 150 pp., and 13 *beautiful plates, executed in tinted lithography, leather back, uncut.* £2. 2s.
A handsome volume, interesting to the Architect and Archæologist.

GENOA; with Remarks on the Climate, and its Influence upon Invalids. By HENRY JONES BUNNETT, M.D. 12mo, *cloth.* 4s.

Heraldry, Genealogy, and Surnames.

CURIOSITIES OF HERALDRY, with Illustrations from Old English Writers. By MARK ANTONY LOWER, M.A., Author of "Essays on English Surnames;" *with illuminated Title-page, and numerous engravings from designs by the Author.* 8vo, *cloth.* 14s.

"The present volume is truly a worthy sequel (to the 'SURNAMES') in the same curious and antiquarian line, blending with remarkable facts and intelligence, such a fund of amusing anecdote and illustration, that the reader is almost surprised to find that he has learned so much, whilst he appeared to be pursuing mere entertainment. The text is so pleasing that we scarcely dream of its sterling value; and it seems as if, in unison with the woodcuts, which so cleverly explain its points and adorn its various topics, the whole design were intended for a relaxation from study, rather than an ample exposition of an extraordinary and universal custom, which produced the most important effect upon the minds and habits of mankind."—*Literary Gazette.*

"Mr. Lower's work is both curious and instructive, while the manner of its treatment is so inviting and popular, that the subject to which it refers, which many have hitherto had too good reason to consider meagre and unprofitable, assumes, under the hands of the writer, the novelty of fiction with the importance of historical truth."—*Athenæum.*

PEDIGREES OF THE NOBILITY AND GENTRY OF HERTFORDSHIRE. By WILLIAM BERRY, late, and for fifteen years, Registering Clerk in the College of Arms, author of the "Encyclopædia Heraldica," &c. &c. Folio, (only 125 printed.) £1. 5s. *(original price £3. 10s.)*

GENEALOGICAL AND HERALDIC HISTORY OF THE EXTINCT AND DORMANT BARONETCIES of England, Ireland, and Scotland. By J. BURKE, Esq. Medium 8vo, SECOND EDITION, 638 *closely printed pages, in double columns, with about 1000 arms engraved on wood, fine portrait of JAMES I, and illuminated title-page, cloth.* 10s. *(original price £1. 8s.)*

This work engaged the attention of the author for several years, comprises nearly a thousand families, many of them amongst the most ancient and eminent in the kingdom, each carried down to its representative or representatives still existing, with elaborate and minute details of the alliances, achievements, and fortunes; generation after generation, from the earliest to the latest period.

ENGLISH SURNAMES. An Essay on Family Nomenclature, Historical, Etymological, and Humorous; with several illustrative Appendices. By MARK ANTONY LOWER, M.A. 2 vols., post 8vo, THIRD EDITION, ENLARGED, *woodcuts, cloth.* 12s.

This new and much improved Edition, besides a great enlargement of the Chapters contained in the previous editions, comprises several that are entirely new, together with Notes on Scottish, Irish, and Norman Surnames. The "Additional Prolusions," besides the articles on Allusive Arms, and the Roll of Battel Abbey, contain dissertations on Inn signs, and Remarks on Christian Names, with a copious INDEX of many thousand Names. These features render "English Surnames" rather a new work than a new edition.

"A curious, ingenious, and amusing book. Mr. Lower brings considerable knowledge to bear, both in his general history of the use of Surnames in England, and in his chapters on the different ways in which particular classes of names have originated from names of places, occupations, dignities, offices, personal and mental qualities, &c."—*Spectator.*

"Mr. Lower has gone to work in the true spirit of antiquarian discovery, and a most amusing and instructive book he has produced."—*Brighton Herald.*

"A curious work, and got up, moreover, with that commendable attention to paper and typography which is certain to make a book 'tak the eye.' . . . . . . Mr. Lower has been ' at a great feast of languages, and has stolen more than the ' scraps.' He both instructs and entertains."—*John Bull.*

INDEX TO THE PEDIGREES AND ARMS contained in the Heralds' Visitations and other Genealogical Manuscripts in the British Museum. By R. SIMS, *of the Manuscript Department.* 8vo, *closely printed in double columns, cloth.* 15s.

An indispensable work to those engaged in Genealogical and Topographical pursuits, affording a ready clue to the Pedigrees and Arms of nearly 40,000 of the Gentry of England, their Residences, &c. (distinguishing the different families of the same name in any county), as recorded by the Heralds in their Visitations between the years 1528 to 1686.

"This work will be very acceptable to all who have occasion to examine the MSS alluded to, whether for study, amusement, or professionally; those who have experienced the toilsome labour of searching, with the help only of the existing very imperfect Catalogues, can appreciate the perseverance and accurate examination necessary to produce such an Index as that just published by Mr. Sims; it will be an indispensable companion to the Library table of all students in genealogical pursuits, and those engaged in the History of Landed Property."—*Journal of Archæological Institute for September,* 1849.

ROLL OF ARMS OF THE REIGN OF KING EDWARD II. Edited by Sir HARRIS NICOLAS; to which is added, an "Ordinary" of the Arms mentioned by Jos. Gwilt, Esq. 8vo, *cloth.* 4s. 6d. (*original price* 10s. 6d.) On LARGE PAPER, 4to, *cloth,* 10s. (*original price* 21s.)

CALENDAR OF KNIGHTS; containing Lists of Knights Bachelors, British Knights of the Garter, Thistle, Bath, St. Patrick, the Guelphic and Ionian Orders, from 1760 to 1828. By F. TOWNSEND, *Windsor Herald.* Post 8vo, *cloth.* 3s. (*original price* 9s.)
A very useful volume for Genealogical and Biographical purposes.

THE SLOGANS OR WAR-CRIES OF THE NORTH OF ENGLAND, by M. AISLABIE DENHAM; with an Introduction on their Supposed Origin, by JOHN FENWICK; and Observations on Martial Mottoes, by W. HYLTON LONGSTAFFE. Post 8vo, *elegantly printed, with Coats of Arms, Seals, &c.,* sewed. 6s. 6d.

GENEALOGISTS' MANUAL; or Guide to the various Public Records, Registers, Wills, Printed Books, and other Documents necessary to be consulted in tracing a Pedigree. With particulars of the days and hours each Office or Registry is available, the charges made, the objects and dates of their Records, &c. &c.; the whole carefully compiled from Returns made expressly for this work; together with other Tables and Calendars useful to the Antiquary, Topographer, and Conveyancer. By MATTHEW COOKE. Thick 12mo, *cloth.* 6s. (*nearly ready.*)

Fine Arts.

PLAYING CARDS.—Facts and Speculations on the History of Playing Cards in Europe. By W. A. CHATTO, author of the "History of Wood Engraving," with Illustrations by J. JACKSON. 8vo, *profusely illustrated with engravings, both plain and coloured, cloth.* £1. 1s.

"The inquiry into the origin and signification of the suits and their marks, and the heraldic, theological, and political emblems pictured from time to time, in their changes, opens a new field of antiquarian interest; and the perseverance with which Mr. Chatto has explored it leaves little to be gleaned by his successors. The plates with which the volume is enriched add considerably to its value in this point of view. It is not to be denied that, take it altogether, it contains more matter than has ever before been collected in one view upon the same subject. In spite of its faults,

it is exceedingly amusing; and the most critical reader cannot fail to be entertained by the variety of curious outlying learning Mr. Chatto has somehow contrived to draw into the investigations."—*Atlas.*
"Indeed the entire production deserves our warmest approbation."—*Lit. Gaz.*
"A perfect fund of antiquarian research, and most interesting even to persons who never play at cards."—*Tait's Mag.*
"A curious, entertaining and really learned book."—*Rambler.*

HOLBEIN'S DANCE OF DEATH, with an Historical and Literary Introduction, by an Antiquary. Square post 8vo, *with 63 Engravings,* BEING THE MOST ACCURATE COPIES EVER EXECUTED OF THESE GEMS OF ART, *and a frontispiece of an ancient bedstead at Aix-la-Chapelle, with a Dance of Death carved on it, engraved by Fairholt, cloth.* 9s.

"The designs are executed with a spirit and fidelity quite extraordinary.—They are indeed most truthful."—*Athenæum.*

"Ces 53 Planches de Schlotthauer sont d'une exquise perfection.—*Langlois, Essai sur les Dances des Morts,* 1852.

CATALOGUE OF THE PRINTS which have been Engraved after Martin Heemskerck. By T. KERRICH, *Librarian to the University of Cambridge.* 8vo, *portrait, bds.* 3s. 6d.

CATALOGUE OF PICTURES, composed chiefly by the most admired Masters of the Roman, Florentine, Parman, Bolognese, Venetian, Flemish, and French Schools; with Descriptions and Critical Remarks. By ROBERT FOULIS. 3 vols. 12mo, *cloth.* 6s.

MEMOIRS OF PAINTING, with a Chronological History of the Importation of Pictures by the Great Masters into England since the French Revolution. By W. BUCHANAN. 2 vols. 8vo, *bds.,* 7s. 6d. (*original price* £1. 6s.)

HISTORY OF THE ORIGIN AND ESTABLISHMENT OF GOTHIC ARCHITECTURE, and an Inquiry into the mode of Painting upon and Staining Glass, as practised in the Ecclesiastical Structures of the Middle Ages. By J. S. HAWKINS, F.S.A. Royal 8vo, 11 *plates, bds.* 4s. (*original price* 12s.)

Popular Poetry, Tales, and Superstitions.

THE NURSERY RHYMES OF ENGLAND, collected chiefly from Oral Tradition. Edited by J. O. HALLIWELL. The FOURTH EDITION, enlarged, with 38 Designs, by W. B. SCOTT, *Director of the School of Design, Newcastle-on-Tyne.* 12mo, *illuminated cloth, gilt leaves.* 4s. 6d.

"Illustrations! and here they are; clever pictures, which the three-year olds understand before their A, B, C, and which the fifty-three-year olds like almost as well as the threes."—*Literary Gazette.*

"We are persuaded that the very rudest of these jingles, tales, and rhymes, possess a strong imagination nourishing power; and that in infancy and early child-

hood a sprinkling of ancient nursery lore is worth whole cartloads of the wise saws and modern instances which are now as duly and carefully concocted by experienced *littérateurs*, into instructive tales for the *spelling* public, as are works of entertainment for the reading public. The work is worthy of the attention of the popular antiquary."—*Tait's Mag.*

POPULAR RHYMES AND NURSERY TALES, with Historical Elucidations. By J. O. HALLIWELL. 12mo, *cloth.* 4s. 6d.

This very interesting volume on the Traditional Literature of England, is divided into Nursery Antiquities, Fireside Nursery Stories, Game Rhymes, Alphabet Rhymes, Riddle Rhymes, Nature Songs,

Proverb Rhymes, Places, and Families, Superstition Rhymes, Custom Rhymes and Nursery Songs; *a large number are here printed for the first time.* It may be considered a sequel to the preceding article.

OLD SONGS AND BALLADS.—A Little Book of Songs and Ballads, gathered from Ancient Music Books, MS. and Printed, by E. F. RIMBAULT, LL.D., F.S.A., &c., *elegantly printed* in post 8vo, pp. 240, *half morocco.* 6s.

"Dr. Rimbault has been at some pains to collect the words of the Songs which used to delight the Rustics of former times."—*Atlas.*

ROBIN HOOD.—The Robin Hood Garlands and Ballads, with the Tale of "The Little Geste," a Collection of all the Poems, Songs, and Ballads relating to this celebrated Yeoman; to which is prefixed his History, from Documents hitherto unrevised. By J. M. GUTCH, F.S.A. 2 vols. 8vo, *with numerous fine woodcuts, &c., by Fairholt, extra cloth.* £1. 1s. (original price £1. 10s.)

Two very handsome volumes, fit for the drawing-room table.

BALLAD ROMANCES. By R. H. HORNE, Esq., Author of "Orion," &c. 12mo, pp. 248, *cloth.* 3s. (original price 6s. 6d.)

Containing the Noble Heart, a Bohemian Legend; the Monk of Swineshead Abbey, a ballad Chronicle of the death of King John; the three Knights of Camelott, a Fairy Tale; The Ballad of Delora, or the Passion of Andrea Como; Bedd Gelert, a Welsh Legend; Ben Capstan, a Ballad of the Night Watch; the Elfe of the Woodlands, a Child's Story.

"Pure fancy of the most abundant and picturesque

description. Mr. Horne should write us more Fairy Tales; we know none to equal him since the days of Drayton and Herrick."—*Examiner.*

"The opening poem in this volume is a fine one, it is entitled the 'Noble Heart,' and not only in title but in treatment well imitates the style of Beaumont and Fletcher."—*Athenæum.*

SIR HUGH OF LINCOLN: or an Examination of a curious Tradition respecting the JEWS, with a Notice of the Popular Poetry connected with it. By the Rev. A. HUME, LL.D. 8vo. 2s.

ESSAY ON THE ARCHÆOLOGY OF OUR POPULAR PHRASES AND NURSERY RHYMES. By J. B. KER. 2 vols. 12mo, *new cloth.* 4s. (original price 12s.)

A work which has met with much abuse among the reviewers, but those who are fond of philological pursuits will read it now it is to be had at so very moderate a price, and it really contains a good deal of

gossiping matter. The author's attempt is to explain every thing from the Dutch, which he believes was the same language as the Anglo-Saxon.

MERRY TALES OF THE WISE MEN OF GOTHAM. Edited by JAMES ORCHARD HALLIWELL, Esq, F.S.A. Post 8vo. 1s.

These tales are supposed to have been composed in the early part of the sixteenth century, by Dr. Andrew Borde, the well-known progenitor of Merry Andrews.

"In the time of Henry the Eighth, and after," says Ant-A-Wood, "it was accounted a book full of wit and mirth by scholars and gentlemen."

SAINT PATRICK'S PURGATORY; an Essay on the Legends of Hell, Purgatory, and Paradise, current during the Middle Ages. By THOMAS WRIGHT, M.A., F.S.A., &c. Post 8vo, *cloth.* 6s.

"It must be observed that this is not a mere account of St. Patrick's Purgatory, but a complete history of the legends and superstitions relating to the subject, from the earliest times, rescued from old MSS. as well as from old printed books. Moreover, it embraces a singular chapter of literary history ntted by Warton and all former writers with whom we are acquainted; and we think we may add, that it forms

the best introduction to Dante that has yet been published."—*Literary Gazette.*

"This appears to be a curious and even amusing book on the singular subject of Purgatory, in which the idle and fearful dreams of superstition are shown to be first narrated as tales, and then a[pp]lied as means of deducing the moral character of the age in which they prevailed."—*Spectator.*

NOBLE AND RENOWNED HISTORY OF GUY, EARL OF WARWICK, containing a Full and True Account of his many Famous and Valiant Actions. Royal 12mo, *woodcuts, cloth.* 4*s.* 6*d.*

PHILOSOPHY OF WITCHCRAFT, (*Chiefly with respect to Cases in Scotland*). By J. MITCHELL, and J. DICKIE. 12mo, *cloth.* 3*s.* (*original price 6s.*) A curious volume, and a fit companion to Sir W. Scott's "Demonology and Witchcraft."

ACCOUNT OF THE TRIAL, CONFESSION, AND CONDEMNATION of Six Witches at Maidstone, 1652; also the Trial and Execution of three others at Faversham, 1645. 8vo. 1*s.* These Transactions are unnoticed by all Kentish historians.

WONDERFUL DISCOVERY OF THE WITCHCRAFTS OF MARGARET and PHILIP FLOWER, Daughters of Joan Flower, near Bever (Belvoir), executed at Lincoln, for confessing themselves Actors in the Destruction of Lord Rosse, Son of the Earl of Rutland, 1618. 8vo. 1*s.* One of the most extraordinary cases of Witchcraft on record.

Bibliography.

BIBLIOTHECA MADRIGALIANA.—A Bibliographical Account of the Musical and Poetical Works published in England during the Sixteenth and Seventeenth Centuries, under the Titles of Madrigals, Ballets, Ayres, Canzonets, &c., &c. By EDWARD F. RIMBAULT, LL.D., F.S.A. 8vo, *cloth.* 5*s.*
It records a class of books left undescribed by Ames, Herbert, and Dibdin, and furnishes a most valuable Catalogue of Lyrical Poetry of the age to which it refers.

THE MANUSCRIPT RARITIES OF THE UNIVERSITY OF CAMBRIDGE. By J. O. HALLIWELL, F.R.S. 8vo, *bds.* 3*s* (*original price* 10*s.* 6*d.*) A companion to Hartshorne's "Book Rarities" of the same University.

SOME ACCOUNT OF THE POPULAR TRACTS, formerly in the Library of Captain Cox, of Coventry, A.D. 1575. By J. O. HALLIWELL. 8vo, *only* 50 *printed, sewed.* 1*s.*

CATALOGUE OF THE CONTENTS OF THE CODEX HOLBROOKIANUS. (A Scientific MS.) By Dr. John Holbrook, Master of St. Peter's College, Cambridge, 1418-1431). By J. O. HALLIWELL. 8vo. 1*s.*

ACCOUNT OF THE VERNON MANUSCRIPT. A Volume of Early English Poetry, preserved in the Bodleian Library. By J. O. HALLIWELL. 8vo, *only* 50 *printed.* 1*s.*

BIBLIOTHECA CANTIANA. A Bibliographical Account of what has been published on the History, Topography, Antiquities, Customs, and Family Genealogy of the COUNTY of KENT, with Biographical Notes. By JOHN RUSSELL SMITH, in a handsome 8vo volume, pp. 370, *with two plates of facsimiles of Autographs of 33 eminent Kentish Writers.* 5*s.* (*original price* 14*s.*)—LARGE PAPER 10*s.* 6*d.*

Miscellanies.

NEW FACTS AND VERIFICATIONS OF ANCIENT BRITISH HISTORY. By the Rev. BEALE POSTE. 8vo, *with engravings, cloth.*

THOMAS SPROTT'S (*a monk of Canterbury, circa* 1280) Chronicle of Profane and Sacred History. Translated from the original MS., on 12 parchment skins, in the possession of Joseph Mayer, Esq., of Liverpool. By Dr. W. BELL. 4to, *half bound in morocco, accompanied with an exact Facsimile of the entire Codex, 37 feet long, in a round morocco case,* PRIVATELY PRINTED, *very curious.* £2. 2*s.*

TONSTALL (Cuthbert, *Bishop of Durham*), Sermon preached on Palm Sunday, 1539, before Henry VIII, *reprinted* VERBATIM *from the rare edition by Berthelet in* 1539. 12mo, 1*s.* 6*d.* An exceedingly interesting Sermon, at the commencement of the Reformation, Strype in his Memorials has made large extracts from it.

LAPPENBERG'S HISTORY OF ENGLAND, under the Anglo-Saxon Kings. Translated by BENJ. THORPE, *with Additions and Corrections, by the Author and Translator.* 2 vols. 8vo, cloth. 12s. (*original price* £1. 1s.)

"Of modern works I am most indebted to the History of England by Lappenberg, the use of which, more particularly in conjunction with the translation given by Thorpe, and enriched by both those scholars, affords the best and surest guide in penetrating the labyrinth of early English History."—*König Aelfred und seine Stelle in der Geschichte Englands, von Dr. Reinold Pauli.*—Berlin, 1851.

LETTERS OF THE KINGS OF ENGLAND, *now first collected* from the originals in Royal Archives, and from other authentic sources, private as well as public. Edited with Historical Introduction and Notes, by J. O. HALLIWELL. Two HANDSOME VOLUMES, post 8vo, *with portraits of Henry VIII and Charles I, cloth.* 8s. (*original price* £1 1s.)

These volumes form a good companion to Ellis's Original Letters.

The collection comprises for the first time the love letters of Henry the VIII. to Anne Boleyn in a complete form, which may be regarded perhaps as the most singular documents of the kind that have descended to our times; the series of letters of Edward VI. will be found very interesting specimens of composition; some of the letters of James I, hitherto unpublished, throw light on the murder of Overbury, and prove beyond a doubt the King was implicated in it in some extraordinary and unpleasant way: but his letters to the Duke of Buckingham are of the most singular nature; only imagine a letter from a so vereign to his prime minister commencing thus; "My own sweet and dear child, blessing, blessing, blessing on thy heart-roots and all thine." Prince Charles and the Duke of Buckingham's Journey into Spain has never been before so fully illustrated as it is by th documents given in this work, which also includes the very curious letters from the Duke and Duchess of Buckingham to James I. *Forming an essential com panion to every History of England.*

WALES.—ROYAL VISITS AND PROGRESSES TO WALES, and the Border Counties of CHESHIRE, SALOP, HEREFORD, and MONMOUTH, from Julius Cæsar, to Queen Victoria, including a succinct History of the Country and People, particularly of the leading Families who Fought during the Civil Wars of Charles I., the latter from MSS. never before published. By EDWARD PARRY. *A handsome 4to volume, with many wood engravings, and fine portrait of the Queen, cloth.* £1. 1s.

HUNTER'S (Rev. Joseph) HISTORICAL AND CRITICAL TRACTS. Post 8vo. 2s. 6d. each.

I. Agincourt; a contribution, towards an authentic List of the Commanders of the English Host in King Henry the Fifth's Expedition.
II. Collections concerning the Founders of New Plymouth, the first Colonists of New England.

III. Milton; a sheaf of Gleanings after his Biographers and Annotators.
IV. The Ballad Hero, "Robin Hood," his period, real character, &c., investigated, and, perhaps, ascertained.

ARCHERY.—The Science of Archery, shewing its affinity to Heraldry, and capabilities of Attainment. By A. P. HARRISON. 8vo, sewed. 1s.

ILLUSTRATIONS OF EATING, displaying the Omnivorous Character of Man, and exhibiting the Natives of various Countries at feeding-time. By a BEEF-EATER. Fcap. 8vo, *with woodcuts.* 2s.

ELEMENTS OF NAVAL ARCHITECTURE; being a Translation of the Third Part of Clairbois's "Traité Elémentaire de la Construction des Vaisseaux." By J. N. STRANGE, Commander, R.N. 8vo, *with five large folding plates, cloth.* 5s.

LECTURES ON NAVAL ARCHITECTURE; being the Substance of those delivered at the United Service Institution. By E. GARDINER FISHBOURNE, Commander, R.N. 8vo, *plates, cloth.* 5s. 6d.

Both these works are published in illustration of the "Wave System."

NEW YORK IN THE YEAR 1695, with Plans of the City and Forts as they then existed. By the Rev. JOHN MILLER. *Now first printed.* 8vo, bds. 2s. 6d. (*original price* 4s. 6d.)

THOUGHTS IN VERSE FOR THE AFFLICTED. By a COUNTRY CURATE. Square 12mo, sewed. 1s.

POEMS, partly of Rural Life, in National English. By the Rev. WILLIAM BARNES, author of "Poems in the Dorset Dialect." 12mo, *cloth.* 5s.

WAIFS AND STRAYS. A Collection of Poetry. 12mo, *only 250 printed, chiefly for presents, sewed.* 1s. 6d.

MIRROUR OF JUSTICES, written originally in the old French, long before the Conquest, and many things added by ANDREW HORNE. Translated by W. HUGHES, of Gray's Inn. 12mo, *cloth.* 2s.

A curious, interesting, and authentic treatise on ancient English Law.

CONTRIBUTIONS TO LITERATURE HISTORICAL, ANTIQUARIAN, and METRICAL. By MARK ANTONY LOWER, M.A., F.S.A., Author of "Essays on English Surnames," "Curiosities of Heraldry," &c. Post 8vo, woodcuts, cloth. 7s 6d

CONTENTS.

1 On Local Nomenclature.
2 On the Battle of Hastings, an Historical Essay.
3 The Lord Dacre, his mournful end; a Ballad.
4 Historical and Archæological Memoir on the Iron Works of the South of England, *with numerous illustrations.*
5 Winchelsea's Deliverance, or the Stout Abbot of Battayle; in Three Fyttes.
6 The South Downs, a Sketch; Historical, Anecdotical, and Descriptive.
7 On Yew Trees in Church-yards.
8 A Lyttel Geste of a Greate Eele; a pleasaunt Ballade.
9 A Discourse of Genealogy.
10 An Antiquarian Pilgrimage in Normandy, *with woodcuts.*
11 Miscellanea, &c. &c. &c.

There is a good deal of quaint and pleasing reading in this volume. Mr. Lower's jokes are of the oldest—as befits the pleasantries of an antiquary,—but, on the whole, we seldom meet with more readable antiquarian essays than these. Most of them have been printed elsewhere. One, on the South Downs, contains the best of the new matter. The author is at home on the wide expanse of these chalk ranges. He speaks with knowledge of the picturesque villages enclosed in their secluded nooks,—of the folk-lore and legends of old days which still abound amongst the sequestered inhabitants, and of the historical associations which render celebrated many spots otherwise of little interest.—*Athenæum.*

Most of the papers in this volume have already appeared in periodicals, and in the Collections of the Sussex Archæological Society. They are well worthy of being printed in a collected form. The account of the Battle of Hastings and the memoir on the Southern Iron Works contain matter of historical value, in addition to their local interest in connexion with the topography and archæology of Sussex. Among the papers now printed for the first time that on the South Downs is the most important, and will be read with much interest, both for the information it contains and the pleasing style in which it is written. There are some charming descriptions of scenery, and acceptable notices of the history, traditions, and customs of the district. Among the minor contributions in the volume, the paper on Local Nomenclature is full of valuable suggestions. Altogether it is a volume of very agreeable and instructive reading.—*Lit. Gas.*

HANDBOOK to the LIBRARY of the BRITISH MUSEUM, containing a brief History of its Formation, and of the various Collections of which it is composed; Descriptions of the Catalogues in present use; Classed Lists of the Manuscripts, &c.; and a variety of Information indispensable for the "Readers" at that Institution; with some Account of the principal Public Libraries in London. By RICHARD SIMS, of the Department of Manuscripts, Compiler of the "Index to the Heralds' Visitations." Small 8vo, pp. 438, *with map and plan, cloth.* 5s

It will be found a very useful work to every literary person or public institution in all parts of the world.

What Mr. Antonio Panizzi, the keeper of the department of printed books, says *might be done.* Mr. Richard Sims, of the department of the manuscripts, says *shall be done.* His Hand-book to the Library of the British Museum is a very comprehensive and instructive volume. I have the sixtieth edition of "Synopsis of the Contents of the British Museum" before me—I cannot expect to see a sixtieth edition of the *Hand-book,* but it deserves to be placed by the side of the Synopsis, and I venture to predict for it a wide circulation.—*Mr. Bolton Corney, in Notes and Queries,* No. 213.

A GRAMMAR of BRITISH HERALDRY, consisting of "Blazon" and "Marshalling," with an Introduction on the Rise and Progress of Symbols and Ensigns. By the Rev. W. SLOANE EVANS, B.A. 8vo, *with 26 plates, comprising upwards of 400 figures, cloth.* 6s.

One of the best introductions ever published.

A PLEA FOR THE ANTIQUITY OF HERALDRY, with an Attempt to Expound its Theory and Elucidate its History. By W. SMITH ELLIS Esq., of the Middle Temple. 8vo, *sewed.* 1s 6d

A FEW NOTES ON SHAKESPEARE, with Occasional Remarks on the Emendations of the Manuscript-Corrector in Mr. Collier's copy of the folio, 1632. By the Rev. ALEXANDER DYCE. 8vo, *cloth.* 6s

Mr. Dyce's Notes are peculiarly delightful, from the stores of illustration with which his extensive reading not only among our writers, but among those of other countries, especially of the Italian poets, has enabled him to enrich them. All that he has recorded is valuable. We read his little volume with pleasure and close it with regret.—*Literary Gazette.*

A FEW WORDS IN REPLY TO MR. DYCE'S "FEW NOTES ON SHAKESPEARE." By the Rev. JOSEPH HUNTER. 8vo, *sewed*. 1s

THE GRIMALDI SHAKESPEARE.—Notes and Emendations on the Plays of Shakespeare from a recently-discovered annotated copy by the late JOSEPH GRIMALDI, Esq., Comedian. 8vo, *cuts*. 1s

A humorous Squib on the late Shakespeare Emendations.

SHAKESPEARE'S VERSIFICATION and its apparent Irregularities explained by Examples from early and late English Writers. By the late WILLIAM SIDNEY WALKER, formerly Fellow of Trinity College, Cambridge; edited by W. NANSON LETTSOM, Esq. Fcp. 8vo, *cloth*. 6s.

A PHILOLOGICAL GRAMMAR, grounded upon English, and formed from a comparison of more than Sixty Languages. Being an Introduction to the Science of Grammars of all Languages, especially English, Latin, and Greek. By the Rev. W. BARNES, B.D., of St. John's College, Cambridge. Author of "Poems in the Dorset Dialect," "Anglo Saxon Delectus," &c. 8vo, pp. 322, *cloth*. 9s

TIM BOBBIN'S LANCASHIRE DIALECT, with his Rhymes and an enlarged Glossary of Words and Phrases, used by the Rural Population of South Lancashire. By SAMUEL BAMFORD. 12mo, the second edition, *cloth*, 3s 6d

BRITANNIC RESEARCHES: or, New Facts and Rectifications of Ancient British History. By the Rev. BEALE POSTE, M.A. 8vo, (pp. 448) *with engravings, cloth*. 15s

The author of this volume may justly claim credit for considerable learning, great industry, and, above all, strong faith in the interest and importance of his subject. . . . . On various points he has given us additional information and afforded us new views, for which we are bound to thank him. The body of the book is followed by a very complete index, so as to render reference to any part of it easy : this was the more necessary on account of the multifariousness of the topics treated, the variety of persons mentioned, and the many works quoted.—*Athenæum*, Oct. 8, 1853.

The Rev. Beale Poste has long been known to antiquaries as one of the best read of all those who have elucidated the earliest annals of this country. He is a practical man, has investigated for himself monuments and manuscripts, and we have in the above-named volume the fruits of many years' patient study. The objects which will occupy the attention of the *reader* are—1. The political position of the principal British powers *before* the Roman conquest—under the Roman dominion, and struggling unsuccessfully against the Anglo-Saxon race; 2. The geography of Ancient Britain; 3. An investigation of the Ancient British Historians, Gildas and Nennius, and the more obscure British chroniclers; 4. The ancient stone monuments of the Celtic period; and, lastly, some curious and interesting notices of the early British church. Mr. Poste has not touched on subjects which have received much attention from others, save in cases where he had something new to offer, and the volume must be regarded, therefore, as an entirely new collection of discoveries and deductions tending to throw light on the darkest as well as the earliest portion of our national history.—*Atlas*.

COINS OF CUNOBELINE and of the ANCIENT BRITONS. By the Rev. BEALE POSTE, B.C.L. 8vo, *plates, and many woodcuts, cloth* (*only 40 printed*). £1.8s

BARONIA ANGLIA CONCENTRATA ; or a Concentration of all the Baronies called Baronies in Fee, deriving their Origin from Writ of Summons, and not from any specific Limited Creation, showing the Descent and Line of Heirship, as well as those Families mentioned by Sir William Dudgale, as of those whom that celebrated author has omitted to notice; interspersed with Interesting Notices and Explanatory Remarks. Whereto is added the Proofs of Parliamentary Sitting from the Reign of Edward I to Queen Anne; also *a Glossary of Dormant English, Scotch, and Irish Peerage Titles, with references to presumed existing Heirs.* By Sir T. C. BANKS. 2 vols. 4to, *cloth*. £3. 3s NOW OFFERED FOR 15s

A book of great research by the well-known author of the "Dormant and Extinct Peerage," and other heraldic and historical works. Those fond of genealogical pursuits ought to secure a copy while it is so cheap. It may be considered a Supplement to his former works. Vol. ii, pp, 210-300, contains an Historical Account of the first settlement of Nova Scotia, and the foundation of the Order of Nova Scotia Baronets, distinguishing those who had seisin of lands there.

RETROSPECTIVE REVIEW (New Series); consisting of Criticisms upon, Analysis of, and Extracts from curious, useful, valuable, and scarce Old Books. Vol. 1, 8vo, pp. 436, *cloth.* 10s 6d

₊ Published Quarterly at 2s. 6d. each Number.—No. VII is published this day.

CONTENTS OF No. V.

1 Sir William Davenant, Poet Laureate and Dramatist, 1673.
2 Cooke's "Poor Man's Case," 1648.
3 Old English Letter-writing; Angel Day's English Secretary, 1592; W. Fulwood's Enemy of Idlenesse.
4 The Old Practice of Gardening; Thos. Hyll's Briefe and Pleasaunt Treatise, 1563.
5 English Political Songs and Satires, from King John to George I.
6 Medieval Travellers in the Holy Land.
7 The Athenian Letters, by Lord Hardwicke and others.
8 The Writings of Wace the Trouvère.
ANECDOTA LITERARIA.—Pepy's Directions for the Disposition of his Library; A Legendary Poem of the 15th Century, the Story laid at Falmouth, in Cornwall: both now first printed.

CONTENTS OF No. VI.

1 Drayton's Polyolbion.
2 Penn's No Cross No Crown.
3 Lambarde's Perambulation of Kent.
4 Philosophy of the Table in the Time of Charles I.
5 Russia under Peter the Great.
6 Life and Works of Leland, the Antiquary.
7 The Decay of Good Manners.
8 Stephen's Essayes and Characters, 1615.
ANECDOTA LITERARIA.—The Child of Bristow, a Metrical Legend. Now first printed.

The title of this Review explains its objects. It is intended to supply a place unfilled in our periodical literature, and this first number is very satisfactory. The papers are varied and interesting, not overlaid by the display of too much learning for the general reader, but showing sufficient research and industry on the part of the writers to distinguish the articles from mere ephemeral reviews of passing publications. In the prospectus the editor says "It is our design to select, from the vast field of the literature of the past, subjects which are most likely to interest modern readers; we shall lay before them from time to time, essays on various branches of the literature of former days, English or foreign; we shall give accounts of rare and curious books; point out and bring forward beauties from forgotten authors; and tell the knowledge and opinions of other days." The design is well carried out in this number, and will, no doubt, be further developed as the work advances. It is to be published quarterly, at a very moderate price, and will, we have no doubt, prove a successful undertaking.—*Atlas.*

REMAINS OF PAGAN SAXONDOM, principally from Tumuli in England. Drawn from the Originals. Described and Illustrated by JOHN YONGE AKERMAN, Fellow and Secretary of the Society of Antiquaries. 4to, *parts* 1 to 9. 2s 6d each (*Pt.* 10 *in the press*).

The plates are admirably executed by Mr. Basire, and coloured under the direction of the Author. It is a work well worthy the notice of the Archæologist.

WILTSHIRE TALES, illustrative of the Manners, Customs, and Dialect of that and Adjoining Counties. By JOHN YONGE AKERMAN. 12mo, *cloth.* 2s 6d

We will conclude with a simple, but hearty recommendation of a little book which is as humourous, for the drolleries of the stories, as it is interesting as a picture of rustic manners.—*Tallis's Weekly Paper.*

Mr Akerman's WILTSHIRE TALES embody most of the provincialisms peculiar to this county and the districts of other counties lying on its northern borders, and possess the additional recommendation of preserving the old songs (and the airs to which they are sung), which are still to be heard at most harvest houses and other merry makings,—the well-known "Here's a health to our meester," and a "A pie upon the pear tree top" among the rest. Both to the philologist, therefore, and to the general reader, the book is an interesting one.—*Salisbury and Winchester Journal.*

HISTORY AND ANTIQUITIES OF THE TOWN OF MARLBOROUGH, and more generally of the entire Hundred of Selkley in Wiltshire. By JAMES WAYLEN, Esq. Thick 8vo, *woodcuts, cloth.* 14s

This volume describes a portion of Wilts not occupied by Sir R. C. Hoare and other topographers.

SIGILLA ECCLESIÆ HIBERNICÆ ILLUSTRATA. The Episcopal and Capitular Seals of the Irish Cathedral Churches illustrated. By RICHARD CAULFIELD, A.B. 8vo. Part I—CASHEL and EMLY, *with 12 engravings,* sewed. 1*s* 6*d*

ULSTER JOURNAL OF ARCHÆOLOGY : conducted under the superintendence of a Committee of Archæologists at Belfast. Handsomely printed in 4to, *with engravings. Published quarterly. Annual Subscription, 12s.* (*Not sold in single Nos.*) *Nos.* 1 *to* 5 *are ready.*

DESCRIPTIVE CATALOGUE OF THE COLLECTION OF ANTIQUITIES, and other Objects Illustrative of Irish History, exhibited in the Belfast Museum, at the Meeting of the British Association, Sep. 1852, with Antiquarian Notes. 8vo, *sewed.* 1*s* 6*d*

ANTIQUITIES OF SHROPSHIRE. By the Rev. R. W. EYTON, Rector of Ryton. Royal 8vo, *with plates.* Parts I to III. 5*s* each. *Published Quarterly.*

The Work will extend at least to five volumes or twenty parts. Any subscriber will be at liberty to withdraw his name after the publication of any fourth part or completed volume.

ANTIQUITIES OF THE BOROUGH OF LEEDS, described and illustrated. By JAMES WARDELL, Esq. 8vo, 16 *plates, mostly coloured.* 7*s* 6*d*—LARGE PAPER. 12*s*

HISTORICAL ACCOUNT OF THE CISTERCIAN ABBEY of SALLEY, in Craven, Yorkshire, its Foundation and Benefactors, Abbots, Possessions, Compotus, and Dissolution, and its existing Remains. Edited by J. HARLAND. Royal 8vo, 12 *plates, cloth.* 4*s* 6*d*

A DESCRIPTIVE ACCOUNT OF LIVERPOOL, as it was during the last Quarter of the Eighteenth Century, 1775—1800. By RICHARD BROOKE, Esq., F.S.A. A handsome vol. Royal 8vo, *with illustrations, cloth.* £1. 5*s*

In addition to information relative to the Public Buildings, Statistics, and Commerce of the Town, the Work contains some curious and interesting particulars, which have never been previously published, respecting the Pursuits, Habits, and Amusements of the Inhabitants of Liverpool during that period, with Views of its Public Edifices.

A GUIDE TO LYNTON AND PLACES ADJACENT, IN NORTH DEVON, including Ilfracombe. By T. H. COOPER. 12mo, 5 *plates,* and *Map of North Devon, cloth.* 3*s* 6*d*

HISTORY OF GREAT YARMOUTH, containing the Origin, Foundation, and History of that Ancient Borough ; and an Account of its Government, Incorporation, Liberties, and Franchises ; with a Description of the Public Buildings, Churches, Convents, and other Religious Houses of the Middle Ages, &c. Compiled by HENRY MANSHIP, Town Clerk temp. Queen Elizabeth. Edited by CHARLES JOHN PALMER, F.S.A. Thick vol., post 4to, pp. 456, *with* 11 *illustrations, half bound.* £1. 1*s*

ARCHÆOLOGICAL MINE, a Magazine in which will be comprised the History of Kent, founded on the basis of Hasted. By A. J. DUNKIN. 8vo, Parts 1 to 12. *Published Monthly.* 8*d* each.

DUNCUMB'S (Rev. John) HISTORY AND ANTIQUITIES of the County of Hereford. 2 vols. 4to, *portraits and plates, new, in boards.* £1. 4*s* *Hereford,* 1801-12

This is the only History of the County published. This copy contains five additional sheets (the Hundred of Greytree) and the Index to the Second Volume, which are wanting in all the Subscribers' copies.

HISTORY OF OREGON AND CALIFORNIA and the other Territories on the North West Coast of America, accompanied by a Geographical View and Map and a number of Proofs and Illustrations of the History. By ROBERT GREENHOW, *Librarian of the Department of State of the United States.* Thick 8vo, LARGE MAP, *cloth.* 6s (pub. at 16s)

HISTORY OF ANGLING LITERATURE, and on Matters connected with Fish and Fishers from the earliest period, to which is added a General Bibliography of Books on Angling. By an ANGLER. Fcp. 8vo, *cloth.* 5s (nearly ready).

CHRISTMASTIDE, its History, Festivities, and Carols. By WILLIAM SANDYS, Esq., F.S.A., in one handsome vol. 8vo, ILLUSTRATED WITH 20 ENGRAVINGS AFTER THE DESIGNS OF J. STEPHANOFF, *cloth.* 14s

Its title vouches that *Christmastide* is germane to the time. Mr. Sandys has brought together, in an octavo of some 300 pages, a great deal of often interesting information, beyond the stale gossip about "Christmas in the olden time," and the threadbare make-believes of jollity and geniality which furnish forth most books on the subject. His carols too, which include some in old French and Provençal, are selected from numerous sources, and comprise many of the less known, and more worth knowing. His materials are presented with good feeling and mastery of his theme, and for excellent taste and appropriateness in binding, without extreme costliness, the book is a model. On the whole, the volume deserves, and should anticipate, a welcome.—*Spectator.*

JUST IMPORTED.

HISTOIRE DE L'ARCHITECTURE SACRÉE du quatrième au dixième siècle dans les anciens évechés de GENÈVE, LAUSANNE et SION. Par J. D. BLAVIGNAC, Architecte. One vol. 8vo, pp. 450, and 37 plates, and a 4to Atlas of 82 *plates of Architecture, Sculpture, Frescoes, Reliquaries, &c. &c.* £2. 10s

A VERY REMARKABLE BOOK, AND WORTH THE NOTICE OF THE ARCHITECT, THE ARCHÆOLOGIST, AND THE ARTIST.

COPENHAGEN—THE TRAVELLER'S HANDBOOK TO COPENHAGEN and its Environs. By ANGLICANUS. 12mo, *with large Map of Sealand, Plan of Copenhagen, and Views.* 12mo, *cloth.* 8s

ANTIGUEDADES PERUANAS, por MARIANO EDUARDO DE RIVERO, *Director del Museo Nacional de Lima,* y Dr. JUAN DIEGO DE TSCHUDI (*author of Travels in Peru*). 4to, pp. 342, *with woodcuts,* and folio volume of COLOURED PLATES, *bds.* £5. 5s

A description of remains discovered in the sites of ancient cities and temples in Peru, those objects which arrested the attention and excited the wonder of the philosophic Humboldt, when investigating the physical features of that remarkable country. The illustrative plates, executed at Vienna, from the drawings of the Artist, are among the marvels of lithography. They comprise representations of mummified bodies, prepared in the manner peculiar to the Peruvians, vases of grotesque form and characteristic idols in terra cotta and the precious metals, textile fabrics, weapons of a very remote period, and view of temples and buildings, which, for symmetry and beauty, may vie with those of Greece and Asia Minor in the dawn of civilisation, all executed with a spirit and truthfulness unsurpassed by any work of the kind that has come under our notice.—*Literary Gazette,* Jan. 8, 1853.

ESSAI HISTORIQUE PHILOSOPHIQUE et Pittoresque sur les Danses des Morts. Par E. H. LANGLOIS; suivi d'une Lettre de Leber, et une note de Depping sur le même sujet, publié par Pottier et Baudry, 2 vols, royal 8vo, *with 54 plates of Death's Dance of various ages, also many vignettes,* sewed, £1. 1s

LA ROMAINE, ou HISTOIRE, LANGUE, LITTERATURE, OROGRAPHIE, statistique des Peuples de la Langue d'Or, Adrislicus, Vallaques, et Moldaves, resumés sous le nom de Romans. Par J. A. VAILLANT, 3 vols, 8vo sewed, 18s.

VOYAGES, Relations, et Memoires originaux pour servir à l'Histoire de la Decouverte de l'Amerique, publiés pour la première fois en Français. Par H. TERNAUX-COMPANS. 20 vols. 8vo, both Series, and complete. *Sewed,* £3. 10s

A valuable collection of early voyages and relations on South America; also translations of unpublished Spanish MSS., principally relating to Old and New Mexico.